Knechel and Salterio's *Auditing: Assurance and Risk* is an innovative book that takes a wide ranging approach to the auditor's assessment of an organization's environment and business risk. The new edition is a valuable update of this approach.

David Hay,
The University of Auckland Business School, New Zealand

Two features set this textbook apart from many others. First, it is truly global in scope. Second, it goes beyond definitions and explanations of how audits are performed. It challenges students to think critically, at a higher level, with excellent examples and thoughtful cases. Great textbook!

Pamela R. Murphy,
Stephen J.R. Smith School of Business,
Queen's University, Canada

Knechel and Salterio guide students through an accounting landscape full of challenges. This fourth edition is updated in many ways—including the major changes in Auditor Reporting.

Arnold Schilder,
Chairman, International Auditing and Assurance
Standards Board (IAASB), USA

Auditing

Focusing on auditing as a judgment process, this unique textbook helps readers strike the balance between understanding auditing theory and how an audit plays out in reality.

The only textbook to provide complete coverage of both the International Auditing and Assurance Standards Board and the Public Company Accounting Oversight Board, *Auditing* reflects the contemporary evolution of the audit process. New additions to the book include expert updates on key topics, such as the audit of accounting estimates, group audit, and the Integrated Audit.

Supplemented by extra on-line resources, students using this established text will be well-equipped to be effective auditors and to understand the role of auditing in the business world.

W. Robert Knechel is the Frederick E. Fisher Eminent Scholar in Accounting at the University of Florida, USA. He is currently the Director of the *International Center for Research in Accounting and Auditing* (ICRAA). He holds honorary faculty appointments at the University of Auckland, New Zealand, and KU Leuven, Belgium.

Steven E. Salterio is the Director of the CPA Centre for Governance, the PWC/O'Neill Faculty Research Fellow in Accounting, and a Professor of Business at the Stephen J. R. Smith School of Business, Queen's University, Canada. He is a Fellow of the Chartered Professional Accountants of Ontario (formerly the Institute of Chartered Accountants of Ontario).

Auditing

Assurance and Risk

Fourth Edition

W. Robert Knechel and Steven E. Salterio

Routledge
Taylor & Francis Group

NEW YORK AND LONDON

Please visit the companion web site for this title at:
www.routledge/cw/knechel

Fourth edition published 2017
by Routledge
711 Third Avenue, New York, NY 10017

and by Routledge
2 Park Square, Milton Park, Abingdon, Oxon OX14 4RN

Routledge is an imprint of the Taylor & Francis Group, an informa business

© 2017 Taylor & Francis

First edition published by South-Western College Pub 1998
Second edition published by South-Western College Pub 2001
Third edition published by Thomson/South-Western 2007

Library of Congress Cataloging in Publication Data
A catalog record for this book has been requested

ISBN: 978-1-138-69277-0 (hbk)
ISBN: 978-1-138-69279-4 (pbk)
ISBN: 978-1-31553-173-1 (ebk)

Typeset in Myriad Pro by
Servis Filmsetting Ltd, Stockport, Cheshire

Printed and bound in the United States of America by Sheridan

To my wife, Anna, and children, Abigail, Martina and Andrew who, collectively, are an ongoing source of inspiration, encouragement, and tolerance of my efforts.

—W. Robert Knechel

To my spouse Leslie and my son Alexander who support, encourage, and tolerate my efforts to be a strong academic and a loving spouse and father.

—Steve Salterio

Table of Contents

Chapter 4: The Audit Process

Chapter 5: Understanding the Client's Industry and Business: Strategic Analysis and Management Controls

Chapter 6: Understanding the Client's Industry and Business: Processes and Process Controls

Chapter 7: Risk Mitigation and the Audit: Internal Control over Financial Reporting In A GAAS Audit

Chapter 8: Internal Control over Financial Reporting In an Integrated Audit

Chapter 9: Inquiry and Analytical Evidence Including Auditing of Accounting Estimates

Chapter 10: Designing Substantive Tests: Responses to Residual Risks

Chapter 11: Audit Testing for the Sales and Customer Service Process

Chapter 12: Audit Testing for the Supply Chain and Production Process

Chapter 13: Auditing Resource Management Processes

Chapter 14: Completing the Audit I: Final Evidence Aggregation and Analysis

Chapter 15: Completing the Audit II: Audit Reporting

Chapter 16: The Ethical Auditor: Factors Affecting Auditor Decision Making

CHAPTER 1

Assurance and Auditing

Outline

- Introduction
- Information, Business, and Global Capital Markets
- The Role of Auditing in an International Economic System
- The Demand for Assurance: Integrity, Trust, and Risk
  - o Incentives
  - o Ethical Principles
  - o The Role of Corporate Governance
  - o The Role of the External Auditor
- Differentiating Assurance, Attestation, Auditing, and Accounting
  - o The Nature of Assurance and Attestation Engagements
- The Auditing Profession and Regulation
  - o Entering the Profession: Education, Training, and Certification
  - o Organizational Forms of Public Accounting Firms
  - o Regulating the Auditing Profession
- Knowledge and Skills Needed by Auditors in the Twenty-First Century
- The Plan of this Book
- Summary and Conclusion
- Bibliography of Relevant Literature

Learning Goals for this Chapter

1. Introduce the role of audit and assurance in the global economy.
2. Examine critically the background forces that affect the twenty-first century audit.
3. Introduce the role of the professional accountant.
4. Introduce the public accounting firm and its role in the global economy.
5. To describe the plan of this book and how it maps to the audit of financial statements.

Introduction

To live is to make decisions. Informed decisions should be based on information that is objective, relevant, reliable, and understandable. But how does an individual making a decision know that he or she has reliable information? In a nutshell, this question captures the nature of the problem that justifies the study of auditing and assurance. In today's global business environment in which all sorts of data is transmitted on a real-time basis, decision makers worry that the information they have available will *not* be objective, relevant, reliable, or understandable. Indeed, information can be incorrect because someone makes an accidental mistake, or it can be intentionally manipulated for someone's benefit. We have seen in the accounting crisis at the turn of the century and continuing into the fiscal crisis that has plagued the world since 2007–08, individuals and organizations who rely on information that is misleading, incomplete, or confusing may make decisions that lead to unexpected and/or unacceptable outcomes. These outcomes can range from bankruptcy at the individual or firm level to a freeze of the global economy with a lack of trust in counterparties to a transaction.

While being relatively blasé about everyday routine decisions, people and organizations rarely accept information at face value when a critical decision depends on it. People and organizations are especially wary when the information comes from a source that may have questionable motivations (e.g., a salesperson). Buyers read consumer reports before making a major purchase, shoppers compare prices on-line, employers obtain multiple references about a job candidate, and candidates for a corporate acquisition are subjected to extensive due diligence. Regardless of the decision being made, people and organizations need useful information about their options. Ideally, they would like assurance that they will make their decision based on information that is, in fact, objective, relevant, reliable, and understandable. However, in many areas of economic life, alternative sources of information are either not available, or not available at a reasonable cost, to an individual or organization making a decision. Hence, the need for assurance arises endogenously, that is, from within the economy itself. In order to ensure that information is supplied so as to enable markets to work effectively and efficiently, some information is required from firms by law and regulation. Assurance on that information is required whenever the information provider might bias the information for their own advantage. Accounting information is the main focus of this text, but there are many other examples of the need for assurance over information, some of which we will also explore.

Information, Business, and Global Capital Markets

Investors in today's global marketplace have more choices than ever as to how to invest capital. A multitude of options elevates the importance of high quality information used to make investing decisions. An important source of information to all investors is the periodic—always annually but in some countries also quarterly or semi-annually—financial statements prepared by publicly listed companies. Furthermore, the availability of real-time information about competitive pressures and environmental forces that threaten the value of an investment provides investors with a better understanding of the risks surrounding their investments. Consider a few of the information risks that investors face when making decisions based on financial reports:

- Information may be *biased* to entice an investor to purchase shares in a company that is intentionally overvalued. Accounting procedures that accelerate revenues and slow down expenses are common "tricks" for pushing earnings to higher levels.

- Information may be *irrelevant,* emphasizing facts that appear important but are unrelated to the future prospects of the company. The marketing of new stock issues may involve claims about future prospects that are hard to evaluate and tangential to the operations of the organization.

- Information may be *inaccurate*. There are any number of reasons why information may be incorrect by accident or through intentional manipulation by the management of a company.

- Information may be thought to be *"sensitive"* so a company may decide to hide it from outsiders, especially if the information will have a negative impact on the company's market valuation. For example, a company may not want to disclose that much of its profits come from transactions with affiliated companies.

- Information may be *complex* hence difficult to understand or decipher. Some companies may deliberately report complex transactions, such as mark to market items as derivatives and hedges, or have complex activities such as defined benefit pension accounting that can be presented in ways that confuse investors.

Any of these conditions may lead to poor decisions if the investor is unaware of the low quality of the information being used. The role of the auditor is to reduce these risks for people who use the information. It is sometimes claimed that sophisticated individuals or organizations like investment analysts do not need such information as they do enough work on their own to ensure that their recommendations are well based. The crises of the last two decades should disabuse all but the most fervent believer in the abilities of analysts to correct for these potential biases. Indeed, the fiscal crisis has shown that even regulators, who have the power to carry out their own investigations, can be misled by self-serving information provided by firms and individuals.

Virtually any information provided by one party to another can be subject to an "audit" if the recipient of the information is concerned about its objectivity, relevance, or reliability. In this book, we focus on situations where an independent third party evaluates financial statements to ensure that they are prepared in accordance with established criteria such as Generally Accepted Accounting Principles (GAAP). So why is an audit of financial statements important to the stakeholders of an organization? At least four general reasons explain the natural demand for auditing:

1. Managers of an enterprise may get sloppy or behave in inappropriate ways if they are not subject to independent scrutiny. An audit helps keep

management honest and motivated since they know that they are being examined and reported on to others.

2. Many stakeholders (employees, casual investors, politicians, and so forth) might not have sufficient expertise to evaluate the quality of financial statements. An audit provides this assurance in an efficient and effective manner.

3. Reliable financial reports, in general, reduce an organization's cost of capital. Since potential investors and their intermediaries use audited information to help make their investment decisions, reducing the risk of unreliable information reduces the risk of surprises and improves investment decisions.

4. Investors and creditors want "insurance" against significant errors or fraud associated with financial statements. Auditors provide a reasonable level of assurance that information received by capital providers is reliable, while maintaining that they do not guarantee that the financial statements are accurate. However, on rare occasions when fraud is uncovered, investors and creditors typically take legal actions against auditors because they believe that the presence of an audit constitutes a virtual guarantee about the quality of information in much the same way that an insurance policy would operate. The insurance versus assurance debate is played out in courtrooms around the world but it is a most pressing issue for companies that can be sued in the US legal system where there is a much greater reliance on the courts to determine the "line in the sand" between assurance and insurance.

The combination of the risks of unreliable information and the benefits of an audit create a natural demand for auditing and related services that arises as a result of economic forces, human nature, and the need to make informed decisions. In other words, the demand for auditing has its roots in the capitalist market system, and some level of auditing would exist even if there were no legal requirements for firms to have an audit. In this book, we specifically examine the audits of financial statements and the role of auditors in maintaining fair and active capital markets as well as providing assurance over the financial statements of important non-public entities such as private companies and not-for-profit entities.

The Role of Auditing in an International Economic System

The demand for auditing is not a new development dependent on modern economic conditions. In ancient times, some auditors worked for the government and sometimes doubled as tax collectors. The auditing profession as we know it today dates from the 1800s and developed as a result of the economic and political forces of the time. Britain was a major economic power as a result of its industrial prowess, far-flung colonial empire, and strong navy. Consequently, the economic base of the country's wealth was scattered all over the world. At the same time, wealth was typically controlled by individuals, families, or family-run banks, who hired local caretakers to run the day-to-day operations of their widespread interests. A major concern of these wealthy and powerful individuals was that their distant assets were properly maintained and utilized by local caretakers. The early emphasis of auditing was on asset stewardship, meaning verification of the existence and proper handling of assets. As a result, auditing professionals tended to follow the assets, often to some ports-of-call that, at the time, were considered very exotic (like Cleveland, Ohio, in the US).

In that same period of time, these wealthy individuals, families, and banks, as well as other nascent entrepreneurs, wanted the protection of limited liability so they could raise capital for such useful enterprises as railways and canals. Limited liability meant that the total loss to an investor would be the amount they invested in the company and they could not have their personal assets seized if the company's debts exceeded its ability to pay. However, prior history with the corporate form of organization had caused British lawmakers to ban the incorporated company in the 1720s (e.g., "Google" the story behind the South Seas Bubble) with some notable exceptions (e.g., the British East India Company). In the 1830s and 1840s as the exceptions became more and more numerous a new social compact was formed. The British government allowed the formation of limited liability companies on a routine basis subject to the requirement that they file audited financial statements even if the company was not open to public investment. Thus was born what became known as the statutory audit of financial statements, one that is required in order to obtain the right to have limited liability attached to the investment in the stock of a company.

Hence, both economic and political considerations laid the foundation for auditing in the Anglo-Saxon world. During the short period of global dominance of those countries from the 1850s to 1950s auditing spread to most of the rest of the developed world and increasingly in the developing and underdeveloped economies.

This early model of auditing started to change, especially in the US, in the early years of the 1990s. The breakup of the large investment trusts like Standard Oil in the US led to the need for any large corporation to have sources of equity beyond what the small number of wealthy individuals and US banks could provide. Hence, an increasing number of companies issued common shares to the general public leading to a new class of investors in the middle class being formed in what previously had been a mostly wealthy oriented activity. Due to this expanded shareholding, the role of both accounting and auditing began to change because outside investors were more concerned with future profitability than stewardship of specific assets. Hence, new approaches to accrual accounting were developed, along with refocusing auditing on the results of accrual accounting (in other words, the income or earnings rather than the assets on the balance sheet). Profitability became the basis for assessing and predicting share values, and measuring and verifying financial results became the dominant concern of accountants and auditors.

As such, modern business enterprises have a great deal in common whether they manufacture cars, sell food, provide healthcare, or loan money. These similarities include the need to procure capital, acquire productive assets, sell products or services, collect payment from customers, and, eventually,

When a customer logs on to Amazon.com or any of its country-specific affiliated sites to shop for books, music, movies, and a dizzying array of other products and services, they are accessing the computerized information system of Amazon. That is, the customers are effectively inside the information system of Amazon. Further, Amazon not only hosts its own stores but is providing a platform for other stores to establish an Internet presence. This creates both opportunities and challenges for Amazon. First, such access serves to improve customer service and reduce administrative costs as customers can place orders, check on order status, store items for future purchase, process returns and provide feedback, all without the intervention of a human employee. However, Amazon would not want customers, and even more so the competitors that it also hosts, to roam electronically around the entire IT system so electronic boundaries must be put in place (for example, retail customers should not be allowed to change posted price lists but stores that Amazon hosts must be able to change their prices at will). Given the power of technology, those boundaries can be placed at various locations within the electronic world of Amazon and are not relegated to the front door, or checkout counter, as would be the case in a traditional "bricks and mortar" retailer.

provide adequate returns to investors. The specifics of operations, however, may vary dramatically from business to business and even more so between companies in different industries. For example, capital may be obtained by borrowing money from a bank or by selling common stock in a public offering; products may be manufactured or purchased from another vendor; and sales may be made through retail outlets, catalogs, telemarketing, or the Internet.

Large and small business enterprises, not-for-profit entities, and governmental organizations all need relevant and reliable information since the quality of decision making at all levels is directly affected by the quality of information used to make decisions. All organizations have some type of accounting and information system. In some organizations, the accounting system is highly sophisticated and complex. In these cases, computerized databases may be used to capture desired information which can then be sorted, aggregated, and reported in different ways depending on the needs of the audience. In other organizations, the accounting system may be rather informal, going down to the most basic level of a check book and shoe box of receipts, although such informal "systems" are disappearing with the rise of very low cost accounting software that can be run on a laptop computer. Regardless of the circumstances though, the need for reliable information is important[i].

Furthermore, businesses operate in a global, real-time marketplace in which developing and maintaining a competitive advantage has become increasingly difficult. The cycle of reporting and using information has become increasingly dynamic, almost fluid, to the extent that users of information are looking for ways to understand not only how well an organization is performing now but also how well it can be expected to perform in the future. This task is made more complex by the reduction in barriers between countries, industries, and market participants. As companies become more and more innovative in their production and distribution processes, even boundaries between organizations become blurred. For example, just-in-time inventory systems necessitate an extensive degree of integration between the information systems of two or more companies. In fact, technology has the power to make traditional boundaries virtually invisible.

Adding further complexity to technology developments are changes in the ways businesses conduct some of their basic operations. Many independent organizations are linked with strategic partners such that the performance and actions by one party will impact the performance of other parties. These relationships often are complex and involve organizations in different countries and/or industries. To illustrate, consider a Japanese automotive company that manufactures vehicles in Canada for sale in North America. Some of the parts and components will be manufactured by suppliers in Canada while others will be manufactured in Japan, Thailand, the US, or Mexico and shipped to Canada. The information needs for this company are highly complex. First, the company must design vehicles based on projected consumer preferences, technological developments, and regulatory requirements. The company must forecast sales to make decisions related to facility location, production planning, coordination with suppliers, labor management, and distribution. Furthermore, given the degree of integration with suppliers, unforeseen disruptions anywhere in the supply chain can result in an expensive factory shutdown (e.g., floods in Thailand in 2011 disrupted production for Toyota all over the world). Finally, the company must know where to move completed vehicles to maximize the efficiency of product sales and distribution.

In short, access to good information can be used to acquire wealth and power; lack of good information may lead to failure. Accountants who oversee the company's information systems, and auditors who audit the financial statements, are uniquely positioned to increase the usefulness of information which ultimately contributes to the economic growth of a society.

The Demand for Assurance: Integrity, Trust, and Risk

As discussed in the last section, the history of auditing suggests that it arises both naturally from economic activity and is in part a social contract between the government and entrepreneurs who want the advantages of limited liability. To illustrate this view more concretely, consider a company that wishes to obtain a bank loan in order to purchase equipment. Normally the company will have to provide financial statements to the bank as well as other information about its assets. The bank may be willing to loan money to the company but will protect itself against the risk of being misled by charging a risk premium in the form of higher interest rates. Sometimes, the bank will also require a personal guarantee by the owner that negates limited liability for the bank as a creditor. The bank will forgo some of this risk premium and may not require a personal guarantee of the owner if the company agrees to submit audited financial statements that report the results of operations and the financial status at the end of the year. Some accounting academics have reported that this interest rate reduction alone may be as great as 50 basis points (½ percent).[1]

Consider another typical business story: In the early stages of a start-up business, the founder may supervise everything and perform the most critical tasks. If the business is successful, two things happen. First, it gets bigger so that more help is needed and some management responsibility must be turned over to others. Second, the transactions of the company become more numerous and more complicated. For example, the company may lease some of its locations using long-term leases or extend employee benefits to include health insurance and retirement benefits. The natural result of growth means the owner can no longer directly observe all actions and decisions and give them his personal approval. By the time the business reaches this stage, the owner no doubt wishes to have his personal assets protected from creditors by having limited liability. Furthermore, he or she may not have the expertise to evaluate the handling of complicated transactions such as long-term leases and employee benefits. As this growth continues, he or she will become more dependent on performance reports prepared by managers and accountants. Hence, the owner must be concerned with the accuracy of those reports. The managers preparing the reports may accidentally make mistakes, or may intentionally misstate the results to show their own performance in a positive light.

These illustrations highlight the need for integrity and trust in economic activities. A lack of trust may cause potential market participants to avoid getting involved in situations where integrity may be lacking. A bank will not loan funds to a person it does not trust and an owner will not employ individuals of questionable character. A used car dealer may *say* that a specific car is reliable and free from problems, but in the absence of an independent confirmation that it has not been in a past accident or that its parts are not defective or worn out, a buyer is unlikely to trust the dealer completely. At best, the buyer will offer a low price for the car; at worst, the buyer will go somewhere else.

Management reports their performance to owners and other interested parties in the annual financial statements. However, managers are subject to two potentially offsetting forces that might influence the likelihood that they will misstate financial results for their own benefit: (1) incentives for showing good performance, and (2) ethical principles that emphasize honest dealing. **Incentives** refers to motivational forces such as bonuses or contingent compensation that may push a manager to work hard to achieve goals and objectives, but may also motivate an individual to lie or employ accounting "tricks" when the goals are not met. **Ethical principles** provide a counterweight to perverse incentives by defining norms of behavior or conduct for individuals and organizations that define inappropriate actions and activities.

Incentives

Why do organizations create incentives? Normally the goal is to increase the individual manager's commitment to achieving the broad goals of the organization. Monetary and non-monetary incentives have been found to lead, on average, to better individual decisions and greater overall productivity. However, the key words are "on average better" allowing for a wide range of behavior that may not be in the best interests of third parties (e.g., investors). This results from an uneven distribution of information among individuals making it difficult for third parties to observe the behavior of managers. **Information asymmetry** occurs when one party (e.g., the supplier of information) knows more about the quality of the information provided (in other words, reliability) than another party (the user of the information). Third parties are aware of the possibility that others may misrepresent information or take advantage of circumstances for personal gain so a certain degree of distrust will arise among parties in an economic relationship. Economists have identified two situations where incentives and information asymmetry combine to create potentially dysfunctional distrust: (1) **adverse selection**, and (2) **moral hazard**.

Adverse selection exists when a buyer of products or services cannot distinguish between good and bad alternatives. Is that car really reliable? Is that restaurant really as good as they advertise? Can I believe the information on the job candidate's resume? Are these financial statements really prepared in accordance with GAAP? In all these examples, the seller (management) knows more about the product/service (financial statements) than the buyer (investor/creditor) does. If the buyer or investor or creditor is uncomfortable enough with this information asymmetry, he or she may walk away from any association with the seller—no car sales, no dinners, no jobs, no loans, no investment.

Furthermore, even if a company is a valuable investment with excellent future prospects, potential investors may only be willing to offer a low price for the company's shares if they cannot discriminate good quality from a poor quality investment. In the extreme, the market for the company's shares may collapse if there are no buyers willing to trust management. To avoid this possibility, management has an incentive to provide trustworthy information about the company so that prospective buyers can sort out good investments from bad. This need creates an economic role for assurance about the reliability of information, thus the need for an auditor. Adverse selection in the financial reporting context usually refers to whether investors have credible information for determining if an investment is "good" or "bad." Absent such information, investors will reduce the price they are willing to pay for a company's stock, avoid a company's securities altogether, or even avoid an entire market (e.g., stock exchanges in countries infamous for their level of corruption).

The second problem related to information asymmetry is **moral hazard**, which refers to how individuals (managers) behave when their actions cannot be observed by other stakeholders, or when they are not held accountable for their decisions by those to whom they report. To illustrate, if a manager knows that his or her actions cannot be directly observed by the owners of the company, he or she may have an inclination to "goof off" or to consume corporate resources for his or her own personal benefit (such as expensive and unnecessary travel, fancy meals, corporate funded transportation, club memberships, or low interest personal loans). The less likely the owner is to observe this behavior, the more likely it is to occur and to result in problems. These inappropriate behaviors—at least from the owner's perspective—are referred to as **shirking**. Moral hazard in financial reporting refers to situations where owners do not have enough reliable and trustworthy information to evaluate whether management is doing a good job or not.

The owner is not without recourse, however. Knowing full well that the manager cannot be observed at all times, the owner will then be inclined to pay the manager less for his or her services. The cost of inappropriate behavior by the manager and the manager's loss of earnings attributable to the owner's distrust are often referred to as **agency costs**. Accurate and trustworthy information about the manager's actions provides a way in which to avoid agency costs. Hence, it can be argued that the manager has incentives to hire an independent auditor to report on the quality of the financial information.

Ethical Principles

Ethical principles influence the willingness of individuals, particularly managers, to take part in inappropriate activities that can arise as a result of information asymmetry. To determine if a decision has an ethical dimension, an individual can simply ask: "If this action were to appear on the front page of the local paper, would I be ashamed or concerned?" Ethical behavior by individuals comes from their own internalization of what is ethical, based in part on the behavioral norms of society and the organization. Consequently, ethical principles and their interpretation can vary widely from person to person. There are a variety of philosophical perspectives that expound on the nature and value of societal norms:

- **Utilitarianism** involves making those decisions that will result in an increase in the benefits to some while doing no harm to others.
- **Golden Rule** involves making decisions that result in treating others in a manner in which the individual making the decision would like to be treated.
- **Theory of Rights** suggests that the rights of a decision maker and other parties should be equally balanced in making a decision.
- **Theory of Justice** suggests that decisions should treat all stakeholders fairly, impartially, and equitably.
- **Enlightened Self-Interest** involves making decisions in all parties' long-term self-interests and avoiding a short-term focus that might harm others.

Although these perspectives differ in what they emphasize, the norms that follow from each perspective facilitate ethical decision making. Individual norms may be further affected by the organization that employs an individual. Consequently, it is important for stakeholders to understand how an organization approaches the ethical dimension of its decisions, communicates the need for ethical considerations throughout the organization, and implements decisions that are consistent with reasonable standards of ethical behavior. Again, however, the priority that individuals will give to ethical norms depends on many factors and can lead to a wide range of behaviors given the circumstances of an organization.

In principle, individuals can react in one of three ways when they encounter a situation in which decisions may be ethically questionable. One easy reaction is to do nothing, that is, to *remain loyal* to those making unethical decisions by choosing to actively or passively collude in the unethical practices (e.g., many employees at Enron participated in the company's unethical practices, often enriching themselves, or knew about them and did nothing). Indeed, some individuals exhibit a level of organizational or interpersonal loyalty that disguises the fact (even to them) that they have been complicit in unethical behavior. Another response would be to *exit from the situation*, that is, to quit because of unethical decisions but without informing others who have a legitimate stake in the practices of the organization. Finally, the response that is often the most difficult to pursue is to *voice concern* or to warn others about unethical practices (e.g., a whistleblower who informs others in authority of unethical practices). In other words, the individual actively tries to rectify the unethical organizational practices albeit normally involving a personal cost[(ii)].

Full and complete disclosure of information about the performance of an organization goes a long way to discourage unethical decisions because few people are willing to undertake actions that will make them look bad (or worse, guilty) if the public were to find out. Hence, managers who have ethical norms that enable them to recognize ethical dilemmas are less likely to take advantage of information asymmetry and are more likely to do the "right" thing when confronted with an ethical dilemma.

The Role of Corporate Governance

The problems related to adverse selection, moral hazard and ethical breakdowns are so important to the stakeholders of most organizations that a system for dealing with these risks has developed over time, referred to as **corporate governance**. Corporate governance involves oversight of management's activities, including establishing strategy, conducting operations to achieve strategic objectives and manage risks, and communicating effectively with key stakeholders. A system of corporate governance usually includes the Board of Directors, committees of the board such as the Audit Committee and Compensation Committee, the internal auditor, and the external auditor.

Most public companies elect those charged with corporate governance using a process in which shareholders vote (with the number of votes normally equaling the number of common shares owned) on who will serve on the Board of Directors. Ideally, most board members will be from outside the company but some members may have executive positions within the company (called insiders or executive directors) or other economic links with the organization. Directors who also serve as the external legal counsel, or are senior executives with a significant supplier of the company, are referred to as "gray directors" because they are neither insiders nor outsiders in the strictest sense but their economic future is related in part to that of the firm whose board they serve on.

An important Board of Directors' subcommittee is the Audit Committee whose role is to monitor on behalf of the board and shareholders management's financial reporting process. In most Anglo-Saxon countries the board's Audit Committee consists of at least three board members who are not considered insiders. Other countries have similar rules; these frequently call for only the majority of the Audit Committee members to be outsiders. A common responsibility of the Audit Committee is to hire, terminate and determine the compensation of the external audit firm on behalf of the Board of Directors and shareholders. This is a legal requirement for publicly traded companies in the US and is increasingly required elsewhere in the world. Typically, the Audit Committee is briefed on the audit plans of both the external audit firm and the company's own internal auditors, receives all correspondence from auditors during the engagement, and assists in resolving accounting or other disagreements between auditors and management.

Given the importance of the Audit Committee for fostering reliable financial reporting, the criteria for being a member may be higher than for simply being a member of the Board of Directors. In the US, each member of the committee must be financially literate, with one member being a financial expert. To be **financially literate**, a committee member must be able to read and understand financial statements appropriate for the complexity associated with the organization. To be a **financial expert**, a committee member must have served an accounting role or supervised accountants in a previous or current position such that it can be expected that he or she would have an in-depth understanding of the organization's financial statements. Ultimately, the ability of the external auditor to communicate with the Audit Committee is critical to conducting an effective audit because the interests (iii)**EXAMPLE**

In 2004, Deloitte & Touche LLP became concerned by accounting policies established by the CFO of Molex, Inc. Further, the CEO admitted to having signed the letter of representations (relating to the audit) without having first read the document. Based on these and other issues, Deloitte demanded that the Board of Directors of Molex terminate both the CEO and the CFO. When the board decided against such action, Deloitte & Touche resigned as auditors. Only after the board yielded and demoted both the CEO and CFO was the Audit Committee able to retain a new auditing firm, Ernst & Young LLP.

of the auditor and the Audit Committee are likely to be the same, that is, to produce reliable financial reports.[2 (iii)]

Another important part of a public company's corporate governance is the Compensation Committee of the Board of Directors. This committee is charged with overseeing executive compensation and to provide reports to the shareholders about the amount and nature of compensation given to individuals. These committees have been under scrutiny in the US because of the allegedly excessive compensation packages offered to senior executives in the form of salary, bonuses, and stock-based compensation.

Internal auditors are employed by the company itself and are seen as a key component of corporate governance oversight in larger companies. Internal auditors as company employees are primarily responsible for monitoring on behalf of senior management and the Board of Directors the effectiveness and efficiency of operations, including the reliability of processes that handle information within the organization. The existence, extent, and quality of internal auditing activities directly affects the quality of internal control within the organization. This role is considered so important that in the US, under the provisions of the Sarbanes-Oxley Act, large public companies are required to have an internal audit function that reports to the Audit Committee of the Board of Directors.

Although all of these mechanisms are helpful in reducing problems related to adverse selection and moral hazard, there are limitations on their effectiveness. Internal auditors work for the company's managers they audit, hence the effectiveness of board oversight is dependent on the quality of information they receive from management for evaluating management. Not exactly an independent nor impartial view. Thus, external auditors play a critical role in the system of corporate governance because they are independent and provide assurance about the quality of information available to the board and investors. While a more robust check on managers than internal auditors, under the current system of engaging audit firms, company managers have a significant say on which audit firm is hired and how much they are paid either directly or indirectly via advice to the Audit Committee or board.

The Role of the External Auditor

Since incentives may push managers into actions or decisions that are undesirable to other stakeholders, and because personal and organizational ethical principles are an incomplete or uneven brake on undesirable practices, a role develops naturally in capital markets for an auditor to reduce the effects of information asymmetry and questionable ethics. More specifically, providers and users of information may agree to bring in a third-party to evaluate the extent to which information is objective, relevant, reliable, and understandable. The **auditor** is considered a trusted arbiter of the information. To be useful, however, an auditor must be free of conflicts of interest with the supplier and user of the information, possess adequate expertise, be able to evaluate the reliability of the information, and understand the context in which the information is being conveyed.

However, auditors are people too, and they face incentives that may cause them to act in an unethical fashion. Given British history that required an external audit as part of the contract that led to incorporation and limited liability, the payment of the external auditor was made by the firm being audited in order to satisfy its filing requirements with legal authorities. When the role of the auditor changed to become more of a guardian of third parties, like shareholders, the decision was made to continue with the prior practice of the auditor being paid by the company being audited. At the time it was thought that the adherence of auditors to profession-based Codes of Conduct, as well as the relative scarcity of auditors, would encourage an auditor to quit a client that wanted something done that was not in accordance with GAAP, thus mitigating the negative incentives to auditors of being hired and compensated by client management. However, as companies became larger and accounting firms had more of their revenue dependent on a few large clients, it also became more costly for an auditor to "fire the client." As a result, external auditors faced increasing cost constraints and time pressure imposed by client management. These incentives and pressures may tempt auditors to act in ways that are unethical. Market pressures on the auditing profession in the 1990s led to an unprecedented level of competition among assurance firms. The resulting downward pressure on audit fees led to two potentially devastating developments: (1) reduced audit effort on individual engagements due to low profitability of the audit, and (2) an increased emphasis on cross-selling by audit partners of non-assurance services for generating fee growth (consulting) and enhancing firm profitability.

One firm that went too far in both directions was Arthur Andersen, which faced crippling lawsuits arising from audit failures associated with its audits of Waste Management, Sunbeam, Global Crossing, WorldCom, and Enron. In the latter case, Andersen was indicted for failing to follow up on questionable accounting practices at the energy company, known for its high level of intangible assets and complex transactions. Making matters worse, the partner on the engagement pled guilty to obstruction of justice for his role in encouraging the shredding of documents that were likely to be subpoenaed in connection with the Enron engagement. The loss of confidence in Andersen that followed the firm's conviction on felony charges trapped the firm in an oubliette of its own making and eventually led to dissolution of the firm during 2002. The reversal of that conviction in 2005 was a pyrrhic victory given that the firm itself had ceased to exist and given that, while a new trial could have been held, there was no public interest reason for the government to prosecute a bankrupt entity.

The Andersen audit of Enron hopefully taught audit firms a powerful lesson—*no amount of revenue can justify abdicating or appearing to abdicate an auditor's professional responsibilities.* Considerable emphasis throughout this book will be placed on the need for the auditor to recognize the effects of the inherent conflicts of interests that arise as a result of the audit firm being paid by the client as well as other ethical dilemmas and deal with them properly when they arise. Because of the importance of ethical decision making by auditors, both the accounting profession and society have rules and regulations to help auditors to recognize ethical problems and to react appropriately.

Differentiating Assurance, Attestation, Auditing, and Accounting

Before going further, we need to define some terms more precisely. Assurance and auditing are very broad concepts, and go beyond the basic audit of financial statements. While the concept of assurance is fundamental to auditing, not all accountants agree as to what constitutes an engagement to provide assurance. For example, evaluating the reliability of corporate performance reports or the effectiveness of management in complying with legal regulations could both be considered assurance services. Currently, the most general and succinct definition of **assurance services** is suggested by the American Institute of Certified Public Accountants (AICPA 1996 Report of the Special Committee on Assurance Services):

> Independent professional services that improve the quality of information, or its context, for decision makers.

Although this definition is not an official standard of the profession, it suggests a broad range of professional services that an accountant/auditor can provide to a variety of clients and clearly pertains to the reliability of information[iv].

Assurance services can also apply to a large set of general decision making issues. For example, assurance providers can address questions about the relevance of information used in making decisions, the viability of a company's business plan, the appropriateness of its business processes, the effectiveness of its attempts to reduce risks, and the quality of its decision processes. Although the boundary is a bit fuzzy, assurance services do not include engagements to provide advice aimed at directly improving the profitability of the organization (such as consulting).

The International Federation of Accountants (IFAC) through its International Auditing and Assurance Standards Board (IAASB) addressed the issue of assurance services in a narrower fashion than the AICPA did in the US. The *International Framework on Assurance Engagements* (Supplement 2014 p. 74) defines an assurance engagement as:

> An assurance engagement is an engagement in which a practitioner aims to obtain sufficient appropriate evidence in order to express a conclusion designed to enhance the degree of confidence of the intended users other than the responsible party about the outcome of the measurement or evaluation of an underlying subject matter against criteria.

AUTHORITATIVE GUIDANCE & STANDARDS

Throughout the remainder of the textbook, authoritative guidance that enhances descriptions of standards in the text will be included in text boxes in this format. Since this book is written to be applicable for auditing courses taught in a variety of pedagogical approaches in a variety of contexts, these boxes help illustrate that each topic in the text is consistent with International Standards on Auditing created by the International Auditing and Assurance Standards Board (IAASB) as well as those standards issued by the US based Public Company Accounting Oversight

Board (PCAOB). As the US Auditing Standards Board is converging IAASB standards, we do not separately discuss them in this text. Standards are not embedded within the text each time the topic is mentioned but rather are set in boxes similar to this one. This approach reinforces the idea that an audit complies with the standards but is not driven by the standards.

International Standards make the distinction between: (1) a direct reporting engagement, and (2) an attest engagement. In a ***direct reporting engagement***, the practitioner measures and evaluates information directly.[3] The nature of the measurement or evaluation is provided to the intended users in an assurance report. For example, the audit firm PWC counts and reports the votes for the Academy Awards. The process of counting votes represents a direct reporting engagement.

AUTHORITATIVE GUIDANCE & STANDARDS

*IAASB International Standards on Assurance Engagements (***International Framework for Assurance Engagements,** *ISAE 3000* **Assurance Engagements Other than Audits or Reviews of Historical Financial Information***) and on Related Services (ISRS 4400* **Engagements to Perform Agreed-Upon Procedures Regarding Financial Information***) and PCAOB Interim Standard AT 101* **Attest Engagements** *and AT 601* **Compliance Attestation** *provide professional standards in this area. The IAASB has dedicated resources to develop specific assurance services standards on such areas as greenhouse gas emissions statements (ISAE 3410* **Assurance Engagements on Greenhouse Gas Statements***) and is considering other specific area standards. The PCAOB has so far not ventured into assurance or attestation standards beyond adopting the legacy AICPA Auditing Standards Board (ASB) existing standards as of 2003 as part of their set of standards.*

Attestation is the process of providing assurance about the reliability of specific information provided by one party to another. Attestation focuses on a specified assertion that is made in writing. The professional who is providing an attestation does not usually generate original information since that is the responsibility of the party reporting the information. The attester is simply adding his or her opinion about the reliability of the information. Figure 1.1 shows attestation as a subset of assurance engagements. An attest service cannot be a direct reporting engagement[(v)].

The most common form of attestation pertains to the verification of financial reports. As a result, auditing and "accounting" are integrally entwined. More specifically, **accounting** is the process by which information about an activity or enterprise is identified, recorded, classified, aggregated, and reported. Most often, the information of interest relates to the monetary effects of economic events that have an impact upon the enterprise. ***Financial accounting*** refers to the specific process of identifying, recording, classifying, aggregating, and reporting the information that is required for external purposes that has historically been called ***generally accepted accounting principles*** (GAAP).

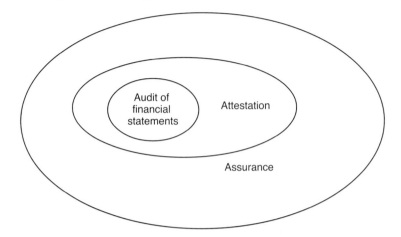

Figure 1.1 *Relationship between Assurance, Attestation, and Financial Statement Auditing*

Financial accounting is a subset of the total information that is generated by a business enterprise. In the US, the Financial Accounting Standards Board (FASB) issues standards for financial reporting that must be followed by all public companies headquartered in the US and in many cases, but not all, companies that are registered with the US Securities and Exchange Committee (SEC), the regulator of US stock markets. Most countries in the rest of the world follow GAAP as defined by the International Accounting Standards Board (IASB), often with some allowances for local differences as determined by national standard setters. In Europe, IASB standards are required for all entities traded on stock exchanges and for group accounts but local GAAP may continue to be used for individual country based subsidiaries. To reduce the chance of confusion, increasingly audit reports have to include a reference to the exact source of GAAP (e.g., FASB, IFRS, national accounting standards, etc.) that were used to prepare the financial statements.

Auditing is the process of providing assurance about the reliability of the information contained in a financial report prepared by management in accordance with GAAP. Management generates the financial reports based on its interpretation of GAAP and the external auditor examines them in accordance to what we will call **generally accepted auditing standards** (GAAS), suggests changes to client management where the auditor believes GAAP has not been applied correctly, and reports to the shareholders the results of the audit. In the world outside the US, IAASB, a group established by the International Federation of Accountants, establishes GAAS albeit with an allowance for local adaption where national audit standard setters or legislation requires. In the US there are two sources of GAAS. For public companies registered with the US SEC (including companies that are headquartered anywhere in the world but traded on US stock exchanges) the PCAOB is the source of GAAS. For private companies and other entities in the US, The American Institute of Certified Public Accountants' (AICPA) Auditing Standards Board (ASB) creates GAAS for private companies and other entities in the US. To make matters somewhat simpler, going forward all standards set by the AICPA's ASB will converge to those of the IAASB resulting in fewer GAAS differences in audits of international and US-based non-public clients. Hence, to simplify presentation we will not refer to the AICPA's current ASB standards. The standards referred to in the text boxes "**Authoritative Guidance & Standards**" will include both the IAASB and the PCAOB standards including the PCAOB interim standards based on the AICPA ASB standards that the PCAOB adopted in 2003. Finally, the PCAOB recently adopted a new organizational format, including renumbering, for its auditing standards. We will note these new standard numbers in brackets following the current title of the PCAOB standard.

The Nature of Assurance and Attestation Engagements

Although the range of potential assurance services that an accountant can provide is very broad, there are some general guidelines as to when an accountant should or should not provide specific services. In general, an auditor or public accountant should only undertake an *assurance engagement* when three conditions are met:

1. He or she has adequate knowledge of the context in which assurance is to be given.
2. The subject matter of the assurance can be examined with an objective evaluation process.
3. The assurance provider must be independent and objective in regards to the information and its context.

Examples of assurance services that are commonly provided by auditors and public accountants include:

*   *Environmental audits* to test compliance with environmental laws and regulations.
*   *Ethics audits* to evaluate management's compliance with the norms of ethical decision making.
*   *Software audits* to test the reliability of commercial software.
*   *Royalty audits* to determine proper amounts for licensing fees or royalty payments.
*   *Utilization audits* to verify key operating data such as occupancy rates or attendance levels.
*   *Investment performance audits* to verify yields on managed portfolios and mutual funds.
*   *Cost audits* to verify data used in computing reimbursements under cost-sharing contracts.

The general criteria for offering *attestation services* are somewhat more specific than an assurance engagement. In an attest engagement, a public accountant is engaged to issue a written communication that expresses a conclusion about the reliability of a written assertion made by one party to another (as illustrated in Figure 1.2). To offer such services, the accountant should meet four basic conditions:

1. There must be an assertion being made by one party, the accuracy of which is of interest to another party. This assertion may be quantitative or qualitative in nature.

Figure 1.2 *Three parties involved in an attest engagement*

2. There must exist agreed-upon and objective criteria that can be utilized to assess the accuracy of the assertion. All parties must agree as to how the assertion is to be evaluated using a common unit of measure and measurement technology.

3. The assertion must be amenable to verification by an independent party. That is, the accountant must be able to obtain adequate, diagnostic evidence to support or refute the assertion being made.

4. The accountant should prepare a written conclusion about the accuracy of the assertion(s).

AUTHORITATIVE GUIDANCE & STANDARDS

IAASB International Standards on Assurance Engagements (**International Framework for Assurance Engagements**, *ISAE 3000* **Assurance Engagements Other than Audits or Reviews of Historical Financial Information**) *and PCAOB Interim Standard AT 101* **Attest Engagements** *and AT 601* **Compliance Attestation** *provide professional standards in this area.*

These conditions clearly apply to the audit of financial statements, which can be considered a special form of attestation engagement. Indeed, we will be spending most of the rest of this book seeing how these conditions apply to the audit of financial statements.

Beyond these general guidelines, specific legal and regulatory constraints may limit the assurance and attestation services that an accountant can offer, or limit to whom some services may be offered. One very important limitation is on the provision of consulting services to audit clients. Drawing the line between assurance and consulting services can be problematic, but the general trend in practice and regulation is to severely limit the types of services than can be provided to an audit client, although the same service might be offered to non-audit clients without restriction.

The Auditing Profession and Regulation

The avoidance of future "Enrons" and other accounting and audit failures was the focus of both accounting and auditing standard setters around the world in the first decade of this century. The second decade has been dominated by improving accounting and auditing so as to avoid future "fiscal crises" that led to the downfall of the banking sector in many Western countries in 2007–09. Consequently, a wide variety of rules govern the public accountant. The accounting profession regulates itself to some extent but it is also subject to extensive government regulation, either directly in national/state/province laws or via regulatory bodies that receive their mandate from the state. The nature and form of self- and government regulation varies from country to country but is generally focused on the need to maintain the integrity of the profession and the trust society has in auditors. Areas affected by regulation include requirements for entering the profession, the organization of accounting firms, and the process for updating and modifying the rules under which professionals are governed. Each of these is discussed in turn below.

Entering the Profession: Education, Training, and Certification

The process for becoming a licensed public accountant varies by country. Almost all countries require: (1) a minimum level of education, (2) testing of applicants, (3) work experience, and (4) continuing post-professional education. Generally, to be a public accountant one needs to be technically competent, independent, and have good judgment. There is also a need for deep understanding of financial statements and generally accepted accounting principles. To practice public accounting and conduct an audit, an auditor needs to be a licensed certified public accountant (CPA), a chartered accountant (CA), chartered professional accountant (also denoted CPA) or hold the appropriate level of certification consistent with the rules of a country. Adequate knowledge of relevant GAAP(s) is implicit for anyone holding a professional accounting certification (such as a CA or CPA). Some countries have a single professional body of accountants who can do audits (such as CPAs in the US), whereas others have competing professional groups that can legally conduct an audit (e.g., in Australia both CPAs and CAs can perform audits). The International Accounting Education Standards Board (IAESB), another Board established by IFAC, is mandated to develop minimal standards for accounting and auditing education around the world as well as recommendations for the minimum work experience required. See Table 1.1 for minimum international standards in these areas.

AUTHORITATIVE GUIDANCE & STANDARDS

IFAC's International Accounting Education Standards Board (IAESB) provides guidance on the minimal education standards that it suggests its member bodies enact as part of pre-professional education and experience requirements as well as post-qualification as a professional accountant continuing education requirements. Member bodies (e.g., AICPA, CPA Australia, Institute of Chartered Accountants in England and Wales, etc.) undertake their best efforts to have these standards incorporated into the legislation that allows professional accountants in their country to call themselves CPAs, CAs or other such titles. As the professional accounting designation is normally given as a result of a regulatory process, individual countries as well as individual states or provinces within decentralized countries might well have provisions that are greater than the minimum level established by IAESB.

Organizational Forms of Public Accounting Firms

The accounting and auditing profession is organized into self-selected groups of professionals that form professional services firms. Although audits require extensive work by individual professionals, most are performed by

Table 1.1 *Selected international accounting education standards requirements*

Pre-professional education (International Education Standard (IES) 1 and 2)	• Entrance into the pre-professional accounting program should be the equivalent of entry into a recognized university degree program.
	• Must include elements of general education.
	• The professional accountancy knowledge component of prequalification education should consist of at least two years of full-time study (or the part-time equivalent).
	• Students should pursue a degree in accounting, or a professional qualification, to gain this knowledge. The content of professional accounting education should consist of:
	  o Accounting, finance and related knowledge;
	  o Organizational and business knowledge; and
	  o Information technology knowledge and competences.

Professional skills (IES 3)	Individuals seeking to become professional accountants should acquire the following skills: (a) Intellectual skills; (b) Technical and functional skills; (c) Personal skills; (d) Interpersonal and communication skills; (e) Organizational and business management skills.
Professional values, ethics, and attitudes (IES 4)	Ethics education should include: (a) The nature of ethics; (b) Differences of detailed rules-based and framework approaches to ethics, their advantages and drawbacks; (c) Compliance with the fundamental ethical principles of integrity, objectivity, commitment to professional competence and due care, and confidentiality; (d) Professional behavior and compliance with technical standards; (e) Concepts of independence, skepticism, accountability, and public expectations; (f) Ethics and the profession: social responsibility; (g) Ethics and law, including the relationship between laws, regulations, and the public interest; (h) Consequences of unethical behavior to the individual, to the profession, and to society at large; (i) Ethics in relation to business and good governance; (j) Ethics and the individual professional accountant: whistle-blowing, conflicts of interest, ethical dilemmas and their resolution.
Practical experience (IES 5)	• The period of practical experience in performing the work of professional accountants should be a part of the pre-qualification program. This period should be long enough and intensive enough to permit candidates to demonstrate they have gained the professional knowledge, professional skills, and professional values, ethics and attitudes required for performing their work with professional competence and for continuing to grow throughout their careers. • Minimum of 3 years with up to 12 months credited for specific integrated professional accounting education.

Entrance Examinations (IES 6)	The assessment of professional capabilities and competence should:
	(a) Require a significant proportion of candidates' responses to be in recorded form;
	(b) Be reliable and valid;
	(c) Cover a sufficient amount of the whole range of professional knowledge, professional skills, and professional values, ethics and attitudes for the assessment to be reliable and valid; and
	(d) Be made as near as practicable to the end of the pre-qualification education program.
Continuing Professional Education and Development (IES 7)	Requirements with respect to continuing professional development can include:
	(a) Complete at least 120 hours or equivalent learning units of relevant professional development activity in each rolling three-year period, of which 60 hours or equivalent learning units should be verifiable.
	(b) Complete at least 20 hours or equivalent learning units in each year.
	(c) Track and measure learning activities to meet the above requirements.

teams of licensed public accountants working within larger accounting firms. In general, there are four types of accounting firms in most countries:

1. *Local*: Sole practitioners or small accounting firms that mostly serve small businesses and not-for-profit organizations in local communities. These firms perform relatively few full-scale audits. They often provide basic accounting services (bookkeeping) and may have a heavy emphasis on tax and other consulting services.

2. *Regional:* Regional accounting firms usually consist of multiple offices of the same firm in one region of a country. These firms typically serve mid-size clients, including publicly owned companies on a relatively limited basis. These firms tend to offer a full array of accounting, taxation and consulting services.

3. *Emergent international:* Emergent international accounting firms generally comprise loose federations of national accounting firms. They often start as federations of regional firms in one country and gradually became integrated national firms. They may have some international integration as well. They tend to compete for small-to-medium size public company audits and medium-to-large private company audits. The largest firms in this category are BDO (with various local affiliates such as BDO Seidman in the US and BDO Spicers in New Zealand) and Grant Thornton.

4. *International:* International accounting firms perform a wide range of services for organizations of many sizes; however, these firms specialize in publicly owned organizations, many of which are multinational. The dominant four firms in this category are Deloitte, Ernst & Young (rebranding as EY as this book is being written), KPMG, and PwC—commonly referred to as the **Big Four.** The number of these firms has been reduced from eight to four over the last twenty-five years.[4]

The hierarchy within an accounting firm is usually based on relative levels of experience among the professional staff. At the top of a firm are the partners. Newly hired employees are referred to as associates or staff and are closely supervised as they learn to apply their academic knowledge in a practical setting. Staff accountants typically perform basic auditing tests, with senior staff assigned more complex audit tests and limited supervisory responsibilities for junior staff. Individuals will usually be promoted to manager in four to six years, taking on many key responsibilities for running the day-to-day operations of an engagement, planning the audit, supervising and reviewing the work of associates, and resolving routine audit issues. Senior managers perform activities that may lead to promotion to partner such as client development, resolution of complex audit issues, and collection of fees. Managers deemed qualified are voted as partners by the existing partners of the firm. Partners have a claim to net revenues of the accounting firm but also are liable for partnership losses. Some firms also have a permanent position called "principal" or "associate partner" for people that are more skilled and experienced than managers but who will not be admitted to the partnership of the firm either by their own choice or by firm policy.

One effect of structuring accounting firms as partnerships is the potential legal liability that may arise if professionals within the firm provide substandard services, that is, audits that do not meet the profession's standards of quality. The most visible and unfortunate form of a breakdown in audit quality occurs when an auditor certifies a company's financial statements that turn out to be misleading or fraudulent. In such circumstances, the individual auditor and the firm may be held accountable by the legal system. Sometimes, the partners in the firm must pay large settlements to stakeholders who relied on misleading financial statements. To protect against high levels of personal liability, many firms form **limited liability partnerships** (LLP) or **limited liability corporations** (LLC), which provide some protection for individual partners against the mistakes made by others in their firm.

Regulating the Auditing Profession

Following Enron and other audit failures in the US, the US Congress passed the Sarbanes-Oxley Act of 2002, which regulated the auditing profession for public companies by stripping the profession of its ability to self-regulate and self-assess its quality control in the area of public company audits replacing it with the PCAOB, which is charged with supervising and regulating audit firms and their practices. Additionally, the Sarbanes-Oxley Act of 2002 changed some of the common practices of the US-based accounting profession. For example, audit firms were prohibited from performing certain non-audit related services for their audit clients that they had previously been allowed to provide (e.g., information systems consulting). As a result, at most public companies, those charged with corporate governance reacted by limiting auditors to the audit engagement only, regardless of whether other services were allowable under the law.

The PCAOB regulates who can conduct audits of publicly traded companies in the US. An audit firm that wishes to audit publicly traded companies must register with the PCAOB and be subject to inspection by PCAOB review teams. Inspections are performed on an annual basis if the firm audits 100 or more US SEC registered clients or every third year if it audits fewer than 100 clients. Most regional, all emergent international, and all international firms are registered firms, whereas most local firms are not registered.

In many other countries, accounting firms perform audits in accordance with GAAS as established by the IAASB. In some cases, the standards of the IAASB are supplemented with oversight by a local authority, such as CPA Canada's Auditing and Assurance Standards Board. Fraud and audit failures around the world (such as Parmalat in Italy and Barclay's in the United Kingdom) suggest that enhanced scrutiny of the auditor is likely to continue. Yet most other countries to date have resisted the level of government regulation that is now the hallmark of the US audit profession, albeit there have been recent moves in Europe by the European Commission to take a much more active role in the audit market.[5]

The move toward two major bodies of auditing standards on a worldwide basis is particularly lauded by international auditing firms who have previously had to comply with rules from many jurisdictions (such as PCAOB standards for publicly owned companies, ASB standards for privately held US companies, IAASB standards for many non-US companies, and local standards for companies in some countries). Furthermore, by concentrating standard setting in fewer organizations, more resources can be devoted to developing the best possible auditing standards, with a significant reduction in the redundancy of standard setting across multiple jurisdictions.

Knowledge and Skills Needed By Auditors in the Twenty-First Century

During the past decade, the auditing profession underwent an unprecedented number of rapid changes, particularly in the US. The 1990s started with many of the largest global accounting firms implementing new audit approaches that emphasized a deep understanding of a client's business environment and risks relating to a company's strategies and processes in order to facilitate the assessment of risks related to financial reporting. This shift occurred partially in response to frauds that occurred in the late 1980s and early 1990s that were not detected by auditors because of an insufficient understanding of how organizations operated within their respective industries. Furthermore, the technology boom of the 1990s that accompanied the shift to an information age changed the way information is created, processed, and communicated. Also complicating matters was the increase in highly complex transactions such as financial derivatives. Taken together, these developments increased the challenges facing auditors in verifying financial reports.

This textbook describes auditing within the context of current economic, regulatory, and global conditions. The conduct of a financial statement audit has become increasingly complex and the skill set necessary to perform effective and efficient audits has expanded greatly in recent years. The critical skills and knowledge needed by auditors are far ranging. The materials in the book and its on-line supplements are developed to provide exposure to a wide range of issues in auditing. More specifically, this book will help students to:

- Develop an understanding of the role of auditing and corporate governance in ensuring reliable financial reporting and appropriate behavior by stakeholders.
- Understand how organizations design and carry out corporate strategies that affect financial reporting.
- Evaluate how business processes and strategic alliances that affect financial reporting are designed and implemented.
- Assess the effect of external forces on organizations in an international marketplace.
- Assess how internal forces create risk within an organization.
- Evaluate control responses to organizational risks.
- Integrate business knowledge about an organization with accounting knowledge to develop expectations about financial reporting.
- Link an understanding of an organization's business risks to concerns about financial reporting and the need for audit testing.
- Develop critical thinking, ethical reasoning, and problem solving skills to enable careful, objective analysis of audit issues.

The Plan of the Book

In this chapter we have started to develop an understanding about the environment in which the audit takes place. Chapters 2 and 3 expand on this discussion by examining what is meant by risk in the corporate environment and then discussing how the audit acts as a risk management activity that focuses on the auditor's key responsibilities of prevention and detection of financial statement fraud and an assessment of the ability of the entity to continue as a going concern.

We then move into the key information gathering and analysis process that enables the auditor to determine the extent of his or her audit of a particular client. We explain how the auditor obtains an in-depth knowledge of the client's business starting from gathering basic factoids about the business (Chapter 4) to an in-depth understanding of the client's strategy (Chapter 5) to understanding how the client puts its strategy into effect (Chapter 6). Throughout these chapters we identify the key means that management uses to control the risks associated with developing and implementing its strategy including both management controls and process controls always keeping in mind that the auditor's goal is to identify risks of material misstatement for the audit of the financial statements.

After thoroughly understanding the business and how its risks relate to the risk of material misstatement, we then delve into internal controls over financial reporting. Chapter 7 focuses on internal controls over financial reporting that are applicable to all audits, whereas Chapter 8 focuses on the additional examination of internal control that needs to take place if an auditor is going to issue an opinion on the effectiveness of internal controls over financial reporting. The latter opinion is required by the Sarbanes-Oxley Act of 2002 for all companies from anywhere in the world that are registered with the United States Securities and Exchange Commission to trade on any US based stock exchange, subject to a permanent exemption for US traded public companies that meet the requirements to be considered a small issuer (generally less than $100 million in market capitalization).

Chapter 9 then highlights two of the most important and controversial tools that are in an auditor's toolkit: analysis (also known as analytical procedures) and inquiry of client management. These tools, when properly employed, can provide high quality audit evidence about the state of the client's internal controls and about the amounts in the financial statements. Yet these very tools that can be cost effective to use in the modern audit are also subject to much concern from regulators as sloppy use of them has been associated with significant under auditing of clients that turned out to have materially misstated financial statements and ineffective internal controls.

Chapter 10 lays the basis for the next section of the textbook as it summarizes the evidence that has been collected to the start of testing of internal control effectiveness at the business process level. In other words, now that the client's environment has been understood, its control system assessed and documented, how does the auditor carry out an effective and efficient set of tests to ensure himself or herself that the controls are working to the extent that the auditor is relying on them or reporting on their effectiveness as well as the fact that the financial statements are not materially misstated? Chapter 10 thus introduces the considerations needed for planning substantive tests of the financial statements. This lays the basis for a detailed exposition of the tests of the client's implementation of internal controls, and substantive tests of financial statement accounts, balances and disclosures in Chapters 11, 12 and 13. Chapter 11 focuses on the accounts, balances and disclosures associated with the sales and customer service business process, and Chapter 12 focuses on the supply chain and production processes. Chapter 13 considers the resources management processes, including property, plant and equipment, as well as financial management, including financial assets and liabilities of the client.

Chapters 14 and 15 focus on the audit reporting process with Chapter 14 focusing on summarizing the audit evidence that has been collected to date as well as the auditor's processes for ensuring that the audit work has been completely and competently carried out. Chapter 15 focuses on the content of the audit report (or reports when reporting on effectiveness of internal control over financial reporting), as well as the various communications that the auditor must make to those charged with governance of the client firm. Chapter 15 also discusses the complexities that are found in audits of larger clients that are composed of many auditable entities and whose reporting is done on a consolidated basis across an entire group of companies.

The final section of the book features two key topics that can be introduced at any point in the course. Chapter 16 focuses on professional ethics and legal considerations that are associated with auditing. Chapter 17 gives a more in-depth introduction to audit sampling techniques that are employed for both tests of controls and for substantive tests of details beyond the preliminary material introduced in the main part of the text.

Summary and Conclusion

As a result of the Sarbanes-Oxley Act in the US and regulatory changes in other parts of the world, the role of those charged with corporate governance has been increasingly emphasized. To focus the attention of management more directly on the quality of financial reporting, executives determined to be culpable in the production of fraudulent reports will now receive mandatory prison sentences in certain situations. These events have helped the accounting profession in several ways. First, those charged with governance are paying higher fees, albeit not willingly, and increasingly returning to their cost reduction approach, to auditors to ensure that situations such as Enron do not happen again. Second, the scope of auditing is expanding to accommodate new regulations and, more importantly, to reduce the likelihood of the auditor issuing an incorrect opinion. Consequently, accounting firms have seen increases in revenues and demand for personnel that are unprecedented in the first decade of this century, albeit the recession invoked by the Global Fiscal Crisis of 2007–09 has somewhat dented that demand in recent years. Third, it is unlikely that in the foreseeable future the audit will be perceived as a commodity or unessential service to be given to the lowest bidder without consideration of audit quality as it often was in the 1990s. Fourth, the assertion that historical cost-based financial statements are irrelevant and auditors are an anachronism is unlikely to be made again soon!

All of this indicates that the need for assurance is more important than ever for decision makers, particularly for users of financial information in today's complex, real-time global marketplace. Organizations that provide information that is accompanied by independent assurance help maintain stable international capital markets. To provide such assurance, auditors should possess a set of skills that will facilitate the decision processes needed to properly conduct an engagement. For the most part, we will focus on the audit of financial statements, and the remainder of this book is designed to introduce and illustrate the most critical of those skills as well as the institutional and regulatory aspects that determine how audits are performed.

We provide coverage of promulgations by both the IAASB and the PCAOB in the rest of this book. While the audit process described in this book is not dependent on either set of standards, we believe that auditors worldwide need to be familiar with both sets of standards. Many non-US public companies are registered with the US SEC so non-US auditors need an understanding of PCAOB standards. US auditors need to understand international standards since many non-publicly traded clients are audited under the standards of the AICPA ASB, which are being harmonized with the standards of the IAASB. As a result, the largest international audit firms have pushed to have a single audit methodology on a worldwide basis that facilitates compliance with both sets of standards. Our book delivers the best of both standard setting worlds while emphasizing that an audit is much more than a compliance activity that can be done with a cookbook mentality.

Bibliography of Relevant Literature

Research

Blackwell, D. W., T. R. Noland, and D. B. Winters. 1998. The Value of Auditor Assurance: Evidence from Loan Pricing. *Journal of Accounting Research*. 36(1): 57–70.

Copeland Jr., J. E. 2005. Ethics as an Imperative. *Accounting Horizons*. 19(1): 35–43.

Elliott, R. K. 1995. The Future of Assurance Services: Implications for Academia. *Accounting Horizons*. 9(4): 118–127.

Mautz, R. K. and H. A. Sharaf, 1961. *The Philosophy of Auditing*. American Accounting Association Monograph No. 6, Sarasota, FL: American Accounting Association.

Zeff, S. 2003. How the US Accounting Profession got to Where it is Today, Part I *Accounting Horizons*. 17(3): 189–205.

Professional Reports and Guidance

American Institute of Certified Public Accountants. 1994. *Improving Business Reporting—A Customer Focus: Report of the AICPA Special Committee on Financial Reporting (Jenkins Committee)*. New York: AICPA.

American Institute of Certified Public Accountants. 1996. *Report of the AICPA Special Committee on Assurance Services (Elliott Committee)*. New York: AICPA.

Auditing Standards

IAASB (International Audit and Assurance Standards Board). *International Framework for Assurance Engagements*.

IAASB *International Standards on Assurance Engagements*. ISAE 3000 "Assurance Engagements Other than Audits or Reviews of Historical Financial Information."

IAASB, *International Standards on Assurance Engagements*. ISAE 3410 "Assurance Engagements on Greenhouse Gas Statements."

IAASB. *International Standards on Related Services*. ISRS 4400 (previously ISA 920) "Engagements to Perform Agreed-Upon Procedures Regarding Financial Information."

IFAC. International Accounting Education Standards Board (IAESB). 2014. *Handbook of International Education Pronouncements*. New York: International Federation of Accountants.

IFAC. International Ethics Standards Board for Accountants (IESBA). 2015. *Handbook of Code of Ethics for Professional Accountants*. New York: International Federation of Accountants.

IFAC. International Auditing and Assurance Standards Board (IAASB). 2015. *Handbook of International Quality Control, Audit, Review, Other Assurance, and Related Services Pronouncements*. New York: International Federation of Accountants.

PCAOB (Public Company Accounting Oversight Board). 2003. *Interim Standards on Attestation.* Washington DC.

PCAOB *Interim Standard,* AT 101, "Attest Engagements."

PCAOB. *Interim Standard,* AT 601, "Compliance Attestation."

SOX Sarbanes-Oxley Act - Library of Congress. 2002. House Resolution Number 3763, An Act to protect investors by improving the accuracy and reliability of corporate disclosures made pursuant to the securities laws, and for other purposes (*The Sarbanes-Oxley Act of 2002*). www.libraryofcongress.gov.

Notes

1   Blackwell, D. W., T. R. Noland, and D. B. Winters. 1998. The Value of Auditor Assurance: Evidence from Loan Pricing. *Journal of Accounting Research.* 36(1): 57–70.
2   It is also the auditor's responsibility for companies selling securities on US stock exchanges to evaluate the effectiveness of the Audit Committee in carrying out its responsibilities, which can be challenging given the role the Audit Committee now has in hiring and terminating the auditor.
3   Alternatively, the auditor might obtain a representation from a responsible party that has measured and evaluated the relevant information but which cannot be communicated directly to the intended users.
4   According to Stephen Zeff, a prominent accounting historian, the term "Big 8" was made popular in a 1960 article in *Fortune* magazine (see Zeff, S. 2003. How the US Accounting Profession got to Where it is Today, Part I *Accounting Horizons.* 17(3): 189–205).
5   See the European Commission's proposals at http://ec.europa.eu/internal_market/auditing/reform/.

CHAPTER 2

Managing Risk
The Role of Auditing and Assurance

Outline

Learning Goals for this Chapter

1. Describe the objectives of the auditor in carrying out an audit of financial statements.

2. Identify the business risks that occur in firms.

3. Explain how business risks affects the audit of the firm's financial statements.

4. Describe the concepts underlying the enterprise risk management (ERM) framework.

5. Relate the ERM concepts to internal control over financial reporting.

6. Recognize key aspects of the audit and assurance regulatory environment.

7. Examine how auditing and assurance standards aid auditors in carrying out their audits.

Introduction

The financial statements have been the primary focus of auditors for more than 150 years. Accounting standards and auditing technology have become increasingly complex, but the purpose of the audit has not changed—to provide an opinion about the fairness of periodic financial reports. The need for a financial statement audit arises naturally from the needs of external stakeholders, especially investors and creditors, for reliable information about an organization's financial status and performance. Although organizations are able to release this information through various channels (such as corporate web sites or press releases), formal financial statements continue to be the most effective and efficient mechanism for communicating corporate performance to a wide range of stakeholders. Furthermore, stakeholders want to know if the financial information they receive is reliable. Reliable financial reporting is facilitated by the use of established accounting rules as verified by an external auditor and described in the auditor's report.

AUTHORITATIVE GUIDANCE & STANDARDS

International Standards on Auditing are established by the International Auditing and Assurance Standards Board (IAASB). These standards grew out of attempts to harmonize various national auditing standards known historically as generally accepted auditing standards (GAAS). Outside the US, and for non-public companies in the US, International Standards on Auditing (ISAs) form the basis for local auditing standards with supplementary guidance and standards provided by local standard setters. For example, since 2005 the US-based American Institute of Certified Public Accountants' (AICPA) Auditing Standards Board (ASB) has been converging its pre-existing standards to ISAs.

Audits of publicly listed companies in the US are conducted under Auditing Standards (ASs) issued by the Public Company Accounting Oversight Board (PCAOB), which are a mixture of new standards set by the board and legacy standards promulgated by the AICPA's ASB that were in force when the PCAOB was created in 2003. In other words, the ASB standards that existed in 2003 are "frozen" until amended by the PCAOB for audits of publicly listed companies in the US. Thus, the changes made by the ASB to its standards since 2005 do not apply to audits of US publicly listed companies unless the PCOAB incorporates those changes in its new standards.

The auditor's overall objective is to determine if the financial statements of an organization are fairly and consistently reported in accordance with what has been known historically as generally accepted accounting principles (i.e., GAAP). To reach that conclusion, the auditor must obtain sufficient evidence to support the conclusion that the financial results and position are reported appropriately. An audit has four broad objectives:

1. To ensure that financial statements are presented in accordance with GAAP.

2. To deter and, if need be, detect material fraudulent financial reporting carried out by an organization's management.

3. To evaluate the likelihood that the organization will continue as a going concern.

4. To report the conclusions from those evaluations to interested stakeholders.

In addition, a fifth objective exists for audits of public companies registered with the US Securities and Exchange Commission (SEC) for trading of securities in the US:

5. *Evaluate and report to stakeholders about the effectiveness of the internal* controls over the processes by which financial reports are generated.[1]

As the financial statements are the result of a complex process of capturing, classifying, aggregating, and reporting information, the apparently straightforward objectives of the auditor are quite challenging in practice. The purpose of this chapter is to introduce the related concepts of risk and risk management as they pertain to stakeholders with an interest in an organization. An organization faces a variety of different risks and adopts different strategies to mitigate the potential impact they may have on operations, performance, compliance with legal mandates, and the quality of financial reporting. Given their unique focus on the reliability of financial statements, auditors have a special regard for managing financial reporting risks. However, auditors are also concerned with risk management in its broadest sense because any risk that can negatively impact an organization has the potential to influence the results reported in the financial statements and the auditor's planning and conduct of the audit. Audit standard setters and regulators have developed standards that provide guidance to auditors on how to carry out their responsibilities.

Risk Management in a Business Enterprise

The Nature of Risk

To understand the role of auditing and assurance, it is first necessary to understand the nature of risk in a business enterprise and how an organization can mitigate or reduce risks. For the moment, we will adopt a general definition of **risk**:

> A threat to an organization that reduces the likelihood that the organization will achieve one or more of its objectives.

Threats from the competitive environment may prevent an organization from achieving its growth and profitability objectives. Serious problems can occur when employees or management take improper or incompetent actions that adversely affect the organization. Management can make bad decisions or employees can squander or steal corporate assets. Problems can also arise from ineffective efforts to deal with risk, such as management's failure to identify and properly react to changes in the business. From an auditor's perspective, problems within the organization may result in inaccurate information processing, lead to noncompliance with regulatory constraints, allow fraudulent activities to occur, or suggest a risk of failure for the business. Furthermore, inaccurate processing of information can lead to poor decisions, increased operating costs, diminished asset values, and unreliable reports to significant stakeholders.

Risk comes in many forms, and we will discuss numerous types of risk in great detail throughout this text. However, one risk that is particularly relevant to auditors and will be mentioned frequently is *information risk*, which is defined as the risk that information used in decision making is inaccurate or insufficient. Public company financial statements represent a sizeable category of information used by a clearly identified group of decision makers: Investors. Misstatements in financial statements can occur in a number of ways, but an important distinction is made by auditors between errors, mistakes or unintentional inaccuracies and fraud, dishonesty or intentional manipulation. One purpose of the audit is to reduce the information risk associated with financial statements by reducing the likelihood that the financial statements include either type of misstatement.

Enterprise Risk Management

Efforts to manage risk are becoming increasingly proactive in many organizations, with a focus on avoiding problems before they occur, and minimizing their impact when they are unable to prevent them. To better ensure that risk is addressed by senior management and the Board of Directors, organizations adopt *enterprise risk management* (ERM) as a formal process designed to identify potential events that may affect the entity, to manage risks to be within its risk appetite, and to provide reasonable assurance regarding the achievement of entity objectives.[2]

ERM is considered an iterative, continuous process that involves identifying, assessing, and managing key risks that threaten an organization's strategic, operational, compliance, and reporting objectives across all levels and units. Effective risk management under the ERM principles recognizes that:

- Risks affect organizations in various ways (e.g., achieving strategy, performing effectively, reporting faithfully, and complying with regulations fully).
- Risks are interrelated (e.g., one risk event may trigger other risk events).
- Risks can only be managed through intervention by management or other stakeholders.

Furthermore, the more serious the risk, the more vigorous the intervention that will be needed in order to achieve the desired results. However, intervention in the case of one risk may create unintended consequences, often in the form of new or increased risks in other areas. For example, management can reduce the risk of customers defaulting on their obligations by refusing to grant credit. However, if all credit sales are banned by the company, it may find that its risk of going out of business has been increased dramatically as it loses customers to competitors. This cause and effect relationship necessitates that management adopt a cost/benefit view of their response to risk and balance the direct and indirect consequences of intervening to manage a specific set of risks. One US-based organization, the Committee of Sponsoring Organizations (COSO), has become the de facto international thought leader on how enterprises can proactively manage their risks.

Figure 2.1 illustrates the COSO view of enterprise risk management. One side of the cube represents the different levels at which risk management can be applied: entity, division, unit, or subsidiary. Another side of the cube emphases the sources of the risks: strategic, operations, reporting and compliance with laws and regulations. The third side of the cube presents the eight components of an enterprise risk management approach:

1. *Internal environment:* The organization's general philosophy and approach to risk management.

2. *Objective setting:* The set of organizational objectives to be supported through risk management. The top of the cube represents the four types of objectives that might be relevant to risk management: strategic, operations, reporting, and compliance.

3. *Event identification:* The circumstances and events that represent potential risks that are relevant to the organization's objectives. Identifying situations and events that may negatively affect an organization is the first step in dealing with potential problems.

4. *Risk assessment:* The identification and evaluation of potential risks that emanate from the identified events. Management must prioritize risks in order to determine which ones are most critical at any point in time.

5. *Risk response:* The organization's basic plan for avoiding, accepting, reducing, or sharing risks.

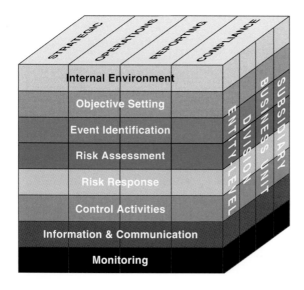

Figure 2.1 COSO'S 2004 enterprise risk management— integrated framework Framework (*Source:* Enterprise Risk Management—Integrated Framework, *Committee of Sponsoring Organizations of the Treadway Commission. 2004, AICPA, Jersey City, NJ.)*

6. *Control activities:* Specific activities undertaken by an organization to reduce risk. Examples of control activities are discussed in detail below.

7. *Information and communication:* An organization needs information to effectively respond to risk, and the production and distribution of relevant and timely information will determine the effectiveness of risk management.

8. *Monitoring:* Because circumstances change for any organization, the continuous evaluation of risk management efforts is necessary to assure its effectiveness over time.

Although all components of risk management are important, the **internal environment** is critical because it lays the foundation for all other elements of risk management. Specifically, the internal environment reflects the attitudes, approach, and competence of management towards enterprise risk management. If owners can hire competent and honest management whose personal goals are aligned with the owners, many other forms of control may be reduced. However, control is inherently limited by the quality and integrity of people working within the organization. Undue reliance on management to "do the right thing" often creates incentives and opportunities to act contrary to the objectives of the owners, even if management had no initial intent to do so. Furthermore, even the best run company can occasionally stumble with bad decisions. Consequently, elements of control implemented only through management are rarely adequate for reducing risks to an acceptable level.

Since there may be different ways to deal with a specific risk, management must design a portfolio of risk responses that is consistent with their appetite for risk. Figure 2.2 illustrates common ways of managing risks by avoiding it (e.g., leaving the line of business), sharing it (e.g., insurance), monitoring it (i.e., measuring it and determining if it becomes unacceptable and then take one of the other options), or accepting it as part of the cost of doing business. More formally stated, organizations can approach risks by:

(i)**EXAMPLE**

A bank may decide to not issue loans in certain countries due to problems with currency volatility and political stability.

- *Avoidance:* The organization may attempt to avoid some risks by carefully circumscribing their activities (e.g., avoiding certain markets or products(i)).

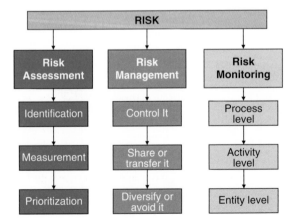

Figure 2.2 *What to do with risk*

Source: *Adapted from Business Risk Assessment. 1998 – The Institute of Internal Auditors*

- *Acceptance:* Some risks may be accepted as an inevitable, unavoidable result of business decisions[(ii)].

- *Sharing:* Risk sharing involves transferring, at a cost, all or part of a set of risks to another party. Examples of the ways in which risks may be shared with other organizations include insurance (paying premiums), strategic alliances (dividing profits), and/or hedging transactions (incurring financial fees[(iii)(iv)]).

- *Reduction:* An organization may attempt to reduce many risks by designing and implementing proactive policies, procedures, and processes[(v)(vi)].

In general, it is management's job to decide which approach to adopt for any specific risk. The approaches are not mutually exclusive and can be used in combination to reduce risks to an acceptable level. **Control activities** refer to any actions taken by a company or individual to reduce the likelihood or significance of risk. However, very few risks can be reduced to zero, no matter what approaches or combination of approaches are selected.

Control Activities for Compliance Risks

A special interest to auditors is how a client firm manages compliance and regulatory reporting risks associated with government regulations and oversight. Regulatory reporting risks are managed by identifying internal decision makers who are responsible for significant regulatory mandates, and then providing them with relevant and reliable information so that they can monitor conditions related to those mandates. Most organizations have a process in place to focus on the core regulatory requirements they face (e.g., regulations of the US Food and Drug Administration related to the development of new pharmaceutical products).

One emerging area of reporting and compliance risks for organizations that can involve the auditor is **corporate social responsibility reporting (CSR)**. Under CSR, organizations follow established criteria for reporting information about the sustainability of the organization and its impact on the environment. For example, as of 2015, over 8,000 international organizations issued reports in accordance with the Global Reporting Initiative (GRI) on risk management activities and performance across key areas that impact investors, employees, customers, suppliers, communities, governments, and the environment.[3] Some firms have these reports audited—but not always by accounting firms—and there is a growing demand by stakeholders for audits to increase in number and scope.[4]

Control Activities over Financial Reporting Risks

Auditors are most explicitly interested in the risk management activities that directly impact the financial statements upon which the auditors are issuing an opinion. These activities are referred to as **internal controls over financial reporting**. Determining which parts of ERM comprise internal control over financial reporting can be challenging because many information systems integrate controls relating to operations and compliance with controls that relate to information processing and reporting. With the emphasis on **entity level controls** in recent professional pronouncements, an auditor's interest

[(ii)]**EXAMPLE**

A company that manufactures trendy clothing recognizes that tastes and styles can change quickly and accept that as an inherent element of its product market.

[(iii)]**EXAMPLE (STRATEGIC ALLIANCE)**

An organization that produces motion pictures might reduce the risks associated with costs of producing, marketing, and distributing a motion picture by partnering with another studio. In exchange, both studios agree to share the revenues from the project.

[(iv)]**EXAMPLE (FINANCIAL HEDGING)**

An organization sells its product in various overseas markets, usually getting paid in the local currency. Given that the company is not an expert in foreign currency speculation, it may wish to protect itself against unfavorable swings in currency exchange rates. This can usually be accomplished through the use of financial derivatives linked to currency trading markets.

[(v)]**EXAMPLE**

A bank may protect itself against default by formally reviewing loan applications from prospective borrowers (a process), obtaining a credit report on the borrower (a procedure) and/or requiring borrowers to pledge collateral for a loan (a policy).

An organization's Board of Directors engages an auditor to examine financial statements to reduce the risk that they (and shareholders) will receive inaccurate information about a company's activities and results.

in risk management at the entity level has increased. In general, internal controls over financial reporting are the subset of controls that help ensure accurate and reliable processing, storing, and reporting of information relating to transactions, accounts, and financial statement aggregation.

AUTHORITATIVE GUIDANCE & STANDARDS

PCAOB Auditing Standard AS 2201 (formerly known as AS No. 5) **An Audit of Internal Control over Financial Reporting that is Integrated with An Audit Of Financial Statements** *describes* **entity level controls** *broadly as including the control environment, controls to prevent management override of other controls, the company's risk assessment process, information processing controls, controls that monitor results of operations, and controls that monitor the effectiveness of other controls. ISA 315* **Identifying and Assessing the Risk of Material Misstatement through Understanding the Entity and Its Environment** *does not use the term but describes the same set of controls in paragraphs 12 to 25.*

Currently, most organizations use COSO's 1992 report, *Internal Control— Integrated Framework*, which is a forerunner of the 2004 ERM framework, as the basis for evaluating internal control over financial reporting. In 2013, COSO issued an update of that framework to integrate the *Internal Control-Integrated Framework* even closer with its ERM framework. Indeed, the cube design of Figure 2.3 harkens to the ERM cube. The key differences are the ERM framework explicitly includes strategic activities and objective setting, whereas the internal control framework focuses on the five components of internal control over financial reporting that are a subset of the eight components of the ERM framework:

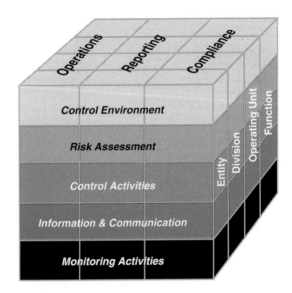

Figure 2.3 COSO'S 2013 internal control—integrated framework used as basis for addressing internal control over financial reporting

- *Control environment* (part of the *internal environment*): The general environment in which internal controls operate, including the attitudes and competence of management and employees of the organization.

- *Risk assessment:* The activities the organization performs to identify, assess, and prioritize risks. A breakdown in identifying or prioritizing risk will probably have a negative impact on the performance of the organization.

- *Control activities:* The activities the organization performs to reduce the effect of risk on its performance. The range of possible control activities in any organization is extremely broad and depends on the nature of the environment and risks that are of concern.

- *Information and communications:* The production and distribution of information necessary for effective internal control.

- *Monitoring:* The oversight of internal control to determine if it is effective.

In 2006 COSO issued a version of **Internal Control—Integrated Framework** targeted at special issues that arise in smaller companies.[5] While other countries have internal control frameworks that the SEC has stated might also be acceptable for US public company audits, (e.g., the UK's Turnbull Combined Code or Canada's Criteria of Control [COCO] Framework), many international companies that are registered with the US SEC base their evaluations on COSO and then ensure compliance with local frameworks if deemed necessary. Indeed, many national securities regulators recommend that companies evaluate and report to their stakeholders about their firm's internal controls employing the COSO framework even if they do not require the auditor to audit that assessment[vii].

As is the case for controlling risk in general, internal controls over financial reporting may be imposed at different levels within an organization. First, the basic attitude towards reliable financial reporting is set at the management level. The **control environment** is the component of the organization's internal environment that reflects management's attitude about internal control over financial reporting, including both intentional and unintentional misstatements or misleading disclosures. The control environment is a necessary condition for effective internal control over financial reporting in the long term. The control environment is particularly important in times of organizational stress because errors or fraud are more likely to occur when conditions are difficult (e.g., rapid growth, pressure to meet earnings forecasts, industry downturns, shortages of competent employees[viii][ix]).

The second level of internal control is within the internal business processes that include embedded controls over financial reporting. In general, these controls encompass the activities designed to assure that transactions occurring in a business process are properly recorded, classified, and maintained. Controls help address the risk that transactions are lost or misstated, as well as help ensure that accounting accruals are reasonable. Many process controls are embedded in automated information systems. Other process controls include authorization, the division of responsibilities among different employees, and reviews of transactions. In the past, auditors have frequently considered these controls in detail when planning an audit of financial statements[x][xi].

[vii]**EXAMPLE**

Canadian Securities Regulators require that Boards of Directors report on management's assessment of the design and effectiveness of the implementation of firm's internal controls over financial reporting in the Management Discussion & Analysis section of the annual report, a regulatory document for which the board must take explicit responsibility for the accuracy and completeness. The vast majority of such companies cite the Internal Control-Integrated Framework as the basis for making these assessments.

[viii]**EXAMPLE**

Senior management establishes separate codes of conduct for its employees and international supplier network to ensure that unacceptable behaviors are avoided and risks are not taken outside of pre-established guidelines. For example, a company may establish rules against offering or accepting bribes in order to facilitate transactions but it may not cover "facilitation payments" to third parties who then pay the bribes, a now common practice among some firms according to Transparency International that tracks bribery in many second and third world countries.

Traditionally, the auditor needed to understand the internal controls only to the extent necessary for the auditor to carry out the audit of the financial statements in an efficient and effective manner. However, in the last two decades the auditor's mandate has evolved such that the auditor needs to understand the internal controls over financial reporting, including the design of controls and whether they have been placed in operation. The extent to which the auditor needs to examine placement of controls in operation varies across different audit regimes as will be discussed later in this chapter.

Implications of Risk Management for Financial Performance

Risk management should be approached as a systematic and continuous process, whether in the context of enterprise risk-management or internal control over financial reporting. Risk management is iterative—control is a temporary state, not a permanent condition, depending on current circumstances. Consider the sequence of steps in risk management as depicted in Figure 2.4. The critical starting point for effective risk management is identifying and understanding the important risks of the organization (I). A risk that is not identified cannot be reduced or controlled. Once the risk is identified and analyzed, then management can decide how to best cope with the potential problem: avoid, accept, share, or reduce (II). Monitoring

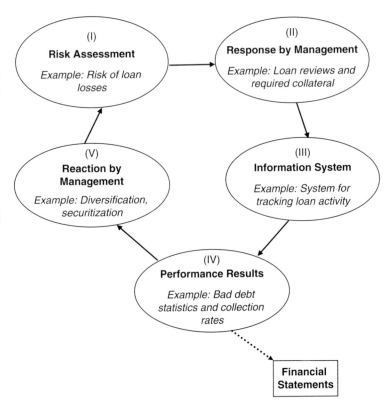

Figure 2.4 The elements of the risk management process relevant to the auditor

of risk and the effectiveness of management's response often requires an information system (III) that provides reliable performance results for subsequent evaluation (IV). If the performance results are acceptable, management may not need to take any further action; however, if results indicate current or future problems, management may want to step in and undertake other actions, in other words, continuous improvement (V).

To illustrate, consider a community bank based in south Florida back in 1990. A major risk of all banks is that they will make loans to individuals who will not be able to make the payments in the future (I). In order to reduce the risk of bad debts, most banks implement a number of formal processes and policies to screen potential borrowers before making a loan, and for monitoring a borrower's condition after a loan has been approved. For example, the bank may require that all loans to individuals are secured by collateral such as real estate or similar property. With such a policy in place, the bank may feel that it has adequately reduced the risk of a loss occurring in the event of default—the bank will then foreclose on the property and recover the loan balance (II).

Now, consider how events that occurred in Florida in 1994 may have affected this bank: Hurricane Andrew ripped a path of destruction through south Florida, the first hurricane to do so in fifty years, and a distressingly large number of people lost their homes and businesses, many of whom had mortgages at the bank. Many borrowers were unable to make the payments on their loans, and most of the collateral that was pledged to support the loans had been destroyed in the storm. Although some insurance proceeds were available to homeowners, most homeowners' policies provide for little or no coverage for flood damage. As a result of these events, the bank's financial performance suffered greatly, with a large increase in delinquent and defaulted loans (III, IV). The bank may have been unlucky, or it may have failed to adequately consider the risk of a hurricane hitting Florida, effectively adopting the strategy of *accepting* this risk.

Assuming the bank survived the economic wreckage, management had to give serious thought about how to mitigate this type of risk in the future. One reaction was to *reduce* the risk by changing the loan approval policy so as to get assurance that homes pledged as collateral were built to survive a hurricane or were located a safe distance from the ocean. Another reaction was to *insure* the risk by transferring some mortgage loans to other investors. For example, mortgage loans in Florida could be swapped for agricultural loans in Iowa and/or consumer product loans in New York (V). This allowed the bank to diversify its loan portfolio and reduce its risk from any single catastrophic event like a hurricane. For example, US real estate data dating back to the early 1960s showed there had never been a collapse in the creditworthiness of US mortgages across such diverse markets as Florida, Texas, and California. When a quartet of hurricanes again hit Florida in 2004, the impact on banks and their loan portfolios was much less severe than experienced in 1994.

Loan swapping was such a success to manage risk, many banks got involved with such swaps and a formal nationwide (and eventually, international) market developed to pool such loans. Banks could then sell "tranches" of the pool to help diversify their risk and as a form of investment for financial institutions, pension funds, and individuals. Transferring the risks of loans to others eventually developed into a very successful new market opportunity for banks involving the bundling of mortgages, consumer loans, and credit cards balances into a new type of investment instrument referred to as a "loan securitization." These instruments facilitated the buying and selling of investments in pools of loans by banks and individuals. However, as is the case with all attempts to control one risk, another risk increased.

Eventually, the bundling of loans, or parts of loans, led to the development of extremely complicated derivative contracts known as **Collateralized Mortgage Obligations (CMOs),** or more generally, **Asset Backed Commercial Paper (ABCP)**, which bond rating agencies often rated as being highly secure (often approaching the same security as government debt). It was sold as a highly liquid short-term investment where investors could "park" spare cash for short periods of time so it could earn more interest than a conventional term deposit or other liquid investment. In the summer of 2007, significant concerns began to arise about the quality of the assets on which CMOs and ABCP were based. This was the start of the so-called Global Financial Crisis (GFC). Suddenly these investments could only be sold at a significant discount from face value (30 percent to 60 percent) if they could be sold at all. Essentially, these securities became extremely illiquid and led to large write-downs by many financial institutions, leading to the fiscal crisis of 2008–09 and the resulting bail-outs of financial institutions the world over.

So, we see from the events that transpired over fifteen years, that the banking sector's attempts to deal with one set of risks (concentration risk) actually led to the creation of an entirely new set of risks (financial derivatives) that turned out to be far-reaching, returning the bank to Step I of the risk management process (recognizing risks). Unfortunately, as with the banks in Florida in 1994, there were many institutions that did not recognize the risk from these CMOs and ABCP and did not have a plan to deal with the liquidity risk when it struck. Hence, the need for ongoing alertness to risk is highlighted yet again.

The ability of management to effectively manage risk is of direct concern to the owners of an organization because it is their investment that is ultimately at risk. Hence, the entire risk-management process is relevant to the conduct of the audit because it can inform the auditor's judgments, for example, about the collectability of loans that are recorded in the financial records. Even in the absence of such a direct link to a specific financial statement account, the extent of firm risk may also be of interest to the auditor because it has a pervasive influence of the culture and activities of the organization, reflecting the general competence of management to "run" the company and influencing the overall aggressiveness of the firm's accounting and willingness to "bend the rules" to achieve its objectives.

Need for External Assurance as a Component of Risk Management

At the most mundane level, the external audit examines the information in the financial statements in accordance with established professional or regulatory mandated standards. The primary attribute that makes external auditing valuable is that it is designed to provide an *objective* check on the reliability and fairness of financial information. However, external auditors can and do provide assurance over other aspects of an organization. For example, assurance about the effectiveness of internal control over financial reporting is valuable to both owners and managers. Owners benefit because they obtain corroborative evidence that control is operating effectively, and managers benefit because they obtain feedback on how to improve internal control over financial reporting for their own purposes. Auditors are uniquely qualified to provide such assurance because they possess the professional skills to provide highly diagnostic services, while maintaining objectivity.[6]

Table 2.1 illustrates how the risk management process parallels the audit process. The audit process begins with an evaluation of the goals and risks of the organization, which requires a deep understanding of the industry and the strategic positioning of others in the industry. This is followed by an evaluation of management's responses to those risks including the design and implementation of internal processes. Execution of management's plans and processes requires reliable performance measurement and reporting that

Table 2.1 *Relationship between risk management and audit*

Process Step	Management Perspective	Auditor Perspective
Risk Assessment	Management identifies and evaluates risks that can have a negative impact on the organization. Each risk is evaluated based on the likelihood of it occurring and the significance of its impact.	The auditor is concerned that management has identified all potentially critical risks and assessed their significance accurately. Missing or under-appreciated risks will not be effectively managed.
Response by Management (Risk Control and Mitigation)	Management makes choices about how to respond to specific risks. Choices include avoidance, acceptance, insurance, or reduction. Risk reduction involves designing business processes to address groups of related risks. Internal policies and procedures are designed to guide the actions of individuals within the organization.	The auditor assesses whether management's responses to risks are likely to be effective. The more effectively management exercises control, the fewer problems the auditor will expect to observe during the course of the engagement.
Information Reliability	Information systems are designed to provide appropriate performance measurement data to assess the past, present, and future likelihood or significance of various risks.	The auditor assesses the reliability of information processing and reporting. Much of the information that an auditor needs comes from internal processes. The more reliable the information, the fewer problems the auditor can expect during the engagement.
Performance Results	Information is generated on a periodic basis for management review. Performance measures should indicate how the organization has performed, as well as provide early warning for potential problems.	Performance measurement information gives the auditor a basis for judging management's control of risks. Data measured over a period of time will indicate when conditions change or risks arise that may lead to problems during the engagement.
Reaction by Management	Management reacts to performance data and decides whether adjustments are needed in strategic decisions, business plans, or business processes as a result of existing circumstances or potential future problems.	The auditor judges management's willingness and ability to react to changes in conditions or risks. If reactions are inadequate, the auditor may expect problems to be revealed by the audit and may offer assistance.

can be used to evaluate the performance of key processes and management activities, along with tests of the effectiveness of control activities. Finally, performance information is used as feedback to assist management to reduce reporting and compliance risks. Overall, effective risk management processes and feedback enable long-term improvement of the organization.

This process is iterative and continuous. Traditionally, auditors have focused on the question of information reliability, primarily constrained by the objectives of financial reporting. However, to develop a sufficient understanding of the risks related to financial reporting, it is important that an auditor understand aspects of the organization's enterprise risk management that go beyond financial reporting. Since effective management requires the effective execution of *all* components of risk management, the auditor should consider the overall effectiveness of management's actions and responses to risk.

A general rule of thumb is that any business risk that is not effectively controlled can impact the conduct of the audit. A company with weak operations or ineffective risk management is unlikely to be successful in the long run and can present difficult challenges for the conduct of the audit. Indications of ineffective risk management include:

- Lack of a formal enterprise risk management process.
- Failure to monitor strategic risks.
- Failure to adequately respond to identified risks.
- Lack of reliable performance measurement data.
- Inadequate information for monitoring processes.
- Failure to respond to signs of problems and visible threats.

These are signs of potential risk from the point of view of the auditor. Consequently, the auditor needs to monitor the action/measurement/reaction cycle described in Table 2.1 and assess the likelihood, significance, and potential impact of specific risks within the client.

Role of Rules, Regulations, and Standards on Risk in the Audit

Over the long history of the auditing profession, various forms of self and external regulation have attempted to improve the reliability of financial reporting and the quality of auditing. Today auditing standards are established internationally by the International Audit and Assurance Standards Board (IAASB) and then adopted by national auditing standard setters with such supplementary standards and guidance that are considered necessary for local needs. In the US this general approach is followed for the audits of companies that are not registered with the SEC as IAASB standards are substantially being adopted by the AICPA's Auditing Standards Board. For public companies registered with the US SEC auditing standards are established by the Public Company Accounting Oversight Board (PCAOB) and these auditing standards are mandated for all public companies subject to the SEC's jurisdiction no matter where in the world they are headquartered.

Both of these sets of standards have evolved from what historically have been called **generally accepted auditing standards** (GAAS). Standards that have evolved from GAAS are probably the most important in the day-to-day life of the auditor because the standards cover the conduct of the audit and the form of the report.

Two other sets of standards also play a substantial role in establishing who can audit firms and how the auditor carries out the audit: (1) ethical standards, and (2) quality control standards. Ethical standards address who can perform an audit and how auditors should behave, whereas quality control standards pertain to procedures and practices within the public accounting firm to ensure that the firm applies auditing standards and ethical standards consistently across all relevant audit engagements.

Auditing Standards

The nature of standards applicable to an audit depends on the nature of the engagement. We will follow the convention throughout this book of referring to the audit of financial statements without an accompanying report on effectiveness of internal control as a **GAAS Audit** and refer to the audit of financial statements with an accompanying report on effectiveness of internal control over financial reporting as an **Integrated Audit.**

GAAS Audit

The overall objective of an auditor is to:

> Obtain reasonable assurance about whether the financial statements as a whole are free from material misstatement, whether due to fraud or error, thereby enabling the auditor to express an opinion on whether the financial statements are prepared, in all material respects, in accordance with an applicable financial reporting framework.
>
> (ISA 200 paragraphs 11–12)

All audits involve an examination of the information included in the financial statements. The focus of this part of the audit is on the numbers and disclosures included in the financial report, which are evaluated against accounting standards. Regardless of how the numbers are generated, and how sophisticated the client's accounting system, the auditor must do his or her best to verify that the financial statements are accurate, complete, and reasonable given the circumstances of the company.

The basic approach for conducting all audits requires that an auditor have adequate expertise and training to perform the audit of a specific client consistent with the circumstances of the engagement. This may include industry knowledge that is relevant to the specific client. Furthermore, an auditor should maintain an independent attitude about the client and not be biased in favor or against a particular client (known as professional skepticism). Finally, the audit should be executed with a degree of care that is appropriate for a professional and recognizes that professional judgment is involved in carrying out all steps of the audit. All of these relate to reducing the risk to users that the auditor will become biased in favor of management's version of the financial statements. See Box 2.1 "Conducting A GAAS Audit."

BOX 2.1 CONDUCTING A GAAS AUDIT

General qualifications and conduct

- *Audit performed by persons having adequate training and proficiency.*
- *Auditors must maintain independence in mental attitude.*
- *Auditors must exercise due professional care.*

Audit fieldwork (also known as examination)

- *The audit must be properly planned and where assistants are used they should be properly supervised.*
- *Auditor must gain a sufficient understanding of the entity, including internal control, to plan and conduct the audit.*
- *Auditor must obtain sufficient, competent evidence.*

Reporting audit result

- *Auditor must express an opinion on the financial statements as a whole.*
- *Auditor must indicate those situations where generally accepted accounting principles (GAAP) are not consistently applied.*
- *Auditor must evaluate the adequacy of disclosures.*
- *Auditor must state whether statements were prepared in accordance with GAAP.*

Fieldwork describes approaches taken to an audit engagement that need to be performed so as to acquire sufficient evidence to support the conclusions reached by the auditor. This requires that the auditor carry out adequate planning and supervision of the engagement, obtain an understanding of a client's business environment including its risks and related system of internal control, and obtain evidence that supports the accuracy of the financial statements. The second point is particularly important because all audits involve some level of evaluation of the quality of the internal accounting system that generates financial information. For the purposes of this chapter we describe internal control over financial reporting as the subset of enterprise risk management that pertains to the processes and procedures that management has established to:

- Maintain records that accurately reflect the company's transactions.
- Prepare financial statements and footnote disclosures for external purposes and provide reasonable assurance that receipts and expenditures are appropriately authorized.
- Prevent or promptly detect unauthorized acquisition, use, or disposition of the company's assets that could have a material effect on the financial statements.

During the control tests the auditor can find evidence that pertains to:

- Prevention of fraud or errors.
- Reliability of significant accounting numbers and disclosures.
- Potential sources of breakdowns in controls.

This evidence then affects how the auditor gathers other evidence about whether the financial statements are in accordance with the relevant accounting standards as well as the contents of any auditor report over the effectiveness of internal controls in an Integrated Audit.

AUTHORITATIVE GUIDANCE & STANDARDS

Understanding control activities over financial reporting risks is an important job of all auditors even if they do not have to issue a formal report. ISA 315 establishes guidance for assessment of internal controls where no separate reporting is involved.

The reporting phase of the audit highlights communication of the auditor's findings to interested parties. An audit report for a GAAS audit should include the following information:

1. Types of opinion and basis for that opinion, including any matters that the auditor deems necessary to emphasize in the report:

   - In general, an auditor can provide a "positive" report on an engagement when the auditor is convinced that the financial statement assertions are supported by the evidence that the auditor has obtained, and that all matters have been measured and disclosed as required by the underlying accounting standards—the measurement and finanical reporting criteria.

   - Measurement and financial reporting criteria: For an audit of financial statements, the basis for evaluation are the accounting standards under which the financial statements are prepared. Historically these were referred to as generally accepted accounting principles (GAAP). Given the emergence of multiple sets of accounting principles, the most prominent of which are International Financial Reporting Standards (IFRS) and Financial Accounting Standards Board (FASB) standards, the auditor now refers explicitly to the set of accounting principles that the financial statements have been prepared under. In addition to these well-known sets of financial reporting standards, many countries have specific accounting standards for government entities, not-for-profit organizations, and less complex accounting standards for private companies that do not sell securities to the public.

2. Responsibilities of management and those charged with governance for the financial statements:

   - To prepare the financial statements in accordance with GAAP (as discussed above and in the text book).

   - Assess the entity's ability to continue as a going concern.

   - Identify those who have oversight of management with respect to these responsibilities.

3. Auditor responsibilities for the audit of financial statements:

   - State the audit's objective of reasonable assurance, what reasonable assurance means, and describe materiality.

   - State that the audit involves professional judgment and that there are risks of not detecting material misstatements and especially there are higher risks for not detecting such misstatement with respect to fraud.

- State the limited goal of examining internal control for the purposes of carrying out the audit, not to provide an opinion on internal control effectiveness.

AUTHORITATIVE GUIDANCE & STANDARDS

The movement away from auditors referring to "generally accepted accounting principles" in their reports toward specific reference to the set of accounting standards employed to evaluate the fairness of the financial statements has emerged over the last 20 years. The consolidation of multiple national accounting standard setters into two major private sector standard setters, the International Accounting Standards Board (IASB) and the US Financial Accounting Standards Board (FASB) hastened this movement to be explicit about which set of standards were being employed by the auditor. ISA 700 **Forming an Opinion and Reporting on Financial Statements** *calls such accounting frameworks as general purpose framework. There are many differences in the degree of disclosure mandated by the two major accounting standard setters and to a lesser extent, but still significant, differences in how substantively certain items should be measured in the financial statements, or indeed, whether they should be measured at all. Where these matters affect the audit we will discuss them further later in this book. In general we will continue to refer to the accounting standards that the auditor employs to evaluate financial statements as GAAP.*

Integrated Audit

From an auditor's perspective the Integrated Audit can be segmented into two separate phases: (1) examination of the effectiveness of internal control over financial reporting, and (2) examination of the financial statements (i.e., the same as a GAAS Audit as outlined above.) The auditor's additional responsibility in an Integrated Audit is to evaluate and test the effectiveness of internal control over financial reporting as of the end of the fiscal year. The effort required to evaluate internal control is much more extensive in an Integrated Audit as it starts with an assumption that all public companies should have strong internal control over all significant process and accounts in the financial statement. In fact, the development of a reliable financial reporting system is considered a fundamental responsibility of management in order to prevent, or detect and correct, material misstatements prior to issuing financial statements. The starting point of an Integrated Audit is management stating that they:

- Formally accept the responsibility for the effectiveness of the company's internal control over financial reporting.
- Have evaluated the effectiveness of the company's internal control over financial reporting using suitable criteria (e.g., COSO's internal control framework).
- Support its evaluation with sufficient evidence, including documentation.
- Provide a written assessment about the effectiveness of the company's internal control over financial reporting as of the end of the fiscal year.

AUTHORITATIVE GUIDANCE & STANDARDS

The US PCAOB has issued AS 2201 (formerly AS 5) for firms under its jurisdiction that have to issue such a report over a firm's internal controls.

The auditor's approach normally emphasizes entity level controls as the effectiveness of these "big picture" controls may well effect the amount of testing the auditor will do of other controls. The auditor then moves to the control over significant accounts and disclosures so as to ensure that the audit covers all such accounts. The auditor tests controls that are important for significant transactions, accounts, and disclosures across all significant business process. The nature and extent of control tests depends on the nature of the controls that management has implemented and should focus on the most sensitive (i.e., risky) areas of the financial reporting system. Finally, the auditor reports to the shareholders via the Board of Directors about the auditor's assessment of the internal control over financial reporting either integrated into the auditor's report over the financial statements or as a separate standalone report that features references to the financial statement audit report.

Ethical Standards

A great deal of individual judgment goes into the conduct of an audit so it is important that auditors make choices and decisions that are consistent with the professional and ethical principles of the profession. Ethical standards have been developed to guide auditors in their decision making so as to avoid many common sources of bias or ethical breakdowns. The International Federation of Accountants requires that all member bodies (e.g., the AICPA in the US) have a professional code of conduct that defines the standards of ethical behavior for a professional accountant. These standards cover topics such as the responsibilities to clients and the public, professional integrity, and the nature of professional independence and objectivity. Some of the key provisions that are found in the IFAC's *Code of Ethics for Professional Accountants* are summarized in Table 2.2. Ethical standards exist to protect the user against risk of poor behavior by auditors by requiring a high standard of professional behavior. They also guide auditors as to what is acceptable professional behavior with regard to clients and the public. In this chapter we emphasize two important ethical principles that have a direct effect on the conduct of the audit: (1) objectivity and independence, and (2) professional skepticism.[7]

Objectivity and Independence

One of the core ethical principles of a professional auditor is to be objective, which the IFAC *Code of Ethics Section 120* defines as "A combination of impartiality, intellectual honesty and a freedom from conflicts of interest." [page 17] If public accountants are perceived as biased, non-objective, or self-serving, their value as potential assurance providers is essentially eliminated. A closely related concept to objectivity is independence which the IFAC's *Code of Ethics Section 290* defines as composed of two parts:

Table 2.2 *An overview of issues addressed in a code of ethics for professional accountants*

Code of Ethics Topic	General Requirements
Integrity (Section 110)	Auditors must be straightforward and honest in all professional and business relationships. Integrity also implies fair dealing and truthfulness. Auditors cannot violate laws or regulatory requirements, knowingly mislead clients or users, or make intentionally biased decisions. In particular, auditors cannot knowingly misstate facts.
Objectivity (Sections 120 and 280)	Auditors cannot compromise their professional or business judgments because of bias, conflict of interest, or the undue influence of others.
Professional Competence and Due Care (Section 130)	Auditors must maintain professional knowledge and skill at the level required to give competent professional service and to follow applicable technical and professional standards. The auditor must carry out all services carefully, thoroughly and on a timely basis.
Confidentiality (Section 140)	Auditors must protect the confidentiality of client information and cannot use such knowledge for their personal advantage or the advantage of third parties. Auditors may disclose client information only after receiving permission from the client, permitted by law or unless directed by a court official, peer review or regulatory inspection, when required by technical standards or ethics requirements.
Professional Behavior (Section 150 and 250)	Auditors must comply with all relevant laws and regulations and avoid any actions that may discredit the profession. All marketing and promotional activity needs to be honest and truthful without making exaggerated claims or disparaging references to the work of others.
Conflicts of Interest (Section 220)	Auditors need to take steps to identify proactively potential conflicts of interest and development procedures to assess the threats so as to apply safeguards necessary to eliminate the threats or reduce them to an acceptable level.
Fees and Other Types of Remuneration (Section 240)	Auditors may not accept fees that are conditional upon outcome of the engagement. [Note: In some countries contingent fees may be accepted for non-audit services provided the firm does not also perform the audit and discloses the arrangement.]
Gifts and Hospitality (Section 260)	Auditors may only accept gifts or hospitality offered by clients that a reasonable and informed third party, weighing all the specific facts and circumstances, would consider trivial and inconsequential.
Independence (Sections 290 and 291)	Auditors have a set of specific items that are deemed as so great a threat to independence that they are prohibited (e.g., firm member with a financial interest in client). Further, auditors must comply with a conceptual framework to judge threats to their independence in mind and appearance through a three step process of: (1) identify threats to independence; (2) evaluate the significance of the threats identified, and (3) apply safeguards, when necessary, to eliminate the threat or reduce it to an acceptable level.

"independence in appearance" and "independence in mind or fact." If auditors are perceived to be biased by third parties, they are said to lack *independence in appearance*. Formally stated independence in appearance is defined as:

> The avoidance of facts and circumstances that are so significant that a reasonable and informed third party would be likely to conclude, weighing all the specific facts and circumstances, that a firm's, or a member of the audit or assurance team's, integrity, objectivity or professional skepticism has been compromised.
>
> (290.6)

Whether auditors are actually independent or not is referred to as *independence in mind or fact*, defined as "the state of mind that permits the expression of a conclusion without being affected by influences that compromise professional judgment, thereby allowing an individual to act with integrity, and exercise objectivity and professional skepticism" (290.6). In general, independence in fact is a state of mind for the auditor that is closely related to the ethical concept of objectivity.

AUTHORITATIVE GUIDANCE & STANDARDS

Codes of ethics or professional conduct are promulgated by various professional accounting bodies around the world. The International Federation of Accountants' (IFAC) **Code of Ethics for Professional Accountants** *provides international guidance that is frequently adopted by national, state, or provincial accounting bodies. These bodies can level penalties for violation of their specific code provisions, including expulsion from membership of the professional bodies. In some countries this results in the inability to audit as without membership in a professional accounting association, the accounting designation is lost. Other countries have national, state, or provincial regulators that issue the license to practice public accounting and additional specific actions may be needed prior to the withdrawal of the license to practice.*

Some countries view objectivity as requiring that the public accountant be independent in appearance, whereas other countries view a public accountant's independence in appearance as demonstrating he or she is objective. In any case, a lack of independence can undermine not only an auditor's professional reputation and stature but also the value of the audit in general. As a result, many regulations have been developed to foster the appearance of independence among auditors. These rules dictate conditions under which an auditor would *not* be considered to be independent and thus potentially biased. There are five general conditions that undermine independence in appearance:

1. Having a financial interest in the client: An auditor (or his or her immediate family) cannot own shares in a client nor have a significant investment in a mutual fund owning shares of a client's stock.

2. Having a family relationship with employees, management, or owners of the client: Auditors are not independent of clients where a relative is on the Board of Directors or holds an executive position with the client.

3. Performing work that is the responsibility of management: Auditors cannot authorize transactions, approve journal entries to correct the financial statements, or perform accounting procedures to support journal entries.

4. Auditing work that was originally completed by the auditor or the firm: Auditors cannot assess the effectiveness of internal control over financial reporting for an information system designed or installed by the same accounting firm.

5. Providing services to a client that are incompatible to the objectives of the external audit: Auditors cannot serve as the legal counsel for an audit client, recommend client products or services to other audit clients, or recruit executives for a client.

Professional Skepticism

An "auditing mind-set" requires that an auditor maintain an attitude of ***professional skepticism*** if he or she is to fulfill his or her responsibility to external users of financial statements, especially to investors in public companies.[8] Professional skepticism requires that the auditor base judgments on solid evidence and avoid being misled by casual appearances or the personality of management. Professional skepticism is a state of mind that helps auditors remain objective, and requires a questioning mind and a critical assessment of evidence. While working closely with management and other corporate employees, auditors must maintain an attitude of professional skepticism when they evaluate information from and about the people they deal with on a daily basis. Professional skepticism requires a balanced view of people and organizations and is based on the assumption that management is neither honest nor dishonest until evidence proves otherwise; in other words, the auditor remains neutral.

Auditors are often subject to subtle influences that may undermine professional skepticism without the auditor realizing it. Client personnel are often friendly and pleasant, so it becomes difficult for the auditor to look at them as potentially incompetent or fraudulent. Even documentary evidence that has been forged or altered will look good on its face. Thus, auditors may be unknowingly influenced by what they see or hear during the course of the audit in ways that undermine their ability to be skeptical. Ultimately, failure to live up to the professional and ethical standards expected of the auditing profession will damage the reputation of the individual auditor, their firm, and the profession.

Quality Control Standards

The final area of professional regulation and standards relates to how an accounting firm operates. Although not directly related to the conduct of a single engagement, policies and procedures within an accounting firm determine the circumstances under which audits are conducted. For example, the way that professionals are compensated, auditors are assigned to engagements, and the quality of audits is monitored could all influence how a specific engagement is conducted. Thus, the profession provides guidance to accounting firms about the appropriate way to run their audit practice. These standards are referred to as quality control standards. The IAASB Quality Control Standards are summarized in Table 2.3. In addition, various countries' regulatory bodies also have standards or rules for quality control in public accounting firms.

AUTHORITATIVE GUIDANCE & STANDARDS

The IAASB has established International Standards on Quality Control No. 1 **Quality Control for Firms that Perform Audits and Reviews of Financial Statements, and Other Assurance and Related Services Engagements** *to deal with a public accounting firm's responsibilities for its system of quality control. In addition, the IAASB ISA 220* **Quality Control for an Audit of Financial Statements** *provides specific guidance for the auditor about quality control procedures for an audit of financial statements. The US PCAOB has adopted the AICPA's Auditing*

Table 2.3 *Elements of a system of quality control**

Elements of Quality Control	Requirements
Leadership responsibilities for quality within the firm	Policies and procedures designed to promote an internal culture recognizing that quality is essential in performing all engagements. Senior officials in the firm such as the chief executive officer (or equivalent) assume ultimate responsibility for the firm's system of quality control.
Relevant ethical requirements	Policies and procedures should be established to provide the firm with reasonable assurance that people at all organizational levels comply with relevant ethical requirements especially to maintain independence and perform all professional responsibilities with integrity and objectivity.
Acceptance and continuance of clients and specific engagements	Policies and procedures should be established for deciding whether to accept or continue with a client in order to provide reasonable assurance that the firm will not associate with a client whose management lacks integrity, that the required professional services can be competently provided in compliance with relevant ethical requirements and to identify potential conflicts of interest and the resolution.
Human resources	Policies and procedures for assigning personnel to engagements should be established to provide the firm with reasonable assurance that the firm has sufficient personnel with competence, capabilities and commitment to ethical principles necessary to perform engagements in accordance with professional standards and enable the firm to issue reports that are appropriate for the circumstances.
Engagement performance	Policies and procedures should be established to provide reasonable assurance that the work performed meets all appropriate professional standards and legal and regulatory requirements with an emphasis on carrying out appropriate consultations with experts.
Monitoring	Policies and procedures for a monitoring process should be established to provide the firm with reasonable assurance that the procedures relating to the other elements of quality control are relevant, adequate, and operating effectively.

* From ISQC No. 1 and ISA 220. Similar guidance is provided by PCAOB AS 1220 and Interim Quality Control Standards.

Standards Board's Statements on Quality Control Standards as its **Interim Quality Control Standards** *and has specifically developed AS 1220 (formerly known as AS No. 7)* **Engagement Quality Review** *that sets out requirements for the audit partner who carries out an audit engagement quality review.*

Quality control standards require that the firm has procedures in place to monitor and maintain independence, manage professional personnel, review client relationships, and support and monitor engagement quality. Many firms have dedicated personnel to monitor new authoritative guidance in accounting and auditing to ensure that firms adapt to new standards that affect the conduct of the audit. A firm should implement monitoring processes to ensure that its personnel follow professional standards and firm policies when accepting and conducting an audit. An important element of quality control is the process by which individual actions and decisions are reviewed by others. A typical audit involves several layers of review:

- Detailed review of all working papers prepared by subordinates by a superior on the engagement.
- General review of critical working papers by senior managers or partners on the engagement.
- A general review of working papers by a second partner, who is not otherwise involved in the engagement.
- Detailed review of a sample of engagements on an annual basis as part of an overall quality review.

Firms should follow up identified quality weaknesses and take steps to rectify these weaknesses with procedural changes, training, and communications with personnel throughout the firm. Again, these standards provide protection for the users of audit reports against the risk of poor quality audits, but can also be seen as providing guidance to auditors as to what they must do to meet the standards of the profession and avoid charges of poor audit quality auditing.

Summary and Conclusion

Public accountants can perform a wide range of assurance services that would be relevant to the management of risks in an organization. In essence, the value of assurance is directly proportional to the extent of risk reduction that can be achieved relative to a set of objectives for individual stakeholders. The audit of financial statements is the most common form of assurance engagement performed by auditors, and the service subject to the largest portion of professional standards and regulations. The objective of an audit of financial statements is to provide an opinion about the fairness of reported financial position and results based on generally accepted accounting principles. This traditional GAAS Audit of financial statements has now been supplemented for publicly listed companies in the US with a more extensive

Integrated Audit that, in addition to the opinion on the financial statements, contains the auditor's report on the effectiveness of these controls. These engagements build on the skill set that the auditor has developed in carrying out the audit of financial statements.

Bibliography of Relevant Literature

Relevant Research

Ballou, B. and D. Heitger. 2005. Practical Enterprise Risk Management: A Building Block Approach to Implementing COSO 2004. *Management Accounting Quarterly.* 6(Winter): 1–10.

Beasley, M., J. Carcello, and D. Hermanson. 1999. *Fraudulent Financial Reporting: 1987–1997. Committee of Sponsoring Organizations of the Treadway Commission.* www.coso.org.

Blackwell, D., T. Nolan, and D. Winters. 1998. The Value of Auditor Assurance: Evidence from Loan Pricing. *Journal of Accounting Research.* 36(Spring): 57–70.

Cohen, J. R. and R. Simnett. 2015. CSR and Assurance Service: A Research Agenda. *Auditing: A Journal of Practice and Theory.* 34(1): 59–74.

Kinney, W. R., Jr., and R. D. Martin. 1994. Does Auditing Reduce Bias in Financial Reporting? A Review of Audit Adjustment Studies. *Auditing: A Journal of Practice and Theory.* Spring: 149–156.

Mayhew, B. W., and J. E. Pike. 2004. Does Investor Selection of Auditors Enhance Auditor Independence? *The Accounting Review.* 79(3): 797–822.

Newman, D. P., E. R. Patterson, and J. R. Smith. 2005. The Role of Auditing in Investor Protection. *The Accounting Review.* 80(1): 289–314.

Relevant Professional Accounting Reports

Sundem, G. L., R. E. Dukes, and J. A. Elliott. 1996. *The Value of Information and Audits.* New York: Coopers & Lybrand.

Relevant Professional Standards

Committee of Sponsoring Organizations of the Treadway Commission (COSO). 1992. *Internal Control—Integrated Framework*, Vol. 1–4. New York: COSO.

Committee of Sponsoring Organizations of the Treadway Commission (COSO). 2004. *Enterprise Risk Management—Integrated Framework.* New York: COSO.

Committee of Sponsoring Organizations of the Treadway Commission (COSO). 2006. *Internal Control—An Integrated Framework: Guidance for Smaller Public Companies.* New York: COSO.

Committee of Sponsoring Organizations of the Treadway Commission (COSO). 2013. *Internal Control-Integrated Framework*, Vol. 1–4. New York: COSO.

Criteria of Control Committee. 1995. *Guidance on Control*. Toronto: Canadian Institute of Chartered Accountants.

Criteria of Control Committee. 1995. *Guidance for Directors – Governance Processes for Control*. Toronto: Canadian Institute of Chartered Accountants.

IAASB International Standards on Auditing (ISA) No. 200, "Objectives and Principles Governing an Audit of Financial Statements."

IAASB *International Standards on Auditing* (ISA) No. 220, "Quality Control for an Audit of Financial Statements."

IAASB *International Standards on Auditing* (ISA) No. 315, "Identifying and Assessing the Risks of Material Misstatement through Understanding the Entity and Its Environment."

IAASB *International Standards on Auditing* (ISA) No. 700, "The Independent Auditor's Report on General Purpose Financial Statements."

IFAC IAASB *Staff Questions and Answers*. 2011, "Professional Skepticism in an Audit of Financial Statements."

IFAC. International Ethics Standards Board for Accountants (IESBA). 2015. *Handbook of Code of Ethics for Professional Accountants*. New York: International Federation of Accountants.

IFAC. International Auditing and Assurance Standards Board (IAASB). 2015. *Handbook of International Quality Control, Audit, Review, Other Assurance, and Related Services Pronouncements*. New York: International Federation of Accountants.

PCAOB 2003. *Interim Quality Control Standards*.

PCAOB 2007. *Auditing Standard 2201 (formerly No. 5)*, "An Audit of Internal Control Over Financial Reporting That Is Integrated with An Audit of Financial Statements."

PCAOB 2009. *Auditing Standard 1220 (formerly No. 7)*, "Engagement Quality Review."

PCAOB 2014. *Rules of the Board* Section 3. "Auditing and Related Professional Practice Standards."

PCAOB 2012. *Staff Audit Practice Alert No. 10,* "Maintaining and Applying Professional Skepticism in Audits."

Turnbull Committee. 1999. *Internal Control—Guidance for Directors on the Combined Code*. London: Institute of Chartered Accountants in England and Wales.

Notes

1   PCAOB *Auditing Standard 2201 (formerly known as AS No. 5)*, "An Audit of Internal Control Over Financial Reporting That Is Integrated with An Audit of Financial Statements."

2   Committee of Sponsoring Organizations of the Treadway Commission (COSO). 2004. *Enterprise Risk Management—Integrated Framework* provides the definition.

3   http://database.globalreporting.org accessed on October 4, 2015.

4   For more information, J. R. Cohen and R. Simnett. 2015. CSR and Assurance Service: A Research Agenda. *Auditing: A Journal of Practice and Theory.* 34(1): 59–74.

5   To help smaller public companies in the US better comply with the requirements of COSO's 1992 internal control framework, in 2006 COSO issued *Internal Control: An Integrated Framework: Guidance for Smaller Public Companies*, which was intended to help companies with fewer resources than larger organizations implement effective internal control over financial reporting.

6   In the US, the external auditor is now required by the Public Company Accounting Oversight Board (PCAOB) to report on the effectiveness of internal control over financial reporting. We will discuss this internal control effectiveness audit in depth in Chapter 8 and refer to it as needed in other chapters.

7   The IFAC *Code of Ethics for Professional Accountants* is discussed in more detail in Chapter 16.

8   Professional skepticism has become a very "hot" issue for auditing standard setters. See IAASB's Questions and Answers on "Professional Skepticism in an Audit of Financial Statements" and the PCAOB's Staff Alert 10 "Maintaining and Applying Professional Skepticism in Audits."

CHAPTER 3

The Building Blocks of Auditing

Outline

- Summary and Conclusion
- Bibliography of Relevant Literature

Learning Goals for this Chapter

1. Identify and explain the set of financial statement and internal control assertions that auditors test as part of an audit.
2. Describe the three major concepts underlying the audit process—risk, materiality, and evidence.
3. Integrate audit risk concepts with concepts of business risk.
4. Understand and apply the concept of materiality in auditing.
5. Describe the various types of audit evidence the auditor can collect to support the opinion.
6. Explain how the auditor gathered evidence affects the components of audit risk.
7. Explain the interrelationships between risk, materiality, and evidence.
8. Recognize and describe the set of responsibilities the auditor has in an audit.

Introduction

Management and auditors have separate, but complementary, responsibilities related to the production and release of audited financial statements. Management is responsible for preparing the financial statements, meaning that it decides what information will be included. Management also has the responsibility to implement and maintain an adequate system of documents and records that enable the preparation of the financial statements. As part of this system, management should implement controls that provide assurance that information (especially financial reporting information) is being properly captured, recorded, and reported.

The auditor's primary professional responsibility is to plan the audit so as to provide reasonable assurance that there are no significant misstatements in the financial statements.[1] The auditor can never know with certainty whether financial statements are fairly presented. Consequently, the audit engagement is planned to obtain enough evidence to support the auditor's conclusions. Identifying the facts that must be examined, assessing the risk that information may be erroneous, obtaining evidence about the accuracy of information, and reaching an overall conclusion involves a very complex and time consuming process that must be carefully planned if the auditor is to avoid making mistakes. The purpose of this chapter is to introduce and describe the basic building blocks of the auditor's analytical process which, when completed, will support the auditor's conclusion about the fairness of the financial statements.

An Overview of the Auditor's Role

As noted above, the primary responsibility of the auditor is to conduct the audit so that he or she has reasonable assurance that errors and fraudulent misstatements are detected and corrected. Reasonable assurance for an audit engagement is defined as "a high, but not absolute, level of assurance."[2] Auditors are not providing a guarantee that all significant misstatements will be discovered because they cannot evaluate every transaction or account balance in detail. Furthermore, management can collude with employees to conceal misstatements or instruct subordinates to override otherwise effective control systems such that auditors might fail to find existing misstatements.

AUTHORITATIVE GUIDANCE & STANDARDS

This chapter provides an overview of the fundamental concepts of an audit. Important topics covered in this chapter are included in standards that apply to a wide range of topics including the nature of assertions (ISA 315 **Understanding the Entity and Its Environment and Assessing the Risks of Material Misstatement**, *ISA 500* **Audit Evidence**; *AS 1105 [formerly AS 15]* **Audit Evidence**); *the risk of material misstatement and the quality of internal control over financial reporting (ISA 315, AS 2201 [formerly AS 5]* **An Audit of Internal Control Over Financial Reporting that is Integrated with An Audit of Financial Statements**), *fraud (ISA 240* **The Auditor's Responsibilities Relating to Fraud in an Audit of Financial Statements**; *PCAOB AS 2401 [formerly Interim Standard AU 316]* **Consideration of Fraud in a Financial Statement Audit**[3]); *materiality (ISA 320* **Materiality in Planning and Performing an Audit**; *AS 2105 [formerly AS 11]* **Consideration of Materiality in Planning and Performing an Audit**), *and audit evidence (ISA 500; AS 1105).*

Auditors distinguish between different types of financial misstatements. **Errors** are unintentional misstatements or omissions of financial information. Errors may be caused by incorrect processing of information, incorrect estimates, mistakes in the application of accounting principles, or incomplete disclosure. Fraudulent misstatements are intentional misstatements, or omissions of amounts, or disclosures in financial statements to deceive users. **Fraudulent misstatements** can result from the alteration or forgery of documents and records, omission or misrepresentation of key facts, or misuse of accounting principles. The difference between an error and a fraudulent misstatement is the existence or absence of "intent." All organizations and all accounting systems are subject to mistakes. On the other hand, fraudulent misstatements occur when one or more persons try to achieve personal or organizational goals at the expense of other stakeholders of the organization.

Fraud is further distinguished by the nature of the misstatement or omission. Fraudulent financial reporting involves management or other parties intentionally manipulating information in the financial statements (sometimes called management fraud[(i)]). If the fraud involves employee theft

(i)EXAMPLE

An overstatement in ending inventory usually results in an understatement of cost of goods sold and an overstatement of net income. Due to this relationship, the artificial inflation of inventory balances is a common technique to boost reported income artificially. This is known **as fraudulent financial reporting**.

Lapping is a situation where incoming cash receipts from customers are appropriated by an employee. This theft is then hidden by posting the customer's account as being paid at a later date using cash receipts from other customers. The net result is that today's receipts are stolen and tomorrow's receipts are posted to today's customers. This process must continue indefinitely or until the funds are returned. This is known as **misappropriation of assets.**

of entity assets, it is referred to as misappropriation of assets (sometimes called employee fraud(ii)). Typical examples of minor employee fraud are theft of petty cash funds or small tools. Embezzlement occurs when an executive steals corporate assets on a large scale and leaves others to absorb the loss. This type of problem is more common in small companies in which owners or managers obtain funds from customers or investors and then disappear before delivering the goods or developing the business.

AUTHORITATIVE GUIDANCE & STANDARDS

The concept of reasonable assurance is critical to conducting an effective audit. Standards on planning (ISA 300 **Planning an Audit of Financial Statements**; *AS 2101 [formerly AS 9]* **Audit Planning***) and assessing risk and materiality (ISA 320; AS 2101) both stress the importance of planning an audit to attain reasonable assurance. These standards imply that reasonable assurance should be a high level of assurance (ISA 200* **Overall objectives of the independent auditor and the conduct of the audit in accordance with international standards on auditing**; *AS 1101 [formerly AS 8]* **Audit Risk***).*

The public generally expects that an auditor will ferret out all errors and fraud in a client. The reality of auditing is a bit more complex, however. As a practical matter, an auditor focuses on errors and fraudulent financial reporting because they directly affect the financial statements and are often highly significant. Auditors are less concerned with misappropriation of assets because the amounts involved tend to be small and often have little direct impact on the financial statements unless the culprit tries to hide the theft by manipulating the accounting records. Professional standards require that the audit be planned so as to provide reasonable assurance that significant errors or fraudulent misstatements will be detected, regardless of their cause. Professional standards also acknowledge that a well-planned audit may not detect all fraudulent misstatements, especially those involving collusion among multiple persons or forgery of documents.

If a client is registered with the US SEC to issue equity or debt securities, the auditor also must obtain reasonable assurance that management's system of internal control over financial reporting is effective. Although auditors have always paid attention to internal control to some degree, it was up to the auditor to decide how much reliance to place on internal control during the course of the audit. Rules promulgated by the PCAOB have made the evaluation of internal control a responsibility that is the equal of the audit of the financial results for publicly traded companies in the US. Consequently, auditors in an **Integrated Audit** now devote a great deal of time and energy in the audit of those companies to internal control over financial reporting, and auditors are required to issue an opinion on the effectiveness of the client's internal control over financial reporting. This report on internal control effectiveness at year end, along with a report on the audit of the financial statements for the year, are the results of the Integrated Audit.

Management's Assertions

The starting point for an auditor is to identify the information that is to be subject to the auditor's attention and that is subject to potential misstatement. The focus of the audit is on assertions made by management about its financial results and internal control system. The auditor's task is to determine whether the assertions can be believed.

Financial Reporting Assertions

A financial statement audit is designed to assess the fairness of management assertions about financial results. Figure 3.1 depicts the key conceptual elements of the audit process. Each of these elements will be defined in turn. The key point to note is that Figure 3.1 represents the thought process that the auditor undertakes in each and every audit. The context, details, and requirements may change, but the logical process is essentially the same.

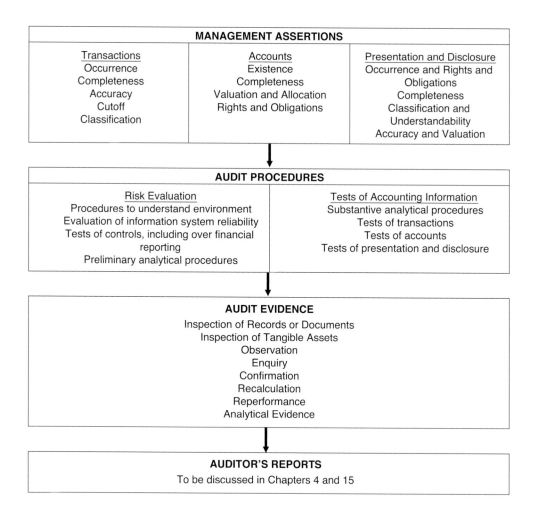

Figure 3.1 Concepts Underlying the Audit Process

In the context of an audit, assertions represent the set of information that the preparer of information (management) is providing to another party. Financial statements represent a very complex and interrelated set of assertions. At the most aggregate level, the financial statements include assertions such as "total assets as of December 31 are $30 billion," "net income for the year is $125 million," and "gross margin is 35 percent." Each of these assertions is interesting in its own right, but each can also be decomposed into a more refined set of assertions. For example, the statement about total assets can be decomposed into separate statements about cash, receivables, inventory, and so forth. Similarly, an assertion about net income can be broken into more detailed statements about revenues and expenses.

Although readers of financial statements tend to focus on highly aggregated assertions about profit margins, income, and assets, financial statements implicitly reflect a number of specific assertions made by management. For example, management implicitly asserts that recorded assets and liabilities exist and that transactions actually occurred; there are no unrecorded assets, liabilities, or transactions; the organization actually owns the assets reported; and the valuation, presentation, and disclosure of assets, liabilities, and transactions is in accordance with GAAP. Auditors decompose broad assertions into a detailed set of statements referred to as **management assertions** (or **financial statement assertions**), separated into three categories: (1) transactions, (2) accounts, and (3) presentation and disclosure:[4]

Management Assertions about Transactions

- *Occurrence*—Transactions and events that have been recorded have occurred and pertain to the entity.
- *Completeness*—All transactions and events that should have been recorded have been recorded.
- *Accuracy*—Amounts and other data relating to recorded transactions and events have been recorded appropriately.
- *Cut-off*—Transactions and events have been recorded in the correct accounting period.
- *Classification*—Transactions and events have been recorded in the proper accounts.

Management Assertions about Accounts

- *Existence*—Assets, liabilities, and equity interests exist.
- *Rights and obligations*—The entity holds or controls the rights to assets, and liabilities are the obligations of the entity.
- *Completeness*—All assets, liabilities, and equity interests that should have been recorded have been recorded.
- *Valuation and allocation*—Assets, liabilities, and equity interests are included in the financial statements at appropriate amounts and any resulting valuation or allocation adjustments are appropriately recorded.

Management Assertions about Presentation and Disclosure

- *Occurrence and rights and obligations*—Disclosed events and transactions have occurred and pertain to the entity.

- *Completeness*—All disclosures that should have been included in the financial statements have been included.

- *Classification and understandability*—Financial information is appropriately presented and described, and information in disclosures is clearly expressed.

- *Accuracy and valuation*—Financial and other information is disclosed fairly and at appropriate amounts.[5]

These assertions are considered to be the basic building blocks of accounting information and can be used to decompose specific transactions, account balances, or presentation and disclosure items into components that can be readily tested by the auditor. The auditor is responsible for verifying that all important management assertions related to transactions, accounts, and line items and disclosures in the financial statements are reasonable, that is, free of significant misstatement.[6] A key point to keep in mind is that these assertions do not necessarily correspond directly with a specific statement made by the provider of information and some may only be implied by the information provided.

AUTHORITATIVE GUIDANCE & STANDARDS

ISA 315 (A110–A112) groups management assertions according to the three components of financial reporting—classes of transactions, accounts, and presentation and disclosure. These standards also suggest that auditors should consider assertions made by management for the financial statements taken as a whole (e.g., ISA 315). Auditors are not precluded from considering management assertions from a different perspective as long as the alternative approach addresses all assertions described in the standard. The PCAOB in AS 1105 continued with the traditional classification of what it calls "financial statement assertions": existence or occurrence, completeness, valuation or allocation, rights and obligations, and presentation and disclosure.

To illustrate, consider the financial statements of a manufacturing company. The process of acquiring materials is critical to most manufacturers. Table 3.1 illustrates the nature of management's assertions related to purchases and inventory. For transactions, management asserts that all inventory purchases *occurred*, the recorded transactions are *complete* (none were overlooked), recorded amounts are *accurate*, purchases occurred before the end-of-period *cut-off* date, and all journal entries were recorded in the proper account *classifications*. For inventory accounts, management asserts that inventory actually *exists* and is *complete* (no amounts omitted). Potential problems arise when inventory is out on consignment or when shipments are in transit. In these cases, the company may include inventory for which it has no *rights* because title belongs to another party. The *valuation* assertion for inventory must take into account the pricing method being

Table 3.1 *Management Assertions for Purchases and Inventory*

Assertions	Example
Transactions Assertions	
Occurrence	Recorded purchases of inventory actually took place.
Completeness	All actual purchases of inventory were recorded.
Accuracy	Purchases were recorded at the appropriate amounts (e.g., all prices and quantities were accurately computed).
Cutoff	All recorded purchases occurred in the current period.
Classification	All purchases of inventory were recorded in the proper accounts (e.g., inventory debited and accounts payable credited).
Account Assertions	
Existence	All items included in the list of inventory exist in the quantities indicated.
Completeness	All existing inventory has been included in inventory counts.
Rights and Obligations	Items that have been included in inventory are owned by the client firm who has the right to sell or pledge the items.
Valuation and Allocation	Inventory is properly priced using an acceptable method and considering the application of the lower-of-cost-or-market rule.
	Inventory transactions, as affected by sales and purchases, have been recorded in the proper period.
	Inventory has been accurately compiled and summarized and agrees with the recorded account balance.
Presentation and Disclosure Assertions	
Occurrence and Rights and Obligations	The line item of merchandise inventory includes only valid inventory accounts that reflect actual purchased and produced inventory, all of which is owned by the client.
Completeness	The line item of merchandise inventory includes all inventory accounts.
Classification and Understandability	The significant accounting policies footnote clearly describes the inventory method used (e.g., FIFO [first-in, first-out] adjusted for lower-of-cost-or-market), and the inventory footnote properly segregates raw materials inventory, work-in-process inventory, and finished goods inventory.
Accuracy and Valuation	The merchandise inventory line item properly sums all inventory accounts net of reserves for obsolescence.

used (e.g., FIFO [first-in, first-out]) and current market conditions affecting the lower-of-cost-or-market. Finally, management also makes assertions related to the disclosures about purchases and inventory in the financial statements, including that they are *understandable*.

Internal Control Assertions

Management is responsible for establishing effective internal control over financial reporting whether in the context of a GAAS Audit or an Integrated Audit. Formally, internal control over financial reporting is defined as:[7]

> A process designed by, or under the supervision of, the company's principal executive and principal financial officers … and effected by the company's Board of Directors, management, and other personnel, to provide reasonable assurance regarding the reliability of financial reporting … for external purposes in accordance with generally accepted accounting principles and includes those policies and procedures that:

1. Pertain to the maintenance of records that, in reasonable detail, accurately and fairly reflect the transactions and dispositions of the assets of the company;

2. Provide reasonable assurance that transactions are recorded as necessary to permit preparation of financial statements in accordance with generally accepted accounting principles, and that receipts and expenditures of the company are being made only in accordance with authorizations of management and directors of the company; and

3. Provide reasonable assurance regarding prevention or timely detection of unauthorized acquisition, use or disposition of the company's assets that could have a material effect on the financial statements.

While management is always responsible for internal control, there is no standard approach for establishing and evaluating the effectiveness of internal control over financial reporting. In an Integrated Audit setting, management must choose and employ an appropriate control framework. To be suitable, the PCAOB requires that an internal control framework should be: (1) unbiased, (2) subject to consistent measurement, (3) comprehensive, and (4) relevant. For all settings other than an Integrated Audit, management does not have to explicitly adopt an internal control framework, albeit it is difficult to develop a comprehensive set of internal controls without at least some guiding principles.

There are three primary frameworks for evaluating internal control over financial reporting that are generally accepted in practice. The first framework, *Internal Control–Integrated Framework*, was developed by the Committee of Sponsoring Organizations (COSO) in 1992. COSO expanded this framework in 2006 to also focus on the special needs of smaller public companies.[8] As the COSO framework is specifically endorsed in the US by the PCAOB, we will discuss it further when we discuss internal control in depth in Chapters 7 and 8.[9] In 2013 COSO updated *Internal Control–Integrated Framework* and made the framework broader than the 1992 Framework's focus on internal control over financial reporting. Companies had until December 2014 to transition to the new framework. Other frameworks include *Guidance on Control*, developed by the Canadian Institute of Chartered Accountants' (CICA) Criteria of Control Committee (COCO), and the *Turnbull Combined Code*, developed in the United Kingdom. The COCO and Turnbull approaches have a broader view of control the than 1992 COSO framework and incorporate elements of enterprise risk management. Whereas the COCO and Turnbull frameworks focus on monitoring and improving control, the COSO framework is oriented toward evaluating internal control. However, improving internal control necessitates using a framework for detecting control weaknesses; therefore, the different approaches have a great deal of overlap.

In addition to adopting a framework, in companies where an Integrated Audit is required, management must publicly accept responsibility for the effectiveness of the company's internal control over financial reporting; evaluate the effectiveness of the internal control over financial reporting using the chosen framework; support its evaluation with sufficient evidence, including documentation; and present a written assessment of the effectiveness of internal control over financial reporting as of the end of the company's most recent fiscal year. Furthermore, the control system must be comprehensive enough to provide reasonable assurance that the management assertions in the financial statements are reliable. Auditors in a GAAS Audit do not require that companies carry out such an evaluation or make such a report. As we will see in Chapter 4, auditors as part of their engagement letter require management take explicit responsibility for sufficient internal control so that an audit of financial statements can be undertaken.

The Pervasive Concepts of Auditing: Risk, Materiality, and Evidence

Management assertions reflect the start of the audit process but how does the auditor determine whether management's assertions are accurate? We start our discussion of the audit process by focusing on a key phrase that occurs frequently in the discussion of the audit process—***reasonable assurance***. Subjectivity is inherent in the audit process as evidenced by commonly encountered terminology such as "significant," "important," "sizeable," "likely," and "probable." Although aggravatingly imprecise, these terms reflect that the auditor must deal with uncertainty in many different forms. The notion of reasonable assurance comprises three concepts that are pervasive to the conduct of an audit: risk, materiality, and evidence.

Risk, as pointed out in Chapter 2, is fundamental to all auditing because it reflects the reality that an auditor can never be completely certain that the assertions he or she is auditing—regardless of whether they pertain to single accounts, the overall financial statements, or internal control over financial reporting—are free of omissions or misstatements. That condition is why much of the previous discussion used terms such as "reasonable" and "likely." Auditors define many different types of risk. Misstatements may or may not be present, but the audit must be planned to enable the auditor to provide reasonable—not absolute—assurance that any existing misstatements that would matter to outside users of the financial statements are discovered and removed from the assertions and disclosures that comprise the financial statements.

Materiality is the term used to describe the significance of financial statement information to decision makers. Information is material if it is probable that its omission or misstatement would influence or change a decision. More formally, materiality is defined in the International Accounting Standards Board The Conceptual Framework for Financial Reporting as:

> Information is material if its omission or misstatement could influence the economic decisions of users taken on the basis of the financial statements. Materiality depends on the size of the item or error judged in the particular circumstances of its omission or misstatement, thus, materiality provides a threshold or cut-off point.
>
> (paragraph 30)

Materiality is a matter of professional judgment as to what is significant or important in the context of the financial statements being audited. Unfortunately, the definition of materiality is open to interpretation and there are no regulatory or generally accepted standards for determining what is, or is not, material in a given engagement or particular set of circumstances. Consequently, the implementation of materiality rests firmly with the professional judgment of the practitioner conducting an audit.

Audit evidence is any information that gives the auditor an indication whether an assertion is reasonable or not. Evidence comes in many forms and can provide strong or weak support for the fairness of assertions, depending on the circumstances of an engagement. A key goal of the audit is to obtain sufficient appropriate evidence on which to base an opinion about the financial statements. Unfortunately, evidence is often incomplete or subject to interpretation. The auditor must make explicit decisions about how to obtain sufficient evidence that provides reasonable assurance that there are no material misstatements in the financial statements, and that satisfies generally accepted auditing standards. The general rule that most auditors adopt is that they will concentrate their efforts looking at conditions that are most likely to lead to problems and/or misstatements.

The three concepts of risk, evidence, and materiality interact during the course of the audit to guide the appropriate conduct of the audit. An auditor will gather more evidence for a client who is considered to be high risk than for a client who is considered to be low risk. At the same time, the auditor's perception of materiality will affect the risk of the client. If the materiality threshold is low (that is, small errors are important) the auditor will have to gather more evidence because it is harder to find small errors than large errors. In short, the auditor gathers evidence to determine the risk that a material misstatement exists in one or more assertions made by the client's management. The more evidence the auditor obtains, the lower the risk that there are undetected material errors in the assertions being examined.

Risk Concepts in Auditing

Although auditors deal with many forms of risk during the course of an engagement, three broad types of risk are of paramount interest to the auditor: client business risk, auditor engagement risk, and audit risk.

Client Business Risk

Client business risk reflects the possibility that an organization will experience adverse outcomes as a result of economic conditions, events, circumstances, or management action/inaction. As noted in Chapter 2, business risks are identified, analyzed, and mitigated through enterprise risk management. Auditors are also concerned with client business risks because such risks shed light on the effectiveness of the client's ERM framework, and they may eventually have an impact on the company's financial statements. Business risks may arise from the complexity of the environment and/or changes in the organization, though a failure to recognize the need for change may also give rise to risk. For example, organizations may suffer adverse outcomes from the failure of new products, inadequate market development, or from flaws in execution that lead to economic losses or impairment of reputation.

Some risks may result in the need for significant adjustments to the financial statements. When a tsunami in the Indian Ocean struck two luxury Le Méridien resorts in Thailand in December 2004, both resorts closed for an extended period. This event was a great human tragedy and also had a severe economic impact on many businesses, including the hotel. An auditor would assess whether the insurance on the properties was sufficient to cover the losses associated with the property, as well as the lost business at the damaged properties. The issue is whether any losses sustained are large enough to be material to the hotel chain and, if so, whether the company has fairly reflected such actual and expected losses in its financial statements.

In response to alleged improprieties and lack of professionalism in the conduct of some audits, the SEC prohibited Ernst & Young from accepting any new clients for a six-month period. Ernst & Young did not perceive that the actions in question warranted this punishment. Nevertheless, in an effort to minimize its losses, the firm accepted the ruling while protesting its innocence.

Most client business risks will eventually have an effect on the results reported in the financial statements. However, some business risks can have an immediate effect on a class of transactions, account balance, or disclosure. For example, risk arising from a shrinking customer base due to industry consolidation may lead to questions about the valuation of receivables (which may not be collected) and/or inventory (which may not be sold(iii)).

Auditor Engagement Risk

Auditors and audit firms are also susceptible to their own form of business risk since they choose which organizations to take on as clients. **Engagement risk** refers to the risk the audit firm is exposed to due to loss or injury from litigation, adverse publicity, or other events arising in connection with the audited financial statements. Such risk may exist even if the audit is conducted according to professional standards. The concept of engagement risk recognizes the possibility that the audit firm may suffer a loss from association with a client even though the firm complies with all relevant professional standards and issues the appropriate audit report based on the evidence available at the time of the audit. Possible manifestations of engagement risk include:

1. Litigation. If the audit firm is sued because the client goes bankrupt or has committed fraud or an illegal act, often the audit firm will suffer an economic loss even if it wins the case. The costs of litigation, even in the case of the auditor's successful defense, can more than wipe out any profit earned by the firm on the original engagement. These costs are mitigated in some countries where the plaintiff must pay the costs of the defendant auditor. Even in these cases the costs are often assessed on schedules that do not reflect the audit firm's full out of pocket defense costs, let alone its opportunity costs.

2. Regulatory penalties. Audit firms may be subject to fines or other penalties if they are associated with a failed client or a client involved in fraud or intense regulatory scrutiny (e.g., material restatements of financial statements(iv)).

3. Loss of professional reputation. If the firm becomes associated with an enterprise that has a poor reputation, it may lose future clients because more reputable organizations do not want to associate with the firm—that is, they do not want to suffer guilt by association(v).

4. Lack of profitability. After an auditing firm completes an engagement, it may discover that the fee that a client is willing to pay is inadequate to cover the costs of providing audit services. Unless there is a good reason for continuing the association, the firm would prefer not to undertake engagements that are not profitable.[10]

Audit Risk

Audit risk is considered at both the overall engagement level and the account balance level. It is defined as the likelihood that an auditor will render an incorrect opinion on the financial statements in spite of the effort expended to conduct the audit effectively. More formally, audit risk is defined as the likelihood or probability that the auditor will conclude that all material assertions made by management are true when, in fact, at least one material assertion is incorrect. Audit risk can be decomposed into two component risks: (1) risk of material misstatement, and (2) detection risk.

Risk of Material Misstatement

Accounting misstatements—whether unintentional errors or intentional frauds—arise from many sources. Transaction processing can be inaccurate, transactions can be lost or omitted from the accounting system, results can be falsified, assets can be stolen or lost, inappropriate accounting policies may be selected, or accounting estimates may be manipulated. Hence, the auditor must consider the ***risk of material misstatement,*** which is defined as "the risk that the financial statements are misstated prior to audit."[11] At the financial statement level, the risk of material misstatement pertains to the financial statements as a whole and reflects the joint effect misstatements may have across a number of assertions. The risk of material misstatement also applies to classes of transactions, specific accounts, and individual disclosures, and is a function of:

- Business risks associated with the client's industry, strategy, business model, and business processes.

- Susceptibility of assets to theft.

- Ease with which information can be manipulated.

- Information processing risks associated with high-volume, routine transactions.

- Challenges associated with accounting for non-routine or complex transactions.

- Risks associated with judgments made while determining accounting estimates.

- Limitations (e.g., cost, competence, and so forth) that prevent internal controls over financial reporting from preventing or detecting all material misstatements.

AUTHORITATIVE GUIDANCE & STANDARDS

The concepts of risk are referenced in many standards including some overarching standards (ISA 200; AS 1101). Other standards that are more focused on risk considerations during a financial statement audit are focused on identifying risks (ISA 320, AS 2105), assessing risk of material misstatement (ISA 315, AS 2210 [formerly AS 12] **Identifying and Assessing the Risks of Material Misstatement**), *performing procedures in response to assessed risks (ISA 330* **The Auditor's Responses to Assessed Risks,** *AS 2201, AS 2301 [formerly AS 13]* **The Auditor's Responses to Risks of Material Misstatement**).

The auditor cannot directly influence the risk of material misstatement in the current period because it is considered an attribute of the accounting system and internal control over financial reporting that the company has currently

(v)EXAMPLE

In the 1950s, large auditing firms would not accept Las Vegas casinos as clients due to their unsavory links with organized crime. Now that casinos are often owned by large, public companies, auditors are willing to take them on as clients. In recent years, on-line gambling sites have reputedly had similar problems in engaging auditors.

A credit manager is responsible for reviewing credit applications from new customers in order to reduce the risk of bad debts. If the credit manager does not get credit reports on new customers, credit may be granted to customers that have previously defaulted on obligations and eventually leading to the customer's balance being written off. This weakness in internal control may lead to a material misstatement in the current financial statements (such as an inadequate allowance for bad debts). The auditor may provide advice on how to rectify this problem in the future, reducing the risk of material misstatement in future audits.

in place. In future years, auditors may influence the risk of misstatement by encouraging management to strengthen areas of the accounting system that are considered to be at risk. If management responds to the auditor's advice and implements effective controls, the risk of material misstatement is likely to be reduced for future audits(vi).

The risk of material misstatement can be further decomposed at the assertion level into two components: inherent risk and control risk. **Inherent risk** is defined as the risk that misstatements might occur *if there were no internal controls*. However, this risk only exists in theory because we also know all entities have at least some internal controls that will prevent and/ or detect at least some potential misstatements. **Control risk** reflects the likelihood that the controls present in the system will not prevent or detect a material error in the financial statements. Past experience has demonstrated that auditors have difficulty separating inherent risk from control risk so the broader concept of risk of material misstatement (previously called joint assessment by some firms) has become more common in practice, although some firms continue to split the concepts as part of their formal audit approaches.

Detection Risk

The primary task of an auditor is to search for and uncover misstatements in the financial records. The risk that an auditor may fail to discover an existing misstatement is **detection risk**, more formally defined in ISA 200 as, "The risk that the auditor will not detect a material misstatement that exists in an assertion." Detection risk is a function of the effectiveness of the audit procedures performed and the interpretation of the resulting evidence. Detection risk cannot be reduced to zero because the auditor usually does not examine all transactions, account balances, or disclosures. Furthermore, the auditor may fail to perform the appropriate audit procedure, misapply an audit procedure, or misinterpret the results.

Materiality

The question "does it matter?" reflects the essence of materiality. When an auditor encounters potential problems during the course of the audit, he or she has to anticipate whether other stakeholders will consider the impact of the problem on the financial statements to be important. Judgments about materiality are often about "scale." For example, if a cash drawer is $5.00 short, an error or theft may have occurred, but the auditor is unlikely to be concerned since the amount is small in the context of the total balance sheet. At the other extreme, an account such as inventory usually represents a large portion of total assets for a manufacturing or merchandising company, as well as the largest expense on the income statement (i.e., cost of goods sold). Therefore, if inventory is misstated by 50 percent, most auditors would agree that the impact on both the balance sheet and income statement would be "material." For other accounts, such as prepaid insurance, an error of 50 percent of the balance may be immaterial, unless management has intentionally misstated the balance. Whether an "error" is "material" then depends on a number of possible factors.

Quantitative Materiality

When planning the audit, the auditor considers the magnitude of an error that would make the financial statements materially misstated. If a company is going to round off its financial results to the nearest million dollars, then it is easy to see that materiality must be at least $500,000—anything smaller would not even create a "rounding" error. How large the materiality threshold should be is subject to a great deal of judgment and auditors have developed numerous rules of thumb for setting an initial materiality level.

AUTHORITATIVE GUIDANCE & STANDARDS

Materiality is one of the most important judgments that an auditor must make, and standards discuss important considerations regarding the concept (ISA 320, AS 2105), although they do not stipulate a preferred method of determining materiality. For publicly traded US companies, the SEC issued Staff Accounting Bulletin (SAB) No. 99 that essentially prohibits any consideration of materiality for known misstatements, meaning that auditors must require clients to correct any known misstatements except for trivial amounts that are very small relative to overall materiality.

Generally, a reasonable guideline for materiality is 5 to 10 percent of net income for a business making a profit (not showing losses) or 1 to 3 percent of net assets for a not-for-profit organization. However, auditors may select other bases or percentages for establishing materiality if they have a good reason. For example, an auditor who believes that readers emphasize revenues or gross margin as the basis for evaluating an organization may use something along the lines of 3 percent of revenues or 10 percent of gross margin for materiality.

The auditor should also consider the possibility that numerous small misstatements could have a material *aggregate* effect on the financial statements. For example, an error in a month-end procedure could lead to a material misstatement if it is repeated each month. The auditor considers materiality at both the overall financial statement level and in relation to individual account balances, classes of transactions, and disclosures. Auditors should consider materiality both for current period misstatements in isolation, and for prior misstatements that were uncorrected because they were not deemed to be material but might be material when combined with current year misstatements.

Qualitative Materiality

The auditor should also consider qualitative aspects of materiality, that is, the nature of a misstatement may be more important than its size. Some subjective reasons why an auditor might consider a small misstatement to be material include:

- Fraud: The discovery of fraud is always considered to be important because it indicates problems with management's integrity and credibility.
- Violations of debt covenants: Misstatements that allow a company to avoid technical default may be important since violating a debt covenant may mean renegotiating the entire debt agreement.
- Missing earnings targets: Failing to achieve earnings equal to or superior to analysts' forecasts, even by a penny a share, may cause an extreme drop in the market capitalization of a company.
- Hitting incentive goals: If management and/or employees have incentive-based compensation contracts, misstatements that allow them to achieve their goals can be material[vii].

In some situations, the concept of materiality may not be quantifiable at all. For example, incomplete or improper disclosures may be considered to be "material" if they have the potential to mislead users of the financial statements. Similarly, failure to disclose a breach of regulatory requirements might be considered a material disclosure "error[viii]."

The concept of materiality has been greatly abused in recent years. In some cases, auditors have relied on an arbitrary level of materiality to allow revenue and associated profits to be intentionally shifted between time periods in order to meet analysts' forecasts of earnings per share. Typically, this behavior has been rationalized by keeping intentional misstatements small, that is, below materiality. Because the behavior is presumed to affect the decisions of stakeholders interested in the company—otherwise, why do it—it is difficult to argue that such misstatements "don't matter." Some regulatory bodies have taken steps to remove an auditor's ability to use materiality as justification for actions that are taken simply to appease management. The SEC specifically prohibits the use of materiality as a basis for not following generally accepted accounting principles—they require that all known errors in the financial statements be corrected, except those that are clearly trivial.

Evidence Collection in Auditing

An auditor's conclusions about the fairness of financial statements must be based on a convincing body of evidence. In terms of auditing standards, the auditor must gather sufficient competent evidence on which to base an opinion. An auditor follows a well-understood process for obtaining the requisite evidence, conditional on the environment, circumstances, and risks of the client. The process of gathering information and evidence about the client's activities, risks, and results is divided into two main phrases: (1) risk assessment, and (2) tests of accounting information (refer to Table 3.2).

Risk Assessment

To inform the auditor about the various types of risks related to the audit engagement and to aid in developing criteria for what is to be considered material, auditors assess current conditions within an organization.

Table 3.2 *Collection of Audit Evidence*

Type of Procedure	Resulting Audit Evidence	Relationship with Financial Statement Errors
Procedures to Assess Risk		
Understanding an organization's environment, strategies, and plans	Enquiries Observation Inspection of documents Analysis	Indication of errors is very indirect. The procedures indicate the risks from the environment that can adversely affect the organization and the reliability of management and information systems in general, but does not indicate whether specific transactions or accounts are correct.
Understanding information system design, reliability and effectiveness	Enquiries Observation Inspection of documents Analysis	Indication of errors is indirect. Breakdowns in the information system and controls over transaction flows may or may not result in an error in a transaction or account. Frequent breakdowns increase the likelihood that errors occur and go undetected by the organization.
Preliminary analytical procedures	Analysis Enquiries	Indication of errors is indirect. The procedures indicate circumstances that appear to be unusual and could arise from misstatements or errors.
Procedures to Test Accounting Information		
Substantive analytical procedures	Analytical evidence	Indication of errors or fraud is indirect. The procedures indicate accounts that appear to have unusual balances which may be due to a misstatement.
Tests of transactions	Inspection of documents Recalculation and reperformance Enquiry	Indication of errors or fraud in a *transaction* is direct; indication of an error or fraud in an *account* is indirect since the problem may have been detected and corrected at a later date or may have reversed by the end of the year.
Tests of accounts	Inspection of tangible assets Inspection of documents Recalculation Confirmation Enquiry	Indication of errors or fraud is direct based on auditor inspection of assets, documentation of specific items, and recalculation of numerical values and/or confirmation of information provided by third parties.
Tests of presentation and disclosure	Inspection of documents Confirmation Enquiry Recalculation	Indication of errors or fraud is direct based on a review of the disclosures or may be indirect in the case of the examination of related documents from which disclosures are derived.

Information that is necessary for understanding the context of the audit is gathered by means of procedures that help the auditor to:

- Understand an organization's environment, objectives, strategies, and risks.
- Understand the design, reliability, and effectiveness of enterprise risk management and internal control over financial reporting.
- Perform preliminary analytical procedures.

These procedures will be discussed in much more detail in later chapters, but it is important to understand how they influence the conduct of the audit.

Understanding an Organization's Environment and Risks

One of the first tasks during an engagement is to develop an understanding of the client's environment, including the external forces influencing the organization (e.g., regulation, competition); its business objectives and strategies for achieving them; the design of its internal activities and processes; the nature of its information system; and the types of transactions that occur. This information is critical for understanding the risks that threaten the organization, and it provides a framework for interpreting the organization's financial results. Additionally, the auditor tries to develop a comprehensive understanding of the risks that are most critical to the organization, paying careful attention to how these risks likely impact the financial statements[ix].

Understanding Risk Management and Internal Control over Financial Reporting

Every organization devotes substantial resources to managing risks and safeguarding itself from errors and fraud in the accounting system. The more effective management is at reducing its risk, the fewer problems the auditor can expect to encounter during the engagement. Of most interest to the auditor is the effectiveness of the internal controls over financial reporting. For example, the auditor might want to know that inventory purchases are being properly authorized, that sales clerks are checking the price of merchandise being sold, and that credit card charges are being properly validated. If these control activities are systematically and rigorously followed, there is less of a chance that sales will be processed incorrectly. Auditors use tests of system reliability, often called **tests of controls**, to assess the quality of transaction processing and measure the risk that transactions may be processed incorrectly[x].

Preliminary Analytical Procedures

Auditors usually have a great deal of quantitative data available to help assess the significance of risks facing an organization. This data may be financial or nonfinancial in nature and can be used to develop a greater understanding of the company and expectations about its economic condition. Auditors are required to look at the preliminary financial results during the course of the year, or right after the end of the fiscal year, in order to identify potential problem areas where the results are inconsistent with the known circumstances of the company, or where they just don't make sense given the risk profile of the company. In short, the auditor looks for initial warning signals that results may be out of line, or possibly misstated[xi].

Tests of Accounting Information

Once an auditor has assessed the risk of material misstatements, the next step is to perform specific tests of reported results. Auditors may perform a broad range of tests at this point dependent on their risk assessments, the assertions at risk, and the type of evidence that is available. In general, there are four different types of tests applicable to accounting information:

- **Substantive analytical procedures:** The comparison of quantitative relationships among account balances and other indicators to an auditor's expectations. If an auditor's expectations are not met (e.g., the relationships exhibit unusual patterns), additional evidence is gathered to identify whether misstatements exist[(xii)].
- **Tests of transactions:** The verification of the details of specific transactions[(xiii)].
- **Tests of accounts:** The examination of the details that comprise a year-end balance[(xiv)].
- **Tests of presentation and disclosure:** Review and examination of the disclosures in the financial statements for clarity and completeness[(xv)].

Numerous specific examples of these types of procedures are identified and described in later chapters. It is important to keep in mind that the design of these tests depends on the nature of the assertion or account being examined and the level of detection risk the auditor wishes to achieve.

Types of Audit Evidence

All audit procedures create audit evidence which facilitates the auditor's evaluation of the accuracy and completeness of management assertions that comprise the financial statements. Auditors should be aware that many of these forms of evidence are now collected with the assistance of information technology. When utilizing information generated from client automated systems, auditors should ensure that data used as evidence is reliable. This normally requires that an engagement team member have special expertise in information technology controls. Regardless of the underlying procedure that generates the evidence, there are seven general categories of evidence used by auditors:

- **Inspection (or Examination) of Tangible Assets:** Evidence obtained from the firsthand inspection of tangible assets by the auditor. This type of evidence is very reliable but can be used only for assets that are available for inspection. This type of evidence is particularly good for verifying the existence of assets[(xvi)].
- **Confirmation:** Written or oral evidence received from third parties who are independent of the client and believed to be unbiased. This type of evidence is considered to be highly reliable and is particularly useful for verifying the existence or completeness assertions[(xvii)].
- **Inspection (or Examination) of Records or Documents:** Evidence obtained from the examination of the client's written records or documents in the client's possession. This is also referred to as "vouching" a transaction. This type of evidence is easy to obtain and can support all assertions in the financial statements. However, because it is obtained from the client, its reliability should be established through other procedures.
- **Observation:** Visual evidence obtained by the auditor by witnessing client activities while they are in progress. This type of evidence can be used in the absence of a "paper trail" for processing transactions, and is often used for tests of controls.[12] [(xviii)]

[(xii)]**EXAMPLE**

The revenue for a hotel chain can be estimated by multiplying the number of rooms in each of the hotels by the average occupancy rate for the hotel and the average room charge per night. If the auditor computed result is reasonably close to the recorded amount for revenue on the hotel chain's books, the auditor would consider that evidence in forming an opinion that the account is free of material error.

[(xiii)]**EXAMPLE**

To ensure the occurrence of sales, an auditor selects a sample of recorded sales transactions and tests them by examining the supporting sales invoice, shipping documentation, and customer purchase order.

[(xiv)]**EXAMPLE**

To test the existence and valuation of the work in progress account for a manufacturer, the auditor can observe the raw and semi-processed inventory during the inventory observation in addition to detailed testing of how costs are transferred into the work in progress account.

[(xv)]**EXAMPLE**

To test the understandability of an organization's disclosures about long-term debt, the auditor can inspect the footnotes to ensure they are clear, concise, and do not use complex terminology to mislead users.

The existence of tangible assets such as inventory, plant and equipment, investment securities, and cash can be physically verified.

(xvii)**EXAMPLE**

Typical confirmation evidence comes from customers who confirm receivable balances, banks who confirm deposit balances (and loans), attorneys who confirm details of litigation (possible contingent losses), and suppliers who confirm balances owed (accounts payable).

(xviii)**EXAMPLE**

Companies typically restrict access to computer facilities to avoid unauthorized use and modification of computer records. The auditor might observe the physical security over computer equipment to determine if access is actually restricted and observe authorized personnel performing the necessary procedures to gain access.

(xix)**EXAMPLE**

The accuracy of an invoice can be checked by re-performing the procedures that the client follows such as entering the price and quantity of a sale and then recalculating taxes, discounts, and transaction totals. The total of the transaction can then be traced to the proper accounting records such as a sales journal and/or customer receivable ledger.

- **Recalculation and/or Re-performance:** Computational evidence obtained by verifying summary totals (e.g., adding up individual transaction amounts to arrive at the total account balance) or re-performing client procedures. Traditionally, auditors referred to recalculation as "footing" or "running a tape." Today, the mechanical steps of adding accounts are normally performed through the use of computer software (i.e., computer-assisted audit techniques or CAATs) that can check the accuracy of account activity[xix].

- **Analytical Evidence (or Analysis):** Auditor comparison of expected balances or relationships to actual financial and nonfinancial data. Unexpected relationships often are due to unusual circumstances that are inconsistent with the auditor's expectations for an account or class of transactions. Evidence based on analysis often involves examining the relationships among important account balances, percentages or ratios for unexplained variations that might indicate that an error has occurred. Another form of analytical procedures is *scanning* client records for the existence of any unusual amounts or entries[xx].

- **Client Enquiry:** Evidence obtained from written and oral representations made by management or other client personnel. This evidence is usually obtained in response to questions raised by the auditor. Client enquiry is often a starting point for gathering further evidence. Client enquiries are very important for assessing current conditions within an organization, but will usually need to be corroborated with other types of evidence. In evaluating the strength of the evidence, the auditor must assess the credibility of the source[xxi].

AUTHORITATIVE GUIDANCE & STANDARDS

The types and competence of evidence are discussed in auditing standards on audit evidence (ISA 500, AS 1105). These standards do not require that the auditor gather specific types of evidence, however, except in very narrow circumstances (e.g. receivables confirmations ISA 505 **External Confirmations**, *PCAOB AS 2310 [formerly Interim Standard AU 330]* **The Confirmation Process**).

Competence of Audit Evidence

When selecting procedures to address specific management assertions, the auditor will consider the risk assessments related to the assertion and the materiality of the assertion relative to the overall financial statements. With this in mind, the auditor will then determine how competent the evidence needs to be in order to satisfy the auditor's goal for detection risk. If the desired detection risk is low, the auditor will want a great deal of competent substantive evidence; if desired detection risk is high, the auditor may examine fewer transactions or utilize somewhat less effective procedures that are easier to perform or are less time consuming.

How does an auditor know the competence or quality of the evidence from a specific audit procedure? There are a number of characteristics that the auditor can consider in order to understand the competence of audit evidence.

- **Degree of relevance:** Is the evidence obtained from a procedure relevant to the assertion being examined? If the auditor wishes to know if inventory exists, the best way to find out is to physically observe the inventory on hand and count the items. Of course, physical observation will not tell the auditor whether or not the items in the warehouse are actually owned by the client.

- **Independence of the provider:** Is the source of the evidence independent of the company, or is it subject to possible manipulation by the company? Information obtained from a person outside the client's company is usually considered to be superior to that received from an insider. An outsider is assumed to have no vested interest in the outcome of the audit, whereas an insider may try to sway the auditor's opinion in order to advance his or her own goals.

- **Degree of auditor's direct knowledge:** Is the evidence directly observable at its source by the auditor? "Seeing is believing" is an adage that clearly applies to auditors. Again, the best way to determine if inventory is present is to look at it. Supplier invoices may indicate how many items of inventory the client acquired, but this type of documentary evidence is only second-best to direct physical examination of the inventory[xxii].

- **Qualifications of the provider:** Is the source of the evidence qualified to provide evidence that is accurate? When receiving evidence from another person, the auditor must consider the competence of the provider. For example, the best person to provide information to the auditor about a pension plan is probably an actuary. Similarly, the best person to provide information about the value of real estate is an appraiser.

- **Degree of objectivity:** Is the evidence ambiguous or open to interpretation? Audit evidence is rarely clear-cut in its support of an assertion. This is especially true for the valuation assertion. For example, a company may provide extensive evidence concerning sales debits and cash credits to a customer's account. However, how does the auditor determine if the net balance is actually collectible? Does the evidence that a customer has paid his or her bill in the past imply that he or she will continue to pay the bill? The evaluation of such evidence bears directly on the recorded value of receivables but is potentially ambiguous.

- **Quality of internal recordkeeping:** How reliable is evidence generated from the company's accounting system? Auditors make great use of the client's internal recordkeeping system. In every audit, transaction vouching is a common audit procedure performed in many account areas, especially as related to the existence and completeness assertions. However, the use of internal company documents to support audit conclusions presumes that those documents are accurate. If the system is weak and internal documents are potentially inaccurate, the auditor may need to obtain other forms of evidence for some assertions.

[xx] **EXAMPLE**

Depreciation expense can be estimated from other facts known to an auditor. The auditor could divide depreciation expense by the average balance in plant assets (buildings and equipment). If this percentage seemed reasonable based on the auditor's prior expectation, the auditor might conclude that depreciation expense is reasonably accurate. If the computed value seems out of line, it may be due to the use of an imprecise estimate, a change in asset mix, a change in accounting principle, or an accounting error. The auditor then plans further tests when the value is not in line with expectations.

[xxi] **EXAMPLE**

An auditor might ask the credit manager why a specific receivable was written off as a bad debt, ask the marketing manager to explain why sales results are down from prior years, or ask the plant foreman what procedures the company uses to approve the purchase of equipment.

(xxii)EXAMPLE

A famous audit fraud was perpetrated by a manufacturer of disk drives for personal computers who was able to fool the auditors into thinking that the warehouse was full of inventory by placing bricks into disk drive boxes, shrink-wrapping the boxes, and stacking them in the warehouse. The auditor failed to realize the charade when physically examining the inventory. "Seeing is believing" only when the auditor knows what he or she is looking at!

Figure 3.2 illustrates the typical hierarchy of evidence based on the above attributes. In general, the auditor will try to obtain more competent evidence (the "best" evidence) when desired detection risk is low for an assertion. When detection risk is moderate or high, the auditor will usually be satisfied with evidence considered "good." However, the auditor will rarely be totally satisfied with evidence classified as "weak" unless the account or assertion in question has turned out to be immaterial or has very low residual risk.

To illustrate the trade-off of the quality of evidence and risk, consider the procedures to test assertions related to accounts receivable for two different levels of risk as described in Table 3.3. The preparation of the aged trial balance by the client is more risky because the preparer is not independent. Selecting 100 accounts to confirm is better than selecting 25 accounts because the larger sample provides more extensive evidence. Client restrictions on the selection of customer accounts interferes with the independence of the evidence and reduces its competence. Confirmations sent to businesses will usually be more reliable than those sent to retail customers because other businesses are more likely to have accounting systems that allow them to respond accurately to the confirmation request. Finally, confirming accounts before year end provides less competent evidence because the connection between the confirmation results and the year-end balance is less objective than direct year-end confirmation would provide.

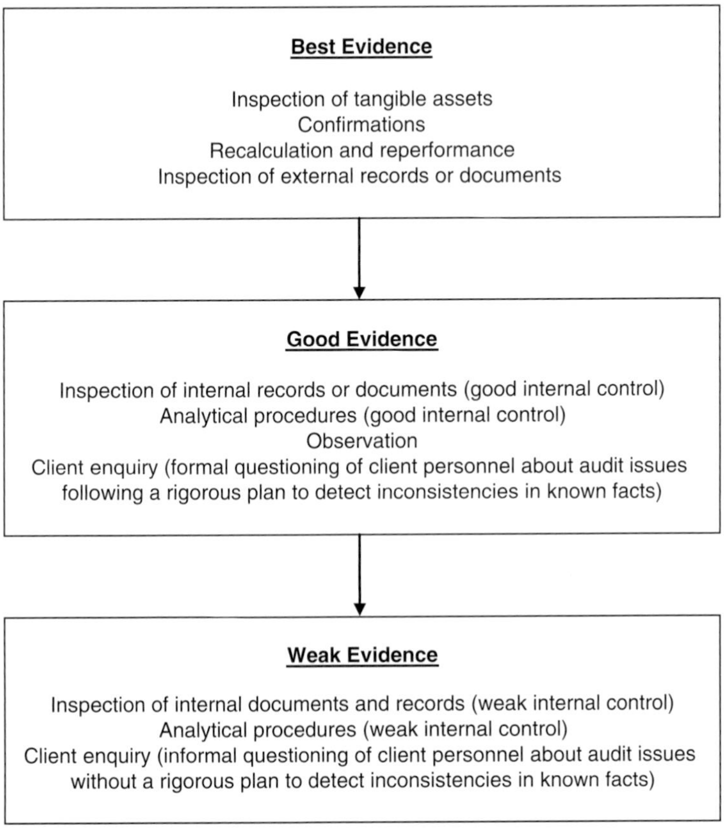
Best Evidence
Inspection of tangible assets
Confirmations
Recalculation and reperformance
Inspection of external records or documents
Good Evidence
Inspection of internal records or documents (good internal control)
Analytical procedures (good internal control)
Observation
Client enquiry (formal questioning of client personnel about audit issues following a rigorous plan to detect inconsistencies in known facts)
Weak Evidence
Inspection of internal documents and records (weak internal control)
Analytical procedures (weak internal control)
Client enquiry (informal questioning of client personnel about audit issues without a rigorous plan to detect inconsistencies in known facts)

Figure 3.2 *Hierarchy of Audit Evidence*

Table 3.3 *Trade-Off of Detection Risk and Audit Evidence*

Low Detection Risk/High Audit Effort	High Detection Risk/Low Audit Effort
Aged trial balance for receivables prepared by the auditor.	Aged trial balance for receivables prepared by the client's personnel.
100 customer accounts randomly selected and confirmed.	25 customer accounts randomly selected and confirmed.
No client restrictions placed on population of accounts to confirm.	A few accounts omitted from confirmation by request of the client.
Accounts to be confirmed pertain to other businesses.	Accounts to be confirmed pertain to retail consumers.
Customer accounts confirmed as of 12/31 (for fiscal year end of 12/31).	Customer accounts confirmed as of 11/1 (for fiscal year end of 12/31).

The Interrelationship of Risk, Materiality, and Evidence

There is a complex interaction between the level of materiality and the level of audit risk and, together, risk and materiality influence the amount of evidence that an auditor may need to collect on an engagement. This relationship leads to two general, but very important, observations:

1. **High risk of material misstatement implies the need for high levels of audit effort.** Since risk of material misstatement is not under the control of the auditor, and can only be estimated based on the auditor's experience and knowledge of the client, an auditor will gather more evidence in situations where the risk of material misstatement is deemed to be high.

2. **Low audit risk via low detection risk is achieved through high levels of audit effort.** An audit that results in a low level of audit risk can be achieved through planning an audit with low detection risk. Low detection risk audit plans are achieved by the auditor collecting more evidence during the course of the audit[xxiii].

The auditor's assessment of materiality and audit risk may be different at the time of initially planning the engagement and at the time of evaluating the results of audit procedures. This could be because of a change in circumstances or because of a change in the auditor's knowledge. For example, if the audit is planned prior to period end, the auditor will anticipate the results of operations and the financial position. If actual results of operations and financial position are substantially different, the assessment of materiality and audit risk may also change. Additionally, the auditor may, in planning the audit work, intentionally set the acceptable materiality level at a lower level than is necessary so as to reduce detection risk and to provide a margin of safety when evaluating the effect of misstatements discovered during the audit. In general, almost everything the auditor does during the course of the audit is designed to provide the appropriate balance between audit risk, materiality, and audit evidence.

[xxiii]**EXAMPLE**

Inventory is usually a critical component of the financial statements of a manufacturing company. It is also a complex area to audit given the nature of cost accounting and allocation and the continual movement of inventory assets. As a result, an auditor will usually consider the processes and activities surrounding inventory to be important to the audit and potentially high risk. This perspective leads the auditor to devote significant resources to the audit of transactions, accounts, or disclosures related to inventory.

Auditor Responsibilities

In summary, the auditor has four primary responsibilities related to the conduct of the audit: (1) to plan the audit so as to have reasonable assurance that errors and fraudulent misstatements will be detected and corrected, (2) to evaluate (GAAS Audits) and report (Integrated Audits) on the effectiveness of internal control over financial reporting, (3) to evaluate the potential for illegal acts on the part of the client, and (4) to evaluate the likelihood that the company will continue as a going concern.

Reasonable Assurance about Errors and Fraudulent Misstatements

As noted in the previous chapter, auditors gather evidence sufficient in amount and competent in content to provide financial statement users with reasonable assurance that financial statements are free of significant misstatements. Auditors distinguish between different types of possible financial misstatements: errors and fraudulent misstatements. The former are considered accidental and unintentional while the latter reflect intentional actions by employees within a client and may involve misappropriation of assets or fraudulent financial reporting. The distinction between the two types of fraud may be minimal. For example, if a manager's annual bonus is based on the sales for the period, he or she might intentionally accelerate January sales into December so that they can be counted in the current year (even though the earnings process is not complete and the goods are not delivered until January). This clearly represents fraudulent financial reporting because the financial statements are being intentionally misstated. What may be less obvious is that this also reflects misappropriation of assets because the manager is acquiring corporate assets (in the form of a bonus) to which he or she is not entitled.

Auditors are expected to plan and conduct the audit to detect and correct both types of errors. However, due to the potential significance of fraud and the effect on shareholders and others, auditors must follow specific standards for assessing and following up on the possibility of fraudulent misstatements. However, an audit may not be able to detect all fraudulent conditions. To do so, an auditor would have to plan and conduct an engagement differently if the detection of all fraud was the primary goal. Such an audit is called a **forensic audit** and requires an extensive body of evidence that is cost prohibitive in the absence of strong suspicions of the occurrence of fraud. For example, in a forensic audit all documents are considered to be potentially fraudulent until proven otherwise. To direct auditors' attention to the possibility of fraud on each audit engagement, team members are required to discuss the potential ways fraud could occur at the client during the planning phase of the engagement. This meeting, called a **brainstorming** session, is intended to help develop an audit plan that adequately accounts for potential fraud. Thus, the auditor's standard of due care in planning the audit is based on a healthy dose of professional skepticism combined with procedures that provide reasonable assurance of detecting significant errors and fraud. Given the seriousness of fraud, auditors may use, or be required to use by standards setters or regulators, more forensic audit procedures in the future than they currently use. Of course, such a requirement will increase the costs of doing an audit.

The responsibilities of the auditor regarding potential fraud are summarized in Figure 3.3. If an auditor expects that fraud has occurred at a client, he or she should investigate and obtain evidence about the facts of the situation. If the

---

The auditor's responsibility is to plan the audit to provide reasonable assurance that material errors and fraudulent misstatements will be detected including:

• Exercise adequate professional skepticism.
• Investigate whether risk factors are present that indicate a higher than average risk of material misstatement.
• Discuss with audit team explicitly how fraud or other material misstatement might occur in this specific client, how earnings management attempts might lead to fraud, and how the audit team would uncover indications of fraud or other material misstatement.

If sufficient risk factors are present to indicate a higher than average risk of material misstatement due to errors and fraudulent misstatements, the auditor should:

1. Assign more senior staff to the audit and review all audit work more carefully.
2. Reduce the predictability of the audit by changing the nature or timing of audit procedures. Some examples include:

  • Increase the extent of testing of large and unusual transactions.
  • Follow up on significant unexpected account fluctuations.
  • Investigate significant discrepancies in transactions with outsiders.
  • Examine transactions with missing or inadequate documentation.
3. Heighten professional skepticism in areas where there can be material managerial judgments. Some examples include:

  • Examine transactions involving senior management in detail.
  • Question whether accounting principles are being misused.
  • Inquire about errors known to the client but not rectified.
  • Investigate unauthorized transactions.

If an error or fraudulent misstatement is detected during the course of the audit, the auditor should:

• Document the nature of the problem.
• Determine if the misstatements are errors or fraudulent transactions. Then:

  • Consider implications for other aspects of the audit, including possible withdrawal.
  • Discuss the matter with management at the appropriate level for action.
  • Refer matters to auditor's legal counsel and suggest the client involve their legal counsel.
• Have the client adjust the statements for all material errors and fraudulent misstatements.
• If the client will not adjust the statements, issue a qualified or adverse report.
• Inform the Audit Committee.

Figure 3.3 Auditor Responsibility for Detecting and Reporting Error and Fraud (Based on ISA 240.)

auditor concludes that fraud has occurred, the facts should be presented to management at a level that is high enough in the organization to intervene, at least one level above the level at which the auditor suspects that the fraud is taking place. Any financial statement effects should also be corrected. If management refuses to rectify the fraud, or is itself involved in the fraud, the auditor should inform the Audit Committee of the Board of Directors and consider issuing a negative audit report (discussed later) or resign from the engagement. The auditor should also consider whether there is a legal responsibility to report the fraud to appropriate government authorities.

Internal Control Over Financial Reporting

In Integrated Audits involving clients that are publicly owned and registered with the SEC in the US, the auditor is also responsible for evaluating the quality of internal control over financial reporting and issuing a report concerning the effectiveness of the system. Indeed, rules promulgated by the PCAOB have made the evaluation of internal control a responsibility that is equal to the audit of the financial results for publicly traded companies in the US. Consequently, auditors now devote a great deal of time and energy to the audit of internal control over financial reporting and are required to issue an opinion on its effectiveness. The report is issued as of the end of the fiscal year in conjunction with the audit report on the financial statements.

Illegal Acts By Clients

AUTHORITATIVE GUIDANCE & STANDARDS

The underlying standards are not the focus at this time. In latter chapters we will consider in more detail the specifics of these standards (ISA 250 **Consideration of Laws and Regulations in an Audit of Financial Statements***; PCAOB AS 2405 [formerly Interim Standard AU 317]* **Illegal Acts by Clients** *and ISA 570* **Going Concern***; PCAOB AS 2415 [formerly Interim Standard AU 341]* **Consideration of an Entity's Ability to Continue as a Going Concern***). For the present, the key is to understand, in broad terms, what the overall set of auditor responsibilities are.*

Another situation that an auditor occasionally encounters is when a company commits an illegal act—a violation of laws or government regulations committed by individuals on behalf of the company. For example, if a manager orders toxic waste from the production process to be dumped in a nearby river, he is probably committing an illegal act. Illegal acts that the auditor looks for do not include personal misconduct by the entity's personnel. Furthermore, illegal acts carried out by employees can be distinguished from employee fraud (that is, misappropriation of assets) by noting that illegal acts are actions on behalf of the company at the expense of "society," whereas employee fraud represents actions on behalf of an individual at the expense of the company. This distinction may become hazy in some situations, particularly those involving securities laws and fraudulent financial reporting.

For example, if a company intentionally misstates earnings prior to "going public," it may have committed fraud and other illegal acts.

Illegal acts can be further classified by the impact they have on accounting and financial reporting. Violations of tax or financial reporting laws can have a direct and material impact on financial reports. Many other laws and regulations apply primarily to the operations of an organization rather than financial or accounting functions, such as environmental regulations. Such laws may be far from the purview of the auditor but can have an indirect and potentially significant impact on the financial statements since violations may lead to fines and penalties.

What are the auditors' responsibilities for detecting illegal acts that have been committed by client personnel? In general, the auditor has a greater responsibility for illegal acts that are direct and material to the financial statements. However, an auditor is not considered to be a legal expert, and thus determination of whether an action is legal may be beyond his or her professional judgment. If the auditor knows that certain laws are important to the operations of a client firm and that significant violations may have occurred, the audit should be planned to provide reasonable assurance that these violations are appropriately reported in the financial statements. Auditors are also expected to obtain the advice of a qualified legal expert when necessary[xxiv].

If evidence comes to the attention of the auditor that an illegal act may have occurred, the auditor is required to investigate the situation. Once the auditor understands the facts, the matter should be referred to management at a level high enough to allow corrective action. If the client fails to undertake corrective action, the auditor should consider resigning from the engagement. As a practical matter, the auditor is most concerned with circumstances that may necessitate recognition of a contingent liability for fines and penalties. The auditor would typically not refer the matter to legal authorities unless required by law. In any case, the auditor would be foolish not to discuss the matter with their own legal counsel. A summary of the auditor's responsibility regarding illegal acts is presented in Figure 3.4.

Assessment of Going Concern

As part of the engagement, the auditor evaluates the ability of the organization to continue as a going concern over the next year. Generally, auditors focus on several key issues when evaluating whether there is substantial doubt about the entity's ability to continue as a going concern. Auditors consider the ability of an organization to generate sufficient cash flows to meet obligations by evaluating liquidity ratios and cash flow projections. Further, auditors evaluate trends relating to sales, expenses, and asset management to develop an understanding about the organization's financial stability. Consistent failure in attaining realistic business objectives are also an indicator of possible problems. Finally, litigation issues should be evaluated since significant legal exposures could bring the going concern assumption into doubt.

If the weight of evidence is such that the auditor has substantial doubts that the company can survive the next twelve months, and in the absence of mitigating circumstances (discussed in Chapter 14), an explanatory paragraph is added to the auditor's opinion describing the conditions leading to this

[xxiv]EXAMPLE

Government rules define the attributes of a safe and healthy work environment. Evaluating possible violations of those laws is outside the expertise of most auditors and generally such violations would not be important to the financial statements. Other laws outside the auditor's range of expertise include laws related to environmental protection, food and drug safety, and equal opportunity hiring. However, violations of these laws may lead to sizeable fines for an offending company.

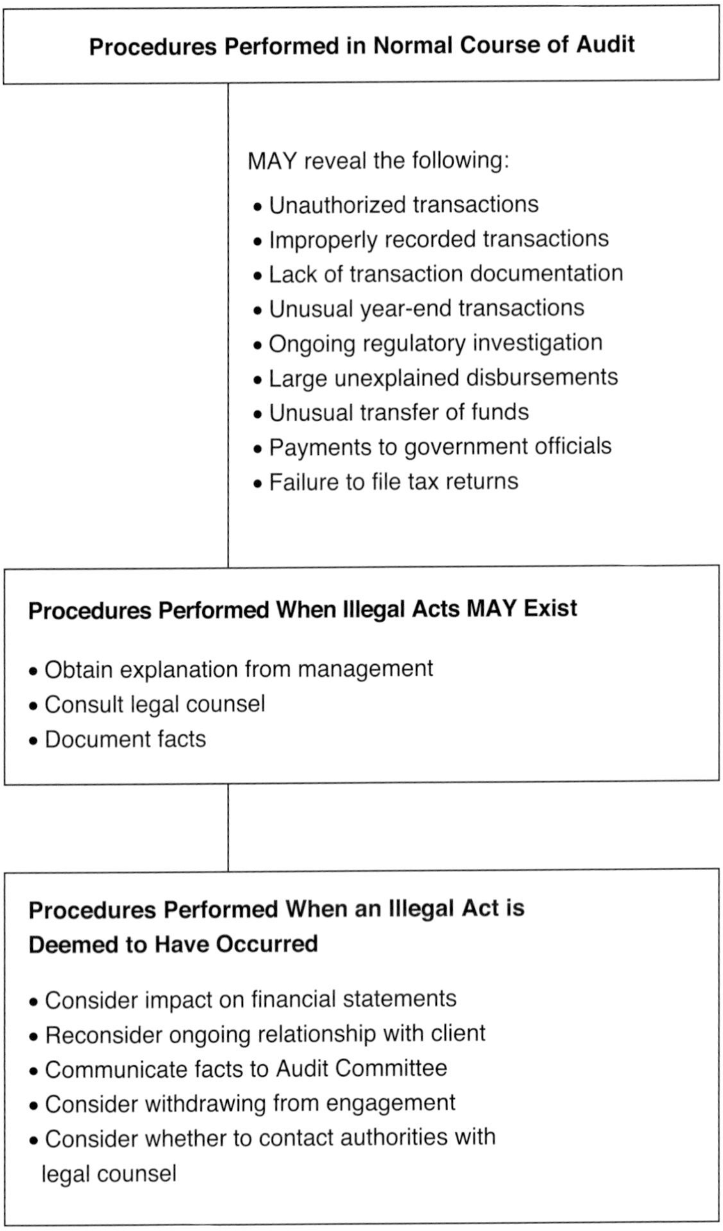

Procedures Performed in Normal Course of Audit

MAY reveal the following:

- Unauthorized transactions
- Improperly recorded transactions
- Lack of transaction documentation
- Unusual year-end transactions
- Ongoing regulatory investigation
- Large unexplained disbursements
- Unusual transfer of funds
- Payments to government officials
- Failure to file tax returns

Procedures Performed When Illegal Acts MAY Exist

- Obtain explanation from management
- Consult legal counsel
- Document facts

Procedures Performed When an Illegal Act is Deemed to Have Occurred

- Consider impact on financial statements
- Reconsider ongoing relationship with client
- Communicate facts to Audit Committee
- Consider withdrawing from engagement
- Consider whether to contact authorities with legal counsel

Figure 3.4 Auditor's Responsibility for Detecting Illegal Acts by Clients (Based on ISA 250.)

determination. Auditors are supposed to be conservative in making this assessment. As a result, organizations that receive an explanatory paragraph for substantial doubt about being a going concern often do not actually fail. Auditors face a trade-off in making this determination because such conditions can strain relations between an auditor and client management; however, the auditor's responsibility to users of the financial statements necessitates such conservativeness whenever substantial doubt exists. Most countries require auditors to alert readers of the financial statements that there is a going concern issue disclosed in the notes to the financial statements[xxv].

Summary and Conclusion

In this chapter we have introduced the critical building blocks of auditing. Management assertions about the financial statements and internal controls provide the basis for the auditor's examination. Next, we introduced the critical concepts of audit risk, materiality, and audit evidence. Finally, we illustrated how an auditor uses audit procedures to assess risk and obtain evidence as to the fairness of the overall financial statements. Proper understanding and development of these building blocks of auditing are necessary for an auditing firm to be effective and to minimize the possibility of performing a substandard audit or rendering the wrong opinion on the financial statements. In the subsequent chapters, the building blocks of the audit are applied in detail to the audit once we have set the context in which the audit occurs. With this understanding of the auditor's responsibilities we now turn to consider how the auditor decides to accept new clients and continue their association with existing clients.

Bibliography of Relevant Literature

Research

Blokodijk, H., F. Drieenhuizen, D. A. Simunic, and M. T. Stein. 2003. Factors Affecting Auditors' Assessments of Planning Materiality. *Auditing: A Journal of Practice & Theory.* 22(2): 297–307.

Brody, R. G., D. J. Lowe, and K. Pany. 2003. Could $51 Million be Immaterial when Enron Reports Income of $105 million? *Accounting Horizons.* 17(2): 153–160.

Kinney, W. R., Jr., and R. D. Martin. 1994. Does Auditing Reduce Bias in Financial Reporting? A Review of Audit Adjustment Studies. *Auditing: A Journal of Practice and Theory.* Spring: 149–156.

Messier, W. F. Jr., N. Matinov-Bennie, and A. Eilifsen. 2005. A Review and Integration of Empirical Research on Materiality: Two Decades Later. *Auditing: A Journal of Practice & Theory.* 24(2): 153–187.

Nelson, M. W., S. D. Smith, and Z.-V. Palmrose. 2005. The Effect of Quantitative Materiality Approach on Auditors' Adjustment Decisions. *The Accounting Review.* 80(3): 897–921.

Newman, D. P., E. Patterson, and R. Smith. 2001. The Influence of Potentially Fraudulent Reports on Audit Risk Assessment and Planning. *The Accounting Review* 76(1): 59–80.

Tuttle, B. M. Coller and R. D. Plumlee. 2002. The Effect of Misstatements on Decisions of Financial Statement Users: An Experimental Investigation of Auditor Materiality Thresholds. *Auditing: A Journal of Practice & Theory.* 21(1): 11–28.

(xxv)**EXAMPLE**

The following is an excerpt from Ernst & Young's 2003 Auditor's Report for US Airways, which describes an example of substantial doubt about going concern:

> The accompanying consolidated financial statements have been prepared assuming that the Company will continue as a going concern. As discussed in Note 2 to the consolidated financial statements, the Company's significant recurring losses and other matters regarding, among other things, the Company's ability to maintain compliance with covenants contained in various financing agreements as well as its ability to finance and operate regional jet aircraft and reduce its operating costs in order to successfully compete with low cost airlines, raise substantial doubt about its ability to continue as a going concern. Management's plans in regard to these matters are described in Note 2 to the consolidated financial statements. The accompanying consolidated financial statements do not include any adjustments that might result from the outcome of this uncertainty.

The Company subsequently filed for bankruptcy protection and was later acquired by AmericaWest Airlines and then renamed US Airways Group.

Auditing Standards

Committee of Sponsoring Organizations of the Treadway Commission (COSO). 1992. *Internal Control—Integrated Framework*. New York: COSO.

Committee of Sponsoring Organizations of the Treadway Commission (COSO). 2006. Internal *Control—An Integrated Framework: Guidance for Smaller Public Companies*. New York: COSO.

Committee of Sponsoring Organizations of the Treadway Commission (COSO). 2013. *Internal Control—Integrated Framework*. New York: COSO.

IASB, International Accounting Standards Board, 2010, The Conceptual Framework for Financial Reporting.

IAASB *International Standards on Auditing (ISA)* No. 200, "Overall objectives of the independent auditor and the conduct of the audit in accordance with international standards on auditing."

IAASB *International Standards on Auditing (ISA)* No. 240, "The Auditor's Responsibilities Relating to Fraud in an Audit of Financial Statements."

IAASB *International Standards on Auditing (ISA)* No. 250, "Consideration of Laws and Regulations in an Audit of Financial Statements."

IAASB *International Standards on Auditing (ISA)* No. 300, "Planning an Audit of Financial Statements."

IAASB *International Standards on Auditing (ISA)* No. 315, "Understanding the Entity and Its Environment and Assessing the Risks of Material Misstatement."

IAASB *International Standards on Auditing (ISA)* No. 320, "Materiality in Planning and Performing an Audit."

IAASB *International Standards on Auditing (ISA)* No. 330, "The Auditor's Responses to Assessed Risks."

IAASB *International Standards on Auditing (ISA)* No. 500, "Audit Evidence."

IAASB *International Standards on Auditing (ISA)* No. 505, "External Confirmations."

IAASB *International Standards on Auditing (ISA)* No. 570, "Going Concern."

IFAC. International Auditing and Assurance Standards Board (IAASB). 2015. *Handbook of International Quality Control, Audit, Review, Other Assurance, and Related Services Pronouncements*. New York: International Federation of Accountants.

PCAOB. *Auditing Standard* 1101 (formerly No. 8), "Audit Risk."

PCAOB. *Auditing Standard* 1105 (formerly No. 15), "Audit Evidence."

PCAOB. *Auditing Standard* 2101 (formerly No. 9), "Audit Planning."

PCAOB. *Auditing Standard* 2105 (formerly No. 11), "Consideration of Materiality in Planning and Performing an Audit."

PCAOB. *Auditing Standard* 2201 (formerly No. 5), "An Audit of Internal Control over Financial Reporting that is Integrated with An Audit of Financial Statements."

PCAOB. *Auditing Standard* 2210 (formerly No. 12), "Identifying and Assessing the Risks of Material Misstatement."

PCAOB. *Auditing Standard* 2301 (formerly No. 13), "The Auditor's Responses to the Risks of Material Misstatement."

PCAOB. *Auditing Standard* 2310 (formerly *Interim Standard* AU 330), "The Confirmation Process."

PCAOB. *Auditing Standard* 2401 (formerly *Interim Standard* AU 316), "Consideration of Fraud in a Financial Statement Audit."

PCAOB. *Auditing Standard* 2405 (formerly *Interim Standard* AU 317), "Illegal Acts by Clients."

PCAOB. *Auditing Standard* 2415 (formerly *Interim Standard* AU 341), "Consideration of an Entity's Ability to Continue as a Going Concern."

SEC, *Staff Accounting Bulletin* No. 99, "Materiality."

Notes

1 The auditor has other specific responsibilities, which are discussed in Chapter 4.
2 ISA Glossary of terms and ISA 200.
3 The US PCAOB adopted as Interim Standards all standards of the AICPA's ASB as of April 16, 2003, to the extent that new PCAOB standards do not supersede them. In 2015 the PCAOB incorporated both the standards it had passed and these Interim Standards based on the 2003 ASB standards into one new codification (i.e., a numbering system). We will refer to this new codification (that contains four numbers) consistently in the text and where warranted shall also mention the preceding standard number (PCAOB standards were numbered 1–18 and Interim ASB standards had three numbers) as it normally takes several years for a new codification to become common language to all auditors, causing confusion to students who only know the new numbering system.
4 Previously, the IAASB defined only five management assertions to be applied across classes of transactions and accounts. Accordingly, auditing textbooks and accounting firms translated the five types of assertions into a broader class of audit objectives in order to facilitate the planning and collection of audit evidence. With the expansion and clarification of management assertions across three categories (transactions, accounts, and presentation and disclosure), there is no longer a need for an additional layer of audit objectives, essentially the objectives of the audit are to ensure that appropriate evidence is gathered to support management assertions for all three categories of financial reporting.
5 Source: ISA 500 *Audit Evidence*, IFAC 2014.
6 The term material means that the assertion must be significant enough to affect the decisions of a reasonable user (materiality is discussed in more detail later in this chapter).
7 COSO (1992), *Internal Control—Integrated Framework*, Definition of Terms.
8 To address the concerns of smaller public companies in 2006 COSO issued *Internal Control: An Integrated Framework: Guidance for Smaller Public Companies*. COSO is part of the Treadway Commission on Fraudulent

Financial Reporting formed in response to major frauds in the US in the late 1980s. The "organizations" are the primary organizations in the US representing public accountants, financial executives, managerial accountants, internal auditors, and academics.

9 COSO issued a document on enterprise risk management in 2004 that expands the 1992 framework on internal control. However, organizations are likely to continue to use the 1992 framework as a basis for internal control over financial reporting because of its restrictiveness, making it easier to utilize when only responsible for internal control over financial reporting, and not other aspects of enterprise risk management (e.g., strategic and operations risks). The new COSO 2013 *Internal Control–Integrated Framework* continues the tradition of internal control frameworks being considered as complementary to COSO's ERM framework we discussed in Chapter 2.

10 Firms will occasionally undertake an engagement knowing that they will not earn their normal profit margin. This can occur in the case of charitable organizations, such as the audit of United Way. It can also occur when the firm is using the audit as a "loss leader" in order to gain entry into a specific audit market (e.g., a geographic region or specialized industry), where significant spin-off work in tax and permitted management consulting is expected, or where the possibility exists that future fees will grow enough to justify the near-term losses. This practice is not recommended for most public company audits as regulatory scrutiny could increase substantially.

11 ISA 200 "Objectives and Principles Governing an Audit of Financial Statements."

12 The distinction between inspection (also known as examination) and observation can sometimes be confusing. Inspection/examination focuses on evaluating or seeing the tangible assets, records, or documents, whereas observation focuses on witnessing activities or business processes as they take place in operations.

CHAPTER 4

The Audit Process

Outline

- Introduction
- Client Acceptance and Retention
  - o Factors Affecting Client Acceptability
  - o Communication with the Predecessor Auditor
  - o To Accept or Not?
  - o Engagement Letters
- Preliminary Planning
  - o Obtain a General Understanding of the Client
  - o Becoming Familiar with the Organization's Strategic Plan
  - o Obtain a High Level Understanding of Information Processing Systems
  - o Identify New, and Review Known, Problem Areas that May Affect Audit Planning
    - Review Board Minutes
    - Review Preliminary Financial Statements
    - Identify Key Accounting Policies
  - o Consider Special Circumstances that May Affect Audit Planning
    - Related Party Transactions
    - Need for Specialists
    - Use of Internal Auditors
  - o Discuss and Assess Fraud Risk and the Risk of Material Misstatement
- An Overview of the Audit Process
- Communicating the Results of the Audit
  - o GAAS Audit Opinions
  - o Integrated Audit Opinions including Effectiveness of Internal Control over Financial Reporting
- Summary and Conclusion
- Bibliography of Relevant Literature

Learning Goals for this Chapter

1. Recognize the factors that an auditor must take into consideration when making the decision to accept or retain a client.

2. Identify the basic knowledge needed for an auditor to begin to plan the audit of financial statements.

3. Become familiar with the fraud triangle and the elements that compose the incentives, attitudes, and rationalization that can lead to fraud.

4. Comprehend the logical flow for an audit of financial statements with and without an audit of the effectiveness of internal control over financial reporting.

5. Understand and be able to prepare a simple unqualified auditor's report and develop an awareness of alternative reports that an auditor can issue.

Introduction

An audit is a complex but systematic process. Although the overall audit process often follows a general methodology determined by the audit firm that intends to ensure an audit that is compliant with professional and regulatory standards, every client is unique and the process must be tailored to fit the circumstances of each client. Given the potential variation in the audit process from client to client, auditors and other stakeholders want to be confident that the quality of an audit does not vary. If an audit is done well, information risk is minimized, the efficiency of capital allocations and investment decisions are improved, and the economy benefits. If done poorly, stakeholders will be subject to an excessive level of information risk and may suffer economic losses as a result of decisions made while relying on inaccurate or incomplete financial information.

The purpose of this chapter is to introduce the auditor's primary professional responsibility to provide reasonable assurance that there are no significant misstatements in the financial statements. The auditor can never know with certainty whether financial statements are fairly presented. Consequently, the engagement is planned to obtain enough evidence to support the auditor's conclusions. We start by discussing the acquisition and retention of clients. We continue with a broad overview of the preliminaries of an audit, give an overview of the audit process as developed in this book, and provide an initial look at the output of the audit—the auditor's report(s). In general, the topics discussed in this chapter pertain to all audits. As previously noted, the primary difference between the two main types of audits (GAAS Audits and Integrated Audits) is the extent to which the auditor formally evaluates and reports on the effectiveness of internal control over financial reporting.

Client Acceptance and Retention

Auditors provide services to clients in return for fees. Therefore, to succeed and grow, auditors need to obtain a client base that generates fees adequate to cover the costs of professional services and office overhead. Auditors rarely wish to turn away prospective clients or to drop current clients, but involvement with dishonest clients can have dire consequences for the auditor. One way to think about this trade-off is that clients produce revenues for an auditor, but business failures or accounting problems not discovered by an auditor can lead to very high costs to the auditor in the form of litigation expenses, regulatory fines, or revenue losses due to a decline in professional reputation. In other words, partners in an audit firm weigh the revenues earned from desirable clients against the potential problems that may occur if the auditor becomes involved with a bad client.

AUTHORITATIVE GUIDANCE & STANDARDS

IAASB's International Standards on Quality Control 1 **Quality Control for Firms That Perform Audits and Reviews of Historical Financial Information and Other Assurance and Related Service Engagements,** *and ISA 220* **Quality Controls for Audits of Financial Statements** *requires that auditors consider whether the firm has the competence, capabilities, and resources to undertake a new engagement from a new or an existing client as part of its quality control system. Similar requirements are found in PCAOB Interim Quality Standard QC 20* **System of Quality Control for a CPA Firm's Accounting and Auditing Practice,** *as well as AS 1110 (formerly Interim Standard AU 161)* **Relationship of Auditing Standards to Quality Control Standards,** *AS 1201 (formerly AS 10)* **Supervision of the Audit Engagement,** *and AS 1220 (formerly AS 7)* **Engagement Quality Review** *provides similar guidance for Integrated Audits.*

Consequently, auditors screen prospective clients and re-evaluate current clients as a matter of professional necessity. Client integrity is by far the most important aspect of screening new and current clients. An auditor wants to know a great deal about a client before agreeing to undertake an audit engagement or to renew an existing engagement. The auditor's main concern is avoiding prospective clients and continuing with current clients that could cause the firm to suffer a loss. There are five broad steps that an auditor should perform when deciding whether to accept or retain a client:

1. Obtain background information about the client.
2. Determine if the preconditions for an audit exist.
3. Evaluate the risk factors or changes in risk factors associated with the client.
4. Decide on the acceptability or retention of the client as part of the audit firm-wide risk portfolio.
5. Obtain an engagement letter.

Factors Affecting Client Acceptability

Box 4.1 "Preconditions for an Audit" on the following page identifies the issues that the auditor needs to consider when considering whether a potential client is appropriate for the firm. These are referred to as the preconditions of the audit and, with a few exceptions, the inability to meet these conditions indicate that an audit cannot be undertaken for this client. These preconditions include:

- Existence of an acceptable accounting framework under which the management will prepare the financial statements (e.g., International Financial Reporting Standards).

- Existence of a sufficiently robust internal control set to enable financial statements to be prepared.

- Willingness of management to cooperate with the auditor so that the auditor may comply with appropriate professional auditing standards.

AUTHORITATIVE GUIDANCE & STANDARDS

IAASB's ISA 210 **Agreeing to Terms of Audit Engagements** *lays down a set of principles that must be met as preconditions for an auditor to accept an audit engagement. The PCAOB AS 1301 (formerly AS 16)* **Communication with Audit Committees** *provides similar guidance for US registered public company auditors.*

BOX 4.1   PRECONDITIONS FOR AN AUDIT

- *Determine whether the financial reporting framework to be applied in the preparation of the financial statements is acceptable. Factors that are relevant include:*
  - o *The nature of the entity.*
  - o *The purpose of the financial statements.*
  - o *Whether law or regulation prescribes the applicable financial reporting framework.*
  - o *Financial reporting standards established by organizations that are authorized or recognized to promulgate standards. These include:*
    - *International Financial Reporting Standards (IFRSs) promulgated by the International Accounting Standards Board.*
    - *International Public Sector Accounting Standards (IPSASs) promulgated by the International Public Sector Accounting Standards Board.*
    - *Accounting principles promulgated by an authorized or recognized standards setting organization in a particular jurisdiction, provided the organization follows an established and transparent process involving deliberation and consideration of the views of a wide range of stakeholders (e.g., Financial Accounting Standards Board in the US).*
- *Obtain the agreement of management that it acknowledges and understands its responsibility:*
  - o *For the preparation of the financial statements in accordance with the applicable financial reporting framework.*
  - o *For internal control as management determines is necessary (or required in the US for public companies) to enable the preparation of financial*

statements that are free from material misstatement, whether due to fraud or error.

o *To provide the auditor with:*

- *Access to all information of which management is aware that is relevant to the preparation of the financial statements.*

- *Additional information that the auditor may request from management for the purpose of the audit.*

- *Unrestricted access to persons within the entity from whom the auditor determines it necessary to obtain audit evidence.*

Assuming that these preconditions are met, and normally these are routine matters in the vast majority of audits, the auditor turns to more practical issues related to whether the auditor can carry out the audit. Box 4.2 "Factors Affecting the Acceptability and Retention of Clients" identifies seven such issues. The first two factors are under the control of the auditor and, given enough time, can often be resolved. The availability of appropriate expertise will depend on the size of the audit firm and the experience and training of the firm's professional staff. Audit firms are often able to shift personnel, hire new staff, and work overtime to service a new client. A current lack of independence may be more troublesome but can also be resolved in most situations. A common situation in which an auditor may lack independence is when the auditor has a financial interest in the prospective client (e.g., the auditor's partners own stock in the company). If the financial interest can be removed, the independence concern will be resolved.[1]

BOX 4.2 FACTORS AFFECTING THE ACCEPTABILITY AND RETENTION OF CLIENTS

A. Factors within the control of the auditor

1. *Expertise and staffing: Does the audit firm have the requisite staff available who possess or can obtain the needed expertise for completing the audit engagement including: (1) industry expertise; (2) regulatory and reporting knowledge; (3) experts for specialized areas; (4) individuals available to do quality review; and (5) can meet reporting deadlines?*

2. *Independence: Is the audit firm independent of the client so as to be able to provide an opinion that is both seen to be and is unbiased or objective?*

B. Factors that must be evaluated by the auditor about the client

3. *Integrity: Do the client's principal owners, management, and those charged with governance of the company possess adequate integrity so that the audit firm can be reasonably assured that they are not committing material fraud and/or illegal acts?*

4. *Reputation and image: Does the client company have a poor reputation such that the audit firm's association with the client could be embarrassing or detrimental to the audit firm? Is there any indication the company is engaged in money laundering?*

5. *Accounting practices: Does the company have a positive attitude about complying with professional accounting standards so as to present a full and accurate portrait of the company's financial performance and status in their financial statements? What is client management's commitment to the internal control environment and operations of controls?*

6. *Financial status: Is the company in danger of ceasing operations in the near-term due to extremely poor performance or other factors?*

7. *Profitability: Can the audit firm earn a reasonable profit as a result of accepting and completing the audit engagement? Or, is the client (management or those charged with governance) aggressively concerned with keeping the audit fee low?*

Two of the characteristics of the client that should be evaluated by the auditor prior to accepting an engagement are of special concern. There is little argument among auditors that the most important issue that must be addressed for each client is management's integrity. In most circumstances, if client management lacks integrity, an audit cannot be performed that will provide reasonable assurance that the financial statements are fairly presented. If the client management is not actively and openly cooperating with the auditor, the auditor has a high risk that incorrect conclusions will be reached about the accuracy of the financial statements and, when required, the effectiveness of internal control over financial reporting.

The other point of particular interest is the client's financial status. Public accounting firms prefer to avoid clients that are on the verge of bankruptcy. An incidence of bankruptcy often leads to litigation against the auditor because: (1) investors believe that the auditor should have informed them of the impending bankruptcy, and (2) the bankrupt firm has few assets left but the auditing firm has the resources to finance a settlement (the so-called "deep pockets" effect). Another reason relates to the profitability of the engagement because audit firms currently earn most of their profits from repeat audit engagements. The initial audit of a company entails a large start-up cost on the part of the auditors as they gain familiarity with the client. As a result of this large one time start-up cost, the audit firm may not price the audit to realize a profit in the first year of the engagement or indeed, cover all its direct costs. Therefore, a short-term relationship (i.e., a client that only stays with an audit firm for one or two years) in the current pricing environment for audit services cannot be justified given current audit pricing norms relative to the initial engagement cost.

How does an auditor obtain the information needed to assess the factors identified in Box 4.2 "Factors Affecting the Acceptability and Retention of Clients"? In many cases, the starting point is based on the auditor's existing knowledge of a company, as well as the reputation of management, via accounts in the popular press and the business media or prior experience with the client. The firm will also conduct discussions with the management of the client that may provide suggestions for other sources of information. Typically, the auditor will contact the client's bankers and attorneys for information about the client's business dealings. The firm may also contact investment firms, other business acquaintances, employees of the firm, and mutual friends.

For new clients, the firm may also undertake more formal investigations by conducting media research for stories about the company, obtaining Dun & Bradstreet or credit reports, and hiring a professional investigator to delve into the background of key executives and shareholders[i].

Communication with the Predecessor Auditor

An auditor that is new to an engagement is required by ethical rules as well as auditing standards to contact the predecessor auditor when one exists. The incoming auditor should first get permission from the prospective client to talk to the predecessor auditor; otherwise, client confidentiality restrictions will preclude the former auditor from discussing the client. Once client permission is obtained and communicated to the predecessor, the predecessor is required by professional auditing and ethical standards to respond to reasonable inquiries from the successor. If the prospective client refuses permission to contact the predecessor auditor, or places restrictions on what the predecessor can discuss with the potential new auditor, the auditor should consider the ramifications of this refusal, particularly as they relate to the issue of client management integrity. Some of the issues that should be discussed with the predecessor are:

- The reasons for the auditor change.
- The nature of any disagreements the predecessor had with management.
- The identification of important risk areas, including internal control weaknesses.
- Any prior experience with fraud or illegal acts.
- Arrangements for gaining access to the predecessor workpapers from the prior-year audit.

AUTHORITATIVE GUIDANCE & STANDARDS

Communication with a predecessor auditor is required under ISA 510 **Initial Audit Engagements—Opening Balances** *and Section 210 of IFAC* **Code of Ethics***. This guidance is intended to prevent clients from replacing one audit firm with another that is likely to be more cooperative in allowing accounting practices that the first auditor rejected. It should be noted that communication with a predecessor auditor may be difficult or impossible in certain countries due to legal restrictions or practices. PCAOB AS 2610 (formerly Interim Standard AU 315)* **Initial Audits—Communications between Predecessor and Successor Auditors** *contains similar requirements for US public company auditors.*

To Accept or Not?

In the majority of situations, the auditor is going to eventually reach the conclusion that a prospective client is acceptable or decide to retain an existing client—but only if the anticipated revenues over the length of the engagement exceed the foreseeable costs. In most cases, if a major

[i]EXAMPLE

With the development of more sophisticated on-line search engines and data bases, investigating a company and its executives is getting easier. Without leaving the office, an auditor can usually explore the company's web site, its regulatory filings, media reports about the company, market performance and analyst ratings, the nature of its products and competition, quality reviews of its products, outside activities of its executives (through links to other organizations), and current issues affecting the industry. Such data searches are now considered standard procedures by large accounting firms.

In previous editions of this text we listed AIG as a company that most auditors would love to have as a client. However, the story of AIG has not been pretty since its high flying days in early 2006. Since then there has been the replacement of a high profile CEO due to one accounting scandal and the near bankruptcy of the company due to over-exposure to certain sub-prime mortgages and derivatives products in the US housing market melt-down of 2007. These were the same forces that led to the failure of Lehman Brothers in 2008. Indeed, an early warning sign of trouble in February 2008 was the fact that the auditor, PricewaterhouseCoopers (now known as PWC), forced AIG to increase its investment loss provision by a factor of more than four (from just under $1 billion to over $4.5 billion) in less than sixty days and forced the company to admit there was a material weakness in its internal control over this area.

KPMG was sued by its former client Xerox over alleged problems that occurred during the conduct of its audit in the early years of this century.

multinational company, such as General Motors, Royal Dutch Shell, or ING, requests an auditor's services, it is highly unlikely that many auditors would refuse the engagement. However, today's auditor examines even these types of organizations carefully[ii].

Even a company with a long and successful history is not immune to accounting and other problems that can have an adverse impact on the auditor[iii]. To avoid such problems, the auditor needs to carefully develop an understanding of the client. In the rare situations where serious conditions are revealed by the auditor's preliminary analysis and cannot be resolved, the auditor should forgo the engagement, declining to audit a new client or resigning from the audit of an existing client.

Engagement Letters

Upon determining that a client is acceptable (or will be retained by the firm), both parties should agree to the terms of the engagement. At this point, the firm prepares an engagement letter to be signed by the client. This letter serves as a contract between the public accounting firm and the company and explicitly states the terms of the engagement. The primary advantage of using an engagement letter is to avoid future misunderstandings between the client and the firm. This can minimize the chance that the client is unhappy about the services rendered or that the firm will not be able to recover amounts billed for services rendered. The minimum content requirements for a good engagement letter include:

(a) The objective and scope of the audit of the financial statements;

(b) The responsibilities of the auditor;

(c) The responsibilities of management;

(d) Identification of the applicable financial reporting framework for the preparation of the financial statements; and

(e) Reference to the expected form and content of any reports to be issued by the auditor and a statement that there may be circumstances in which a report may differ from its expected form and content.

An example of an engagement letter is included in Box 4.3 "Example of an Engagement Letter for a GAAS Audit". The key elements include:

1. Addressee: Typically the Board of Directors, the Audit Committee, or the Shareholders of the company. For an Integrated Audit, the PCAOB requires that the engagement letter must be signed by the chair of the Audit Committee on behalf of the client.

2. Identification of the service to be rendered: The service in this case would be a financial statement audit and a brief description of the nature of that service. Other services that are intended in conjunction with the audit (e.g., preparation of regulatory reports) should also be identified. For an Integrated Audit, the letter would indicate that the auditor will also conduct an examination of the effectiveness of internal control over financial reporting.

3. Specification of the respective responsibilities of the auditor and management.

4. Constraints, if any, on the audit firm, such as timing of access to client facilities and accounting records. These constraints are present on rare occasions and generally should be imposed by circumstances rather than by management or else the question of whether an audit can even be performed should be revisited.

5. Deadlines: The dates when reports are due should be explicitly stated along with general guidelines for the timing of the audit work.

6. Description of any assistance to be provided by the client staff: the client's personnel typically prepare some schedules (such as bank reconciliations) and retrieve documents from the files. This assistance should be described in the letter. If the assistance is not provided and the auditors must complete the work themselves, this section of the letter would provide justification for additional billings to the client.

7. Interactions with specialists, internal auditors, and the predecessor auditor needed to conduct the audit.

8. Disclaimer that an audit is not designed to detect all forms of fraud or illegal acts.

9. A description of the basis for fees: This may include a fixed fee or an estimate of fees based on expected completion time and billing rates of personnel assigned to the engagement.

10. Ownership and accessibility of the auditor's files to outsiders.

BOX 4.3   EXAMPLE OF AN ENGAGEMENT LETTER FOR A GAAS AUDIT*

Smith & Brown

Chartered Professional Accountants

(Date)

Mr. George Jones, Chair

Board of Directors

Dear Mr. Jones:

[The objective and scope of the audit]

You have requested that we audit the financial statements of Johnson Pharmaceuticals, Inc., which comprise the balance sheet as at December 31, 20X4, and the income statement, statement of changes in equity, and cash flow statement for the year then ended, and a summary of significant accounting policies and other explanatory information. We are pleased to confirm our acceptance and our understanding of this audit engagement by means of this letter. Our audit will be conducted with the objective of our expressing an opinion on the financial statements.

[The responsibilities of the auditor]

We will conduct our audit in accordance with International Standards on Auditing

(ISAs). Those standards require that we comply with ethical requirements and plan and perform the audit to obtain reasonable assurance about whether the financial statements are free from material misstatement. An audit involves performing procedures to obtain audit evidence about the amounts and disclosures in the financial statements. The procedures selected depend on the auditor's judgment, including the assessment of the risks of material misstatement of the financial statements, whether due to fraud or error. An audit also includes evaluating the appropriateness of accounting policies used and the reasonableness of accounting estimates made by management, as well as evaluating the overall presentation of the financial statements.

Because of the inherent limitations of an audit, together with the inherent limitations of internal control, there is an unavoidable risk that some material misstatements, including those due to fraud, may not be detected, even though the audit is properly planned and performed in accordance with ISAs. In making our risk assessments, we consider internal control relevant to the entity's preparation of the financial statements in order to design audit procedures that are appropriate in the circumstances, but not for the purpose of expressing an opinion on the effectiveness of the entity's internal control. However, we will communicate to you in writing concerning any significant deficiencies in internal control relevant to the audit of the financial statements that we have identified during the audit.

[The responsibilities of management and identification of the applicable financial reporting framework.]

Our audit will be conducted on the basis that management and those charged with governance acknowledge and understand that they have responsibility:

(a) For the preparation and fair presentation of the financial statements in accordance with International Financial Reporting Standards;

(b) For such internal control as management determines is necessary to enable the preparation of financial statements that are free from material misstatement, whether due to fraud or error; and

(c) To provide us with:

   (i) Access to all information of which management is aware that is relevant to the preparation of the financial statements such as records, documentation and other matters;

   (ii) Additional information that we may request from management for the purpose of the audit; and

   (iii) Unrestricted access to persons within the entity from whom we determine it necessary to obtain audit evidence.

As part of our audit process, we will request from management and those charged with governance, written confirmation concerning representations made to us in connection with the audit.

We expect to conduct our examination according to the following time table:

	Start	Finish
Preliminary tests	9/11/20x4	9/30/20x4
Management letter on internal control		10/10/20x4
Year-end testing	2/1/20x5	3/3/20x5
Final audit report and financial statements		3/15/20x5

During the examination, assistance will be supplied by your personnel including the preparation of detailed account schedules, preparation of such reconciliations as are needed, and provision of needed documents and records. Timely assistance with these matters will help us complete the engagement on time and reduce the audit fee.

Our fees are based on hourly rates for various personnel that we will assign to the engagement. The total fee will be based on the amount of time needed to complete the tests and procedures that we deem necessary. You will also be billed for out-of-pocket costs such as travel, typing, copying, etc., which are necessary for us to satisfactorily complete the engagement. We expect that our total fees will not exceed $20,000 and we will bring to your attention any circumstances that would cause our fees to exceed that amount.

Please indicate your agreement with these arrangements by signing and returning one copy of this letter.

Respectfully,

Roberta Smith, Partner

Accepted by: _____   Date: _____

---

*If an Integrated Audit were required all references to International Standards on Auditing as well as International Financial Reporting Standards would be replaced by PCAOB audit standards and FASB financial accounting standards. Recently the SEC has permitted the submission of IFRS based financial statements for non-US based SEC registrants. In addition, in an Integrated Audit the letter would include language outlining the understanding with the client about effectiveness of internal control over financial reporting and related reporting as part of the engagement.

The auditor should always obtain an engagement letter or an acknowledgement that the terms and conditions of a previous year's engagement letter continue. In the past, public accounting firms have faced a number of landmark lawsuits that arose from misunderstandings over the level of service being provided by the firm.

AUTHORITATIVE GUIDANCE & STANDARDS

Standards (ISA 210) addressing communications between the auditor and client expressly require engagement letters be prepared. For many public accounting firms this is interpreted as annual requirement for all clients. The PCAOB AS 1301 has similar requirements for US registrants' auditors.

Preliminary Planning

The term "preliminary planning" refers to the auditor's actions during the early stages of the engagement, be it for a current or new client. The auditor's preliminary planning has two broad purposes: (1) to obtain background information about the client that will assist in the efficient and effective planning of the engagement, and (2) to identify potential problem areas that will require special attention during the engagement.

AUTHORITATIVE GUIDANCE & STANDARDS

Standards (ISA 300 **Planning an Audit of Financial Statements, AS 2101 [formerly AS 9] Audit Planning***) address the details of audit planning and the preliminary planning discussed in this chapter would be a subset of the overall set of matters the auditor will consider in developing a complete and detailed audit plan.*

Obtain a General Understanding of the Client

The logical starting place for preliminary planning is obtaining a general understanding of the client and its business. The nature of the information that the auditor should accumulate at this point is summarized in Box 4.4 "Analyzing a New Client: Ten Key Questions after the Preconditions for Audit Are Met" (see next page). A great deal of the information for understanding the client will have been gathered as part of the client acceptance process (or in prior years). This information can be supplemented with discussions with company personnel who deal with various aspects of the business, particularly areas outside of the accounting department. Further information can be obtained through discussions with industry specialists within the accounting firm. Other procedures for obtaining a sufficient understanding of the client and its environment include:

- Reviewing the regulatory environment of the client.
- Obtaining or developing a business model of the client that includes such components as the products, markets, customers, resource suppliers, alliance partners, processes, and external forces of the client (to be discussed in Chapter 5).

- Touring key plants and facilities of the client.
- Obtaining and reviewing company policies and procedures, particularly mission statements and codes of conduct.
- Obtaining and reviewing significant contracts and other legal documents.
- Identifying related parties.
- Evaluating the need for assistance from specialists.
- Considering the role of the client's internal audit department, if one exists, within the client's control system and with respect to their ability to assist to the auditor.

BOX 4.4   ANALYZING A NEW CLIENT: TEN KEY QUESTIONS AFTER THE PRECONDITIONS FOR AUDIT ARE MET

1. *What are the company's products? Who are the company's customers? What are its markets?*

2. *What is the company's strategy for developing and maintaining a sustainable competitive advantage over its competition?*

3. *What is the nature of the company's operating cycle, i.e., how do they produce, market, and deliver the product or services?*

4. *What are the key processes and activities of the operating cycle?*

5. *What is the nature and composition of the company's asset base and sources of financing?*

6. *What is the nature of the company's strategic relationships with outside organizations or companies?*

7. *How sophisticated is the company's information system(s) that is used to record the activities of each of the elements of the operating cycle?*

8. *What is the company's attitude and strategy for generating reliable accounting information?*

9. *What financial reporting information needs to be generated and reported by the information system(s)?*

10. *What are the critical risks that the auditor should be aware of that suggest reported financial information will not fairly present actual business results?*

Becoming Familiar with the Organization's Strategic Plan

Early in the engagement, the auditor should determine the organization's strategic plan and its source of sustainable competitive advantage. Every organization has a strategy for attaining its goals, although the strategy may not always be formally stated or the result of a rigorous strategic planning process. A company has two broad strategic decisions to make: (1) Do they want their products to be low cost or highly differentiated, and/or (2) do they want to target a broad or narrow group of consumers? The better an organization understands and articulates its strategy, the more likely it is to be successful as it undertakes actions to advance the selected strategy. An

A company with an incoherent or inappropriate strategy for product development is likely to encounter failures in introducing new products. A famous example of a new product failure based on an inappropriate strategy was the introduction of a new formula for Coca-Cola in the 1980s. The new formulation was designed to make the soda sweeter and superior to Pepsi in direct taste tests. A funny thing happened though—hard-core Coke drinkers hated the new formula and exercised their market power. The company quickly reintroduced the original formula under the label Coke Classic and eventually discontinued "New Coke." A similar product failure occurred at Pepsi when it introduced Crystal Pepsi in the 1990s because it believed customers would find clear cola more refreshing—they did not. Such failures generally result in low margins or losses and often lead to accounting problems arising from impairments to plant assets and inventory.

organization that lacks a coherent strategy is less likely to be successful in the long run and may present some difficult challenges to the auditor[iv].

As a general rule, organizations in the growth or decline phase of their life cycle tend to have more challenging business risks which create comparable challenges for the auditor. For example, a rapidly growing company will strain the capacity of its systems and abilities of its personnel, increasing the likelihood of problems within the organization, including strains on the accounting system. The auditor will need to assess whether the organization's strategy is likely to lead to success and whether it is being executed effectively. A poor strategy or weak execution will impact on the financial results, either in the current or future periods. We discuss the issue of strategy in detail in Chapter 5.

Obtain a High Level Understanding of The Information Processing Systems

Another important area for the auditor to address is management's overall attitude and approach for obtaining reliable information and financial reporting. As previously noted, management is responsible for establishing a reliable information system. The auditor should identify the key information systems used within the organization. Eventually, critical information systems will have to be evaluated by the auditor. Systems that are weak or informal may increase the risk of material misstatement associated with the processing of transactions or stored master records. Furthermore, such problems may indicate potentially severe weaknesses in internal control over financial reporting. Finally, weaknesses in information processing may make it difficult for the auditor to obtain evidence that is needed to verify some management assertions (e.g., documents may be inaccurate), causing the auditor to change the approach the auditor uses to gain evidence that supports the financial statement assertions.

Identify New and Review Known Problem Areas that May Affect Audit Planning

An important purpose of preliminary planning is to highlight potential problem areas or risk factors in the audit. Some of these risk factors will have a broad impact on the reliability of the financial statements whereas others will be more isolated, having an impact on individual transactions or accounts. Some of the procedures that are helpful to the auditor at this point include:

- Discuss prior-year problems with the management and, with a new client, the predecessor auditor.
- Review minutes of significant corporate governance related (e.g., meetings of the Board of Directors and key board committees) and management meetings (e.g., strategic planning).
- Obtain and review preliminary financial statements.
- Identify key accounting policies.

We discussed communications with predecessor auditor earlier. Further details about the other procedures are presented below.

Review Board Minutes

An important part of an audit engagement is the review of the Board of Director minutes for all meetings conducted during the year. The board often discusses significant events and transactions that impact the organization, including major acquisitions and disposals, serious litigation matters, strategic risks, executive performance, and strategic initiatives. Furthermore, only the board can declare dividends, making the board minutes the primary source of audit evidence for testing dividends declared and payable. For an Integrated Audit, the Audit Committee of the Board of Directors is required by PCAOB rules to accept direct responsibility for hiring, firing, and compensating the auditor, so having direct access to both board members and board minutes should be relatively easy. Because of the importance of the issues discussed in the board minutes, a restriction on the auditor's ability to access board records should be considered a limitation on the auditor's ability to assess needed audit evidence and might affect the nature of the auditor's report.

Review Preliminary Financial Statements

A review of the pre-audit preliminary financial statements will give the auditor a quick picture of the client's financial situation. Is the client profitable? Is the client growing? What is its asset base? How does it finance its operations? Are there any unusual circumstances or results that suggest a heightened risk level? Although the auditor cannot obtain a complete understanding of the client based on this type of cursory review, it will provide some insight into what to expect as the audit is planned and executed.

Identify Key Accounting Policies

Evaluating significant accounting policies used by the client is also important. Management's accounting choices can reveal much about its attitude towards financial reporting and internal control. Although aggressive accounting by itself does not indicate problems with management, consistently aggressive choices that maximize or accelerate revenue and minimize or defer expenses suggests the possibility that management is more interested in "looking good" than in providing high quality information about the firm's financial results. Aggressive accounting choices combined with other risk factors such as an excessive emphasis on compensation contingent on achieving aggressive growth or income targets could indicate higher risk of material misstatement. Ultimately, the auditor must evaluate whether the accounting choices made by management are appropriate and adjust the planned evidence collection process in light of these management choices.

Auditing standards also require the auditor to evaluate the reasonableness of accounting estimates made by management. The *IFAC Handbook* (Glossary of Terms) defines an **accounting estimate** as "an approximation of a financial statement element, item or account." Such estimates include reserves for uncollectible receivables or loan losses, net realizable value of assets, contingent liabilities, and the stage of completion of work in progress inventory. These estimates can have a pervasive impact on the financial statements, and the auditor must identify potential issues associated with estimates early in the engagement. Management is responsible for developing these estimates, including determining when estimates are needed, designing a system to gather information needed to make the estimate, making assumptions about likely future events, and calculating the estimate. Furthermore, management is responsible for evaluating the reasonableness of prior estimates, including any adjustments to reflect new information that renders previous assessments inaccurate. The auditor's objective is to evaluate whether all needed estimates have been made, whether they are reasonable, and whether they are in accordance with generally accepted accounting principles.

Consider Special Circumstances that May Affect Audit Planning

Some special circumstances can have a significant impact on the planning of the audit engagement and should be addressed as part of the preliminary planning process. These circumstances are singled out for the auditor's attention because they have the potential to pervasively affect the conduct of the engagement. We will discuss three areas of concern at this point: (1) the existence of and nature of transactions with related parties, (2) the need for specialists to aid in gathering audit evidence, and (3) the use of internal auditors to make the audit process more cost efficient.

Related Party Transactions

AUTHORITATIVE GUIDANCE & STANDARDS

ISA 550 **Related Parties** *and PCAOB 2410 (formerly AS 18)* **Related Parties** *address the detail the auditor's need to understand how management has identified related parties and transactions with such parties as well as the auditor's responsibilities to detect related party transactions that have not been identified by management.*

Related party transactions are defined as transactions between two parties who share some common interest. Related party transactions are common for many organizations (e.g., selling goods between parent companies and subsidiaries) and, in most cases, reflect legitimate business decisions by the company. However, they are a prime area for accounting manipulations and should be looked at carefully by the auditor. For example, much of the fraud at Enron was perpetrated through related party transactions.

Accounting standard setters have specified reporting standards applicable to related party transactions. These standards give numerous examples of related parties, including:

a) a parent company and its subsidiaries;

b) subsidiaries of a common parent;

c) trusts for the benefit of employees, such as pensions and profit-sharing trusts that are managed by or under the trusteeship of the enterprise's management;

d) principal owners, management, or members of their immediate families;

e) affiliates.

The accounting standards require specific disclosures when a company has related party transactions. One of the auditor's concerns about related party transactions is that they are not represented in the financial statements as being arm's-length in nature since the pricing of such transactions may not represent the fair market value that would be paid to third parties for the same goods or services. The related party accounting standards (e.g., IAS 24 Related Party Disclosures) presume that the readers of the financial statements will make the judgment about the appropriateness of such transactions for themselves, as long as the transaction and its terms are fully disclosed in the financial statements.

It is management's responsibility to identify related parties, however the auditor needs assurance as to the completeness of this process so as to know the identity of related parties in a particular engagement. This identification must occur during preliminary planning so that the entire audit team are alert for transactions with such parties if one comes to their attention during the audit process. If a related party transaction is detected, the auditor must investigate the transaction, examine supporting documentation, and verify the accuracy of required disclosures. If the financial statement disclosure is in conformity with GAAP, the auditor need perform no further work on the matter. If disclosure is not adequate or is misleading (e.g., by implying that the transaction is actually an arm's-length transaction when it is not), the auditor should ask management to make appropriate changes to the disclosures or adapt the auditor's report (e.g., consider a qualification—see the last section of this chapter) to reflect the incomplete accounting.

Need for Specialists

The auditor may need to consult with specialists to verify the accuracy of some financial statement assertions. Examples of specialists who may be needed on an engagement include:

- Engineer: To verify the stage of completion of electronic components.
- Real Estate Appraiser: To appraise realizable value of real estate used as collateral for loans.
- Actuary: To evaluate the funding requirements and future cash flows associated with pensions or post-retirement health costs.
- Attorney: To evaluate the likely disposition of contingent losses from litigation.
- Geologist: To verify the existence of natural resources being held for future extraction, such as oil and metals.

It is important that auditors identify the situations where such specialists may be needed on an engagement as early as possible. In some cases, the specialist may need to perform certain activities on specific dates, such as examine the inventory on hand as of year-end. In all cases, the specialist should be called in as soon as possible to allow adequate time to complete the necessary work.

The auditor should arrange for the services of an appropriate specialist who should be competent, as evidenced by appropriate professional certification and an upstanding reputation, and be independent of the client, albeit in some cases the auditor can satisfy themselves by using a specialist who is employed by the client. The auditor should have a clear understanding with the specialist as to the specific information needed by the auditor and the form of report that the specialist will issue. The auditor should also strive to understand the assumptions, the computational approach, and the data utilized by the specialist in his or her decision process. In many cases, the auditor will test the accuracy of the input data that the specialist uses for his or her calculations. If the specialist's findings provide support for the financial statement assertions being addressed (e.g., valuation of pension obligations), the auditor can accept these findings as competent evidence in support of the related management assertions.

AUTHORITATIVE GUIDANCE & STANDARDS

Standards provide specific guidance when auditors use others outside of the engagement team to help conduct the audit. Standards for the work of specialists (ISA 620 **Using the Work of an Auditor's Expert;** *PCAOB AS 1210 [formerly Interim Standard AU 336]* **Using the Work of a Specialist***) and internal auditors (ISA 610* **Using the Work of Internal Auditors;** *PCAOB AS 2605 [formerly Interim Standard AU 322]* **Consideration of the Internal Audit Function** *and for internal control testing PCAOB AS 2201 [formerly AS 5]* **An Audit of Internal Control Over Financial Reporting That Is Integrated with An Audit of Financial Statements***) generally allow for auditors to rely on their work when performed by qualified individuals and properly supervised and reviewed by auditors on the engagement team.*

Use of Internal Auditors

Another condition that may pervasively affect the auditor's engagement planning is the existence of an internal audit department within the client. The existence of an internal audit department is now required by the SEC for registrants in the US, and is encouraged in many other countries or required as a stock exchange listing requirement. Some internal auditors perform many of the same tests and procedures that an external auditor performs. If an internal audit staff exists, the external auditor may be able to utilize the personnel and the efforts of that group. The key concerns that the external auditor should address are whether the internal auditors are knowledgeable, objective, and sufficiently independent of management to generate unbiased evidence. Knowledge can be evaluated by reviewing the company's hiring and training practices as evidenced by the level of education, experience, and certification of the internal audit staff. The auditor will review the work performed by the internal auditors and evaluate its quality, especially if it is to be used as part of the evidence in support of the financial statement assertions. Objectivity usually depends on the level of management to whom the internal auditors report. Ideally, the internal auditors should report to the Audit Committee (and are required to do so for public companies in the US). In some organizations, the internal auditors may report to lower level management, such as the controller, in which case the objectivity and independence of the internal auditors may be open to question.

When the internal auditors are found to be knowledgeable and objective, their work can be relied upon by the external auditor when planning his or her own tests. Specifically, internal auditors can be used to assist in obtaining an understanding of the client's system, to make various risk assessments, and to perform some tests. Many of these tests may be directly related to the internal auditor's own audit plans or may be specifically requested, planned, and directed by the external auditor. All work performed by internal auditors should be thoroughly reviewed by the external auditor. Rules of the PCAOB allow internal auditors to perform some of the procedures required to test internal controls, as long as the external auditors' work provides the principal evidence for the auditor's opinion on control effectiveness.

Discuss and Assess Fraud Risk and The Risk of Material Misstatement

An important objective of preliminary planning is to assess the risk of material misstatement associated with fraud. A key procedure for the audit team is to hold a "brainstorming session" involving all engagement personnel who will take a significant role in the audit engagement. The discussion of potential ways that fraud could occur is required under standards related to the auditor's responsibilities to detect fraud when it occurs. Both academic evidence and observations from the PCAOB suggest that auditors are having great problems in implementing this requirement as it needs to be done early in the audit to be effective, yet it must also include all key engagement personnel (including Information Technology, tax, and other relevant specialists).[2] Further, for it to work, the "prior beliefs the audit team members have that management is honest and has integrity" (PCAOB AS 2401) must be set aside in order to contemplate ways that fraud might be committed.

AUTHORITATIVE GUIDANCE & STANDARDS

ISA 240 **The Auditor's Responsibilities Relating to Fraud in an Audit of Financial Statements** *and PCAOB AS 2401 (formerly Interim Standard AU 316)* **Consideration of Fraud in a Financial Statement Audit** *are the standards that most explicitly address fraud in the conduct of an audit. However, given the increased standard setter and regulator attention to fraud, references to fraud appear throughout the professional standards and are now thoroughly integrated into all proposed new and revised standards (e.g., ISA 315* **Identifying and Assessing the Risks of Material Misstatement through Understanding the Entity and Its Environment,** *320* **Materiality in Planning and Performing an Audit,** *330* **The Auditor's Responses to Assessed Risks** *and 500* **Audit Evidence;** *PCAOB ASs 2101, 2105 [formerly AS 11]* **Consideration of Materiality in Planning and Performing an Audit,** *2201, 2210 [formerly AS 12]* **Identifying and Assessing Risks of Material Misstatement,** *2301 [formerly AS 13]* **The Auditor's Responses to the Risks of Material Misstatement** *and 2810 [formerly AS 14]* **Evaluating Audit Results**). *These issues will be considered* *in more depth throughout the book. At present the objective is to become sensitized to the issues related to financial statement fraud.*

The likelihood of fraud occurring at a specific client is evaluated using the Fraud Triangle (Figure 4.1), which illustrates the three conditions that reflect a heightened risk of fraud: Incentives, Opportunities, and Attitudes. The next 3 boxes provide more detail on each element of the Fraud Triangle and outlines the issues that should be considered and discussed by the audit team related to the possibility of fraudulent financial reporting. First, management may have some incentive to commit fraud. Figure 4.1 outlines how incentives in the form of desires or needs on the part of senior management (e.g., greed), or pressures on management to improve the performance of the organization may lead managers to be open to committing fraud. Second, there could be an opportunity to commit fraud. Box 4.5 "Fraud Risk Factors: Incentives and Pressures" shows that opportunities to commit fraud usually arise when an organization has ineffective or incomplete internal controls, weak monitoring, poorly designed and executed processes, or a rapidly changing environment. Third, management (and potentially those charged with governance) may be able to rationalize that they are justified when committing fraud. Box 4.6 "Fraud Risk Factors: Opportunities" shows how otherwise decent people's attitudes can turn toward fraud so that the behavior is acceptable, maybe even necessary, in a given situation. Such an attitude usually means that the perpetrator believes what he or she is doing is all right or will never be discovered.

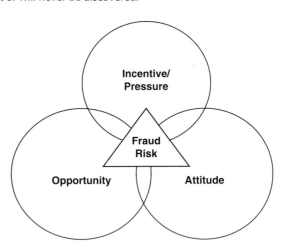

Figure 4.1 *The Fraud Triangle*

BOX 4.5 FRAUD RISK FACTORS: INCENTIVES AND PRESSURES*

Incentives and pressures on management and those charged with governance can arise from:

The personal financial situation of management or those charged with governance is threatened by the entity's poor financial performance as a result of their having:

- *Significant financial interests in the entity.*
- *Significant portions of their compensation (e.g., bonuses, stock options, and earn-out arrangements) being contingent upon achieving aggressive targets for stock price, operating results, financial position, or cash flow.*
- *Significant personal guarantees of debts of the entity to third parties.*

There is excessive pressure on management or operating personnel to meet financial targets established by those charged with governance, including sales or profitability incentive goals.

Incentives for management and those charged with governance to commit fraud occur when:

Financial stability or profitability is threatened by economic, industry, or entity operating conditions such as:

- *High degree of competition or market saturation, accompanied by declining margins.*
- *High vulnerability to rapid changes (e.g., such as changes in technology, product obsolescence, or interest rates).*
- *Significant declines in customer demand and increasing business failures in the industry or overall economy.*
- *Operating losses making the threat of bankruptcy, foreclosure, or hostile takeover imminent.*
- *Recurring negative cash flows from operations or an inability to generate cash flows from operations while reporting earnings and earnings growth.*
- *Rapid growth or unusual profitability especially compared to that of other companies in the same industry.*

Pressures on management and those charged with governance to commit fraud occur when:

Excessive pressure exists for management to meet the requirements or expectations of third parties such as:

- *Profitability or trend level expectations of investment analysts, institutional investors, significant creditors, or other external parties (particularly expectations that are unduly aggressive or unrealistic), including expectations created by management in overly optimistic press releases or annual report messages.*
- *Need to obtain additional debt or equity financing to stay competitive.*
- *Marginal ability to meet exchange listing requirements or debt covenant requirements.*
- *The perceived or real adverse effects of reporting poor financial results on significant pending transactions, such as business combinations or contract awards.*

---

* Based on ISA 240 and PCAOB AS 2401.

BOX 4.6   FRAUD RISK FACTORS: OPPORTUNITIES*

Opportunities that make it easier to commit fraud include:

The nature of the industry or the entity's operations provides opportunities to engage in fraudulent financial reporting including:

- *significant related party transactions not in the ordinary course of business or with related entities not audited or audited by another firm;*
- *a strong financial presence or ability to dominate a certain industry sector that allows the entity to dictate terms or conditions to suppliers or customers that may result in inappropriate or non-arm's length transactions;*
- *assets, liabilities, revenues, or expenses based on significant estimates that involve subjective judgments or uncertainties that are difficult to corroborate;*
- *significant, unusual, or highly complex transactions, especially those close to period end that pose difficult "substance over form" questions;*
- *significant operations located or conducted across international borders in jurisdictions where differing business environments and cultures exist;*
- *use of business intermediaries for which there appears to be no clear business justification;*
- *significant bank accounts or subsidiary or branch operations in tax-haven jurisdictions for which there appears to be no clear business justification.*

There is ineffective monitoring of management as a result of:

- *the domination of management by a single person or small group without compensating controls;*
- *ineffective oversight by those charged with governance over the financial reporting process and internal control.*

There is a complex or unstable organizational structure, as evidenced by:

- *difficulty in determining the organization or individuals that have controlling interest in the entity;*
- *overly complex organizational structure involving unusual legal entities or managerial lines of authority;*
- *management incentive plans contingent upon achieving targets relating only to certain accounts or selected activities of the entity;*
- *high turnover of senior management, legal counsel, or those charged with governance.*

Internal controls are deficient as a result of:

- *inadequate monitoring of controls, including automated controls and controls over interim financial reporting;*
- *high turnover rates or employment of ineffective accounting, internal audit, or information technology staff;*
- *ineffective accounting and information systems, including significant weaknesses in internal control.*

---

* Based on ISA 240 and PCAOB AS 2401.

BOX 4.7 FRAUD RISK FACTORS: ATTITUDES/ RATIONALIZATIONS*

Attitudes and rationalizations that may lead management and others to be more open to committing fraud include:

(a) Management and those charged with governance have ineffective communication, implementation, support, or enforcement of the entity's values or ethical standards, or the communication of inappropriate values or ethical standards.

(b) Non-financial management's excessive participation in or preoccupation with the selection of accounting principles or the determination of significant estimates.

(c) Known client management history of violations of securities laws or other laws and regulations, or claims against the entity, its senior management, or those charged with governance alleging fraud or violations of laws and regulations.

(d) Management's excessive interest in maintaining or increasing the entity's stock price or earnings trend.

(e) Management's public commitments to analysts, creditors, and other third parties to achieve aggressive or unrealistic forecasts.

(f) Management failing to correct known significant weaknesses in internal control on a timely basis.

(g) Management's interest in employing inappropriate means to minimize reported earnings for tax-motivated reasons.

(h) Low morale among senior management.

(i) The owner-manager making no distinction between personal and business transactions.

(j) Recurring attempts by management to justify marginal or inappropriate accounting on the basis of materiality.

(k) The relationship between management and the current (or predecessor) auditor is strained, as exhibited by the following:

   o frequent disputes with the current (or predecessor) auditor on accounting, auditing, or reporting matters;

   o unreasonable demands on the auditor, such as time constraints regarding the completion of the audit or the issuance of the auditor's report;

   o formal or informal restrictions on the auditor that inappropriately limit access to people, information, or the ability to communicate effectively with those charged with governance;

   o domineering management behavior in dealing with the auditor, especially involving attempts to influence the scope of the auditor's work or the selection or continuance of personnel assigned to or consulted on the audit engagement.

*Based on ISA 240 and PCAOB AS 2401.

In 2002, the SEC indicted John Rigas and several members of his family for committing fraud at Adelphia, the cable company started by Rigas. The fraud involved several facets, including the diversion of company funds for personal expenditures such as open market stock purchases by the Rigas family; purchases of timber rights to land in Pennsylvania; construction of a golf club for $12.8 million; repayments of personal margin loans and other Rigas family debts; and purchases of luxury condominiums in Colorado, Mexico, and New York City for the Rigas family. Rigas and his sons had the opportunity to divert these funds through collusion and the ability to override controls. The incentive likely was driven by the need to pay for their high level of personal spending. The attitude associated with the fraud likely was that all of the Adelphia funds were essentially the Rigas' to spend because they founded and developed the Company.

The issues identified in Figures 4.1 and the previous 3 boxes provide many concrete illustrations of incentives, opportunities, and attitudes that in combination may lead to fraudulent financial reporting. Note that it is relatively rare for the isolated existence of one or two of these fraud indicators to be indicative of an increase in fraud risk. It is the pattern of reinforcing incentives/pressures, opportunity, and attitude changes and rationalizations that come together to create an increased risk of fraud. Careful consideration of this set of figures is strongly encouraged as this material is vital to understanding the pervasive concern about fraud that permeates through the modern audit(v).

An Overview of the Audit Process

Having discussed the *logical* process of performing an audit in Chapter 3, and the impact regulatory and professional context in Chapter 2, we now introduce the practical *sequence of* activities that comprise the audit engagement. This sequential process, illustrated in Figure 4.2, will serve as the organizing structure for Chapters 5 to 15. Initially, an auditor must reach the decision to accept or retain a client (I) and that was discussed in this chapter. The remainder of the engagement can then be loosely divided into two phases: risk assessment and evidence gathering. The risk-assessment phase involves obtaining evidence about current conditions and assessing the risks facing the organization (II). Some of these risks may suggest that the financial statements may be materially misstated. The auditor performs three types of activities to assess and measure these risks:

1. Understand a client's business and industry and conduct a strategic analysis to identify potential risk areas in the engagement (IIa is discussed in Chapters 5 and 6).

2. Understand how internal controls are embedded into client's business processes and evaluate the effectiveness of internal control to enable the auditor to determine the likelihood that risks will be mitigated, reducing the likelihood that they will affect the substance of the financial statements. The procedures performed during this phase of the audit provide the evidence necessary for a GAAS Audit (IIb is discussed in Chapters 6 and 7) and form a strong foundation to evaluate the effectiveness of internal control over financial reporting as part of an **Integrated Audit** (Chapter 8).

3. Perform preliminary analytical procedures to identify unusual conditions that have arisen that may indicate significant risk conditions and/or the potential for errors in the financial statements (IIc is discussed in Chapter 9).

After evaluating current conditions and risks, the auditor reaches some preliminary conclusions about internal control over financial reporting and the financial statement assertions made by management. Based on these conclusions, the auditor can prepare a plan for gathering the remaining evidence necessary to evaluate the financial statement assertions (III is discussed in Chapter 10). Following the audit plan, the auditor gathers and interprets evidence in all of the important areas of the audit (IV). The audit is loosely decomposed into key business processes to be examined. We use

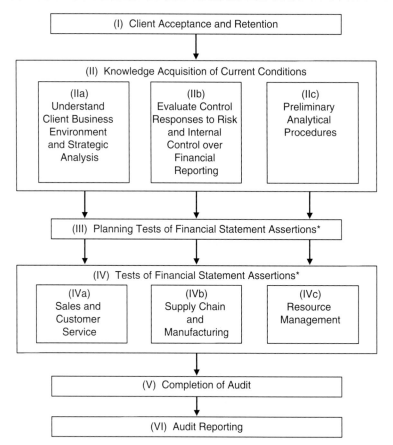

Figure 4.2 Overview of the Audit Process

Including, in an Integrated Audit, management assertions about the effectiveness of internal controls over financial reporting.

the idea of the value chain (i.e., how do firms compete to create value for their customers from the goods or services they provide) and the following separate major business processes are discussed in this text:

- Sales and customer service (IVa is discussed in Chapter 11) including brand management.
- Supply chain and production process (IVb is discussed in Chapter 12).
- Resource management processes (IVc is discussed in Chapter 13) including research and development and mergers and acquisitions.

The processes that require the attention of the auditor depend on the circumstances of the client and the risk assessments made in the knowledge acquisition phase of the audit (II). The final aspects of the audit involve completing the documentation and interpreting the evidence, finalizing conclusions about financial information, and preparing the appropriate report to be issued (V and VI are developed in detail in Chapters 14 and 15, with VI being briefly introduced in the next section of this chapter).

An important point to remember is that while the audit process depicted in Figure 4.2 appears to be linear, in practice it is iterative, meaning that information obtained at any stage in the process may necessitate a return to an earlier phase for reconsideration of previous conclusions[vi].

[vi]**EXAMPLE**

If an examination of sales and customer service and related tests of sales transactions reveals a higher risk of material misstatement than was expected, the auditor may need to readdress his or her risk assessments for revenue accounts, reconsider effectiveness of internal control over financial reporting for sales transactions, and consider the impact on additional evidence needed to complete the audit of customer service activity.

The sequential audit process helps ensure that auditors develop a sufficient understanding of the entity and its environment, including internal control over financial reporting, such that a plan for gathering sufficient, competent evidence to support transactions, accounts, and financial statements (including disclosures) can be developed. The nature, extent, and timing of the procedures utilized in an audit are based to a large extent on the results of analyses performed by the auditor (II and III). These detailed analyses enable the auditor to focus audit effort on transactions, accounts, and aspects of the financial statements most at risk of being materially misstated (IV).

Communicating the Results of the Audit

After gathering all the evidence needed to determine if management's assertions about financial statements are fairly stated, the auditor issues a formal report stating the nature of his or her conclusions. The actual form of the audit report has changed greatly over the past one hundred and fifty years, and further significant changes are occurring as this text is written. Auditing standards are specific about the form of the report that should be used under different circumstances since the public report is essentially a legal document. The key part of the report has always been the auditor's opinion (sometimes called the auditor's certification) of the

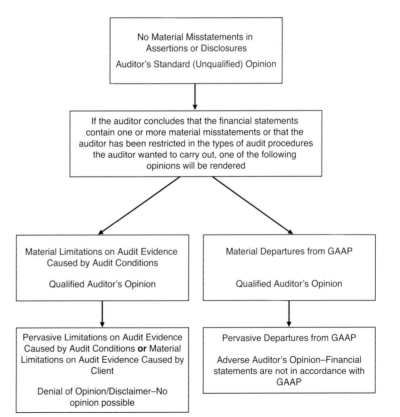

Figure 4.3 Hierarchy of the Auditor's Reporting Options: GAAS Audit

general purpose financial statements and their compliance with generally accepted accounting principles (GAAP) such as IFRS or FASB accounting standards. If all management assertions associated with material amounts are reasonable, the auditor can conclude that the financial statements are fairly presented in accordance with GAAP. If any management assertion associated with a material amount is not supported to the auditor's satisfaction, the auditor cannot conclude that the financial statements are fairly presented.

There are four general types of auditor's opinions depending on the outcome of the audit process and the conclusions reached by the auditor about whether the financial statements are materially misstated. The hierarchy of these reports is illustrated in Figure 4.3 and described below. Each of these types of reports could be combined with the report over internal control effectiveness in the Integrated Audit as discussed in the next section.

GAAS Audit Opinions

AUTHORITATIVE GUIDANCE & STANDARDS

The auditor's reports for a **GAAS Audit** *are discussed in ISA 700* **Forming an Opinion and Reporting on Financial Statements** *with modifications to the unqualified reports discussed in ISA 705* **Modifications to the Opinion in the Independent Auditor's Report** *and matters that need to be emphasized in ISA 706* **Emphasis of Matter Paragraphs and Other Matter Paragraphs in the Independent Auditor's Report.** *ISA 701* **Key Audit Matters** *adds requirements for the auditors of publicly listed companies to disclose the most significant matters that affected the audit of the current year's financial statements. Each of these reporting options will be discussed in detail in Chapter 15. For entities in the US that are not public companies, the AICPA's Auditing Standards Board has adopted analogous standards (with limited differences to allow for US reporting needs) following the same numbering system as ISAs.*

For a *GAAS Audit,* the standard (unqualified) auditor's report is used when the auditor concludes that the evidence obtained supports the fairness and completeness of all material management assertions. The opinion paragraph is arguably the most important part of the report. It is so important that the entire report is often referred to as the auditor's "opinion." In the latest changes to the auditor's report the opinion paragraph about whether the financial statements are fair is now the first paragraph of the auditor's report. The wording of an unqualified opinion is as follows:

> We have audited the financial statements of ABC Company (the Company), which comprise the statement of financial position as at December 31, 20X1, and the statement of comprehensive income, statement of changes in equity and statement of cash flows for the year then ended, and notes to the financial statements, including a summary of significant accounting policies. In our opinion, the accompanying financial statements present fairly, in all material respects, the

financial position of the Company as at December 31, 20X1, and (*of*) its financial performance and its cash flows for the year then ended in accordance with International Financial Reporting Standards (IFRSs).

The key words in the opinion are "present fairly" and "in all material respects." An alternative formulation of the opinion used in much of the world replaces "present fairly" with "give a true and fair view of." The report does not say that the financial statements are absolutely correct. Such a conclusion would be unwarranted due to the inherent uncertainty underlying the audit process. The criteria used for reaching a conclusion about fairness are clearly stated to be the specified accounting framework (normally IFRS or FASB accounting standards). If the auditor does not feel that he or she can issue a standard unqualified opinion, one of the following three alternative reports will be used.

Modification of the Auditor's Opinion

There are three types of auditor's reports that are considered as modifications to the auditor's standard opinion. Each signals that the auditor is not issuing an unqualified opinion on the financial statements and explains the reasons for departing from the "standard" auditor's opinion.

Qualified Opinion: A qualified report is issued when the auditor feels that he or she is unable to conclude that the assertions are completely reliable or fair. This can typically occur for two reasons: (1) scope limitations, and (2) departures from the accounting framework. For scope limitations, the auditor is unable to obtain enough evidence to form an opinion often due to conditions beyond the control of the client and auditor. One example where this might occur is if the auditor is unable to observe the quantity of inventory on hand at the end of the year because the auditor is replacing one who had to resign the engagement after year-end (e.g., the predecessor audit firm loses its license to carry out audits). In the case of departures from the accounting framework, the auditor concludes that the company has violated one or more standards for some significant assertion or set of assertions included in the financial statements. Such a violation may occur because the company fails to correct material misstatements uncovered by the auditor, omits a required disclosure, or uses an unacceptable accounting method (e.g., capitalizing research expenditures). However, the auditor is confident that the disclosures about the qualification made either by the client or in the auditor's report are extensive and clear enough that the nature and magnitude of the departure can be understood by the reader of the financial statements, and the overall financial reports can be interpreted in a meaningful manner.

Denial of Opinion (or Disclaimer): In a denial of opinion or disclaimer, the auditor states that no opinion can be expressed. A denial of opinion may be issued in the case of a scope limitation that has a pervasive impact on the financial statements. In such a situation, the auditor is unable to obtain convincing evidence about the reliability of the assertions and/or disclosures in the statements. For scope limitations one of the more important considerations is whether the limitation was arbitrarily imposed by the client (e.g., management prohibits the auditor from observing inventory). Under this set of circumstances it is much more likely that the auditor will disclaim an opinion then in situations where the scope limitation came from sources other than management (e.g., the former audit firm going out of business during the year of audit hence not allowing the new auditor to observe opening inventory). A disclaimer can also be issued if there is a conflict of interest between the auditor and client such that he or she cannot render an independent professional opinion (e.g., after the audit was commenced it came to the auditor's attention that a significant client subsidiary employs someone as a key financial official who is a close relative to one of the office's audit partners).

Adverse Auditor's Opinion: An adverse opinion is issued when the auditor concludes that the financial statement assertions are largely incorrect or misleading. An adverse opinion means that the violation of accounting standards results in such a pervasive effect on the financial statements (e.g., the company does not make year-end adjusting entries), that the financial statements "do not present fairly" the financial status of the organization. Such opinions are extremely rare, however, because the auditor will usually resign (or be fired) in situations that are this extreme. However, when an auditor resigns under these conditions, the auditor may be perceived as "allowing" the action to continue by not requiring a client to correct a GAAP violation or issuing an adverse opinion. The laws of various countries determine if or when an auditor is allowed to resign instead of reporting with an adverse opinion.

Integrated Audit Opinions including Effectiveness of Internal Control over Financial Reporting

In an **Integrated Audit**, the auditor issues an opinion on the financial statements conformance with GAAP but in addition provides an opinion on the auditor's assessment about the effectiveness of the client's internal control over financial reporting. The audit opinion on the financial statements in an Integrated Audit can, but is not required to, appear as the first paragraph of the auditor's report along with the auditor's conclusions about the effectiveness of internal control over financial reporting.

As noted in Chapter 3 management should test the design and operations of its system of internal control over financial reporting (ICOFR). These tests are done to support management assertions about internal control effectiveness. This testing may reveal one or more **control deficiencies**, which arise when the design or operation of the system does not prevent or detect misstatements on a timely basis.[3] If management identifies a deficiency, the next step is to evaluate the materiality of the deficiency. A **material weakness** is a deficiency, or a combination of deficiencies, such that there is a reasonable possibility that a material misstatement of the company's financial statements will not be prevented or detected on a timely basis. A **significant deficiency** is less severe than a material weakness yet important enough to merit attention by those responsible for oversight of the company's financial reporting, this normally being the Audit Committee of the company's Board of Directors.

AUTHORITATIVE GUIDANCE & STANDARDS

PCAOB AS 2201 provides the basic guidance on how to prepare audit reports in an **Integrated Audit** *with an emphasis on the internal control over financial reporting effectiveness report part of the opinion. PCAOB AS 3101 (formerly Interim Standard AU 508 which incorporated PCAOB AS 1* **References in Auditor's Reports to the Standards of the Public Company Accounting Oversight Board) Reports on Audited Financial Statements** *deals with the opinion on the financial statements that forms part of the Integrated Audit opinion. Significant more detail about these reporting issues will be provided in Chapter 8 (on internal control effectiveness) and Chapter 15.*

Auditors issue an opinion on the effectiveness of ICOFR based on their testing of controls. Based on the evidence that is available about the effectiveness of internal control, an auditor can issue either an unqualified opinion or an adverse opinion. The auditor's opinion on internal control is unqualified, if he or she concludes that ICOFR is effective in all material respects. The opinion is an adverse one if the auditor concludes that ICOFR is not effective due to at least one material weakness. In addition, the auditor has the ability to report scope limitations imposed either by circumstances or by the client. In an ICOFR audit, the only option when there is a scope limitation is for the auditor to disclaim an opinion. Hence, unlike the opinion on financial statements, there are no "qualified" opinions, either ICOFR is effective or not (resulting in an adverse opinion), and the auditor has had no scope limitation or does have a scope limitation (resulting in a disclaimer of opinion). If the auditor discovers a significant deficiency in controls that is not considered to be a material weakness, then the auditor is responsible for ensuring that the Audit Committee is informed about it in writing. A significant control deficiency by definition does not warrant an adverse auditor's opinion about the overall effectiveness of internal control.

An example of an unqualified opinion over the auditor's test of the design and operations of the internal control system over financial reporting combined with an unqualified opinion over the financial statements as required in an Integrated Audit is:

> In our opinion, the financial statements referred to above present fairly, in all material respects, the financial position of W Company as of December 31, 20X8 and 20X7, and the results of its operations and its cash flows for each of the years in the three-year period ended December 31, 20X8 in conformity with accounting principles generally accepted in the United States of America. Also in our opinion, W Company maintained, in all material respects, effective internal control over financial reporting as of December 31, 20X8, based on [*Identify control criteria, for example, "criteria established in Internal Control – Integrated Framework issued by the Committee of Sponsoring Organizations of the Treadway Commission (COSO) 2013."*].

This combined opinion (internal control over financial reporting effectiveness and financial statement audit) in one report, is the most common form of reporting employed in an Integrated Audit. As will be discussed further in Chapter 15, the auditor can also present the opinion in two separate reports—an opinion on the financial statements and an opinion on the effectiveness of internal control over financial reporting. However, the same public accounting or audit firm must prepare both reports and cross reference them to each other in order to meet the reporting requirements of the PCAOB.

Summary and Conclusion

In this chapter we have considered the auditor's professional responsibilities from two perspectives, his or her role in society and as a businessperson who has to make the business analyses that accompany the client acquisition and retention decision. After acquiring a new client, or deciding to retain an existing client, the auditor undertakes preliminary planning of the audit. This involves general consideration of a client's strategy, information processing and related parties, as well as the possible need by the auditor for specialist assistance with evidence gathering or the nature of the auditor's reliance on the client's internal auditors either as part of management's internal control system or as assistants to the external auditor in performing the external audit. Preliminary planning mostly involves gathering basic factual information about the client as a precursor to more detailed analysis during the remainder of the audit. We concluded the discussion with a brief overview of the result of the audit process, the auditor's report both in a GAAS audit and in an Integrated Audit.

Bibliography of Relevant Literature

Relevant Research

Ayers, S. and S. E. Kaplan. 1998. Potential Differences between Engagement and Risk Review Partners and their Effect on Client Acceptance Judgments. *Accounting Horizons.* 12(2): 139–153.

Beaulieu, P. R. 2001. The Effects of Judgments of New Clients' Integrity upon Risk Judgments, Audit Evidence and Fees. *Auditing: A Journal of Practice & Theory.* 20(2): 85–100.

Gendron, Y. 2001. The Difficult Client-Acceptance Decision in Canadian Audit Firms: A Field Investigation. *Contemporary Accounting Research.* 18(2): 283–310.

Johnstone, K. M. 2000. Client Acceptance Decisions: Simultaneous Effects of Client Business Risk, Audit Risk, Auditor Business Risk, and Risk Adaptation. *Auditing: A Journal of Practice & Theory.* 19(1): 1–26.

Johnstone, K. M. and J. C. Bedard. 2003. Risk Management in Client Acceptance Decision. *The Accounting Review.* 78(4): 1003–1025.

Krishnamoorthy, G. 2002. A Multistage Approach to External Auditors' Evaluation of the Internal Audit Function. *Auditing: A Journal of Practice & Theory.* 21(1): 95–122.

Trompeter, G. M., T. D. Carpenter, N. Desai, K. L. Jones and R. A. Riley Jr. 2013. A Synthesis of Fraud-Related Research. *AUDITING: A Journal of Practice & Theory* 32(Supplement 1): 287–321.

Wilks, T. J. and M. F. Zimbelman. 2004. Decomposition of Fraud-Risk Assessments and Auditors' Sensitivity to Fraud Cues. *Contemporary Accounting Research*. 22(3): 719–745.

Auditing Standards

Committee of Sponsoring Organizations of the Treadway Commission (COSO). *Internal Control—Integrated Framework*. AICPA, 1992.

Committee of Sponsoring Organizations of the Treadway Commission (COSO). *Internal Control—An Integrated Framework: Guidance for Smaller Public Companies*. AICPA, 2006.

Committee of Sponsoring Organizations of the Treadway Commission (COSO). *Internal Control—Integrated Framework*. AICPA, 2013.

IASB. *International Accounting Standard* (IAS). No. 24. "Related Party Disclosures."

IAASB *International Standards on Auditing (ISA)* No. 210, "Agreeing to Terms of Audit Engagements."

IAASB *International Standards on Auditing (ISA)* No. 220, "Quality Controls for Audits of Financial Statements."

IAASB *International Standards on Auditing (ISA)* No. 240, "The Auditor's Responsibilities Relating to Fraud in an Audit of Financial Statements."

IAASB *International Standards on Auditing (ISA)* No. 300, "Planning an Audit of Financial Statements."

IAASB *International Standards on Auditing (ISA)* No. 315, "Identifying and Assessing the Risks of Material Misstatement through Understanding the Entity and Its Environment."

IAASB *International Standards on Auditing (ISA)* No. 320, "Materiality in Planning and Performing an Audit."

IAASB *International Standards on Auditing (ISA)* No. 330, "The Auditor's Responses to Assessed Risks."

IAASB *International Standards on Auditing (ISA)* No. 500, "Audit Evidence."

IAASB *International Standards on Auditing (ISA)* No. 510, "Initial Audit Engagements—Opening Balances."

IAASB *International Standards on Auditing (ISA)* No. 550, "Related Parties."

IAASB *International Standards on Auditing (ISA)* No. 610, "Using the Work of Internal Auditors."

IAASB *International Standards on Auditing (ISA)* No. 620, "Using the Work of an Auditor's Expert."

IAASB *International Standards on Auditing (ISA)* No. 700, "Forming an Opinion and Reporting on Financial Statements."

IAASB *International Standards on Auditing (ISA)* No. 701, "Key Audit Matters."

IAASB *International Standards on Auditing (ISA)* No. 705, "Modifications to the Opinion in the Independent Auditor's Report."

IAASB *International Standards on Auditing (ISA)* No. 706, "Emphasis of Matter Paragraphs and Other Matter Paragraphs in the Independent Auditor's Report."

IAASB *International Standards on Quality Control (ISQC)*. No. 1 "Quality Control for Firms That Perform Audits and Reviews of Historical Financial Information and Other Assurance and Related Service Engagements."

IFAC. International Ethics Standards Board for Accountants (IESBA). 2015. *Handbook of Code of Ethics for Professional Accountants*. New York: International Federation of Accountants.

IFAC. International Auditing and Assurance Standards Board (IAASB). 2015. *Handbook of International Quality Control, Audit, Review, Other Assurance, and Related Services Pronouncements*. New York: International Federation of Accountants.

PCAOB. *Auditing Standard* 1101 (formerly No. 8), "Audit Risk."

PCAOB. *Auditing Standard* 1105 (formerly No. 15), "Audit Evidence."

PCAOB. *Auditing Standard* 1110 (formerly *Interim Standard* AU 161), "Relationship of Auditing Standards to Quality Control Standards."

PCAOB. *Auditing Standard* 1201 (formerly No. 10), "Supervision of the Audit Engagement."

PCAOB. *Auditing Standard* 1220 (formerly No. 7), "Engagement Quality Review."

PCAOB *Auditing Standard* 1210 (formerly *Interim Standard* AU 336), "Using the Work of a Specialist."

PCAOB. *Auditing Standard* 1301 (formerly No. 16), "Communications with Audit Committees."

PCAOB. *Auditing Standard* 2101 (formerly No. 9), "Audit Planning."

PCAOB. *Auditing Standard* 2105 (formerly No. 11), "Consideration of Materiality in Planning and Performing an Audit."

PCAOB. *Auditing Standard* 2201 (formerly No. 5), "An Audit of Internal Control over Financial Reporting that is Integrated with An Audit of Financial Statements."

PCAOB. *Auditing Standard* 2210 (formerly No. 12), "Identifying and Assessing the Risks of Material Misstatement."

PCAOB. *Auditing Standard* 2301 (formerly No. 13), "The Auditor's Responses to the Risks of Material Misstatement."

PCAOB. *Auditing Standard* 2310 (formerly *Interim Standard* AU 330), "The Confirmation Process."

PCAOB. *Auditing Standard* 2401 (formerly *Interim Standard* AU 316), "Consideration of Fraud in a Financial Statement Audit."

PCAOB. *Auditing Standard* 2405 (formerly *Interim Standard* AU 317), "Illegal Acts by Clients."

PCAOB *Auditing Standard* 2410 (formerly No. 18), "Related Parties."

PCAOB. *Auditing Standard* 2415 (formerly *Interim Standard* AU 341), "Consideration of an Entity's Ability to Continue as a Going Concern."

PCAOB *Auditing Standard* 2605 (formerly *Interim Standard* AU 322), "Consideration of the Internal Audit Function."

PCAOB *Auditing Standard* 2610 (formerly *Interim Standard* AU 315), "Initial Audits—Communications between Predecessor and Successor Auditors."

PCAOB *Auditing Standard* 2810 (formerly No. 14), "Evaluating Audit Results."

PCAOB *Auditing Standard* 3101 (formerly *Interim Standard* AU 508 incorporating PCAOB *Auditing Standard* No. 1, "References in Auditor's Reports to the Standards of the Public Company Accounting Oversight Board."), "Reports on Audited Financial Statements."

PCAOB. *Release* No. 2007-001 January 22, 2007. Observations on Auditors' Implementation of PCAOB Standards Relating To Auditors' Responsibilities With Respect To Fraud.

PCAOB. *Statement on Quality Control Standards* (SQCS) QC 20, "System of Quality Control for a CPA Firm's Accounting and Auditing Practice."

Securities and Exchange Commission (SEC). 1999. Staff Accounting Bulletin No. 99, "Materiality."

Notes

1 While professional standards do not address the issue of previous investments by an auditor in a current client, it is also possible that such investments have a residual effect on an auditor's independence in fact.
2 Trompeter, Carpenter, Desai, Jones and Riley Jr. (2013) A Synthesis of Fraud-Related Research. *AUDITING: A Journal of Practice & Theory* 32(Supplement): 287–321 and PCAOB (2007) Observations on Auditors' Implementation of PCAOB Standards Relating To Auditors' Responsibilities With Respect To Fraud.
3 The three definitions (control deficiency, material weakness, and significant deficiency) are based on the definitions in AS 2201.

CHAPTER 5

Understanding the Client's Industry and Business

Strategic Analysis and Management Controls

Outline

Learning Goals for this Chapter

1. Describe why auditors need to "understand the client's business."
2. Understand how strategic management tools are useful for risk identification.
3. Apply the strategic management tools to identify strategic risks.
4. Analyze how the identified risks affect risk of material misstatement.
5. Identify management controls that are used to reduce identified strategic risks.
6. Identify tests for effectiveness of management controls over strategic risks.
7. Evaluate the effectiveness of management controls on reducing audit risks.

Introduction

In Chapter 4, we discussed client acceptance and retention, provided an introduction to audit planning, gave an initial look at the end result of the audit process—the auditor's report—and introduced Figure 5.1, which provides an overview of the audit process that will be followed in this text. This chapter focuses on the procedures to develop an understanding of a client's industry and business (IIa). Although a basic acquaintance with the client and its industry is included as part of preliminary audit planning, this chapter provides more depth of analysis in order for the auditor to develop a thorough understanding of the client. This understanding conditions all parts of the audit from the controls that will be tested through to the substantive tests that will be performed. The depth of evaluation undertaken with respect to a client's industry and business will vary, depending on the size of the organization, the complexity of its industry and business, and the heterogeneity of its business units. Nonetheless, it is critical for the auditor to document his or her understanding of the business so as to be able to clearly demonstrate that audit judgments are based on a full understanding of the client.

This knowledge acquisition and risk assessment phase of the audit process is critical for most organizations since virtually all auditing and financial reporting problems that an auditor encounters have a basis in unique aspects, operations, or circumstances affecting the client. Failure to obtain an adequate understanding of the client and its risks may cause the auditor to plan or conduct the audit in an ineffective manner, to misinterpret or miss-evaluate the evidence collected, and, hence, reach inappropriate conclusions about the financial statements being examined.

This chapter is the first of two that will discuss techniques for acquiring knowledge of current conditions of the client and its industry. Risks can arise from a multitude of sources, and success or failure depends on how the organization responds to the forces impacting its industry or business. Failure to understand the dynamic, complex environment in which a client

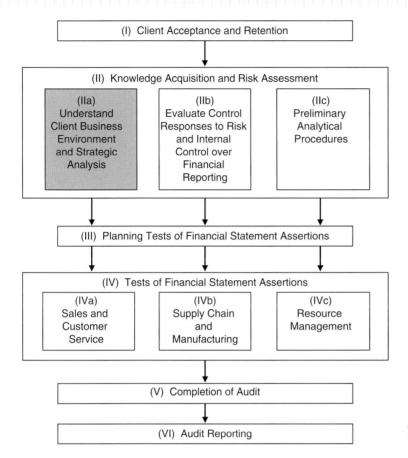

Figure 5.1 Overview of the Audit Process

exists could lead the auditor to develop inaccurate expectations relating to financial reporting, or to misunderstand the economic reality underlying the financial statements. Our approach is truly a top-down approach to planning an audit as we first learn ways of determining the major business risks that affect the client. We will call these risks "strategic risks" to separate them from the other categories of risk we discuss in this book. Strategic risks, if not properly controlled, can result in threatening the reliability of the financial statements directly via valuations and estimates or the viability of the organization, or indirectly via management motivations to conceal poor operational outcomes via "accounting tricks" so the company appears to be more successful than it actually is when viewed through the financial statements.

In this chapter we focus on the tools and techniques that the auditor can use to understand the broader social and economic environment in which the client operates and the forces in its industry. We see how the client intends to survive and thrive in this environment via its strategy as implemented through its business model. We carefully examine these risks because they can be related directly or indirectly to weaknesses in internal control or misstatements in the financial statements. We introduce management controls as the means that management uses to limit its strategic risks. Auditors test these management controls as part of their assessment of the control environment. If management controls are effective their existence may reduce the need for the auditor to conduct more detailed tests of internal controls over financial reporting (see Chapter 7).

In Chapter 6 we focus on how businesses control strategic risks through the development of business processes and demonstrate how auditors identify the process risks and operational controls embedded in these processes. Understanding business processes and their controls is important since almost all routine financial recording of transactions and balances is built into these business processes. In other words, financial accounting transactions do not take place in systems that are separate from the business processes but are deeply embedded in those processes. If those processes are well controlled the data contained in the financial records has a better chance of being complete and accurate. Chapter 7 refines our discussion specifically addressing internal controls over financial reporting that are embedded in these business processes and the accounting function.

AUTHORITATIVE GUIDANCE & STANDARDS

This chapter is designed to help auditors address the standards for understanding an entity and its environment leading to the auditors risk assessment (ISA 315 **Identifying and Assessing the Risks of Material Misstatement through Understanding the Entity and Its Environment** *and AS 2210 [formerly AS 12]* **Identifying and Assessing Risks of Material Misstatement**). *None of the various standards require a particular method to obtain this understanding of the entity's environment and develop the risk assessment. However, utilizing our approach provides an answer to one of the most frequently asked questions by auditors about gaining this knowledge, how much knowledge of the client is enough?*

Knowledge Acquisition for Risk Assessment

All organizations exist to create value for their stakeholders, be they customers, employees, shareholders, or managers. The ability of an organization to create and sustain its value depends on its interactions with a vast network of individuals, entities, and external forces. Every organization exists in a complex network of relationships that affect the markets in which it operates, the alternatives it might pursue, the risks it faces, and the likelihood of achieving its objectives. In order to understand the risks an organization faces, it is first important to understand this network and the way an organization creates value.

Every organization has an internal environment that interfaces with the external environment that is outside of its control. The internal environment represents the activities within the organization. These activities are generally referred to as business processes, and we will be discussing business processes in great detail throughout this book. Serving as a buffer or interface between the internal environment and the external environment is the company's strategic management activities. **Strategic management** comprises the activities of senior management related to developing, communicating, and revising the goals and plans of the organization. In general, strategic management reflects the decisions that an organization makes regarding how it will interact with the external environment via monitoring competitors, negotiating with suppliers, targeting customers, and searching for market opportunities. In effect, strategic management reflects the overall guidance and control of the organization. The efforts to foster desired behavior of personnel, monitor key performance measurements, and control interactions with the external environment are also part of strategic management.

AUTHORITATIVE GUIDANCE & STANDARDS

ISA 315 and AS 2201 (formerly 5) **An Audit of Internal Control Over Financial Reporting That Is Integrated with An Audit of Financial Statements** *and AS 2210 require the auditor to carry out a risk assessment process with the goal of determining the risk of material misstatement at the financial statement and management assertion level.*

The external environment consists of local and global economic links that can impact the organization. Local links may be regional or national depending on the industry. The difference between local and global environments can be blurry. In general, the local environment may be defined by physical vicinity, or may be more broadly considered to be the region in which economic forces and rules of behavior are considered to be "typical" for the enterprise. The global environment reflects the region of economic activity in which different rules, norms, culture, or approaches to business may apply[i].

To fully understand a client's industry and business, it is useful to take a top-down view as reflected in Figure 5.2, which illustrates the approach that

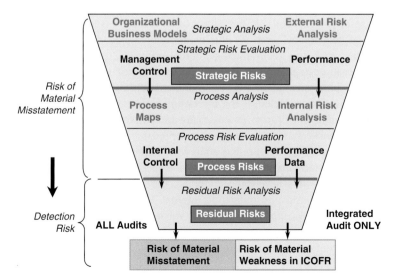

Figure 5.2 A Top-Down Perspective for Understanding a Client's Business

we will adopt in this book. We will start with a very broad perspective of an organization and the risks that it faces, and filter the analysis down to a few residual risks that are considered significant to the audit. The acquisition of knowledge about a client has three broad phases: (1) strategic analysis with a focus on external concerns, (2) process analysis with a focus on internal concerns, and (3) audit analysis that links client business risks to the objectives of the audit. The last step is critical because it links the risk analyses to the risk of material misstatement, planning tests of controls, and planning the testing of management assertions about the financial statements.

Strategic Risk Analysis

The first component of Figure 5.2, strategic analysis, helps the auditor identify the position of the organization relative to external agents and stakeholders. We will use a tool referred to as an ***Organizational Business Model*** to capture our factual understanding of the strategic conditions of the organization. Strategic analysis helps the auditor to identify the threats to the organization that emanate from the external environment. Many of these risks will have an impact on the way the auditor conducts the engagement. We use a technique referred to as ***external risk analysis*** to identify and categorize external risks. We will refer to ***client business risk*** as any external (strategic) or internal (process) threat that could affect the ability of an organization to achieve its objectives. Once strategic risks are identified, we further evaluate those risks by considering management's efforts to mitigate these risks through the use of management controls and business processes. Upon completion of the strategic analysis, the auditor will have obtained an extensive set of evidence about the organization's current risks.

Process Risk Analysis

The second level of analysis in Figure 5.2 involves the examination of internal processes, which represent the allocation of resources (such as personnel, capital, technology) used by the organization to conduct its business. Business processes represent the internal efforts of the organization to advance its goals and respond to strategic risks. We will use a ***process map*** to capture information about the operations and information flows of internal business processes including the accounting transactions and balances that are affected by the process. Processes are also a potential source of risk due to the financial statement effects that can arise due to failure of internal controls over financial reporting embedded in the processes. ***Internal risk analysis*** will facilitate the identification and categorization of process risks. Once process risks have been identified, the auditor can then evaluate the risks by considering mitigating internal controls and quantifying the extent of the risks. Process risk analysis will be discussed in more detail in later chapters. Of particular interest to the auditor is the risk of a material misstatement occurring in a process and the related internal controls over financial reporting.

Residual Risk Analysis

The final step of our analysis is to assess the nature of residual risks that pose a significant threat to the organization. Not all risks represent immediate problems—either because they are adequately controlled and mitigated or conditions are not currently conducive for the risk to cause damage to the organization. A **residual risk** is a strategic or process risk that is either uncontrolled by the organization or exhibits quantifiable warning signals that the risk may create problems for the organization in the near future.

Auditors are concerned with residual business risks because they represent the most likely source of problems for the company and are a likely source of problems that need to be reflected in the financial statements. However, some residual business risks are part of doing business and, as such, have little or no importance to the audit. As a result, careful thought is needed to distinguish among different risks because what appears not to be directly relevant for the audit might turn out to be of great relevance in judging asset impairment, going concern issues, the likelihood of contingent losses, or other matters. Some significant residual risks reflect conditions where the auditor will need to focus more attention in the audit. When an organization is effectively managed and highly controlled, it is less likely to exhibit the types of problems that result in audit problems, such as misstated financial reports, fraud, or bankruptcy. However, low residual business risk does not automatically translate into a low risk of material misstatement across all accounts and disclosures because management incentives or unreliable accounting systems may still result in errors or fraudulent financial reporting[ii].

Understanding a Client's Objectives and Strategies to Achieve Objectives

Analyze the Organization's Strategic Plan

One very important question that an auditor should address early in the audit is the nature of the organization's overall objectives and strategies for achieving those objectives, and its source of sustainable competitive advantage. Every organization has a strategy for attaining its objectives, although the strategy may not always be formally stated. The better an organization understands its objectives and strategies, the more likely it is to be successful. An organization that lacks effective strategic management is less likely to be successful in the long run.

Any company has two basic strategic positioning decisions to make: (1) Does it want its products to be low cost or differentiated from the average product or service offering, and (2) does it want its products or service to appeal to a broad or narrow group of consumers? These two considerations define four basic positioning strategies for any company:

1. Low Cost Strategy: This business strategy focuses on producing at the lowest possible cost for a large market allowing the business to set a price below that of the competition and still be profitable. The

[ii]EXAMPLE

A sudden increase in customer complaints may indicate that product quality has deteriorated, even though the production process has not changed and there are no internal indications of problems. Such a signal may indicate a residual risk that needs consideration by the auditor. Why? It may indicate an inventory valuation issue or that allowances for sales returns may not follow historic patterns— both of which might have material effects on the financial statements if realized.

(iii)**EXAMPLE**

Wal-Mart's strategy is to be the lowest-cost, brand market retailer in every market in which it competes. The company achieves its cost advantage with tight cost controls, superior inventory selection and management, and world-class distribution. Although companies have attempted the same strategy, they have not been able to keep pace with Wal-Mart and have suffered serious setback (bankruptcy, in the case of K-Mart).

(iv)**EXAMPLE**

In a world of multi-national package delivery companies such as FedEx and UPS, in most cities in the world there are small local package delivery companies that provide low-cost within-city package delivery services, often using personal vehicles that are temporarily branded with the name of the courier service. They compete on cost and focus solely on local delivery with no connections outside a small well-defined geographic area.

(v)**EXAMPLE**

Holt Renfrew in Canada and Nordstrom in the US are retailers that provide unparalleled customer service while charging a premium price. The companies are legendary for the lengths their employees will go to meet the desires of customers. Such service comes at a higher cost than many comparable retailers but also generates superior margins.

product or service will be mass-produced with few special features ("no frills"). Demand for the product is likely to be price sensitive.[1] Success often depends on efficient production and generating economies of scale where unit costs are reduced as production increases. Distribution costs need to be tightly managed and there will be minimal advertising or R&D(iii).

2. Low-Cost Niche Strategy: This business strategy focuses on being a low-cost producer but for a product that has a small well-identified market. Many of these companies are small and have limited opportunities to develop brand recognition(iv).

3. Differentiation Strategy: This business strategy focuses on producing products or services with unique features often along the quality dimension for different segments of a broad market. Price is usually not a primary factor to the company's target market. Differentiation can also be achieved through superior customer service, flexible delivery, and extensive warranties. Research and innovation is often important for staying ahead of the competition(v).

4. Differentiation Niche Strategy: This business strategy focuses on producing unique products and services but for small well-defined markets. While many of these organizations are small, as in the case of low-cost niche, some companies develop well-known brands because of the exclusivity of offering high-priced products(vi).

AUTHORITATIVE GUIDANCE & STANDARDS

ISA 315 requires auditors to understand objectives and strategies and the business risks that may result in a misstatement of the financial statements. PCAOB AS 2210 has similar but less comprehensive requirements.

The Impact of Strategic Positioning Decisions

A company's strategic decisions will have a direct effect on the characteristics of the organization. Decisions about markets to enter, products to produce, technology to develop, operating processes to implement, and resources needed are all affected by the basic strategic choices made by the organization. A major challenge for management is to develop business processes that are consistent with the strategy and that effectively advance the organization's goals. Some examples of how internal processes may be affected by strategic decisions are presented in Table 5.1. An allocation of personnel and resources that is inconsistent with overall objectives or strategies employed is unlikely to lead to success.

The activities, risks, and financial statements associated with different strategic choices can be quite different. Management in the low-cost company will focus on making processes more efficient whereas management in a differentiated company will search for new and better ways to provide value to the customer. More specifically, a low-cost strategy

Table 5.1 *The Impact of Strategic Positioning on Selected Internal Business Processes*

Operational Area	Low Cost Strategy	Differentiation Strategy
Acquisition of Materials	• Resources acquired at the lowest possible cost • Order large quantities to obtain volume discounts • Purchases may be delayed until desired prices can be achieved • Maximize the efficiency of distribution and storage	• Purchase the best quality materials, at higher cost if necessary • Storage and distribution designed to maintain quality of materials and products in a cost effective but not necessarily lowest cost manner.
Production	• Emphasis is on achieving operating efficiencies • Striving for economies of scale • Optimize labor/capital trade-offs	• Emphasize product quality, even at the cost of high rates of wastage, rejects and rework
New Product Development	• Research and development, if any, focuses on process efficiency • Little focus on new product innovation • Focus on following industry leaders with proven products	• Continual research to develop better products with more features • Goal of developing new products that better meet needs of customers
Human Resources	• Minimize costs by avoiding unions, using temporary employees, structuring tasks for unskilled labor • Outsource less critical tasks • Tightly control benefits	• Hire the best employees given the quality demands of the organization • Superior pay scales and benefits
Information Technology	• Information system used to minimize costs	• Information system used to maximize revenue by identifying market opportunities
Branding and Marketing	• Minimal, or low cost mass advertising and promotions	• Extensive, focused and expensive marketing including advertisements

suggests that efficient operations are critical because the control of costs is vital to the organization's success. Under a differentiation strategy, however, cost of production is less significant and the ability to create innovative new products and features is critical, suggesting that the product development process is crucial. As we will see, these differences would lead the auditor to focus on different aspects of these organizations.

The Impact of Strategic Risk Assessment on Financial Statements and the Audit

Auditors should evaluate the risks associated with an organization's strategic positioning. In general, auditors look for evidence that managers have made bad or uninformed decisions, misused or misallocated resources, or poorly communicated or utilized information, all of which reduce the likelihood that the organization will succeed in the long term and such consequences may need to be reflected in the current period financial statements (e.g., asset impairments). The auditor's role is not to second guess management but to

(vi)**EXAMPLE**

Maserati S.p.A., now part of the Fiat family, continues to produce a few thousand cars each year in its plant located in Modena, in the Po Valley of northern Italy. These cars, even the entry level, are expensive with a $70,000 (US) at a minimum, quickly moving to vehicles in the $100,000s (US) so they appeal to a very limited portion of car buyers.

look for signs that business risks have been incurred that need to be reflected in the financial statements or business risks that may motivate management to attempt "accounting fixes" to poor organizational performance. Regardless of the strategic position adopted, each of the options available to an organization has potential risks. Some of these risks are described in Table 5.2. These risks will be heightened when strategic management of an organization is weak. Potential indications of weak strategic management include:

- Management's failure to articulate strategy so as to align the goals and activities of various segments of the organization.
- Failure to anticipate and react to potential threats.
- Poor execution of strategy.
- Inflexibility and lack of organizational response in dealing with diverse objectives and activities.
- Inadequate planning for carrying out strategic decisions.
- Inadequate resources to carry out strategic plans or mismatching resources and objectives.

Unreliable or unavailable information can cause significant problems in strategic management, especially if poor information leads to missed opportunities, unidentified threats, and poor coordination. With regard to accounting and the financial statements, the auditor will need to consider the organization's life cycle and strategic decisions when planning and conducting the audit. As a general rule, organizations in the growth or decline phase of their life cycle tend to have more challenging business risks and also create comparable challenges for the auditor[vii].

Table 5.2 *Business Risks Associated with Strategic Positioning Choices*

Risks of Adopting a Cost Leadership Position	Risks of Adopting a Differentiation Position	Risks of Adopting a Broad or Narrow Market Focus
Cost leadership may not be sustainable due to: - Imitation by competitors - Changes in technology that allow competitors to reduce costs	Differentiation may not be sustainable due to: - Imitation by competitors - Changing customer tastes put less value on the attributes of differentiation	The target market becomes unattractive due to: - Imitation by competitors - The target segment shrinks or becomes too small to be profitable
Customers demand more features while expecting low prices.	The cost of providing differentiated features exceeds the price point customers are willing to pay, effectively limiting the extent of differentiation that can be offered	Competitors with a broad market focus threaten a narrow market because: - The differences between segments are narrow or disappear. - The quality/performance of broad market products and services improve
Multiple competitors approach the limits of cost minimization by focusing on smaller market segments leaving no room for a broad cost leader that attempts to service many segments	Differentiation becomes smaller, segment-specific, leaving no room for a broad differentiator to service multiple segments	Narrow markets are segmented into even smaller markets by competitors who have an advantage (cost or quality) in the smaller segments

Strategic positioning decisions (such as low cost or differentiation) related to the various resources and processes of the company will also have a direct impact on the audit. For example, a manufacturer adopting a differentiation strategy is likely to have more expensive inventory, larger margins, greater costs of spoilage, more expensive equipment to be amortized, more skilled labor with better compensation and benefits, greater rates of quality rejects, and more comprehensive warranties—all of which will affect the results reported in the financial statements. These differences will also influence the client's business risk. Furthermore, the strategic differences need to be considered by the auditor when making decisions about how to conduct the audit. Weak strategic management and questionable strategic decisions will ultimately have an impact on reported financial results and may affect the risk of material misstatements in the financial statements[viii].

Organizational Business Models

To evaluate further the business risks that the company faces, the auditor identifies and describes the key external links between the company and other companies, individuals, entities, and organizations. This factual description of the company's environment can be organized into an **Organizational Business Model**. A business model of a client provides an auditor with a snapshot of the business, emphasizing how the client adds value to its economic environment, utilizes business processes to achieve its strategic objectives, and identifies and reacts to external threats to the organization. The business model also provides a structure for identifying key audit issues that will need significant attention during the audit. The overall purpose of using these models is to obtain appropriate knowledge about a client, its risks and responses, and the implications for the auditor.

Components of an Organizational Business Model

The components of an Organizational Business Model are depicted in Figure 5.3, which reflects the basic approach we will take for analyzing the environment of a client. There are six components:

- Markets, customers, and products: All businesses are formed to market specific products (or services) to targeted customers. Markets represent the discernible economic segments in which an organization chooses to compete. They can be defined by geographic region, nature of product, or level of service provided. Each market includes a targeted set of potential customers. Customers may be undifferentiated or identified by individual traits (such as wealth, level of education, and other demographics). Products (or services) are the source of revenues and represent the source of exchange transactions between customers and the company. Determining when revenue is to be recognized is a key accounting issue. The number of markets, products (or services), and customers making up the different business lines of an organization are a key source of complexity in a business model.

[vii]**EXAMPLE**

Virtek Vision, a precision laser company based in Waterloo, Ontario, Canada, expanded rapidly in the late 1990s, going from being a focused niche supplier of laser marking systems for the manufactured-home industry to broad-based producer of laser related products in the aviation and biotechnology industry (in addition to its traditional business). During this transformation, it increased its employee base by 200 percent and severely strained its management systems. In 2004, it shed the biotechnology division and downsized its workforce substantially (including terminating both the president and the chief financial officer). With a return to a more focused strategy it returned to profitability in 2007 and in the spring and summer of 2008 it became the target of numerous takeover bids. As a result, the stock went from $0.38 to $1.20 in value in less than four months.

Many retailers offer in-house credit cards to customers (such as Target and Future Shop). Customers who would normally use Visa or MasterCard are encouraged to sign up for the store card by the offer of a one-time discount on merchandise. On one hand, if the retailer can get customers to use the store credit card, the retailer saves the fees that would be paid to other credit card companies, and may also generate incremental interest income on customers' unpaid balances. On the other hand, the company is also accepting a certain amount of credit risk for delinquent customers. The retailer may also absorb significant data security risks as evidenced by hackers stealing information on thousands of accounts from Target in 2013. In planning the engagement of a retailer with its own credit card operations, the auditor would need to evaluate the process of issuing credit cards, recording and accruing interest income, and recognizing bad debts. Another strategy for a retailer is to form an alliance with Visa or MasterCard in which customers earn rewards by using the company's exclusive version of the card (an example is Starbucks' Visa Duetto card, which earns customers 1 percent in-store credit). The company avoids the financial risks associated with the card but encourages repeat customers and enhances its brand name.

- Competitors: An external organization that is targeting a similar set of markets, customers, and products is a direct competitor. Competition may also be indirect in that relevant competitors who appear to be in different industries are often chasing the same customer resources (usually time and money, often described as "wallet share"). Competitors directly affect the ability of an organization to survive and thrive (i.e., as a "going concern").

- Resources and suppliers: Every organization needs resources to advance its objectives. Obvious resources include tangible assets such as facilities and inventory. However, resources of many types can affect the organization. Resources are frequently portrayed in balance sheet accounts whose value has to be checked for impairment or otherwise marked to market. Labor, capital, and technology are all important to an organization and each is obtained from a different set of suppliers, involve different processes within an organization, and generate a different set of risks.

- Internal processes: Resources within an organization are allocated to business processes that perform important tasks and activities to achieve corporate objectives and minimize strategic risks. Internal processes are involved in producing the goods or services provided by the organization and are often the source of many routine accounting transactions. We take the view that accounting systems do not exist independently of the business but are deeply embedded in these internal business processes. These processes will be discussed in more detail in Chapter 6 as well as Chapters 11 to 13.

- External agents: Various influences outside an organization have a direct impact on its ability to succeed (again with implications for "going concern" assessments) even though they may not have direct economic links or dealings with the organization. For example, the government is responsible for regulation and taxation, both of which can have effects on key financial statement accounts (e.g., income tax expense). Lifestyle trends and other seasonal factors might influence demand. To the extent external forces have an impact on the organization, they should be considered part of the economic network even though the linkages may be indirect and subtle.

- Strategic partners: Strategic partners represent external entities with which the company has a formal relationship in order to advance joint objectives. Although the partners are independent and may represent potential adversaries (e.g., different airlines), they agree to work together in order to obtain mutually beneficial results (code sharing on specific flights) or to reduce the threat from a shared risk. A key identifying characteristic of a strategic partner is the interconnectedness of organizations such that if one is successful, the other is successful. Accordingly, auditors should pay careful attention to the process for selecting, monitoring, and terminating strategic partner relationships as these relationships are often key to continuing as a "going concern".

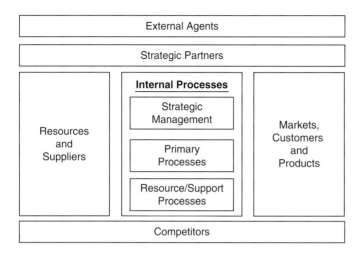

Figure 5.3 *A Generic Organizational Business Model*

AUTHORITATIVE GUIDANCE & STANDARDS

ISA 315 and AS 2210 require auditors to understand the nature of the entity, including (as described in the standards' appendices) the nature of revenue sources; products or services and markets; conduct of operations; alliances; suppliers of goods, services, and labor; and industry, regulations, and other external factors.

An Example of an Organizational Business Model

A simplified example of an organizational business model for a publishing company is presented in Figure 5.4. Although a publisher will have many direct competitors, indirect competition can have a significant impact on the likelihood of an organization achieving its goals. An important external element is the media (both traditional and social), which can push or pan a book and have a significant impact on the title's sales (consider, for example, the impact of Oprah's book club). The most significant strategic partners are authors, who can also be considered suppliers, and bookstores (both traditional and e-book retailers), which can also be considered customers. Obviously, the absence of respected, successful authors or lack of promotion of titles by bookstores (both in store and on-line) will have an adverse effect on a publisher. In fact, author development and marketing are probably the most critical internal processes for a publisher. Relationships with printers, e-book formatters and editors (an e-book layout needs to be considerably different than a print book layout in order to take advantage of the format), and successful authors are probably the most critical supplier links.

By identifying the key market participants and their relationship to the client, the auditor is able to make a first step toward understanding the source and nature of potential risks affecting the organization and the audit of the financial statements. Much of the information and transaction flows within an organization involve one or more of the elements depicted in the

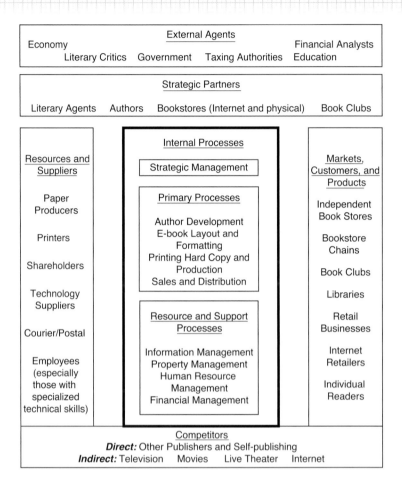

Figure 5.4 Organizational Business Model for Publishing Company

organizational business model. For example, sales, receivables, cost of goods sold, inventory, cash collections, and bad debts involve transactions with customers, whereas fixed assets, accounts payable, accrued liabilities, and various expenses involve transactions with suppliers. Continuing with the publishing example, a number of transactions that might be of interest to the auditor can be identified:

- Transactions with printers: The nature of long-term printing contracts creates risks related to quality, timeliness, and confidentiality. The auditor may need to analyze the exposure to potential losses on long-term purchase commitments and related disclosures. This analysis requires an understanding of the reasons for the relationship, the relative power of the parties, and the terms of the contract.

- Sales arrangements with bookstores: Bookstores (both physical and on-line) typically have the right to return unsold books, which can create potential problems of publisher revenue recognition.

- Placement on e-book retailer sites: The fees charged by different sites can vary greatly for web site listing, placement in search engine, and a percentage of sales that is charged by the retailer.

- Contracts with authors: Contracts with authors need to be examined to determine the proper recognition of unpaid royalties. Calculation of royalties is complicated by the right of return that bookstores can exercise long after the end of a fiscal period. Furthermore, the process of negotiating author contracts raises risks of overpaying or missing out on the next Stephen King. Large author advances need to be analyzed for recoverability.

Although accounting issues are always important to the auditor, the impact of strategic risks may be much more pervasive and important to the auditor than a narrow focus on a single accounting issue. These broader auditor concerns include judging asset impairment, going concern, likelihood of contingent losses, and other such matters all of which have material effects on the financial statements. We now turn to techniques for analyzing strategic risks in this broader context.

Risk Assessment: Strategic Risks

The next step in the process of understanding a client's business is to perform *external risk analysis*. This involves identifying and assessing the possible threats to success that confront an organization. Figure 5.5 depicts a generic structure for performing risk analysis.

Macro-Environmental Forces (PEST Factors)

Macro-environmental forces will rarely have a direct economic link to the organization's financial statements but, nevertheless, can present serious threats since they can have an effect on the environment in which the company must operate. Example of these forces are captured by the so-called PEST factors:

- Political-Legal (P): Labor, worker safety, anti-discrimination, and environmental laws can all have a significant impact on an organization. Compliance with laws may be complex and expensive, but noncompliance may be even more costly to an organization. Many laws and regulations are industry-specific, and compliance may be quite challenging when an organization has international activities. Political threats can lead to

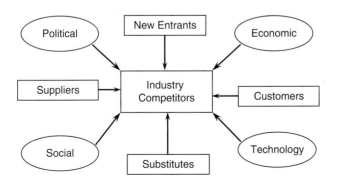

Figure 5.5 Risk Assessment: External Threats to Business Organizations

Many countries have trade barriers related to agricultural products. When a potato fungus infected potatoes from a Canadian agricultural company, the US refused to admit any Canadian potatoes until it was shown that the disease was limited to the single company. Similarly, when "mad cow" disease afflicted cattle in the UK, other countries refused to admit beef shipments from British farmers, many of whom were driven to the verge of bankruptcy.

The decisions of key political actors in the US in 2008 to let Lehman Brothers go into bankruptcy had effects far beyond the investment banking sector where that firm was situated. The resulting implosion of the short-term credit market led many organizations to the brink of bankruptcy even though they had little to do directly with this sector.

Fast food franchises are often dependent on a ready supply of unskilled, minimum wage labor. In boom times in the oil fields of Northern Alberta when overall unemployment was running at 2 percent or less, individuals were able to choose from multiple job offers. Hence, fast food operators were offering free housing and high hourly wages to attract employees.

behaviors by organizations that might be counterintuitive. For example, antitrust concerns may make an industry leader hesitant to merge or acquire a competitor, even though the combination would increase shareholder value[ix][x].

- Economic (E): Economic threats relate to general or regional trends in economic conditions that can have an adverse effect on an organization. Risks can arise from a change in interest rates, unemployment, energy prices, inflation, foreign currency fluctuations, and the general economic cycle. Industries such as banking, real estate, and automobiles are sensitive to small increases in interest rates that affect consumer spending[xi].

- Social (S): There are a multitude of cultural attitudes, opinions, lifestyles, and social pressures that can have an impact on an organization. Employee attitudes toward overtime, customers' attitudes toward specific products (such as tobacco), population shifts and demographics, levels of education, and quality of life concerns can all create problems for an organization. Social problems are complicated when the organization's activities are international. Large multinational corporations often face pressure to acknowledge their responsibilities to key societal stakeholders, such as local communities, employees, and environmental concerns[xii].

- Technological (T): Risk arising from technology typically relates to the rate of innovation in an industry and the risk of being stuck with the wrong or insufficient technology. Technology can affect many facets of an organization, including the manner in which it conducts its basic operations, processes information, markets its products, designs its manufacturing processes, and develops new products. Technology can be used as a source of competitive cost advantage within the manufacturing process[xiii].

See the first four rows of Table 5.3 for questions an auditor might ask to learn more about the PEST factors.

Industry Forces (Porter's Five Forces)[2]

Industry forces can be more readily seen as directly related to the organization's financial reporting as they often have direct effects on financial statement items such as sales and cost of goods sold, and can impact many accounting estimates such as the obsolescence on inventory. The five important industry forces affecting a company are often referred to as "Porter's Five Forces":

1. Competitors: The most immediate risk to a business is the threat that competitors will erode or steal a company's market share by offering superior products, better service, or better prices. Most companies are very cognizant of what their competitors are doing, and actively plan strategies for coping with those threats. These threats and plans to counter the threats can have a direct impact on such accounts as sales, warranty expenses, advertising, marketing expenses, etc[xiv].

2. Potential entrants: Another threat is the possibility that new competitors will enter the market. Rapidly growing or highly profitable industries tend to quickly attract new competitors. The threat from potential competitors

Table 5.3 *Potential Indicators of External Threats to a Business Organization*

Category of Risk	Potential Indicators of Risk
Political	How susceptible is the organization to changes in: • tax laws and/or tax jurisdictions? • international trade regulations? • domestic regulations, including labor laws, consumer protection, lending rules and/or environmental regulation? Is the industry a: • target for antitrust attention? • subject to wage and/or price controls? Does the organization or industry receive favorable regulatory treatment?
Economic	Is the organization more or less susceptible than others to: • changes in general economic conditions? • changes in the money supply and inflation? • changes in the labor pool and levels of unemployment? • changes in energy costs? • changes in commodity markets? • changes in capital markets? How is the organization affected by the economic cycle?
Social	Is the organization more or less: • dependent on the supply of educated and trained skilled labor? • of interest to non-government organizations that might be critical of it? Does the industry have a negative reputation with consumers? To what extent is the industry affected by changes in life styles? Do workplace expectations of employees affect labor relations? How do forthcoming demographic changes affect the organization?
Technological	Is the organization more or less dependent on scientific advancement? Are technology advantages subject to protection from competition? How rapidly is key technology it uses changing? What is the: • rate of new product introductions in industry? • level of automation and prospects for future change? • appropriate level of R&D relative to current activity?
Suppliers	Do suppliers have significant bargaining power? Are inputs: • differentiated? • subject to disruption? • available in adequate quality? Can inputs be substituted for in case of shortage? Is the input a specialized market niche for the supplier? Are switching costs to new suppliers high? Are there few potential suppliers? Can suppliers integrate downstream into your market space? Is the supplier's transaction volume significant to the supplier?

(Continued)

[xii]**EXAMPLE**

Attitudes towards employee rights can be particularly tricky for an organization. Americans are accustomed to working overtime and on weekends, whereas Europeans typically work less overtime. In many countries (such as Sweden), employees expect high levels of benefits and management consideration that are less prevalent in the US (such as in-house day care, vacations, maternity leave, and cafeterias). Canadians have almost double the number of long weekends each year compared with Americans, and have, on average, a week more of paid vacation. A company that wishes to open a factory in another country needs to be very careful to consider local employment practices in the planning of the facility. The US practices towards maternity leave (many organizations offer six weeks of unpaid maternity leave and there are no national standards in this area) would be unacceptable in other parts of the world.

EXAMPLE

In 2009, the New York Times *proclaimed Twitter as the "the fastest-growing phenomena on the Internet." The possibility for responses at the spur of the moment that could violate the most strict control policies are endless, including leaking financial information, passwords, etc. It took many firms years before they realized the potential threat this could present and by the time this issue was dealt with other forms of social media interaction had taken hold.*

(xiv)**EXAMPLE**

Grocery chains often get into price wars over common purchases (such as bread, milk, and butter). Since much of a grocery chain's costs are fixed, grocers search for ways to reduce employee and distribution costs. Wal-Mart became the largest grocer in the US in a short time by (1) utilizing the hypermarket format in which grocery products serve as loss leaders for higher margin products in the store, and (2) leveraging its efficient distribution processes to keep costs lower than the competition.

Table 5.3 *(Continued)*

Category of Risk	Potential Indicators of Risk
	Does the input affect the differentiability of resulting products and services? Is adequate skilled labor available at a reasonable cost? Is adequate capital available at a reasonable cost?
New Entrants or Substitutes	Are there low barriers to entry? Are switching costs by customers to new suppliers low? Does inadequate capacity currently exist? Are current profit levels likely to attract new entrants? Is the market susceptible to fragmentation? Do potential entrants have: • superior technology? • a cost advantage? Are new entrants nimble and flexible?
Customers	Do buyers have: • significant bargaining power? • low switching costs? • superior market information? Do buyers need customized products or services? Are transaction costs for buyers low? Is the buyer dependent on the product or service? Can buyers integrate upstream into the organization's market space? Are buyers: • price sensitive? • brand or fad conscious? • profits too low to sustain their activities? • open to substitution of products and services? • sensitive to pressure from their customers?
Competition	Does a competitor have: • superior product or service? • a cost advantage? • superior brand identification? • possess proprietary technology? • favorable access to resources? • a legal or regulatory advantage? Are switching costs low for customers? Does a competitor get preferential treatment in distribution channels? Are competitors nimble and flexible? Can competitors adjust volume levels easily? Can competitors get new products and services to market quickly?

depends on the level of barriers to entry such as economies of scale in production, brand loyalty, switching costs, technology restrictions, costs to exit and enter markets, and capacity issues at the industry level. These threats can have a direct impact on such accounting matters as inventory obsolescence, asset valuation, and impairments[xv].

3. Substitute products: Products that have been extremely profitable can eventually or indeed suddenly, be driven off the market due to changes in technology and the introduction of substitutes. This type of threat may be direct (e.g., the substitution of MP3 files for compact discs, or the decline in landline telephones as the world converts to a wireless network) or due to forces affecting other markets (e.g., decline in expense account driven business in hotels and restaurants as more meetings are conducted via teleconferencing). Determinants of the threat from substitutes include substitute quality, cost, switching costs, and buyer loyalty to original product[xvi].

4. Suppliers: Serious effects on an entity's profitability arise from the costs of its inputs both human and material. The seriousness of potential threats from suppliers will depend on:

   o   The degree of specialization required for inputs (especially complex components).

   o   The concentration and monopoly power of potential suppliers.

   o   The existence of substitute inputs.

   o   The degree of cooperation among suppliers that could lead to uniform pricing[xvii].

5. Customers: The degree of bargaining power of customers or their fickle tastes may constitute a threat. The seriousness of threats from customers will depend on the level of customer volume in relation to total entity sales, the ability of buyers to access pricing information from other customers, and brand recognition for key parts of the product (e.g., the inclusion of an Intel chip and Windows software are probably more important to most computer purchasers than the brand of a computer with the exception of Apple). These threats can have a direct impact on such accounting matters as inventory obsolescence, asset valuation and impairment[xviii].

See the last four rows in Table 5.3 for questions that the auditor might pose to help him learn about industry forces. To further help understand the nature of strategic risks, we now discuss how risks originating in the external environment can affect the internal operations of the organization, and ultimately the audit of financial statements.

Strategic Risk Assessment Implications for the Audit

Several examples of strategic risks an organization might face are presented in Table 5.4. Although these risks are not specific to any single organization, they illustrate the potential range of strategic risks that can arise from various sources. However, not all risks will be of equal importance to management or the auditor.

A common technique to assess and document the relative importance of a large number of risks is in a ***risk map*** as illustrated in Figure 5.6. The significance of a business risk can be assessed along two dimensions: (1) the

[xv]**EXAMPLE**

The inventor of carry-on wheeled luggage that has a hidden, extractable pull handle enjoyed a short but highly profitable period before other imitators were able to get their own versions to market. The wheeled luggage market had low barriers to entry because the costs of switching production capacity was low for the established manufacturers who already had brand loyalty and established distribution channels. Furthermore, the wheel technology was not sufficiently unique to be legally protected from imitators. Consequently, the original inventor found margins and market share being quickly eroded by cutthroat competition.

[xvi]**EXAMPLE**

SAP is one of the largest suppliers of enterprise resource planning systems based on business processes. Installation of an SAP application is costly, complex, and time consuming, and requires significant internal computing assets. Some analysts now believe that SAP-type installations will be made obsolete or unnecessary by the more recent trend toward Internet-based software referred to as "cloud computing." If this trend develops rapidly enough, sales of traditional SAP products may be squeezed and organizations with significant SAP-related assets may need to consider whether their value is impaired.

Table 5.4 *Risk Assessment: Examples of Strategic Risks and Potential Audit Implications*

Strategic Business Risk/Threat	Source of Threat	Potential Audit Implications
SR1: Competitors begin offering extended warranty protection on products.	Competitors	• Audit Risk: Increase in warranty commitments may require that warranty expense estimates be increased above historical patterns.
SR2: Competitors are rapidly increasing the rate paid to key senior accounting and management personnel.	Competitors	• Control Environment: Reliability of decision-making and information processing may decrease with employee turnover. • Audit Risk: Allocations of labor costs may need to be revised based on relative changes in salary levels. • Audit Risk: Accruals for benefits may need to be increased.
SR3: Top-grade raw materials are in extremely short supply due to bad weather conditions in producing regions.	Suppliers	• Audit Risk: Wastage and spoilage rates may need to be increased in standard costing formulas. • Audit Risk: Valuation problems related to purchase commitments may exist. • Control Environment: Pressure to cut corners to meet customer demand.
SR4: Customer industries are in a recession.	Economic, Customers	• Audit Risk: Receivables may not be collectable at historic rate and allowance for uncollectable may need to be increased. • Client Viability: Shrinking customer base.
SR5: Consumer tastes have changed, necessitating improved functionality and quality in company products.	Social, Customers	• Client Viability: Loss of market share. • Audit Risk: Inventory on hand may become obsolete or out of favor so that carrying values may not be realizable. • Control Environment: Pressure to hit sales targets to protect jobs and/or bonuses.
SR6: The preferred distribution channel for the company's product changes from retail locations to internet, telemarketing, and home delivery.	Technology, Customers	• Audit Risk: Existing distribution channels may need to be shut down with resulting restructuring cost (layoffs, asset disposal). • Viability: Inability to adapt on a timely basis.
SR7: New entrant to the market is technologically superior to current products.	Technology, New Entrants	• Audit Risk: Inventory valuation may need to be reduced to lower-of-cost-or-market due to obsolescence or excess quantities. • Client Viability: Loss of market share.
SR8: Government imposes new regulations on distribution of a company's product.	Social, Political	• Client Viability: Loss of market share if not adaptable. • Audit Risk: Inventory valuation may need to be reduced to lower-of-cost-or-market due to obsolescence or excess quantities. • Control Environment: Efforts to circumvent regulations to meet sales targets.
SR9: Activists protest the company's approach to R&D.	Social	• Audit risk: Valuation of capitalized development costs if associated product demand drops. • Control Environment: Efforts to hide or disguise nature of R&D.
SR10: Foreign currency fluctuations squeeze profit margins on international sales.	Economic	• Audit Risk: Proper treatment of exchange gains and losses. • Audit Risk: Accounting treatment of financial derivatives.
SR11: Manufacturing facilities become non-competitive due to age and inability to upgrade processes	Technological	• Audit Risk: Impairment of fixed assets. • Client Viability: Tightening margins leading to losses, if prices cannot be increased.

Audit implications are based on the four classifications in Figure 5.7. Expectations about financial statement effects are discussed in more detail in Chapter 9 on preliminary analytical procedures and Chapter 14 on business measurement.

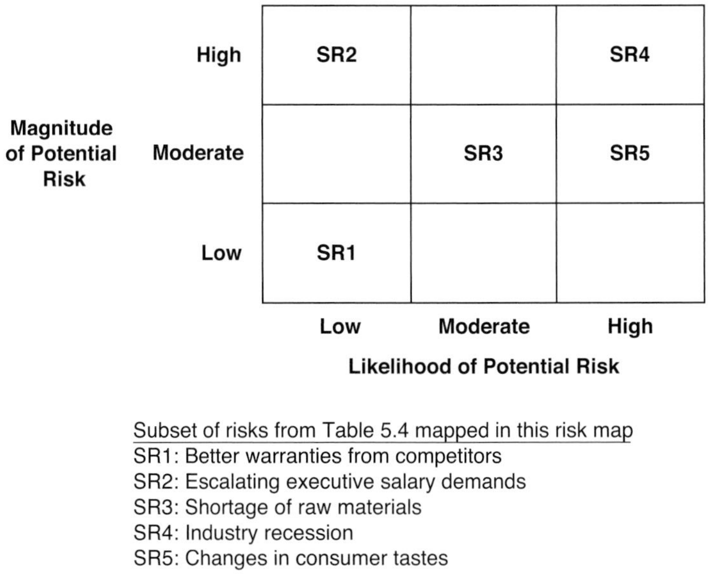

	High	SR2		SR4
Magnitude of Potential Risk	Moderate		SR3	SR5
	Low	SR1		
		Low	Moderate	High

Likelihood of Potential Risk

Subset of risks from Table 5.4 mapped in this risk map
SR1: Better warranties from competitors
SR2: Escalating executive salary demands
SR3: Shortage of raw materials
SR4: Industry recession
SR5: Changes in consumer tastes

Figure 5.6 Risk Assessment: Prioritizing Strategic Risks on a Risk Map

likelihood of the risk causing negative outcomes for the organization, and (2) the magnitude of negative outcomes if the problem actually occurs. Only the first five risks in Table 5.4 are included to keep the graph manageable in appearance, but all eleven risks would normally be assessed and ranked if they pertain to a specific organization.

Risks that are classified in the lower left corner are considered to be less serious because they are unlikely to pose serious problems for an organization. The more risk moves up and to the right, the more serious it would be considered. In the diagram, *SR4*, an industry recession, is clearly the most significant, and the one management would likely focus on most. *SR1*, improved warranties from competitors, might be ignored by management (that is, accepted) due to its relative insignificance. The balancing of *SR2* (escalating labor rates) and *SR5* (changing consumer tastes) is challenging to management because they each rate highly on one dimension, and management's responses would depend on the circumstances of each risk. In most organizations, risks with low likelihood and high impacts (*SR2*) are addressed on an exception or crisis basis.[3] Risks that are small in magnitude but may occur frequently (*SR5*) are usually addressed within routine processes and procedures.

Once strategic risks have been prioritized, the auditor should then consider the implications the risks have for planning and conducting the audit. Figure 5.7 illustrates four types of issues that can arise from any given risk:

1. Expectations: Knowledge of a risk condition will influence what an auditor expects to see in the financial results. For example, knowing that a competitor has triggered a price war would cause the auditor to expect a slowdown in revenue growth and tightening margins. The company may not wish to match price decreases but could respond by increasing service levels, thus increasing costs and squeezing

Figure 5.7 Risk Assessment:
Potential Audit Implications of
Business Risks

*Beginning in 2004 and
continuing to the start of the
recession of 2008, a number
of circumstances combined to
cause a significant increase in
worldwide oil prices. Early on,
businesses directly dependent
on oil, such as utilities and
airlines, found their profit
margins significantly reduced.
To the extent oil is a cost
component of a product, the
large increase could have a
significant impact on production
costs and potentially threaten
the existence of financially
weak organizations. As prices
remained high, the entire
automotive industry in the
US with its emphasis on large
gas guzzling vehicles began
to flounder. The subsequent
collapse of oil prices during the
2008 recession did not help as
consumers seemed to believe
that the relief from high gas
prices was only temporary.
This constant fluctuation
between relatively price and
low oil prices cannot only affect
inventory values of oil and oil
based products but also profit
margins of airlines, vehicle
manufacturers, etc.*

margins. The ability of the auditor to formulate expectations is especially important in carrying out analytical procedures as discussed in Chapter 9.

2. Client Viability: If a risk is severe enough, it may indicate that an organization is no longer viable given its current business plan and target market. If the problem is critical, the company may not be a going concern and the auditor will have to consider the possibility of bankruptcy. Even if the problem is of a long-term nature, the auditor may need to consider whether financial disclosures adequately reflect the situation. Auditor requirements to consider whether the client has the ability to continue as a "going concern" for a year or more beyond the date of the financial statements are considered in Chapter 14.

3. Audit Risks: Some risks provide evidence that certain financial statement assertions may be inaccurate. For example, threats from competitors or new entrants can result in lost sales. If inventory is obsolete as a result of the threat, there may be a problem with inventory valuation. If entire factories depend on the manufacture of an obsolete product, there may be a broader problem with asset impairments that the auditor should consider. These risks lead to the auditor needing to design direct tests of management's assertions and are covered in Chapters 11 to 13.

4. Control Environment: Some threats put pressure on the control environment in such a way that management may feel that the only response is to undertake inappropriate actions. Such stresses and pressures are important to auditors because management may use accounting manipulation to disguise economic failures (as occurred at Enron and WorldCom). These affect the auditor's assessment of internal control, whether it be in a GAAS Audit or to reach an opinion on control effectiveness in an Integrated Audit. The control environment is considered further in Chapters 7 and 8.[4 (xix)(xx)]

Table 5.4 provides a number of examples of the possible implications of the identified strategic risks. To illustrate, consider the risk that buyers will change their preferences for the distribution channel of a product (*SR6*). A product that has been sold through retail outlets may become more attractive if it is sold through the Internet with direct home delivery. This change creates risk for a company because customers may turn to competitors. Computer supplies are a market where this phenomenon is occurring. The effect on internal activities could be extensive: The nature of sales and product delivery will change, shifting to a more technology-based approach. Logistics and distribution will be seriously affected as the company shifts from bulk delivery to retail outlets to small parcel, multiple-destination shipping. Customer service may need to provide dedicated resources to handle customer questions, complaints, and problems that were traditionally handled in-store (such as an 800 phone number and well-designed FAQs on-line). Technology and tangible resources are also affected because of the equipment and system needs of setting up the new sales and distribution system.

The discussion of business risks and management responses is important for auditing because their impact on "economic reality" needs to be properly reflected in the financial statements. In our example, a change in distribution channels may raise questions about the impairment of assets that are used in the "old" channel. Furthermore, if the changes are radical enough, the organization may need to undertake significant restructuring that may result in the layoff of some personnel, the relocation and retraining of other employees, and the disposal of assets. All of these outcomes will create issues that the auditor must examine in order to assure that they are appropriately reflected in the financial statements.

Many of the audit implications suggested in Table 5.4 are general in nature. The audit process requires a much more detailed understanding of overall audit risks, but the analysis of business risks tells the auditor a great deal about the nature of a company and the industry in which it operates. By the time the auditor has completed this analysis, he or she should have an extremely deep understanding of the client, its market position, the factors that will determine its success, and the risks it faces. If this were all that was obtained from the analysis, it would be useful. However, the auditor's understanding of a client's risk profile also provides extremely helpful insight into the organization's control environment and the risk of material misstatement in areas affected by significant client business risks. In turn, these insights help the auditor to plan and conduct the audit of the financial statements.

AUTHORITATIVE GUIDANCE & STANDARDS

Understanding an entity and its environment by performing a strategic analysis helps auditors in assessing the risk of material misstatement for the entity on an overall basis (ISA 315, AS 2210), and is particularly mentioned as important for the auditor in assessing fraud risk (ISA 240 **The Auditor's Responsibilities Relating to Fraud in an Audit of Financial Statements**, *AS 2301 [formerly 13]* **The Auditor's Responses to the Risks of Material Misstatement** *and AS 2401 [formerly* Interim Standard *AU 316]* **Consideration of Fraud in a Financial Statement Audit***).*

(xviii)**EXAMPLE**

In the 1990s, General Electric failed to deliver a sufficient inventory of light bulbs at year end to The Home Depot. Founders Bernie Marcus and Arthur Blank responded by ceasing any business with GE in the future. Although GE developed a significant presence at The Home Depot in other product lines, only Philips light bulbs were sold at The Home Depot during the tenure of Marcus and Blank.

(xix)**EXAMPLE**

WordPerfect was the largest selling word processing package for personal computers in the early 1990s. It was developed and sold by a relatively small independent company based in Utah, which was purchased by Corel—an Ottawa-based Canadian company. However, WordPerfect was surpassed by Microsoft's Word, not because it was a clearly superior product, but because of the marketing power and installed base of Microsoft. Corel built a suite of software around other independent programs (such as Quattro spreadsheets). In the end, Microsoft dominated and WordPerfect lost significant market share, resulting in significant losses to Corel.

Stock options create a potential incentive for executives to manipulate earnings. The value of the options is tied to the price of a company's stock. Therefore, management will be harmed if bad news causes the price of the stock to drop significantly. This could cause management to try to hide bad results through accounting tricks. During the 2005 trial of Bernie Ebbers, former CEO of WorldCom (now part of Verizon), witness and former CFO Scott Sullivan alleged that Ebbers instructed him to ensure that earnings forecasts were achieved using any trick necessary because of the ramifications to the executive's personal wealth should the price of WorldCom's stock fall. Sullivan claimed that this pressure led him to undertake the largest fraud in US history.

The manager responsible for overseeing production may get a weekly report that details production costs by product line and manufacturing process, including an analysis of cost variances. If costs are going up rapidly, this information may be useful for assessing and countering risks that affect the organization's supply chain.

Management Controls

As seen in Figure 5.2, management controls and performance data are used by management to limit and monitor strategic risks. Hence, effectively implemented controls and management monitoring of performance data reduces the risks associated with financial reporting as it means there will be early recognition and management of emergent problems, i.e., problems that if left unattended could have major effects on the financial statements.

Management control systems are "the systems that are used to maintain or alter the pattern in organizational activities."[5] ***Management controls*** are the activities undertaken by senior management to promote effective decision making and efficient business activities, while mitigating strategic risks. Management controls tend to focus on overall effectiveness and efficiency within an organization rather than on details of individual activities or transactions, but without such controls it is unlikely that internal controls at the activities or transactions level would be effective. Most management controls are designed to provide an overall indication that processes and activities are functioning properly.

Types of Management Controls

Management controls that may be relevant for the audit include:

- Top-level reviews.
- Direct activity by management.
- Performance indicators and benchmarking.
- Independent management oversight and monitoring.

Top-Level Reviews: These controls involve senior management periodically reviewing the results of operations against forecasts and budgets and quickly following up on potential problems. The more frequent and in-depth these reviews, the less likely it is that large business threats will remain undetected. The quality and effectiveness of top-level reviews will depend on the timeliness, reliability, and relevance of the information used during the review process. Biased or incomplete information will undermine the ability of management to perform such reviews(xxi).

Direct Activity by Management: Managers at various levels (executive, functional, or activity) who are directly responsible for managing specific business processes are often in the best position to quickly identify problems while they are still small. To be effective, managers need to receive performance information on a timely basis. Management's effectiveness will then depend on their ability to spot problem areas and react appropriately to early warning signals. Information for management analysis should be disaggregated enough to provide details by product or service line, location, type of customer, or other relevant dimension in order to identify potential problems. For this reason, an auditor should communicate directly with managers to understand how risks are handled within a business process(xxii).

Performance Indicators and Benchmarking: The use of diagnostic indicators based on operating and financial data is a potentially powerful tool for monitoring the status of an organization. This tool is made even more powerful if relevant benchmarks are available. A benchmark is simply a target level or standard of comparison for an indicator of interest, such as the delinquency (late payment or non-payment) rate on receivables. Benchmarks can be based on an analysis of prior results, predefined best-case results, or competitors' results. A well-designed indicator may be very useful for highlighting problems at an early stage. The use of benchmarks is discussed in detail in Chapters 9 and 14[xxiii].

Independent Management Oversight and Monitoring: Control is most effective if exercised by someone who is independent of the operations or activities being controlled. Management is usually in the best position to exercise independent oversight for most activities within the organization. Segregating incompatible duties is one element of establishing independent control within an organization (to be discussed in more detail in Chapter 7). More importantly, however, is the need for managers who are responsible for reviewing and controlling a process or activity to be distinct from the individuals who are charged with executing the process or activity. For example, unfavorable budget variances may not be followed up appropriately unless brought to the attention of someone who is independent of the process creating the variances[xxiv].

Evaluating Management Controls

In order to assess the effectiveness of management controls, the auditor must identify which management controls, if effectively implemented, mitigate specific risks. The auditor may review procedures manuals, periodic reports, and internal audit testing in order to evaluate how effective management is in identifying, monitoring, and controlling risk. In most situations, a key step is interviewing personnel who are assigned the responsibility of dealing with critical risks. Key personnel responsible for managing risk typically include senior management, such as the CEO, CFO, COO, and senior-level vice presidents (e.g., a senior VP-Strategy). Those charged with risk management responsibility should be able to answer the following questions:

- How do you identify risks that need to be addressed?
- How do you assess and prioritize the significance of risks?
- What information and reports do you use to monitor important risks? Who produces the information? How reliable and timely is the information?
- How do you decide what action to take in response to an identified risk?
- When are superiors or personnel from other areas involved in responding to a risk?
- How responsive are others to risks you identify?
- Are resources adequate (time, budget, qualified personnel) for effectively responding to risks on a timely basis?

An important part of evaluating management control is to identify the appropriate person to question. Upper and middle management in different departments will be responsible for different aspects of managing risk. In addition to interviewing the senior manager ultimately responsible for managing risk, the auditor should discuss controls with the person(s) who are

J. D. Power and Associates collects data on customer satisfaction for all major automobiles sold in the US and Canada. Because the company is independent of the manufacturers, the customer satisfaction ratings it publishes are highly respected. A good rating is actively pursued by the car companies. The Canadian Automobile Association and Consumers Union also provides independent ratings on dependability, safety, and repairs for most major car companies. These rating agencies provide very important benchmarks for car manufacturers who wish to maintain and enlarge their market share. Significant changes in ratings can alert management to problems with their product and may also provide evidence to the auditor about potential problems in production or design processes.

Ever wonder why, when returning an item to a retail store like The Home Depot, you have to go to a special area at the front of the store to return it? The goal of this segregation of roles is to separate those who are selling the item from those giving refunds for its return. Also, by having returns all done at one site in a store right near the entry point it is easy to station a supervisor there at all times who can approve the returns while undertaking other managerial roles.

closest to the risk in the process. These people are often referred to as **process owners** because they are responsible for managing a process within the organization. In many cases, the appropriate people to interview are outside the accounting and finance area and may be in such diverse functions as research and development, personnel, or manufacturing. By talking to many people about the same risks, and obtaining supporting documentation whenever possible, the auditor can develop a relatively complete picture of the quality of management controls[xxv].

A common characteristic of effective management control is the need for reliable, timely, and appropriate information. The process of preparing and monitoring reports must be reliable. Information used in a monthly budget analysis is more likely to be reliable if generated from the main accounting system by the data processing department than if it is generated by a manager using a desktop spreadsheet of his or her own design. Furthermore, using the wrong information to monitor a process could unknowingly lead to undesirable results[xxvi].

For each significant risk identified by the auditor, consideration should be given to any management controls that may exist to mitigate the risk. If a strategic risk has significant implications for the audit, then the related controls are also relevant to the conduct of the audit. The relationship between management controls and audit planning is illustrated in Table 5.5 for several management controls. Consider the first item, monitoring competitors' actions. This procedure is very important for managing the risk that competitors introduce new products, reduce prices, or improve service without warning. This risk could affect revenue levels, margins, inventory valuation, service costs, and selling expenses, depending on how the company responds. To evaluate whether management is effective, the auditor could examine the periodic reports that management uses and evaluate the nature and timeliness of management's responses. Furthermore, the reports may provide information that is directly relevant to assessing the valuation of inventory[xxvii].

Evidence of Management Controls Mitigating Risk

Numerous controls that management performs on a routine basis may provide useful information for the auditor during the course of the engagement. Particularly strong controls can be tested by the auditor and may serve as a source of audit evidence. Although management controls may appear to be effective, an auditor must also obtain evidence to support the conclusion that controls are effective. An auditor cannot simply reduce assessments of risk of material misstatement based on the auditor's intuition or management's unsupported claims about the controls the company has in place. The auditor needs to obtain sufficient and appropriate evidence to justify the conclusion that risks are less significant than initially believed. This evidence is often obtained through **tests of controls** and some examples of tests that might be used to test control effectiveness are included in Table 5.5. In order for management controls to be effective they must be well designed so as to limit or reduce the risk they are intended to control. A poorly designed control will not reduce the risk[xxviii].

Table 5.5 *Management Controls and Implications for the Audit of Financial Statements*

Management Control	Audit Evidence Needed to Test Control Effectiveness	Potential Impact of Evidence about Control on Audit Overall	Potential Impact on Tests of Financial Statement Assertions
The company monitors its main competition to estimate their time-to-market for new products. The effectiveness of marketing is also assessed relative to the competition.	The auditor can obtain and review reports from the marketing department concerning time-to-market and quality of advertising and promotions.	The market data may provide a leading indicator of potential competitive problems and evidence of new product or advertising failures.	Indications of failed products or marketing campaigns may raise questions of asset impairment or inventory obsolescence.
A company prepares annual sales, expense, and expenditure budgets and monitors variances on a monthly basis. Corrective action, when needed, is initiated on a timely basis.	The auditor can obtain copies of the annual budgets and monthly variance reports. Handling of the variances should be discussed with appropriate personnel.	The monthly variance reports identify unusual conditions or developments that may indicate increasing risks or accounting problems.	Minimal, unless results from analytical evidence suggest accounting problems that impact specific financial reporting items.
A company maintains and enforces a policy on management conflicts-of-interest. All management personnel must complete a conflict-of-interest report every year.	The auditor can discuss conflict-of-interest policies with management, review a selection of conflict-of-interest reports and verify follow-up and resolution of apparent conflicts.	Minimal.	The conflict reports may indicate related party or other transactions that should be disclosed. Valuation of such transactions may need to be verified.
The company prepares weekly sales reports which track turnover by product lines and geographic region.	The auditor can obtain the weekly reports (or a sample) and review them for proper review and follow-up by appropriate personnel.	The weekly reports provide analytical evidence about the valuation of inventory. Quantities in weekly reports may be used to reconcile inventory counts per perpetual records.	Inventory turnover statistics can indicate items that the auditor should count and examine during the year end testing of inventory assertions.
The controller monitors past due receivables on a monthly basis, and follows-up on any accounts that are 60 days past due. Account write-offs must be approved by both the controller and the CFO.	The auditor can discuss the monitoring process with the controller and review reports used or prepared by him. Also, a sample of past due accounts can be reviewed for proper disposition.	The controller's reports provide analytical evidence about the collectible of accounts.	The controller's reports identify transactions and/or accounts that may require in-depth analysis at year end.
The company uses the internal audit department to perform periodic compliance review of key regulations.	The auditor can obtain copies of the internal audit programs, work product, and reports. Documents should be reviewed for unusual conditions.	Minimal.	The internal audit reports may reveal conditions to be disclosed or may lead to the recognition of a contingent liability for fines or penalties.

Auditors can gather evidence to support conclusions about the design effectiveness of management controls by means of:

- Client inquiries: by conducting discussions with multiple individuals about the same risks or controls, the auditor may obtain insight into how effective management controls really are. We discuss effective client inquiries in Chapter 9.

EXAMPLE

During the course of the audit of a mid-size European bank, the audit team identified foreign exchange risk as very important to the bank. To control currency risks, the senior management of the bank established a policy limiting the amount of exposure (assets, loans, guarantees) in specific currencies. In assessing this control, the auditor discovered that the information for monitoring currency positions was maintained by a clerk using a personally designed spreadsheet with manual input from currency traders whenever they remembered to notify the clerk of currency trades. The clerk did not really understand the purpose of the procedure, nor did she have authority to influence the bank's day-to-day activities. Consequently, the bank's risk exposure was much larger than believed because senior-level management failed to ensure that management controls were effective.

- Observation: The auditor may be able to observe actual work effort in real time and form an opinion as to the appropriateness, competence, and reliability of management controls.

- Review of documentation: Because many management controls rely on periodic reports, the auditor should obtain copies of any reports or documents that provide evidence about management's efforts to control specific risks.

To be effective, controls not only need to be well designed to reduce or limit risks but they also need to be put into effect. Auditors can acquire evidence to support conclusions about the operational effectiveness of management controls using variants of the above three techniques as well as:

- Tests of control implementation: Evidence about the reliability of the data going into the reports used by management to control specific risks should be obtained so as to ensure the reliability of the reports. The standards used to determine out of control conditions should also be evaluated by auditors, sometimes involving experts to assess how diagnostic those standards would be at detecting material out of control events. A sample of the reports should be discussed with appropriate management, and the auditor should obtain evidence that indicates how actual problems were addressed (e.g., what does management actually *do* with the information in the reports?(xxix)).

Limitations of Management Control

Although management controls are an effective way to respond to many strategic risks, there are also a number of conditions that can lead to ineffective management control. When such conditions exist, risk may not be reduced or may be much higher than expected because of management's incorrect (but comforting) belief that effective controls are in place. The effectiveness of management control can be limited by the following:

- **Failure by Employees to Internalize the Organization's Mission and Objectives:** Individuals responsible for specific functions within the organization can operate effectively only when they fully understand the mission and objectives of the organization and accept their role. Failure to ensure that the message is internalized at all levels can lead to unproductive or harmful behavior.

- **Inaccurate or Out-of-Date Assumptions:** In framing a response to external risks, management often has to make assumptions about the environment. These assumptions may be at odds with actual conditions or may become inflexible in the face of changing conditions. Controls based on flawed assumptions will be less effective than expected.

- **Undue Focus on Current Conditions:** It is very easy for management to get caught up in the pressure of current challenges and fail to adequately consider future plans. Without a clear vision of the future, current actions may turn out to be inadequate or counterproductive in the future.

- **Rigid Organizational Structure:** External conditions tend to be fluid but internal lines of authority tend to be fixed and slow to change.

This mismatch can lead to an organizational structure appropriate for yesterday's challenges but inadequate for the current/future environment.

- **Failure to Enforce Accountability:** Management control within an organization is based on the assumption that members of the organization will be held accountable for their actions. Failure to enforce accountability can undermine performance.
- **Communication Breakdowns:** Any significant breakdown in communication is likely to undermine the efficiency and effectiveness of an organization. The frequency and severity of communication failures will have a direct impact on whether management controls are effective.
- **Top Management Failure:** In most major accounting frauds, it is the top management of a company that is the source of control failure. Indeed, one analysis of the Securities and Exchange Commission's enforcement actions in the US found that the vast majority of frauds were instigated by the senior managers who had responsibility for the control system's design and monitoring.

The auditor should discuss these possible conditions with management and the Audit Committee and determine if any of these problems are likely to occur. If the auditor feels that some or all of these conditions currently exist, the quality of management control could be significantly weakened.[6]

Linking Strategic Risks to Business Processes

As we noted above, rarely do management controls by themselves reduce strategic risks to a level acceptable to the organization's managers. Indeed, most of the response to strategic risks lies in how the managers design the organization's processes. Hence, in the next chapter we link the effects of the observed strategic risks to the internal business processes within the organization. Business processes are designed to facilitate the strategy of the company, to interact with the external elements of the environment, and to minimize the potential impact of threats from external sources. Auditors need to be able to link threats from strategic sources to business processes and the financial statements in order to use this knowledge to plan audit procedures to reduce the risk of misstatements, whether due to fraud or error, in the financial statements. The following three scenarios give an introduction to this linkage that we will deal with in more detail in subsequent chapters.

1. Threats from competitors and potential entrants are most likely to affect sales, product delivery, branding, and customer service. These threats may create downward price pressure that, in turn, may require the organization to innovate the way it delivers products and develops new brands, and to consider new marketing efforts. For example, competitive pricing and the bundling of service contracts with products may raise issues related to accounting for revenue and inventory.

2. Threats from suppliers are most likely to affect supply chain management and production. Supplier threats affecting the quality or supply of

(xxvi)**EXAMPLE**

A telemarketing company implemented a system to monitor telephone sales representatives that emphasized the number of successfully completed calls per work shift. This created an incentive for the salespeople to get on and off a call quickly once they had gotten the details of an order. However, the company discovered that customer satisfaction was deteriorating and revenue growth was below targets. Management soon realized that the performance measure put too much emphasis on speed and not enough on answering customer questions. Furthermore, marketing research has demonstrated that it is easier to get additional revenue from an existing customer than it is to obtain a new customer. The company changed its performance measurement system to emphasize customer satisfaction and revenue per successful call. Sales growth resumed and customers were more satisfied.

(xxvii) EXAMPLE

Evidence of "coordinated" price movements is apparent in the retail gasoline market in many communities. Often, one gas chain implements a price cut in a certain region, which is quickly followed by similar cuts by other gasoline companies that are in direct competition. Similarly, one gasoline company may announce price increases, but competitors may not choose to follow, and the company initiating the increase is usually forced to retract the price increase. Collusion is often suspected as a result of this apparent coordination, but, in reality, the commonality of pricing is probably the result of extensive competition. Given the large number of local markets in which a gasoline company may operate, matching competitors' prices requires active and continuous monitoring of the prices charged by competitors. The management response in this situation is dependent on timely, reliable information from the external environment.

(xxviii) EXAMPLE

To reduce the risk that customers will not be able to pay their accounts when due, a credit check is often performed by the company granting credit. If the sales person is the one who is supposed to carry out the credit check, and no documentation is available from the credit bureau to show that the check was carried out, this control is not well designed to reduce the risk that a customer cannot pay the bills when due.

raw materials may have an impact on the number of suppliers utilized, the willingness to pay transportation costs for dispersed suppliers, manufacturing changes needed to adjust for changes in the quality of materials (resulting in higher rates of wastage or spoilage during production), or after-market service (resulting in higher warranty costs due to guaranteed repairs).

3. Threats from customers are most likely to affect sales, logistics and distribution, and customer service. Internet marketing and telemarketing combined with the ability of suppliers to do direct home delivery may replace retail outlets, changing the nature of distribution and the fixed asset base needed by the company. This could result in the need to recognize asset impairments.

Well-designed processes reduce the potential impact of strategic risks by standardizing the organization's response to external stimuli and coordinating operations to manage those risks. Accordingly, key information systems for most organizations are designed to accommodate effective and efficient business processes. There are a large number of processes that are embedded in an organization, and problems occurring within one process can have an adverse effect on other processes. Furthermore, breakdowns within a business process will often have a direct effect on the organization's financial statements through not capturing completely the transactions the process is designed to deal with, impair the value of assets, or create new liabilities for the organization as a result of its breakdown. The challenge to the auditor is to identify the processes that have the most potential impact on the auditor's assessment of risk of material misstatement and the consequent effects on the financial statements. We start to deal with those challenges in Chapter 6.

Summary and Conclusion

This chapter introduced a systematic approach to understanding a client's business and industry, strategy, operations and activities, risk, and potential audit implications arising from those conditions and circumstances. The analysis is based on a model that facilitates the identification and summarization of important information about an organization. The Organizational Business Models describe the client's role in its industry. The strategic risk assessment performed in this chapter combined with our examination of management controls and testing of those controls are useful starting points for assessing risk of material misstatement. In addition, identified strategic risks are analyzed to determine how they impact the conduct of the audit of specific accounts and transactions. In the next chapter, we discuss business processes in more detail and expand our risk assessment to include process risks. In later chapters we will see how these strategic and process risk assessments are combined into the auditor's assessment of risk of material misstatement, which then informs both the audit of financial statements and, where required, the audit of internal control over financial reporting effectiveness.

Bibliography of Relevant Literature

Relevant Research

Ballou, B., C. E. Earley, and J. S. Rich. 2004. The Impact of Strategic-Positioning Information on Auditor Judgments about Business Process Performance. *Auditing: A Journal of Practice & Theory*. 23(2): 71–88.

Knechel, R., S. Salterio and N. Kochetova-Kozloski. 2010. The Effect of Benchmarked Performance Measures and Strategic Analysis on Auditors' Risk Assessments and Mental Models. *Accounting Organizations and Society*. 35(3): 316–333.

O'Donnell, E. and J. J. Schultz, Jr. 2005. The Halo Effect in Business Risk Audits: Can Strategic Risk Assessment Bias Auditor Judgment about Accounting Details? *The Accounting Review*. 80(3): 921–940.

Porter, Michael, 1980. *Competitive Strategy: Techniques for Analyzing Industries and Competitors*. New York: The Free Press.

Porter, Michael. 1985. *Competitive Advantage: Creating and Sustaining Superior Performance*. New York: The Free Press.

Porter, Michael and Victor Millar. 1985. How Information Gives You Competitive Advantage. *Harvard Business Review*. July–August: 149–160.

Robert Simons, The Strategy of Control, *CA Magazine*, March 1992, p. 44.

Auditing Standards

Committee of Sponsoring Organizations of the Treadway Commission (COSO). *Internal Control—Integrated Framework*. AICPA, 1992.

Committee of Sponsoring Organizations of the Treadway Commission (COSO). *Internal Control—An Integrated Framework: Guidance for Smaller Public Companies*. AICPA, 2006.

Committee of Sponsoring Organizations of the Treadway Commission (COSO). *Internal Control—Integrated Framework*. AICPA, 2013.

IAASB *International Standards on Auditing (ISA)* No. 240, "The Auditor's Responsibilities Relating to Fraud in an Audit of Financial Statements."

IAASB *International Standards on Auditing (ISA)* No. 315, "Identifying and Assessing the Risks of Material Misstatement through Understanding the Entity and Its Environment."

IFAC. International Ethics Standards Board for Accountants (IESBA). 2015. *Handbook of Code of Ethics for Professional Accountants*. New York: International Federation of Accountants.

IFAC. International Auditing and Assurance Standards Board (IAASB). 2015. *Handbook of International Quality Control, Audit, Review, Other Assurance, and Related Services Pronouncements*. New York: International Federation of Accountants.

PCAOB. *Auditing Standard* 2201 (formerly No. 5), "An Audit of Internal Control over Financial Reporting that is Integrated with An Audit of Financial Statements."

(xxix)**EXAMPLE**

Inventory order systems often have parameters set that trigger a report that specific quantities of a good in inventory reach a level that requires emergency reordering in order to satisfy demand. However, this control will not be effective at reducing out of stock risks if managers do not take timely action to authorize additional purchases or authorize expedited delivery.

PCAOB. *Auditing Standard* 2210 (formerly No. 12), "Identifying and Assessing the Risks of Material Misstatement."

PCAOB. *Auditing Standard* 2301 (formerly No. 13), "The Auditor's Responses to the Risks of Material Misstatement."

PCAOB. *Auditing Standard* 2401 (formerly *Interim Standard* AU 316), "Consideration of Fraud in a Financial Statement Audit."

Notes

1 Economists use the term price elasticity to describe how price sensitive a product is. Elastic demand suggests that consumers are price sensitive; inelastic demand suggests customers do not care very much about price. Obviously, the more elastic demand is, the less ability a company has to raise prices without losing significant revenue.

2 M. Porter. *Competitive Strategy*. New York, Free Press. 1980.

3 For severe risks, crisis management policies and procedures generally include setting up a crisis management team dedicated to designing a response plan for most any crisis that heavily involves public and media relations, CEO involvement, formal channels of communication, business continuation processes, and customer and supplier interaction, among others.

4 A fifth category can be broadly conceived as auditor identification of business related issues that the client management should address. Pointing out to the client management (via a management letter that is discussed in Chapter 15) that it needs to deal with certain operational or strategic issues that are discovered during the audit is appreciated by management and is totally acceptable under auditor independence rules as long as the auditor is not seen as providing consulting advice. For non-public entities, identification of these issues is seen as a very valuable side benefit from the audit and can also lead to the audit firm providing permitted consulting services to these non-public company clients as long as auditor independence is not threatened by their provision.

5 Robert Simons, The Strategy of Control, *CA Magazine,* March 1992, p. 44.

6 In audits of non-public companies, such as private company audits and audits of not-for-profit organizations, the audit firm employing personnel not involved in the audit may also be able to assist the company in designing and implementing a response to risk. For public companies the level of assistance, beyond the identification of risks that may be provided by the audit firm, is dependent on national regulations about the nature and type of non-audit services that a public accounting firm can offer its audit clients. For US SEC registrants, there are relatively few such services that can be offered.

CHAPTER 6

Understanding the Client's Industry and Business

Processes and Process Controls

Outline

- Summary and Conclusion
- Bibliography of Relevant Literature

Learning Goals for this Chapter

1. Understand the role of business processes in limiting strategic risks.
2. Describe how business processes can be analyzed using value chains.
3. Link the strategic risks and the organization's responses, management controls and business processes, to audit implications.
4. Describe how to document a business process employing a process map.
5. Understand the nature of risks that might be found in a business process.
6. Understand how management implements process controls that ensure processes reduce risks.
7. Describe basic information processing controls and their role in reducing process risks.
8. Integrate process controls testing with management control testing as part of an auditor's strategy to assess the risk of material misstatement.
9. Employ the analysis of strategic risks, management controls and business processes, to determine the nature and extent of residual risks in an organization under audit.

Introduction

In Chapter 5, we examined a client's external environment for the purpose of understanding its source of competitive advantage, identifying potential threats to its success and the management controls that are employed in mitigating those risks. As we noted in the previous chapter, strategic risks often have a direct effect on a company's internal operations. The execution of a company's strategy and its ability to cope with strategic threats depends critically on the manner in which it organizes its internal operations. Management allocates its available resources (e.g., employees, tangible assets, financial resources) into **business processes**. Well-designed processes reduce the potential impact of strategic risks by standardizing the organization's response to external stimuli and coordinating operations to manage those risks. Accordingly, key information systems for most organizations are designed to accommodate effective and efficient business processes. There are a large number of processes that are embedded in an organization, and problems occurring within one process can have an adverse effect on other processes. Furthermore, breakdowns within a business process will often have an effect on the organization's financial statements. The challenge to the auditor is to identify the processes that have the most potential impact on the audit.

AUTHORITATIVE GUIDANCE & STANDARDS

Understanding the business processes put in place to implement and monitor the implementation of a company's strategy helps the auditor to assess the risk of material misstatement for financial statement assertions (ISA 315 **Identifying and Assessing the Risks of Material Misstatement through Understanding the Entity and Its Environment;** *AS 2110 [formerly 12]* **Identifying and Assessing Risks of Material Misstatement***). Further, internal controls over financial reporting are usually embedded in individual business processes since the accounting system is part of the operations of the business (ISA 315, AS 2201 [formerly No. 5]* **An Audit of Internal Control Over Financial Reporting that is Integrated with An Audit of Financial Statements***). Consequently, an understanding of the key processes within a business is the starting point for evaluating internal controls over financial reporting.*

Processes pertain to the full scope of activities within the organization, ranging from strategic planning at the level of senior management, to budgeting and accounting by professional accounting staff, to marketing and sales by account managers, to housekeeping by custodial staff. Regardless of the level at which an activity is performed, virtually all processes have a dual purpose: (1) to advance the objectives of the organization, and (2) to minimize the risks of not achieving those objectives (i.e., to control or mitigate the risks). The importance of strategic planning, accounting, and marketing may be self-evident, but the potential problems of excess dust in the computer room that could cause system disruptions, or dirty bathrooms in a restaurant that could disgust customers, can elevate a mundane activity such as housekeeping to a level of importance. Process failure can be just as harmful to an organization as poor strategic planning[(i)].

Internal Operations and Business Processes

Continuing with our top-down approach, we next examine business processes. Conditioned on what we already know about the strategic environment of the company and its management controls, our goal is to evaluate whether internal execution of plans and activities is mitigating the risks faced by the organization. To organize our examination we use value chain analysis. This framework describes how the internal structure of the organization creates value for stakeholders by designing processes to carry out the operations and activities of an entity in an effective and controlled manner. A generic value chain for organizations that manufacture, distribute, or sell tangible products is depicted in Figure 6.1. We add to the normal depiction in corporate strategy of a value chain by explicitly linking the processes in the chain to the financial accounting transactions and estimates that occur as a result of the activities in the value chain.[1] Following Michael Porter's value chain analysis we separate business processes into *primary processes*, performed to directly create value in the form of a product or service, and *support*

[(i)]**EXAMPLE**

A small regional burger chain in Western Canada was shut down for 10 days when it was found that staff at one location were spreading a highly contagious virus. The problem was that the organization had no procedures for monitoring sick employees. The owner-manager voluntarily closed all locations until remedial training and disinfection were completed. Hence, the news stories changed from a focus on the illnesses caused by the chain to the "concerned owner" who put the health of customers ahead of the profits of his burger chain. When the chain reopened, customers came back in a rush, and the company avoided repercussions that might have led to bankruptcy if management's response had been less assertive.

processes, performed in order for the organization to function properly but having an indirect effect on the creation of product value.[2]

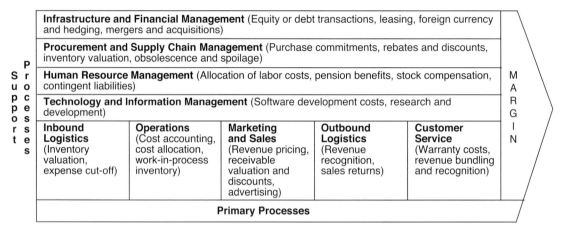

Figure 6.1 *Generic Value Chain for Typical Organization That Sells Product and Impact on Financial Reporting of the Various Processes*

Primary Processes

The primary processes for an organization represent its efforts to take a group of inputs and create an output that has value from the perspective of a customer. Thus, primary processes represent the direct activities that need to take place to move the product to the customer. There are five types of primary processes for organizations that manufacture, distribute, or sell tangible products:

1. **Inbound Logistics:** These processes consist of the *physical activities* by which the organization obtains, stores, and manages input to the production, warehousing, or retail process. Examples of activities included as part of inbound logistics are materials handling, warehousing, and purchase returns. The complexity of inbound logistics will depend on:

   o The volume and range of inputs needed for production.

   o The mode and timing of resource deliveries.

   o The need to control resources once they are received.

   o The method of inventory management employed (e.g., just-in-time inventory).

   o The process for handling purchase returns.

   Accounting and audit issues associated with inbound logistics include the completeness and valuation of incoming inventory as well as the timing of expenses and liabilities[(ii)].

2. **Operations:** These processes enable the company to *transform inputs* into a product (or service) that can be sold to customers. They include machining, assembly, packaging, and testing. They may also include certain maintenance activities directly related to the operating process. The complexity of operations will depend on:

   o The extent resources are transformed by the organization (production).

   o The need to control and manage inventory levels.

o   The complexity of product costing (e.g., large overhead allocations).

o   The extent and costs of by-products, waste, rework, and so forth.

Accounting and audit issues associated with operations include the costing of goods and services, which in turn depends on various cost allocations (such as indirect labor, service departments, depreciation, and amortization[(iii)]).

3. **Marketing and Sales:** These processes develop brand recognition, create demand for the company's products, manage customer relations, and initiate sales. They include advertising, selecting a distribution channel, maintaining a sales force, and setting prices. The complexity of marketing and sales activities depends on:

o   The scope of brand development activities (e.g., international, regional, local).

o   The nature of promotion (e.g., Internet advertising, television/print media, product placement).

o   The extent of differential pricing.

o   The form of sales contact with customers (e.g., personal contact, telemarketing, Internet-based).

o   The selection of distribution channel.

Accounting and audit issues associated with marketing and sales include revenue recognition as affected by the terms of sale (e.g., rights of return) and the collectability of receivables[(iv)].

4. **Outbound Logistics:** These processes involve delivering the products and services to customers. They also include activities related to order processing following initial order entry. The complexity of outbound logistics will depend on:

o   The nature of the product or service being delivered.

o   The form of delivery (e.g., via retail outlet, company-owned trucks, independent shippers, the postal system).

o   Transfer of title of goods (e.g., consignment, FOB-shipping point).

o   The contractual arrangements with customers (e.g., long-term construction contracts, rights of return for unsold merchandise).

Accounting and audit issues associated with outbound logistics include the cut-off of sales, the timing of revenue recognition, and the extent of sales returns[(v)].

5. **After Sales Service:** These processes are performed by the company after goods and services have been delivered, including installation, training of customer personnel, and repairs. The complexity of service activities will depend on:

o   The complexity of installation and use of a product.

o   The extent and nature of warranty coverage.

o   The role of customer follow-up in developing repeat customers.

o   The existence of extended service contracts, often bundled with the product itself.

[(iii)]**EXAMPLE**

Repackaging and redistributing merchandise manufactured by other producers is significantly less complex than the manufacturing processes used to build an automobile, televisions, or mobile phones.

[(iv)]**EXAMPLE**

Products or services that are subject to differential pricing raise complexity in recording sales because different customers and transactions will be charged different prices. Airlines are notorious for their complex system of pricing, which changes regularly, often in real time, as the internal reservation systems continuously monitor load factors on each route the airline flies. As a result, airlines have become very effective at maximizing their revenue per flight.

[(v)]**EXAMPLE**

Products sold on consignment raise difficult accounting and audit issues because the merchandise is not in the possession of the owner and can be mistaken for actual sales. Further, when a sale of consigned merchandise occurs, the owner may not be notified on a timely basis, further complicating the accounting for sales transactions and revenue.

   o The process of performing repairs and part replacement (e.g., independent repair shops versus in-house experts).

Accounting and audit issues associated with service activities include contingent costs (such as warranties) and the timing of revenue recognition under extended service contracts or when service contracts are bundled with product sales(vi).

The relative importance of each primary process will depend on the company's operations and the strategic decisions that management has made concerning the way it will conduct business. For example, two retailers may make very different choices about their distribution channel, which will have a big impact on the nature of outbound logistics. These choices affect how accounting and control systems are designed and the risks associated with these design choices.

Support Processes

There are four basic types of support processes that are considered necessary to the creation of value by the company but are not linked directly to the production, distribution, or sale of a product or service. Many of the support processes described below focus on obtaining the resources needed by the organization to keep its primary activities operating effectively and efficiently, e.g., capital, materials, equipment, labor, and technology. Often these processes result in the creation of capital assets or period expenses.

1. **Infrastructure and Financial Management:** These activities are often referred to as "corporate overhead." They include general management, accounting, corporate governance, treasury, tax planning, and strategic management. These activities can be extremely important to the auditor because many are directly relevant to the conduct of the audit and may result in highly material transactions. Examples of transactions that would be of interest to the auditor include acquiring financing, entering into long-term leases, acquiring other companies, or executing investment and hedging transactions. Most importantly, the financial statements are generated within the accounting sub-process.

   There are many audit issues that might arise from these processes as the process includes the creation of the financial statements. Hence, issues relating to period ending journal entries, many accounting estimates that are required on a quarterly or annual basis (e.g., impairment tests), the controls over the financial statement preparation process including consolidation issues (if any) are all found in this process. Many of the major frauds that have occurred in the last century have occurred in this process using "top level" journal entries near the end of the audit and the financial statements can be employed to quickly change the overall financial picture of the organization.

2. **Procurement and Supply Chain Management:** These activities relate to the arrangements made to acquire materials, supplies, and other tangible inputs that are used throughout the organization. Most of the inputs will be received through inbound logistics and utilized during operations.

Procurement activities tend to be present throughout an organization even though a single official purchasing department may exist for inputs directly related to production. Given that the procurement process often commits the organization to acquiring goods from outsiders, the process is of interest to the auditor in terms of the authorization of transactions and the recognition of liabilities.

Audit issues that might arise from this process include purchase commitments, estimates of asset impairments, and estimates associated with inventory valuation or problems with defective materials. Furthermore, the purchasing process is an area of high risk for fraud or misappropriation of assets because of the ability of purchasing agents to receive kickbacks from vendors in exchange for favorable treatment[vii].

3. **Human Resource Management:** These activities involve the acquisition of human resources, primarily the recruiting, hiring, training, retention, evaluation, and compensation of employees. The acquisition and management of human resources supports the entire value chain. Problems in human resource development will almost always create problems for other primary or support activities. The way that an organization manages its personnel will reveal much about its overall competence and its attitudes towards honest business dealings, accurate and reliable information systems, and the potential for delivering quality goods and services.

Audit issues that might arise from this process include allocations of direct and indirect labor costs, liabilities associated with compensation or benefits (e.g., pensions, post-retirement benefits, and stock option plans), or estimates of contingent liabilities that may arise from improper employee policies, procedures, or behavior (e.g., sexual harassment or discrimination).

4. **Technology and Information Management:** These activities involve the acquisition of technological or knowledge-based resources. This set of activities can be examined at three levels:

   o Research and development for new products.

   o Research and development applied to primary activities and related business processes, such as robotic assembly lines developed to replace labor.

   o Research and development applied to support activities, such as the development and analysis of benchmarking databases for strategic planning purposes and improvements in information systems.

Audit issues that may arise from this process include the proper recognition and allocation of research and development costs, problems related to system failures, system upgrades or changeovers, especially in enterprise resource planning systems that feature organization-wide, integrated systems[viii].

A value chain for an organization that provides services would generally have three primary processes—customer/client acquisition, service delivery, and post service support. A service based organization would normally have the same four support processes albeit Human Resource

[vii] EXAMPLE

Purchase commitments to be fulfilled in the future must be monitored for their market value. If prices decline below the level specified in the purchase commitment, the company may need to recognize a loss on the commitment. The accounting and auditing becomes even more complicated if the risk of changes in future pricing is managed through financial derivatives.

[viii] EXAMPLE

Research and development costs are generally not capitalized under current FASB accounting standards. However, there are exceptions in US accounting standards for software costs that may apply to many of the internal process research activities that a company may pursue. An example could be the development of superior point of entry sales software to reduce errors by sales clerks.

Management and Technology and Information Management often are considered key parts of service delivery rather than supporting processes. This view is a result of the fact that services need to be delivered by appropriate people and often involve a high level of IT involvement in the delivery of the services.

No matter what the type of organization, all processes are potentially critical to the success of an organization and may be relevant to the conduct of the audit. An auditor's chief concern is determining which processes are critical for an organization in meeting its objectives and managing its most important strategic risks, regardless of whether they are primary or support processes.

Linking Strategic Risks to Business Processes

Chapter 5 presented a number of examples of strategic risks from various sources and introduced management controls over these risks. In this chapter, we add to that analysis by linking the identified risks to specific business processes. Building on Table 5.4 from Chapter 5, Table 6.1 illustrates the relationship among business risks, business processes, management controls, and audit implications for a sample of common strategic risks. For each risk, we identify the processes that are most likely to be affected by the risks and related controls.

There is a predictable relationship among the sources of strategic risks and the internal activities, transactions, and accounting estimates that are affected by the risk. For example, threats from suppliers are most likely to affect inbound logistics and procurement and supply chain management. We see an example of this type of risk involving raw materials (*SR3*). Threats from customers are most likely to affect outbound logistics, marketing and sales, and service activities (*SR5*). Threats from substitutes and new entrants are most likely to affect marketing and sales or technology and information management (*SR7*). Finally, although marketing and sales or after sales service are probably the most obvious areas where competitors may impact the company, competitors might influence other risks such as competition for skilled human resources (*SR2*).

The audit implications suggested in Table 6.1 are the same as presented in the prior chapter. However, with the explicit link to management controls, the auditor will be able to make informed judgments about the significance of individual risks. In Chapter 5, we specifically discussed the risk that a company will select an inappropriate or ineffective distribution channel. To reduce this risk, management can undertake timely market research and monitor technology trends that might have an impact on the company's distribution chain. Furthermore, challenging managers to question the accepted wisdom in an organization can be an effective way to protect the company from hubris.

If risks are considered less significant due to the presence of effective management controls, the auditor will next develop an approach for testing

Table 6.1 *Strategic Risks, Management Controls, and Audit Implications: Some Examples*

Strategic Risk/Threat	Source of Threat	Activity Likely to be Affected	Potential Management Controls	Potential Audit Implications
SR1: Competitors begin offering extended warranty protection on products.	Competitors	After sales service	• Policy for responding to competitors' actions. • Established market research procedures for early identification of market trends. • Reliable and timely data on actual warranty costs.	• Audit Risk: Increase in warranty commitments may require that warranty expense estimates be increased above historical patterns. • Control environment: System for tracking warranty costs.
SR2: Competitors are rapidly increasing the rate paid to key senior accounting and management personnel.	Competitors	Human resources Infrastructure and financial management	• Senior management review of personnel policies. • Hiring, promotion, and compensation processes that are fair and responsive to market conditions. • Reliable and timely data on payroll costs.	• Control Environment: Reliability of decision making and information processing may decrease with employee turnover. • Audit Risk: Allocations of labor costs may need to be revised based on relative changes in salary levels. • Audit Risk: Accruals for benefits may need to be increased.
SR3: Top-grade raw materials are in extremely short supply due to bad weather conditions in producing regions.	Suppliers	Inbound logistics Operations Procurement and supply chain management	• Timely monitoring of long-term sources of supplies. • Reliable and timely data on input costs. • Established long-term supply relationships and commitments.	• Audit Risk: Wastage and spoilage rates may need to be increased in standard costing formulas. • Audit Risk: Valuation problems related to purchase commitments may exist. • Control Environment: Pressure to cut corners to meet customer demand.
SR4: Customer industries are in a recession.	Economics, Customers	Marketing and sales Outbound logistics	• Active management of customer accounts. • Reliable and timely data on industry trends, payment history and problem accounts. • Benchmarking of delinquency rates against competitors.	• Audit Risk: Receivables may not be collectable at historic rate and allowance for uncollectable may need to be increased. • Client Viability: Shrinking customer base.
SR5: Consumer tastes have changed, necessitating improved functionality and quality in company products.	Social, Customers	Operations Technology and information management Marketing and sales	• Market research. • Consumer focus groups. • Forward thinking research efforts. • Creating an environment of innovation and risk taking.	• Client Viability: Loss of market share. • Audit Risk: Inventory on hand may become obsolete or out of favor so that carrying values may not be realizable. • Control Environment: Pressure to hit sales targets to protect jobs and/or bonuses.

(Continued)

Table 6.1   *(Continued)*

Strategic Risk/Threat	Source of Threat	Activity Likely to be Affected	Potential Management Controls	Potential Audit Implications
SR6: The preferred distribution channel for the company's product changes from retail locations to Internet, telemarketing and home delivery.	Technology and information management, Customers	Marketing and sales Outbound logistics Technology and information management	• Market research. • Monitoring of technological developments. • Timely management retreats and creative thinking exercises.	• Audit Risk: Existing distribution channels may need to be shut down with resulting restructuring cost (layoffs, asset disposal). • Audit Risk: Ongoing client viability: Inability to adapt on a timely basis.
SR7: New entrant to the market is technologically superior to current products.	Technology and information management, new entrants	Marketing and sales	• Top-level reviews of market trends by senior marketing managers. • Market surveys. • Reverse engineering of competitor products. • Product innovation and research. • Monitoring technology trends in industry.	• Audit Risk: Inventory valuation may need to be reduced to lower of cost or market due to obsolescence or excess quantities. • Audit Risk: Ongoing client viability due to loss of market share.
SR8: Government imposes new regulations on distribution of a company's product.	Social, political	Marketing and sales Outbound logistics	• Monitoring and proactive involvement in regulatory activity on a timely basis. • Innovation and research. • Monitoring technology trends affecting industry.	• Audit Risk: Ongoing client viability due to loss of market share if not adaptable. • Audit Risk: Inventory valuation may need to be reduced to lower of cost or market due to obsolescence or excess quantities. • Control environment: Develop controls to provide assurance that the organization complies with new regulations. • Control Environment: Efforts to circumvent regulations to meet sales targets.
SR9: Activists protest the company's approach to R&D.	Social	Technology and information management	• Proactive involvement with activist causes. • Charitable work in community. • Monitoring technology trends in industry.	• Audit Risk: Capitalized development costs may not be recovered if product performance suffers • Control Environment: Efforts to hide or disguise nature of R&D.

Strategic Risk/Threat	Source of Threat	Activity Likely to be Affected	Potential Management Controls	Potential Audit Implications
SR10: Foreign currency fluctuations squeeze profit margins on international sales.	Economic	Infrastructure and financial management Marketing and sales Outbound logistics (billing)	• Establish and monitor active hedging program. • Consider setting up subsidiaries in foreign countries. • Reassess transfer pricing policies. • Establish information system to monitor exposure.	• Audit Risk: Proper treatment of exchange gains and losses • Audit Risk: Accounting treatment of financial derivatives. • Control environment: Develop control systems to enable early and accurate identification of risks associated with hedging foreign currency exposures.
SR11: Manufacturing facilities become non-competitive due to age and inability to upgrade processes	Technological	Operations Technology and information management	• Monitor current technology trends. • Benchmark production costs against competition. • Establish forward thinking strategic plan.	• Audit Risk: Impairment of fixed assets. • Audit Risk: Client viability if tightening margins leading to losses and/or if prices cannot be increased.

the controls that will justify the auditor's conclusions about risk. The evidence needed to support the conclusion that management controls are effective will depend on the nature of the control and the information flow relevant to the procedure. After completing the analysis of risks and related controls and obtaining required corroborative evidence, the auditor will be able to determine which risks pose a continuing and significant threat to the organization.

The auditor documents conclusions about the effect of control on identified risks using a risk map as illustrated in Figure 6.2. Arrows indicate a reduction in the significance of a risk. Risks for which the auditor believes management

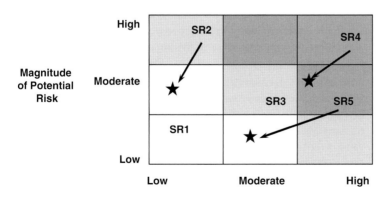

Legend:
SR1: Better warranties from competitors
SR2: Escalating executive salary demands
SR3: Shortage of raw materials
SR4: Industry recession
SR5: Changes in consumer tastes

Figure 6.2 *Impact of Management Control Activities on Risk Assessments*

has an effective response can be downgraded in significance. However, the auditor must collect evidence that these processes and controls are working as intended over the entire period the auditor wants to rely on them. For example, changes in consumer tastes (*SR5*) may be effectively addressed through market research and innovation, whereas escalating executive salaries (*SR2*) may be addressed through proactive personnel policies and industry benchmarking. Although the risk of an industry recession (*SR4*) is largely beyond the control of management, certain procedures can be taken to minimize the effect of a recession on the company's performance. However, in this case, the auditor has concluded that management's response does not significantly reduce the effect of the risk and it remains characterized as a potential residual risk.

An Overview of Process Analysis

Some processes will be more important than others in the audit of a specific client and, in most clients, technology and information management (including the financial reporting sub process) will be critical. We define an ***audit-sensitive process*** as a process that is critical to the conduct of the audit and that is likely to have a significant impact on the evidence that an auditor collects during the course of the engagement. Audit-sensitive processes are expected to be the main source of residual risks within the audit. A process can be considered to be audit-sensitive if it meets any of the following conditions:

1. **Process Critical to Achieving Strategic Objectives:** Some processes are vital to the success of the organization because they comprise the set of activities that are the source of the organization's competitive advantage. Failure within these processes will generally lead to failure for the organization as a whole. For example, in a biotech company, research drives the organization's overall success and is therefore considered a critical process. The auditor needs to understand these processes because they reflect the organization's ability to respond to critical external threats, which determines the viability of the organization (i.e., going concern, asset impairment).

2. **Process with Extensive External Interactions:** Other processes involve important and sizable interactions with outside parties, and often generate a large volume of small transactions or a few highly significant transactions. These processes are significant to the auditor because of the value of the transaction flows. Examples include mergers and acquisitions, capital market activities, financing activities (e.g., leasing), and facility expansion.

3. **Process with High Business Risk:** Processes that are subject to a high degree of risk and where problems are most likely to occur within an organization are also audit-sensitive. A process can be considered high risk because it is highly complex, involves significant management judgment, is expected to exhibit weak internal control, experiences unusual transactions, involves related parties, may lead to liabilities that are not currently recorded (i.e., contingent liabilities), or has a prior history

of problems. High-risk processes are of interest to the auditor because resulting business problems often manifest themselves as complex accounting issues or auditing problems.

Audit-sensitive business processes often meet more than one of these conditions. Given that developing a competitive advantage typically involves consciously accepting a certain amount of risk in dealing with customers or capital markets, auditors spend a great deal of time analyzing a relatively small number of business processes that meet all three conditions[(ix)].

AUTHORITATIVE GUIDANCE & STANDARDS

Internal controls over financial reporting are in part embedded in individual business processes since the accounting system is designed in part to capture the transactions that occur in the operations of the business (e.g., ordering products, paying employees, making sales etc.). Consequently, an understanding of the key processes within a business is the starting point for evaluating internal controls over financial reporting (ISA 315 and AS 2201).

The auditor identifies audit-sensitive processes for the purpose of determining which processes should be examined in detail during the course of the engagement. Once the audit-sensitive processes are identified, the auditor will need to gather a great deal of information about each process. We will use two tools to assist in our analysis of processes: (1) ***process map*** (to document the facts and circumstances surrounding a specific process), and (2) ***internal threat analysis*** (to analyze process risks).

Process Maps

Once an audit-sensitive process is identified, the next step is to gather information to develop an understanding of how the process affects financial reporting. To systematically gather accurate, relevant information, the auditor will conduct interviews with personnel involved in the process, including the managers responsible for the process. A ***process map*** has four components: (1) process objectives, (2) process activities, (3) information flows, and (4) the accounting impact of transactions.

We will illustrate process analysis using human resource management. This process includes recruiting and hiring personnel, setting work hours, training, payroll processing, and employee evaluation. It also includes the activities for terminating an employee, which may occur as a result of voluntary departures, layoffs, retirement, death, or disability. The human resource management process is likely to be a critical process in most companies. The process does not include the actual duties assigned to personnel that are performed as part of other processes. The accounting implications of human resource management range from mundane payroll processing and payments to employees to much more complicated issues related to retirement benefits and incentive compensation.

[(ix)]**EXAMPLE**

One of the most important competitive advantages for an oil exploration company is its process for identifying and extracting oil reserves. The most serious risk is that it will not find adequate reserves of oil or natural gas to justify the high cost of exploration. The uncertainty surrounding such endeavors raises serious questions about the valuation of assets related to exploration, the potential viability of the company, and the value of discovered reserves. Oil exploration companies strive to minimize the potential impact of these risks with their corporate structure (often forming as limited partnerships rather than corporations), with investments in improved exploration technology, and by lobbying for special tax treatment. An auditor would have a difficult time assessing the financial reporting risks of such a company without evaluating the oil exploration process in detail.

Process Objectives

The first element of the process map is identification of the objectives relevant to a process. The top panel of Figure 6.3 illustrates the objectives for human resource management. Process objectives represent an explicit statement of what the process is trying to achieve. Ideally, process objectives should link to broader strategic goals. For example, if the company has adopted a low-cost strategy, then many processes will have a related objective of minimizing costs within the process.

In general, the objective of human resource management is to assure that the organization has an adequate employee base with the skills that are needed to execute the organization's plans and activities. Examining the process map for human resource management (Box 6.1 "Process Map: Human Resource Management"), we see that process objectives include assuring an adequate supply of labor with the appropriate skill and training to fulfill key jobs within the organization. Also of importance is the need to evaluate and compensate employees commensurate with their value to the organization. Furthermore, an organization wants to carefully manage turnover, retaining desirable employees but terminating undesirable employees in a fair and legally justifiable manner. Workplace conditions, employee treatment, and wrongful terminations can all cause severe problems for an organization. Poor management of human resources can have a devastating impact on the entire organization because all processes require appropriate personnel.

BOX 6.1   PROCESS MAP: HUMAN RESOURCE MANAGEMENT

Process Objectives

- *Identify and acquire adequate human resources.*
- *Attract and hire highly skilled, loyal, and motivated employees.*
- *Provide adequate training for employees.*
- *Establish policies and procedures for managing, evaluating, and compensating employees.*
- *Effectively manage employee turnover.*
- *Comply with workplace health and safety regulations.*
- *Compile, process, and report information necessary for process improvement*

Process Activities

- *Identify human resource needs.*
- *Authorize hiring.*
- *Recruiting.*
- *Hiring.*
- *Training and motivation.*
- *Payroll processing.*
- *Employee evaluation.*
- *Promotion and changes to compensation.*
- *Employee termination.*

Process Data Streams

Information Feeds
- Strategic plans and budgets.
- Recruitment needs and hiring requests.
- Position descriptions.
- Work force regulations.
- Tax regulations.
- Union contracts.
- Labor market statistics and demographics.

Information Generation
- Personnel files.
- Tax forms.
- Employment contracts.
- Human resource procedures.
- Performance evaluations/reviews.
- Contract revisions.
- Training schedules.
- Payroll data and costs.
- Payroll tax remittances.

Accounting Impact of Activities

Routine Transactions
- Recruiting and hiring expenses.
- Payroll.
- Benefits.
- Payroll taxes.
- Training costs.
- Employee retirements.

Non-routine Transactions
- Pensions, health care, and other post-retirement costs.
- Bonuses.
- Employee terminations.
- Employee deaths.
- Disability claims.
- Employment litigation.

Accounting Estimates
- Pension accruals.
- Postretirement benefit accruals.
- Self-insured medical or workers' compensation obligations.

Process Activities

Process activities reflect the discrete actions and steps that are performed within the process to achieve process objectives. There are numerous types of activities that can be performed within a process:

- Decision making.
- Physical actions (e.g., training employees, converting raw materials).
- Information gathering, processing, and communication.
- Process monitoring and improvement.
- Accounting for transactions and estimates.

Most processes involve a large number of activities that, in turn, comprised numerous detailed steps. A challenge to the auditor is to decide what level of detail is needed for the analysis. The auditor wants to analyze process actions at a level of detail that allows the identification of key risks related to the objectives of the process and effect on the financial statements. The description of process activities should be adequate to describe how the process starts, how it terminates, and key procedures in between.

The second panel of Box 6.1 "Process Map: Human Resource Management" illustrates the activities performed as part of the human resource management process. These activities depend on the various strategic and process decisions that an organization makes, such as where to locate, how much to automate, and how to compensate employees. Key human resource activities for most organizations include:

- Identifying human resource needs: The organization continually assesses its personnel needs including number, type, and qualifications of factory workers and service providers, administrative staff, and professional and management personnel.

- Authorizing the hiring of personnel: Management approves the initiation of a process to fill identified positions that satisfy specific needs. Management also authorizes general guidelines for compensation and benefits for a position.

- Recruiting: The search for employees takes many different forms and depends on the types of skills that are needed. The hiring of entry level factory or service workers is different from hiring professional staff or senior management. Negotiation of individual compensation and benefits is also considered part of the recruiting process unless it is predetermined by union contract or legal constraint.

- Hiring: Administratively, adding a new employee to payroll involves a number of detailed steps. An employment agreement that stipulates compensation and benefits must be prepared. Payroll deductions are authorized for things such as taxes, insurance coverage, and pension contributions. Maintenance of accurate and up-to-date personnel files is an important aspect of this activity.

- Training and motivation: Organizations promote employee competence with training and educational support. They promote appropriate behavior and discourage undesirable behavior with a statement of core values and code of personal conduct, backed up with appropriate enforcement of firm policies. The control environment of the company depends critically on this training.

- Payroll processing: Paying people on a periodic basis is a routine but complex set of activities. Numerous inputs are needed to process payroll including hours worked, pay scales, payroll deductions, and tax withholding. This information is used to compute payroll amounts for the employees in the organization. Disbursements are made by check or electronic funds transfer. Proper accounting for all of this activity is an important part of the process.

- Employee evaluation: Employee performance should be evaluated periodically. The evaluations can be used to improve performance, justify promotions, or terminate poor performers. Incentives for employees to commit fraud often arise from disgruntled employees who believe that their contribution has been overlooked or that they have been unfairly evaluated.

- Employee pay and benefit adjustments: Employment arrangements with individuals change over time. Promotions and pay increases should be reviewed and authorized by appropriate levels of management.

- Employee termination: Employees leave an organization for a number of reasons: new jobs, life changes (e.g., new partners), death, disability, and involuntary termination. Each of these situations must be handled in a different fashion. Many forms of employee termination involve employee payments (e.g., pension, severance pay). Some terminations can lead to lawsuits if not handled properly.

Complexity in HR management arises for many reasons, including the wide variety of employment opportunities within the organization, the diverse sources of qualified personnel, the terms of employment and compensation, and the variety of reasons for employee terminations. Furthermore, current trends in employment practices increase this complexity. Temporary employment, telecommuting, flex-time, and outsourcing all affect the way in which employees are hired and managed. Compensation arrangements such as stock options, and benefits such as maternity leave and in-house day care, affect the cost of labor. Also, changes in employees' attitudes about loyalty and work-life balance affect the relationship between employees and the company. Finally, employment regulations continue to evolve in areas such as employment discrimination, accommodation of disabilities, privacy, workplace harassment, and worker safety. Failure to adequately consider these regulations can leave an organization with an inadequate workforce or exposed to litigation and fines[x].

Information Flows

Processes use, produce, and transform information. The third panel of Box 6.1 "Process Map: Human Resource Management" lists the information needs and outputs of the human resource management process. The auditor needs to understand the nature and reliability of information flows within a process for three reasons:

1. *Information within a process will have a direct impact on the financial statements:* Information about transactions is initially captured within a process and then transformed through various internal systems. If that information is not reliable, the risk of financial statement misstatement is higher.

2. *Information provides the auditor assurance about the effectiveness of a process:* If key information is missing, untimely, or unreliable, actions taken within the process are less likely to be effective. For example, if a credit manager lacks access to external credit reports, the auditor could conclude that risks associated with credit approval are high.

3. *Information provides the auditor evidence about the significance of process risks:* By tracking key performance measures over time, the auditor (and management) can identify when a process may be inefficient or ineffective. For example, sales managers may monitor on-time delivery statistics to be warned when deliveries are slow, which could lead to a loss of customer goodwill. Such information may provide the auditor with an excellent source of analytical evidence concerning risks that may impact the audit.

Key information used in the human resource management process includes job descriptions and hiring authorizations, legal regulations, personnel data, payroll records, tax information, and training and work schedules. Auditing standards require that the auditor obtain a basic understanding of the flow of

[x]EXAMPLE

Many organizations outsource some of their noncritical processes and related personnel. Facilities maintenance, delivery and shipping, and transaction processing activities are areas where outsourcing has become common. The organization benefits by gaining more control over its human resources by turning what is often a fixed cost component of operations into a variable cost that can be easily adjusted as personnel needs change. The primary disadvantage is that the company gives up some control over personnel hiring and assignments that could lead to quality problems and additional tax or legal complexities. Customer call centers are a common example of outsourcing. When call center operations were first outsourced, they usually were turned over to a telecommunication service company who established a centralized site in the US. Subsequently, many outsourced call centers were also off-shored to places like India and the Philippines. A backlash from customers and politicians has caused some companies to return some of their call center operations to the US and using this return as a source of competitive advantage.

transaction data and related internal control so the auditor should consider the reliability of relevant information systems. Some information systems will connect directly to accounting and the financial statements (e.g., sales journal entries, inventory changes) whereas others are useful as a potential source of analytical evidence (e.g., customer ratings and satisfaction). Further, some systems operate independently from each other, whereas other systems are linked across processes or even companies. If an important information system is highly automated, it may be necessary for the auditor to use an information technology specialist to evaluate the design and reliability of the system.

Accounting Impact of Process Activities

The final element of the process map is identification of the accounting transactions and estimates that are affected by the activities within the process. This provides a direct link to the financial statements being examined. As a general rule, the more effective a process is on an overall basis, the more likely that transaction processing within the process will be accurate and reliable. Auditors classify process activities into two categories that affect accounting: (1) accounting transactions, and (2) accounting estimates. The first category may be broken down into routine and non-routine transactions. This classification is important because each transaction type may have different effects on the financial statements and may exhibit different risks of misstatement.

Routine Transactions: These transactions reflect events and circumstances that occur on a regular and systematic basis. Routine transactions drive most processes because they reflect normal activity that occurs on a daily basis. Most companies invest heavily in controls over routine transactions, and often use automated systems to process routine transactions in a highly reliable manner. Failure on the part of a company to effectively and efficiently control routine transactions likely will lead to process or even business failure. Also, because of the emphasis by management on routine transactions and the presence of automated controls, these transactions are harder to manipulate by individuals wishing to commit fraud. However, the auditor cannot ignore routine transactions because, cumulatively, they usually have a highly material effect on the financial statements. Furthermore, they are often the source of period-end adjustments that can be manipulated for fraudulent purposes.

The key transactions related to human resource management are identified in Box 6.1 "Process Map: Human Resource Management." Employees are usually paid on a periodic basis, e.g., every two weeks. The emphasis of payroll processing is on the periodic preparation of payroll and the proper classification of the expenditures. The detailed steps for processing payroll are indicated in Table 6.2. Hourly employees use physical or electronic *time cards* to check in and out of work to record hours worked. Hourly employees may also complete a *time report* or *job ticket* that describes exactly what they did during a given pay period. This information is needed to assure that payroll expenditures can be debited to the appropriate expense or asset account. Salaried employees do not need to complete time cards but are often asked to complete a periodic time report.

Table 6.2 *Summary of Payroll Activities*

PROCESS/Activity	Documents	Journals, Ledgers, and Records Used	Typical Journal Entry
Hiring: Recruiting new employees based on company needs and policies.	Employment application (internal)	Job descriptions and guidelines	
Personnel: Maintain accurate records on all personnel including pay rates, deduction authorization, tax information, and fitness reports.	Pay rate authorizations (internal) Tax forms (external) Deduction authorizations (external)	Employee master file	
Employee time reporting: Employees report time spent on job-related activities with frequency and level of detail dependent on nature of employment.	*Hourly workers:* Time cards (internal) Job tickets (internal) *Salaried workers:* Time report (internal)		
Payroll preparation: Payroll costs are computed and disbursements are prepared.	Check (internal) EFT authorization (internal)	Payroll register Labor distribution report	
Payroll distribution: Payroll disbursements are delivered to employees, by check, cash, or direct deposit.		*(Documents may be provided by service organization if payroll processing is outsourced)*	
General accounting: Payroll expenditures and liabilities are recorded in the appropriate accounts.	Journal entry ticket (internal) Tax forms (internal)	General ledger	Dr. Payroll Expenses Dr. Assets (inventory) Cr. Cash Cr. Accrued Liabilities

Payroll computations are based on hours worked, authorized wage and salary scales, and appropriate deductions. Gross payroll reflects total wages earned prior to deductions; net payroll reflects the amount actually paid to an employee after considering all mandatory and voluntary deductions. Employee **paychecks** or direct deposit documents are prepared, approved, and distributed to the employees.[3] Payroll information is summarized in a **payroll register**, including gross pay, taxes, deductions, and net pay, which becomes the basis for making entries to the general ledger and preparing payroll tax returns that are filed with various taxing authorities (e.g., local, state/provincial, and federal/national governments).

Non-routine Transactions: These transactions reflect events or circumstances that do not occur on a regular or frequent basis, and may involve complex calculations or require significant judgment on the part of management. Examples might include purchase of new facilities, introduction of new products, or negotiating a new union contract. Because these transactions are infrequent, information systems may not be structured to process them reliably. Furthermore, non-routine transactions often arise when a process does not operate as planned. For example, disposing of underperforming assets, discontinuing product lines, terminating contracts, or repossessing assets are usually non-routine events for an organization. However, these events are often associated

For a retail operation, sales returns are probably considered a relatively routine transaction and can be highly automated, even though such transactions are less common than the initial recording of sales. To compensate for the slightly less routine aspects of sales returns, many retailers may require that they be processed by supervisors rather than clerks, or processed at a special counter. In contrast, many industries have very few sales returns, so they would then constitute a non-routine transaction. Consider the builder of commercial aircraft —the idea of a sales return is unlikely. However, price adjustments for production deficiencies and delays might be a common transaction in such an environment.

with unforeseen developments that management might be tempted to underreport in the financial statements. Because of these conditions, the risks of error and misrepresentation are higher than for routine transactions. Determining whether a specific transaction is routine or non-routine requires judgment by the auditor[xi]. The key event of the human resource process is the completion of service by the employees. Each day, hour, and minute that an employee works adds to the amount of the company's liability to that employee. However, because payroll costs are usually recorded when employees are paid (i.e., on a periodic basis), a timing issue can arise when the end of a fiscal period does not coincide with the end of a pay period. This also applies to payroll taxes and other personnel expenses such as vacation time that accrue but may be paid much later. Examples of other non-routine transactions arising in human resource management include payments for employee termination, disability, or litigation.

Accounting Estimates: Accounting estimates involve judgment on the part of management and typically pervade the financial statements. Estimates are not transactions in the typical sense because they might not be associated with a specific event. However, estimates may be the most critical accounting aspect of a process because management bases the decision on how to account for estimates primarily on their opinions and knowledge relating to the underlying facts and events. The use of estimates is a powerful tool for managing earnings or bolstering the level of performance reported in the financial statements should management want the financial statements to reflect a specific outcome. In practice, it is hard to argue with a process manager who asserts that the current recorded level of an estimate is consistent with his extensive industry experience. However, most of the major accounting frauds of the twentieth century involved accounting estimates, highlighting to auditors the need to evaluate estimates very carefully.

The financial statements contain numerous estimates related to the realizability of asset values, the market value of investments, the present value of obligations, and the likelihood of loss contingencies. Such estimates present a challenge to the auditor because their ultimate resolution depends on uncertain future events. Lacking a crystal ball, the auditor must make a best guess about future outcomes and their impact on current financial statements. Further, the best source of information about the resolution of these events is the organization's management who have an unknown bias toward achieving a desired outcome. Examples of estimates related to human resource management include pension and post-retirement benefit accruals.

The risk of an estimate being misstated is directly affected by its complexity, the availability and reliability of data used to make the estimate, the nature of assumptions used, and the degree of uncertainty surrounding future events. Warranty costs on small appliances that have been manufactured for a long time without significant production changes will be relatively easy to estimate as long as the client accurately records actual warranty costs as they arise. This historical data can be extremely useful for supporting reasonable estimates of future warranty claims. In contrast, environmental liabilities arising from the clean-up of toxic land sites may be extremely difficult to estimate due to the long lead time of the clean-up process, uncertainty surrounding who pays and how much, the changing nature of clean-up technology, changing trends in regulatory assessment, and potentially biased input from management.

The auditor's objective is to test management assertions associated with estimates. Most of the evidence needed to evaluate accounting estimates is obtained during the review of key processes and related information flows. Typical audit procedures include analysis of significant business risks, inquiry about client procedures for dealing with estimates, analytical procedures applied directly to the results of the estimation process, and evidence obtained from other tests that may be pertinent to the reasonableness of estimates (e.g., evidence of obsolescence from observing the physical condition of inventory). For particularly difficult estimates, internal information may be supplemented with industry statistics or outside experts may be needed (e.g., actuaries, engineers). We will discuss the work required by the auditor in auditing estimates in more detail in Chapter 9.

Risk Assessment: Process Risks

One of the reasons an auditor prepares a process map is to provide a framework for analyzing the risks associated with a process. Many of the strategic risks discussed in Chapter 5 can have a direct impact on potential risks within individual processes. An economic recession (an external event) may cause customers to be slow in paying their bills, which directly relates to customer service. Problems with suppliers will have an impact on internal operations and procurement. In this section, we will discuss the types of risks that can arise within a process and how they might lead to significant residual risks that affect the audit.

The purpose of *internal threat analysis* is to assess the impact of process risks on the organization. There are three components to internal threat analysis: (1) risk identification, (2) risk response (e.g., controls), and (3) risk monitoring. Column 1 of Table 6.3 identifies numerous risks that might occur as part of human resource management. Process risks can emanate from many sources. For example, external developments in technology can have a direct impact on the technology of specific processes by making existing systems obsolete. Other process risks will be unique to individual processes, for example the risk of incorrectly processing loan payment transactions is primarily a financial management problem. Our focus in this chapter is to analyze the specific risks that arise in business processes. To facilitate our discussion, we will discuss the eight categories of internal risk identified in Table 6.4.

People Risks

Managerial Risk: Risk can occur when a process is not adequately managed or clear lines of authority and accountability are lacking. The efficiency and effectiveness of a process is dependent on a proper balance between manager responsibilities, competence, experience, and incentives. Managers who lack appropriate authority, proper training, or adequate experience are more likely to make mistakes. For example, managers lacking information

Table 6.3 *Risk Assessment: Human Resource Management*

Process Risks	Potential Audit Implications
PR1: Lack of personnel with appropriate skills.	• Expectations: High levels of process errors and related costs. • Viability: Risk of failure if critical skills missing. • Control environment: Lack of personnel may cause processes to be ineffective or segregation of duties to be bypassed.
PR2: Excess or unneeded personnel.	• Expectations: High overhead or administrative costs. • Audit risk: Proper allocation of excess labor costs, especially if related to production (standard costs).
PR3: Discriminatory employment practices.	• Audit risk: Contingent liabilities due to litigation. • Control environment: Attitudes of management and employees toward fellow employees may have implications for approach to financial reporting.
PR4: Excess costs of recruiting and hiring.	• Expectations: High overhead or administrative costs. • Audit risk: Cost allocation, especially related to production.
PR5: Errors in payroll authorizations (pay rates, taxes, time).	• Audit risk: Errors in payroll related transactions and accounts. • Control environment: Heightened control risk related to payroll transactions. • Client need: Improved procedures for payroll authorizations.
PR6: Errors in payroll processing.	• Audit risk: Errors in payroll related transactions and accounts. • Control environment: Heightened control risk related to payroll transactions. • Client need: Improved procedures for payroll processing.
PR7: Low employee morale.	• Expectations: Increased costs related to poor worker performance, e.g., direct labor or product defects. • Control environment: Disgruntled employees may be ineffective or act against interests of company.
PR8: Violations of employment laws.	• Audit risk: Contingent liabilities due to fines and penalties. • Control environment: May indicate attitudes toward regulation in general (including financial reporting). • Client need: Process improvement to assure compliance with labor laws.
PR9: Failure to provide adequate feedback or training for improvement.	• Control environment: Disgruntled employees may be ineffective or act against interests of company.
PR10: Unplanned loss of critical personnel or excessive turnover.	• Viability: Risk of failure if critical personnel depart. • Control environment: If losses are critical to financial reporting, there may be a pervasive effect on levels of control risk.

technology expertise may think that IT controls are reducing a risk when they are not effective at doing so. Performance incentives can create unforeseen problems if not properly aligned with the objectives of the process. Risk may also arise if there is a lack of procedures, policies, and decision limits within a process. For example, an organization may establish maximum credit limits that can be assigned by a credit manager or maximum price discounts that can be granted by a sales manager.

Ethics Risk: The auditor should examine a process for indications that there is a lack of integrity or ethical behavior by individuals. Given that people

Table 6.4 *Process Risks Types and Sources*

People Risks		
Managerial Risk	**Ethics Risk**	**Human Resource Risk**
Lines of authority	Management fraud	Competence
Performance incentives	Employee theft	Performance incentives
Institutional constraints	Illegal acts	Hiring and retention
Competence	Unethical behavior	Training and development
	Unauthorized actions	Required skills

Direct Process Risks	
Operational Risk	**Information Risk**
Quality of products	Reliability of information
Cost of processes	Quality of performance measurement
Cycle time	Timeliness of information
Efficiency	Relevance
Capacity usage	Completeness
Repairs and maintenance	Dissemination and reporting
Resource utilization and wastage	
Process failure	
Process interruption	

Indirect Process Risks		
Technology Risk	**Planning Risk**	**Regulatory Risk**
System reliability	Budgeting and planning	Labor laws
System adequacy	Incentives	Tax laws
System security	Adequacy of resources	Environmental laws
Process efficiency	Performance measurement	Health and safety regulations
System changes		Product licensing

bring their attitudes about ethical behavior with them from outside the organization, this risk follows from risks associated with social attitudes and the market for labor. The auditor should consider whether the company is alert to potential unethical behavior and whether it actively strives to avoid conflicts of interest and illegal actions by employees. The auditor's evaluation of the organization's control environment is an important predictor of whether individuals at the process level perceive that unethical behavior will be tolerated or even encouraged. The auditor should consider conditions that might cause otherwise honest individuals to behave in questionable ways.

Human Resource Risk: The effectiveness and efficiency of most processes will be dependent on the quality of staff personnel assigned to the activities of the process. The auditor should consider whether staff have the qualifications, competence, and training to adequately perform their duties. The quality of personnel is directly affected by conditions in the market for labor and is influenced by a company's approach to recruiting, compensation, training, and supervision. If any of those functions are performed poorly, the quality of a process may deteriorate because disgruntled employees can negatively impact a process. Although auditors are often uncomfortable judging individuals, the assessment of employee competence and attitudes is an important element of process risk assessment.

Direct Process Risks

Operational Risk: This risk category pertains to the execution of the basic activities within a process and encompasses the potentially wide range of things that can wrong within a process. Potential operational risks relate to:

- *Quality:* Is the process subject to unacceptable rates of defects, mistakes, or errors?
- *User satisfaction:* Are users of the process unhappy after the process is complete?
- *Cycle time:* Do processes take too long to execute?
- *Obsolescence/impairment:* Does the process depend on obsolete equipment, technology, or practices?
- *Shrinkage:* Is there excess waste in the process (e.g., time, materials)?
- *Capacity:* Does the process have too much or too little capacity for the work flow?
- *Process failure:* Are there excessive breakdowns or work stoppages in the process?
- *Process linkages:* Are connections/links to other processes (including external parties) subject to problems?

Operational risks tend to be unique to a specific process. However, many of these risks are dependent on the nature of other process risks, especially people risks. In fact, the visible manifestation of people risks may be in the form of operational risk. For example, if employees are not adequately trained, quality, cycle time, or customer satisfaction may deteriorate.

Information Risk: Numerous problems can arise in the absence of accurate and reliable information about a process. Reliable information is needed for decision making, to monitor process activity, and to evaluate performance. Of particular importance to the auditor is the reliability of transaction processing. Given that most accounting transactions are initially identified, captured, and measured during process activities, information risks may have a direct impact on the risk of material misstatements in financial reports. The reliability of information processing will depend on a number of factors, including the design of the system, the reporting structure, the dependence on information technology, reliance on external providers of information technology (software, hardware, and service bureaus), the accessibility of information, and control over changes to information processing.[4]

Indirect Process Risks

Regulatory Risk: Most organizations are subject to a wide variety of external regulations that impact different processes in an organization. Employment laws affect human resources; worker safety and environmental laws place boundaries on production practices; consumer protection laws may influence sales efforts; and securities regulators can dictate financial and accounting practices. The auditor should identify the forms of regulation that affect a process and assess the likelihood that the organization can comply. Lack of compliance with appropriate regulations opens the organization to fines and penalties, and may harm its reputation.

Technology Risk: Every process has elements of technology, and the role of IT in most processes is increasing rapidly. Technology risks can arise from the external environment, as when new advances render internal systems obsolete, or internally, as when research and development initiatives fail to produce desired results. The auditor should consider whether technology has been appropriately utilized to achieve the objectives of a process, including sufficient automated controls. The design and installation of new systems creates special challenges to an organization. Technology can affect a process in a number of ways:

- *Execution of a process:* The design of a process is often dictated by the technology available. For example, technology can affect manufacturing (e.g., robots can make welds, apply paint, or install parts in a car) and the execution of transactions (e.g., credit cards can be verified by "swiping" the card through a reader).

- *Information processing:* The manner in which information is captured and processed is dependent on technology. Manual entry of a sale into a cash register is different than scanning bar codes on merchandise. Enterprise resource planning systems allow companies to link data across processes and facilitate the integrated analysis of results for the entire organization.

- *Process monitoring:* The cost of monitoring a process is declining as the power of technology increases. Most cars now have a large number of different sensors for monitoring potential problems ranging from low fuel levels to whether a door is open. Production processes are no less amenable to electronic monitoring, which creates enormous potential for the auditor to assess the effectiveness and efficiency of processes in real time. A sensor in an automotive assembly line that detects that door installations are slightly misaligned helps the company detect a problem before it has resulted in a number of defective vehicles.

Planning Risk: Issues related to planning that can have a negative impact on a process include budgeting, scheduling, resource and cash needs, and financial reporting. In essence, planning risk reflects the possibility that resource allocations do not match the needs of specific processes. If plans and budgets are unreasonable or unrealistic, they can cause dysfunctional performance. For example, if production demands exceed process capacity, it is likely that quality problems will arise as the components of the process (e.g., equipment and labor) are pushed beyond their intended endurance levels. If excess attention is devoted to inappropriate performance measures, employees may focus on activities that are reflected in the performance measures at the expense of other important activities. Perhaps even more serious is when too much emphasis is placed on performance measures within a single business process at the expense of performance across business processes, leading to better process performance but poorer performance for the organization overall.

Assessing Process Risks

After developing a process map, the auditor then assesses the related process risks. Poorly trained, dishonest, or unmotivated personnel can have serious ramifications for the effectiveness and efficiency of the organization. Problems in human resource management may often be revealed by problems in other processes, and may be especially important in service organizations. Internal threat analysis for human resource management (Table 6.3) highlights ten representative—but incomplete—risks. Key risks pertain to hiring the appropriate labor force in a cost effective manner (*PR1, PR2, PR3, PR4*), managing the workforce for best results (*PR7, PR8, PR9, PR10*), and assuring accurate information processing related to payroll (*PR5, PR6*). Different organizations may have different risks. The last two are most significant to the audit because they directly affect financial reporting.

As a last step, the auditor then assesses the potential impact of each identified process risk in order to determine if any are likely to consitute a residual risk. Whether a risk needs to be controlled depends on how it affects the performance of the organization. For our analysis, let's assume that the company is a software company that is owned and managed by a small group of friends who dropped out of their university to start up the business. It has been generally successful and is rapidly growing and evolving in a very competitive environment. Within this context, the small sample of human resource risks is plotted in a risk map (Figure 6.3).

In the example, *PR10,* the risk of unplanned loss of key personnel, is considered the most significant risk. In different ways, *PR5* (risk of errors in payroll authorizations), *PR1* (lack of personnel with appropriate skills), and *PR9* (failure to provide training or feedback) are also very important risks.

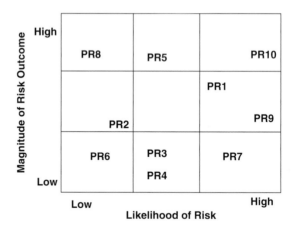

Figure 6.3 Assessment of Process Risks for Human Resource Management

Legend

PR1: Lack of personnel
PR2: Excess personnel
PR3: Employment discrimination
PR4: Excess recruiting costs
PR5: Errors in payroll authorizations
PR6: Errors in payroll processing
PR7: Poor morale
PR8: Illegal employment practices
PR9: Inadequate training
PR10: Loss of critical personnel

Risks *PR2, PR3, PR4,* and *PR6* are considered to be relatively insignificant unless subsequent performance indicates a rising problem. Finally, the remaining risks (*PR7, PR8*) could be significant under some conditions. The potential implications of the individual risks are summarized in Table 6.3 (second column). The relatively high level of significance for *PR10, PR5, PR1,* and *PR9* make them candidates to be residual risks so their implications take on an increased importance for the auditor.

Process Control Activities

After identifying process risks, an auditor will then consider how process controls might affect those risks. While a full discussion of the role of internal control in a GAAS Audit is the topic of the next chapter, we will introduce some basic process controls in this chapter. Recall that management can choose to accept, avoid, share, or reduce risks. Process control activities tend to focus on specific risks within a process, although one control activity may mitigate multiple risks. Continuing our analysis of human resources, column 2 of Table 6.5 indicates a number of process controls that might be used to control risks that were identified in Table 6.3. Control at the process level should reflect the organization's broader strategic decisions. For example, the control environment at the corporate level will manifest itself in attitudes toward careful performance of assignments, implementation of control procedures, and reporting relationships at the process level. Finally, monitoring procedures for the entire organization, such as the internal audit function, will also affect individual processes.

Table 6.5 *Internal Threat Analysis: Human Resource Management*

Process Risks	Controls Linked to Risks	Performance Measures
PR1: Lack of personnel with appropriate skills.	• Formal job descriptions for all positions. • Systematic approach to recruiting. • Monitor market and demographic conditions. • Establish strategic relationships with potential suppliers of labor (e.g., universities, schools, head hunters).	• Number of unfilled positions. • Time-to-fill vacant positions.
PR2: Excess or unneeded personnel.	• Planning and budgeting procedures. • Formal assessment of labor needs. • New positions approved by appropriate management. • Procedures for reassigning excess personnel to different functions.	• Employee chargeable time. • Employee down time. • Unassigned personnel.
PR3: Discriminatory employment practices.	• Establish and monitor hiring policies and procedures. • Interviews with those who turned down offered positions. • Exit interviews with employees leaving the company. • Establish communication channel for work force complaints.	• Labor force demographics. • Frequency of complaints from recruits. • Frequency of complaints from employees.

(Continued)

Table 6.5 *(Continued)*

Process Risks	Controls Linked to Risks	Performance Measures
PR4: Excess costs of recruiting and hiring.	• Establish budget for recruiting. • Monitor recruiting costs. • Appropriate approval of recruiting functions. • Appropriate approval of hiring bonuses and moving cost allocations.	• Cost per new hire. • Bonuses paid to new hires. • Moving costs per new hire. • Ratio of acceptances to offers.
PR5: Errors in payroll authorizations (pay rates, taxes, time).	• Obtain written authorizations for all payroll adjustments. • Changes in payroll authorizations are properly authorized. • Overtime approved in advance.	• Number of processing errors. • Dollar value of pay discrepancies. • Frequency of discrepancies in employment documents.
PR6: Errors in payroll processing.	• Maintain and update master payroll files on a timely basis. • Process payroll on a timely basis. • Use time cards to report time worked. • Use time reports to allocate labor costs. • Review all time cards, reports and payroll records. • Use prenumbered payroll documents in sequence. • File tax reports on a timely basis.	• Number of processing errors. • Number of exceptions caught by system. • Size of transaction adjustments
PR7: Low employee morale.	• Monitor employee satisfaction. • Belief systems (e.g., core values, mission statement). • Institute programs for improving morale (e.g., business casual dress codes, special functions, work-life balance programs).	• Employee absenteeism. • Employee satisfaction.
PR8: Violations of employment laws.	• Establish formal policies and procedures for hiring and work place behavior including acceptable internet use policies. • Establish appropriate privacy policies with respect to employee information. • Monitor work force behavior. • Establish communication channel for work force complaints. • Timely and effective response to complaints.	• Number of citations by enforcement agencies. • Percentage of labor force completing training on employment laws. • Frequency of employee complaints.
PR9: Failure to provide adequate feedback or training for improvement.	• Establish formal policies and procedures for employee evaluation. • Require employee signoff on evaluations. • Require management to perform evaluations as part of core duties. • Establish formal policies for employee training.	• Training hours per employee. • Frequency of employee evaluations. • Ratings of training programs. • Percent of employees receiving "poor" evaluations. • Timeliness of required evaluations.
PR10: Unplanned loss of critical personnel or excessive turnover.	• Monitor employee satisfaction. • Monitor and maintain competitive compensation and benefit packages. • Monitor and establish procedures for improving employee morale. • Conduct exit interviews with departing employees.	• Employee turnover rates. • Results from exit interviews. • Turnover rates for key personnel.

AUTHORITATIVE GUIDANCE & STANDARDS

The Sarbanes-Oxley Act requires all US SEC registered public companies to have an internal audit function that reports to the Audit Committee. The Act allows companies the option of outsourcing internal audit to other professional accounting firms, but precludes the firm that performs the external audit of the company from also performing internal audit services.

There are a number of common control activities that an organization can use to minimize process risks. However, each process is unique so a variety of control activities might be effective at preventing or reducing process risks. The auditor must assess the impact of controls when determining whether or not any of the process risks represent significant residual risks that may need additional attention. Furthermore, the existence and effectiveness of these controls may be relevant to the auditor's assessment of control risk related to misstatements in accounting information. There are four general types of process controls that may be relevant to our analysis:

1. Performance reviews.
2. Physical controls.
3. Segregation of duties.
4. Information systems and processing controls.

Performance Reviews

Management can compare actual performance within a process to a set of standards that may include prior results, forecasts, budgets, and external benchmarks, looking for signs that a process is failing to meet its objectives. The effectiveness of performance reviews depends on whether a manager has information available that will provide effective warning when risk conditions have changed. The auditor can use quantitative measures, called **performance indicators**, to assess whether process risks are an immediate threat. The challenge for the auditor is to determine which performance indicators the organization has available and then connect those indicators to specific risks. Column 3 of Table 6.5 indicates a number of performance indicators that might be used to assess risks arising from the human resource management. No single performance indicator provides a complete picture of a process, and many may pertain to multiple risks, so the auditor needs to examine multiple indicators to develop an overall perspective of the process[xii].

Most of the performance indicators are based on information that is generated internally but some may require external data. There are two potential problems the auditor can encounter when examining performance indicators. First, auditors have to rely on the organization to provide appropriate data. The auditor is therefore limited to the data maintained by the client. The lack of appropriate performance indicators provides an indication that management of a process may not be effective. Second, the auditor must have some assurance that the data is reliable. If data is

[xii]EXAMPLE

The risk of late or lost shipments during the sales and delivery process is an important consideration for most retailers. Sales managers will monitor statistics related to on-time delivery to determine if customers are receiving their shipments. Delayed or lost shipments tend to irritate customers, which may lead to a significant drop in customer satisfaction and lost customers. On-time delivery statistics provide an indication whether this particular risk is a problem for the organization.

unreliable, the auditor will have difficulty using performance data as a source of audit evidence.

Physical Controls

Limiting access to assets that are susceptible to defalcation and records that are subject to falsification is an important control. Most people know to keep cash secure, not to allow customers to roam around inventory storerooms, and to keep important documents and securities in a safe place. Locking doors and limiting access to restricted areas within an organization's facilities are highly effective methods for preventing unauthorized use of assets. Limiting access to documents and records is also important because many documents, when properly completed, provide access to assets. For example, assets may be misappropriated by presenting an authentic, but forged, check at a bank.

Most organizations now realize that two important but traditionally overlooked assets that need physical controls are people and information. For example, many businesses take expensive precautions to protect employees and customers, including hiring guards and limiting access to facilities through the use of complex entry controls (e.g., hologram-encoded passes, fingerprint scanners, metal detectors). Similarly, as hackers have become more sophisticated, companies have invested significantly in mechanisms to encrypt data and protect access from unauthorized users (e.g., firewalls). Limiting electronic access may be more important and difficult than physical access.

Segregation of Duties

Adequate segregation of duties within and across processes is extremely important and can significantly strengthen other control activities that are in place. In concept, the segregation of duties is relatively simple—individuals responsible for operational decisions, transaction authorization, maintaining custody of assets, and handling accounting records should not perform any of the other roles. However, determining if an organization has the proper segregation of duties can be difficult because potentially risky combinations of functions may not be easy to discern. Three key failures to segregate duties are:

1. *Failure to segregate asset custody from the accounting function:* Access to both assets and accounting records allows an individual to misappropriate assets and then hide the action by changing the accounting records.

2. *Failure to segregate transaction authorization from asset custody:* If a single individual can authorize improper transactions and get access to the related assets, it is possible to misappropriate assets and cover up the theft. A good example of this type of problem is in payroll: The person who authorizes the hiring of employees should not have access to payroll checks so as to avoid payments to fictitious employees.

3. *Failure to segregate operating functions from accounting functions:* If an operating unit maintains its own accounting records, the personnel

in that unit may have an incentive to bias the information, especially if current performance is poor.

As a result of concerns about segregation of duties, a typical organization creates separate functional groups to perform the accounting function (the controller), handle receipts and disbursements (the treasurer), provide independent monitoring (internal auditing), and design, implement, and maintain computer systems (IT department)[xiii].

Information Systems and Processing Controls

In technology-based system, further consideration should be given to segregation of duties within the IT function. The use of automated systems often creates ways to electronically obtain access to assets or to authorize transactions that could not be accomplished physically. Improper combinations of functions related to information systems can undermine otherwise good segregation of duties. In general, the following information systems activities should be handled separately:

- Systems analyst (responsible for general design of the system).
- Programmer (responsible for writing computer code and testing of the system).
- Computer operator (responsible for actual running of installed system).
- Trouble-shooter (responsible for addressing problems in the system).
- Data librarian (responsible for maintaining computerized files and records).
- Data control group (responsible for internal audit of all computerized functions).

As information systems of various types are employed in nearly all organizations, we now consider the role of information systems and process activity controls. These controls tend to be some of the most detail level controls that are examined by an auditor. An organization will have many policies and procedures in place to assure the proper authorization of activities and to verify the accuracy and completeness of transaction processing. There are two broad categories of processing controls: general controls and application controls.

General Controls

General controls pertain to the manner in which a process is designed and managed.[5] For example, general controls include defining steps and tasks within a process, authorizing decisions, implementing system changes, establishing processing schedules, updating system documentation, and assuring software and data integrity (i.e., file back-up procedures).

Organizations should maintain adequate up-to-date **procedures and systems documentation** either in manuals or on intranet web sites that describe how the activities and control procedures of a process are to be

[xiii]**EXAMPLE**

Have you ever wondered why when you take an unneeded purchase back to The Home Depot that you must line up at a separate department at the front of the store waiting for the one clerk authorized to accept returned goods when there are five cashiers standing nearby doing nothing? While cynically you might suggest this is a way to reduce returns, segregation of duties is also at least partially the blame. The cashier who accepts payments for tools and materials is not allowed to also authorize refunds and doing so is a firing offense. Why? Given the amount of cash the cashiers handle every day, it would be easy for them to authorize a refund for goods that were not really purchased and pocket the funds. Hence, a separate area with a separate cash register near a manager that is set up for refunds.

executed. The documentation should describe the tasks and responsibilities of key individuals in a process, that is, how things are to be done. Procedures documentation should also include a description of the flow of documents and records in the organization, a listing of reports and who receives them, and a chart of accounts. The **chart of accounts** lists and describes the acceptable ledger accounts to be used for recording transactions (a key component of a process map) and is useful for proper classification of transactions occurring with a process.

System documentation for key applications of information technology (IT) is an important form of general control because much of the system's operations are not directly observable by the organization's personnel or the auditor. Because the activities of the automated system are represented by code that may be difficult to decipher, verbal and visual (e.g., flowcharts) descriptions of the system are useful to the auditor. At a minimum, IT documentation should include the following:

- *Systems requirements:* A description of the purpose of the software and the required input and output.
- *Program documentation:* A description of the application logic, computer code, and reliability testing. A particularly important aspect is the description of the procedures for testing, authorizing, and instituting changes to the software.
- *Run instructions:* A description of how the software is to be executed including details on hardware and software configurations, operating schedules, and possible error conditions. Computer application should be capable of flagging input and processing errors and to produce a message (called an **edit listing**) that can be used by management to identify system weaknesses.
- *User instructions:* For mainframe applications, these instructions will primarily be a description of the output and who should receive it. In microcomputer applications, user instructions may be combined with elements of the run instructions.

Application Controls

Application controls pertain to the way in which individual tasks are performed and transactions are handled within a process. For example, procedures for verifying decision authorization and transaction accuracy are common application controls. An auditor will be particularly interested in three types of application controls: (1) **authorization procedures**, (2) **use of documents and records**, and (3) **independent verification procedures**.

Authorization Procedures: Control procedures should be established that provide assurance that only authorized activities are performed. Approval of individual transactions should be performed only by authorized personnel. Authorizations may be either general or specific. **General authorization** allows an individual to execute all tasks or transactions that meet certain criteria. For example, a payroll clerk may be allowed to process payroll deductions for hourly employees but pay rates are set by management.

Specific authorization should be required for any actions that are not subject to general authorization. For example, store clerks may be hired by a store manager based on general qualification criteria established by management (e.g., high school graduate or equivalent).

Use of Documents and Records: The proper design of documents and records is a very important element of internal control and helps assure the reliability of information within a process. The concepts of good document design apply equally to physical documents filled out by hand and to electronic documents that are viewed on a computer screen and completed with input from a keyboard. Documents should be designed so that all pertinent information is entered at the time that the document is completed (which should be when a transaction is being executed). The appropriate input can be specified by indicating what information is to be entered in a document—blank data fields would indicate missing information. Similarly, data entry fields on a computer screen can be used to provide prompts for the data to be entered.

Documents—paper or electronic—that represent transactions should be sequentially *pre-numbered* whenever their use is intended to be sequential (e.g., payroll checks). In that way, the sequence of documents that are actually used can be easily verified. Documents that are generated by the computer can be assigned numbers from a pre-established sequence to facilitate control over the order of transactions. Documents that are not necessarily used in sequence (e.g., employee time cards) can have identification numbers to facilitate cross-referencing to other documents and records.

Documents should be designed for ease of use. This is accomplished for on-line documents using specified data fields, pop-up options, and help screens that are embedded in the software. Documents should provide an indication of what types of authorization are needed for an action to occur or a transaction to be executed. An obvious example of this is a check that requires two signatures and thus has two signature lines. Recent advances in electronic transaction processing allow such authorizations to be performed on-line and in real time.

An important distinction should be made between boundary documents and processing documents. *Boundary documents* are those that are prepared upon execution of a transaction with an external party and provide evidence that a transaction has occurred. *Processing documents* assist in tracking the internal flow of resources and information within the accounting system. To illustrate, consider payroll processing that occurs as part of human resource management. *Time cards* are the boundary document that demonstrates that an employee has worked a certain number of hours and is owed wages. *Payroll checks* are the boundary documents that demonstrate settlement of payables to employees. *Job tickets* are used to keep track of what employees do with their time and facilitate recording the cost of labor in an appropriate expense or asset account.

Independent Verification Procedures: A common method for maintaining reliable information in a system is through independent verification. One type of verification involves direct examination of individual transactions for accuracy or proper approval. For example, a store manager can review time cards for completeness and accuracy. In automated systems, the conversion of data to machine-readable form is a potential problem. Scanning technology has greatly reduced the risk of error during data entry, but manual entry is still common for non-routine tasks. To reduce the risk of errors, the same data may be input twice and then compared. If the two entries do not agree, the item entered will be flagged as an error. This process is referred to as **key verification**. For example, changing the password for accessing computer files (e.g., the PIN code for ATM machines) usually requires entering the new password twice to make sure that the code that is entered is the one intended by the user.

Check digits are another type of verification often used for account codes, parts numbers, or customer accounts. Check digits involve embedding special code digits that represent a mathematical combination of the other digits in an identification number.[6] For example, an employee number may be defined to be eight digits long with the first six digits indicating the employee identification and the last two being the check digits. The two check digits could be the simple sum of the other six digits or may be derived using a more complex formula. For example, assume the first six digits of Mr. Smith's identification number are 983425. The check digits 31 (9+8+3+4+2+5) could be added to form an eight-digit code (i.e., 98342531). The presence of the check digits provides a mechanism for verifying the accuracy of the customer number that is entered for a transaction.

A final type of independent verification involves comparing and **reconciling data** that should be the same but is taken from two different sources. This type of comparison can be made between internal records and external data sources or between two or more internal data sources. Due to the nature of most accounting systems, the same data often appears in more than one set of records. For example, employees are listed alphabetically in a payroll register while payroll checks are listed by check number in a check register. To verify that the data is included properly in both places, total payroll from the payroll register can be reconciled with the payments to employees in the check register. Payments can also be reconciled with the costs charged to specific asset and expense accounts.

Batch controls are used to test sequential processing of data. Typically, a large number of similar transactions are combined and processed as a group. For example, all pay checks issued on a single day could form a batch. The batch is represented by one or more **control totals** that reflect the summation of a common element in the batch.[7] For payroll, the control total could be the total hours worked, the number of disbursements made, the total cash disbursed, the total payroll deductions, etc. Once the control total is established, it can be compared to subsequent totals that are computed as the group is processed. For example, the control total for payroll could be compared with the credit to the cash account to verify that all payments have been recorded. If any of these comparisons revealed a discrepancy, accounting personnel could investigate the cause and make needed adjustments.

Process Controls: Human Resource Management

The accounting implications of human resource management range from basic payroll processing to much more complicated issues related to retirement benefits and incentive compensation. Examples of process risks related to human resource management are presented in the first column of Table 6.5. These risks are intended to be representative rather than comprehensive. As previously discussed, key risks pertain to hiring the appropriate labor force in a cost effective manner (*PR1, PR2, PR3, PR4*), managing the work force for best results (*PR7, PR8, PR9, PR10*), and assuring accurate information processing related to payroll (*PR5, PR6*). Controls that are relevant to human resource management include:

- Establishing authorization and monitoring procedures related to employee hiring, compensation, utilization, raises/promotion, and appropriate behavior.

- Establishing codes of conduct: Management should formally establish core values and a code of conduct, invest sufficient resources to ensure that employees are familiar with them, and punish violators when appropriate.

- Performance reviews or monitoring controls: Management should actively monitor labor market conditions, recruiting and training performance, regulatory compliance, personnel needs and labor costs, and employee morale and workloads.

- Segregation of duties: Incompatible functions in personnel payroll include authorization of new positions and hiring, employee supervision and evaluation, payroll processing and payroll authorization.

- Processing controls: Authorization should be required for creating a position, selecting the person to fill the position, establishing the rate of pay, assigning work schedules (including whether there is paid overtime or not), determining appropriate mandatory and voluntary deductions, and generating payroll checks.

- Physical controls: Physical controls primarily pertain to the accessibility of facilities to personnel and protecting personnel and payroll accounting records.

Of particular importance to the auditor are internal controls over financial reporting that are embedded in the process. Authorizations of employee activities, preparation of paperwork, maintenance of accurate records, reliable processing of payroll related costs and expenditures, and proper handling of payroll taxes and deductions are all important to the auditor because of their direct link to the financial statements. Controls that relate to the valuation of long-term employment obligations (e.g., pensions, health care, and other post-retirement benefits) are also very important, as are controls that minimize potential contingent liabilities due to discrimination, harassment, or wrongful termination. Once management has decided how to respond to identified risks, it also needs to identify performance indicators that measure the significance of each risk. Key indicators can include employee costs (wages, benefits, support, travel, termination) and transaction processing (error rates, processing costs, errors in authorizations), hiring (recruiting costs, unfilled positions), employee utilization (down time, overtime, training, absenteeism), and employee attitudes (morale, turnover).

Control Effectiveness and Residual Risks

The auditor develops a process map and assesses internal threats for the purpose of assessing residual risks that are likely to have a significant impact on the conduct of the audit. Consequently, the risk map for human resource management in Figure 6.3 needs to be updated to reflect internal controls. Consider the following additional facts: (1) the company is very active in monitoring competitors and labor markets and is quite successful at attracting talented employees, (2) the company has excellent employee training and incentive programs, (3) the company uses an outside service organization to process its payroll, and all payments are made electronically, (4) most employees are salaried, and (5) the company has a legal firm periodically review its hiring, promotion, and termination policies and procedures.[8]

If the auditor considers the effect of these management responses on the identified risks, he or she might conclude that some individual risks should shift downward on the risk map. Specifically, the auditor might be able to downgrade *PR1* due to the recruiting experience of the firm, *PR8* due to the legal review, and *PR9* due to an evaluation of the company's training practices. These conclusions are documented in Figure 6.4. However, any such shifts would necessitate that the auditor obtain evidence that the identified control responses are effective.

The auditor should also consider evidence indicating heightened residual risk. Assume that in the course of discussions with client personnel, it is revealed that there is no systematic approach to promotions and pay raises. Employees are often promoted and given hefty bonuses or raises on the whim of one or two of the members of the management team. Paperwork for these actions is often ignored, delayed, or lost. Because changes in pay rates are initiated by the company, they cannot be processed by the outside service center without appropriate supporting documentation; this slipshod approach suggests that there is a significant risk of errors in payroll authorization. These problems would justify maintaining *PR5* at a high level.

As part of the process review, the auditor would also look at the key performance indicators available. Assume the following for our illustration: (1) there are few processing exceptions reported by the outside service center, (2) recruiting costs per new employee are in line with industry levels, (3) employee morale consistently ranks high, (4) open or new positions are filled quickly, (5) training hours per employee exceed the industry average by 10 percent, and (6) employee turnover is higher than the industry and has increased in the past year.

Some of these indicators support the auditor's conclusions about some of the risks documented in Figure 6.4, notably, the downgrading of *PR1* (positions fill quickly) and *PR9* (adequate training occurs). Furthermore, the performance

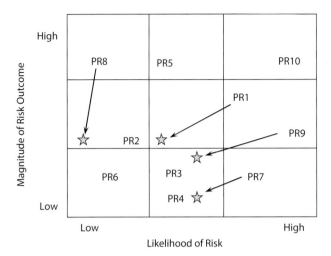

PR1: Lack of personnel
PR2: Excess personnel
PR3: Employment discrimination
PR4: Excess recruiting costs
PR5: Errors in payroll authorizations
PR6: Errors in payroll processing
PR7: Poor morale
PR8: Illegal employment practices
PR9: Inadequate training
PR10: Loss of critical personnel

Figure 6.4 *Effect of Controls and Performance Indicators on Inherent Risks for Human Resource Management*

measures provide evidence to support a downgrade of *PR7* since employee morale is high. However, the increase in employee turnover is a concern and suggests that *PR10* should continue to be considered a potential residual risk. This information will eventually be used to assess audit risks related to human resources and associated financial statement accounts that will influence the nature and extent of audit testing to be conducted by an auditor.

AUTHORITATIVE GUIDANCE & STANDARDS

ISA 315 and AS 2110 require audit teams to have a discussion regarding potential for material misstatements in the financial statements. By completing a risk map that illustrates inherent risks, controls, and residual risks, audit teams would be in a good position to discuss the risk of material misstatement, particularly when comparing residual risks across all business processes being analyzed.

Summary and Conclusion

The purpose of this chapter was to introduce business processes, their related accounting transactions and estimates, and to further develop our approach to risk assessment, this time with a focus on internal process risks. Following our top-down audit approach, we view the internal environment of the business through the framework of a value chain. We described a value chain as a means for identifying audit-sensitive process and showed how various elements of the value chain related to financial statement accounts and transactions. The business processes within the value chain are designed to deliver value to the customer as well as to respond to specific pressures or threats from the external environment. We linked the strategic risk assessments discussed in the previous chapter to explicit business processes that can be impacted by them. These risk assessments are useful for identifying and assessing risks and the processes put in place in response to those risks. Our example based on human resource management process showed both how strategic risks affected it as well as identifying specific process risks and their implications for the audit. We document conclusions in a risk map, indicating risks that can be downgraded due to the existence of effective process controls related to specific risks. The conclusion that risks *PR5* and *PR10* are significant residual risks for human resource management has implications for the conduct of the remainder of the audit. There will probably be other residual risks arising in other processes. We defer further discussion of what the auditor does when a significant residual risk has been identified until Chapter 10, and first turn our attention to a more detailed discussion of internal control over financial reporting using the processes we identified as audit-sensitive to be the ones that internal controls are vital for and need to be tested for effectiveness (Chapter 7).

Bibliography of Related Literature

Research

Armour, M. 2000. Internal Control: Governance Framework and Business Risk Assessment at Reed Elsevier. *Auditing: A Journal of Practice & Theory*. 19(Supplement): 75–82.

Beasley, M. S., J. V. Carcello, and D. R. Hermanson. 1999. *Fraudulent Financial Reporting: 1987–1997 An Analysis of US Public Companies*. Jersey City, NJ: Committee of Sponsoring Organizations of the Treadway Commission.

Farrell, J. 2004. Internal Controls and Managing Enterprise-Wide Risks. *The CPA Journal*. 74(8): 11–12.

Porter, Michael. 1985. *Competitive Advantage: Creating and Sustaining Superior Performance*. New York: The Free Press.

Simons, R. 1992. The Strategy of Control. *CA Magazine*, March, 44–46.

Spira, L. and M. Page. 2003. Risk Management: The Invention of Internal Control and the Changing Role of the Internal Audit. *Accounting, Auditing & Accountability Journal*. 16(4): 640–661.

Auditing Standards

IAASB *International Standards on Auditing (ISA)* No. 315, "Identifying and Assessing the Risks of Material Misstatement through Understanding the Entity and Its Environment."

IFAC. International Auditing and Assurance Standards Board (IAASB). 2015. *Handbook of International Quality Control, Audit, Review, Other Assurance, and Related Services Pronouncements.* New York: International Federation of Accountants.

PCAOB. *Auditing Standard* 2201 (formerly No. 5), "An Audit of Internal Control over Financial Reporting that is Integrated with An Audit of Financial Statements."

PCAOB. *Auditing Standard* 2110 (formerly No. 12), "Identifying and Assessing the Risks of Material Misstatement."

SOX Sarbanes-Oxley Act - Library of Congress. 2002. House Resolution Number 3763, An Act to protect investors by improving the accuracy and reliability of corporate disclosures made pursuant to the securities laws, and for other purposes (*The Sarbanes-Oxley Act of 2002*). www.libraryofcongress. gov.

Notes

1   This approach to understanding how accounting transactions and estimates originate contrasts with many audit texts that focus on the accounting information system almost exclusively ignoring the important link of business activities to the portrayal of those activities in the financial statements.

2   Porter, Michael. 1985. *Competitive Advantage: Creating and Sustaining Superior Performance.* New York: The Free Press.

3   Direct deposit of payroll into employee bank accounts is becoming more common. In a direct deposit system, paper checks are not needed and payroll distribution is performed electronically. However, employees usually receive a pay advice summarizing the gross pay and deductions used to compute net pay deposited to the employee's bank account.

4   A service bureau is an outside organization that provides computing services to other companies, alleviating the need for the companies to maintain their own computing resources. Payroll is probably the most frequently outsourced computing service. Such services are provided by companies that specialize in computing services, and often by banks.

5   The concept of "general controls" was first developed in the context of computerized information systems so many of the examples directly apply to risks associated with computerization of accounting processes. However, the term general controls can be interpreted in a much broader manner and is used in this book to refer to a specific type of control activity occurring within a business process, regardless of whether the actions or steps being addressed relate to computerized information systems.

6   The specification of check digits must be done with care in order to assure that the check digits are unique. Simple summation is not usually the best technique because digits can be transposed—a common mistake—and yield the same check digit, e.g., the computer would accept 98435231 as correct even though 98342531 is the correct code. One way to overcome this problem is to multiply each digit by a unique factor and then add. For

example, 983425 could yield check digits of 90 (1*9 + 2*8 + 3*3 + 4*4 + 5*2 + 6*5).

7   Control totals do not need to be meaningful on their own. Artificial control totals are referred to as hash totals and are useful for verifying account numbers or other identification numbers. For example, a hash total of customer numbers can be computed for all sales transactions in a batch. Then, when the sales are posted to the accounts receivable ledger, a second total of the account numbers posted can be computed. The second total should agree with the control total if the posting process has been performed correctly even though the hash totals do not have any meaning themselves.

8   Employers must comply with numerous state/provincial and national/federal laws applicable to hiring personnel and in some countries local level regulations (e.g., anti-discrimination laws). Auditors must be alert to possible non-compliance with such laws because of the significant penalties and contingent losses that may be imposed on the organization.

CHAPTER 7

Risk Mitigation and the Audit

Internal Control over Financial Reporting in a GAAS Audit

Outline

Learning Goals for this Chapter

1. To define internal control over financial reporting and its components.
2. To relate internal control over financial reporting to process controls.
3. To review the basic financial reporting process.
4. To describe how the elements of internal control fit into the financial reporting process.
5. To understand the application of the auditor's assessment of control risk to evaluating ICOFR.
6. To carry out control risk assessments.
7. To understand how to document internal controls over financial reporting.

Introduction

In Chapter 6 we introduced the basic approach for evaluating risks associated with audit-sensitive business processes. We discussed that a key component of process analysis is the evaluation of internal control activities that mitigate the risks within a process, especially controls over accounting transactions and estimates. This chapter discusses internal controls in more detail and specifically focuses on internal controls designed to reduce the risk of errors in the financial reporting process (see Figure 7.1). More specifically, this chapter deals with **internal controls over financial reporting (ICOFR)** found in business processes that provide reasonable assurance that the financial statements are fairly presented. In this chapter, we consider ICOFR in the context of a GAAS Audit, and extend our discussion of ICOFR to an Integrated Audit in the next chapter.

Much of the auditor's analysis of controls focuses on the reliability of information generated within a business process. Much of the information from a process will eventually be included in the financial statements. Linking the auditor's conclusions about risks derived from process analysis to the risk of misstatement in the financial statements necessitates that the auditor focus on the controls directly related to financial statement assertions. However, if the economic context and business purpose of a transaction is not understood, auditors may fixate on whether the transaction meets the precise rules of GAAP but miss the real implications for the financial statements[i].

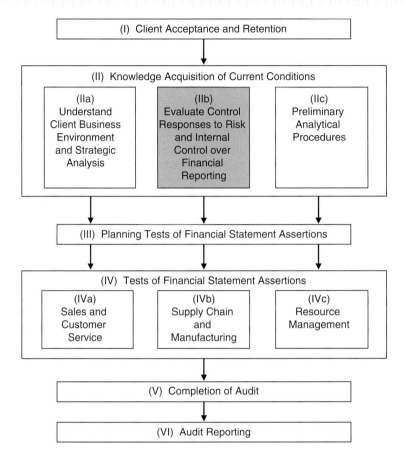

Figure 7.1 An Overview of the Audit Process for a Financial Statement Audit

Using Internal Control to Mitigate Risk

We gave a number of examples of internal controls as applied to the human resource process in the prior chapter. We will now expand and generalize our discussion of internal control. Management has to balance the significance of a risk against the cost of implementing a control response unless required by regulation (e.g., pollution controls). The company can either choose to accept or avoid the risk (if possible) when the cost of control is prohibitive. If cost-effective controls are available, management will choose techniques to reduce the risk or share the risk through insurance or strategic alliances.

AUTHORITATIVE GUIDANCE & STANDARDS

The description of internal control, including its components, used in this chapter are based on ISA 315 **Identifying and Assessing the Risks of Material Misstatement through Understanding the Entity and Its Environment,** *which draws on concepts from COSO's* **Internal Control: An Integrated Framework** *even if not always the same precise wording. ISA 315, in the Applications and Other Explanatory Material section and in Appendix 1, provides a high level summary of the COSO internal control* *framework based on the CPCP 1992 version. COSO has developed a new version of the framework released in 2013. The material presented in this chapter is consistent across the two versions. In the next chapter we will present material that considers in more depth COSO's 2013 framework. Whether ISA 315 is revised to reflect the nuances of the updated COSO framework is not known at this time. It should be noted by US readers that for all audits other than public company audits, the AICPA's Auditing Standards Board has adopted, with minor modification, the ISA 315 control requirements.*

Management's Fundamental Responsibility for Internal Control

Management has a fundamental responsibility to establish internal control over the operational and reporting activities of the company. We first provide a technical definition of internal control and then discuss what an internal control system looks like.

Internal Control Defined

Control in the broadest sense "comprises those elements of an organization (including its resources, systems, processes, culture, structure, and tasks) that, taken together, support people in the achievement of the organizations objectives."[1] Internal controls should be designed to provide reasonable assurance that the organization's objectives are being met. There are three broad objectives of any system of internal control:

1. To improve the effectiveness of management decision making and the efficiency of business processes.
2. To increase the reliability of information (especially financial reporting).
3. To foster compliance with laws, regulations, and contractual obligations.

An organization may use different types of internal control for achieving each of the three objectives—it is the auditor's responsibility to obtain a basic understanding of the controls being used and how they might affect the audit.

There are a number of important attributes of internal control that should be emphasized. First, internal control is a process, meaning it is something the organization does on an ongoing basis. Situations, people, transactions, and risks change, suggesting that internal control monitoring needs to be a continuous activity. Second, internal control is part of management's responsibilities under direction of Board of Directors, and failure to assess risk and design effective controls are deficiencies that suggest ineffective management and, potentially, ineffective board governance. Third, internal controls have inherent limitations that prevent them from eliminating all risks. For example, employees make mistakes, senior management may bypass or override controls, and individuals may collude to commit fraud. Because some problems may not be prevented or detected by controls, the goal of internal control is to provide *reasonable* protection against risks. Internal controls are directly linked to the organization's objectives. Given that a risk is any condition that can cause the organization to not achieve its objectives, internal control can be considered the antidote to risk (i.e., activities that reduce the potential for negative outcomes from risk and increase the ability of the organization to achieve its objectives[(ii)]).

Components of Internal Control

The *Internal Control-Integrated Framework* developed by COSO in 1992 provides a convenient model for designing a well-designed control system. In a GAAS Audit there is no requirement that management adopt such a model to evaluate their own internal controls but for audit purposes the auditor has to have a systematic means to determine and document the degree of control risk associated with the internal controls that management has in place. Hence, the COSO framework provides a convenient means to summarize the overall components of an effective control system. Further, as we will see in Chapter 8, the COSO Framework is integral to nearly all Integrated Audits.

Figure 7.2 summarizes the five components of internal control as defined by COSO: (1) control environment, (2) risk assessment procedures, (3) control activities, (4) monitoring activities, and (5) information and communication. Each element is important for effective risk management. A complete understanding of internal control often provides assurance to the auditor that many risks have been effectively reduced. Control environment, risk assessment, and general monitoring activities were briefly discussed as part of the overall strategic planning of the organization in Chapter 5.

Control Environment: The control environment is commonly referred to as the organization's **_tone at the top_**, which refers to the organization's integrity, attitudes towards ethical dealings and general competence. Senior management usually sets the tone at the top. The control environment

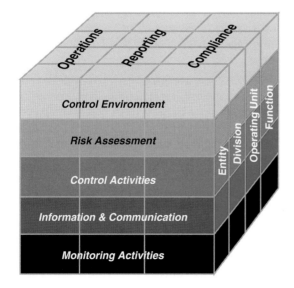

Figure 7.2 COSO'S 2013 Internal Control—Integrated Framework Used as Basis for Addressing Internal Control over Financial Reporting

Source: *Internal Control—Integrated Framework, Committee of Sponsoring Organizations of the Treadway Commission.* 2013, AICPA, Jersey City, NJ

(iii)EXAMPLE

*A number of industries, including software, tobacco, and consumer products, are famous for a sales practice called "**channel stuffing**." Essentially, channel stuffing involves shipping a large volume of merchandise to regular customers near the end of the fiscal year, even if it has not been ordered or requested. These shipments are recorded as sales in the fourth quarter, ensuring that management meets its performance goals. The amount of merchandise that is "stuffed" into the distribution channel will depend on the level of sales needed to reach the sales target. Unfortunately, such shipments may not meet the definition of a sale according to GAAP because much of the merchandise will be returned for credit, often after the end of the audit. The practice reveals a weakness in the control environment. Furthermore, the practice may actually harm the company because the merchandise may have a limited shelf life (e.g., food products) and not be salable upon return.*

is affected by the way in which management grants authority and assigns responsibility because this will have an impact on how decisions are made and the possibility that individuals can take unilateral actions that negatively affect the organization. Without a solid control environment the other components of control are unlikely to be effective. The control environment often is described as the most important element of internal control because of its apparent role in a vast majority of material frauds. For example, a study examining US accounting frauds over a ten-year period showed that 84 percent of all frauds involved the CEO, CFO, or both, emphasizing the importance of strong ethical managers in the top positions setting that tone.[2]

The most important aspects of the control environment are management's attitudes and incentives. If management is unconcerned about policies and procedures that effectively mitigate risks, control risk in the audit will probably be very high no matter how good other elements of internal control appear to be. For example, if management is lackadaisical about enforcing controls, lower-level personnel are unlikely to adhere to a company's policies and procedures.

Management's incentives may also shed light on the control environment. If management is evaluated and rewarded on a contingent basis, individual managers may be hesitant to comply with controls that have a negative impact on the evaluation of their performance. For example, if management is to receive a bonus based on sales volume, they may be less willing to deny credit to risky customers[(iii)].

A number of organizational factors provide indications of the effectiveness of the control environment. Clear lines of authority, responsibility, and performance evaluation are usually indicative of an effective control environment. Management's use of effective monitoring techniques such as budgets, periodic performance reports, and variance analyses are also indicative of a good control environment. Other factors that are important include the existence of a competent and independent internal audit department, and clearly stated and documented personnel policies (e.g., hiring and firing, training, performance evaluation, job descriptions and requirements). A common element of the control environment of public companies is the regular meeting of the Board of Directors and the related Audit Committee.

Auditors can also look at outside influences and constraints imposed on the organization that may affect the control environment. External requirements often cause management to be particularly observant about the policies and procedures in certain areas of their operations. For example, a bank is subject to strict accounting and reporting requirements imposed by government regulatory authorities. As a result, information systems in banks are highly sophisticated and reliable. This does not mean that risk is low in all areas, however, as evidenced by the problems with bad loans that banks, especially in western Canada and the US, experienced in the 1980s and the mortgage loan saga in 2006–9 in the US. As another example, pharmaceutical companies must operate under very strict inventory control regulations to ensure product safety. This may indicate to the auditor that risks related to inventory are relatively low; however, strong controls in one area do not necessarily translate to a good control environment for other risks the company faces.

Risk Assessment: Management should put in place a set of procedures whose purpose is to identify, analyze, and manage risks identified in the firm's environment (Chapter 5) and its business processes (Chapter 6). Identifying a risk that is likely to affect an organization is the critical first step to reducing or managing the risk—a risk that is unknown cannot be controlled. Consequently, it is important for management and the auditor to continually scan the environment for new risks or changing conditions that could increase risk. Common causes of increased risk include new information systems, employee turnover, changes in product lines or operating systems, or corporate restructuring. Significant and rapid changes in an organization or its environment are particularly troublesome because risks arise quickly in such an environment. Furthermore, a company that is experiencing high growth may find that its information and monitoring systems are inadequate for coping with new conditions. Once risks are identified, management should assess the likelihood of their occurrence and the severity of any negative effects that may be experienced.

Risk assessment is an area of internal control that has not received a great deal of attention relative to other elements of internal control. However, this element is critical for an organization as a necessary condition for identifying appropriate risk responses. To help organizations better understand the critical nature of risk assessment, COSO expanded this element greatly when drafting *Enterprise Risk Management—Integrated Framework*. Under the ERM framework, "risk assessment" is considered to consist of four elements: objective setting, event identification, risk assessment, and risk response.

When evaluating an organization's effectiveness at risk assessment, that is, deciding which risks to include and how to determine their significance, auditors should carefully consider each of the four components of risk assessment as they specifically relate to financial reporting:

1. What are the objectives of the process that have financial reporting implications?
2. What risk events could lead to a failure to achieve those objectives?
3. What is the likely impact of those risks?
4. What response has management taken (i.e., accept, avoid, reduce, or share) to address the risks?

By considering the risk assessment process, auditors are in a much better position to understand how risks may impact the financial statements and when material misstatements are likely to occur.

Control Activities: Management must first assess whether controlling a risk has a net benefit to the organization. If management believes that it is cost effective to respond to a risk, then control activities are the actual procedures that are performed to reduce the likelihood or potential impact of the risk in question. There are many types of controls that an organization can use. The design and execution of a control activity is affected by numerous considerations, including the level of personnel exercising control, the extent of automation built into the activity (e.g., manual versus computerized),

Financial institutions that maintain and trade marketable securities, such as bonds, equities, or derivatives, often specify exposure limits for different categories of investments. A bank may wish to hold fewer bonds denominated in Mexican pesos than it would for bonds denominated in Japanese yen. The exposure limits (also known as tolerable risk limits) are a form of general authorization and investment levels that exceed the limits for any given category would be identified and referred to appropriate management for rectification. The ability to monitor actual investment levels across many categories in a highly dynamic trading environment requires continuous real-time information about the financial positions of the firm and the related exposure to foreign currency fluctuations.

the information system in place, and the subjectivity of the risk condition being monitored. Control activities can serve a preventive role, a detective role, or both. A preventive control primarily reduces the likelihood that a risk will occur in the first place therefore reduces the likelihood of a material misstatement. A detective control leads to the discovery of the risk occurring early enough to limit the impact of the risk therefore reducing the amount of any misstatement.

Information and Communication: Internal control can rarely be effective unless an organization has adequate information for monitoring potential risks on a timely basis. Thus the fourth component of internal control is communication, which means that important information is identified, captured and made available to the appropriate persons in the organization. Effective communication is critical to high-quality internal control to ensure that all parties clearly understand their role in the system, and that problems are brought to the attention of the proper level of the organization for corrective action. Information must flow throughout the organization if control is to be effective. Information needs to flow *up* so that management can respond to current conditions. Information must also flow *down* so that staff and employees are aware of the policies and decisions that may affect their individual activities. Finally, information needs to flow horizontally (i.e., *across* functional departments) so that interconnected processes can function effectively and events and transactions can be processed smoothly(iv).

Monitoring: The final component of internal control is monitoring, the process whereby the organization tracks the effectiveness of internal control. Monitoring activities are designed to provide information to management about potential and actual breakdowns in the control system that could allow risks to become serious problems. Normal management and supervisory activities may be considered a form of monitoring, such as when management checks with subordinates to see how things are going. Monitoring can also be a specific activity assigned to a group within the organization. In many organizations, the internal audit department is responsible for monitoring the quality of internal control. Monitoring activities can be performed on an ongoing basis, often using technology to provide a continuous check on information processing. In other situations, monitoring can be based on periodic evaluations of performance over a period of time.

Levels of Control Activity

As noted in earlier chapters, internal control can be exercised at either a management or process level. As discussed in Chapter 5, ***management controls,*** are the activities undertaken by senior management to mitigate strategic risks to the organization, and to promote the effectiveness of decision making and the efficiency of business activities. In general, management controls help to determine the design, implementation, and monitoring of the other components of internal control and include:

- Communicating a belief system (including business objectives) throughout the organization.

- Setting strategic boundaries (i.e., the organization's risk appetite including activities that an organization will not pursue).

- Establishing and enforcing boundaries of behavior (e.g., through formal codes of conduct and acceptable business practices such as tolerable risk limits being enforced).

- Establishing lines of authority and accountability.

- Implementing and executing an enterprise risk management framework to identify, assess, address, communicate, and monitor business risks.

- Allocating resources through the design and execution of business processes.

- Forming strategic alliances to manage strategic risks[(v)].

Process controls refer to the control activities that are performed as part of the various processes within the organization. Process controls are usually performed by staff employees and low-level management but may not be effective if related management controls are not effective. Process controls are generally focused on internal risks within processes and reflect the formal policies and procedures defined by senior management. Also, process controls deal with the reliability of accounting information and compliance with rules and regulations. Traditionally, auditors have examined internal controls over the financial reporting process at this level. However, for greater effectiveness and efficiency, auditors increasingly consider higher level controls that help mitigate a specific risk[(vi)].

AUTHORITATIVE GUIDANCE & STANDARDS

Control activities are described in ISA 315. ISA 315 describes control activities as those related to authorization, performance reviews, information processing, physical controls, and segregation of duties.

Internal Control and Financial Reporting in a GAAS Audit

Internal control over financial reporting may involve control activities employed at multiple levels within an organization including all of the following:

- *Management controls* that relate to selecting accounting personnel, planning the installation of information/accounting systems, authorizing access to journals, and specifying the nature and timing of acceptable transactions.

- *Business process controls* that relate to authorizing specific transactions and capturing information at the point that a transaction occurs (e.g., linking the invoicing system to the sales journal).

- *Monitoring controls* that provide periodic performance reports to process owners and can lead to managerial intervention when problems occur.

- *Financial reporting controls* that relate to estimating accruals, making adjusting entries, and preparing disclosures and reports.

[(v)]**EXAMPLE**

Establishing and enforcing a policy on conflicts of interest for managerial personnel is a common management control. Such a policy is important for minimizing the self-serving behavior of individuals in positions of authority that might increase risks to the organization. A key problem at Enron was that the chief financial officer was also the general partner of many of the entities employed to keep liabilities off the books of Enron. Indeed, what is particularly amazing about this is that Enron's Board of Directors approved this violation of the company's conflict of interest policy.

[(vi)]**EXAMPLE**

Assigning responsibility for making decisions or authorizing transactions to specific individuals is a form of process control. In this way, responsibility can be assigned to individual employees in the event of bad decisions or significant errors. Failure to assign responsibility for authorizing transactions creates a void in a business process that can have a negative impact on its effectiveness. Process outcomes in the absence of assigned authority can be unpredictable. For example, transactions may be approved that don't meet the objectives of the company (e.g., selling to bad credit risks) or potential transactions may be missed because no one has the authority to act in a given situation.

No system of internal control is perfect—errors may be made and fraud may occur even in an organization with outstanding process controls and internal control over financial reporting. Controls that appear to be quite rigorous may fail for a number of reasons. Generally, an organization is only as good as its personnel. If personnel are not competent, mistakes may occur and go undetected. If personnel are not trustworthy, individuals may collude (work together) to undermine the financial reporting process, or management may use its power and prerogatives to circumvent (or override) financial reporting controls. With these limitations in mind, the auditors' understanding of internal control over financial reporting is an important factor for assessing control risk for financial statement assertions. This assessment, in turn, influences how much the auditor will rely on internal controls to detect and prevent material misstatements.

Auditors differentiate between the controls addressing strategic and operating risks and controls that relate to how specific transactions and accounting estimates are recorded within a process. Both are important because internal control over financial reporting is less likely to be effective if other types of process risks are not well managed. Furthermore, analysis of process risks beyond those associated with the financial statements provides a context for evaluating the competence of management, the nature of required reporting for a process, and the context in which to evaluate the appropriateness and reasonableness of transactions, accounts, and estimates affected by a process. Some of these controls may also have implications for many valuations included in the financial statements. However, auditors are only required to test and evaluate the ICOFR when they are relying on them to reduce the risk of material misstatement, hence different audit firms use different approaches to achieve this objective.

In this chapter, we focus on process controls related to internal control over financial reporting, starting from the point where transactions are initiated and initially recorded and culminating with final presentation of the results in the financial statements. We first review the financial reporting process. Next, we discuss the techniques employed by the auditor to gain an understanding of a client's internal control over financial reporting. We then examine specific auditor planning and testing of internal control over financial reporting. We also present a detailed example of how an auditor may evaluate internal control over financial reporting for the purposes of a GAAS Audit.

The Financial Reporting Process

The financial reporting (accounting) process comprises the set of activities used by an organization to capture and communicate financial and other information. These processes are for the most part embedded within other processes with the main exception being the final financial statement preparation, known as "closing the books." The primary purpose of the accounting system is to identify, record, classify, aggregate, and report transaction information. In general, the quality of information and communication will have a direct impact on management's ability to effectively and efficiently manage the resources and activities of the organization.

The financial reporting process generally includes routine and non-routine transactions between an organization and external parties, as well as transactions or transfers within an organization. Increasingly the process also includes adjusting entries needed for accounting estimates (especially fair values) to comply with generally accepted accounting principles. Transactions with external parties represent exchanges involving the receipt and distribution of various types of resources (e.g., cash, materials, equipment, and promises to pay). In most organizations, exchange transactions are voluminous and a formal system is required to make sure each is identified and captured by the system. Events related to accounting estimates may be less obvious but still need to be captured by the system, e.g., a decline in the collectability of receivables. Typically, identifying and recording these circumstances is a greater challenge.

Management assertions, discussed in detail in Chapter 3 and summarized in Table 7.1, reflect the output from the accounting system. Internal control over financial reporting should be designed to provide reasonable assurance that conditions that could lead to material misstatements are prevented or corrected by management. The financial reporting process will vary across companies based on the structure of business processes and the design of the information systems used to process transactions and compile the financial statements. In general, all financial reporting systems are composed of four components:

1. Source documents and transactions.
2. Journals.
3. General and subsidiary ledgers.
4. Financial statements.

In this section, we briefly describe each component as a basis for understanding internal controls over transaction recording and financial reporting.

Source Documents and Transactions

Transactions reflect an exchange, usually with an independent organization. For a sale, a transaction occurs when goods are shipped to another organization or funds are transferred in payment for goods. In an automated system, the accounting process may be triggered by electronic data entry related to these events. For transactions that are not in electronic form, the receipt of documentation indicating a sale or payment may trigger the recognition of a transaction.

Accounting transactions usually generate one or more source documents, whether paper based or electronic. Some examples of documents used to process a sales transaction include:

- *Sales order*: This document represents an order received from a customer and indicates the nature and quantity of items the customer wishes to purchase. These documents are increasingly electronic due to on-line ordering systems.

Table 7.1 *Management Assertions about Financial Reporting*

MANAGEMENT ASSERTIONS
Transactions
• *Occurrence*—Transactions and events that have been recorded have occurred and pertain to the entity.
• *Completeness*—All transactions and events that should have been recorded have been recorded.
• *Accuracy*—Amounts and other data relating to recorded transactions and events have been recorded appropriately.
• *Cut-off*—Transactions and events have been recorded in the correct accounting period.
• *Classification*—Transactions and events have been recorded in the proper accounts.
Accounts
• *Existence*—Assets, liabilities, and equity interests exist.
• *Rights and obligations*—The entity holds or controls the rights to assets, and liabilities are the obligations of the entity.
• *Completeness*—All assets, liabilities, and equity interests that should have been recorded have been recorded.
• *Valuation and allocation*—Assets, liabilities, and equity interests are included in the financial statements at appropriate amounts and any resulting valuation or allocation adjustments are appropriately recorded.
Presentation and Disclosure
• *Occurrence and rights and obligations*—Disclosed events and transactions have occurred and pertain to the entity.
• *Completeness*—All disclosures that should have been included in the financial statements have been included.
• *Classification and understandability*—Financial information is appropriately presented and described, and information in disclosures is clearly expressed.
• *Accuracy and valuation*—Financial and other information is disclosed fairly and at appropriate amounts.

- **Bill of lading:** This document indicates that a shipment has been made and a sale has occurred. Traditionally, this has been a paper document, but transportation companies are increasingly using electronic documents with an electronic signature.

- **Sales invoice:** This document represents a bill to the customer and indicates the quantity of goods shipped, the price, and the payment terms.

Transactions can also arise from internal actions taken by an organization such as asset transfers between locations or internal work effort. Because GAAP requires the use of accrual-based accounting, the accounting system needs to record these activities as part of the financial reporting process. For example, when employees produce work for an organization, there is a corresponding expense and liability for their efforts before payment occurs. Therefore, organizations must develop financial reporting systems that facilitate recognition of payroll accruals at the end of a period (e.g., wages payable).

Journals

Transactions are generally recorded and summarized in either a **general journal** or a specific journal, such as a sales journal, cash disbursements journal, or purchases journal. For example, the **sales journal** represents a chronological listing of all sales transactions. Almost all companies keep their records electronically these days but the names survive from the age of pen and paper. Indeed, fewer and fewer companies keep paper copies of their invoices and some do not even present paper invoices to customers, using electronic communications including government approved postal services (e.g., via e-post provided by Canada Post).

All journal entries, no matter what their source, represent the authorization to increase or decrease an account balance for a specific amount at a specific point in time. For example, a journal entry might be a computer command to change amounts in an accounting database, such as the addition of a new sales record linked to a specific customer. The old manual system analogy would be the totals of specific journals for a specific period of time (e.g., a day) that are summed then entered into the related general ledger accounts (e.g., sales) through a journal entry.

Journal entries are often made in the days and weeks after the end of the period while the "books are still open" so as to record various adjustments and accruals that may reflect the circumstances of the entity at the end of the period, but which may not be known until a few days later. While some period ending journal entries are routine (e.g., recording an accrual for an invoice received after the end of the period but related to services received in the previous period), others are not. Auditors should be particularly concerned about non-routine transactions and estimates recorded by period-ending adjusting entries. While many of these are used to ensure that financial statements comply with generally accepted accounting principles, there is the opportunity for management to include journal entries that may also misstate the final accounting. In many past accounting frauds, perpetrators hid their activities by using adjusting journal entries to move fraudulent entries from accounts where they might be detected to accounts where detection would be more difficult[vii].

Ledgers

Ledgers aggregate the transaction activity on an account basis and indicate the current balance at a point in time. Ledgers include a transaction summary for all authorized accounts. Ledgers are the summation of master files of a computerized accounting information system organized by account balance. The ledger utilized most by auditors is the **general ledger**, which is a summary of the net activity for all accounts contained in the chart of accounts at a point in time (possibly daily). The manual system analog is the ledgers will indicate the final balance of each account after all current journal entries are posted. In both cases, the beauty of double entry accounting is that the ledger accounts are formatted into a **trial balance**, i.e., a listing of the ending balances for accounts in the general ledger, typically classified by financial statement line item. This ensures that the debits and credits equal.

Cendant—a travel and leisure company—perpetrated an accounting fraud that involved fictitious sales transactions recorded throughout the year. The intent of these transactions was to convey the message that the company's customer base was growing rapidly. However, before the auditors investigated the sales transactions at the end of the year, the company would transfer some of the fictitious sales accounts to other (reserve) accounts created to account for reorganization costs. Although this fraud sounds fairly easy to identify, the complexity of the sales transactions and reorganization process employed by Cendant made the detection of the adjusting entries very difficult.

One of the problems encountered in the WorldCom fraud was the reclassification of expenses as an asset, thus removing their effect from the income statement. To be able to reclassify expenses, WorldCom used a fictitious account, called "prepaid capacity." Management first had to add this account to the chart of accounts in the general ledger; otherwise, there would be no account in which to place the debit part of the journal entry which reduced expenses. To understand the nature of this fraud, the auditor would need to examine the credit activity in the expense accounts and the debit activity in the account for the nonexistent asset.

Because many accounts contain a tremendous amount of detailed information about a group of transactions, most companies maintain subsidiary ledgers to break down the account into specific categories. For example, accounts receivable can be broken down by customer by using an ***accounts receivable subsidiary ledger***, which is a listing of all customers and the balances owed. Sales are entered as debits to this ledger and payments are credits with the offsetting credits and debits being electronically posted to other general ledger accounts.[3] Similarly, payables may be disaggregated using an ***accounts payable subsidiary ledger*** and plant, property, and equipment may be disaggregated using a ***fixed asset ledger*** (essentially a listing of all long-lived assets).[4]

Ledgers are important for auditors because financial reporting misstatements and fraud must eventually be included in one or more of the ledgers of the organization in order to affect the financial statements. Careful analysis of ledger activity is needed to understand the nature and effect of a misstatement or fraud in order to correct the problem prior to preparing the financial **statements**(viii).

Financial Statements

Financial statements consist of line items that summarize related account balances conditional on account type, materiality, and GAAP requirements. For example, a company may have a number of different types of long-lived assets such as vehicles, buildings, land, computers, office equipment, and factory equipment. For financial reporting purposes, all these may simply be combined into a single line item: Plant, Property, and Equipment. Accumulated depreciation may be reported separately or netted against the related asset. The process of aggregating accounts into line items may become quite complex for organizations with subsidiaries that must be consolidated with the financial statements of the parent organization. Furthermore, accumulating information to be disclosed in the footnotes can be quite challenging because much of disclosure information is descriptive and may need to be collected manually.

Impact of Information Technology on Financial Reporting

In Chapter 6 we considered the effects of information systems on control activities as part of our understanding of the business process. In this chapter we explicitly look at the ICOFR that can be implemented via an information system. Every client has a different accounting system, ranging from nearly extinct manual bookkeeping to complex enterprise resource planning (ERP) systems that are highly computerized and integrated across functions. Consequently, the auditor must be familiar with the many types of systems used for financial reporting. Although internal control over financial reporting should be active at many levels of the organization, from the Audit Committee to clerks in the accounts payable department, the underlying goal is quite simple: all journal entries, ledger amounts, and financial statement presentations should be free of any material misstatements relating to transactions, accounts, estimates, and disclosures.

Many smaller organizations employ off-the-shelf accounting software that is "locked down" so it is difficult for the organization's management to reprogram the software. In these cases the auditor often ignores the computer system as the auditor can rely on the programming of the software to be accurate and can print out any reports or documents needed to examine all stages of the financial reporting process. For example, the auditor can determine the following:

- Documents are filled out with essential information.
- Journal entries are properly prepared and posted to journals and ledgers.
- Account ledgers are accurately totaled.
- Trial balances are accurate.
- Closing entries are complete and accurate.
- Financial statements are prepared properly.

In essence, a commercial accounting software package allows an auditor to approach the engagement in a manner that is very similar to a manual system.

In highly automated systems, and systems that are customized to a specific client, an auditor may need to include computer experts as part of the audit team. Highly automated accounting systems may possess the following attributes:

- Paper documents may not exist.
- Routine and many non-routine journal entries are generated by the computer.
- Posting and account accumulation is done automatically.
- Reports are available only on-line and are printed out only as requested by managers or the audit team.

In this type of system, most of the accounting process is unobservable, making the use of computer-assisted audit techniques (CAATS) necessary, if not critical, to the successful completion of the audit. CAATS do not change the essential goal of this stage of the audit—ensuring that the ICOFR, both computer and human, are effective[ix].

The current trend of linking information systems across organizations is changing the way that auditors think about process controls. Customers and suppliers use electronic data interface (EDI) to improve the efficiency of transaction processing and to reduce the costs of holding and moving inventory. In an EDI system, major suppliers of an organization directly monitor inventory levels at the customer and determine what and when to ship to the customer. Orders are nearly instantaneous, including the electronic transfer of funds (EFT), and avoid traditional (and cumbersome) procurement processes and documents. Although the use of information technology and general authorization of transactions improves the efficiency of a process, electronic linkages make the supplier and customer much more dependent on each other. Integrated systems are one form of a strategic alliance in which information processing risks of one party become information processing risks of the other party, meaning that auditors must consider such risks for both organizations[x].

[ix] EXAMPLE

Most gasoline in the US is now sold on a self-service basis. Not only does the customer pump his or her own gasoline, but the customer can also pay for the gasoline by simply inserting a credit card into a reader that is built into the pump. With virtually no human intervention, this relatively simple transaction has a multitude of effects:

- *the transaction is recognized as a sale by the gas station by automatically listing the transaction in a computerized sales journal;*
- *gasoline supplies on hand are automatically updated based on the volume pumped by the customer;*
- *a receivable is recognized from the credit card company by the gas station;*
- *the credit card company recognizes a payable to the gas station owner;*
- *the credit card company charges the customer's account for the credit card transaction;*
- *the credit card company recognizes a small fee as revenue based on a percentage of the transaction.*

In short, a large number of accounts are affected in two separate organizations almost simultaneously, with no paper trail being produced, except for a small receipt that the customer may print out at the pump (and likely promptly discards).

The use of EDI and newer Internet-based procurement systems has allowed many companies to adopt just-in-time inventory techniques. Instead of maintaining a large stock of parts and supplies, a manufacturer may rely on its suppliers to monitor its inventory levels and send shipments of needed parts based on production orders. Often, the lead time for such deliveries is short: the Mercedes factory in Alabama that makes the M-class sports utility vehicle requires that suppliers deliver appropriate parts within three hours of an order being placed. The parts are immediately used in the manufacturing process, resulting in virtually no parts supplies being maintained at the Mercedes factory. However, the integrated systems extend information processing risks from the suppliers to Mercedes. Although auditors of the Mercedes plant were not concerned about their information system, they have to be concerned about the situation at their suppliers to ensure that a system breakdown elsewhere would not halt operations at Mercedes.

The nature of errors that can occur in an accounting system will depend on the extent of automation. In a simple computer system with off the shelf accounting software, humans can introduce many types of error due to mistakes made by the individuals processing transactions. As the old computer class saying goes "garbage in, garbage out", i.e., the system is only as good as the people inputting the data. In a complex computerized system, transaction processing is highly accurate so random errors are much less likely to occur, such as in our gas station example above. However, because computer systems often lack flexibility, systematic errors may occur if new or unusual transactions arise that do not meet the parameters specified by the system. Finally, no matter how complex or automatic the transaction processing and accounting are, key estimates are almost always made based on human judgment and intervention. Further, such intervention can lead to data being downloaded into spreadsheets where none of the normal processing controls are in place. Thus, either deliberate or random errors can occur when humans interact with an automated system.

Auditors must be comfortable shifting from one type of system to another given that the objective of obtaining reliable information is the same regardless of the form of the system. Routine transactions tend to be highly automated, whereas non-routine transactions and accounting estimates are more likely to be processed manually. Systems are becoming more complex, and even small organizations are becoming dependent on information technology. The trend towards enterprise resource planning systems (ERPs) and complex systems that link information flows from all the key processes of an organization is changing the way that organizations look at financial reporting. In turn, this trend creates new challenges for auditors who must increase their understanding of new information technologies. For more details about the role of information technology and internal control see Appendix A to this chapter.

The Role of Internal Control over Financial Reporting

Establishing effective internal control over financial reporting is a basic responsibility of management. As noted in Chapter 3, the audit risk model presumes a relationship between the risk that controls fail to prevent or detect a financial statement misstatement (i.e., control risk) and the extent of auditor effort needed to gather substantive evidence about financial statement assertions (detection risk). The extent to which auditors test controls during the course of the audit depends on the auditor's judgments about the quality of internal control, the trade-off between reliance on and auditor testing of internal controls versus the auditor's use of substantive tests to reduce audit risk, and the professional rules applicable to the engagement.

Before the auditor can make the decision about whether to rely on internal controls to reduce the likelihood of material misstatements, the auditor must assess how well designed the internal control system is at an organization. Hence, the auditor needs to determine if there are weaknesses in internal control. Such a weakness is referred to as a **control deficiency** and can arise for two reasons. First, the control is designed, implemented or operated in such a way that it is unable to prevent, or detect and correct, misstatements in the financial statements on a timely basis. Second, a needed control is missing. Determining whether controls have been well designed and implemented can be a challenging and time-consuming task. Determining if a control is needed based on a basic description of the existing system can be very difficult as one has to apply the concepts underlying internal control to the specifics of the client's system.

Management's responsibility includes designing an effective system of internal control over financial reporting so that control deficiencies are minimized. To do so, management designs internal control to:

- *Initiate, authorize, record, process, and report significant accounts and disclosures and related assertions about the financial statements:* Control deficiencies within a process depend on the value, volume, and financial reporting risk associated with process's transactions.

- *Enable selection and application of accounting policies in conformity with generally accepted accounting principles:* Control deficiencies might occur if management fails to properly review and apply new accounting pronouncements in a timely manner.

- *Prevent fraud:* Control deficiencies might occur if management fails to set a proper control environment to prevent and detect fraud.

- *Serve as general controls over information technology or those upon which other significant controls are dependent:* Control deficiencies might occur if management fails to design controls over program development and changes, computer operations, or access to programs or data.

- *Facilitate significant non-routine, non-systematic, or complex transactions:* Control deficiencies might occur if operational or accounting staff are not able to properly handle transactions that do not fit within predetermined routine accounting processes.

- *Facilitate the development of significant accounting estimates including fair values:* Control deficiencies might occur if there is a lack of documentation for complex accounting estimates.

- *Facilitate period-end financial reporting, including preparing financial statements and disclosures:* Control deficiencies might occur if management fails to ensure that the use of journals, ledgers, trial balances and other tools used to produce the final financial statements is appropriate.

The Auditor's Role in Evaluating Internal Control over Financial Reporting

When evaluating internal control over financial reporting, the auditor must understand and evaluate the effectiveness of internal control itself and identify any control deficiencies that might have implications for the conduct of the audit. Table 7.2 summarizes the elements of internal control over financial reporting that are of direct interest to the auditor and the types of information the auditor should consider in evaluating each element.

Table 7.2 Components of Internal Control over Financial Reporting Relevant to the Conduct of the Audit

Control Environment	Risk Assessment	Control Activities	Information and Communication	Monitoring Activities
• Management philosophy and operating style • Organizational structure • Corporate governance • Board committees • Proper lines of communication, authorization, and responsibility • Management control methods • Internal auditing • Personnel policies • External constraints	• Changes in environment • Changes in personnel • Changes in information systems • Rapid growth • New technology • Changes in product lines or operations • Corporate restructuring • Accounting changes	• Performance reviews • Processing controls • Physical controls • Segregation of duties	• Define classes of transactions and events to be captured • Initiate events and transactions • Record events and transactions • Summarize and classify events and transactions • Reporting (financial statements and other)	• Attitudes and competence of senior management and the board • Real time monitoring of ongoing activities • Periodic performance evaluations • Periodic process reviews • Performance of internal auditors

To plan the audit, the auditor must determine the effectiveness of these elements of internal control. The basic steps for evaluating internal control are summarized in Box 7.1 "Steps for Evaluating Internal Control Design and Effectiveness".

BOX 7.1 STEPS FOR EVALUATING INTERNAL CONTROL DESIGN AND EFFECTIVENESS

Plan the Evaluation

• *Materiality considerations.*

• *Fraud considerations.*

• *Multi-location testing considerations.*

Evaluate Management's Control Documentation and Testing

• *Obtain an understanding of management's control documentation.*

• *Obtain an understanding of management's control assessment process.**

• *Evaluate how management determines the controls to be tested (if any).**

• *Evaluate the completeness of management's documentation and the effectiveness of the control as designed.*

• *Evaluate the likelihood that control failures could result in a misstatement.*

• *Obtain an understanding of the results of testing performed by company personnel or third parties.*

• *Evaluate whether management's documentation supports its assessment.**

• *Evaluate Audit Committee effectiveness.**

Obtain an Understanding of Internal Control

- *Identify significant account balances and disclosures.*
- *Identify significant processes and major classes of transactions.*
- *Identify relevant assertions for transactions, accounts, and disclosures.*
- *Understand the financial reporting process.*
- *Perform walkthroughs.*
- *Evaluate design of controls for effectiveness in preventing material misstatements.****
- *Identify controls to test, if any.*

Assess Control Risk for Financial Reporting Assertions

- *For each significant financial statement assertion for each material class of transaction or balance assess control risk as:*
  - o *Maximum;*
  - o *Slightly reduced from maximum (high);*
  - o *Moderate;*
  - o *Low.***

Test the Effectiveness of Internal Control

- *Consider use of the work of others (when allowed).*
- *Establish timing of tests of controls.*
- *Perform tests of controls.*

Assess Operational Effectiveness of Internal Controls over Financial Reporting

- *Based on control design effectiveness and tests of operating effectiveness conclude whether preliminary control risk assessments are reasonable.*
- *If control risk assessments are reasonable—continue with audit plan.*
- *If control risk assessments are not reasonable—consider the nature and extent of changes to be made to the planned substantive tests in the audit plan (or in the extreme consider whether the entity is auditable)*

* Indicates procedures required in an Integrated Audit. However, these procedures can also be used when an Integrated Audit is not required.

** An implicit assumption in an Integrated Audit is that control risk should be evaluated at low in all public company audits, hence tests of controls are required.

*** New requirement in 2006 for all entities that are not SEC registrants reporting under SOX 404 per SAS 109 and ISA 315.

Plan the Evaluation: Planning the evaluation of ICFOR is important in order to identify critical internal controls to be evaluated and potentially tested by the auditor. In making planning decisions, the auditor considers the complexity of the system, materiality, and the risk of fraud. The assessment of materiality will help the auditor to determine the significance of identified control deficiencies. An assessment of the controls that are in place to prevent or detect fraud, including the control environment, are also important in planning because the presence of fraud-related control deficiencies will have a significant effect on the nature and extent of auditor substantive tests of the financial statement amounts and disclosures. In organizations with multiple locations or multiple operating units, auditors need to be careful not to inappropriately generalize from the controls that are in effect at one location or unit to others. It is important to evaluate and test controls in all individually important locations and units.

AUTHORITATIVE GUIDANCE & STANDARDS

Guidance in ISA 315 requires auditors to develop a sufficient understanding of the entity and its environment sufficient to assess the risk of material misstatement, including being able to determine the design effectiveness of internal controls. For controls that the auditor wishes to rely on to reduce the amount of substantive testing the auditor does of the financial statement amounts and disclosures, the auditor must carry out tests of operating effectiveness of controls according to ISA 330 **The Auditor's Responses to Assessed Risks**.

Evaluate Management's Control Documentation and Testing: Understanding how management assesses and monitors the accounting system enhances the auditor's understanding of the entity's internal control over financial reporting. Auditors will usually evaluate the documentation of internal control that is available from management to ensure that the company has identified critical controls related to transactions, accounts, and disclosures. A lack of such documentation would suggest that the control environment of the organization is weak. The auditor also evaluates the design of internal controls to assess the likelihood that control deficiencies could result in a misstatement. This evaluation should include the impact of any **compensating controls**— controls that might help to address apparent deficiencies in the system—and determine if the compensating controls would detect material misstatements if they occurred. Auditors will also consider how management communicates deficiencies to affected parties and the nature of corrective actions that may have been taken to address such deficiencies. Finally, auditors should consider the results of tests of controls performed by internal auditors.

Obtain an Understanding of Internal Control: A critical step in evaluating ICOFR is to determine what controls are in place that ensure transactions, accounts, and disclosures are not materially misstated. As part of this process, auditors use a number of approaches for documenting the financial reporting process of an organization. The three primary techniques are:

1. *Written narrative:* A narrative is simply a written description of the organization's processes and controls. At a minimum, the narrative should include a description of the key processing steps that occur, identification

of all documents and records used in the accounting system, and the identification of relevant control activities that provide assurance that the process is reliable. This information may be included in a process map for particularly important processes. Copies of documents (or key computer screens) may be included as exhibits to the narrative. The description should include discussion of the control environment, risk-assessment process, and specific control activities.

2. *Flowchart:* A flowchart is a diagram of a process describing the key sequential steps in the process. A very simple flowchart can be used to describe the activities in a process map. An example of a system flowchart appears in Figure 7.3 and is discussed in detail later in the chapter. The flowchart should show the source, handling, and disposition of transactions within a process using standardized symbols. The flowchart can be supplemented by brief descriptions where further detail may be needed. Flowcharts have the advantage of providing a general overview of a system. More details about how to create flowcharts are provided in Appendix 2 of this chapter.

3. *Control questionnaire:* A control questionnaire is a series of questions, usually in a yes/no format, about the control activities that could be performed within a specific process. In most cases, a "yes" answer indicates that a control procedure is performed and that a deficiency does not exist. A "no" answer implies that there is no control of the indicated type and that a deficiency may exist depending on whether there are compensating controls. Questionnaires are useful for quickly identifying the control procedures that an organization has in place in key processes. Because a good questionnaire is comprehensive, the auditor is unlikely to overlook any control procedures that might have an impact on the audit. However, a questionnaire rarely provides a coherent picture of internal control and should be used as a supplement to a written narrative or flowchart. Furthermore, since questionnaires are general in nature, it is the auditor's responsibility to consider the unique circumstances of the client being audited.

One procedure that is particularly useful for developing an understanding of the controls in a process is a ***walkthrough***. This procedure involves tracing one (or a few) transaction(s) from origination through the entire information system of the organization, including manual and automated activities, culminating in inclusion in the financial statements. One common misconception about walkthroughs is their role as evidence for an auditor. Because a walkthrough only consists of one test item, it is a very weak test of control effectiveness. Rather, walkthroughs are used to develop a better understanding on how controls are designed and whether they appear to be in operation.

AUTHORITATIVE GUIDANCE & STANDARDS

ISA 315 describes a walkthrough as a procedure that an auditor can perform to gain a sufficient understanding of an entity's internal control design.

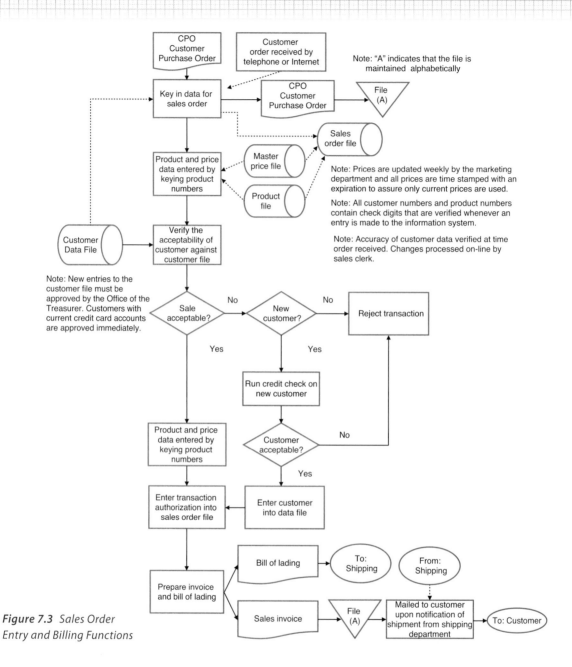

Figure 7.3 *Sales Order Entry and Billing Functions*

Assessing Control Risk

Assess Control Risk for Financial Statement Assertions: The most challenging part of the auditor evaluating internal control is linking the auditor's understanding of the financial reporting system to the risk that material misstatements in the financial statement assertions. After completing the evaluation of internal control the auditor makes a preliminary assessment of **control risk** for significant management assertions. If internal control over financial reporting is well-designed and implemented (i.e., it is a reliable control), the auditor's control risk assessment can be set relatively

Figure 7.3 continued

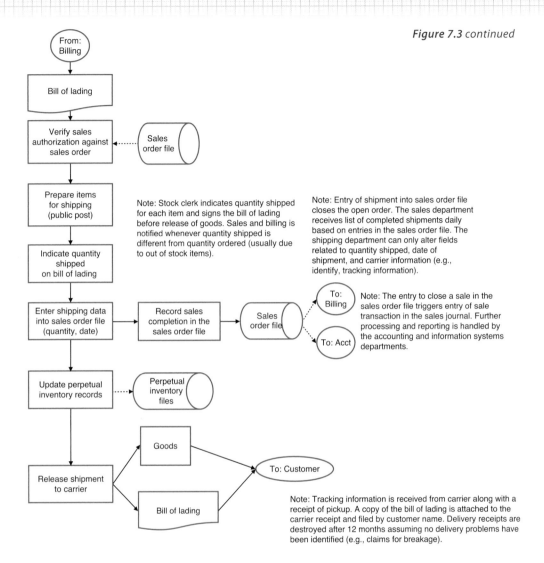

low. Control deficiencies related to specific financial statement assertions may lead to inaccurate information processing and result in misstatements in the financial reports, suggesting that the auditor's assessment of control risk should be higher for some assertions. Conclusions about control risk and whether to rely on internal controls to reduce the risk of material misstatement will eventually influence the conduct of the audit and the nature and extent of substantive audit testing. The auditor's evaluation of control risk depends on two things: (1) the auditor's assessment of internal control system strength, and (2) the degree the auditor intends to rely on the control system to reduce substantive audit testing. In general, auditors use a fourfold classification of assessed control risk:

1. **Maximum**: The auditor decides not to rely on internal control to reduce the risk of material misstatement, hence the auditor's substantive testing will be much more extensive. This results in the auditor facing a substantial amount of risk of material misstatement (i.e., detection risk is set by the auditor at a very low level). However, it is important to note that even

when the auditor sets the control risk at maximum, the auditor is required to gain sufficient knowledge of internal control to evaluate the design effectiveness of the control system. In general, most audits will require some internal control testing, especially on difficult to assess assertions around revenue.

2. **High (reduced below maximum)**: Internal control will be relied on to reduce risk of material misstatement slightly and hence only limited testing of internal controls will be carried out by the auditor. However, given the relatively high risk that material misstatements will not be detected by controls, the auditor will perform extensive substantive tests to reduce detection risk (i.e., the auditor sets detection risk at a low level).

3. **Moderate**: The auditor will rely on the quality of internal control to reduce risks of material misstatement, therefore the auditor does a substantial amount of control testing to ensure the controls are working as intended. However, consistent with the moderate reliance on controls to reduce the risk of material misstatement, the auditor sets detection risk at a moderate level leading to performance of relatively fewer substantive tests compared to when the auditor assesses control risk at a higher level. Nonetheless, a substantial amount of evidence about whether the financial statements contain material misstatements still needs to come from these substantive tests.

4. **Low**: The auditor will rely heavily on the quality of internal control to reduce the risk of material misstatement, therefore the auditor carries out extensive tests of control effectiveness. Given the substantial reduction of the risk of material misstatement obtained from the control system, the auditor may perform relatively fewer substantive tests when there is such an effective control system (i.e., the auditor can set the detection risk at a much higher level as the auditor relies on controls to detect most material misstatements).

The evidence from process analysis and system walkthroughs can be used to justify some reduction in assessed control risk even if other tests of controls are not used. Consequently, control risk for many assertions may be reduced from the maximum level based on the procedures that the auditor has performed during strategic and process analysis. The evidence to support this conclusion will consist of client inquiries about the design of the system, observation of client personnel performing their duties, and limited examination of documentation as part of the system walkthroughs.

In a GAAS Audit the auditor chooses, when the design of the client control system allows for it, whether to test controls to reduce the likelihood of material misstatement or to carry out substantive audit tests that result in the reduction of all significant residual risks to an appropriately low level. Hence, an auditor may set control risk at a maximum level if the auditor concludes that substantive tests will be so effective that no reliance on controls is necessary to form an opinion about the financial statements, even if internal controls are designed effectively and could be tested. In this case, the auditor is essentially ignoring internal control as a source of risk reduction and completely relies on substantive tests of transactions and accounts.

Consequently, an auditor must document why substantive procedures alone reduce audit risk to an appropriately low level before setting control risk at the maximum level.

The approach of not relying on and testing controls is becoming less acceptable in practice as international auditing standards presume that some testing of controls is necessary to reduce audit risk to an acceptable level.[5] Internal controls are an important element of reducing misstatement risk in any organization; hence, they should not be ignored by auditors simply in the name of perceived audit efficiency. However, it is also possible that some systems of internal control are so weak as to justify the auditor's assessment of maximum control risk. The primary procedures needed to support an assessment of maximum control risk are client inquiries, observations, documentation of client activity performed as part of strategic and process analysis, and an assessment of whether the controls are designed to effectively reduce risk of material misstatement, even if they are not being tested for reliance.

Test the Effectiveness of Internal Control: Auditors perform procedures to test and evaluate the effectiveness of internal controls to support the level of reliance they are placing on controls to reduce material misstatements. It should be noted that management may believe, and indeed the control system may actually be, stronger than the level that the auditor decides to rely on. However, it is the auditor's judgment as to the appropriate trade-off between relying on and testing controls versus substantive tests of financial statement assertions when designing the audit.

In evaluating control operating effectiveness, auditors consider whether a control is operating as designed and whether the person performing the control possesses the necessary authority and qualifications to perform the control appropriately. The auditor will perform a variety of procedures to test controls, including inquiry, inspection of records, observation, and re-performance to ascertain whether control activities are consistently and appropriately applied. Inquiry alone (as is common in a walkthrough) is usually not sufficient to conclude whether internal control is effective[(xi)].

The auditor should perform sufficient testing to justify a conclusion to rely on the effectiveness of ICOFR consistent with the audit's objective of reducing the risk of material misstatement to an appropriately low level. The auditor may rely to some extent on the work of others, including company personnel, internal auditors, and third parties working under the direction of management or the Board of Directors (e.g., an inventory count service). In determining the extent to which the work of others is used, the auditor should evaluate the nature of the controls tested, evaluate the competence and objectivity of the individuals involved, and test some of the work performed by others. Two areas in which auditors are generally *not* allowed to use the work of others include (1) testing controls that are part of the control environment, including controls specifically established to prevent and detect fraud, and (2) walkthroughs used to develop a sufficient understanding of internal control over financial reporting.

Assess Operational Effectiveness of Internal Control over Financial Reporting: After completing the planning, walkthroughs, and tests of

[(xi)]**EXAMPLE**

For a retail client, an auditor may perform a number of tests to determine if there is adequate control over cash that is kept in the checkout registers in a store. First, the auditor might review the software that controls access to the cash drawers. For example, the auditor could review who can get into the drawers (clerks, supervisors) and under what conditions (at time of a transaction or to correct an error). Second, the auditor could observe how cashiers handle their cash drawers (e.g., Are they left open? Are unauthorized personnel allowed access?). Third, the auditors could review documentation related to the pickup of cash drawers by individual cashiers at the start of shift and their return to safekeeping at the end of a shift. Fourth, the removal of excess cash can be observed or verified by reviewing documentation and authorizations by cashiers and supervisors. Finally, documentation related to the reconciliation of cash on hand to automatically generated transaction totals (e.g., sales per shift) can be reviewed for accuracy and proper handling.

controls, the auditor should be able to reach a conclusion about the effectiveness of internal control for the level of reliance that the auditor plans to use when setting the nature and extent of substantive tests. The culmination of this work is reflected in the final assessments of control risk reliance. As will be discussed in Chapter 10, when internal controls are found to be ineffective, or less effective than originally expected, the auditor needs to adjust the nature and extent of planned substantive audit procedures that will be carried out. The auditor should also consider how internal control may have changed during the year. Management might be aware of a serious control deficiency early in the year and correct it so it no longer exists by the end of the year. However, the fact that some portion of transactions for the year was processed when a serious control deficiency existed means that misstatements may have occurred. This possibility must be considered when the auditor assesses control risks and planning substantive procedures.

Control Risk and Tests of Financial Statement Assertions

When control risk is assessed by the auditor to be relatively high, there is an increased likelihood of undetected misstatements in financial reports. When control risk is assessed by the auditor to be relatively low, the auditor believes that there is less risk of undetected material misstatements in transactions, accounts, estimates, or disclosures when the control is operating effectively. To achieve a given level of audit risk, auditors need to choose the extent to rely on (and test) a client's controls versus substantive tests of assertions. This decision is driven by the effectiveness of the client's accounting system in preventing and detecting material misstatements and the auditor's choice of how much reliance to place on the system given its presumed level of effectiveness.

Figure 7.4 illustrates several examples of the potential trade-off between reliance on internal control and substantive testing. Moving from left to right, we see that auditors are willing to increasingly rely on evidence concerning internal control over financial reporting (i.e., assessing control risk to be low). This is in parallel to a decreasing reliance on direct evidence about transactions, accounts, and presentation and disclosure. Although the same level of overall audit risk (e.g., 5 percent) is achieved in each scenario, the mix of tests an auditor performs varies a great deal. In cases where a client has relatively weak internal control (i.e., the left-most scenario in Figure 7.4), the auditor must document that substantive evidence alone can support the auditor's opinion.

The Auditor's Control Reporting Responsibilities in a GAAS Audit

Although no formal report is issued on internal control in a GAAS Audit, some matters related to internal control should be communicated to the Audit Committee (or equivalent) of the client. The first step in determining what to report to the client, if anything, depends on which controls are most important to the system. Typically, critical controls are those associated with monitoring

Each column represents a combination of assurance obtained from:

(1) Tests of controls used to support reliance on client controls to minimize the risk of material misstatements related to management assertions about financial reporting.

(2) Substantive tests of transactions, accounts, and presentation and disclosure to identify material misstatements related to management assertions about financial reporting.

In each scenario, 95% assurance is obtained such that there is a 5% level of audit risk of issuing an unqualified opinion when a material misstatement exists.

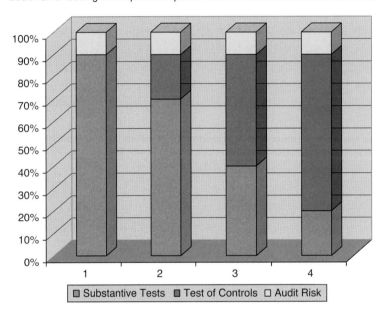

Figure 7.4 *Summary of Combinations of Evidence to Achieve the Same Level of Audit Risk*

the system, preventing or detecting fraud, applying significant accounting policies, handling non-routine transactions, or entering adjustments to the financial statements.

AUTHORITATIVE GUIDANCE & STANDARDS

Reporting auditor discovered control deficiencies to management and those charged with governance is covered by ISA 265 **Communicating Deficiencies in Internal Control to Those Charged with Governance and Management** *and is discussed in more detail in Chapter 15.*

Next, the auditor should assess whether any of the important controls are deficient (i.e., missing or not operating as intended) such that the management or the Board of Directors would consider that they merit attention. The auditor should then communicate to the client the nature of *significant deficiencies*. Determining that a deficiency is significant is a matter of judgment and is not based solely on whether an actual material misstatement has occurred. Rather, this decision is based on the *possibility* of an error occurring in the future. There are several criteria that the auditor might consider when determining if a control deficiency is significant:

- Likelihood of material misstatements in the future financial statements.
- The susceptibility to loss or fraud of the related asset or liability.
- The subjectivity and complexity of determining estimated amounts (e.g., fair values).
- The volume of activity that has or could occur in the account balance or class of transactions exposed to the deficiencies.
- The importance of the controls to the financial reporting process.

If any of these, or a combination of these, conditions are present, it is more likely that the client has a significant control deficiency. Examples of potentially serious deficiencies include:

a. Evidence that the overall control environment is not effective. For example, management does not react to previous reports of significant control deficiencies or the likelihood of fraud has not been reduced to an acceptable level.

b. Management's risk assessment process is ineffective (or absent) such that management is not identifying and addressing risks that are important to the organization's potential success.

c. Actual accounting errors have occurred due to processing errors in the current or prior period.

The standards applicable to a GAAS Audit do not require an auditor to uncover all possible significant deficiencies, but the auditor's process analysis, especially related to process risks and controls, may reveal control deficiencies. In these cases, the auditor has certain reporting requirements. *Significant* deficiencies are required to be reported in writing to those charged with governance whereas minor control deficiencies can be reported in writing or orally to management. The report given to those charged with governance, often the Audit Committee, is separate from the audit report. This is discussed further in Chapter 15.

Other control deficiencies, as well as more general suggestions for the effective conduct of the business, can be reported in a ***management letter*** and often include suggestions on how business processes can be improved. Many of the situations discussed in the management letter will not have an effect on the reliability of the financial statements, but such communications can be an effective method of adding value to the audit and assisting the client in process improvement. The management letter is an excellent opportunity for auditors to demonstrate their expertise as both an accounting and an industry expert. Where a management letter is not employed and auditors orally report important matters to management, auditors should carefully document the communications in their working papers.

An Example of Internal Control Evaluation and Control Risk Assessment

An example of a portion of the sales and distribution process of J. J. Mean Company, a privately owned mail-order bookseller (e.g., Book of the Month

Club), is depicted in flowchart form in Figure 7.3. The sales process consists of three separate activities: sales order entry and billing, shipping, and accounting/data processing. This example does not include marketing and promotions, cash collections, sales returns or customer service, all of which can also be considered part of the sales and distribution process in most companies. This example assumes that the management of information resources (e.g., system design, system programming, and data librarian functions) is independent of the data processing depicted in the flowchart as would be the case in a well-designed control system.

Evaluating Internal Control over Financial Reporting

Processing of transactions is relatively simple in this example. Sales orders are received from potential customers (by phone, mail, or Internet), goods are shipped if they are in stock, customers are billed, and accounting records are updated. The accounts affected by this process are primarily Sales Revenue and Trade Accounts Receivable. The primary documents and records used in the system include: (1) sales orders, (2) sales invoices, (3) bills of lading, (4) a sales journal, and (5) the accounts receivable subsidiary ledger. Sales orders are electronic documents, whereas invoices and bills of lading are both paper (sent to customers) and electronic. The accounting records (sales journal and accounts receivable subsidiary ledger) are electronic but are printed on a periodic basis for review by the controller.

The auditor's task is to analyze the process and related controls and assess the control risk for the financial assertions affected by the process. Figure 7.3 provides documentation of the process and control activities in flowchart form. Additional documentation of control activities can be provided by completing an appropriate control questionnaire as illustrated in Table 7.3. Close examination of the flowchart and the questionnaire reveals a number of control strengths and a few potential deficiencies.

Segregation of Duties: The company seems to have very good segregation of duties. Sales and billing, shipping, and accounting are all independent. Also, there is good segregation within accounting/data processing, which allows independent verification of data entry. However, we can observe one potential deficiency related to the approval of customers:

> D1: There is a lack of segregation in the approval of credit. There should be an independent credit check to make sure that sales are made only to credit-worthy customers and that the pre-authorized credit limits are enforced. This is especially important for new customers.

Although this deficiency is potentially important, it would only be relevant to customers who maintain a personal account with the company. If the deficiency is serious enough, it could lead the auditor to increase the risk of material misstatement for the valuation of receivables. The fact that many customers have credit cards on file transfers much of the collection risk to the credit card companies. This is an example of a compensating control.

Authorization Procedures: Clear procedures exist for authorizing transactions. General authorization is established for customer credit and

Table 7.3 *Control Questionnaire for Sales Transactions—J. J. Mean Company*

Management Assertion	Yes	No	N/A	Comments
Occurrence, Completeness and Accuracy				
1. Customer credit is approved by an appropriate official who is independent of the sales function.		✗		Approval is performed by the sales department and is not independent.
2. Proper procedures exist for approving credit for new customers and changing credit limits for existing customers.	✗			The treasurer's department does credit checks on customers to set credit limits. Many customers have credit card data on file.
3. A master price list is maintained and current prices are entered on sales documents. Standard discount and payment terms are used.	✗			Master price data file is time-stamped so that expired prices are less likely to be used.
4. Proper procedures exist for periodically revising the master price list and assuring the current list is in use.	✗			Master price data file is reviewed and updated weekly by the marketing department, which is independent of sales processing.
5. Shipments can only be made with evidence of proper authorization and access to shipping is limited to prevent unauthorized shipments.	✗			Shipments only occur upon receipt of a completed and approved bill of lading and sales invoice which is verified against approved sales orders.
6. Shipping personnel are segregated from other aspects of sales transaction processing.	✗			
7. Billing personnel are segregated from other aspects of sales transaction processing.		✗		Billings are prepared at same time as sales order is taken by sales clerks. Invoice and pricing is generated electronically. Only potential problem is failure to send invoice to customer.
8. Sales transactions are supported by appropriate documents that indicate approval of the transaction.	✗			The company uses a sales order, sales invoice, and bill of lading, all of which are in electronic form and must be approved for a transaction to be processed.
9. Sales order documents are pre-numbered and accounted for on a periodic basis to assure that all approved sales are executed.		✗		Sales order documents are pre-numbered but approved sales are not reviewed for completion.
10. Sales invoice documents are pre-numbered and accounted for on a periodic basis to assure that all sales are included in summary records.	✗			The sequence of sales invoices is independently verified by the accounting department.
11. Shipping documents are pre-numbered and accounted for on a periodic basis to assure that all shipments are billed.		✗		Bills of lading are pre-numbered but the sequence is not reviewed. Simultaneous preparation of invoice and bill of lading mitigates against unrecorded shipments, however.
12. Shipping and billing documents are matched to properly approved sales orders and reviewed for accuracy.	✗			Computer software prepares all documents based on shared information reducing the risk of inconsistencies across documents and files.
13. Sales documents are processed in the proper time period.		✗		There is a potential delay between shipment and recording of a sale since accounting doesn't post the sale until notified by shipping. Entry is supposed to be daily but no independent verification is done to make sure that posting is timely.

Management Assertion	Yes	No	N/A	Comments
14. Quantities shipped are independently verified, e.g., by double counting.		X		Quantities that are shipped are indicated on the bill of lading. If quantities shipped differ from the initial order (which is the basis of the invoice), excess quantities may be billed if such changes go unnoticed by the billing department.
Cut-off and Classification				
1. Accounting personnel handling sales transactions are independent of other aspects of sales transaction processing.	X			There is good segregation of duties in the accounting/data processing area.
2. Monthly statements are sent to customers.			X	Mailing the invoice separately from the shipment of goods should cause customers to notify the company when shipments go astray.
3. Procedures exist to assure that receivables are posted to the correct customer.	X			Customer numbers include a check digit which is electronically verified.
4. Sales data posted to sales records is reconciled with sales data posted to receivables records.	X			Reconciliation performed by accounting and data processing.
5. Summary records for sales (e.g., sales journal) and receivables (e.g., accounts receivable ledger) are footed and reconciled with the general ledger.	X			All significant records and files are computerized and internally reconciled on a regular basis.

prices. Shipments are only allowed when independent approval has been provided.

Use of Documents and Records: Reasonable documents and records are used in order to facilitate accurate transaction processing. Key documents are sequentially numbered to control their use. Electronic links within the process add assurance that routine transactions will be properly processed. However, the system is less well-suited for situations where quantities shipped do not agree with the initial order, as in the case of out-of-stock items.

D2: A problem may arise when an order is not filled completely. The shipping department adjusts the bill of lading to reflect the amount of the actual shipment and notifies billing of the change. However, this process is informal and may omit some of the changes. This could result in billing for items not shipped.

This deficiency could lead to an increase in the risk of material misstatement for the assertions of occurrence and accuracy as they relate to sales transactions.

Independent Verifications: Several important independent verifications are performed:

• Electronic data processing facilitates accurate processing and verification of transaction information.

• Customer number check digits are automatically verified upon entry to assure posting to the correct customer balance.

• Data entry into the sales journal, accounts receivable ledger, and perpetual inventory file is performed independently and reconciled daily.

- The sequence of sales invoices used is reviewed for completeness.

One independent verification control activity is missing that could affect the reliability of processing of sales transactions, however:

> D3: Sales orders are not reviewed to make sure that all approved sales have actually been filled. Failure to follow up open orders could result in lost revenues.

This deficiency could lead the auditor to increase the risk of material misstatement related to the completeness or cut-off assertions as they relate to sales transactions.

Physical Controls: Access to inventory is limited to shipping personnel and documents and records are stored and filed in the locations that they are used.

Assessing Control Risk

The auditor analyzes the implications of ICOFR for each management assertion (see Table 7.1) and specifically evaluates the effect of known control design deficiencies on control risk. If there are no compensating controls for this specific management assertion in this particular process, then the auditor cannot rely on controls with significant deficiencies. For other controls that are designed appropriately to reduce the risk of material misstatement, at this point in the audit the auditor makes some tentative decisions whether to rely on certain controls to reduce control risk. The final decision to rely on controls occurs after the auditor implements tests of controls. In order to justify a control risk assessment of low and hence supporting the auditor's belief that controls reduce the risk of material misstatement substantially, the auditor must plan and perform extended tests of controls to obtain evidence concerning the effectiveness of controls. Remember that the auditor in a GAAS Audit is testing the proposition that the controls are at least as strong as the auditor intends them to be to reduce risk of material misstatement. The actual controls may be stronger in management's eyes but the auditor is testing for the level of control risk they have decided to rely on in planning substantive tests.

Table 7.4 illustrates the control risk assessments related to our example. There are three control deficiencies evident in the example, which may lead to moderate or high risk of material misstatement for some assertions. Specifically, these deficiencies could cause the auditor to undertake substantive tests of the following management assertions:

1. Valuation (collectability) of customer receivables.
2. Accuracy (quantity of inventory) of sales transactions.
3. Cut-off of sales transactions.

The final decision regarding the significance of these risks will depend on the evidence from the substantive tests. If substantive tests support management assertions, then the auditor's worry about control effectiveness needs to be communicated to management but will not affect the auditor's opinion on the overall financial statements.

Table 7.4 *Analysis of Control Risk and Audit Planning*

Assertion	Auditor's Assessed Control Risk (MAX/H/M/L)	Basis of Conclusions about Control Risk	Audit Implications
Occurrence: Recorded sales transactions (including details such as credit approval, items shipped prices, and payment terms) are authorized and actually occurred.	Moderate	1. Proper authorizations are required but a problem may arise due to poor segregation of duties for the credit check of customers not using credit cards. 2. Proper use of documents and records makes it unlikely that a fictitious sale can be entered into the system. A problem may occur when quantities shipped are different from the quantities initially entered on the sales invoice.	1. Rely on internal control for most transaction attributes (e.g., payment terms and shipping authorization). 2. Perform substantive analytical procedures to verify collectability of receivable balances of non-credit card customers. 3. Perform some substantive tests of transactions to verify that correct quantities are billed to customers.
Completeness: All transactions that have occurred have been recorded.	Low	1. Pre-numbering the bill of lading and simultaneous preparation of the invoice makes it unlikely that sales will be omitted.	1. Test controls. 2. No substantive tests of completeness needed.
Accuracy: Sales transactions are recorded at the proper amount and are correctly summarized and aggregated.	High	1. Lack of independent credit approval may result in sales to high risk customers. 2. Errors could occur when quantity shipped is different from the quantity ordered. 3. Independent processing of sales and receivable data, use of pre-numbered documents and independent reconciliation of posting reduce errors in summarization. 4. Aggregations done by computer.	1. Limited reliance on controls. 2. Perform substantive analytical procedures to verify collectability of receivable balances of non-credit card customers. 3. Perform some substantive tests of transactions to verify that correct quantities are billed to customers. 4. Review a sample of daily activity reconciliations and trace totals for inclusion in the general ledger.
Cut-off: Sales transactions are recorded in the proper period.	Low	1. There is a delay in recording transactions until accounting is notified of transactions and there is no independent verification that sales are recorded on the day of shipment.	1. Substantive tests: Perform cut-off tests on a sample of sales transactions. Compare the posting date per the sales journal to date on the shipping document. If there are a significant number of delays, test transactions at year end for recognition in the proper period.
Classification: Sales transactions are recorded in the proper accounts, ledgers, and journals.	Low	1. Check digits facilitate proper classification of transactions.	1. Test controls likely using CAATS. 2. No substantive tests of classification needed.

Control Risk Assessments and Planned Audit Procedures

The extent of substantive testing of financial assertions that will be performed by the auditor depends on the final assessments of the level of control risk. Based on these conclusions, the auditor adjusts the conduct and scope of the audit in various ways so that detection risk combined with assessed control risk reduces the risk of material misstatements to an appropriately low level. Some adjustments an auditor might make to substantive testing when internal controls are effective include:

- **Selecting different audit procedures:** The auditor has a portfolio of procedures to use to obtain direct substantive evidence about financial statement assertions. If control risk is assessed at a relatively low level, the auditor can choose less time-consuming and less diagnostic procedures. For example, confirmations and physical examination tend to be more reliable audit evidence, but much more costly and time consuming, than documentation and analytical procedures.

- **Adjusting the timing of audit work:** The auditor often has an option as to when to perform audit tests. Substantive tests after the end of the year are usually considered more effective because more evidence is potentially available to the auditor. For example, confirmation of accounts receivable might normally be performed as of December 31, but could be done earlier if control risk is low.

- **Adjusting the extent of testing:** Many audit procedures are performed on a sample basis—that is, not all transactions are examined. When control risk is assessed at a relatively low level, the auditor may be justified in examining fewer transactions related to a process.

As these options illustrate, an auditor has a great deal of flexibility in specifying the procedures to be performed, the number of transactions to examine, the timing of the tests, and the evidence to be gathered. For example, the risk related to quantities shipped may appear to be high. The auditor might test quantities shipped for individual transactions by examining a number of transactions and comparing the quantities shipped per the various documents and records that are affected by the transaction. The auditor could examine 50, 100, or 500 transactions. Obviously, the more transactions that the auditor looks at, the more confident he or she can be that management's assertions about the accuracy of sales are not materially misstated.[6]

Every organization will have different processes, control activities, and control risks. The auditor must conduct the audit in accordance with the actual conditions observed in the organization and its processes. Table 7.5 illustrates how the auditor's approach to understanding internal control and assessing control risk might be different for two different clients, one small and family-owned and one large and publicly traded. This illustration emphasizes the need to consider the unique circumstances of each client because those circumstances can affect the auditor's understanding and evaluation of internal control over financial reporting.

Table 7.5 *Effect of Client Characteristics on the Auditor's Approach to Assessing Control Risk*

	Small, Family-Owned Client	**Large Publicly Traded Client**
Internal Control Environment	*Nature of Management:* The owner is often an active manager in the enterprise. *Auditability:* May be a question if documents and records are not available. *Client Goals:* The owner/manager is usually more concerned with reducing tax liabilities than maximizing reported profits.	*Nature of Management:* The management typically has little direct ownership interest in the enterprise other than in the form of stock incentive plans (and possible incentive compensation). *Auditability:* May be a question if management integrity is in serious question. *Client Goals:* The management is usually concerned with maximizing reported profits.
Risk Assessment Procedures	Risk assessment may be informal, relying mainly on the firsthand knowledge of the owner/manager.	Formal assessment procedures will be used to identify and measure potential risks. This analysis may be performed by internal auditors.
Control Activities	Procedures and segregation of duties may be lacking, due to small number of personnel. Owner involvement may compensate for some control weaknesses.	Procedures tend to be many, formal and complex. Much independent verification may be performed within a computerized system.
Information and Communication (Accounting system)	Tends to be relatively simple with heavy use of manual procedures and independent microcomputer applications.	Tends to be highly sophisticated with heavy use of mainframe computing and networked microcomputer applications.
Monitoring Activities	Monitoring will often be informal due to the direct involvement of the owner/manager.	Formal and sophisticated monitoring procedures on a continuous basis using technology or separate evaluations by internal auditors.
Auditor Documentation	Documentation using a narrative will often be adequate due to simplicity of system(s).	Documentation using flowcharts and questionnaires is advised due to complexity and number of systems.

For purposes of a GAAS Audit, the auditor's impact of the auditor's assessment of ICOFR and its relationship to the testing needed to support the assessment is illustrated and summarized in Table 7.6. We also introduce the relationship of the results of these assessments and tests with the auditor's substantive testing in Table 7.6. We will re-examine the trade-off of internal control testing and substantive testing in more detail in Chapter 10.

Summary and Conclusion

In this chapter, we have discussed the role of internal control over financial reporting in a GAAS Audit while noting that the same fundamental concepts apply to the PCAOB mandated Integrated Audit that we will discuss in Chapter 8. Regardless of the type of audit being performed, the techniques and procedures used to evaluate internal control are essentially the same for all audits. The auditor assesses control risk for management assertions as high, moderate, or low based on the auditor's evaluation of internal control system design, performs tests of controls when reliance on control is set as being below maximum, and designs and adjusts, if need be, the auditor's substantive tests of assertions based on the outcome of the control risk assessment and testing so as to reduce audit risk to the appropriately low level. In general, the better the ICOFR, meaning the fewer significant deficiencies, the less substantive testing the auditor will perform for a given assertion.

Table 7.6 *Relating Conclusions about Internal Control over Financial Reporting to Substantive Testing*

	Control Risk = 100% (Maximum)	**Control Risk < 100%** (Slightly Reduced)	**Control Risk << 100%** (Greatly Reduced)
Conditions Necessary in a GAAS Audit	The auditor assesses that controls are lacking, or tests of ICOFR reveal one or more *significant deficiencies* such that the controls would not detect a material misstatement in the financial statements on a timely basis should they exist. OR The auditor can justify that substantive tests alone are effective for reducing achieved audit risk to an acceptable level. (*Such circumstances would be considered to be rare.*)	The auditor assesses that some key controls are lacking, or tests of ICOFR reveals one or more *significant deficiencies* but that the system would still likely detect some, but not all, material misstatements in the financial statements on a timely basis should they exist. OR Procedures are limited to basic process analysis, client enquiry, walkthroughs and limited observation. Additional tests of controls are not considered appropriate based on the auditor's preliminary assessment of ICOFR	The auditor's assessment and testing of ICOFR reveals no *significant deficiencies.*
Nature of Evidence Required to be Documented in order to Support Conclusions about Internal Control over Financial Reporting and Resulting Assessments of Control Risk	• Client Enquiry: Extensively used to obtain details of control activities. • Observation: Performed to obtain details of control activities.	• Client Enquiry: Extensively used to obtain details of control activities. • Observation: Performed to obtain details of control activities and repeated during different time periods to check for changes. • Documentation: Reviewed on a walkthrough basis to clarify control activities performed.	• Client Enquiry: Extensively used to obtain details of control activities. • Observation: Performed to obtain details of control activities and repeated during different time periods to check for changes. Plus: Tests of Controls • Client Inquiry and Observation: Used to *verify* control activities. • Documentation: Extensively used to see if appropriate control activities were performed. • Accuracy: To test whether reconciliations have been effectively performed and reviewed.

	Control Risk = 100% (Maximum)	Control Risk < 100% (Slightly Reduced)	Control Risk << 100% (Greatly Reduced)
Implication for Planning Substantive Tests of Transactions, Accounts, Estimates, and Disclosures	Reliance on Internal Control to reduce audit risk: *None* Use of Substantive testing to reduce control risk: *Very Extensive*	Reliance on Internal Control to reduce audit risk: *None/Limited* Use of Substantive testing to reduce control risk: *Extensive*	Reliance on Internal Control to reduce audit risk: *Extensive* Use of Substantive testing to reduce control risk: *Minimal*

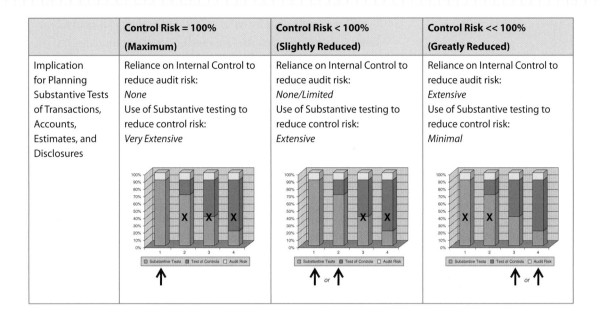

Appendix A: Information Technology and Internal Controls[7]

The objective of an audit and the need to assess risks and understand control are not affected by the extent and nature of information technology used by an organization—the same basic auditing standards and financial reporting objectives apply in all situations. However, the auditor must be aware of the nature of an organization's information technology because the design and operation of systems will have a direct impact on audit risk, the conduct of the audit, the evaluation of processes, and the nature of audit evidence to be gathered.

Impact of Information Technology

A number of differences can be observed in an organization's processes when it is highly computerized and automated. Some of the more significant changes include:

- Computer input/output devices (keyboard, mouse, and printer) replace manual devices (typewriter, pencils, and document imprinting machines).
- Computer screens and electronic images replace paper documents.
- Computer files replace paper journals and ledgers.
- Fiber optics, cable connections, networks, and e-mail replace interoffice mail and fax communications.
- Application software replaces procedures manuals.
- Flexible reporting replaces fixed periodic reporting.
- More data replaces less data.
- Real-time transaction processing replaces batch processing.

- Internal processing may be replaced by service center processing.
- Resident data storage may be replaced by "cloud" data storage.
- Systematic problems become more pervasive than random errors.

Some of these changes may seem mundane. However, because an auditor must be familiar with the risks and controls within a system, all of these changes have potential implications for the audit process. For example, the availability of documentary evidence, the existence of reliable computerized controls, variations in reporting, and the ability to access large volumes of on-line data all have implications for conducting the audit and the nature of evidence that will be available to the auditor for testing specific management assertions.

Probably the most relevant distinction is the last one—the nature of errors that can occur. Prior to extensive computerization, manual processing of individual transactions meant that every single transaction was at risk of improper handling and random errors. With computerization, consistency across transactions is increased. If the system is properly programmed to handle a specific type of transaction, it will be handled in essentially the same way every time. Thus, routine transactions are typically low risk. Problems arise when a transaction falls outside the normal parameters of the system. For example, a transaction may be for an amount larger than the system allows or involve nonstandard terms. In these cases, the system could repeatedly mishandle the transaction if there is no human intervention. Consequently, the risk of random errors in routine transactions is reduced but the risk of systematic errors in unusual transactions may be increased.

Myths Concerning Information Technology and Internal Control

A number of myths have evolved over time concerning the relationship between information technology and internal control. In many cases, these myths result from a serious misunderstanding on the part of auditors of the strengths and limitations of information technology. Often these myths have resulted in the auditor treating computer systems as being unfathomable, causing the auditors to "audit around" the computer, or automatically calling in an IT specialist.

The biggest myth is that control objectives change when an information system is automated. This is not true because the basic definition of internal control makes no reference to technology; it simply refers to the three basic objectives of good internal control:

1. To improve the effectiveness of management decision making and the efficiency of business processes.
2. To increase the reliability of accounting information.
3. To foster compliance with rules and regulations.

These objectives apply regardless of the extent of computerization. Other myths concerning internal control in automated systems include the following:

Myth 1—Information technology is primarily a risk to be controlled: Many auditors perceive that computerized systems increase risk. This perspective fails to consider the increase in control that may be achieved through computerized controls and the processing consistency that can be achieved across transactions. Complex systems may create some new risks for the organization, but the auditor should not overlook the extensive control advantage that can be achieved through computerization of information processes. IT is often a facilitator of control, not a threat to control.

Myth 2—The more complex a technology-based system, the greater the risks: Complexity may tend to increase certain kinds of risks, especially related to interactions between subsystems, networks, data files, and program code, but manual systems or mixed systems are not necessarily of lower risk. Information manipulation and transfer that is performed manually is always subject to corruption; mixed manual-computerized systems often involve manual interfaces where human error can be introduced. Spreadsheets are an area where the use of technology can be both an aid to control and a threat to reliability.

Myth 3—Automated information processing destroys the audit trail: This myth focuses narrowly on a paper-based audit trail. Computerization can actually increase the audit trail for a transaction by using internal references to connect transactions across subsystems in a network. For example, the use of scanning technology to keep track of the location of packages in the FedEx shipping system enhances the ability to follow transaction processing. Similarly, reference numbers can be used to keep track of transactions or events in progress (e.g., confirmation numbers for hotel reservations and cancellations).

Myth 4—Weaknesses observed on an anecdotal basis prove the inability to control complex systems: A few well-publicized system failures are often used as an argument for minimizing system complexity or auditor reliance on a system. This perspective reveals more about the fear of technology than actual system reliability. When a large bank fraud is perpetrated using computer technology, or the phone system in a major city fails due to a software glitch, the popular media tends to overstate the risk and extent of such problems, leading to the myth that complex systems are inherently unstable. In fact, given the pervasiveness of such systems, the relative lack of problems is notable and creates an expectation of perfection that results in overreaction to the rare failure that does occur. On the other hand, complex information systems may be used to perpetrate inappropriate or fraudulent behavior[xii].

Myth 5—Small organizations cannot have good automated controls: A few years ago, computerized systems were synonymous with large mainframe computers and complex application codes. With the increase in computing power now available on the desktop, as well as the related advances in software, even the smallest organization can use technology to establish and operate an automated information system. For a relatively small investment, fairly sophisticated accounting systems can be put in place that provide much of the analytical power and control over processing that was only available in large applications a decade ago. Off the shelf accounting

[xii]**EXAMPLE**

In 2015, Volkswagen embedded software into their diesel powered cars to fool the machines used to rate the fuel economy of those engines. The software allowed the vehicles to mimic compliance with emissions standards when, in reality, they spewed forty times the allowed level of certain pollutants. While this was a business issue for Volkswagen, the accounting implications were significant with the company incurring significant fines, litigation costs, lost value in inventory, and lost brand value.

software may significantly reduce many of the traditional accounting risks within small organizations.

These myths, when taken together, highlight the fact that the introduction of technology is a double-edged sword. It does create some new risks for the organization but often alleviates many other, more significant risks. In general, the introduction of technology in an information system results in improved quantity, quality, and availability of information for use in the organization.

Illustrative Controls in a Computerized Information System

The nature of specific control activities changes in a highly computerized information environment due to new activities and processes being introduced in the more complex information system installed. These changes lead to new risk concerns as well as new opportunities for exercising control over transactions. The following provides some illustrations of control activities in a computerized environment. The details of individual control activities will differ across systems.[8]

Processing Controls

Authorization: There are two aspects of authorization that can be affected by technology. First, technology can lead to standardization of authorization within a process. For example, a grocery store can use scanning technology to link its cash registers directly to the product price database, providing increased consistency and easy modification of current prices. Similarly, on-line approvals of credit card purchases decrease the risk of fraudulent use of credit cards. Second, the design and implementation of the system raises numerous authorization issues. System parameters and changes need to be authorized, often requiring significant design, development, and testing, before systems are allowed to come on-line.

Use of Documents and Records: Documents and records are more and more frequently becoming digital, often with no paper existence at all. Computer screen images are used for data input/output (documents), and computerized data files contain all evidence of transaction processing (records). Consequently, the basic design principles for documents and records apply to digital images as much as paper documents. Data input screens should be well-designed to minimize entry errors, transactions should be prenumbered and cross-referenced to related "documents," and the integrity of data files must be maintained against improper changes or usage.

Controls over file revision and destruction are very important in a computerized environment, especially when master files are periodically updated using data from transaction files. Multiple generations of master files need to be maintained to assure processing accuracy and to protect against hardware or software failures that might corrupt or destroy data, necessitating expensive file reconstruction. File controls such as external and internal labels, the use of read-only files, and file protection rings on tapes are all useful for preventing accidental destruction or corruption of data.

Independent Verifications: Probably the most numerous of computerized controls fall in the area of independent verification, especially as relates to data entry. The range and nature of data entry and transaction controls is quite large and depends on the method of processing being used. Manual data entry, such as keypunching, presents problems that are different from scanning entry or direct data download from an external party (e.g., electronic connections to suppliers). Electronic edit checks tend to replace manual data checks when systems are computerized. Some of the more common verifications are described in Table 7.7.

Other controls include the use of batch control totals, exception reporting, and process controls. Batch controls use summary data over a group of related transactions to verify that the group was accurately processed *in total*. Exception reporting triggers human intervention when a transaction fails some test condition embedded in the system. Processing controls tend to focus on the revision of data included in the organization databases so as to assure long-term reliability and data integrity.

Physical Controls

Access controls in a computerized system take on new meaning, but this is one area where the popular media has properly sensitized people to potential risks. Increased use of the Internet for credit transactions has highlighted the potential dangers of transmitting sensitive economic data electronically. Data encryption reduces the risk of unauthorized interception and use of information that is being transmitted over the Internet. However, the Internet

Table 7.7 *Common Edit Checks in Automated Systems*

Edit Check	Description
Key verification	Duplicate processing of input to identify discrepancies in data entry.
Verification of check digits	Embedding digits into an account code that reflect the numerical combination of other digits in the code which can be tested for internal consistency by the computer
Completeness check	Verification that all required data has been entered
Use of default values	Substitution of default values for key data fields unless explicitly replaced by the user. An example is automated entry of the sales tax percentage during billing processing
Range check	Verification of a value against maximum and minimum limits (e.g., credit limits)
Validity check	Verification of new data against previously entered data maintained in a master file. For example, when new shipments are being entered into the perpetual inventory records the computer can verify that specific part numbers are included in the master database
Sign check	Verification that proper positive or negative values are entered
Referential integrity check	Verification that two data sets that share a common data field have the same items included. For example, if a payroll register includes a specific employee, the inclusion of that person could be tested in related files such as the master payroll file, insurance coverage file and pay rate authorization file
Reasonableness check	Verification that summary totals for a transaction fall within specified guidelines
Sequence check	Verification that transaction identification numbers are used in the proper sequence
Transaction type check	Verification that a transaction is being entered into the proper records. For example, an attempt to improperly enter a payroll transaction into the purchases journal could be prevented

is an open medium and the problems of misuse of data, invasion of privacy, theft of identity, and outright fraud are very real when dealing in a world of electronic commerce (e-commerce).

Access controls can help with both network security and unauthorized entry by outside parties (hackers). Limitations on access can be improved with physical controls such as securing the facilities where computers, data files, and system documentation are maintained, as well as electronic controls, which forestall unauthorized access to the system. Electronic access controls can include the use of passwords and user identifications, scheduled processing that allows access to certain files only at specified times, and dedicated communication channels not accessible to outsiders.

Segregation of Duties

Introduction of technology into information systems tends to result in the need for two-dimensional segregation of duties. Not only must an organization segregate across traditional dimensions (access to assets, accounting for assets, and authorization of assets) but also across the data processing function itself. The segregation within data processing should, at a minimum, provide adequate separation of the system analyst, programmer, computer operator, data librarian, and data control group.

Summary

System computerization is often a mixed blessing to an organization. The fear that computerization of information systems will induce increased risk is usually based on a lack of understanding of the benefits that can accrue from proper utilization of system automation. The objectives of the audit process are not affected by the existence of extensive computerization within an accounting system, but the auditor must be aware that computerization will have a tremendous impact on how a system is designed and operated. Consequently, different risks may become important to the auditor, and the audit plan will be modified to reflect those risks and the evidence available to support management's assertions.

Appendix B: Flowcharting Techniques

Overview of Flowcharting

Flowcharting is an extremely useful technique for documenting activities and transaction processing within an organization. When combined with a narrative description of the system and a completed internal control questionnaire, the auditor can obtain a thorough understanding of how a system operates, which provides a good foundation for making initial assessments of control risk. An example of a simple system flowchart was presented in Figure 7.3.

There are many variations in the way flowcharts are prepared. The purpose of this appendix is to introduce a few of the more common techniques and guidelines for preparing flowcharts. The level of detail to include in the flowchart depends on the objectives of the exercise and the preferences of the preparer. At one extreme, flowcharts can be very broad and general, especially when applied to organization-wide systems. These types of flowcharts are useful when preparing a process map and for identifying the key activities in an organization, the personnel associated with each activity, and the connections among the activities. At the other extreme, flowcharts can be very detailed, depicting the tiniest steps in the process. These flowcharts may be prepared from the perspective of a single department or even a single individual. The example in Figure 7.3 can be considered to be at the moderate level of detail because it encompasses a perspective across departments with some departmental details included.

Key Elements of a Flowchart

All flowcharts consist of three basic components: (1) symbols to represent activities and objects in the system, (2) discrete sections to demarcate responsibilities across departments and individuals, and (3) lines and arrows to represent movement within the system.

Figure 7.5 displays some of the most common symbols used in flowcharts. The definition of flowchart symbols is not completely standardized, and different auditors, firms, and systems analysts may have different variations. Most of the symbols depicted in Figure 7.5 are used in the example documented in Figure 7.3.

The boundaries between areas of responsibility are key elements of a flowchart. Symbols for actions should pertain to a specific department or individual that can be easily identified with a glance at the flowchart. For example, Figure 7.3 depicts three areas of responsibility: sales order entry and billing, shipping, and data processing. By placing the flowchart symbols within a clearly defined area, the flowchart identifies who is performing the activity.

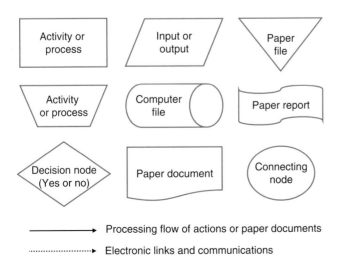

Figure 7.5 *Selected Flowchart Symbols*

Lines and arrows are used to indicate the connections between various objects within the flowchart and the flow of information, documents, and authority. Most commonly, a line with an arrow indicates that paperwork is being sent from one place to another, but lines and arrows can be used to indicate the electronic flow of data as well (e.g., dotted lines). Occasionally, a line/arrow will connect to an object that appears on another page of the flowchart. In that case, the line is taken to the edge of the page and terminated in a circle. The circle indicates an inter-page connection, and the reader should be able to find another circle with the same code on another page of the flowchart where the information flow resumes.

Guidelines for Flowchart Preparation

All well-prepared flowcharts follow a few simple rules which improve interpretation of the flowchart in spite of personal variations in style.

- **Flows should go from left to right and top to bottom:** Flowcharts, like books, are easiest to interpret if they are presented from left to right and from top to bottom. Connections going up or to the left are allowed but should be used sparingly. Such "reverse" flows generally mean that a transaction is being recycled or reprocessed.

- **Origination of all actions and documents should be clearly indicated:** Documents may arrive from outside the organization, be created by someone depicted in the flowchart, or arrive from a part of the organization that is not presented in the flowchart.

- **Termination of all actions and documents should be clearly indicated:** Documents should terminate by leaving the organization, being permanently filed in a department depicted in the flowchart, or being forwarded to a part of the organization that is not presented in the flowchart.

- **Keep it simple:** Flowcharts should be presented in as streamlined a manner as possible to retain the information that needs to be presented. An excessively "busy" or cluttered flowchart can create confusion rather than clarity. The appropriate level of detail is a matter of judgment, but it should be detailed enough to present the activities that are important to the reader. However, it is critical that each step of the process be easily understood by someone who is not familiar with the underlying process.

- **Check for completeness:** A final review should be made to make sure that no significant elements, activities, or connections have been omitted. The preparation of a flowchart tends to be an iterative process, resulting in frequent changes and revisions as more information becomes available and is selected for inclusion in the flowchart.

Auditors use flowcharts to enhance their understanding of the accounting system, transaction processing, and internal control. Although there is no single proper way to prepare a flowchart, the use of the techniques described above will increase the effectiveness and efficiency of preparing flowcharts and understanding the information contained therein.

Bibliography of Relevant Literature

Relevant Research

Ashton, R. H. 1974. An Experimental Study of Internal Control Judgments. *Journal of Accounting Research*. 12(1): 143–157.

Beasley, M., J. Carcello, and D. Hermanson, 1999. *Fraudulent Financial Reporting: 1987–1997. An Analysis of US Public Companies.* New York: Committee of Sponsoring Organizations of the Treadway Commission.

Beasley, M., J. Carcello, D. Hermanson, and T. Neal. 2010. *Fraudulent Financial Reporting 1998–2007: An Analysis of US Public Companies.* New York: Committee of Sponsoring Organizations of the Treadway Commission.

Biggs, S. and T. J. Mock, 1983. An Investigation of Auditor Decision Processes in the Evaluation of Internal Controls and Audit Scope Decisions. *Journal of Accounting Research*. 21(1): 234–255.

Kreutzfeldt, R. W. and W. A. Wallace. 1990. Control Risk Assessments: Do They Relate to Errors? *Auditing: A Journal of Practice and Theory*. 9(Supplement): 1–48.

Mayper, A. G. 1982. Consensus of Auditors' Materiality Judgments of Internal Accounting Control Weaknesses. *Journal of Accounting Research*. 20(2 Part II): 773–783.

Trotman, K. T. and R. Wood. 1991. A Meta-Analysis of Studies on Internal Control Judgment. *Journal of Accounting Research*. 29(1): 180–192.

Willingham, J. J. and W. F. Wright. 1985. Financial Statement Errors and Internal Control Judgments. *Auditing: A Journal of Practice and Theory*. 5(1): 57–70.

Auditing Standards

Criteria of Control Board. 1995. *Guidance on Control*. CPA Canada (formerly the Canadian Institute of Chartered Accountants).

COSO—Committee of Sponsoring Organizations. 1992. *Internal Control: An Integrated Framework*.

COSO—Committee of Sponsoring Organizations. 2013. *Internal Control: An Integrated Framework*.

IAASB *International Standards on Auditing (ISA)* No. 265, "Communicating Deficiencies in Internal Control to Those Charged with Governance and Management."

IAASB *International Standards on Auditing (ISA)* No. 315, "Identifying and Assessing the Risks of Material Misstatement through Understanding the Entity and Its Environment."

IAASB *International Standards on Auditing (ISA)* No. 330, "The Auditor's Responses to Assessed Risks."

SOX Sarbanes-Oxley Act - Library of Congress. 2002. House Resolution Number 3763, An Act to protect investors by improving the accuracy and reliability of corporate disclosures made pursuant to the securities laws, and for other purposes (*The Sarbanes-Oxley Act of 2002*). www.libraryofcongress.gov.

Notes

1   CPA Canada (formerly CICA). Criteria of Control Committee: Guidance on Control, 1995, paragraph 6.

2   Beasley, Carcello, and Hermanson, *Fraudulent Financial Reporting: 1987–1997. An Analysis of US Public Companies* and updated to 2007 in Beasley, Carcello, Hermanson, and Neal. *Fraudulent Financial Reporting 1998-2007: An Analysis of US Public Companies.*

3   The offsetting credit to the debit to accounts receivable would be to sales; the offsetting debit to the credit to accounts receivable would be to cash.

4   Payables may also be disaggregated by a voucher ledger, which essentially lists amounts payable by the date the liability was incurred or is due.

5   The emphasis on requiring that controls normally be tested as part of the audit of financial statements is a change from previous audit practice. Until recently, it was assumed that control risk could be set at maximum for any or all assertions and account classes because substantive procedures alone could efficiently provide all necessary audit evidence. The choice was often justified as a more cost-efficient approach even though testing of internal controls has been encouraged by professional standards for over three decades, but has never been required.

6   An unstated assumption about the performance of audit testing is that the company will correct any mistakes that the auditor detects.

7   There are several excellent textbooks that provide extensive coverage of this topic. The Information Systems Audit and Control Association that grants the Certified Information Systems Auditor (CISA) Designation is another resource in this area. See www.isaca.org/.

8   This overview is not intended to be comprehensive or technical.

CHAPTER 8

Internal Control over Financial Reporting in an Integrated Audit

Outline

- Introduction
- Management's Responsibility for Internal Control
  - o COSO's Internal Control Defined
  - o Components of Internal Control
    - Control Environment
    - Risk Assessment
    - Control Activities
    - Information and Communication
    - Monitoring
    - Integrating Internal Controls
    - Applying the COSO Framework
- Consideration of Internal Control over Financial Reporting in an Integrated Audit
  - o Classifying Control Deficiencies
  - o Requirement for the Auditor to Plan Internal Control Tests
  - o The special role of entity level controls in an Integrated Audit
  - o Assessment of Control Risk: Implications for Tests of Financial Statement Assertions
  - o The Auditor's Reporting Responsibilities in an Integrated Audit
  - o Management Remediation of Material Weaknesses and Auditor Reporting on such Remediation
- Summary and Conclusion
- Bibliography of Relevant Literature

Learning Goals for this Chapter

1. Understand the central role of internal control over financial reporting in an Integrated Audit.

2. Deepen the understanding of the components of internal control under COSO.

3. Integrate the top-down approach to the audit introduced in Chapters 4, 5, and 6 with the COSO internal control components and underlying principles.

4. Develop the ability to apply the COSO *Internal Control-Integrated Framework* to evaluate the system of internal controls over financial reporting (ICOFR).

5. Assess control risk via an evaluation of ICOFR under the COSO Framework.

6. Understand the classification of control deficiencies in an Integrated Audit.

7. Adapt audit plans in light of the findings about ICOFR in an Integrated Audit.

8. Introduce how auditor's design remediation engagements for identified material weaknesses can be undertaken before the next year-end.

Introduction

(i)EXAMPLE

Pre-SOX some balance sheet accounts such as tax liabilities were not subject to extensive internal controls since the client's tax department usually worked closely with the auditor's tax experts to come up with the appropriate quarterly and year end numbers. Under SOX such an approach would lead to an adverse opinion on internal control effectiveness because auditors were perceived as (1) auditing their own work, and (2) fulfilling responsibilities that should reside with management, both conditions being considered a violation of independence standards. Thus, companies rushed to develop well-controlled processes related to the tax computations needed to prepare financial reports.

The US Public Company Accounting Oversight Board (PCAOB) requires the auditor of a public company registered with the US Securities and Exchange Commission (SEC) to evaluate and report on the effectiveness of a company's internal control over financial reporting system (ICOFR). Given that hundreds of firms around the world are registered with the SEC, auditors in many countries have become familiar with PCAOB standards for the Integrated Audit. As noted before, this book features a complete integration of International Auditing and Assurance Services Board (IAASB) and PCAOB audit standards. However, one major difference between a GAAS Audit (i.e., IAASB standards-based) and an Integrated Audit (i.e., PCAOB standards-based) is that in the Integrated Audit the auditor must test and report on the effectiveness of ICOFR. This PCAOB requirement is based on the rationale that all public companies should have strong internal control systems that reduce control risk to a relatively low level for all material classes of transactions and account balances. Management of SEC registrants, except for the very smallest firms (less than $100 million in sales or market capitalization), have little choice but to implement controls over material transactions that directly affect financial reporting because failure to do so will result in an adverse audit opinion about the effectiveness of ICOFR[i].

One purpose of this chapter is to expand on the discussion of COSO's *Internal Control-Integrated Framework* introduced in Chapter 7 to provide the basis for understanding management's responsibilities pertaining to their evaluation and testing of ICOFR in an Integrated Audit. As we discuss the COSO Framework in more detail in this chapter, we relate management responsibilities for the five interrelated components of the COSO Framework to how an auditor—using the audit approach described in Chapters 4, 5 and 6—gathers evidence about the completeness and accuracy of management's assessment of ICOFR. We then introduce the auditor's planning objectives related to internal control assessment; the nature, extent and timing of control testing; and the reporting requirements in an Integrated Audit.

It is important to note that the process to document and evaluate the design of ICOFR, as well as the means employed to test the effectiveness of controls, are essentially the same whether one is carrying out an Integrated Audit or a GAAS Audit. Hence, the material in Chapter 7 is relevant to an Integrated Audit's approach for evaluating ICOFR. The main difference is that in an Integrated Audit, strong ICOFR is expected so control effectiveness must be explicitly tested. Because management is responsible for designing and testing ICOFR, the first part of this chapter explores the COSO Framework that is used by management in evaluating their ICOFR. Knowledge of the COSO Framework is also useful to those carrying out GAAS Audits as it provides a benchmark against which to judge ICOFR effectiveness. We use the second part of this chapter to emphasize the added reporting requirements that an auditor must meet in order to complete an Integrated Audit.

AUTHORITATIVE GUIDANCE & STANDARDS

The requirement for the auditor to formally evaluate ICOFR in an Integrated Audit arises from Section 404 of the Sarbanes-Oxley Act of 2002. This chapter focuses primarily on the guidance provided in PCAOB AS 2201 (formerly AS 5) **An Audit of Internal Control Over Financial Reporting That Is Integrated with An Audit of Financial Statements** *for companies that are publicly traded in the US for reporting on ICOFR at year-end. PCAOB AS 2201 followed an earlier standard, PCAOB AS 2, which it superseded. All considerations in Chapter 7 apply when considering the reliance that is placed on internal control for determining the nature and extent of substantive tests.*

Management's Responsibility For Internal Control

An important premise underlying the Integrated Audit is that management takes formal responsibility for establishing, implementing, and monitoring ICOFR. In order to fulfill this formal responsibility, management must:

1. Explicitly acknowledge responsibility for the effectiveness of ICOFR.

2. Explicitly evaluate the effectiveness of ICOFR using suitable control criteria (e.g., the COSO Framework introduced in Chapter 7 and elaborated on in this chapter).

3. Support the evaluation with sufficient evidence, including documentation of the design of controls related to all relevant assertions.

4. Present a written assessment of the effectiveness of ICOFR supported by tests of controls as of the end of the most recent fiscal year.

Management must follow procedures similar to those described in Chapter 7 to document and assess the effectiveness of internal controls over financial reporting. Management must analyze any control deficiencies that are identified during the course of their evaluation of ICOFR. A control deficiency occurs when the design or operation of any part of the system of ICOFR is insufficient to prevent or detect significant errors or misstatements.

COSO's Internal Control Defined

In Chapter 7, we introduced the five key components of internal control as a means for the auditor to evaluate the design of a system of ICOFR. In this chapter, we delve into the COSO Framework in greater depth to understand the responsibilities of management for evaluating and testing internal controls. In some ways one can consider the COSO Framework being "GAAP" for internal controls. How management does its work of documenting and testing ICOFR will affect how the auditor gathers the information needed to make the auditor's independent control risk assessment and the nature and extent of the auditor's tests of ICOFR to establish the auditor's assessment of effectiveness.

COSO (2013) defines internal control as "a process, affected by an entity's Board of Directors, management and other personnel, designed to provide reasonable assurance regarding the achievement of objectives relating to operations, reporting, and compliance." (COSO Internal Control: Integrated Framework Executive Summary, p. 3). The COSO Framework provides three categories of objectives:

1. Operational objectives pertaining to the effectiveness and efficiency of the entity's operations including operational and financial performance goals and the safeguarding of assets against loss.

2. Reporting objectives pertaining to internal and external financial and non-financial reporting may include reliability, timeliness, transparency and other similar terms set forth by regulators, recognized standard setters, or the entity's own policies.

3. Compliance objectives pertaining to the entity adhering to laws and regulations.

An organization may use different types of internal controls for achieving each of the three categories of objectives. Hence, it is the auditor's responsibility to obtain a basic understanding of the controls being used by a specific client related to specific control objectives.

AUTHORITATIVE GUIDANCE & STANDARDS

AS 2201 defines ICOFR as "a process designed by, or under the supervision of, the company's principal executive and principal financial officers, or persons performing similar functions and effected by the company's Board of Directors, management, and other personnel, to provide reasonable assurance regarding the reliability of financial reporting and the preparation of financial statements for external purposes in accordance with GAAP..."
AS 2201's definition covers only financially related internal controls and is more limited than the COSO internal control definition that management would use if it were to fully implement the COSO Framework as an overall control framework rather than just limiting it to ICOFR. Hence, AS 2201 limits management and auditor responsibilities for assessing ICOFR to those aspects of the COSO Framework that are relevant to AS 2201's objectives.

The COSO Framework emphasizes a number of important attributes of internal control.

- Internal control is a process, meaning it is something the organization does on an ongoing basis. Situations, people, and risks change, suggesting that internal control needs to be a continuous activity. It is a means to an end, not an end in and of itself.

- Internal control is ultimately part of management's responsibilities, and failure to design effective controls is itself a deficiency and suggests ineffective management.

- Internal controls have inherent limitations that prevent them from eliminating all risks. For example, employees make mistakes, senior management may bypass controls, and individuals may collude to commit fraud. Because some problems may not be prevented or detected by controls, the goal of internal control is to provide reasonable assurance, rather than absolute protection, against risks.

- Internal controls need to be adaptable to the entity's structure, as they have to be scaled up or down depending on changes in the overall entity.

Components of Internal Control

As introduced in Chapter 7, there are five inter-related components to controls that support management achievement of three types of objectives which may be applied to the whole entity or individual units within the entity. These multiple dimensions are portrayed in COSO *Internal Control-Integrated Framework* as the cube presented in Figure 8.1. In this chapter, we deepen our understanding of the COSO Framework by linking the Framework first to management's evaluation and testing of control effectiveness and then relate the Framework to the top-down process used by the auditor to gather knowledge of the entity and process controls that support the auditor's testing of the effectiveness of ICOFR.

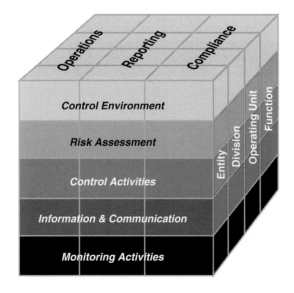

Figure 8.1 *COSO'S 2013 Internal Control—Integrated Framework Used as Basis for Addressing Internal Control over Financial Reporting*

Source: *Internal Control—Integrated Framework, Committee of Sponsoring Organizations of the Treadway Commission.* 2013, AICPA, Jersey City, NJ

Control Environment

In Chapter 7 we introduced an organization's control environment, defined by COSO as "the set of standards, processes, and structures that provide the basis for carrying out internal control across the organization" (COSO 2013, p. 31). The five underlying principles that generally must exist in order for management to determine they have an effective control environment are:[1]

1. The organization demonstrates a commitment to integrity and ethical values.

2. The Board of Directors demonstrates independence from management and exercises oversight of the development and performance of internal control.

3. Management establishes, subject to board oversight and agreement, the overall structure of internal control lines of authority and reporting, and assigns responsibilities to enable the organization to achieve its objectives.

4. The organization demonstrates a commitment to attract, develop, and retain competent individuals whose skills and abilities are in alignment with the needs of the organization's plans and objectives.

5. The organization holds individuals accountable for their internal control responsibilities in the pursuit of the entity's objectives.

Each of these principles are associated with a specific "points of focus" as illustrated in Box 8.1 "Control Environment Principles and Points of Focus". "Points of focus" are described in the COSO Framework as items that "assist management in designing, implementing, and conducting internal control, and in assessing whether the relevant principles are, in fact, present and functioning" (COSO Framework, p. 24). In general, the points of focus are designed to direct management's attention to important conditions and activities that will facilitate an effective control environment.

The auditor's perspective: Auditors who follow the procedures laid out in Chapters 4, 5 and 6 will gain required knowledge about the control

BOX 8.1 CONTROL ENVIRONMENT PRINCIPLES AND POINTS OF FOCUS

Principle 1: Demonstrates Commitment to Integrity and Ethical Values *The organization demonstrates a commitment to integrity and ethical values.*

Points of Focus

- *Setting and consistently communicating from the top of the organization a commitment to integrity and ethics values.*
- *Establishment of standards of conduct both with respect to internal operations of the entity and between the entity and outside parties.*
- *Evidence of adherence to standards of conduct.*
- *Processes to detect and deal with deviations from the standards in a timely manner.*

Principle 2: Exercises Oversight Responsibility *The Board of Directors demonstrates independence from management and exercises oversight of the development and performance of internal control.*

Points of Focus

- *The board identifies and accepts its responsibilities for oversight of management and internal control more generally.*

- *The board evaluates whether it has the skills and expertise needed among its members to enable them to ask probing questions of management and take actions where warranted.*

- *The board has a sufficient (often defined as at least a majority) number of directors who are independent from management and who can be objective in evaluations and decision-making.*

- *The board retains oversight responsibilities (or often delegates it to a committee of the board) for management's design, implementation and conduct of internal control, especially the five interrelated components highlighted in Figure 8.1.*

Principle 3: Establishes Structure, Authority, and Responsibility
Management establishes, subject to board oversight and agreement, structures, reporting lines of authority, and assigns responsibilities to enable the organization to achieve its objectives.

Points of Focus

- *Management and the board consider the various ways that they have organized the business of the entity including operating units, legal entities, geographic organization, and the use of outsourced service providers to support the achievement of the entity's objectives.*

- *Management designs and evaluates lines of reporting for each entity in the organization structure to enable delegation of authority and assignment of responsibility to lower level managers and ensure that management has the information flows both across and up and down the organization to be able to manage the entity.*

- *Management defines, assigns and sets limits on the authority of managers and personnel at various levels in the entity. This includes appropriate segregation of duties and the enforcement of information technology controls and processes to allow only those authorized to have access to the entity's proprietary information.*

Principle 4: Demonstrates Commitment to Competence
The organization demonstrates a commitment to attract, develop, and retain competent individuals whose skills and abilities are in alignment with the needs of the organization plans to achieve its objectives.

Points of Focus

- *Establish policies and practices, at a level of detail necessary for the given level responsibility and authority, consistent with the entity being able to achieve its objectives.*

- Assess whether those assigned and held accountable for the given responsibilities have the competence to carry them out. This may be especially important in areas where there is fast technological change in which one day's leading edge may be tomorrow obsolete skill set.

- Consistent with the strategy employed to achieve the entity's objectives, that the organization have processes to attract, develop, and retain sufficient and competent personnel and external service providers.

- That the organization carry out appropriate succession planning especially for senior management and other mission critical personnel as well as key third party service providers.

Principle 5: Enforces Accountability   *The organization holds individuals accountable for their internal control responsibilities in the pursuit of the entity's objectives. A well-designed internal control system will not be effective unless those that are in the positions that require them to execute the policies and practices including related actions actually do so.*

Points of Focus

- *Mechanisms must be in place to communicate and hold responsible individuals for their performance of internal control activities and to implement corrective action where need be.*

- *That performance measures, incentives, and rewards appropriate for the responsibilities at the various levels of the entity be provided taking into consideration appropriate dimensions of performance and expected standards of conduct with appropriate balancing of short term and long-term entity objectives.*

- *That in evaluating the performance measures and associated incentives and rewards that there is alignment between those incentives and rewards and fulfillment of internal control responsibilities.*

- *That management and the board evaluate and adjust for excessive pressures associated with the achievement of objectives as they assign responsibilities, develop performance measures, and evaluate performance of those in the organization.*

- *That the reward and incentive system provides rewards (or where needed disciplinary action) for (lack of) performance of internal control responsibilities including adherence to standards of conduct and expected levels of competence.*

environment of an organization to enable them to audit management's assertions about ICOFR effectiveness. In particular, the general knowledge of the client's business in Chapter 4, plus the detailed knowledge of the strategic approach and management controls in Chapter 5, provides a basis for evaluating management's assertions about the first three principles supporting the control environment. Understanding the business processes in Chapter 6—especially as illustrated in the human resource management example—provides the auditor with an ability to assess the control environment's fourth and fifth principle[ii].

Risk Assessment

Chapter 7 also introduced the concept of risk assessment as defined by COSO: "a dynamic and iterative process for identifying and assessing risk to the achievement of objectives" (COSO 2013, p. 59). Here, risk is defined as "the possibility that an event will occur and adversely affect the achievement of objectives" (COSO 2013, p. 59). Management either explicitly or implicitly must set risk tolerances (i.e., the level of variation in performance that management can accept and still feel confident that the entity will be able to achieve its broad objectives) at the overall company level and in each of the major business segments. Setting risk tolerances was not part of the original COSO Framework but was added as part of COSO's Enterprise Risk Management framework (see Chapter 2). Indeed, one of the key differences between the two frameworks is that the eight core components of COSO's ERM framework includes setting objectives and associated risk tolerances by management. While the COSO internal control framework does not require evaluation and testing of the process for setting objectives or risk tolerances, it does require that managers evaluate and test the effectiveness of the *risk assessment* process. The evaluation of risk assessment should consider the following four additional COSO principles:

6. The organization specifies objectives with sufficient clarity to enable the identification and assessment of risks relating to objectives.

7. The organization identifies risks to the achievement of its objectives across the entity and analyzes how the risks should be managed.

8. The organization considers the potential for fraud in assessing risks.

9. The organization identifies and assesses changes that could significantly affect the system of internal control.

Box 8.2 "COSO's Risk Assessment: Objectives Principle" highlights the three general classes of objectives that managers should consider under the COSO Framework principle 6. The points of focus for Principles 7, 8 and 9 related to risk assessment are found in Box 8.3 "COSO'S Risk Assessment Principles with Related Points of Focus".

BOX 8.2 COSO'S RISK ASSESSMENT: OBJECTIVES PRINCIPLE

Principle 6: Specifies Suitable Objectives   *The organization specifies objectives with sufficient clarity to enable the identification and assessment of risks relating to objectives.*

Points of Focus

Operations Objectives

- *Reflects Management's Choices—Operations objectives reflect management's choices about structure, industry considerations, and performance of the entity.*

- *Considers Tolerances for Risk—Management considers the acceptable levels of variation relative to the achievement of operations objectives.*

- *Includes Operations and Financial Performance Goals—The organization reflects the desired level of operations and financial performance for the entity within operations objectives.*

- *Forms a Basis for Committing of Resources—Management uses operations objectives as a basis for allocating resources needed to attain desired operations and financial performance.*

External Financial Reporting Objectives

- *Complies with Applicable Accounting Standards—Financial reporting objectives are consistent with accounting principles suitable and available for that entity. The accounting principles selected are appropriate in the circumstances.*
- *Considers Materiality—Management considers materiality in financial statement presentation.*
- *Reflects Entity Activities—External reporting reflects the underlying transactions and events to show qualitative characteristics and assertions.*

External Non-Financial Reporting Objectives

- *Complies with Externally Established Standards and Frameworks—Management establishes objectives consistent with laws and regulations, or standards and frameworks of recognized external organizations.*
- *Considers the Required Level of Precision—Management reflects the required level of precision and accuracy suitable for user needs and as based on criteria established by third parties in non-financial reporting.*
- *Reflects Entity Activities—External reporting reflects the underlying transactions and events within a range of acceptable limits.*

Internal Reporting Objectives

- *Reflects Management's Choices—Internal reporting provides management with accurate and complete information regarding management's choices and information needed in managing the entity.*
- *Considers the Required Level of Precision—Management reflects the required level of precision and accuracy suitable for user needs in non-financial reporting objectives and materiality within financial reporting objectives.*
- *Reflects Entity Activities—Internal reporting reflects the underlying transactions and events within a range of acceptable limits.*

Compliance Objectives

- *Reflects External Laws and Regulations—Laws and regulations establish minimum standards of conduct that the entity integrates into compliance objectives.*
- *Considers Tolerances for Risk—Management considers the acceptable levels of variation relative to the achievement of compliance objectives.*

BOX 8.3 COSO'S RISK ASSESSMENT PRINCIPLES WITH RELATED POINTS OF FOCUS

Principle 7: Identifies and Analyzes Risk   *The organization identifies risks to the achievement of its objectives across the entity and analyzes risks as a basis for determining how the risks should be managed.*

Points of Focus

*   *Includes Entity, Subsidiary, Division, Operating Unit, and Functional Levels— The organization identifies and assesses risks at the entity, subsidiary, division, operating unit, and functional levels relevant to the achievement of objectives.*

*   *Analyzes Internal and External Factors—Risk identification considers both internal and external factors and their impact on the achievement of objectives.*

*   *Involves Appropriate Levels of Management—The organization puts into place effective risk assessment mechanisms that involve appropriate levels of management.*

*   *Estimates Significance of Risks Identified—Identified risks are analyzed through a process that includes estimating the potential significance of the risk.*

*   *Determines How to Respond to Risks—Risk assessment includes considering how the risk should be managed and whether to accept, avoid, reduce, or share the risk.*

Principle 8: Assesses Fraud Risk   *The organization considers the potential for fraud in assessing risks to the achievement of objectives.*

Points of Focus

*   *Considers Various Types of Fraud—The assessment of fraud considers fraudulent reporting, possible loss of assets, and corruption resulting from the various ways that fraud and misconduct can occur.*

*   *Assesses Incentive and Pressures—The assessment of fraud risk considers incentives and pressures.*

*   *Assesses Opportunities—The assessment of fraud risk considers opportunities for unauthorized acquisition, use, or disposal of assets, altering of the entity's reporting records, or committing other inappropriate acts.*

*   *Assesses Opportunities—The assessment of fraud risk considers opportunities for unauthorized acquisition, use, or disposal of assets, altering of the entity's reporting records, or committing other inappropriate acts.*

Principle 9: Identifies and Analyzes Significant Change: *The organization identifies and assesses changes that could significantly impact the system of internal control.*

Points of Focus

*   *Assesses Changes in the External Environment—The risk identification process considers changes to the regulatory, economic, and physical environment in which the entity operates.*

*   *Assesses Changes in the Business Model—The organization considers the potential impacts of new business lines, dramatically altered compositions of existing business lines, acquired or divested business operations on the system of internal control, rapid growth, changing reliance on foreign geographies, and new technologies.*

*   *Assesses Changes in Leadership—The organization considers changes in management and respective attitudes and philosophies on the system of internal control.*

When Section 404 of SOX became effective in 2004 (as implemented in Auditing Standard No. 2 followed by No. 5) auditors faced the challenge of trying to evaluate the effectiveness of client internal control, mostly using the COSO Framework as their criteria. However, one of their most challenging problems was the fact that many companies lacked a systematic approach to risk assessment, a key component of COSO. Nevertheless, in the early years of implementing the audit of ICOFR, auditors rarely flagged this lack of risk assessment as a material weakness, suggesting that the importance of risk assessment to the auditor and the financial statements was underappreciated by auditors and management.

The auditor's perspective: The methods of risk assessment introduced in Chapters 5 and 6 help the auditor to understand an organization's objective setting and risk tolerances. In assessing internal control, the auditor is not second guessing management decisions but is trying to understand the potential effect of the decisions management has made on the effectiveness of ICOFR. The auditor should consider whether management's risk assessment process identifies all risks that are relevant to the information portrayed in the financial statements. Of the three broad sets of management objectives encompassed by principle 6 (see Box 8.2 "COSO's Risk Assessment: Objectives Principle"), the ones that the auditor is most interested in are those pertaining to external financial reporting. However, these objectives are likely to be influenced by objectives related to management's internal controls over compliance with laws and regulations. Further, as highlighted in Chapter 5's discussion about management controls and in Chapter 6's discussion of performance reviews, the auditor utilizes management's internal reporting system in carrying out the audit. Thus, the audit will be affected by those managerial objectives as well. We have introduced how the auditor deals with fraud (principle 8) in Chapter 3 and will consider it further in Chapter 9. Chapter 7 provides the basic approach for the auditor documenting the control systems. Comparing this documentation over time can help the auditor identify any important changes in the system of internal control (principle 9). The material in Chapter 7 about internal control documentation and testing will be elaborated on in Chapters 11 to 13 where we consider various business processes that are audit sensitive(iii).

Control Activities

COSO defines control activities as "actions established through policies and procedures that help ensure that management's directives to mitigate risks to the achievement of objectives are carried out" (COSO 2013, p. 87). Control activities are the "things a company does" to reduce the effect of risk from both an operational and financial reporting perspective. Often, control activities are the first thing that people think of when they hear the term "internal control" because, in many ways, they are the most visible manifestation of good internal control. Principles for establishing effective control activities are:

10. The organization selects and develops control activities that contribute to the mitigation of risks to the achievement of objectives to acceptable levels.

11. The organization selects and develops general control activities over technology to support the achievement of objectives.

12. The organization deploys control activities through policies that establish what is expected and procedures that put policies into place.

See Box 8.4 "COSO's Control Activities Principles and Points of Focus" for points of focus associated with each of these three principles that aid management in assessing whether they have established an effective ICOFR.

BOX 8.4 COSO'S CONTROL ACTIVITIES PRINCIPLES AND POINTS OF FOCUS

Principle 10: Selects and Develops Control Activities   *The organization specifies objectives with sufficient clarity to enable the identification and assessment of risks relating to objectives.*

Points of Focus

* *Integrates with Risk Assessment—Control activities help ensure that risk responses that address and mitigate risks are carried out.*

* *Considers Entity-Specific Factors—Management considers how the environment, complexity, nature, and scope of its operations, as well as the specific characteristics of its organization, affect the selection and development of control activities.*

* *Determines Relevant Business Processes—Management determines which relevant business processes require control activities.*

* *Evaluates a Mix of Control Activity Types—Control activities include a range and variety of controls and may include a balance of approaches to mitigate risks, considering both manual and automated controls, and preventive and detective controls.*

* *Considers at What Level Activities Are Applied—Management considers control activities at various levels in the entity.*

* *Addresses Segregation of Duties—Management segregates incompatible duties, and where such segregation is not practical management selects and develops alternative control activities.*

Principle 11: Selects and Develops General Controls over Technology   *The organization selects and develops general control activities over technology to support the achievement of objectives.*

Points of Focus

* *Determines Dependency between the Use of Technology in Business Processes and Technology General Controls—Management understands and determines the dependency and linkage between business processes, automated control activities, and technology general controls.*

* *Establishes Relevant Technology Infrastructure Control Activities— Management selects and develops control activities over the technology infrastructure, which are designed and implemented to help ensure the completeness, accuracy, and availability of technology processing.*

* *Establishes Relevant Security Management Process Control Activities— Management selects and develops control activities that are designed and implemented to restrict technology access rights to authorized users commensurate with their job responsibilities and to protect the entity's assets from external threats.*

* *Establishes Relevant Technology Acquisition, Development, and Maintenance Process Control Activities—Management selects and develops control activities over the acquisition, development, and maintenance of technology and its infrastructure to achieve management's objectives.*

Principle 12: Deploys through Policies and Procedures *The organization deploys control activities through policies that establish what is expected and procedures that put policies into action.*

Points of Focus

- *Establishes Policies and Procedures to Support Deployment of Management's Directives—Management establishes control activities that are built into business processes and employees' day-to-day activities through policies establishing what is expected and relevant procedures specifying actions.*

- *Establishes Responsibility and Accountability for Executing Policies and Procedures—Management establishes responsibility and accountability for control activities with management (or other designated personnel) of the business unit or function in which the relevant risks reside.*

- *Performs in a Timely Manner—Responsible personnel perform control activities in a timely manner as defined by the policies and procedures.*

- *Takes Corrective Action—Responsible personnel investigate and act on matters identified as a result of executing control activities.*

- *Performs Using Competent Personnel—Competent personnel with sufficient authority perform control activities with diligence and continuing focus.*

- *Reassesses Policies and Procedures—Management periodically reviews control activities to determine their continued relevance and refreshes them when necessary.*

The Auditor's Perspective: We have introduced control activities at the management control level in Chapter 5, at the process control level in Chapter 6, and over financial reporting in Chapter 7. A great deal of the work an auditor does to assess and test internal control focuses on control activities, i.e., the actual activities of exercising control. The auditor will generally be most concerned about the internal controls over financial reporting when doing this testing since they are the focus of the Integrated Audit. However, even general controls can have an impact on the audit, especially if they affect the conditions under which accounting estimates are made, i.e., do managers base estimates on high quality information, using appropriate evaluation models, and subject to good judgment practices and guidelines? Specific applications of control activities will be extensively discussed when we examine individual audit-sensitive business processes in Chapters 11 to 13.

Information and Communication

COSO defines communication as "the continual, iterative process of providing, sharing and obtaining necessary information" (COSO 2013, p. 105) whether it be for internal purposes or external purposes. This information flow can go upward through an organization from process participants to managers, downward through an organization from managers to process participants, horizontally across divisions or units, and outward between the company and relevant external parties. Some of these communications may reflect contractual or legal requirements but most communication exists to facilitate more effective decision making and operations within the company. Information can simply mean data, but in most cases information means data that has been analyzed, combined, and summarized based on needs of the recipients, both internal and external. The principles that support COSO's concept of information and communication processes are:

13. The organization obtains or generates and uses relevant, quality information to support the functioning of internal control.

14. The organization internally communicates information, including objectives and responsibilities for internal control, necessary to support the functioning of internal control.

15. The organization communicates with external parties regarding matters affecting the functioning of internal control.

Box 8.5 "COSO's Information and Communications Principles and Points of Focus" highlights the key points of focus associated with each of these three principles that aid management in assessing whether they have established an effective ICOFR.

BOX 8.5 COSO'S INFORMATION AND COMMUNICATIONS PRINCIPLES AND POINTS OF FOCUS

Principle 13: Uses Relevant Information   *The organization obtains or generates and uses relevant, quality information to support the functioning of internal control.*

Point of Focus

- *Identifies Information Requirements—A process is in place to identify the information required and expected to support the functioning of the other components of internal control and the achievement of the entity's objectives.*

- *Captures Internal and External Sources of Data—Information systems capture internal and external sources of data.*

- *Processes Relevant Data into Information—Information systems process and transform relevant data into information.*

- *Maintains Quality throughout Processing—Information systems produce information that is timely, current, accurate, complete, accessible, protected, verifiable, and retained. Information is reviewed to assess its relevance in supporting the internal control components.*

- *Considers Costs and Benefits—The nature, quantity, and precision of information communicated are commensurate with and support the achievement of objectives.*

Principle 14: Communicates Internally   *The organization internally communicates information, including objectives and responsibilities for internal control, necessary to support the functioning of internal control.*

Point of Focus

- *Communicates Internal Control Information—A process is in place to communicate required information to enable all personnel to understand and carry out their internal control responsibilities.*

- *Communicates with the Board of Directors—Communication exists between management and the Board of Directors so that both have information needed to fulfill their roles with respect to the entity's objectives.*

- *Provides Separate Communication Lines—Separate communication channels, such as whistle-blower hotlines, are in place and serve as fail-safe mechanisms to enable anonymous or confidential communication when normal channels are inoperative or ineffective.*

- *Selects Relevant Method of Communication—The method of communication considers the timing, audience, and nature of the information.*

Principle 15: Communicates Internally *The organization communicates with external parties regarding matters affecting the functioning of internal control.*

Point of Focus

- *Communicates to External Parties—Processes are in place to communicate relevant and timely information to external parties including shareholders, partners, owners, regulators, customers, and financial analysts and other external parties.*

- *Enables Inbound Communications—Open communication channels allow input from customers, consumers, suppliers, external auditors, regulators, financial analysts, and others, providing management and the Board of Directors with relevant information.*

- *Communicates with the Board of Directors—Relevant information resulting from assessments conducted by external parties is communicated to the Board of Directors.*

- *Provides Separate Communication Lines—Separate communication channels, such as whistle-blower hotlines, are in place and serve as fail-safe mechanisms to enable anonymous or confidential communication when normal channels are inoperative or ineffective.*

- *Selects Relevant Method of Communication—The method of communication considers the timing, audience, and nature of the communication and legal, regulatory, and fiduciary requirements and expectations.*

(iv)EXAMPLE

Managing risk usually requires extensive and timely information about the causes and potential consequences of risk. Accounting systems provide many types of information that can be used to assess risk. A marketing manager may receive a weekly or daily report of sales by product line or location in order to detect potential problems in the sales process. A credit manager may receive a weekly or monthly report on delinquent accounts to determine if credit policies and procedures should be changed. A production manager may receive daily or weekly reports on inventory levels to adjust production as appropriate. Failure to have such information available could cause problems to arise in the organization which might impact the financial statements. An unnoticed increase in customer delinquencies calls into question the valuation of receivables while a build-up in inventory balances that goes on without intervention may lead to inventory that cannot be sold and that may need to be written down.

Audit perspective: Information that is communicated externally is an obvious focus of the auditor since much of the information will be incorporated into the annual audited financial statements. Internal information can also be critical to an auditor because it can be used to analyze current risk conditions and provide a basis for many of the auditor's procedures and tests. Chapters 6 and 7 discuss the information needs of an organization and provide the basic approach for implementing the three principles, including documenting the processes via process maps. Further discussions about implementation from the audit perspective are found in more detail in Chapters 11 to 13 when we discuss specific business processes such as sales and customer service(iv).

Monitoring

COSO defines monitoring as management's "activities that assess whether each of the five components of internal control and the relevant principles are present and functioning" (COSO 2013, p. 124). It is important to monitor a system of internal control because conditions change over time, both in the external environment and internally with personnel or system changes. Certainly, changing technology can dramatically change the nature of internal systems, influencing the potential existence and significance of related risks. The principles related to this control component are:

16. The organization selects, develops, and performs ongoing and/or separate evaluations to ascertain whether the components of internal control are present and functioning.

17. The organization evaluates and communicates internal control deficiencies in a timely manner to those parties responsible for taking corrective action, including senior management and the Board of Directors as appropriate.

See Box 8.6 "COSO's Monitoring Principles and Points of Focus" for the points of focus associated with these two principles from the perspective of managers who have to design and operate the control system.

BOX 8.6 COSO'S MONITORING PRINCIPLES AND POINTS OF FOCUS

Principle 16: Conducts Ongoing and/or Separate Evaluations *The organization selects, develops, and performs ongoing and/or separate evaluations to ascertain whether the components of internal control are present and functioning.*

Points of Focus

- *Considers a Mix of Ongoing and Separate Evaluations—Management includes a balance of ongoing and separate evaluations.*
- *Considers Rate of Change—Management considers the rate of change in business and business processes when selecting and developing ongoing and separate evaluations.*
- *Establishes Baseline Understanding—The design and current state of an internal control system are used to establish a baseline for ongoing and separate evaluations.*
- *Uses Knowledgeable Personnel—Evaluators performing ongoing and separate evaluations have sufficient knowledge to understand what is being evaluated.*
- *Integrates with Business Processes—Ongoing evaluations are built into the business processes and adjust to changing conditions.*
- *Adjusts Scope and Frequency—Management varies the scope and frequency of separate evaluations depending on risk.*
- *Objectively Evaluates—Separate evaluations are performed periodically to provide objective feedback.*

Principle 17: Conducts Ongoing and/or Separate Evaluations The organization evaluates and communicates internal control deficiencies in a timely manner to those parties responsible for taking corrective action, including senior management and the Board of Directors, as appropriate.

Points of Focus

- *Assesses Results—Management and the Board of Directors, as appropriate, assess results of ongoing and separate evaluations.*
- *Communicates Deficiencies—Deficiencies are communicated to parties responsible for taking corrective action and to senior management and the Board of Directors, as appropriate.*
- *Monitors Corrective Actions—Management tracks whether deficiencies are remediated on a timely basis.*

AUTHORITATIVE GUIDANCE & STANDARDS

The Sarbanes-Oxley Act of 2002 requires all US SEC registered public companies to have an internal audit function that reports to the Audit Committee. The Act allows companies the option of outsourcing internal audits to public accounting firms or others with the necessary expertise but precludes the firm that performs the external audit from also performing internal audit services for the same client. As a result, Principle 16 of the COSO Framework will normally be supported by the internal audit function for US SEC registered public companies. Internal audit functions are found in most large organizations even if they are not subject to the US SEC mandate as they provide the means for management to exercise its monitoring function.

Audit perspective: Monitoring is often interpreted to mean "internal auditing" but monitoring can come in many forms, including supervisor oversight of processes and employees. For example, some organizations specifically task employees to point out control deficiencies in their area of responsibility. Many forms of monitoring fall into the general category of management controls that were introduced in Chapter 5. They are essential to understanding and assessing the quality of management's monitoring activities in an organization. Chapter 6's process controls, especially performance reviews, are also relevant to an auditor and can be useful for testing the effectiveness of ICOFR as it relates to monitoring activities.

Integrating Internal Controls

One of the key points of emphasis of the COSO Framework is that the five internal control components should not be considered in isolation and need to be integrated with each other. The same point is made about the principles that underlie each component. Management has to exercise judgment in assessing whether each component and the relevant principles is present and functioning in an organization. "Present" is defined by COSO to mean that "components and relevant principles exist in the design and implementation of the system of internal control to achieve specified objectives" (COSO

2013, p. 19). "Functioning" is defined to mean that "components and relevant principles continue to exist in the conduct of the system of internal control to achieve specific objectives" (COSO 2013, p. 19).

In summary, management must demonstrate that the components of internal control are present, functioning, and operating together effectively. For example, policies and procedures are developed and deployed as part of the overall control environment. These policies provide guidance on the design and implementation of control activities intended to mitigate specific risks identified during risk assessment. However, to have the desired effect on risk, the controls must operate effectively. If all this happens, the net result is a control environment and control system that reduces the risk of poor judgments, errors, and fraud. In assessing the integration of the components of internal control, auditors and management utilize essentially the same tools described in Chapter 7 to document the existence of internal control, evaluate the strength of the ICOFR design, and to plan and document tests of the effectiveness of internal control to fulfill their responsibilities related to ICOFR in an Integrated Audit.

AUTHORITATIVE GUIDANCE & STANDARDS

The responsibilities of the auditor (and implicitly for management) for performing (preparing for in management's case) an audit of ICOFR are described in AS 2201. For US SEC registered public companies, management must perform their responsibilities to provide the basis for the auditor's testing of the effectiveness of ICOFR. If management does not fulfill its responsibilities, there is the requirement for an auditor to render an adverse audit opinion on the effectiveness of ICOFR.

Applying the COSO Framework

The introduction of the requirements for an Integrated Audit for publicly listed companies in the US represented a highly controversial and radical change in the responsibilities of auditors. Both management and auditors found it difficult to implement the audit of ICOFR in the early years following SOX, and the costs arising from the Integrated Audit were high. In fact, the average audit fee of a publicly listed company in the US more than doubled between 2001 and 2004, suggesting the magnitude of the start-up costs of implementing Section 404. Auditors could no longer undertake a perfunctory examination of internal control, set control risk at maximum, and then rely almost exclusively on substantive tests of accounts to support the audit opinion. Control risk can still be set at the maximum level in an Integrated Audit but that assessment needs to be based on an explicit analysis of internal control rather than as an excuse to avoid evaluating and testing ICOFR in the name of audit efficiency.

The importance of the audit of ICOFR can be seen in one area that is often considered to be a relatively low priority in many audits: human resource processing and payroll. Historically, while the payroll department may execute many transactions (e.g., issuing paychecks), they are considered to be relatively routine, standardized, and likely to be highly accurate (e.g., employees would probably let it be known quickly if payroll processing was inaccurate). However, breakdowns in hiring such as conducting ineffective background checks, utilizing discriminatory hiring practices, or approving improper benefits can create problems later on in the organization. Further, the human resource process also encompasses some very significant and difficult transactions such as deferred compensation (pensions), benefits (health care), and incentive schemes (contingent compensation such as stock options). In addition, the activities of human resource processing are important because the personnel that are hired through the process will play many critical roles throughout the organization.

A common potential problem in the control environment is that contingent compensation such as stock options can influence individuals to undertake actions and decisions that maximize their employment rewards but may subject the organization to unknown or misunderstood risks. Many of the problems arising during the Global Financial Crisis in 2007–8 can be attributable to misaligned incentives in banks that "encouraged" bank officers to undertake highly risky strategies that were not sustainable when economic conditions began to deteriorate in the US and around the globe.

While those risks played out in many banks, events also revealed that even though most large banks had large risk management operations and formal risk management officers, their approach to risk assessment was not effective in the conditions experienced at the time of the crisis. Prior to the crisis, the risk assessment and management activities of banks were probably considered to be highly effective in the view of the auditors and management. Events revealed this to not be the case, which created huge losses in the financial statements of the banks. And although the banks were subject to the requirements of the Integrated Audit, circumstances revealed significant gaps in the internal control system, which were quite often traceable to poor decision making by key employees.

Additionally, some of the problems in the banks could be traced to poor information and communication across different departments in a bank. While one department was busy securitizing mortgages and selling off much of the loan portfolio so as to obtain the maximum return and reduce risk for the bank, another department would be issuing credit default swaps—a form of investment guarantee—to customers that was bringing the risk back into the bank, but in an off-balance sheet form. In effect, these two activities, while generating significant revenue to the bank, were offsetting the risk and control effects of the other. When the crisis began, this lack of information and communication led to huge losses in both activities.

Overall, human resource processing and management can have a profound effect on the control environment through the incentives given to employees and the quality and honesty of the personnel who are hired. Risk assessment can be influenced through the entire organization if the hiring process does not bring in the appropriate and qualified personnel to work in this complex but critical area. This issue also applies to monitoring. Unless internal auditors are qualified, trained, and supported in their work by senior management and the Board of Directors, their ability to oversee the internal control system will be limited. Failure to monitor employees to identify serious problems such as excessive absenteeism or potential substance abuse can also have a serious effect across the organization. Finally, the ability and willingness to communicate across different areas of an organization could significantly influence the ability of individuals to identify and react appropriately to critical risks. In the end, while control activities in specific processes are clearly important for evaluating whether ICOFR is effective, the auditor needs to give significant consideration to these other aspects of the COSO Framework given the potential pervasive effect any breakdowns may have on the organization as a whole.

Consideration of Internal Control over Financial Reporting in an Integrated Audit

As previously noted, an Integrated Audit as defined by the PCAOB imposes additional requirements on the auditor regarding testing and reporting on ICOFR that exceed the requirements of a GAAS Audit. We now turn our attention to a more detailed discussion of those requirements. Although the techniques for documenting, assessing, and testing internal controls over financial reporting are the same in all audits (see Chapter 7), the introduction of the Integrated Audit has changed the nature of audit planning and execution in general, and has increased the focus on the nature and extent of internal control testing. Furthermore, the Integrated Audit has introduced additional reporting requirements for the auditor.

AUTHORITATIVE GUIDANCE & STANDARDS TERMINOLOGY ALERT

*The PCAOB has not adopted the three-fold classification for management assertions about financial reporting that has been adopted by the IAASB in ISA 200 **Objectives and Principles Governing an Audit of Financial Statements** (see Chapter 7, Table 7.1). The PCAOB continues to use the five financial statement assertions (existence or occurrence, completeness, valuation or allocation, rights and obligations, and presentation and disclosure) that the IAASB embeds in its assertions about transactions, balances, and presentation and disclosure. Hence, to link these five general assertions to specific financial statement transaction streams, balances and presentation and disclosures the PCAOB employs the term "control objective." Control objectives are in substance the same as the more detailed management assertions found in Chapter 7, Table 7.1.*

The PCAOB defines a control deficiency (AS 2201, Appendix A) as follows:

> A **deficiency** in internal control over financial reporting exists when the design or operation of a control does not allow management or employees, in the normal course of performing their assigned functions, to prevent or detect misstatements on a timely basis.

- A deficiency in design exists when (a) a control necessary to meet the control objective is missing, or (b) an existing control is not properly designed so that, even if the control operates as designed, the control objective would not be met.

- A deficiency in operation exists when a properly designed control does not operate as designed, or when the person performing the control does not possess the necessary authority or competence to perform the control effectively.

Control deficiencies under AS 2201 are classified into three categories, as indicated in Figure 8.2, depending on the likelihood of a deficiency leading to a misstatement in the financial statements and the magnitude of misstatement that could occur. A ***material weakness*** is a deficiency in ICOFR, or a combination of deficiencies, such that there is a *reasonable possibility* that a material misstatement of the company's annual or interim financial statements will not be prevented or detected on a timely basis. Material weaknesses often occur when a control is not operating effectively or there is evidence of actual misstatements arising from the deficiency.

A ***significant deficiency*** is a deficiency, or combination of deficiencies, that is less severe than a material weakness, yet important enough to merit attention by those responsible for oversight of the company's financial reporting. Any deficiency that does not meet either of those definitions is, by default, an **insignificant deficiency**. Currently, the PCAOB does not provide an explicit definition for this category, but it was previously defined in the original ICOFR standard as having "either a remote likelihood of leading to a misstatement or the misstatement resulting from the deficiency is inconsequential" (former PCAOB AS 2, now superseded by AS 2201).

AUTHORITATIVE GUIDANCE & STANDARDS— TERMINOLOGY DIFFERENCE ALERT

*Unfortunately, for auditors and auditing students, the PCAOB and the IAASB did not agree on the use of terms over the evaluation of control deficiencies starting with the definition of what a deficiency is. In particular, ISA 265 **Communicating Deficiencies in Internal Control to Those Charged with Governance and Management** uses a twofold classification of control deficiencies instead of the PCAOB threefold classification. Specifically the term "significant control deficiency" is used*

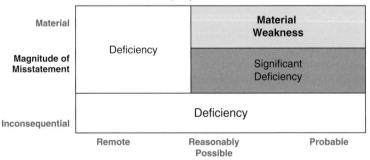

Figure 8.2 *Control Deficiencies in Internal Control over Financial Reporting: Significant Deficiencies and Material Weaknesses*

in a manner by the IAASB that is not consistent with the PCAOB's use of the term. This is elaborated on further in Chapter 15 under the GAAS auditor's reporting responsibilities to those charged with governance about the findings of their internal control evaluation and testing.

Classifying Control Deficiencies

The distinction between classifications of deficiencies requires extensive judgment by both management and the auditor and critically depends on the determination of whether it is "reasonably possible" that an identified deficiency will lead to a material misstatement. The criteria for "reasonable possibility" are not specifically provided by the PCAOB other than the general guidance that "reasonable possibility" for their purposes should follow the definition provided in FASB Statement 5 *Accounting for Contingencies* (FAS 5). Under this standard, an uncertain condition can fall into one of three categories:

a. *Probable.* The future event or events are likely to occur.

b. *Reasonably possible.* The chance of the future event or events occurring is more than remote but less than likely.

c. *Remote.* The chance of the future event or events occurring is slight.

As a result, the criteria in FAS 5 suggest that only remote events are excluded from the classification of material deficiency.

The factors that an auditor should consider when determining if a deficiency is insignificant versus significant or a material weakness are the same as those considered in Chapter 7 for determining if a significant deficiency exists in a GAAS Audit. In other words, both the severity and magnitude of the potential misstatement that might occur determines whether the control deficiency is more than insignificant. Further, auditors in an Integrated Audit are also allowed to consider whether compensating controls are effective. Indicators that a significant deficiency should be considered a material weakness include:

- Identification of any fraud, whether material or not, on the part of senior management.
- Restatement of previously issued financial statements to reflect the correction of a material misstatement.
- Identification by the auditor of a material misstatement of the current financial statements in circumstances that indicate that the misstatement would not have been detected on a timely basis by the company's ICOFR.
- Ineffective oversight by of the company's financial reporting and ICOFR by the company's Audit Committee.

AS 2201 suggests a "prudent official" test when determining if a significant deficiency is a material weakness. That is, the auditor should determine the level of detail and degree of assurance that would satisfy prudent officials in the conduct of their own affairs that would provide reasonable assurance that transactions are recorded as necessary to permit the preparation of financial statements in accordance with GAAP. If the auditor concludes that the deficiencies "might prevent prudent officials" (AS 2201, paragraph 70) from making that conclusion, then it is likely that the deficiency is a material weakness.

Nine large US-based public accounting firms have issued **A Framework for Evaluating Control Exceptions and Deficiencies Version 3**, but they explicitly note this framework cannot substitute for professional judgment.[2] Practice experience has shown that when auditors or management have discovered the existence of a misstatement in the financial statements, even an immaterial one, auditors are able to determine whether a material weakness or a significant deficiency in controls is present. However, barring the discovery of such a misstatement, auditors find it very difficult to classify a deficiency in the operations of a control as a material weakness and find it almost impossible to identify missing controls that would be termed as a material weakness.[3]

Requirement for the Auditor to Plan Internal Control Tests

In an Integrated Audit, the auditor must plan the audit to directly evaluate and test ICOFR for all major accounts and classes of transactions as at year-end. Thus, the auditor's focus on internal control is more extensive, yet also more limited, than what normally occurs in a GAAS Audit. The focus on ICOFR in an Integrated Audit is more extensive given the requirement to test controls over all material classes of transactions and account balances whether or not the auditor intends to rely on the controls in reducing substantive tests. In the GAAS Audit, the auditor only tests controls if they believe that a finding of effective controls would reduce the nature or extent of the substantive tests over account balances.

Further, the controls tested by a GAAS Auditor would normally be in place for the entire year whereas in the Integrated Audit the auditor is only required by AS 2201 to focus on the effectiveness of the control system *at year-end*. As long as the control relied on has been in effect long enough for management to test its implementation, the ICOFR can be found effective at year-end even if there were deficiencies earlier in the year. However, for planning the audit of financial statements, auditors can only rely on testing controls to reduce substantive tests *if the controls are found to be effective over the entire year*. Hence, in spite of any conclusions reached about the effectiveness of ICOFR at year-end, the auditor must evaluate control risk for the entire year just as a GAAS Auditor must do. This full year evaluation could mean that the auditor assesses control risk for the purpose of planning the financial statement audit at or near maximum while also concluding that controls at year end are effective. This could occur if there have been significant changes in the control system over the course of a year to correct previous deficiencies. In summary, three key control considerations have a direct effect on the planning of an Integrated Audit:

1. The auditor must document and consider the effectiveness of internal controls over financial reporting as of year-end for all material classes of transactions and balances (even if substantive testing can provide adequate evidence to support the financial statements).

2. The auditor must test the operating effectiveness of the controls at year-end unless a material weakness exists in the design of the control such that the control cannot prevent material misstatements.

3. The auditor must take into account the length of time a control has been in place if changes were made to the internal control system during the year. However, ICOFR does not need to be in place for the entire year for the auditor to consider the system to be effective at year-end.

The Special Role of Entity Level Controls in an Integrated Audit

AS 2201 introduces a classification of internal controls that is unique to the US—**entity level controls**. AS 2201 does not explicitly define entity-level controls but provides characteristics and examples of such controls. Entity level controls are considered important because, it they are operating effectively, they may reduce the auditor's need to test ICOFR at the process level. Entity level controls are similar in many ways to the concept of management controls that we previously discussed. Entity level controls are normally documented as part of the control environment. However, not all management controls would be considered to be entity level controls. Some entity level controls that are particularly important to the audit of the financial statements include:

- Controls over management override of control activities.
- Controls over the period-end financial reporting process that lead to the financial statements, especially period ending adjusting journal entries.
- Policies that address significant business control and risk management practices.

Controls over management override of controls are important for ICOFR effectiveness for all companies, and may be particularly important at smaller companies because of the higher level of involvement of senior management in the financial reporting process.

Entity-level controls vary in nature and precision—for example, the control environment can have an indirect effect on the likelihood that a misstatement will be detected. Generally, entity level controls do not prevent or detect specific misstatements but increase the likelihood that other control activities are properly performed and hence those activities will prevent or detect specific misstatements. Monitoring controls can work at a level where they can detect breakdowns in process level control activities. Hence, effective entity level controls can warrant some reduction in the testing of more detailed control activities. However, such controls may not be detailed or precise enough to justify a very low level of control risk.

Among the entity level controls, the PCAOB highlight their concern for what they call **_Period-end Financial Reporting Process_** controls. The period-end financial reporting process includes:

- Procedures used to enter transaction totals into the general ledger.
- Procedures related to the selection and application of accounting policies.
- Procedures used to initiate, authorize, record, and process journal entries in the general ledger.

- Procedures used to record recurring and nonrecurring adjustments to the annual and quarterly financial statements.

- Procedures for preparing annual and quarterly financial statements and related disclosures.

In particular, in an Integrated Audit, the auditor should assess the following aspects of these controls:

- Inputs, procedures performed, and outputs of the processes the company uses to produce its annual and quarterly financial statements.

- The extent of information technology ("IT") involvement in the period-end financial reporting process.

- The extent to which management is involved in the year-end process.

- The locations involved in the period-end financial reporting process.

- The types of adjusting and consolidating entries.

- The nature and extent of the oversight of the process by management, the Board of Directors, and the Audit Committee.

The emphasis on entity level controls in AS 2201 arose because the PCAOB believed that the audit firms had responded to the original standard on ICOFR (AS 2 that was in effect from 2003 to 2008) in a way that was excessively detailed, expensive and narrow. AS 2201, on the other hand, was designed to encourage auditors and management to look at ICOFR from a top-down perspective. The purpose of focusing on entity level controls during part of the Integrated Audit ICOFR evaluation was to induce management and auditors to emphasize risk assessment and control so as to lead to a broader view of ICOFR in an organization. The Integrated Audit's renewed emphasis on a top-down, risk-based approach to the audit is fully consistent with this text's approach to auditing as laid out in Chapters 4 to 7.

Assessment of Control Risk: Implications for Tests of Financial Statement Assertions

In an Integrated Audit, conclusions about control risk follow logically from the existence of one or more material weaknesses or significant deficiencies. Furthermore, the evidence needed to support conclusions about control risk is collected as part of the auditor's evaluation and testing of ICOFR. If a material weakness exists, then control risk is likely to be set at a maximum level for one or more assertions. If a significant deficiency exists (but there are no material weaknesses), then some assertions may have slightly reduced control risk. Table 8.1 is a modified version of Table 7.6 from Chapter 7 reflecting the role of ICOFR in an Integrated Audit. Table 8.1 illustrates the relationship between conclusions about ICOFR and substantive testing.

To reduce control risk substantially below maximum for a material class of transactions, there can be no material weaknesses or significant deficiencies at year end in the business process that generates transactions (e.g., the sales and customer service process). However, the auditor must consider the possibility that there may have been deficiencies in internal control at other times during the year that have been remedied by management prior to

Table 8.1 Relating Conclusions about Internal Control over Financial Reporting to Substantive Testing: Integrated Audit

	Control Risk = 100% (Maximum)	Control Risk < 100% (Slightly Reduced)	Control Risk << 100% (Greatly Reduced)
Conditions Necessary in an Integrated Audit	The auditor's assessment and testing of ICOFR reveals the existence of one or more *material weaknesses*.	The auditor's assessment and testing of ICOFR reveals the existence of one or more *significant deficiencies* (but no material weaknesses).	The auditor's assessment and testing of ICOFR reveals no significant deficiencies or material weaknesses.
Nature of Evidence Required to be Documented in order to Support Conclusions about Internal Control over Financial Reporting and Resulting Assessments of Control Risk	• Client Enquiry: Extensively used to obtain details of control activities. • Observation: Performed to obtain details of control activities.	• Client Enquiry: Extensively used to obtain details of control activities. • Observation: Performed to obtain details of control activities and repeated during different time periods to check for changes. • Documentation: Reviewed on a walkthrough basis to clarify control activities performed.	• Client Enquiry: Extensively used to obtain details of control activities. • Observation: Performed to obtain details of control activities and repeated during different time periods to check for changes. ***Plus: Tests of Controls*** • Client Inquiry and Observation: Used to *verify* control activities. • Documentation: Extensively used to see if appropriate control activities were performed. • Accuracy: To test whether reconciliations have been effectively performed and reviewed.
Implications for Planning Substantive Tests of Transactions, Accounts, Estimates, and Disclosures	Reliance on Internal Control to reduce audit risk: *None* Use of Substantive Testing to reduce control risk: *Very Extensive* 	Reliance on Internal Control to reduce audit risk: *None/Limited* Use of Substantive Testing to reduce control risk: *Extensive* 	Reliance on Internal Control to reduce audit risk: *Extensive* Use of Substantive Testing to reduce control risk: *Minimal*

year-end. Deficiencies that only affected part of the year should be explicitly considered when an auditor sets control risk at the assertion level for an area of the audit. If the auditor does not identify any material weaknesses or significant deficiencies during the evaluation of ICOFR throughout the year, it is likely that the auditors will have performed sufficient tests of controls to justify a significant reduction in planned control risk for many assertions. Even if one or more material weaknesses are identified, there may be many assertions that are unaffected by the control deficiencies. For these assertions, the extensive control testing performed by the auditor may justify reduction of planned control risk and therefore allow for a reduction in the amount of substantive testing performed.

AUTHORITATIVE GUIDANCE & STANDARDS

Under AS 2201, auditors are required to perform walkthroughs as part of their testing of the design of internal controls. We described walkthroughs in Chapter 7.

The Auditor's Reporting Responsibilities in an Integrated Audit

In an Integrated Audit, an auditor is required to issue an opinion on the effectiveness of ICOFR in addition to their opinion on the fairness of the financial statements. There are two means of presenting these reports: (1) separate reports on the financial statements and effectiveness of ICOFR, or (2) a combined report of the results of both audits. Both choices will be discussed in more detail in Chapter 15. In either report format the auditor needs to describe the nature and purpose of ICOFR as well as the nature of the audit of ICOFR. In particular, the auditor has to point out that because of inherent limitations of any control system, ICOFR may not prevent or detect all misstatements. Further, the auditor has to caution that projections of any evaluation of ICOFR effectiveness to future periods are subject to the risk that controls may become inadequate because of changes in conditions, or that the degree of compliance with the policies or procedures may deteriorate. As briefly introduced in Chapter 4, auditors can either issue an unqualified or adverse opinion on ICOFR. The auditor does not have the option to issue a qualified opinion on the effectiveness of ICOFR hence the presence of one material weakness results in an adverse opinion on ICOFR effectiveness. The reporting choices are simple: ***unqualified*** if the auditor concludes that ICOFR is effective in all material respects or ***adverse*** if the auditor concludes that ICOFR is not effective due to one or more material weaknesses.

On a rare occasion, an auditor can disclaim an opinion if a **scope limitation** exists, meaning that auditors are unable to gather sufficient evidence to make an informed assessment on internal control. But, if the auditor has become aware of a material weakness in control before determining that there was a scope limitation, the auditor must report that material weakness as part of the disclaimer. If the auditor is disclaiming an opinion, the auditor does not describe what the nature and purpose of an audit of ICOFR as the auditor would normally describe in an unqualified or adverse opinion. The purpose of removing the description of what an audit of ICOFR consists of is to focus the reader on the disclaimer without distraction.

We will discuss in more detail the external reporting requirements of the auditor under an Integrated Audit in Chapter 15. In addition, AS 2201 requires the auditor to communicate in writing to senior management and the Audit Committee both material weaknesses (i.e., deficiencies that are reported publically) and significant deficiencies. Internal disclosures of deficiencies by auditors are usually more detailed than what is provided in the auditor's public report. AS 2201 requires the auditor to make the internal report about ICOFR effectiveness to the Audit Committee prior to issuance of the external audit report on ICOFR. In addition, all control deficiencies that the auditor discovers, even insignificant ones, must be reported to management in writing and the auditor must inform the Audit Committee when such a communication to management has been made. In effect, this makes it likely that the Audit Committee will review all control deficiencies that the auditor has reported. A limited exception may be in extremely large companies where management may summarize the auditor's findings so that the Audit Committee can focus on the most serious deficiencies.

Management Remediation of Material Weaknesses and Auditor Reporting on such Remediation

Once a material weakness is identified by management or the auditor, there is generally a presumption that it will be corrected in the future. This correction is called "remediation." In most cases, it is in the best interests of a company, its management and the board to remediate a material weakness because failure to do so can be considered a sign of an ineffective management and a material weakness unto itself that will cause further adverse reports on ICOFR in subsequent periods. Real consequences for public companies can occur if financial analysts and investors reduce a company's market valuation because management fails to remediate a material weakness. These consequences are especially problematic to companies that plan to raise new equity capital, issue new debt, or enter into other transaction that require a clean audit opinion on both ICOFR and the financial statements.

It is possible for the auditor to undertake a special engagement to verify management's assertion that it has remediated specific material weakness(es) in ICOFR that were previously reported. The auditor must carry out all the steps we have discussed in an audit of the effectiveness of ICOFR but focused only on management's assertion about the remediation of the previously identified material weakness(es). Given that the SEC requires that the auditor issue a quarterly review report on the interim financial statements, it is common that reports about the remediation of ICOFR weaknesses are issued at the same time. As in the year-end report on ICOFR, the report is about the state of internal controls as of a specific date and makes no assurances about the state of the controls over the entire period. However, this is subject to the constraint that the new controls have been in operation long enough for both management and the auditor to gather evidence about their design and the effectiveness of their implementation. The remediation engagement focuses solely on management's assertion about the remediation of the material weakness(es) identified in the previous audit report. The new report explicitly notes that the auditor is not reporting on the effectiveness of ICOFR as a whole at this subsequent report date, only that the company has remediated the material weakness previously reported.

AUTHORITATIVE GUIDANCE & STANDARDS

PCAOB AS 6115 (formerly AS 4) **Reporting on Whether a Previously Reported Material Weakness Continues to Exist**, *provides guidance to auditors who are engaged to render an opinion as to whether a material weakness(es) disclosed in a previous ICOFR effectiveness opinion has been remediated by the client. Normally such a limited focus audit can only take place if the previous auditor continues for the current period, albeit there are provisions for more extensive work to be done if the client has changed auditors.*

Summary and Conclusion

In this chapter, we have discussed the role of ICOFR in the Integrated Audit that is required by the PCAOB for public companies, except the smallest, registered with the US SEC. Under the Integrated Audit, the auditor must issue two opinions: one regarding the effectiveness of a company's ICOFR and the other on the financial statements, although they can be combined into one auditor's report. The auditor's evaluation of ICOFR is illustrated and summarized in Table 8.1. The evaluative techniques and procedures used to test internal controls are essentially the same for all audits. Hence, all of the material in Chapter 7, except for the material about control risk assessment and the reporting of control deficiencies in a GAAS Audit, is relevant to this chapter's documentation, evaluation, and testing of ICOFR. What differs between an Integrated Audit and a GAAS Audit are the objectives of ICOFR assessment, the extent and nature of control testing, and reporting requirements to internal and external users of the financial statements. In both financial statement audits, the auditor will assess control risk for management assertions as maximum, near maximum, moderate, or low based on the evaluation of the internal control system over the entire year, perform tests of controls where necessary in order to justify a decrease in the substantive testing of assertions, and carry out substantive tests of assertions so as to reduce audit risk to the desired level. In general, the better the ICOFR and the longer the period it is in effect, meaning the fewer and less severe the nature of the control deficiencies, the less substantive testing the auditor will perform. We will examine further the trade-offs between the auditor gaining assurance about material misstatements from relying on internal control reliance that is justified by testing versus the auditor's direct substantive testing of management financial statement assertions in Chapter 10.

Bibliography of Relevant Literature

Relevant Research

Kinney, William R., Roger D. Martin, and Marcy L. Shepardson. 2013. Reflections on a Decade of SOX 404(b) Audit Production and Alternatives. *Accounting Horizons* 27(4): 799–813.

Professional Guidance

BDO Seidman LLP, Crowe Chizek and Company LLC, Deloitte & Touche LLP, Ernst & Young LLP, Grant Thornton LLP, Harbinger PLC, KPMG LLP, McGladrey & Pullen LLP, PricewaterhouseCoopers LLP and W. F. Messier Jr. 2004. *A Framework for Evaluating Control Exceptions and Deficiencies Version 3*. December 20. Available on-line at www.grantthornton.com/ portal/site/gtcom/menuitem.91c078ed5c0ef4ca80cd8710033841ca/? vgnextoid=506aa3e0aec36010VgnVCM100000308314a cRCRD&vgnextfmt=default. (accessed March 21, 2006).

Auditing Standards

Criteria of Control Board. 1995. *Guidance on Control*. CPA Canada (formerly the Canadian Institute of Chartered Accountants).

COSO—Committee of Sponsoring Organizations. 1992. *Internal Control: An Integrated Framework*.

COSO—Committee of Sponsoring Organizations. 2013. *Internal Control: An Integrated Framework*.

FASB Financial Accounting Standards Board Statement 5, "Accounting for Contingencies."

IAASB *International Standards on Auditing (ISA)* No. 200, "Objectives and Principles Governing an Audit of Financial Statements."

IAASB *International Standards on Auditing (ISA)* No. 265, "Communicating Deficiencies in Internal Control to Those Charged with Governance and Management."

PCAOB. *Auditing Standard 6115* (formerly No. 4), "Reporting on Whether a Previously Reported Material Weakness Continues to Exist."

PCAOB. *Auditing Standard 2201* (formerly No. 5), "An Audit of Internal Control over Financial Reporting that is Integrated with An Audit of Financial Statements."

PCAOB. *Auditing Standard 2210* (formerly No. 12), "Identifying and Assessing the Risks of Material Misstatement."

SOX Sarbanes-Oxley Act - Library of Congress. 2002. House Resolution Number 3763, An Act to protect investors by improving the accuracy and reliability of corporate disclosures made pursuant to the securities laws, and for other purposes *(The Sarbanes-Oxley Act of 2002)*. www. libraryofcongress.gov.

Notes

1   The following principles are summarized based on Chapter 5 Control Environment of COSO 2013 *Internal Control: Integrated Framework*.

2   BDO Seidman et al, *A Framework for Evaluating Control Exceptions and Deficiencies Version 3*.

3   Kinney, William R., Roger D. Martin, and Marcy L. Shepardson. 2013. Reflections on a Decade of SOX 404(b) Audit Production and Alternatives. *Accounting Horizons* 27(4), 799–813.

CHAPTER 9

Inquiry and Analytical Evidence Including Auditing of Accounting Estimates

Outline

Learning Goals for this Chapter

1. To acquire a depth of understanding about two important audit evidence gathering techniques: client inquiry and analysis (analytical procedures).

2. To recognize the strengths and limitations of client inquiry as an audit evidence collection tool.

3. Introduce ways of gathering inquiry evidence that enhance its reliability.

4. Understand how the role of inquiry and analysis varies across phases of the audit (e.g., planning, substantive testing, and final review).

5. To develop and design analytical procedures appropriate for planning and substantive testing.

6. To illustrate how inquiry and analysis assist in fraud detection.

7. To apply inquiry and analysis to test the reasonableness of management's accounting estimates.

Introduction

One of the things that auditors do is ask lots of questions. In fact, almost everything the auditor does during the course of an audit involves formulating questions and then searching out answers. We have already discussed a number of general categories of questions an auditor asks in an audit: What risks threaten an organization? How does the company respond to risk? Is internal control reliable? Are the numbers accurate? The answers to these questions may be available in the documents and records of a client but, more often than not, the auditor will need to obtain information, clarification, insight, and explanations from client personnel or others who hold the required information. In short, client inquiries are an integral and crucial part of the auditor's tool kit.

Commonly linked to inquiry are various forms of auditor *analysis* (also referred to as *analytical procedures* or *analytical review*). Preliminary analytic procedures (or analysis) refers to the examination of performance results for indications of potential risk or problems within the financial statements. Preliminary analysis may indicate areas of the financial statements where more in-depth audit testing is needed. Inquiry is intrinsically linked to analysis because numbers usually mean little without an explanation of what they represent. Auditors often turn to management to obtain these explanations as a first step to satisfying themselves as to the reasonableness of the numbers.

A classic example of the interplay between analysis and inquiry occurs when the auditor asks management to explain an observed performance result. For example, the auditor may have noted that sales in a specific time period have experienced an unusual increase or decrease. A thoughtful auditor may be curious as to why that has happened. Although nothing untoward may have occurred, the unusual sales pattern catches the attention of the auditor because of the possibility that the results may indicate accounting problems or misstatements. The obvious place to turn for an initial explanation is the management of the company. By discussing the result with management, the auditor can begin to discern the cause of the performance results. However, the manager who is approached may be in a hurry, distracted, misinformed, or devious, so the explanation that is offered may be incorrect or incomplete. It is then up to the auditor to determine if such responses have value as evidence in the conduct of the audit.

The purpose of this chapter is to assist an auditor in conducting analysis and inquiry in an efficient and effective manner. The information provided in the scenario just described will not always be reliable audit evidence, so the auditor needs to develop appropriate skills for sorting out the true and important from the biased and trivial when making client inquiries. In this chapter, we introduce an integrated approach for understanding basic relationships among financial statement and nonfinancial data to facilitate analysis and inquiry. ***Preliminary analytical procedures*** performed at the level of the overall financial statements, or significant business segments, are an important part of the auditor's risk assessment procedures. In essence, an auditor examines financial and other data in order to identify risks and account relationships that seem inconsistent with known economic circumstances (see Figure 9.1).

Auditors are required to perform preliminary analytical procedures as part of audit planning. Furthermore, analytical procedures may be performed

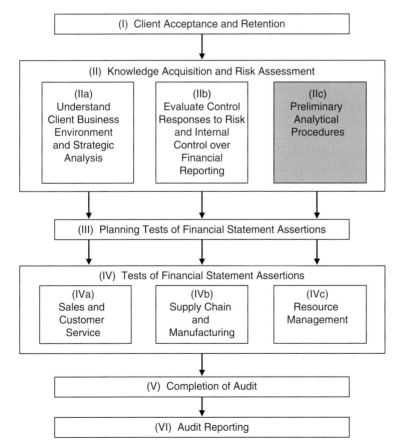

Figure 9.1 *Overview of the Audit Process*

at other stages of the audit, including the testing of account balances (i.e., substantive analytical procedures). Finally, analytical procedures are required as part of the final overview of the audit results (see Chapter 14 for details). We conclude this chapter with two specific examples of using inquiry and analysis in problem areas of auditing, assessing fraud risk and in auditing accounting estimates. In both of these areas inquiry and analysis are vital for gathering evidence necessary for successful completion of the auditor's task.

AUTHORITATIVE GUIDANCE & STANDARDS

*This chapter emphasizes two commonly used types of evidence gathering: inquiry and analytical procedures. Standards on audit evidence (ISA 500 **Audit Evidence**, PCAOB AS 1105 [formerly 15] **Audit Evidence**) cover both analysis and inquiry; however, a separate standard (ISA 520 **Analytical Procedures**, PCAOB AS 2305 [formerly Interim Standard AU 329] **Substantive Analytical Procedures**) provides additional guidance on analytical procedures.*

A Traditional View of Inquiry Evidence

Formally, **inquiry** involves seeking appropriate information from knowledgeable persons located within or outside the entity. There has never been an audit performed that did not incorporate extensive inquiries of management and others. However, in recent years, inquiry has taken on a greater importance to auditors for a number of reasons. For example, risk analysis is most effectively performed by talking to a large number of people with insight about the organization. Second, much of the information needed in an audit is the personal knowledge of individuals and is often not documented in any formal or systematic manner. Third, tangible evidence about events, circumstances, and decisions may be lacking, especially in a computerized environment.

Inquiry, however, is rarely an adequate source of evidence by itself as management responses to inquiries may be naïve, overly optimistic, misinformed, or intentionally misleading. In extreme situations, management may lie to the auditor. Consequently, the responses to client inquiries should rarely be taken at face value. The auditor needs to gather other evidence to corroborate explanations provided by management that are critical for evaluating whether the financial statements are free of material misstatements.

Overreliance on evidence from inquiry or gullible acceptance of management responses to inquiries have created problems for auditors in the past, often leading to severe audit problems, exposure to litigation, and damage to auditor reputations. Although inquiry is a common source of *information* in an audit, professional standards make it clear that inquiry is the least reliable source of audit *evidence*, especially if the responses to inquiries come from members of senior management[i].

[i]EXAMPLE

In the ZZZZ Best fraud, entrepreneur Barry Minkow created a carpet cleaning and insurance restoration company in which almost every customer was nonexistent and every recorded revenue transaction was fake. Virtually all information in the financial statements was fraudulent, resulting in unreasonable financial ratios and unrealistic business process measures. However, Minkow was able to fool the auditors on the engagement mostly through his slick ability to persuade the auditors with his clever answers to inquiries, many of which were not followed up by the auditors (or were followed up with limited corroborative evidence).

Inquiry is not a discrete step in the auditor's process of collecting evidence like other audit procedures such as examining a specific transaction's documentation or confirming customer accounts. Rather, inquiry permeates the audit and is reflected in both formal interviews that are planned in advance and informal discussions with management. Indeed, a rigorous auditor is never "off-duty" when in the presence of client personnel. The auditor should always be alert for the opportunity to gain additional insights from client management or other personnel through informal or, even, accidental conversations.

Professional standards have always recommended that information obtained from management inquiries be corroborated by other evidence due to the inherent unreliability of management's answers. As a result, auditors normally supplement and corroborate evidence from inquiry with evidence obtained through observation, documentation, or confirmation procedures. Although inquiries are not usually corroborated with additional inquiries of client personnel, there are situations in which information obtained from multiple sources within the organization can be compared for consistency. However, unless inquiries are conducted as part of a rigorous plan for collecting evidence, the reliability of individual responses should be viewed skeptically[(ii)].

A Rigorous Approach to Obtaining Inquiry Evidence

Figure 9.2 illustrates the five major attributes that may affect the quality of inquiry evidence. The planning and conduct of client inquiries should consider all five attributes to obtain the best possible evidence:

1. The interviewee: Does the interviewee have the appropriate knowledge, and can he or she be expected to be honest in providing information?
2. The interviewer: Does the interviewer have an appropriate attitude, knowledge of the area to be discussed, and appreciation for the context of the discussion?
3. Conduct of the interview: Is the discussion scheduled at an appropriate time with well-thought-out objectives and issues to discuss?
4. Documenting findings: Have interviewee responses (verbal and nonverbal) been evaluated and adequately captured in the audit documentation?
5. Integrating and synthesizing the meaning of inquiry evidence: Does the information confirm expectations, corroborate other audit evidence, or raise red flags about the issues discussed?

Each of these steps should be given consideration when developing a rigorous interview program for obtaining inquiry evidence and are discussed in more depth below.

Planning Client Inquiries

Before inquiries occur (and probably before fieldwork begins), the audit team should identify situations in the audit where rigorous inquiry evidence will

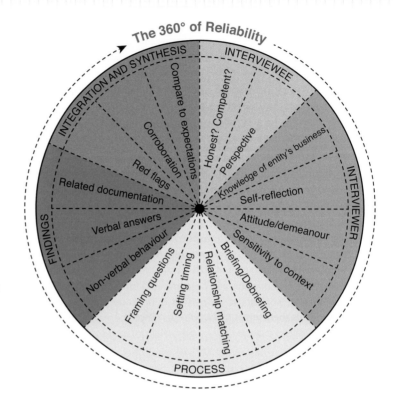

Figure 9.2 *A Rigorous Approach to Inquiry*

Source: *CICA Research Report "Audit Inquiry: Seeking More Reliable Evidence from Audit Inquiry"* Canadian Institute of Chartered Accountants, 2000. p. 30

be needed and develop an interview plan for the *formal* inquiry phase of the audit. Some examples where formal inquiries are encountered in the audit include:

- Obtaining an understanding of a client's environment and activities.
- Discussing the design and operation of processes with client personnel.
- Identifying important changes in the client's internal or external environment.
- Discussing risks and controls with client personnel.
- Evaluating the nature of performance results with management.
- Identifying key accounting policies, assumptions, and estimates.
- Discussing possible future plans of the organization.

An important audit decision is determining the appropriate client personnel to interview. If the questions to be discussed involve the financial reporting process, interviews with accounting personnel are appropriate. However, when trying to understand the reasonableness of transactions and balances, auditors should find client personnel who are responsible for conducting the underlying business activities. Although finding and interviewing operating personnel can be intimidating, these employees will have a better understanding of the business than accounting personnel because they are directly involved in executing transactions. Further, they usually have less accounting knowledge and are less likely to bias their answers in a way to make results appear better than they really are. To the extent possible, auditors should speak with operating personnel without accounting personnel present. Interviews with operating managers need to use terms and jargon with which they are comfortable—that is, "talk their language."

Planning considerations include matching the appropriate members of the audit team with client personnel to be interviewed and ensuring that interviewers have the appropriate background knowledge of the client to conduct the interview effectively. In general, audit partners will conduct interviews with the Audit Committee, CEO, and CFO; audit managers will interview senior managers, especially those in charge of key business units; and junior auditors will interview client accounting personnel and lower-level operational managers. To enhance learning and the effectiveness of the interview process, a more junior auditor should accompany a more senior auditor and act as a note taker if the interview is to be lengthy or broad-ranging. This mentoring arrangement allows the more experienced auditor to focus on the meaning of client responses, manage the flow of the interview, note and interpret the non-verbal reactions of client personnel, and draw out nuances of client's responses without the distraction of taking notes of the conversation. In addition, inexperienced auditors can learn to conduct effective interviews themselves by observing others[iii].

Although it can and should be preplanned, an interview should not consist of a list of standardized questions. An auditor may schedule an interview with a set of generic questions but should also be willing to let the interviewee take the conversation in directions that could turn out to be relevant to the auditor. The interview should be customized to the client's particular situation, drawing on knowledge from previous audits and knowledge of the client's industry. Furthermore, the auditor must consider the language to be employed in the interview. Approaching the interviewee with a view to understanding his or her world is one of the keys to establishing effective rapport and in eliciting meaningful responses. Box 9.1 "Preparing Interview Questions" provides some guidance on how questions should be prepared prior to an interview.

BOX 9.1 PREPARING INTERVIEW QUESTIONS

- *Use terminology the interviewee understands.*
- *Stay within the area of the interviewee's work responsibilities (formally or informally).*
- *Have the interviewee tell "a story" about what you want to know, instead of using a formal question and answer structure:*
  - o *Tell me about your system for receiving goods?*
        <<instead of>>
  - o *Does the shipper sign the receiving report?*
- *Phrase questions to elicit information, not suggest an answer:*
  - o *What do you think is causing the decrease in inventory turnover this year?*
        <<instead of>>
  - o *Inventory turnover decreased this year. Is it due to {interviewer suggestion}?*

[iii]EXAMPLE

A senior manager from an international accounting firm shared this actual encounter with one of the co-authors recently. He was touring the central warehouse of a client that is a retailer of bed and bath products with the warehouse manager. The controller insisted on accompanying the senior manager and warehouse manager on the tour. During the tour, the accounting senior manager asked about the layout of the warehouse, causes of bottlenecks, additional activities when deliveries were late, and so forth. The warehouse manager provided much information about the need for extra employees and expensive costs associated with overnight deliveries using alternative carriers, among other things. The controller acted as if he were unaware of all of these additional costs and tried to blame the manager for not ensuring that these costs were properly recorded. Finally, near the end of the tour, the senior manager asked the warehouse manager about the room off to the side of the warehouse that was full of inventory. The warehouse manager commented that it was full of inventory that was never going to be sold, so they found a place to get it out of the way. The controller, without missing a beat, reached up and slapped the warehouse manager on the back of the head. The inventory in that room was listed on the books at full cost.

(iv)**EXAMPLE**

One type of inquiry that auditors often perform is to ask management to explain an unexpected result in an analytical procedure, say an unexpected fluctuation in gross margin. Management's normal tendency is to provide a single cause as the explanation and both audit researchers and PCAOB practice inspections have shown that auditors are too willing to accept that first explanation even if does not explain the entire fluctuation. Audit researchers have shown that a simple but powerful method to deal with this tendency is to cue the auditor to consider not only the plausibility of the explanation but its sufficiency to cover the entire amount of the unexpected result.[1]

- *Always be neutral in wording your questions:*
  - o *What happens if a sales order does not get input into the system?*

    <<instead of>>
  - o *What happens when your people lose a sale because they are not paying attention?*
- *Don't show off your own expertise/knowledge:*
  - o *What causes your inventory turnover to be lower in the summer?*

    <<instead of>>
  - o *Based on my experience at other car dealerships I assume that inventory turnover is generally lower in the summer, right?*

Conducting Client Inquiries

When conducting a formal interview, the auditor should be clear about what is to be discussed, stay on topic (unless follow-up is needed or important tangential issues arise), and respect the interviewee's time. To the extent possible, the audit team should plan interviews to take place at a time convenient to client personnel when they are not under unusual time pressure. Interviews should be planned so they take place at separate times with a manager's supervisors, colleagues, and subordinates with little chance that the manager has time to coordinate responses. The auditor should also consider interviews with other client employees in different parts of the organization to corroborate responses from multiple sources. Consistency of client responses enhances the reliability of evidence obtained through inquiry. If one finds puzzling contradictions or implausible responses, this should alert a skeptical auditor to delve deeper into the area in question, often through the use of other audit procedures(iv).

The information gleaned from interviews should be documented in a manner that captures the key points in an understandable fashion so that the information can be shared with other members of the audit team. Furthermore, regular audit team meetings should be scheduled to candidly share what has been learned through inquiry. Audit partners benefit from this debriefing process because they may grasp the significance of some information that may have eluded less experienced personnel. Also, these discussions can help inexperienced auditors to understand potentially worrisome information by putting it in the broader context of the audit and client. Often it is only through discussion among members of the team that patterns of inconsistent responses emerge or non-verbal cues can be meaningfully interpreted.

AUTHORITATIVE GUIDANCE & STANDARDS

ISA 500 and AS 1105 are very clear about the need to corroborate inquiries. The standards note that "the auditor should perform audit procedures in addition to the use of inquiry to obtain sufficient appropriate audit evidence. Inquiry alone ordinarily does not provide sufficient appropriate audit evidence to detect a material misstatement at the relevant assertion level" (ISA 500).

An excellent opportunity for discussion among team members is during the mandatory brainstorming session when the risk of material misstatement and fraud are discussed by the audit team. If team members observe that company personnel provide contradictory or inconsistent answers to critical questions, the audit team should consider increasing its assessment of the risk of fraud or material misstatement. At a minimum, the auditor should gather enough evidence to reconcile the apparent inconsistencies, possibly with evidence obtained from procedures other than inquiry. If the contradictions are severe enough, more formal interviews may be conducted, possibly by specialists in forensic auditing, or other rigorous procedures may be used to gather additional evidence. For all interviews, the auditor should consider possible sources of evidence that might corroborate the evidence from inquiry. Some examples include:

- Viewing documentary evidence maintained by the interviewee or other personnel that supports the inquiry evidence.

- Examining third-party documents or data that reinforces the information obtained through inquiry.

- Consulting industry experts who provide context about information and evaluate the reasonableness of evidence from inquiry[(v)].

Introduction to Analysis

The complement to inquiry evidence is analysis. Analysis encompasses the use of quantitative tools and analytical procedures to facilitate decisions, evaluate performance, and signal risk conditions affecting an organization. Analysis is frequently utilized as part of the strategic and process analyses performed during the engagement. Management itself uses many forms of analysis to monitor and assess its success and the extent of risks it faces. An auditor's analysis can be used to corroborate evidence from inquiries about the client's operations and activities[(vi)].

The process of performing analytical procedures is relatively simple in concept but complex in practice. The auditor selects a measurement of interest (e.g., concerning a risk, account balance, or process attribute), generates an expectation about the item, and compares that expectation to actual results. If the expectation and the actual outcome are significantly different, the auditor needs to obtain an explanation of the unusual variation. If unexpected results cannot be adequately explained, the auditor could conclude there may be significant residual risks associated with the performance measure being examined, which could affect the subsequent conduct of the audit.

AUTHORITATIVE GUIDANCE & STANDARDS

ISA 520 and AS 2210 (formerly 12) **Identifying and Assessing Risks of Material Misstatement,** *AS 2810 (formerly 14)* **Evaluating Audit Results** *require auditors to perform analytical procedures at the beginning of the audit to identify issues and at the end of the engagement as a last big-picture look. Although analytical procedures are not required to be used*

[(v)] **EXAMPLE**

In the Enron fraud, one of the allegations about Arthur Andersen's audit work was that the firm did not properly follow up on answers to inquiries related to the special purpose entities (SPEs) that were established to move debt off Enron's books, while simultaneously enabling key officers to profit from the transactions (through the receipt of Enron stock to cover any losses associated with the SPEs). Although there were several partners at Andersen who were uncomfortable with the SPEs, the auditors would have had a better chance of unraveling the fraud had they utilized more third party documents and outside financial experts to follow up on these issues.

[(vi)] **EXAMPLE**

An auditor with a strong understanding of the client's business and industry including the key non-financial performance indicators in that business is in a much better position to detect accounting manipulations than an auditor who does not have that knowledge. The level of sophistication that an auditor with a solid analysis of the client's operating processes and how they must work in order for the company to be profitable will be more likely to detect both fraud and error at the financial statement level than those that do not have such knowledge according to recent accounting research.[2]

as substantive tests, they are frequently used for this purpose (ISA 520, AS 2305), albeit there is some controversy over the effectiveness of such tests versus other substantive tests.

Analysis can be used in numerous phases of the audit: as a planning tool or a risk assessment procedure to guide the audit or to allocate resources to potentially problematic areas, as a substantive test (substantive analytical procedure) that signals potential material misstatements, as an overall test of reasonableness of the financial statements near the end of the audit, and to inform the going concern judgment the auditor must make (discussed in more detail in Chapter 14). There are a number of differences in the use of analysis among these stages: (1) the level of detail utilized in the analysis, (2) the precision of the expectations developed prior to carrying out the analysis, and (3) the nature and extent of the follow-up work carried out by the auditor when there is a difference from expectation. Hence it is very important to understand the level of detail necessary to conduct an effective analysis. Table 9.1 summarizes the differences in using analysis at each of the various stages of the audit[vii].

Table 9.1 *Analysis at Various Audit Phases*

Audit Stage	Level of Analysis and Precision of Expectations	Follow-Up when Expectations are not Met
Preliminary or planning analytical procedures (also known as risk assessment procedures)	**Level of analysis** • Financial statement level. • Significant operating segments level. • Legal entity level. **Precision of expectation** • Tends to be more general such as "increasing trend" or "same as last year".	• Seek explanations from client management. • Plan additional audit tests to corroborate those explanations. • Note differences for follow-up at later in the audit.
Substantive analytical procedures	**Level of analysis** • At a segment or sub-segment level often focused on a particular account or set of accounts. • Could be product line, geographic area, individual store or factory. **Precision of expectation** • Must be able to precisely quantify in advance a level of tolerance for variation from expectation that is acceptable.	• Seek explanations from client management, especially operating management. • Plan additional substantive tests of details to support client explanations of the direction of observed discrepancies and the amount of the discrepancies. • Consider alternative reasons for the expectation not being met, including possibility of deliberate misstatement, and carry out further audit tests with added professional skepticism.
Overall or end of audit analytical procedures (including evaluating going concern issues)	**Level of analysis** • Financial statements taken as a whole and perhaps all reportable operating segments as per the notes to the financial statements. **Precision of expectation** • Assessment of reasonableness in light of knowledge gathered to date in audit. • Consider further whether anything at this stage suggests a "going concern" issue.	• Obtain additional explanations from client management if needed. • Maintain professional skepticism about management's responses. • Conduct additional audit testing if unable to resolve inconsistency between client explanation and actual results based on the available evidence.

We will introduce several analysis techniques that are used by auditors to obtain analytical evidence about risks, processes, and accounts. The computation of numbers is not the goal of analysis; it is merely the means to an end. The purpose is to obtain a better understanding of what is happening to the company and to highlight areas where risks are significant or financial results are unexpected, unusual, or possibly erroneous (or even fraudulent). Although very useful, none of these techniques are sufficient if used in isolation and should be combined with effective client inquiries and, possibly, other substantive procedures depending on the seriousness of the findings.

Preliminary Analytical Procedures Example

Preliminary analytical procedures are used at the audit planning stage (see details in Chapter 4). Use of analytical procedures at this stage is likely to be characterized by simple expectations such as comparisons to the previous years, adjusted for current economic activity and client specific information that has come to your attention over the past year. The further the auditor has completed the strategic and process analysis (described in Chapters 5 and 6) before carrying out these procedures the more precise the auditor's expectations can be and the more reliance that can be placed on preliminary analytical procedures as evidence.

To illustrate the basic approach to preliminary analytical procedures carried out at a very early stage in the audit, consider the following descriptive data for accounts receivable and sales:

	20x7	20x8
Accounts receivable (net)	$6,000	$8,000
Receivables/assets	18.5%	17.9%
Sales revenue	$50,000	$65,000
Sales growth	19%	30%

This illustration shows sales have increased significantly. Receivables also have increased but not at a pace commensurate with sales. We can compute an interesting ratio using the above data called Days-to-Collect, which indicates how long it takes for the company to turn receivables into cash receipts:[3]

Days-to-Collect	43.8 days	44.8 days

We see that the speed of collection has slowed down slightly, that is, customers are not paying their bills as fast in 20x8 as they did in 20x7. This could be the result of natural fluctuations in the company's operations or could occur for a number of specific reasons:

- The company has loosened its credit standards and is selling to riskier customers.
- The industry is in a recession, and all customers are paying more slowly.
- The company has changed its policy of writing off bad debts.
- There is an error (or fraud) related to receivables.

AUTHORITATIVE GUIDANCE & STANDARDS

ISA 520 and AS 2305 specify that analysis involve comparing the results of the analysis to auditor expectations as to what the results should be. Even when auditors use simple analytical procedures (such as comparison to last year), they should first develop expectations. For example, comparing current and prior year results is only appropriate when there is an expectation that the numbers will be the same under a stable operating environment.

The first explanation is unlikely because we expect that loosening sales credit in a period of rapid sales growth would lead to proportionally more rapid growth in receivables—the opposite of what is suggested by the raw data. The rapid sales growth also seems to belie the recession explanation. Regarding the third possible explanation, the auditor may inquire about the company's policy for writing off bad debts but must keep in mind that it is possible the receivable balance is incorrect. The audit should be conducted to provide reasonable assurance for eliminating the last possibility. As Table 9.1 indicates, preliminary analysis is usually done at the financial statement level, mainly involves year-to-year comparisons, generates inquiries to management, and may lead to changes in the audit plan.

Consider further that if in response to a client inquiry the auditor then learned that the allowance for bad debts was $1,000 at the end of 20×7 but is $800 at the end of 20×8. Typically, an auditor would expect an inverse relationship between the receivable turnover and the allowance for bad debts. When customers are paying more slowly, or other factors affect the recoverability of receivables, the company bears a greater risk that receivables will not be collected. This risk should be translated into a *higher* estimate of bad debts. In other words, given that the receivable turnover has decreased, an auditor would find it *unusual* that the allowance for bad debts has decreased. This is an example of the type of analysis that an auditor should perform during preliminary analytical procedures.

Techniques for Obtaining Analytical Evidence

Auditors have traditionally relied on extensive review of financial statement balances when performing analytical procedures. However, analytical evidence from nonfinancial performance measures is becoming more common and is particularly useful for assessing the performance of processes. There are six basic approaches for performing analytical procedures:

- Basic judgmental methods:
  - o Comparative financial statement analysis
  - o Common size financial statement analysis (or percentage analysis)
  - o Ratio analysis
- Advanced judgmental methods
  - o Cash flow analysis
  - o Nonfinancial performance measurement
  - o Competitive benchmarking

Although each method is individually useful, the auditor cannot interpret a single number or set of numbers in isolation. The appropriate standard of comparison may take many forms: prior-year results, management's budgeted results, an auditor's industry expertise, or results from similar companies. Furthermore, unique facts known about the company must be considered in determining whether a specific performance measure is unusual or not. Thus, much of the interpretation of analytical evidence involves extensive client inquiries. Remember, however, as it is illustrated in Table 9.1, the phase at which analytical procedures are carried out determines the level of analysis (e.g., firm as a whole vs. product line) and the precision of the auditor's expectation of the results before carrying out the procedure (e.g., greater than last year versus a 2.2 percent increase due to industry growth) that is expected to be obtained from those procedures.

Basic Judgmental Methods

Comparative Financial Statement Analysis: The comparison of financial statement balances across time is one of the oldest and most common analytical procedures used by auditors. In general, an auditor is interested in understanding why significant accounts have increased or decreased over time, especially if the change in account balances is extreme or unusual. Accounts that fluctuate in dramatic steps are of most interest. However, although steady growth of revenues by 5 percent per year may not raise many questions, it is not necessarily indicative of low risk.

An example of comparative financial statements is presented in the first four columns of Table 9.2 for a hypothetical company called AMA Autoparts Inc. A few dramatic account changes can be noted immediately:

- The wild swings in the cash balance.
- The doubling of accounts receivable in 20 x 8.
- The reduction in plant assets in 20 x 8.
- The reduction in retained earnings in spite of increasing profits.
- The dramatic growth in revenue.
- The unusual level of dividends.

Tentative explanations for some of the changes in account balances may already be apparent, such as the large dividend explains the drop in retained earnings, but at this point our explanations will be incomplete and mere guesswork without additional information that is obtained through inquiry.

Common-Size Financial Statement Analysis: Common-size financial statement analysis is based on the premise that the relationships among accounts in the balance sheet and income statement are predictable. For example, a typical manufacturing company will have relatively minor cash balances whereas inventory and plant assets will be a large proportion of total assets. Common-size analysis entails transforming all of the data in the balance sheet and income statement into percentages relative to a common denominator. This is accomplished for the balance sheet by dividing each account balance by total assets, yielding the percentage of total assets that is accounted for by each account or group of accounts. A similar transformation

Table 9.2 *An Example of Comparative and Common Size Analysis: Basic Financial Data for Ama Autoparts Inc.*

Balance Sheet

	Audited	Audited	Unaudited	Percentage Analysis		
	20x6	20x7	20x8	20x6	20x7	20x8
Cash	$26,000	$312,000	$10,000	1.47%	14.81%	0.48%
Marketable Securities	100,000	120,000	125,000	5.66%	5.70%	6.04%
Accounts Receivable	525,000	350,000	700,000	29.73%	16.61%	33.82%
Inventory	310,000	310,000	300,000	17.55%	14.71%	14.49%
Prepaid Expenses	60,000	75,000	50,000	3.40%	3.56%	2.42%
Current Assets	1,021,000	1,167,000	1,185,000	57.81%	55.39%	57.25%
Long-Term Investments	275,000	300,000	310,000	15.57%	14.24%	14.98%
Plant and Property	555,000	740,000	640,000	31.43%	35.12%	30.92%
Accumulated Depreciation	(85,000)	(100,000)	(65,000)	−4.81%	−4.75%	−3.14%
Total Assets	1,766,000	2,107,000	2,070,000	100.00%	100.00%	100.00%
Accounts Payable	32,000	110,000	85,000	1.81%	5.22%	4.11%
Wages Payable	28,000	32,000	18,000	1.59%	1.52%	0.87%
Dividends Payable	0	5,000	130,000	0.00%	0.24%	6.28%
Taxes Payable	36,000	55,000	62,000	2.04%	2.61%	3.00%
Current Portion of Debt	150,000	175,000	100,000	8.49%	8.31%	4.83%
Current Liabilities	246,000	377,000	395,000	13.93%	17.89%	19.08%
Mortgage Payable	800,000	625,000	525,000	45.30%	29.66%	25.36%
Total Liabilities	1,046,000	1,002,000	920,000	59.23%	47.56%	44.44%
Common Stock ($10 par)	110,000	150,000	225,000	6.23%	7.12%	10.87%
Additional Paid-In Capital	260,000	345,000	425,000	14.72%	16.37%	20.53%
Retained Earnings	350,000	610,000	500,000	19.82%	28.95%	24.15%
Total Equity	720,000	1,105,000	1,150,000	40.77%	52.44%	55.56%
Total Liability and Equity	1,766,000	2,107,000	2,070,000	100.00%	100.00%	100.00%

Income Statement

	Audited	Unaudited	Percentage Analysis	
	20x7	20x8	20x7	20x8
Sales	4,185,000	6,045,000	100.00%	100.00%
Cost of Goods Sold	(2,565,000)	(4,015,000)	−61.29%	−66.42%
Gross Margin	1,620,000	2,030,000	38.71%	33.58%
Depreciation Expense	(90,000)	(75,000)	−2.15%	−1.24%
Selling Expense	(600,000)	(575,000)	−14.34%	−9.51%
Administrative Expense	(420,000)	(480,000)	−10.04%	−7.94%
Net Operating Income	510,000	900,000	12.19%	14.89%
Interest Expense	(65,000)	(50,000)	−1.55%	−0.83%
Net Income Before Taxes	445,000	850,000	10.63%	14.06%
Income Tax Expense	(175,000)	(365,000)	−4.18%	−6.04%
Net Income	270,000	485,000	6.45%	8.02%

is obtained for the income statement by dividing each nominal account by total sales (or total revenues). An example of this type of transformation is provided in the right-most columns of Table 9.2 for AMA Autoparts Inc.

Simply noting that a company has more receivables or inventory is not very meaningful given that a successful company grows over time. The more important question pertains to which assets have grown fastest (or slowest) and why. In our example, building and equipment has decreased as a percentage of total assets (35.12 to 30.92 percent). In most businesses, plant assets will increase because new facilities are needed as the company grows. At the same time, older equipment may be retired and replaced by newer equipment, which is typically more expensive. These two trends would tend to cause plant assets to grow at a rate commensurate with total asset growth. In our example, we have already seen that plant assets decreased in 20x8. Such an outcome may be the natural result of conditions within the organization (e.g., the company has changed its operations), the result of accounting changes, or an indication that the company has made an accounting error (e.g., failed to capitalize some expenditures that should be treated as assets).

Ratio Analysis: Auditors and financial analysts have traditionally used a number of common ratios to assess the financial performance of a company. These ratios fall into five broad categories:

1. Profitability ratios: These ratios measure the profitability of the company relative to its asset base and revenue stream.

2. Asset management ratios: These ratios measure the company's effectiveness and efficiency at managing various types of assets.

3. Liquidity ratios: These ratios measure the ability of the company to satisfy its obligations in the near term (usually considered to be the next twelve months).

4. Debt management ratios: These ratios measure the ability of the company to manage its capital financing and to satisfy its obligations in the long run.

5. Market value ratios: These ratios measure the company's standing in the eyes of outside investors.

Ratios allow an auditor to link information from the balance sheet to activity in the income statement in order to identify unusual relationships across the financial statements. Thus, ratios may tell an auditor something about an organization that is not apparent from the raw accounting data used in comparative or common-size financial analysis.

The formulas for some commonly used ratios in each of these categories are presented in Box 9.2 "Illustrative Ratios Used in Analysis of Financial Statements." Before discussing these ratios, three points should be noted. First, this list is not intended to be comprehensive. There are many different ratios that may be relevant and important for the evaluation of any given company. For example, additional ratios may be needed to evaluate a company that has a heavy commitment to research and development. Other specialized industries (e.g., banking, insurance, health care) may require an entirely different set of ratios. The second point is that the formulas for computing ratios are intended to be flexible. Data may not be available to compute some of the ratios exactly as stated in Box 9.2 "Illustrative Ratios Used in Analysis of Financial Statements." In these cases, the ratios may need to be slightly modified (e.g., using year end balances rather than average balances). Third, and most importantly in practice, the key to calculating ratios often depends on what you are going to compare the calculated ratios to. If you are going to use an industry benchmark ratio as the base of reference, the computation of a client's comparable ratios should follow the same formula as the industry data base. The efficiency of analytical procedures can be greatly reduced if different methods are used to compute client and industry metrics, e.g., it would be unfortunate to find out that you have spent considerable time trying to determine why your client's level of inventory and costs of goods sold is different than the industry only to realize that you are comparing ratios you calculated based on an average cost approach to inventory to industry ratios calculated based on FIFO inventory.

Table 9.3 presents some key ratios for AMA Autoparts Inc. Profitability ratios reveal that the company was significantly more profitable in 20x8 than in 20x7. Profit margin, which indicates the percentage of each dollar of revenue that is profit, increased from 6.45 percent to 8.02 percent.

BOX 9.2 ILLUSTRATIVE RATIOS USED IN ANALYSIS OF FINANCIAL STATEMENTS

Liquidity Ratios:

Quick Ratio $$\frac{Cash + Marketable\ Securities + Net\ Receivables}{Current\ Liabilities}$$

Current Ratio $$\frac{Current\ Assets}{Current\ Liabilities}$$

Debt Management Ratios:

Payable Turnover $$\frac{Cost\ of\ Goods\ Sold}{Accounts\ Payable}$$

Debt Ratio $$\frac{Total\ Liabilities}{Total\ Assets}$$

Interest Coverage Ratio (Times Interest Earned) $$\frac{Earnings\ before\ Interest\ \&\ Taxes}{Interest\ Expense}$$

Interest Rate Ratio $$\frac{Interest\ Expense}{Average\ Total\ Debt}$$

Asset Management Ratios:

Inventory Turnover $$\frac{Cost\ of\ Goods\ Sold}{Inventory}$$

Receivable Turnover $$\frac{Net\ Sales\ or\ Revenue}{Net\ Receivables}$$

Fixed Asset Turnover $$\frac{Net\ Sales\ or\ Revenue}{Net\ Fixed\ Assets}$$

Total Asset Turnover	$\dfrac{Net\ Sales\ or\ Revenue}{Total\ Assets}$

Average Days to Collect	365/Receivable Turnover
Average Days to Sell	365/Inventory Turnover
Average Operating Cycle	Average Days to Sell + Average Days to Collect
Depreciation Rate	$\dfrac{Depreciation\ Expense}{Net\ Fixed\ Assets}$

Profitability Ratios:

Return on Assets	$\dfrac{Net\ Income + Interest\ Expense \times (1 - Avg\ Tax\ Rate)}{Total\ Assets}$

Return on Equity	$\dfrac{Net\ Income - Preferred\ Stock\ Dividends}{Total\ Common\ Equity}$

Profit Margin	$\dfrac{Net\ Income}{Net\ Sales}$

Market Value Ratios:

Price/Earnings	$\dfrac{Common\ Stock\ Price}{Earnings\ per\ Share}$

Earnings per Share	$\dfrac{Net\ Income\ for\ the\ Current\ Period}{Number\ of\ Common\ Stock\ Shares}$

Market/Book	$\dfrac{Common\ Stock\ Share\ Price}{Common\ Stock\ Book\ Value}$

Dividend Payout	$\dfrac{Dividends\ Paid\ Out}{Net\ Income}$

Book Value per Share	$\dfrac{Total\ Equity\ Attributable\ to\ Common\ Stock}{Number\ of\ Common\ Stock\ Shares}$

The return on assets (usually abbreviated ROA) indicates the magnitude of profits relative to total assets and increased from 15.98 percent to 24.59 percent. ROA is independent of the forms of financing used by the company and is not affected by the extent of debt that a company has issued. The return on equity (abbreviated ROE) measures the profit relative to the amount of equity invested by common shareholders—that is, it factors out the cost of debt. ROE increased from 29.59 percent to 43.02 percent.

Asset management ratios provide an indication of how well a company is utilizing various types of assets. Higher asset management ratios indicate

Table 9.3 *An Example of Ratio Analysis*

Ratio Analysis	20x8	20x7
Liquidity Ratios:		
Quick ratio	2.11	2.07
Current ratio	3.00	3.10
Asset Management Ratios:		
Inventory turnover	13.16	8.27
Receivable turnover	11.51	9.57
Fixed asset turnover	9.95	7.54
Asset turnover	2.89	2.16
Average days to collect	31.71	38.14
Average days to sell	27.74	152.08
Averaging operating cycle	59.45	190.22
Depreciation expense/plant assets	1.24%	2.15%
Debt Management Ratios:		
Payable turnover	41.18	36.13
Debt/assets	44.44%	47.56%
Interest coverage	18.00	7.85
Profitability Ratios:		
Return on assets	24.59%	15.98%
Return on equity	43.02%	29.59%
Return on sales (profit margin)	8.02%	6.45%
Earnings per share	$2.16	$1.80
Market Value Ratios:		
Price/earnings	8.93	12.08
Book value of equity	5.11	7.37
Dividend payout	122.68%	3.70%
Effective tax rate	42.94%	39.33%

more efficient management of assets; for example, a high inventory turnover may indicate that the company makes effective use of just-in-time inventory techniques. However, it is also possible that very high values may indicate problems; in some cases, high inventory turnover may occur because the company maintains too little inventory and loses revenues due to stock-outs or shortages. In our example, the inventory turnover has increased substantially from 8.27 to 13.16. The company may have improved its marketing, it may be experiencing inventory shortages, or an error may have occurred in the recording of the inventory balance at year-end. The auditor must conduct the audit to have reasonable assurance that the cause is not an error or fraudulent transaction.

Liquidity and debt ratios show that the company is more liquid in 20x8 than it was in 20x7. The company is paying its bills faster (i.e., payable turnover went from 36.13 to 41.18), has better interest coverage (18.00 versus 7.85), and lower levels of debt relative to assets (44.44 percent versus 47.56 percent). These results indicate that the company has a stronger financial position than in the prior year.

Advanced Judgmental Methods

Cash Flow Analysis: Most financial statement and ratio analysis is based on accrual accounting numbers. However, a company must also generate positive cash flow over a reasonable period of time, or it will not be able to pay its obligations or satisfy its investors. Companies are required to prepare a Statement of Cash Flows as part of the annual financial report. Accountants usually analyze three components of cash flow: cash from operations, cash from investing activities, and cash from financing activities. Cash from operations refers to the net cash flows generated from the day-to-day activities of the company such as producing and selling inventory. Cash from investing activities reflects the purchase (and sale) of long-lived assets such as plant assets and investments. Cash from financing reflects the sources of financing (debt, equity) and payments to investors and creditors.

Cash flow is not expected to be positive from all three components, but over an extended period the company needs to generate a positive cash flow. The cash flow profile of an organization will generally follow a predictable pattern based on its life cycle. In the early growth stages, most companies will have negative cash flow from operations and significant cash inflows from financing and outflows for investments. In a mature, stable period, the company should have relatively balanced cash flow from all three sources with new financing activity mainly being used to fund replacement of productive assets. In the decline stage, cash flow from operations may still be positive (but reduced), investing activity will slow down and possibly create a positive cash flow as productive assets are sold, and cash will flow out to investors and creditors as the company winds down its operations[(viii)].

Many traditional accounting ratios can be recast as cash flow ratios if desired. For example, many companies report cash flow per share (usually positive) along with earnings per share (almost always lower) in order to communicate their financial health. Similarly, interest coverage can be calculated based on net cash flow rather than earnings. An important cash flow indicator is *free cash flow*. This is usually defined as cash flow from operations less dividends and any capital expenditures needed to maintain *current* capacity.[4] Free cash flow reflects the amount of money the organization has available for expansion, new product development, and to absorb the impact of risk or shocks within the industry. A company with negative free cash flow will need to shrink or shut down eventually.

Nonfinancial Performance Measurement: Many risks, especially within processes, are more effectively measured using nonfinancial measures than traditional accounting numbers. In many industries financial analysts frequently supplement financial information with nonfinancial indicators when evaluating potential investments. For example, financial analysts valuing a professional sports franchise may focus on the franchise win-loss record and the size of local market. Common nonfinancial measures that apply to many manufacturing, retail and service organizations include:

- Market share: This is the percentage of total market consumption that is filled by a specific company or product. A successful company will have a larger market share. An interesting aspect of defining market share is to define the relevant market. Coca-Cola controls a dominant portion of the (ix)**EXAMPLE**

The rate of success for developing new pharmaceuticals is very low, and those that are successful take a long time to bring to the market. On average, the pharmaceutical industry must identify and test 5,000 new compounds in order to obtain a single viable product. Although the success rate is very low, the potential rewards can be huge when success is achieved, especially if the drug is effective against a broad-based disease. The time-to-market can be as long as thirteen years because of the approval process used by government agencies that often requires years of testing for new drugs. In such an environment, small gains in success rates or time-to-market can yield a significant competitive advantage to a pharmaceutical company.

"cola" market or even "soft drink" market. However, if the market is defined as "thirsty people," Coke comes in a distant second to water.

- Customer satisfaction: Long-term success for most organizations depends on providing satisfying experiences to their customers. A drop in customer satisfaction generally leads to reduced revenue and profits.

- Time-to-market for new products: This is the length of time it takes a company to conceive a new product and begin to sell it. The longer it takes to get a new idea to market, the more risk there is that a competitor will get there first, or external developments will cause early obsolescence. The software and media industries are particularly sensitive to time-to-market issues.

- New product success rates: Companies may introduce many new products and multiple product introductions maximize the chance that some of the products will prove successful and profitable. Movie studios, record companies, book publishers, and consumer products manufacturers (e.g., Proctor & Gamble) all use this approach, and improvement in the success rate of new products can have a very positive effect on the company(ix).

Nonfinancial measures are frequently generated by information systems in firms that are not subject to the extensive internal controls that are in place over financial data. Hence, the use by auditors of such measures is dependent on the availability of systematic and reliable data. Before, the auditor relies on such nonfinancial measures, just as with financial data, the auditor needs to consider controls over the reliability of the information. The need for reliable data has created opportunities for organizations to develop and sell the output of proprietary measurement systems (e.g., J.D. Power & Associates report customer satisfaction for automobiles) and independent ratings for products and service (e.g., *Consumer Reports* provides quality assessments for a wide variety of consumer products). Nonfinancial performance measures tend to be industry specific. Some examples of nonfinancial measures include:

- Airlines: On-time percentages.

- Automobiles: Reliability ratings and number of recalls.

- Hotels: Average occupancy rates.

- Internet business sites: Number of hits by web users.

- Telecom mobile phone providers: Churn rate (the number of customers lost versus gained in a period).

- Universities: Student performance statistics, such as graduation rates(x).

Competitive Benchmarking: The evaluation of performance measures is a complex process. In general, some standard of comparison is needed in order to determine if a specific measurement indicates good or bad news. Internal comparisons over time or comparisons with forecasted results (such as budgets) are very useful. Another common approach is to compare a company's performance to outside organizations. This technique is referred to as *competitive benchmarking*.

The two challenges for effective competitive benchmarking are (1) identifying the appropriate external organization to use as a comparison, and (2) obtaining meaningful data for comparison. Organizations in the same industry provide an obvious starting point because they will often

(x)**EXAMPLE**

The Financial Times has a major accounting firm carry out audit procedures on all schools that want to be ranked in their annual rankings of MBA and other graduate programs. Hence, the rise of the use of nonfinancial performance measures has provided an assurance opportunity for audit firms seeking to expand their assurance practice.

have processes that are similar to the client. However, the auditor must be careful to consider differences across companies in the same industry. For example, distribution processes for Amazon.com are significantly different from Barnes & Noble, and one cannot realistically be used as a benchmark for the other. Sometimes, the appropriate benchmark for a process is found in an entirely different industry. For example, LL Bean, a mail-order retailer, has a world class telemarketing operation that could be used as a competitive benchmark for the telemarketing activity in other industries such as insurance or telecommunications.

The problem of obtaining meaningful data is aggravated by the efforts of most organizations to keep information about their internal processes secret. Proprietary internal information is seen as a source of competitive advantage, so that organizations are often unwilling to share data on performance measures. This obstacle is sometimes overcome by using independent third parties such as trade associations and not-for-profit rating agencies to compile sensitive data and then disguise actual results from individual organizations. Nevertheless, acquiring meaningful external benchmarks is a serious challenge for the auditor and management.

A Rigorous Approach to Obtaining Analytical Evidence

When carrying out substantive analytical procedures that could potentially reduce the amount of detailed testing the auditor is going to do, it is likely that the auditor is going to want to adopt a structured approach to obtaining and evaluating the analytical evidence to support his or her conclusions. Evidence standards require that sufficient appropriate evidence be obtained to support the auditor's opinion and the use of analytical procedures as audit evidence has been controversial. Substantive analytical procedures are relatively cheap to perform but substantive analytical procedures only provide an indication that there is a potential problem in an account and provide little direction about whether a problem actually exists. In contrast, most detailed testing provides a starting point to seek out indications of additional problems whereas substantive analytical procedures just lead to formulating a plan for additional substantive tests of details to find the problem. Furthermore, auditors frequently inquire of client management about the reasons for unexpected results, allowing management to mislead the auditor or head off additional investigation.

Performing Structured Analysis

Given the huge volume of performance measures, accounts, ratios, and percentages that an auditor could consider during the course of an audit, it is vital that the auditor adopt a systematic approach to evaluating analytical evidence. Effective and efficient use of analytical evidence requires training and experience. The interpretation of the results from analytical procedures is more an art form than a mechanical process. Nevertheless, the auditor can follow a systematic process that makes the interpretation more effective, as illustrated in Box 9.3 "A Systematic Process for Conducting Substantive Analytical Procedures".

Step 1 is to identify the attribute that the auditor wishes to evaluate. The attribute of interest can be a specific risk, the effectiveness of a process, or a management assertion about a class of transactions or account balance. Step 2, gathering relevant facts, is an important but

---

BOX 9.3   A SYSTEMATIC PROCESS FOR CONDUCTING SUBSTANTIVE ANALYTICAL PROCEDURES

PURPOSE: *To use analytical evidence to identify accounts, risks or process attributes where observed outcomes are inconsistent with the auditor's expectations and which may require further investigation during the course of the audit.*

STEP 1: Identify a process attribute, risk or account to be subject to analysis: *The focus of the analysis needs to be specified. An account balance can be examined to determine if it may contain material misstatement, a specific risk can be measured to determine if it was significant, or nonfinancial process attributes can be examined to see if they are consistent with reported financial results.*

STEP 2: Gather facts relevant to the analysis: *Identify key events, situations or other facts that may have an impact on the interpretation of performance indicators.*

STEP 3: Identify relevant performance measures: *The auditor must decide what attributes to measure. The selection may be self-evident in the case of accounts, but less obvious for risks or process performance indicators.*

STEP 4: Obtain data and perform computations: *Performance measures should be based on reliable data and computational procedures. Hence, steps must be taken to examine controls over data collection and computation, prior to carrying out substantive analytical procedures.*

STEP 5: Impose structure: *Organize the numerical data into logical segments or audit areas that can be separately analyzed for unusual results, events or patterns.**

STEP 6: Analyze: *Analyze each performance measure for deviations from expectations. Reactions to unexpected deviations depend on the nature of the measure and the size of the deviation (i.e., quantitative and qualitative materiality).*

STEP 7: Conclude: *Construct a cohesive explanation of the numerical data, which incorporates all of the data, facts, and circumstances that are known about the company and determine the implications for the conduct of the audit.*

* Step 5 will be discussed in more detail in Chapter 14.

---

often overlooked step. The interpretation of analytical evidence can only be effective when the auditor factors in what he or she already knows about the company, often as a result of client inquiries. Step 3, identifying the appropriate performance measures, may be trivial in the case of a management assertion about an account balance, but may be difficult when the attribute of interest is the company's current competitive condition. First, the attribute or risk may not have an obvious performance measure or the appropriate performance measure may be nonfinancial. Selection of an inappropriate performance measure may yield confusing or inaccurate results. Second, accurate and complete data must be available to determine the value of the performance measure[xi].

Step 4 is computational, and can be facilitated using computer software. Many commercial software accounting packages also generate useful statistics for analysis. The key concern for the auditor is making certain that the data being used and the computational procedures are reliable. It is also vital that the auditor does not rely on the software's default features to flag problems and that the auditor carefully set the parameters of the program when the program generates a list of unexpected fluctuations. Step 5, imposing structure, is helpful for developing an integrated understanding of the company's operations and results. The organization of data into logically related categories helps bring together disjointed data that relates to the same attribute or activity. This topic will be discussed in more detail in Chapter 14.

Step 6 of the analysis is where the auditor's skill, experience, and expertise have the most impact. The ability to integrate a large volume of information into a coherent picture of a client's situation is obtained with training and experience. Probably the hardest part of this process is deciding when the reported results do not meet expectations. Such a decision must draw upon the auditor's knowledge of the company, industry, and specific facts.

As a final step, the auditor should be able to reconcile all the facts that are available, and explain why some performance indicators went up, some went down, and others were stable. In particular, the auditor needs to focus carefully on facts that do not fit the expected pattern. It is these facts that may often be a clue to something far more important. When expectations are met, the auditor has strong evidence about risk levels, process effectiveness, and information reliability. When expectations are not met, additional effort is usually needed for the auditor to determine how these circumstances affect the audit. This analysis must be explicitly tied into our earlier discussion of materiality and tolerable error such that if expectations are not met, what difference from expectations will trigger the auditor's suspicion there might be a material misstatement. This has to be identified beforehand as most people are very good as rationalizing differences away after the differences are known[xii].

The analysis process described above is summarized as a decision flowchart in Figure 9.3. The evaluation of analytical evidence is iterative in nature since the auditor can never know if their expectations are completely reasonable. As new information becomes available, an auditor may revise his or her expectations. At some point, however, the auditor will reach a conclusion as to whether actual conditions and results confirm the expectations, suggesting that the assertion being examined is acceptable, or will identify a discrepancy that will influence the conduct of the audit.

[xii]**EXAMPLE**

The WorldCom auditors are alleged to have done a great deal of analysis based on the expectation that results would be similar to prior years. The problem was that the worldwide telecommunications industry was undergoing a rapid transformation due to excess capacity, and hence expectations that results would be the same as last year were inappropriate. The fact that the auditor observed that important financial items were close to the levels of the prior year should have triggered additional investigation NOT provided the auditor with comfort about the reported results.

[xii]**EXAMPLE**

A strategic business unit of a retail apparel firm showed strong growth in urban areas and weak growth in rural areas when detailed analyses of sales growth and contribution margins by store were undertaken by the auditor. The auditor justified these outcomes as being due to the slump in crop prices. Sounds very convincing, but would the auditor have expected this result in advance if the auditor had considered the growth in population in what were formerly "rural areas" that were becoming increasingly populated with long distance commuters.

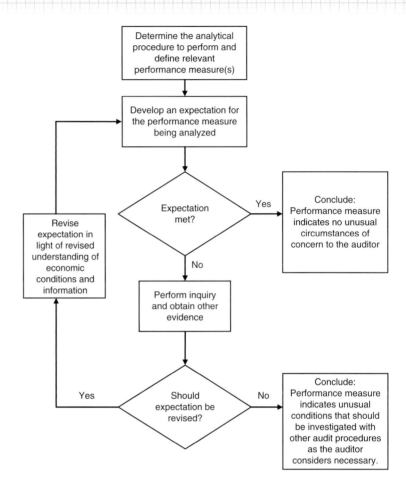

Figure 9.3 Evaluation of Analytical Evidence

Substantive Analytical Procedures

Most of what has been introduced above has been couched in terms of preliminary analytical procedures, and in Chapter 14 we will discuss analytical procedures used to review the financial statements at the end of the audit. In Chapters 11 to 13 we will discuss substantive analytical procedures that are employed in specific audit-sensitive processes to complement or as a substitute for other substantive tests such as tests of details. While the general techniques for analysis introduced above are readily adaptable as substantive tests, the auditor must refine these procedures to have a much tighter level of precision if the auditor intends to rely on them as substantive evidence. The level of precision of substantive analytical procedures can depend on a number of factors. Some specific guidelines to consider include:

- The auditor must carefully specify the transaction or account balance to be the focus of the test before the analysis is performed. Relationships should be based on logical associations (e.g., cause and effect) rather than being based merely on the statistical model that fits best. Further, the documented past relationships should not only be logical but also have a high degree of predictability(xiii).

- The auditor needs to ensure that the data being used for the analysis is reliable, which means that the internal controls over the data processing should be tested at both the design and implementation level or the auditor should perform other procedures that support the completeness and accuracy of the underlying data employed in the procedure.

- The auditor needs to develop their own expectations prior to carrying out the analysis. The more detailed the data used and the more precise the auditor's expectation, the greater the probability that a substantive analytical procedure will detect a misstatement, e.g., weekly data is more detailed than quarterly or annual data, location data is more detailed than division data, and line of business data is more detailed than overall firm data. The greater the level of aggregation of the data and resulting analysis the less able the procedure will be to detect misstatements[xiv].

- The auditor needs to consider the level of precision that the analytical procedure can provide. How much variation from the auditor's expectation used in the analysis is acceptable? The amount of such difference must be considered in light of the tolerable error or materiality that is associated with the transaction stream or account balance that is being tested.

- The auditor should investigate significant deviations from expectations as analytical procedures alone normally cannot confirm the existence of a misstatement. When substantive analytical procedures are being employed, all reasonable explanations—whether from client inquiry or an auditor's own expertise—need to be corroborated by additional evidence. Further, if no explanation can be generated, the auditor may need to perform other audit procedures to ensure that the difference is not the result of an accounting misstatement.

Potential Pitfalls from Using Analysis as Evidence

Analytical procedures can be an extremely useful technique for identifying areas of high risk in the audit. However, the auditor must be careful to avoid some common pitfalls that could lead to a reduction in their usefulness. The most common mistakes made in applying analytical procedures include:

- Simplistic or ill-defined expectations: Analytical procedures are most effective when the auditor generates an independent expectation about an attribute being evaluated (risk, process, or account). Unfortunately, in many situations the auditor may not have a good basis for generating an expectation. For example, auditors may oversimplify their expectations about accounts by using the prior-year balance as the current-year expectation. If the auditor cannot generate a reasonable and logical expectation, the benefit of performing the analytical procedure will be reduced. Expectations should be tied to materiality and tolerable error for account balances and allowable error or deviation rates for tests of internal controls.

- Lack of precision: All expectations involve a range of values that are reasonably likely to occur—the auditor's expectation is just one point in that range. The range of reasonable expectations reflects the margin of error of the estimate and can be quite large. The larger the margin of error, the less accurate will be the analytical procedure. Unfortunately, the auditor rarely knows the true margin of error for a specific performance measure and may end up questioning fluctuations that are normal fluctuations, rather than indicative of an underlying problem, risk, or error. If the range of values is not significantly less than tolerable error or materiality then the analytical procedure is not a good candidate for substantive analytical procedures.

- Lack of reliable data: Auditor expectations will not be reliable if they are based on inaccurate or unreliable data. If the data used for analytical procedures comes from inside the organization, the process that generates the data should be subject to control testing to ensure the data is reliable or, if not, that the data used for the analytical procedure itself is tested to ensure it is reliable. Misleading data will often cause the auditor to develop unreasonable expectations and decrease the precision of the estimation. This problem is potentially compounded whenever an analytical procedure uses data from outside the organization or data that is not controlled effectively within the organization (e.g., nonfinancial information that is processed outside the accounting system).

- Influence of reported outcomes: The auditor often knows the reported outcome for an attribute before performing an analytical procedure. Knowledge of the reported outcome has the tendency to bias the auditor's expectation in the direction of the known value and can potentially reduce the effectiveness of an analytical procedure. This problem commonly arises when the auditor is aware of the unaudited book value for an account that is being analyzed. Professional standards reinforce this problem by requiring that preliminary analytical procedures be performed early in the audit, which can lead an auditor to fixate on the reported value.

- Incomplete or inconsistent explanation of fluctuations: When an auditor identifies an attribute where expectations diverge from reported outcomes, he or she should generate possible explanations for that fluctuation. Fluctuations can occur because of natural business conditions, increased risks, process breakdowns, or accounting errors (or fraud). An auditor may not be aware of many of the possible conditions that could explain the fluctuation. The auditor will only investigate explanations that come to his or her attention; therefore, failure to recognize possible explanations for the fluctuation may lead the auditor to overlook the underlying problem. Furthermore, even when a potential explanation is recognized, the auditor may not realize that it only partially explains the fluctuation.

- Poor pattern recognition: Many performance indicators interact in predictable patterns—that is, they are correlated. Analytical procedures are most effective when the changes in different attributes are recognized as forming a pattern indicative of underlying conditions. Unfortunately, recognizing patterns in a diverse set of data is very difficult for most people.

- Undue reliance on client inquiry: Auditors have a natural tendency to ask management to provide an explanation for any unusual fluctuations observed while performing analytical procedures. As discussed earlier in this chapter, client inquiry is a legitimate source of audit evidence, but the auditor must be careful not to be overly swayed by management's explanations. First, there is always the possibility that the explanation is not accurate or does not explain the entire fluctuation. The auditor should consider other possible explanations for the fluctuations, especially those that might indicate an error or problem. Second, the auditor should obtain independent corroboration of the explanation if possible[xv].

In spite of the potential pitfalls in analytical procedures, they are extremely useful and powerful techniques for the auditor to evaluate the level of strategic and process risks present in the various areas of the audit. Because the results of such procedures frequently lead to inquiry of client management for explanations, it is important that the auditor think carefully about how to approach the managers to get the best possible response to those questions. Familiarity with the potential pitfalls will help the auditor to perform the procedures effectively and efficiently.

Inquiry and Analysis in Assessing Fraud Risk

One area of the audit where analysis and inquiry are particularly important is in assessing the risk of accounting fraud. Although outright material fraud is relatively rare, many of the hints or clues that fraud may exist initially arise during analysis and inquiry. Suspicion of fraud makes an innocuous pattern of financial results appear suspicious, and innocent-sounding client explanations sound furtive. An auditor must always be alert to indications of fraud and should process all evidence from analysis and inquiry with an appropriate degree of skepticism.

When performing analytical procedures, an auditor may encounter a number of circumstances that might indicate a potential fraud. Almost any unusual fluctuation in performance results could be a warning of a deeper problem. In some cases, the *lack* of fluctuations may be even more important. Some examples of circumstances that might alert an auditor to a risk of fraud include:

- Unexplained shortages or adjustments to asset accounts, which could be indicative of theft or embezzlement.
- Excessive costs of materials, which could be indicative of bribes or kickbacks.
- Unusually high number of debit or credit entries, which could indicate fictitious accounting entries.
- Unreasonable expenses, expenditures, or reimbursements, which could indicate improper use of corporate assets or improper rebates.
- Unusual relationships among expense and revenues, which could indicate manipulation of the elements of net income.

[xv] **EXAMPLE**

The PCAOB's critique of US public accounting firms' performance in the period 2004–7 had this to say about problems they found that auditors had in performing analysis: "Inspection teams have identified deficiencies in firms' performance of analytical procedures that the firms intended to be substantive tests, including the failure to

a) develop appropriate expectations, including in some instances the failure to appropriately disaggregate data in order to obtain the necessary level of precision for the expectation,

(b) establish a threshold for differences that the firm could accept without further investigation,

(c) establish a threshold for differences that was low enough to provide the level of assurance that the firm planned to achieve from the test,

(d) test the data that the firm used in the analytical procedures,

(e) investigate significant unexpected differences from the firm's expectations, and

(f) examine other evidence to obtain corroboration of management's explanations regarding significant unexpected differences."
(PCAOB Release 2008–008, p. 15)

AUTHORITATIVE GUIDANCE & STANDARDS

ISA 240 **The Auditor's Responsibilities Relating to Fraud in an Audit of Financial Statements** *and AS 2401 (formerly AU 316)* **Consideration of a Fraud in a Financial Statement Audit** *provide numerous references to the auditor making inquiries to client management and others as well as using analytical procedures to detect the increased possibility of material fraud (or error) in the financial statements.*

(xvi)EXAMPLE

Two of the most widely documented frauds of the late 1980s could have been identified through careful analysis and inquiry. In the previously mentioned case of ZZZZ Best, there was rampant fraud involving false insurance restoration contracts. Evidence was presented during congressional hearings that the market share data that ZZZZ Best offered to the auditors suggested that the company possessed more than 100 percent of the worldwide market for insurance restoration contracts. In another case, Lincoln Savings and Loan in Arizona in the late 1980s, fraud was conducted in part by the company recording market values for land transactions well in excess of the average market values of any land transaction in the area at the time of the transactions. In both frauds, inquiries made by the auditors were met with fraudulent representations by management (and even third parties in the case of Lincoln Savings and Loan). Only with careful analysis comparing data received from the client with industry data could the auditors have been able to detect the inconsistencies in the data.

Some examples of unusual account relationships that might indicate a heightened fraud risk include increased revenue when receivables, inventory, cash flows, or marketing expenses are declining; increased inventory when payables, warehousing, or employee costs are declining; increased inventory activity when unit costs of production are increasing or scrap, waste, or overhead is declining; and increased profits when revenues are stagnant or declining or costs are rising. If the auditor observes these conditions, a full explanation is needed to be sure that client personnel or management are not manipulating accounting results or otherwise behaving in a fraudulent manner[(xvi)].

The conduct of client interviews will be affected if an auditor is suspicious of a client's actions and motivations. The auditor will probably adjust the approach to the interview including adjusting the type of questions asked, the personnel interviewed, and the degree to which statements are corroborated. The key for the auditor is to place an interviewee in a situation where manifestations of discomfort can appear. Most people will become uncomfortable if they have something to hide but are not sure what the auditor knows, what questions will be asked, and how the interview will be conducted. This makes it difficult for a person with something to hide to prepare completely for the interview. Although the auditor will want to establish rapport with the interviewee so as to foster communication, the auditor should not signal too much to the interviewee. Often, important information will be revealed because an interviewee is led to assume that the auditor knows it already and the interviewee tries to explain it or put the information into a context that makes it seem innocuous.

Client personnel with something to hide will usually exhibit any of a number of verbal and non-verbal indications of discomfort. The way a person answers a question may be more revealing of a potential problem than the actual information that is provided. For example, people being less than honest with an auditor may tell less complex stories, use fewer self-references, and use more negative emotion-laden words.[5] Individuals under stress and faced with difficult questions may try to stall the interview by repeating the questions asked, making gratuitous comments about the circumstances of the interview, fawning over the interviewer or feigning interest in his family, or answering a question with a question. The interviewee may also try to bolster his or her own believability by emphasizing his or her own general honesty, implying that others will vouch for them, and denying any knowledge or involvement with questionable activity before such possibilities are raised. Furthermore, a person who is particularly uncomfortable in an interview situation may make excuses for hypothetical behavior, exhibit a selective memory about important information, pretend to be uninterested in the issues at hand, and be reluctant (or in an extreme hurry) to have an interview end. It is important to note that none of these items individually has diagnostic value; it is the combination of several characteristics that is indicative that the interviewee may be lying.

A skilled interviewer with forensic experience can also obtain a great deal of insight from the non-verbal behavior of an interviewee. Body motions, squirming, and use of hands and arms may all provide clues about whether a person is trying to hide something during the course of an interview.[6] In the extreme, the interviewee may become agitated or volatile. In general, an effective interview will keep the interviewee engaged, talking, and helpful. Creating a situation where an interviewee can shut down, justifiably disagree with the interviewer, or end the interview on his or her own terms is unlikely to be helpful to the auditor. Rather, the auditor gains most by having the interviewee speak freely and in a non-confrontational manner.

Routine questions can be used to establish a cordial framework for the discussion. Questions should not be leading in nature, where the appropriate answer is implied in the question, but should encourage open-ended responses. Sensitive questions should be transitioned to carefully, but an auditor can also use a surprise question to elicit an unguarded response. Although a general auditor will never be as skilled at forensic auditing as a fraud expert or criminal investigator, all auditors can be alert to suspicious information that is obtained through analysis and inquiry[(xvii)].

There is no single indicator that is diagnostic of lying, hence, a trained interviewer looks for a pattern of behaviors rather than a single behavior. Furthermore, research has shown that behaviors such as eye contact, blinking, and shrugs are not reliable indicators. Indeed, it has been very difficult to identify classes of trained investigators that can detect deception. Thus, while the auditor should be alert for cues when interviewing management, very low reliance should be placed on the ability of the auditor to detect misrepresentations based on "body language." Hence, the professional requirement to corroborate evidence obtained via inquiry is well justified based on humans' inability to consistently detect lying in responses to their questions.

Inquiry and Analysis for Auditing Accounting Estimates

An area that is becoming increasingly prominent and more challenging for auditors to deal with is the audit of accounting estimates, especially estimates of fair value as accounting standard setters move away from historical cost as the basis for measurement. There are two different types of accounting estimates, each of which brings about a different set of audit issues. One type of estimate relates to the eventual outcome of accounting transactions that have already been recorded. Examples of these would include allowance for doubtful accounts, warranty estimates, inventory obsolescence, depreciation

[(xvii)]**EXAMPLE**

Staff auditors are rarely in a position to ascertain whether an interviewee is lying because interview and interrogation techniques used by forensic auditors require specialized training and experience. However, auditors should be careful to document answers based on representations by management. When answers appear inconsistent, interviewers should carefully document inconsistencies and ask interviewees to reconcile such inconsistencies—being careful not to imply that the interviewee is lying. Interviewers should also carefully note any non-verbal reactions to these requests and subsequent explanations and document them to the best of their abilities. At that point, the manager or partner of the engagement team can consider whether it makes sense to seek further advice from a forensic accountant.

(e.g., salvage values and useful lives), and the outcome of litigation. We will discuss the use of inquiry and analytical procedures for these types of estimates in Chapters 11 through 14 at the appropriate stage of the audit cycle, although the general issues discussed below apply equally to these estimates.

The second type of estimate is a fair market valuation, usually estimated based on the measurement rules in a specific accounting standard and reflective of market conditions prevalent at the measurement date, that is, the estimated market price for a particular asset or liability. For example, an accounting standard may require fair value estimates be based on a hypothetical current arm's length transaction today, rather than the settlement of a transaction at some past or future date. Most prominent among the current accounting standards that require fair market value estimates are those for financial instruments and investments, but could also include goodwill and intangible assets acquired in a business combination.

Inquiry and analysis play a large role in auditing both types of accounting estimates as there are limited tests of details that an auditor can perform on accounting estimates. The key audit problem with accounting estimates is the degree of uncertainty that will vary across different types of estimates and even within a class of estimates. For example, the fair market value of financial instruments traded on a public market in normal trading conditions is relatively straightforward and involves little uncertainty, whereas the allowance for doubtful accounts of a retailer heading into an economic recession may suffer from a great deal of uncertainty.

AUTHORITATIVE GUIDANCE & STANDARDS

ISA 540 **Auditing Accounting Estimates, Including Fair Value Accounting Estimates, and Related Disclosures** *provides numerous references to the auditor making inquiries to client management and others as well as using analytical procedures in the audit of accounting estimates including fair value measurements in the financial statements. PCAOB Standards provides separate standards for auditing accounting estimates (AS 2501 [formerly AU 342]* **Auditing Accounting Estimates***) and a more specific standard for fair value measurements (AS 2502 [formerly AU 328]* **Auditing Fair Value Measurements and Disclosures***).*

In addition to estimation uncertainty the auditor has to deal with the challenge of management bias, either deliberate or unintentional, when preparing an accounting estimate. While management bias is a concern throughout the audit and is a primary reason the auditor has to act with appropriate professional skepticism, accounting estimates are more prone to management bias as the very nature of the estimation process makes it easier for even unintentional optimism to be reflected in the estimates developed. Furthermore, management bias may be difficult to detect on an estimate by estimate basis. Often, management bias can only be detected by considering systematic bias across a range of different types of estimates, e.g., all the estimates made by management tend to increase earnings.

Inquiry may be used to obtain information about many aspects of an accounting estimate including:

- How management identifies those transactions, events and conditions, and changes thereto, that may create a need for accounting estimates to be recognized or disclosed in the financial statements.
- How management makes accounting estimates, including the data and computational model, used in arriving at a specific number for an accounting estimate.
- Relevant controls over the data used in the models and over access to the computational process that generates the model results.
- Whether management has used an expert to assist in developing the estimate and is the expert an employee or independent of client management.
- The key assumptions underlying the accounting estimates.
- Whether there has been, or ought to have been, a change from the prior period in the methods employed in making the accounting estimates, and why.
- Whether management has adequately assessed the effect of estimation uncertainty.

Use of a rigorous approach to inquiry is often one of the few means that the auditor has available to determine the reasonableness of management's assumptions underlying estimates especially when there is no third party data available. In the area of more traditional accounting estimates, interviewing managers that are involved in operational issues who are not necessarily schooled in the answers needed to satisfy accounting rules is one source of information that often goes untapped. For example, an analytical procedure about buildup of inventory (e.g., days' sales in inventory increasing or inventory turnover ratio decreasing) may lead to a series of carefully thought out interviews with financial and operating management[xviii].

Inquiry is also vital in discovering matters that need to be recorded at fair value, especially given that many financial instruments are not necessarily recorded at the time the contract is entered into as no exchange of resources takes place at that time. Here, using the auditor's understanding of the environment and what other entities do in similar situations may lead the auditor to be more persistent in his or her inquiries about the activities of a client.

Analytical procedures also play a large role in audit of fair values as the auditor seeks to find an independent means to confirm the fair value and to quantify the degree of uncertainty surrounding a given estimate (called a point estimate). The auditor's ability to develop and use rigorous models (such as those for valuing derivatives, i.e., the Black-Scholes Option Model) and knowledge of when the auditor needs to employ an independent expert, is important in ensuring that the computational model the client uses is in accordance with the relevant accounting standard.

For all estimates, whether the assessed risk of material misstatement is low or high, the auditor needs to consider whether the appropriate accounting standard has been applied. The auditor must consider:

[xviii] **EXAMPLE**

Interviewing the client's research and product development scientists is one means that an auditor has at his or her disposal to check on management's assertion that the client's high-end technology products are not rapidly approaching obsolescence. Yet frequently auditors ignore this valuable source of technological evidence within the company. Perusal of several US SEC Enforcement Actions against auditors with high tech clients who had overvalued inventory finds that their inquiries were limited to discussions with financial and senior management, both who could be strongly biased in their representations about the valuation of existing inventory.

- Whether management has employed methods for making the accounting estimates that are appropriate.
- Whether they have been applied consistently.
- Whether changes from the prior period in accounting estimates, or in the method for making them, are appropriate in the circumstances.

There are four potential sources of evidence for the auditor to consider when examining estimates:

1. Determine whether subsequent events (occurring up to the date of the auditor's report) provide evidence about the accuracy of the accounting estimate as of the end of the year end.
2. Test how management made the accounting estimate and the data on which it is based, and evaluate whether the method of measurement used is appropriate and the assumptions used are reasonable.
3. Test the operating effectiveness of relevant controls over the accounting estimate, together with appropriate substantive procedures.
4. Independently develop a point or range estimate against which the management's point estimate can be evaluated.

Often the second choice is the one taken by auditors as it is the most similar to the procedures that the auditor employs for traditional accounting estimates like bad debts, inventory obsolescence and similar estimates. However, auditors should think carefully when deciding on which procedures will give them the strongest evidence to ensure that no material misstatements are present in these estimates that can be very material to the financial statements.

If the auditor concludes there is a significant residual risk about one or more estimates, then the auditor needs to carry out additional tests. Additional evidence could come from tests of internal controls (e.g., when the reliability of internal data is in question) or alternative substantive tests (e.g., when the computational methods or level of uncertainty are in question). These will be discussed in Chapter 10. We will discuss in Chapter 14 what happens should the auditor's point estimate and range differ significantly from that of management and how the two would be resolved.

Summary and Conclusion

Inquiry and analysis are common audit procedures that are used throughout the audit. In this chapter, we introduced systematic approaches for obtaining both inquiry and analysis evidence. Although relatively common and easy to perform, inquiry and analysis procedures often require additional corroboration in order to provide meaningful audit evidence about the risk of material misstatement. This chapter discussed how auditors can improve the quality of inquiry and analysis evidence during the course of the audit. In either case, the quality of the evidence obtained from a client depends on the experience and expertise of the auditor conducting the inquiry or analysis. The strength of such evidence can be improved in conjunction with thorough strategic and process analysis during the early stages of the audit.

However, auditors must always be aware of the possibility that inquiry and analysis may produce confusing, incomplete, or misleading evidence and maintain appropriate professional skepticism whenever they conduct such procedures. We conclude our discussion of inquiry and analysis by showing how both tools are important in difficult areas of auditing, assessing fraud risk, and the discovery and audit of accounting estimates, including fair value measurements.

Appendix: Statistical Methods for Obtaining Analytical Evidence

An auditor has two significant problems to consider when using the judgmental analysis techniques discussed above: (1) generating an expectation about an account of interest, and (2) deciding when a fluctuation from that expectation is important enough to require adjustments to risk assessments. The first problem arises because the auditor does not necessarily know what to expect about any given account or variable. Should the account increase? If so, how much should the increase be? The second problem arises because there is no good definition of what constitutes an unusual variation. Is a 5 percent fluctuation important? Is a 10 percent fluctuation important? Statistical regression has been used in recent years to systematize the analysis, reduce these problems, and add rigor to the analytical review process.

Overview of Univariate Regression

Regression is a method of statistical analysis that facilitates the rigorous comparison of data for two or more variables. The primary logic underlying regression is that the value of one variable can be used to predict the value of another variable based on past history and a theoretically sound computational procedure. For example, weather forecasters know that when the barometric pressure changes in certain ways, rain is likely to follow. This relationship is based on observation of weather patterns over many years. Regression can be used to measure the increased likelihood of rain in terms of specific changes in barometric pressure. Such a model improves the quality of weather predictions. However, regression models, like the weather, have a random element that makes it impossible to predict future events with certainty—there is always a margin of error in regression models.

We will use regression to capture the benefit of prior knowledge about a client in a systematic manner. Regression analysis is an effective tool to use in the audit process because analytical procedures often involve comparisons of results over many variables and an extended period of time. Regression analysis is based on a theoretical, linear relationship between two variables as depicted in the following equation:

$$y_i = \alpha + \beta x_i + \varepsilon_i$$

In this equation, y_i is the variable that we wish to estimate, x_i is the variable that we can observe to assist us in developing our expectations, α and β are

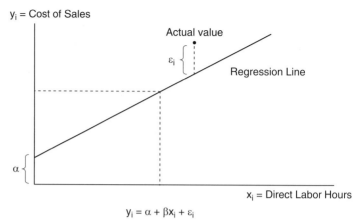

$$y_i = \alpha + \beta x_i + \varepsilon_i$$

Note: The regression line will always pass through the average values of x_i and y_i. This is indicated by the dotted lines intersecting the regression line. Also, α is the intercept of the regression line, i.e., where the line would cross the Y-axis if extended to the left. β is the slope of the regression line. ε_i reflects the dispersion of the scattered points from the regression line.

Figure 9.4 Assumed Linear Relationship for Regression Models

regression parameters that define the relationship between x_i and y_i and ε_i is a random error term that reflects that the relationship is not perfectly predictable.[7] By deriving values for α and β, we can predict the value of y_i given any value of x_i.

An example of the type of linear relationship underlying regression analysis is depicted in Figure 9.4. The straight line shows the relationship between y_i and x_i. Given the random nature of the relationship, the actual data for a given model are scattered around the line. The vertical distance between any single point and the regression line is ε_i. Regression analysis is based on a formula that determines the line that best "fits" a set of observed data.

An Application of Regression Analysis to Auditing

We will use the following six-step process to develop a regression model, develop expectations about an account of interest, and evaluate the results in terms of the audit.

1. Identify the model to be estimated.

2. Obtain the appropriate data.

3. Calculate the regression model.

4. Assess the quality of the regression model.

5. Generate expectations for the variable of interest for the period being audited.

6. Compare regression expectations to actual results.

Identify the Model to be Estimated: The first step in the process is to decide what variable the auditor is going to estimate (y_i, the dependent variable) and the variable that will serve as the basis for generating our expectation (x_i, the independent variable).[8] The context in which regression is to be used is important. First, because of the difficulty of obtaining data to support the regression model, the method is best used for material accounts that have an expected relationship with another variable. Second, a model that is based on logical relationships is easier to understand and interpret. An auditor might believe that sales revenue is related to the phases of the moon, but it would be difficult to make a logical argument that such a relationship exists. Finally, the auditor must be careful to assure that the model being estimated is stable, meaning that it does not change over time. Most applications of regression require the auditor to use historical data from prior periods. If the underlying relationship between x_i and y_i has changed, expectations based on the prior relationship will not be appropriate for the current period.

To illustrate the use of regression analysis, we will look at the hypothetical relationship between cost of goods sold (y_i) and direct labor hours (x_i) in a manufacturing company because they have a predictable relationship, especially if the production process is labor intensive. Other independent variables could be tried if direct labor hours were not expected to have a relationship with cost of goods sold. Examples of other possible independent variables include raw material prices, quantity of raw material, or hours of machine time used in production.

Obtain the Appropriate Data: Once the auditor has decided what variables to include in the model, the next step is to obtain adequate data on which to base the estimates of α and β. We will denote our estimate of α as a and β as b. The more data that is available, the more robust will be the model's predictions (meaning, there will be smaller margin for error). The data for our example is presented in Table 9.4. We will base our estimate of the regression model on data from the 24 months that precede our audit period (20x6 and 20x7). A sample size of 24 data points is the minimum that should be used to estimate a regression model. In many industries, data are collected on a daily or weekly basis, thus allowing a larger sample on which to base the model, which will increase its reliability. Shortly, we will use the results of our analysis to form an expectation about the level of costs of goods sold for the months in the period under audit (20x8). It is important to base the estimates of α and β on data from the period prior to the audit because we want to be able to use the estimated model to *independently* test the current-year results.

The quality of the data used in the estimation model will have a direct impact on the quality of the expectations developed from the model. The input data should be reliable and, ideally, would have been audited in a prior period. The user must be careful not to select data that is inappropriate for the model. Very old data may have been generated when production processes were significantly different and may not be appropriate for the current model. Also, data from multiple factories or locations, even if from the same time period, may not be appropriate if the separate locations have different production processes.

Calculate the Regression Model: Software is generally available to perform the computations needed to derive a regression model. Simple spreadsheet packages like Microsoft Excel include a data analysis package that supports various statistical techniques including linear regression. An example of the output from regression software is depicted in Table 9.5. The first issue related to the regression results is whether the expected relationship between x_i and y_i actually exists. The analysis is not of much use if this relationship is not statistically significant as measured by the value and significance level of the

Table 9.4 *Data Used to Estimate Regression Model Used in a Preliminary Analytical Procedure*

Month	Cost of Sales (Y) (in 000s)	Direct Labor Hours (X) (in 000s)
20x6:		
January	160.31	9.99
February	156.59	8.71
March	170.73	10.54
April	161.33	9.57
May	155.27	8.25
June	145.44	7.18
July	156.95	8.28
August	139.37	6.15
September	130.84	5.73
October	189.88	11.53
November	183.29	11.23
December	162.07	9.38
20x7:		
January	153.52	8.64
February	150.77	8.56
March	178.27	8.93
April	190.25	10.28
May	167.71	7.21
June	181.63	7.06
July	173.46	8.11
August	195.08	11.18
September	169.63	7.22
October	151.87	6.13
November	142.84	5.51
December	183.66	10.97

F-statistic reported in Table 9.5. In our example, the F-value of 27.789 can only occur in less than one in a thousand chances (as indicated by a p-value less than 0.001). Furthermore, both *a* and *b* are significant in the model, with p-values less than 0.001.

Assess the Quality of the Regression Model: Next, the auditor should assess how well the model explains the variation in the historical data. There are four primary measures of the quality of the model. Such measures are often referred to as **goodness-of-fit tests** because they measure how well the linear model represents the underlying data.

1. Coefficient of correlation (r): The higher the value of r, the better the model captures the relationship between x_i and y_i. There is no absolute threshold for evaluating r. A reasonable rule of thumb is that a value of r in excess of 0.50 is an acceptable model on which to develop expectations about y_i. Values of r in excess of 0.90 are considered to be excellent. In our example, the r-value of 0.747 is acceptable.

Table 9.5 *Excel Output of Regression Results for Cost of Sales Regressed on Direct Labor Hours*

Correlation coefficient (r)	0.747				
Variance explained (r²)	0.558				
Standard Error (S)	11.776				
Observations (n)	24.000				
	df	**SS**	**MS**	**F**	**P-Value**
Regression	1.000	3853.805	3853.805	27.789	0.001
Residual	22.000	3050.971	138.681		
Total	23.000	6904.776			
	Coefficients	**Standard Error**	**t Stat**	**P-value**	
Intercept a	103.611	11.819	8.766	0.001	
Direct Labor Hours b	7.096	1.346	5.272	0.001	

2. Variation explained (r^2): An alternative way to look at the goodness of fit is to consider r^2 (often referred to as "r squared") as a measure of the amount of variation in the linear regression that is captured by the model. In our example, 55.8 percent of the variation in the data is explained by the relationship between cost of goods sold and direct labor hours. Again, this appears to be acceptable.

3. Standard error (S): Standardized errors are useful for measuring the dispersion of the actual results around the predicted values. The smaller of these values, the better the model fits the data. A large standard error indicates that the data naturally varies over a very wide range, and may mean that the model will have limited use for making predictions; that is, the margin of error will be large. The standard error in our example is 11.776.

4. Standard error of the estimate (S'): S' is calculated by dividing S by the square root of the number of observations. In our example, S' = 11.776 is divided by the square root of 24, which yields 2.41. One way to judge whether S' is small enough to be useful is to compare it to materiality for the account being examined. If S' is no more than half of materiality, the regression model is probably adequate for audit testing purposes. If S' is larger than half of materiality, then the model could identify random errors that would appear to be significant to the auditor but which are simply random deviations inherent in the model, in which case, the model will not be able to distinguish between possible accounting misstatements and random deviations.

Generate Expectations for the Dependent Variable: Given that the regression model fits the data well enough, the values of *a* and *b* can then be used to generate expectations of y_i for the audit period as long as we know the corresponding values of x_i. The equation used to estimate current year values for costs of goods sold based on the results reported in Table 9.5 is:

Cost of Sales = 103.61 + 7.096 (Direct Labor Hours)

Table 9.6 *Results of Regression Predictions*

20x9 Month	(1) Cost of Sales (Y) (in 000s)	(2) Direct Labor Hours (X) (in 000s)	(3) Projected Cost (Y') (in 000s)	(4) = (1) - (3) Residual (in 000s)	(5) = (4)/S' Standardized Deviation
January	206.61	14.05	203.33	3.28	1.36
February	152.61	7.02	153.41	(0.80)	(0.33)
March	167.50	8.84	166.33	1.17	0.49
April	145.68	5.62	143.47	2.21	0.92
May	153.23	6.92	152.70	0.53	0.22
June	153.80	6.78	151.71	2.09	0.87
July	158.41	7.51	156.89	1.52	0.63
August	194.73	12.89	195.09	(0.36)	(0.15)
September	202.83	13.99	202.90	(0.07)	(0.03)
October	191.82	12.09	189.41	2.41	1.00
November	186.57	9.58	171.59	14.98	6.22
December	215.66	15.75	215.40	0.26	0.11

The expectations generated from this equation are presented in Table 9.6, Column (3) "Projected Costs." Care must be exercised to limit expectations from the model to the general range of values that are present in the estimation period. For example, the most extreme values for x_i during the estimation period are 5.51 and 11.53. Expectations will be most accurate as long as the values of x_i stay within or close to that range. Using a value of 100 for x_i would probably lead to a meaningless prediction since that level of labor has not been previously observed.

Compare Regression Expectations to Actual Results: The expectations of the regression model will rarely, if ever, come out exactly equal to the observed values for y_i. The difference between predicted and actual values should be computed and inspected for any unusual results that the auditor might wish to investigate. In the example, all but one of the residuals fall below 3.28 (see column (4), "Residual"). The November residual is rather large at 14.98; hence, it seems so unusual that it heightens the inherent risk of the account, and requires further investigation. At this point, the auditor can take advantage of the regression results to make statements about the likelihood that residuals are the result of random errors (as embodied in ε) or are possible misstatements. Before doing this, it is important to understand that regression analysis is based on the assumption that random errors (ε) are **normally distributed** (the so-called bell shaped curve) with a mean of zero and constant variance, which we can infer from the data. Furthermore, auditors should assume that the error terms across time are uncorrelated, meaning that the value of ε in one month does not influence the value in another month.

We start by "standardizing" the residuals by dividing each by S'. By dividing S' into the residuals based on our current year data, we get a number called the standardized deviation. We know from basic probability theory that approximately 95 percent of the random deviations will fall within about two standard deviations of zero.[9] At 95 percent probability, cost of goods sold can have standardized deviations that range as high as 2.0 just by random chance, without the account having any misstatements or other problems. Similarly, 80 percent of the random deviations will fall within about 1.3 standard deviations of zero. The last column reports the standardized deviation from zero for each of our predictions. Only November has a standardized deviation in excess of 2.00.

The result for November may be explained by unusual circumstances. For example, a labor strike or extreme weather conditions may have affected operations, causing cost of goods sold to be much higher than would have been expected given the observed level of direct labor hours. Another possibility is that the company has made an error in the accounting records in that month that is disrupting the expected relationship captured in the regression model. At this point, the auditor will need to decide what to do to follow up on the unexplained deviation. Until the deviation is adequately explained, residual risk is considered significant and the auditor should consider increasing risk assessments for assertions related to the cost of goods sold. The auditor may obtain additional evidence for cost of goods sold in November to be sure that the deviation is not the result of an error. The regression model provides a powerful signal of unusual conditions, but ultimately, it is up to the auditor to investigate and resolve the uncertainty of the conditions.

Consideration of Key Assumptions

The previous discussion illustrated how regression analysis can be used to facilitate audit planning by signaling conditions that may not be consistent with the auditor's expectations as captured in a regression model. However, the auditor must be aware of the potential problems that can arise when using regression:

- Too few data points: The size of the standard error is a direct function of the sample size (n) used to estimate a and b. If there are too few observations, S and S' may be too large to allow for accurate predictions. Also, this may result in a small value for r and a corresponding lower value for r^2, which does not seem to happen in this case even though we have a relatively small number of observations (24).

- Non-normal error term: The interpretation of the standardized deviations in Table 9.6 is based on the assumption that ε is normally distributed. If this is not the case, then the results could be biased. Regression software generally tests for this potential problem and provides a warning message if the normality assumption is violated. There are numerous techniques for fixing this problem if necessary. Normally, this would involve a consultation with a specialist in the firm trained in statistics.

- Non-constant variance: Regression analysis assumes that the variables in the sample have constant variance over the period of estimation. Violation of this assumption will lead to biased results. Regression software generally tests for this potential problem, and there are numerous techniques for fixing this problem. Again, this problem would lead the auditor to consult with a specialist in statistics. As a first test, we examine the plotted predicted versus actual data (see Figure 9.5).

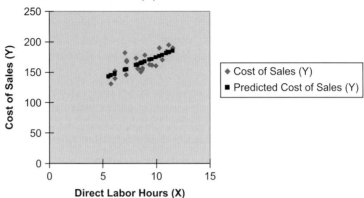

Direct Labor Hours (X) Line Fit Plot

Figure 9.5 *Linearity and Non-Constant Variance Assumption Tested*

- Autocorrelation: This problem occurs when ε has a drift or pattern that emerges over time. For example, ε may tend to grow, in which case the error terms are not considered to be independent. This is a difficult problem to deal with and will definitely require consultation with an expert statistician.

Regression analysis can be a powerful tool for the auditor to gather evidence and assist in assessing risks. However, regression should only be used when it is appropriate and the auditor must be careful that the underlying assumptions are not violated. If used properly, however, the analysis of the residuals or the standardized deviations can improve the effectiveness and efficiency of the audit.

Bibliography of Relevant Literature

Research

Anderson, U., and L. Koonce. 1998. Evaluating the Sufficiency of Causes in Audit Analytical Procedures *Auditing: A Journal of Practice & Theory.* 17(1): 1–12.

Anderson, U., K. Kadous, and L. Koonce. 2004. The Role of Incentives to Manage Earnings and Quantification in Auditors' Evaluations of Management-Provided Information. *Auditing: A Journal of Practice & Theory.* 23(1): 11–28.

Cohen, J. R., G. Krishnamoorthy, and A. M. Wright. 2000. Evidence on the Effect of Financial and Nonfinancial Trends on Analytical Review. *Auditing: A Journal of Practice & Theory.* 19(1): 27–48.

DePaulo, B. M., J. J. Lindsay, B. E. Malone, L. Muhlenbruck, K. Charlton, and H. Cooper. 2003. Cues to Deception. *Psychological Bulletin.* 129(1): 74–118.

Glover, S. M., J. Jiambalvo, and J. Kennedy. 2000. Analytical Procedures and Audit-Planning Decisions. *Auditing: A Journal of Practice & Theory.* 19(2): 27–46.

Newman, M. L., J. W. Pennebaker, D. S. Berry, and J. M. Richards. 2004. Lying Words: Predicting Deception from Linguistic Styles. *Personality and Social Psychology Bulletin.* 29(5): 665–675.

O'Donnell, E. and J. J. Schultz Jr. 2005. The Halo Effect in Business Risk Audits: Can Strategic Risk Assessment Bias Auditor Judgment about Accounting Details? *The Accounting Review.* 80(3): 921–940.

Professional Reports and Guidance

CICA (now CPA Canada) Research Report. 2000. *Audit Inquiry: Seeking More Reliable Evidence from Audit Inquiry.* Canadian Institute of Chartered Accountants (now CPA Canada).

Auditing Standards

IAASB *International Standards on Auditing (ISA)* No. 240, "The Auditor's Responsibility to Consider Fraud in a Financial Statement Audit."

IAASB *International Standards on Auditing (ISA)* No. 500, "Audit Evidence."

IAASB *International Standards on Auditing (ISA)* No. 520, "Analytical Procedures."

IAASB *International Standards on Auditing (ISA)* No. 540, "Auditing Accounting Estimates, Including Fair Value Accounting Estimates, and Related Disclosures."

IFAC. International Auditing and Assurance Standards Board (IAASB). 2015. *Handbook of International Quality Control, Audit, Review, Other Assurance, and Related Services Pronouncements.* New York: International Federation of Accountants.

PCAOB. *Auditing Standard* 1105 (formerly No. 15), "Audit Evidence."

PCAOB. *Auditing Standard* 2210 (formerly No. 12), "Identifying and Assessing the Risks of Material Misstatement."

PCAOB. *Auditing Standard* 2305 (formerly *Interim Standard* AU 329), "Substantive Analytical Procedures."

PCAOB. *Auditing Standard* 2401 (formerly *Interim Standard* AU 316), "Consideration of Fraud in a Financial Statement Audit."

PCAOB. *Auditing Standard* 2501 (formerly *Interim Standard* AU 342), "Auditing Accounting Estimates."

PCAOB. *Auditing Standard* 2502 (formerly *Interim Standard* AU 328), "Auditing Fair Value Measurements and Disclosures."

PCAOB. *Auditing Standard* 2810 (formerly No. 14), "Evaluating Audit Results."

PCAOB. *Release 2008–008* "Report on the PCOAB's 2004, 2005, 2006, and 2007 Inspections of Domestic Annually Inspected Firms."

Notes

1 U. Anderson and L. Koonce. 1998. Evaluating the Sufficiency of Causes in Audit Analytical Procedures *Auditing: A Journal of Practice & Theory.* 17(1): 1–12.

2 E. O'Donnell and J. J. Schultz Jr. 2005. The Halo Effect in Business Risk Audits: Can Strategic Risk Assessment Bias Auditor Judgment about Accounting Details? *The Accounting Review.* 80(3): 921–940.

3 Formulas for Days-to-Collect and other ratios are discussed later in this chapter.

4 Free cash flow also reflects the effect of debt financing. Under FASB accounting standards interest payments are subtracted directly from cash flow from operations whereas International Accounting Standards offer more flexibility in its placement on the Statement of Cash Flows.

5 Newman et al. 2004. Lying Words: Predicting Deception from Linguistic Styles. *Personality and Social Psychology Bulletin.* 29(5): 665–675.

6 DePaulo et al. 2003. Cues to Deception. *Psychological Bulletin.* 129(1): 74–118.

7 The random error in the regression equation (ε_i) is expected to have an average of zero.

8 Regression analysis can be applied in situations where there is more than one independent variable. That is, the dependent variable of interest may be related to a number of independent variables that could be included in the regression model if adequate data is available. A regression model with more than one independent variable is called a **multiple regression**. The underlying computations and checks for assumption appropriateness for multiple regression models are more complex than the univariate model we use in this book, but the process and interpretation of the results are essentially the same.

9 The number of standard deviations is called a ***t-statistic***, and its value depends on the size of the sample used to estimate the regression model. If the sample is very large, then the distribution of random deviations will approximate the ***normal distribution***, in which case 95 percent of the random deviations will fall within 1.96 standard deviations of zero. The smaller the sample, the larger the t-value becomes. For our sample of 24, 95 percent of the random deviations will fall within 2.074 standard deviations of zero. If the sample size was only 12, the corresponding t-value would be 2.228. Standardized tables exist that provide the t-statistic for any sample size and for any probability level.

CHAPTER 10

Designing Substantive Tests
Responses to Residual Risks

Outline

Learning Goals for this Chapter

1. Review management assertions about financial statement, the audit risk model and materiality that was introduced in Chapter 3.

2. Integrate and synthesize the risks identified in Chapters 4, 5, 6, and 7 employing the audit risk model.

3. Apply the audit risk model to plan substantive tests of account balances and transactions.

4. Consider the concept of performance materiality and tolerable error relating them to materiality.

5. Apply the various materiality concepts to aid in planning substantive tests of financial statement account balances and transactions.

6. Apply the concepts of sufficiency and appropriateness of audit evidence to aid in developing a substantive audit testing program for account balances and transactions.

7. To develop an initial substantive testing plan at the overall level and segment it into audit-sensitive processes and account balances.

8. Understand the special considerations that the auditor needs to be aware of in planning substantive tests of accounting estimates.

Introduction

In previous chapters, we discussed how understanding an organization's strategic position, plans, risks, controls, and processes are critical for the performance of an effective audit of financial statements. After carrying out the strategic and process analysis, including tests of controls where controls will be relied upon (or mandatory tests in the Integrated Audit), the auditor possesses a substantial set of evidence about conditions within the organization and has identified strategic risks, process risks, and any significant deficiencies in internal control over financial reporting that are relevant to the financial statement audit. The internal controls over financial reporting provide indirect evidence about management's assertions and represents evidence on how well processes, especially financial controls, reduce the risks of material misstatement. In this chapter, we link our previous risk analysis directly to the auditor's tests of the management assertions that comprise the financial statements (Figure 10.1). In essence, information gathered during the knowledge acquisition and risk assessment stage of the audit provides an informed view about client business and audit risks, especially about the risk of material misstatement. Any significant risk that remains at this point in the audit is referred to as **residual risk**. At this stage, the auditor will assess whether these residual risks have any implications for the risk of material misstatement in the financial statements.

The purpose of this chapter is to describe how the assessment of the risk of material misstatements influences decisions about the direct auditor tests of transactions, accounts, and presentation and disclosures to be performed. Specifically, we discuss the planning that is needed to obtain sufficient evidence to support an opinion about the financial statements using **substantive audit tests**. Decisions concerning the evidence to be gathered about specific assertions and the allocation of audit resources

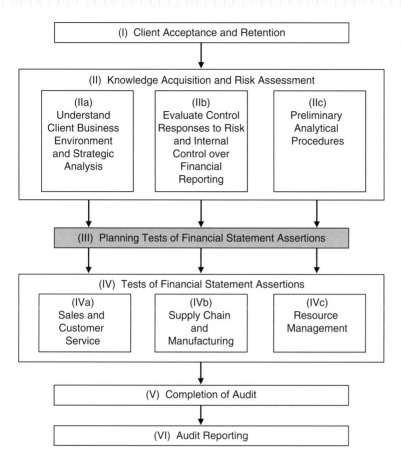

Figure 10.1 *Overview of the Audit Process*

across segments of the financial statements are reflected in an ***audit program*** for substantive testing.

Assertions, Risks, and Evidence Revisited

The general concepts underlying the auditor's decision process were described in Chapter 3, including the concepts of management assertions, audit procedures, and audit evidence. Ultimately, the auditor must issue an opinion about the fairness of the financial statements and related disclosures in accordance with generally accepted accounting principles (or internationally known as an applicable financial reporting framework). However, most of the evidence obtained during knowledge acquisition, including tests of controls, is indirectly linked to financial statement assertions and disclosures. Control tests provide evidence that internal control processes are working as designed but control tests only support the auditor's assessed level of control risk. Control tests do not provide evidence that the reported results are actually in accordance with GAAP; they do reduce the risk of a material misstatement. However, an auditor is required to perform some level of substantive testing on all material accounts, transactions and disclosures regardless of how effective the controls are judged to be by the auditor.

The challenge for the auditor is to take his or her accumulated knowledge and to use it to formulate conclusions about specific information included in the financial statements. Substantive tests may be minimal if internal controls are strong and the risk of material misstatement is low, or can be extensive if internal controls are weak and the risk of material misstatement is high. The management assertions that are embedded in the financial statements are summarized in Box 10.1 "Management Assertions Regarding the Financial Statements." The auditor may determine that some assertions are more significant than others for specific transactions, accounts, financial statement items, or disclosures based on client specific issues that have been revealed during the earlier phases of the audit. Furthermore, the auditor may have reached differing conclusions about the risk of material misstatements affecting specific assertions based on the information available from strategic and process analysis, especially the analysis and testing of internal controls over financial reporting. Ultimately, the auditor needs to obtain sufficient appropriate evidence to support a conclusion that management assertions are in accordance with GAAP.

Additional evidence will also be needed to verify specific assertions or disclosures, but the nature and extent of that evidence varies based on the

BOX 10.1 MANAGEMENT ASSERTIONS REGARDING THE FINANCIAL STATEMENTS

Management Assertions about Transactions

- Occurrence (also known as existence)—*Transactions and events that have been recorded have occurred and pertain to the entity.*

- Completeness—*All transactions and events that should have been recorded have been recorded.*

- Accuracy—*Amounts and other data relating to recorded transactions and events have been recorded appropriately.*

- Cut-off (also known as timing)—*Transactions and events have been recorded in the correct accounting period.*

- Classification—*Transactions and events have been recorded in the proper accounts.*

Management Assertions about Accounts

- Existence—*Assets, liabilities, and equity interests exist.*

- Rights and obligations (also known as ownership)—*The entity holds or controls the rights to assets, and liabilities are the obligations of the entity.*

- Completeness—*All assets, liabilities, and equity interests that should have been recorded have been recorded.*

- Valuation and allocation—*Assets, liabilities, and equity interests are included in the financial statements at appropriate amounts and any resulting valuation or allocation adjustments are appropriately recorded.*

Management Assertions about Presentation and Disclosure

- Occurrence (existence) and rights and obligations—*Disclosed events and transactions have occurred and pertain to the entity.*

- Completeness—*All disclosures that should have been included in the financial statements have been included.*

- Classification and understandability—*Financial information is appropriately presented and described and information in disclosures is clearly expressed.*

- Accuracy and valuation—*Financial and other information is disclosed fairly and at appropriate amounts.*

---

residual risk of material misstatement. At this point, the auditor has a variety of substantive procedures from which to choose: (1) substantive analytical procedures, (2) tests of transactions, and (3) tests of accounts including presentation and disclosure. The auditor must consider both the costs and quality of the evidence needed; however, audit scandals such as WorldCom and Parmalat highlight why the auditor should not place undue emphasis on minimizing the cost of evidence. The selection and mix of tests will vary across segments of the audit due to different residual risks. In general, the more significant and risky an assertion, the more important it is that the auditor obtain high quality evidence.

AUTHORITATIVE GUIDANCE & STANDARDS

This chapter elaborates on the implications of many of the standards discussed in earlier chapters associated with the risk assessment process. The main standards discussed in the chapter include audit evidence (ISA 500 **Audit Evidence**, *AS 1105 [formerly 15* **Audit Evidence***], audit risk and materiality (ISA 320* **Materiality in Planning and Performing the Audit**, *ISA 315* **Identifying and Assessing the Risks of Material Misstatement through Understanding the Entity and Its Environment**, *AS 2105 [formerly 11]* **Consideration of Materiality in Planning and Performing an Audit**, *AS 2210 [formerly 12]* **Identifying and Assessing the Risks of Material Misstatement**), *and performing audit procedures (ISA 330* **The Auditor's Responses to Assessed Risks**, *AS 2301 [formerly 13]* **The Auditor's Responses to the Risks of Material Misstatement**).

Analyzing Residual Risks Identified from Strategic and Process Analysis

Figure 10.2 summarizes the process the auditor used to acquire an understanding of the client's business environment, risks, and controls. The output of this process is a set of residual risks that the auditor believes are potentially significant to the organization. A residual risk can be significant if the potential likelihood or magnitude of a negative outcome is high and the organization has failed to effectively mitigate the risk. It is possible that the auditor will discover residual risks that have no current or near future implications for the financial statements and will just note them in the file as items to watch in future years[i].

Auditors for a large retail chain noted that management was not forthcoming about the reasons for their abnormal profits compared with others in the industry, and were very secretive about everything they did even to the point of not disclosing gross margin (not a required disclosure under local GAAP). The auditor's strategic analysis suggested that the client was attempting a low cost, broad based, differentiation strategy combined with elements of a multiple niche based strategy. All of this was supported by regionalized supply chain management that was optimized for each region but not necessarily for the company as a whole. Nonetheless, despite this residual risk, the auditors could draw few if any implications for the financial statements for several years as whatever it was the company was doing seemed to be working. Working that is, until the company grew too large to be effectively managed through its awkward structure. At that point, problems abounded, significantly affecting the financial statements, including inventory write-downs, obsolete fixed assets, and impaired goodwill.

Figure 10.2 Identifying Residual Risks

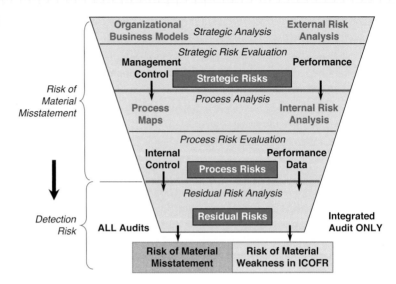

As we discussed in Chapter 5, residual risk analysis can impact an audit in any, or all, of the following four ways:

1. **Condition expectations:** A residual risk analysis can condition the auditor's expectations about financial results that can then be compared against actual outcomes to determine if financial reports are consistent with underlying economic circumstances (e.g., develop expectations for analytical procedures).

2. **Raise concerns about viability:** A residual risk analysis can raise concerns about the ability of an organization to continue in operation (i.e., going concern issues).

3. **Increase control risk:** A residual risk analysis can indicate that there are stresses within the control environment that may negatively impact individual behavior (i.e., increasing the organization's susceptibility to employee or financial reporting fraud).

4. **Increase risk of material misstatement:** A residual risk analysis may provide evidence that specific management assertions at the process level need to be examined closely, that is, there is an increased risk of material misstatement requiring extensive substantive tests for the accounts related to that process.

Of particular interest is whether there are indications that the risk of management assertions being misstated has increased. If so, the risk of material misstatement should be set at a higher level so that the assertion is subject to more extensive substantive tests. Substantive tests are "audit procedures designed to detect material misstatements at the assertion level" (ISA 330 4 (a)).

To illustrate, consider the analysis of human resource management discussed in Chapter 6. In that residual risk analysis, we concluded that there were two risks that could qualify as significant residual risks. Referring to Figure 10.3 (see also Chapter 6), we see that eight of the ten risks were either assessed as being low initially, or were reduced to an acceptable level by controls

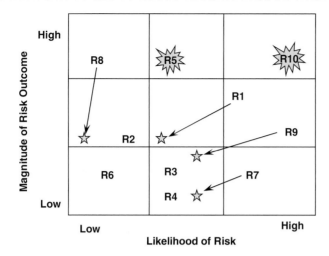

Where: R1 = Lack of appropriate skills
R2 = Excess personnel
R3 = Discriminatory employment practices
R4 = Excess recruiting/hiring costs
R5 = Errors in payroll authorizations
R6 = Errors in payroll processing
R7 = Low employee morale
R8 = Violations of employment laws
R9 = Inadequate training and feedback
R10 = Loss of critical personnel or unplanned turnover

Figure 10.3 Residual Risk Analysis for Human Resource Management

(indicated in the Figure with arrows and stars). The remaining residual risks, errors in payroll authorizations (*R5*) and loss of critical employees (*R10*), remain in the high risk area of the risk map, implying that they could have a significant negative impact on the company. The auditor should analyze the implications of each of these risks as they relate to the conduct of the audit. Some of the possible implications of these risks are summarized in Table 10.1.

Notice that the implications of the two risks are quite different. The risk of errors in payroll authorization is primarily a process risk and has a direct effect both on internal control over financial reporting and on the risks of material misstatement for related transactions. The auditor will probably increase tests of internal control and payroll transactions in response to this risk. The auditor can only assess whether the effect is material with additional testing, but there is a good chance that any resulting errors will be small given the small size of individual payroll transactions unless there is a systematic programing error.

The other risk, loss of personnel, is more strategic in nature so its implications are less directly related to the financial statements. The risk may mean little in the course of the audit, or it could have a pervasive effect on the audit, especially if the control environment is undermined by employee turnover. In the extreme, if the client's success is dependent on the personnel who depart, various assets may need to be evaluated for impairment and the question of whether the company is a going concern could become important. If the remaining personnel are unable to obtain good performance results, they may be motivated to manipulate the financial statements to hide poor results, even to the extent of committing fraud[(ii)].

(ii)**EXAMPLE**

Nortel Networks Inc. was once one of the world's largest providers of telecommunications systems. It delayed its regulatory filings starting in 2003, and had to restate its financial statements in the period 2003 to 2006 three times. One of the key causes identified for these ongoing problems was lack of sufficient personnel with appropriate knowledge, experience and training. In the end these problems caused Nortel to lose the confidence of the market and eventually led to the company filing for bankruptcy.

Table 10.1 *Risk Assessment: Human Resource Risks*

Implication	R5: Risk of errors in payroll authorizations	R10: Risk of loss of critical personnel or unplanned turnover
Expectations	Unclear since direction of potential errors is unknown.	(1) Increased payroll costs due to an increase in recruiting and hiring activity, as well as increases in personnel costs due to hiring new personnel. (2) If personnel critical to the strategy of the organization leave (e.g., in R&D, sales, production), overall performance may be negatively affected, which could affect one or more areas of the financial statements.
Going concern	Minimal.	Likelihood of failure may increase if personnel critical to the strategy and processes of the organization leave unexpectedly.
Risk of material misstatement	Errors in pay rates, withholding or benefits can lead to errors in wage-related expenses and liabilities (*accuracy of transactions*).	Probably minimal, however, if overall performance is affected, valuation issues may arise related to inventory and other assets (*valuation and allocation of accounts*). If loss results in turnover of key accounting personnel who are not readily replaceable or a change in the "tone at the top" this could increase risk of material misstatement substantially.
Control environment	Indicates that internal control over financial reporting related to payroll may be ineffective (i.e., significant deficiency or material weakness).	Overall control environment of the organization might be negatively affected depending on the personnel who depart (e.g., executives in the accounting or financial area).
Client control recommendations	Improved internal control over payroll-related record-keeping and authorizations	Client may need to look into succession planning, training or morale development, or compensation arrangements.*

* The auditor can point this out to the client, typically in the form of a management letter. Indeed, it may be required in an Integrated Audit if the "tone at the top" and/or the qualifications of the accounting personnel are changed due to turnover. In most audits it would be inappropriate for the auditor to directly assist the client in improving these areas of their operations since such work would be considered a potential violation of auditor independence by providing human resource consulting of key accounting or control personnel.

The Audit Risk Model

We have noted that the substantive tests of management assertions about financial reporting depend on the residual risks identified by the auditor. The *audit risk model* is used by an auditor to facilitate the planning of substantive tests by decomposing the concept of audit risk into its constituent parts. We have previously defined the term audit risk as "the likelihood or probability that the auditor will conclude that all material assertions made by management are true when, in fact, at least one assertion is incorrect." Auditing standards actually present a slightly more formal definition:

> **Audit risk:** *The risk that the auditor expresses an inappropriate audit opinion when the financial statements are materially misstated.*

(ISA Glossary of Terms)

Two attributes of this definition should be emphasized. First is the idea that the auditor has reached an incorrect conclusion about the financial statements. Saying that the statements are presented fairly when they are not could cause the auditor to suffer losses from litigation, fines, or reputation damage, particularly if the auditor was negligent in not finding misstatements in the financial report. Second, the concept of materiality, which was defined in Chapter 3, is an integral part of the definition. The auditor is concerned only with misstatements that would influence the decisions of potential readers of the financial statements. However, determining materiality within an engagement is a significant challenge to auditors.

In theory, audit risk can vary from 0 percent (complete certainty that financial statements do not contain material misstatements) to 100 percent (complete certainty that financial statements contain material misstatements), with 50 percent indicating perfect uncertainty. However, auditors design engagements to provide a reasonable level of assurance that financial statements are free of material misstatement. Given that **reasonable assurance** implies a high level of assurance, and a low probability of misstatement, most auditing firms require that engagements are conducted at a relatively low level of audit risk, usually no higher than 5 percent. Because an auditor cannot perform tests on all transactions and accounts, and because significant judgment is required for many financial statement assertions, conventional wisdom suggests that an audit cannot be performed with an audit risk level below 1 percent. Thus, for most firms, audit risk is established somewhere along the following continuum.

1%	3%	5%
Near complete certainty that financial statements do *not* contain material misstatements	High level of certainty that financial statements do *not* contain material misstatements	Reasonable certainty that financial statements do *not* contain material misstatements

In practice, the costs associated with moving below 1 percent typically are quite high relative to the reduction in audit risk. Conversely, 5 percent is probably the highest probability that can or should be accepted while still providing a high level of assurance.

Risk of Material Misstatement

Risk of material misstatement is the risk that the financial statements are materially misstated prior to the audit. Risk of material misstatement can also be phrased at the assertion level: the risk that an assertion contains a material error prior to carrying out audit tests. The risk of material misstatement at the assertion level can be separated into two highly interrelated parts: inherent risk and control risk.

Inherent risk is described as the likelihood that a management assertion may be misstated before considering the effect of internal controls. Inherent risk is affected by a number of factors. Some of the more important factors are described in Table 10.2. Many of these risk factors are explicitly considered

Table 10.2 *Inherent Risk Factors Affecting Overall Level of Risk of Material Misstatement of the Financial Statements*

Inherent Risk Factor	Effect on Risk of Material Misstatement	
	Higher Risk Condition	**Lower Risk Condition**
Nature of client's business and industry	Cyclical, evolving, declining, overly competitive, recent frauds uncovered, threatened regulation.	Stable or mature.
Integrity of management	Dubious (especially if there is a prior record of accounting manipulation).	Respected. Trustworthy.
Client ownership and/or management motivations	Need to satisfy challenging budget goals, existence of contingent bonus or option plans, and undue emphasis on reducing tax liabilities.	Budgets are realistic and readily met, management compensation is not highly contingent on results, lack of prior tax authority sanctions.
Results of prior-year audits	Frequent errors found in prior-year engagements.	Few errors found in prior-year engagements.
Tenure of auditor	Initial audit engagement with new client and little client-specific knowledge.	Repeat and ongoing audit engagement with extensive client specific knowledge with proper audit firm attention being paid to appropriate professional skepticism.
Existence of related parties	Many related party transactions that raise valuation and disclosure problems.	Few related party transactions.
Frequency of transactions	Unusual transactions for which the client lacks the expertise or accounting system to record the transactions accurately.	Frequent homogeneous transactions whose handling is automated and electronic, and where a well-designed system handles transactions efficiently on a regular basis.
Subjectivity of transaction values	Transaction requiring judgment to assign a value.	Easily determined exchange price for transaction.
Susceptibility to defalcation	Assets easily stolen or misdirected.	Assets that cannot be easily moved or misappropriated.
Size of balance/ Number of transactions	Many non-routine transactions.	Large number of transactions.

during the strategic and process analysis performed by the auditor. In general, the presence of a risk factor does not mean that the related assertion(s) and account(s) are misstated; rather, the presence of a risk factor means that the risk of misstatement is higher than it would be if the factor was not present. Some of these risk factors are pervasive to the entire engagement (e.g., honesty of management), whereas others may only affect a small subset of assertions or accounts.

Some of the risk factors listed in Table 10.2 may be counterbalancing. For example, a large account with frequent transactions is more likely to have mistakes because the volume of transactions implies that there is more opportunity for something to go wrong. At the same time, the client will have a great deal of experience handling a transaction that occurs frequently and will devote significant internal control resources to ensuring that mistakes are not made in that process. This latter point highlights the interrelatedness of inherent risk and control risk.

The client motivation factor listed in Table 10.2 deserves further discussion. A critical element of assessing inherent risk is determining the potential motivations of management, which may wish to increase profits so that the market value of the company's stock increases, making management's stock options more valuable. The mere presence of a stock option plan is not bad; indeed, most public companies have them, but the risks deepen if an inappropriate mix of compensation is offered such that management is induced to artificially inflate profits. This risk factor requires a keen understanding of management's attitudes towards inflating profits and the inherent risk of the engagement depends on whether management attempts to cash in on the options by manipulating accounting results. In a similar vein, if a company is small and family-owned, the owners may be interested in keeping profits low so that the company can minimize its tax bill. In this situation, the auditor must then be aware of the potential motivation to intentionally understate income.

Control Risk can be described as the likelihood that internal control will not prevent or detect a misstatement in a management assertion. Factors affecting control risk are examined during the auditor's strategic and process analysis, and many of the factors that affect inherent risk also affect control risk, as was illustrated in the previous discussion of inherent risk. Management integrity and the control environment are particularly important for assessing control risk, over and above the factors discussed in inherent risk. If the auditor suspects that management is less than completely honest, the risk of material misstatement could become extremely high.

AUTHORITATIVE GUIDANCE & STANDARDS

For US SEC registered public companies auditors must test internal controls over financial reporting as at year-end unless there is a material weakness in the design of the control such as to make it ineffective even if implemented. However, AS 2201 **An Audit of Internal Control Over Financial Reporting that is Integrated with an Audit of Financial Statements** *does not require that auditors test internal control effectiveness for the entire year under audit, but only as of year-end. Hence, the control risk assessment and the cost effectiveness of internal control tests for the entire year versus the evidence obtained from substantive tests decision still affects auditors in the Integrated Audit.*

A significant deficiency (or a significant deficiency and material weakness under the Integrated Audit) in internal control over financial reporting is likely to have a significant influence on control risk. A company with no material weaknesses or significant deficiencies may have low control risk, which will then influence the level of the risk of material misstatement. However, in GAAS Audits auditors may decide they want to do minimal testing of internal control and may set control risk at maximum if they can justify that substantive procedures alone will result in audit risk being reduced to an appropriately low level.

Detection Risk

Detection risk is the risk that the auditor will not detect a material misstatement that exists in the financial statements, or more specifically, in a financial statement assertion. Detection risk is set at an appropriate level conditional on the auditor's knowledge acquisition and risk assessment procedures, including evaluation of internal controls over financial reporting. That is, detection risk is the likelihood that substantive tests fail to detect an existing misstatement. A failure of substantive tests can occur for any combination of the following four reasons:

1. **Inadequate planning:** An auditor may not plan or perform the substantive audit procedure(s) necessary to detect an existing misstatement.

2. **Sampling omissions:** Auditors cannot look at every transaction; thus, an existing misstatement may not be discovered because it is not among the sample of transactions that are examined.

3. **Procedural errors:** An auditor may not apply a substantive procedure correctly or may not recognize an error even when an erroneous transaction is selected for testing. This problem may result from poor supervision and review of work of junior auditors, but can occur at any level in the engagement team.

4. **Improper corrective actions:** Even when an auditor identifies an erroneous transaction, there is a possibility that the auditor's response will be inappropriate (intentionally or unintentionally). For example, an auditor may decide not to correct an error (often referred to as "waiving the adjustment") or not adequately extrapolate a known error to the entire population (e.g., an audit test that finds three errors in a sample of 100 transactions suggests that there are likely to be many more unknown errors in the entire population of transactions[iii]).

Inadequate planning, procedural errors, or improper corrective actions are potentially severe problems for auditors because they represent a breakdown in the auditor's planning or judgment. The auditor tries to control these problems through compliance with GAAS, training and supervision of personnel, and careful review of work by experienced auditors. The auditor attempts to control sampling risk through careful selection of transactions to be tested.[1] While sampling omissions are an inherent part of the audit process and can never be avoided entirely, they have rarely been the primary cause of an audit failure.

Applying the Audit Risk Model

The components of audit risk indicate that three events must happen for a material misstatement to affect the financial statements. First, a misstatement

[iii]**EXAMPLE**

In the past, a common practice among auditors was not to correct a detected misstatement because the amount in question was not considered "material." In one infamous case involving the W. R. Grace Company, an intentional manipulation of earnings to defer current profits to future years amounting to $60 million was not corrected in the financial statements because the auditor felt that it was not material. Regardless of the magnitude of the number, however small or incidental, the fact that the misstatement emanated from an intentional action by management should have been enough to make the matter material to the auditor. Indeed, this allegedly immaterial misstatement allowed the company to meet forecasted earnings for the quarter, thus maintaining the value of the stock, which would most likely have dropped if the EPS target was not met.

(error or fraud) must be generated. Second, internal controls fail to prevent the misstatement, or detect the misstatement once it has occurred. Third, the misstatement remains undiscovered, or uncorrected, after the auditor performs substantive tests. If all three of these events occur, a material misstatement will affect the financial statements and an auditor may issue the wrong opinion.

A way to look at these relationships is with the audit risk model. The audit risk model should be thought of as an aid to understanding how various factors affect the amount of substantive testing done in an audit. Although the audit risk model is a mathematical formula, its use is more conceptual than computational, and auditors would generally not try to apply it as tool for calculating risk. Rather, the model provides guidance as to a general level of substantive testing that is needed given the conditions of a client. Specifically, the model relates the components to overall audit risk as follows:

$$AR = RMM \times DR \qquad (1)$$

where AR refers to audit risk, RMM refers to risk of material misstatement, and DR refers to detection risk. Although newer audit standards increasingly suggest that inherent and control risk should be considered jointly, the two interrelated components of RMM can be substituted into the model:

$$AR = (IR \times CR) \times DR \qquad (2)$$

where IR refers to inherent risk and CR refers to control risk. The components of audit risk focus on management assertions; therefore, this equation helps us understand how RMM impacts DR because the nature and extent of substantive tests performed by the auditor are conditional on the assessment of IR and CR.

Looking at the individual components of the audit risk model, we know that RMM is not controlled by the auditor and must be assessed as part of strategic and process analysis. The auditor's understanding of current conditions, risks, and controls provides a solid foundation for making such assessments as they relate to specific management assertions included in the financial statements. That is, the auditor must analyze the strategic and process risks of the organization, evaluate the accounting system that the client is using, and determine the risk that the system will generate material misstatements that go undetected by the internal controls.

DR is the only risk that is under the direct control of the auditor. If the auditor wishes to have a low detection risk, he or she must conduct extensive substantive tests of specific management assertions (normally tests of transactions, accounts, and presentation and disclosure). If the auditor decides that a higher level of DR is acceptable, then the auditor is willing to reach a conclusion about the fairness of financial statement based upon less substantive evidence, possibly substituting substantive analytical evidence for other substantive tests.

The terms of the risk model can be rearranged to emphasize the role of detection risk in planning substantive testing:

$$DR = \frac{AR}{RMM} \qquad (3)$$

Substituting the components of RRM yields:

$$DR = \frac{AR}{(IR \times CR)} \tag{4}$$

The revised form of the model tells us that DR will be lower when AR is lower or RMM is higher. The opposite is also true—DR will be higher when AR is higher or RMM is lower. Given that higher DR implies the need for less evidence about financial assertions, and lower DR implies a need for more evidence, different values for detection risk translate into different sets of substantive audit procedures.

The benefit of using the audit risk model for planning substantive tests is that it provides guidance about the appropriate level of detection risk given the established level of AR and the assessed level of RMM. It also allows the auditor to focus on specific management assertions where risk of misstatement is most severe. However, auditors must also be aware that the guidance from the model is only as good as the auditor's risk assessments. Assessing the risk of material misstatement as low can justify a higher level of detection risk and less substantive testing, so it is critical that the assessment of RMM be based on firm and defensible evidence from strategic, process, and internal control analysis.[2]

Setting Audit Risk

Should an auditor perform the audit to a 5 percent risk level? A 3 percent risk level? A 1 percent risk level? A number of factors will influence the auditor's decision. In general, the auditor will prefer lower audit risk whenever the potential cost of issuing an incorrect opinion is large. An incorrect opinion may lead to lost engagements, negative publicity, or litigation. Loss of even one lawsuit can expose auditors to millions of dollars of damages. Thus, the more likely the auditor is to face such sanctions in the event of audit errors, the lower the desired audit risk will be. As a result, many auditing firms have a formal policy of setting audit risk the same for all engagements.

One factor the auditor should consider in setting desired audit risk is the number of external users who will be relying on the financial statements. The more external users there are, the larger the number of people who will be adversely affected if the auditor issues an incorrect opinion. The number of potential users of the financial statements is related to the size of the client, the distribution of its ownership's interests, whether the stock is publicly traded, and the nature and extent of its debt financing. The desired audit risk used to plan an audit will usually be much lower for a large publicly traded company than for a small single-owner retail store because the auditor's exposure is much greater.

AUTHORITATIVE GUIDANCE & STANDARDS

US audit standards (AS 1101 [formerly 8] **Audit Risk***, AS 2101 [formerly 9]* **Audit Planning***) include all components of the audit risk as described in this chapter—the international standards (ISAs 315, 330) do not include* *the explicit model but state the auditor may wish to use a mathematical model that in general terms expresses the general relationship among the components of audit risk (ISA 200 A36* **Overall Objectives of the Independent Auditor and the Conduct of an Audit in Accordance with International Standards on Auditing***). Both sets of standards requires auditors to assess the risk of material misstatement and perform a combination of procedures (e.g., ISA 330, AS 2210, AS 2301) to achieve an appropriate level of audit risk.*

Another factor to consider when setting desired audit risk is the likelihood that the client organization will suffer financial difficulties in the near future. A company that goes bankrupt shortly after the auditor issues an opinion on the financial statements exposes the auditor to potential litigation. In assessing this possibility, the auditor should examine the client's financial status, its methods of financing, the competence of management, and the nature of the industry. Other factors that may have an impact on the desired audit risk are the auditor's professional attitudes about the level of assurance to be obtained during the engagement, the auditor's attitudes towards risk, and the overall experience and competence of the auditor.

A factor that may affect assessment of audit risk, *but should not*, is the extent of competition among auditors. There have been cases in the past where an auditor has cut back on the amount of audit work performed, and thus the amount of evidence obtained, because competition among auditing firms decreased the fee for the engagement to a point where a reasonable profit could not be earned by performing the needed work. In these cases, a greater risk level was accepted by the auditor in order to justify less evidence gathering, resulting in a reduction of the engagement cost. Such strategies are not consistent with professional standards and are potentially costly to the auditor in the long run (e.g., lost clients or litigation). In the end, it is the auditor's high level of commitment to being a professional, including the willingness to embrace strong ethical values, which provides the best protection for users of audited financial statements.

Materiality
Overall Materiality

A key concept underlying the audit of financial statements and the audit risk model is materiality, which was defined in Chapter 3 as "the magnitude of an omission or misstatement of accounting information that, in light of surrounding circumstances, makes it probable that the judgment of a reasonable person relying on the information would have been changed or influenced by the omission or misstatement." The concept of materiality is important to auditors because it has a direct impact on the amount of effort auditors must expend during the course of an engagement. Remember, the smaller the magnitude of misstatement that is considered to be important, the harder the auditor will have to look in order to be sure that no such misstatements exist. Finding a needle in the proverbial haystack is harder than finding a hockey stick.

As discussed in Chapter 3, the materiality threshold is subject to a great deal of judgment, and auditors have developed numerous rules of thumb for setting an initial quantitative materiality level. The challenge for auditors is that the definition of materiality is necessarily vague as it depends on client-specific risks and does not provide a strict formula for quantifying the size of misstatement that is important. Virtually every reader of financial statements will have a different idea as to what constitutes a material misstatement. Generally, standard setters suggest net income or net assets as the base for establishing quantitative materiality, with percentages between 5 and 10 percent for net income and 1 and 3 percent of net assets.

Auditors may select some other justifiable basis for establishing materiality, however. For example, an auditor who believes that readers of the financial statements focus on revenues or gross margin may use 3 percent of revenues or 10 percent of gross margin for materiality. For biotech companies that generate little or no profits or revenues in the conventional sense, gross research and development expenditures may be a more appropriate base for planning purposes. Other bases that might be appropriate in specific circumstances include current assets, net working capital, total assets, total revenues, gross profit, total equity, and cash flows from operations. Auditors have also developed industry-specific measures of materiality such as:

(a) Not-for-profit organizations: ½–2 percent of total expenses or total revenues; 3 percent of net assets.

(b) Mutual fund industry: ½–1 percent of net asset value.

(c) Real estate industry when an entity owns income-producing properties: 1 percent of revenue.

To illustrate the auditor's challenge in setting quantitative materiality, consider two companies with the following financial results:

	ABC Company	**XYZ Company**
Net income (loss)	$600,000	$20,000
Total assets	3,000,000	3,000,000
Net assets	750,000	750,000
Sales	3,000,000	1,000,000

AUTHORITATIVE GUIDANCE & STANDARDS

Standards (ISA 320, AS 2105) note that materiality for specific items in the financial statements that could impact decisions made by users might be lower than overall materiality. Two examples provided in the standards are research and development expenses for a pharmaceutical manufacturer and financial performance of a newly acquired subsidiary.

What would be considered a material misstatement for each of the companies? As noted, a common rule of thumb is to set materiality equal to 5 percent of net income. This would result in a materiality level of $30,000 for ABC and $1,000 for XYZ. Do these results seem reasonable? For ABC, $30,000 may be about right since that represents 1 percent of total assets and

4 percent of net assets. For XYZ, $1,000 seems quite small and represents only 0.03 percent of total assets. Most auditors would conclude that this value is too low given the general concerns of the readers of the financial statements. So what materiality level is appropriate for XYZ Company? One possibility is to use $30,000, as was done for ABC Company, as this represents 1 percent of total assets. This choice may not be wise, however, because a $30,000 misstatement, if it remained undetected, would change a small loss into a small profit. Knowing that a company actually has a net loss (albeit small) would be important to most readers of the financial statements and should be taken into consideration by the auditor independent of the quantitative level of materiality. Therefore, materiality should be no larger than $20,000 for XYZ Company.

Performance Materiality

Auditing standard setters in recent years have become more concerned with the concept of materiality given widespread reports of its abuse as a reason for auditors to not insist that a client adjust their financial statements. However, small errors can have a serious impact on how financial results are interpreted. One approach taken by standard setters is to require that auditors reduce overall materiality for the fact that undetected misstatements might combine with those that are detected to exceed overall materiality. Hence, auditors are now also required to set "performance materiality," defined for a GAAS Audit as "the amount or amounts set by the auditor at less than materiality for the financial statements as a whole to reduce to an appropriately low level the probability that the aggregate of the uncorrected and undetected misstatements exceed materiality for the financial statements as a whole" (ISA 320). Research suggests that depending on the assessed risk of undetected errors, the auditor is setting performance materiality at amounts of 50 percent to 75 percent of materiality with higher levels of performance materiality reflecting lower risks. In some ways this discussion is like discussions in the 1970s about planning materiality versus evaluative materiality with the idea that the auditor would set planning materiality to a lower level than the amount of error the auditor was willing to tolerate in the final financial statements, resulting in more audit work. In any case, post implementation reports about this new requirement suggest that it is perceived by practitioners as one of the most difficult of the new ISAs to implement.

AUTHORITATIVE GUIDANCE & STANDARDS
TERMINOLOGY ALERT

ISA 320 introduces another terminology difference between a GAAS Audit and Integrated Audit. "Performance materiality" is the ISA term that means "the amount or amounts set by the auditor at less than materiality for the financial statements as a whole to reduce to an appropriately low level the probability that the aggregate of the uncorrected and undetected misstatements exceed materiality for the financial statements as a whole" (ISA 320). The goal of standard setters appears to be to build in a margin for small errors that might add up to a material error. AS 2105 uses the term "tolerable misstatement" to describe the same concept. Neither standard specifies a relationship between materiality and performance materiality/ tolerable misstatement calling it a matter of professional judgment as to how the auditor reduces the overall materiality to performance materiality/ tolerable misstatement.

Audit practitioners often employ rules of thumb of between 50 percent and 75 percent of overall materiality when setting performance materiality depending on the risk associated with the client. Hence, in our example above, the auditor for ABC Company would reduce the $30,000 materiality to say $21,000 if controls were reasonable or to $15,000 if controls were weak. For XYZ Company where we concluded that materiality could reasonably be set at $20,000, the same rule of thumb would result in performance materiality of $15,000 or $10,000 depending on the quality of the controls.

Qualitative Considerations in Setting Materiality

Possibly more important than the level of quantitative materiality are the qualitative factors that surround a potential misstatement of financial results. In judging an actual misstatement, context matters a great deal. Qualitative factors that may be important when setting the overall level for planning materiality include:

- **Misstatements Relative to Segment or Interim Results**: An error may not seem significant when compared with overall financial results for a fiscal year. However, investors also look closely at segment data and interim results. If a misstatement has a significant impact on such information, it might be considered material in spite of its small impact on the annual results.

- **Nature of Misstatements**: Fraudulent transactions are considered extremely significant regardless of the amount of the misstatement. Auditors often adopt a "where there's smoke there's fire" view when dealing with potential fraud, which makes the discovery of a single fraudulent transaction extremely important, even if it is immaterial in amount[iv].

- **Nature of Contractual Constraints**: The auditor should be aware of any contractual or legal limits that may be affected by the financial results of the company. Misstatements that cause violations of debt covenants, or that disguise actual violations of such covenants, are important even if small in amount[v].

- **Trends are Important:** Reported results that indicate a significant change in the trend of results over time are important. A small decrease in sales or net income may be considered to be important. Misstatements that alter the direction of trends in the financial results of the company, or change a loss to a gain or vice versa, are important even if the amounts are small.

- **Meeting or Exceeding Incentive Goals:** If management or employees have incentive-based contracts, misstatements that allow them to achieve their goals should be considered material[vi].

[iv]**EXAMPLE**

Many instances of fraudulent financial reporting start relatively small. For example, a company may hold open the sales journal for a day or two at the end of the year in order to record a few more dollars of sales to meet its sales targets. However, such situations tend to become more serious over time. Furthermore, managers that are detected committing a small fraud are often willing or forced to escalate their fraudulent activity in future periods often to cover up the problems created by the initial smaller fraud.

[v]**EXAMPLE**

Debt covenants may require a minimum level of working capital or a maximum debt/ equity ratio, or regulators may require a certain minimum level of equity capital (e.g., for banks or insurance companies). Misstatements that allow a company to appear to be in compliance should be considered material.

- **External Expectations:** If the broad market expects certain outcomes, misstatements that confirm or refute those expectations may have a significant impact on the market[(vii)].

In the past, securities regulators have raised serious concerns about the materiality judgments made by auditors when evaluating potentially material misstatements. Although not establishing any new standards, recent statements by securities regulators have highlighted the importance of considering qualitative factors in assessing materiality, including the importance to investors of the matter being evaluated, the impact of misstatements on management compensation, and the impact of a misstatement on trends and earnings levels. Furthermore, materiality is not an appropriate justification for failing to correct a discovered misstatement of any magnitude—even though most accounting pronouncements explicitly note that the required standards do not apply to immaterial transactions. Indeed, for US-registered public companies, all auditor-proposed adjustments to correct errors must be posted by the client management irrespective of materiality except in the case where they are obviously trivial.[3] To conclude, setting materiality requires careful analysis and sound judgment because the auditor's decisions concerning materiality early in the audit have a direct impact on subsequent testing.

Allocation of Materiality to Accounts

Many auditors decompose materiality and performance materiality into smaller pieces applicable to specific audit areas or accounts. In practice, the amount of materiality assigned to individual accounts is often called another term, such as **tolerable error,** which refers to the amount of error that an auditor can tolerate in a specific account before it is considered to be materially misstated. Tolerable error can differ for each account because some accounts are more susceptible to error or are more significant to the overall financial results of the organization. The profession does not have formal rules for determining tolerable error for account balances, but two generally accepted guidelines are often used:

- Tolerable error for an account or class of transactions should be less than the overall materiality/performance materiality level.[4]

- The sum of tolerable error across all accounts and classes of transactions may equal or exceed materiality.

AUTHORITATIVE GUIDANCE & STANDARDS TERMINOLOGY ALERT

Professional standards (ISA 320, AS 2105) advocate allocating materiality (or performance materiality/tolerable misstatement) to individual accounts and classes of transactions. However, standards uses the same term to describe these allocated amounts at the account and classes of transaction level as it does for the overall materiality (or performance materiality/ tolerable misstatement) at the financial statement level. Hence, many practitioners have adopted terms like "tolerable error" to differentiate the allocated materiality at the account or class of transaction level.

[(vi)]EXAMPLE

In a famous Canadian case, Nortel, the Board of Directors had—at management's instigation—passed a "Return to Profitability" bonus plan that was especially generous to senior managers. However, the quarter before this plan came into effect, profitability would have been achieved but for the numerous income decreasing accruals made by managers after the end of the quarter. In the next quarter, after the bonus plan came into effect, these income decreasing accruals were reversed and Nortel paid out large bonuses to celebrate its return to profitability. When discovered, these accruals led to numerous financial accounting restatements and significant litigation against the audit firm that had previously expressed unqualified opinions.

[(vii)]EXAMPLE

The valuation of equities is very sensitive to the ability of a company to meet or exceed the consensus earnings forecasts that are published by analysts. Failure to meet earnings forecasts by even a penny can have a dramatic impact on the price of a stock. Consequently, management is very much aware of the level of forecasted earnings. A misstatement that allows a company to meet such forecasts could be considered material even if the amount is small.

The process of allocating materiality/performance materiality/tolerable error is a matter for professional judgment. One of the key means of demonstrating well thought out professional judgment is to show that the allocation is coherent in the context of a specific client. For example, one would not have the same level of tolerable error for a very large account balance versus an account balance that is relatively small nor the same tolerable error if controls were being relied on versus an account where controls were not being tested. Some considerations that go into allocating materiality include:

- Size of the account or class of transactions.
- The complexity of the transactions or account balance.
- Risk of material misstatement that has been assessed by the auditor for the account or class of transactions.

There are situations, normally related to conducting an efficient cost-effective audit under competitive fee pressure, where the auditor may wish to have the sum of tolerable errors exceed materiality. In general, increasing the sum of allocated tolerable error means that the auditor is willing to tolerate larger errors in some accounts, which would increase the overall risk that a material misstatement will remain undetected. However, this need not increase *overall* audit risk if one of the following two conditions is met:

1. **Offsetting Errors Affecting Net Income:** Errors in different accounts may be offsetting, meaning that the error in one account increases net income while the error in another account decreases net income. The net error is not material so the use of higher tolerable error levels does not increase overall audit risk.

2. **"Unused" Tolerable Error:** Error equal to or in excess of tolerable error is unlikely to occur in all accounts. Increasing tolerable error may not increase audit risk as long as actual error in some accounts is less than the tolerable error. In such a case, the sum of *actual* errors would be less than overall materiality even though the sum of tolerable errors exceeds materiality.

Overall, tolerable error is a mechanism for planning and conducting an audit performed by a team of auditors who are simultaneously examining multiple accounts. If tolerable error is not defined by an auditor, audit differences in different accounts may be deemed to be individually immaterial. However, the summation of individually immaterial errors could result in the financial statement being materially misstated on an overall basis. By utilizing a careful process for establishing and allocating tolerable misstatement, auditors decompose materiality to an account level. Regardless of the amount of tolerable error utilized, total audit differences across all accounts must be combined and the net effect on earnings must be less than overall materiality in order for the auditor to conclude that the financial statements are free of material misstatement.

Determining the Nature, Extent, and Timing of Substantive Testing

Once the auditor has made all the necessary risk and materiality assessments, he or she is ready to design the substantive audit program that will guide the testing of assertions regarding transactions, accounts, and presentation and disclosures. At this point, the auditor must make a number of decisions for each significant management assertion:

- What audit procedures should be performed?
- When should the procedures be performed?
- If sample-based testing is used, how many transactions or what percentage of the account balance should be examined?
- If sample-based testing is used, which transactions in the account should be examined?

These questions refer to the ***nature, extent, and timing*** of substantive testing. The answers to the four questions for all significant management assertions will serve as the basis for the audit program for substantive testing of transactions, accounts, and presentation and disclosure. The structure of the audit program will be discussed in more detail below. Suffice it to say that the final audit program for substantive testing must provide adequate evidence concerning all material assertions in the financial statements conditional on the risks identified during strategic and process analysis. However, the audit program is continually subject to revision as new information comes to the auditor's attention.

Appropriateness of Audit Evidence

When selecting procedures to address specific management assertions, the auditor will consider the risk assessments related to the assertion and its materiality relative to the overall financial statements. With this in mind, the auditor will then determine how strong or persuasive the evidence needs to be in order to satisfy the auditor's goal for detection risk. If the desired detection risk is low, the auditor will want a great deal of sound substantive evidence; if desired detection risk is high, the auditor may utilize smaller samples with the same procedures or substitute substantive analytical procedures for some substantive tests of transactions or accounts. We use the term ***appropriateness*** to describe the strength or persuasiveness of audit evidence.

AUTHORITATIVE GUIDANCE & STANDARDS

Standards (ISA 500, AS 1105) explain what constitutes evidence in a financial statement audit.

There are seven types of audit evidence, first introduced in Chapter 3, which an auditor can acquire, create, or obtain as the case may be:

1. Inspection (also known as physical examination) of tangible assets.
2. Confirmation of accounts or transactions with third parties.
3. Inspection (also known as vouching) of client records or documents.
4. Observation of client activities and processes.
5. Recalculation or reperformance of client computations.

6. Analytical evidence (also known as analytical procedures or more generally, analysis).

7. Client inquiry.

How does an auditor know the appropriateness or quality of the evidence obtained from a specific audit procedure? There are a number of characteristics that the auditor can consider in order to understand the appropriateness of evidence.

- **Degree of Relevance:** Is the evidence relevant to the assertion being examined? If the auditor wishes to know if year-end inventory exists, the best way to find out is to inspect the tangible inventory on hand and count the items. Of course, inspection of the tangible inventory will not tell the auditor whether or not the items in the warehouse are actually owned by the client, nor will it help the auditor to know if inventory is properly valued at historic cost.

- **Independence of the Provider:** Is the source of the evidence independent of the company, or is it subject to possible manipulation? Information obtained from a person outside the client is usually considered to be superior to that received from an insider. An outsider is assumed to have no vested interest in the outcome of the audit, whereas an insider may try to sway the auditor's opinion in order to advance his or her own goals.

- **Degree of Auditor's Direct Knowledge:** Is the evidence directly observable at its source by the auditor? The adage "seeing is believing" clearly applies to auditors. Again, the best way to determine if inventory is present is to look at it—this process is often called the "kick test." Supplier invoices may indicate how many items of inventory the client acquired, but this type of documentary evidence is only second-best to direct physical examination.

- **Qualifications of the Provider:** Is the source of the evidence qualified to provide reliable evidence? When receiving evidence, the auditor should consider the competence of the provider. For example, the best person to provide information to the auditor about a pension plan is probably an actuary. Similarly, the best person to provide information about the value of real estate is an appraiser.

- **Degree of Objectivity:** Is the evidence open to interpretation so that support for an assertion is ambiguous? Audit evidence is rarely clear-cut in its support of an assertion; this is especially true for the valuation assertion. For example, a company may provide extensive evidence concerning sales debits and cash credits to a customer's account. How does the auditor determine if the net balance is actually collectible? Does the evidence that a customer has paid his or her bill in the past imply that he or she will continue to pay his bill? The evaluation of such evidence bears directly on the recorded value of receivables but is potentially ambiguous.

- **Quality of Internal Control:** How reliable is evidence generated from the company's accounting system? Auditors make great use of the client's internal recordkeeping system. In every audit, vouching of documents is a common audit procedure performed for many classes of transactions, especially as related to the validity and completeness assertions. However, the use of internal company documents as audit evidence presumes that those documents are accurate. If internal control is weak and internal documents are potentially inaccurate, the auditor may need to obtain other forms of evidence.

- **Specificity of Evidence**: Given that analytical procedures and client inquiry are heavily utilized by auditors, the care with which these procedures are planned impacts the appropriateness of the evidence. Analytical procedures are based upon client data and communications and are used to assess whether results confirm the auditor's expectations. Thus, the more specific the foundation for the expectation and the more precise the computations, the more appropriate the evidence. Also, conducting client inquiry without carefully considering the incentives of the client increases the auditor's susceptibility to being fooled by self-serving information.

Figure 10.4 illustrates the typical hierarchy of evidence based on the above attributes. In general, the auditor will try to obtain more appropriate evidence (the "best" evidence) when desired detection risk for an assertion is low. When detection risk is moderate or high, the auditor will usually be satisfied with evidence considered "good." However, the auditor will rarely be totally satisfied with evidence classified as "weak" except to corroborate other "good" or "strong" evidence.

To illustrate the trade-off of the quality of evidence and risk, consider the procedures to test accounts receivable for different levels of risk as described

BEST

Inspection of Tangible Assets
Confirmation
Inspection of Externally Generated Documentation
Reperformance

↓

GOOD

Inspection of Internal Documentation (strong process controls)
Observation
Analytical Procedures (reliable internal information system and
well specified expectation and procedure)
Carefully Planned Client Enquiry

↓

WEAK

Inspection of Internal Documentation (weak process controls)
Client Enquiry (little or no planning of approach)
Analytical Procedures (poor internal information system or poorly
specified expectation or procedure)

Figure 10.4 Hierarchy of Evidence Reliability

Table 10.3 *Trade-Off of Detection Risk and Audit Evidence*

Auditor Sets Detection Risk at Low = High Audit Effort	Auditor Sets Detection Risk at High = Low Audit Effort
Client Conditions	
Auditor sets low detection risk due to a high assessed risk of material misstatement due to either high inherent risk that controls cannot reduce to a low level, ineffective controls, or the decision to set control risk as maximum. Hence, there is the need for a high level of substantive audit tests.	Auditor sets high detection risk due to the low assessed risk of material misstatement due to having effective internal controls that reduce the assessed level of inherent risk and control risk to a low level. The assessment must be supported by appropriate control tests. Hence, there can be fewer substantive audit tests.
Effect on Substantive Testing	
Aged trial balance for receivables prepared by the auditor.	Aged trial balance for receivables prepared by the client's personnel and reviewed by auditor.
25 largest customer accounts plus 100 customer accounts statistically selected and confirmed with results analyzed employing appropriate statistical methods.	50 customer accounts judgmentally selected across various customer characteristics (e.g., large balances, small balances, etc.) and confirmed with results analyzed judgmentally.
No client restrictions placed on population of accounts to confirm.	A few accounts omitted from confirmation by request of the client.
Accounts to be confirmed pertain to other businesses.	Accounts to be confirmed pertain to retail consumers.
Customer accounts confirmed as of 12/31 (for fiscal year end of 12/31).	Customer accounts confirmed as of 11/1 (for fiscal year end of 12/31).

in Table 10.3. The preparation of the aged trial balance by the client personnel is higher risk because the preparer is not independent. Selecting 125 accounts to confirm is better than selecting 50 accounts because the sample has a greater chance of detecting existing errors. Client management's restriction on the selection of customer accounts interferes with the independence of the evidence and reduces its appropriateness. Confirmations sent to businesses will usually be more reliable than those sent to retail customers because a business is likely to have an accounting system that allows it to respond accurately to the confirmation request. Companies utilizing electronic data interchange with suppliers often have the capability to send electronic confirmations that can be routed directly to the auditor. Finally, confirming accounts before year end provides weaker evidence because it is less timely than direct year-end confirmation.

An Example: Linking Residual Risk Assessments to Tests of Management Assertions

To illustrate the links between strategic and process risks and tests of management assertions, let's consider the example of an electronics company that specializes in high performance sound equipment. The company's strategy is to differentiate its product based on quality. In order to succeed, the company needs to develop and manufacture products that are of higher quality and superior reliability than its competitors, and for which it can charge a premium price. Given the company's strategy, significant threats can arise from its supply chain if vendors are unable to provide components and raw materials that are of sufficient quality to meet the company's performance specifications. The company might try to mitigate this risk at the strategic level by establishing alternative sources of supply, vertically integrating, or forming alliances with key suppliers.

Failure to obtain an adequate supply of high-quality inputs will have an impact on the products and processes of the electronic company. The manufacturing process could be affected by problems in the supply chain for a number of reasons:

- Disruptions in deliveries (especially if the process operates on a just-in-time basis).
- Down time or retooling of equipment originally designed to utilize higher quality inputs than currently available.
- Waste due to the disposal of unacceptable units or materials.
- Defects and rework due to deterioration of the quality of outputs.

The company normally will try to mitigate each of these risks through various entity level controls and procedures. For example, on-site inspections can occur at the supplier for materials utilized on a just-in-time basis, penalty clauses in performance contracts with suppliers can be enforced, assembly and production processes can be adjusted to compensate for lower quality inputs, and new suppliers can be obtained when specialized tooling is not involved. Furthermore, the level of these risks should be measured through the use of several performance indicators, including on-site inspection ratings, delivery statistics, factory operating statistics, production waste and defect rates, customer complaints, and warranty claims.

For the purposes of our illustration, assume that the company has implemented all of the entity level controls indicated above and is monitoring the indicated performance measures. The controls seem to be operating effectively except for deliveries from one specific supplier of a complex component. This supplier has recently been late with deliveries and on-site inspection ratings have been lower than past periods. As a result, the electronics company has suffered delays and been forced to reconfigure some assembly processes. In general, performance measures indicate that deliveries are occurring on time from all other suppliers, there is no indication of increased rejection of deliveries, and the supply chain has not been disrupted. Other performance measures indicate an increased rate of defects, customer complaints, and warranty claims, however. These facts, taken together, could cause the auditor to conclude that there is an increased residual risk of delayed and inferior components.

The auditor would next link the conclusions about residual risks to specific audit implications and assertions that may exhibit an elevated risk of material misstatement. There are at least two account areas where an increased risk of material misstatement arises as a result of these conditions, one fairly obvious and one not so apparent:

1. Warranty Expense (the obvious): The increased level of customer complaints, warranty claims, and defects indicates that the supply chain problems are negatively affecting product quality. This suggests that the management assertions of completeness and valuation of warranty expenses and the

associated liability may have increased risk of material misstatement, and the allowance for warranties may have to be higher than in the past.

2. Inventory (the not-so-obvious): Due to production delays and reconfiguration of the assembly process, the valuation of work-in-process and finished goods inventory may be inaccurate. Because the costs of delays and changing production processes are considered an indirect manufacturing cost, the company's overhead allocations and standard costs may be inaccurate, causing the management assertion of valuation of inventory to have increased risk of material misstatement.

Given that these assertions have a higher risk of material misstatement, the auditor selects appropriate tests of transactions and accounts to achieve a suitably low detection risk for each assertion. For testing the completeness and valuation of warranty expense and liability, the auditor could undertake some or all of the following *substantive* tests:

Analytical procedures

• Obtain historical data on warranty claims by product and develop a projection of future claims based on changes in current conditions. Compare the projection to the recorded balance of claims and determine if it is adequate.

• Compare company claims history to industry trends and patterns.

Tests of details

• Obtain listings of warranty claims for the quarters during the prior year (or two) to benchmark current performance results.

• Review warranty claims being filed after the end of the fiscal year and verify that the pattern of claims is consistent with recorded balances.

• Test the recognition and valuation of a sample of actual claims to determine if they are accounted for properly.

For testing the valuation of inventory, the auditor could use some or all of the following substantive tests of details:

• Review production cycle times (or variances) and determine if unusual patterns or trends are apparent. Increased cycle times could be associated with increased production costs—both labor and overhead.

• Review the overhead allocation and standard cost computations for products affected by the supplier in question.

• Obtain documentation in support of the data used in the standard cost computations (for example, vendor invoices and receiving reports).

• Trace the cost of process down time and reconfiguration (i.e., cost variances) into the overhead allocations and standard cost calculations.

Not all of these substantive tests may be needed in order to obtain sufficient evidence. The actual selection of procedures will depend on the level of detection risk for the assertions. In general, the auditor should obtain enough evidence to be assured that the high residual risk that was identified in the process is not resulting in material misstatements in the related management assertions for the financial statements.

Developing the Audit Plan for Tests of Management Assertions

The preparation of an audit plan for substantive testing requires that the auditor judgmentally select the best set of procedures to be performed in order to obtain sufficient, appropriate evidence that the financial statements are fairly presented. Recall that the auditor can use substantive analytical procedures or tests of transactions, accounts, and disclosure details. An important part of the **audit program** is the list of the substantive procedures that the auditor has decided to perform, typically classified by account area (e.g., transactions cycle or business process) and assertion. The relationship among audit procedures and types of audit evidence is summarized in Table 10.4. Different procedures provide evidence of different quality so the auditor must carefully match the quality of the evidence to the detection risk for an assertion.

Table 10.4 *Relationship between Audit Procedures and Audit Evidence when Planning Substantive Tests of Financial Statement Assertions*

Type of Audit Procedure	Type of Audit Evidence Obtained	Relationship of Evidence to Possible Financial Statement Errors
Substantive Analytical Procedures	Client Enquiries Analytical Procedures	Indirect: Unusual results may be due to error or non-error causes. The actual cause of an unusual discrepancy must be determined using other procedures.
Tests of Details: Transactions	Client Enquiries Observation Inspection of Documents Recalculation/ Re-computation	Direct and Indirect: Actual errors can be detected in the transactions that have been examined. Actual errors indicate the likelihood that errors may have occurred in other transactions not examined.
Tests of Details: Account Balance	Client Enquiries Inspection of Documents Recalculation/ Re-computation Confirmation Inspection of Tangible Assets	Direct: Actual errors can be detected in year-end balances.
Tests of Details: Presentation and Disclosure	Client Enquiries Inspection of Documents Recalculation/ Re-computation Confirmation	Direct: Actual errors can be detected in financial statement line items or footnote disclosures.

AUTHORITATIVE GUIDANCE & STANDARDS

Standards describe both the preliminary planning process (ISA 300
Planning an Audit of Financial Statements *and AS 2101) we discussed*
in Chapter 4 as well as the process to develop a detailed substantive audit
plan (ISA 330 and AS 2301) that we discuss in this chapter.

Selecting Effective and Efficient Audit Procedures to Test Assertions

Recognizing that an auditor will try to follow the basic strategy of obtaining sufficient, appropriate evidence, in the most efficient and least costly manner, Figure 10.5 depicts the various approaches that the auditor can adopt for preparing the audit program. The Figure picks up the audit process at the point where the auditor has completed the strategic and process analyses, assessed risk of material misstatement including determining the degree of reliance on internal controls, tested internal controls in light of the determined amount of reliance and is ready to complete the audit plan.[5] Now the auditor has to take that analysis and plan the approach to substantive testing that the auditor will follow to reduce residual risks to an appropriately low level so as to support the audit opinion:

1. Assess risk of material misstatement for an assertion at a high level based on high inherent risk and high or maximum control risk. Under this option, the auditor plans the engagement assuming that inherent risk is too high to allow reliance on internal control or that no assurance can be obtained from internal control (note that this option should be utilized only in exceptional cases when testing internal control is deemed too costly relative to benefits or the client has no effective controls).

2. Assess risk of material misstatement for an assertion at a reduced level based on the procedures performed during strategic and process analysis including the testing of controls over the financial reporting process. The auditor either has conducted, or plans to conduct, walkthroughs and limited tests of controls as part of process analysis.

3. Assess risk of material misstatement for an assertion at a low level based on low inherent risk and low control risk. To justify this risk reduction, the auditor should conduct extensive walkthroughs and tests of controls as part of process analysis, including testing controls over the financial reporting process.

The analysis in Figure 10.5 highlights the conditional nature of substantive tests. After establishing risk of material misstatement for significant assertions, the auditor will perform substantive analytical procedures based on fairly precise expectations about appropriate performance measurements derived during strategic and process analysis. Finally, the auditor will perform adequate tests of details (i.e., transactions, accounts, and disclosures) to complete the engagement and obtain the remaining evidence that is required to render an opinion on the financial statements. Depending on existing evidence, the extent of substantive tests of details of transactions or accounts can range from extensive to minimal. Six possible outcomes

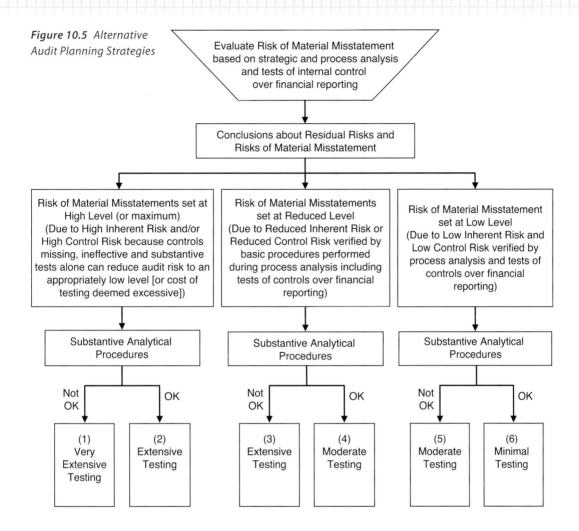

Figure 10.5 *Alternative Audit Planning Strategies*

to the auditor's planning process are summarized in Table 10.5. Each set of conditions is a unique combination of control risk, analytical evidence, and tests of details of transactions or accounts.

Segmenting the Audit Plan

The auditor needs to divide the audit into manageable segments given that different processes affect different assertions in different ways. Indeed, in large multinational organizations the auditor begins this process by dividing the client organization into a series of auditable entities as a precursor to auditing the consolidated entity. One efficient way to segment the auditable entity into smaller pieces is by business process as it allows the auditor to readily apply the knowledge gained from the strategic and process analysis to the financial statement accounts, transactions and disclosures. Many auditors will follow the financial accounting recording process by segmenting the audit by accounting transactions cycles whereas others will divide by financial statement account type. In all cases the knowledge gained in the strategic and process analyses needs to be brought to bear. We adopt the

Table 10.5 *Summary of Alternative Audit Planning Outcomes (Assuming a Given Level of Audit Risk)*

Outcome (see Table 10.6)	Extent of Substantive Tests of Details (Accounts or Transactions)	Auditor Set Detection Risk	Reliance on Substantive Analytical Procedures	Reliance on Tests of Details
(1)	Very extensive substantive tests	Very Low	Low	Very High
(2)	Extensive substantive tests	Low	Moderate	High
(3)	Extensive substantive tests	Low	Low	High
(4)	Moderate substantive tests	Moderate	Moderate	Moderate
(5)	Moderate substantive tests	Moderate	Low	Moderate
(6)	Minimal substantive tests	High	Moderate	Low

approach of segmenting the audit by business process and then identifying the accounts affected by a given process.

In this book, we will discuss the following processes, all of which are broken down into sub-processes for conducting an audit:[6]

- **Sales and Customer Service:** This process deals with customers. It includes activities such as marketing, sales order entry, product delivery, pricing, billing, and cash receipts. The accounts affected by this process include cash, receivables, inventory, cost of goods sold, and selling expenses. See Chapter 11.

- **Supply Chain Management and Manufacturing Conversion:** This process deals with acquiring the resources needed for production and converting them into a product or service. It includes activities such as purchasing, receiving, manufacturing, and cash disbursements. The accounts affected by this process include inventory, accounts payable, and cost of goods sold. See Chapter 12.

- **Human Resource Management:** This process acquires, manages, and compensates human resources. The accounts affected include production costs, accrued liabilities, employee benefits, and equity (e.g., stock options). Introduced in Chapters 6 and 7, our discussion of this process is completed in the Appendix to Chapter 13.

- **Facilities Management:** This process acquires, utilizes, and maintains fixed physical assets such as factories, vehicles, and retail locations. The accounts affected include most fixed assets, depreciation, production costs (for cost allocation), accounts payable, and asset-based obligations (such as mortgages or leases). See Chapter 13.

- **Financial Resource Management:** This process obtains capital for the organization, makes financial investments (other than mergers and acquisitions), and manages cash flow. The accounts affected include long-term debt, equity, long-term investments, financing expenses, and investment revenue. See Chapter 13.

Each process has its own objectives, risks, controls, and performance measures that the auditor should evaluate as part of strategic and process analysis. Each process interfaces with different accounts in the financial statements. The auditor needs to understand which processes can affect which accounts, link residual risks from the process to management assertions, and plan substantive tests based on the assessments of risk and materiality and the availability of evidence. Table 10.6 provides an overview of how significant business processes link to specific elements of the financial statements. Segmentation of the audit in this way provides complete coverage of the information in the financial statements and becomes the basis for finalizing the plan for testing assertions of transactions, accounts, and disclosures.

Table 10.6   *Relationships among Accounts and Processes*

| Account or Class of Transactions | Core Processes | | Resources Management Processes | | |
	Sales and Customer Service (1) [Chapter 11]	Supply Chain and Production [Chapter 12]	Facilities [Chapter 13]	Human Resources [Chapter 6, 7 and 13]	Capital and Investment [Chapter 13]
Assets					
Cash and short-term investments	Cash receipts	Cash payments	Cash payments	Cash payments	Cash receipts, Cash payments, Trading securities
Receivables	Sales, Receipts, Returns, Bad debts				Investment income
Inventory	Cost of goods sold	Purchases, Production, Inventory valuation	Depreciation (product cost)	Direct labor costs	
Plant, property and equipment including accumulate depreciation			Purchases of tangible assets, Asset disposals, Depreciation, Leased assets		
Investments					Purchase investments, Sell investments
Liabilities					
Accounts payable		Vendor payables			
Accrued liabilities (2)	Commissions	Indirect overhead costs	Maintenance, Utilities, Leases	Wages, Benefits, Payroll taxes,	Interest, Dividends, Income taxes, Deferred tax
Debt and borrowed funds			Mortgage payable		Borrow funds, Repay debt
Paid in equity capital					Sales of equity, Repurchase of equity
Retained earnings					Dividends, Net income

(Continued)

Table 10.6 *(Continued)*

| Account or Class of Transactions | Core Processes | | Resources Management Processes | | |
	Sales and Customer Service (1) *[Chapter 11]*	Supply Chain and Production *[Chapter 12]*	Facilities *[Chapter 13]*	Human Resources *[Chapter 6, 7 and 13]*	Capital and Investment *[Chapter 13]*
Income and Expense					
Sales, revenue and gains	Sales		Asset disposals		Investment income and gains
Cost of goods sold	Cost of goods sold	Costs of production, Cost allocation	Depreciation (product cost)	Direct labor costs	
Depreciation expense			Depreciation (period cost)		
Selling, general and administrative expenses			Maintenance, Utilities, Operating leases	Wages and related expenses	Interest expense
Tax expense (3)	Sales taxes		Property taxes	Payroll taxes	
Other Disclosures/Accounts					
Other (4)	Vendor rebates	Purchase commitments, Waste and spoilage	Interest capitalization, Impairments, Leasehold Improvements	Stock options, Pensions and post-retirement benefits	Off balance sheet items, Investment impairments

Notes: (1) Shaded cells indicate accounts and process that have no direct link under normal circumstances.
(2) Most prepaid current assets arise from the same sources as accrued liabilities.
(3) Income tax expense, income taxes payable and deferred taxes would be determined in a separate process.
(4) Most intangible assets are related to "other" business process such as "research and development" (patents), "brand management" (trademarks) or "mergers and acquisitions" (goodwill).

The Substantive Audit Program

The preparation of the plan for testing management assertions requires the auditor to draw upon all of his or her knowledge of the client organization. This knowledge includes the auditor's own prior experiences, as well as the risk assessments and other facts derived from the analysis of the client's environment and activities. Before an audit commences, the auditor will have some expectations of where problems are likely to occur and which accounts are most important based on a general understanding of the client's industry and prior-year audits. As a result, auditors often follow general guidelines when planning substantive testing, which are modified based on the actual results obtained during strategic and process analysis and the resulting residual risks.

Table 10.7 illustrates the relationships between risk of material misstatement and extent of substantive tests for the key management assertions associated with the accounts of a merchandising or manufacturing engagement. Accounts receivable and inventory are usually accounts with high risk of material misstatement. In both cases, the auditor is concerned with the occurrence of transactions and valuation of accounts so the amount of audit

Table 10.7 *Typical Merchandising or Manufacturing Engagement's Accounts and Associated Key Management Assertions Demonstrating the Relationship between Relative Risk of Material Misstatement and Relative Level of Substantive Tests*

Account	Key Management Assertions for Account	Risk of Material Misstatement	Typical Level of Substantive Tests
Cash	Existence Valuation	Low	Low
Accounts Receivable	Existence Valuation	Moderate	High
Inventory	Existence Completeness Rights Valuation	High	High
Land	Valuation Rights	Low	Low
Building	Valuation Rights	Moderate	Moderate
Accumulated Depreciation	Valuation	Low	Low
Investments	Existence Valuation Rights	Moderate	High
Accounts Payable	Completeness Valuation	Moderate	Moderate
Accrued Liabilities	Completeness Valuation	Moderate	Low
Common Stock Equity	Valuation	Low	Low

effort expended in those areas will be relatively high. Other accounts have varying risks of misstatement. Cash, fixed assets, accounts payable, and accrued liabilities usually are assessed as having a moderate risk of material misstatement. Cash is rarely a material account balance, but it is important because of the volume of transactions that flow through the account and the need to strictly control access to cash. Accounts payable and accrued liabilities are often subject to cut-off problems and unrecorded obligations. Fixed assets are usually highly material but may have only a few large transactions in a given period. Land and equity are usually subject to minimal testing since they usually have very few transactions in a given period. Accumulated depreciation often requires only that the appropriate amount has been allocated to expense in the current period. Some investments (especially financial instruments) may have a high risk of material misstatement due to the complexity of transactions, the valuation of securities, and specific disclosure requirements.

The embodiment of the risk assessments and selection of the nature, extent, and timing of audit procedures is the audit program. An example of a substantive audit program for one account, cash and cash equivalents, is presented in Table 10.8 (details of cash account audits are discussed in the Appendix to Chapter 11). The detailed set of procedures in this program is

Table 10.8 *An Illustrative Audit Program: Cash Accounts*

Step	Work-paper Reference	Audit Procedure	Relevant Management Assertion	Performed by whom?	Performed when?
1	A	Conduct a surprise count of cash and receipts on hand in the petty cash fund. Reconcile receipts to proper imprest balance.	Existence Completeness	WRK	12/30/x7
2	A-1-1 A-2-1	Arrange to obtain a bank confirmation as of 12/31/x7 and a bank cut-off statement as of 1/10/x8 for each of the primary disbursement accounts used by the company.	Rights	WRK	12/23/x7
3	A-1 A-2	Obtain a client-prepared bank reconciliation for each bank account as of 12/31/x7. Test each bank reconciliation using the following procedures: • Trace balance per bank to bank confirmation. • Trace balance per books to the general ledger and the cash lead sheet included in the workpapers. • Test the accuracy of the bank reconciliation. • Trace a sample of outstanding checks to the bank cut-off statement for proper clearance and to the cash disbursements journal. Verify that all items are recorded in the proper period. • Trace deposits in transit to the bank cut-off statement for proper clearance and to the cash receipts journal. Verify that all items are recorded in the proper period. • Trace other reconciling items to the appropriate supporting documentation and proper inclusion in the general ledger. • Obtain first and last check numbers used in 20x7 and perform cash disbursement cut-off test. • Prepare adjusting entries for any items requiring correction on the books of the company.	Existence Completeness Valuation	WRK	1/15/x8
4	A-2-2	Prepare a proof of cash for the main disbursement account used by the company.	Existence Completeness Valuation	WRK	1/15/x8

5		Select a sample of cash disbursements and trace to supporting documentation to verify proper processing.	Valuation Existence/ Validity		
6		Select a sample of cash receipts and trace to supporting documentation to verify proper processing.	Valuation Completeness		
7	A-1-1 A-2-1	Review minutes for meetings of the Board of Directors and other management committees for indications of restrictions on cash which should be disclosed. Also review loan agreements and other contracts.	Valuation	WRK	1/15/x8
8	AJE	Review the cash lead schedule and bank reconciliations for any items requiring disclosure, adjustment, or reclassification.	Valuation	WRK	1/15/x8
9		Other procedures deemed necessary due to current circumstances: Describe.	Dependent on procedure		

premised on a high risk of material misstatement for the cash account at this client thus requiring extensive substantive procedures given the need to set detection risk at low. This results in an audit program to generate extensive substantive evidence related to the account details, financial statement presentation, and disclosures associated with the cash and cash equivalent accounts. This program (see column three) includes extensive testing and reperformance of bank reconciliations, surprise cash counts, and extensive work on cash disbursements and receipts over and above what would be done as part of the sales and customer service and the supply chain management processes. Many clients would tend to have lower residual risks associated with the cash account (i.e., strong internal controls over cash to offset the high inherent risk of cash being misappropriated) hence, there would be a need for less substantive tests of cash and cash equivalents.

Substantive audit programs across multiple engagements often have a great deal of similarities. As a result, many firms use automated and standardized programs that are adaptable to specific client conditions, often by means of menu-driven inputs. The auditor must be watchful for circumstances where these programs are not appropriate, especially considering client specific factors that might not be captured in the standard set of planning inputs, and modify the audit approach accordingly. A high-quality audit program for substantive testing has a number of features:

- The audit program for substantive tests should include a comprehensive list of all substantive procedures to be performed, when they are to be performed, and guidelines for selecting the transactions, account balance details, or presentation and disclosure items to examine.

- The audit program for substantive tests should match procedures with management assertions to ensure that all assertions are adequately addressed conditioned on residual risk assessments. The matching of processes and accounts depicted in Table 10.6 helps assure complete coverage of the financial statements.

- The audit program should be easy to revise if new information or evidence becomes available that indicates that the risk assessments or other assumptions underlying the program are not accurate.

- The audit program should provide a mechanism to document the performance of procedures. As the audit program is a comprehensive list of procedures, there should be an indication made on the program as to whether each procedure has been performed, when it was performed, where the procedure is documented, and who did the work.

- Most large audit firms now achieve these goals by using automated systems to generate audit programs based on inputs for a specific client. A comprehensive and accurate audit program provides a record of the audit work performed on the engagement and is an effective control to ensure that all procedures are completed before the audit opinion is issued. Indeed, the latest documentation standards require that the audit program and the results of audit testing be sufficiently documented such that another auditor could re-perform the procedures, including selection of the same individual audited items, and arrive at the same conclusions.

Special Issues Related to Tests of Accounting Estimates

As noted in Chapter 9, accounting estimates, especially those that arise through the need to audit fair value of financial items that appear on the balance sheet, require special consideration by auditors. If the residual risk after carrying out the preliminary inquiries and tests of relevant controls relating to the estimates is anything but low then the auditor has to evaluate how management has assessed the effect of uncertainty on the accounting estimate. Further, the auditor has to evaluate the effect such uncertainty may have on the appropriateness of the recognition of the accounting estimate in the financial statements (as well as the adequacy of related disclosures). In other words, the relative degree of uncertainty with respect to the underlying assumptions that the estimate is based on needs to be considered when assessing whether the recorded estimate may be materially misstated. The auditor has to deal with the residual risks that are other than low through substantive tests so the auditor has to consider:

- Whether management has evaluated alternative assumptions or outcomes, and why it has rejected them, or how management has otherwise addressed estimation uncertainty in making the accounting estimate.

- Whether the significant assumptions used by management are reasonable.

- Management's intent to carry out specific courses of action, and its ability to do so, where relevant to the reasonableness of the significant assumptions used by management or the appropriate application of the applicable financial reporting framework.

In making these assessments the auditor needs to consider the extent and reasonableness of the analysis that management has carried out under alternative scenarios and the quality of the reasoning surrounding their conclusion as to the most appropriate assumptions. In particular the auditor needs to consider whether:

- The individual assumptions appear reasonable.
- The assumptions are interdependent and internally consistent.
- The assumptions appear reasonable when considered collectively or in conjunction with other assumptions, either for that accounting estimate or for other accounting estimates.
- The assumptions appropriately reflect observable marketplace assumptions, in the case of fair value accounting estimates.

AUTHORITATIVE GUIDANCE & STANDARDS

ISA 540 **Auditing Accounting Estimates, Including Fair Value Accounting Estimates, and Related Disclosures** *provides guidance to auditors in this area. PCAOB Interim Standards provides separate standards for auditing accounting estimates (PCAOB AS 2501 [formerly AU 342]* **Auditing Accounting Estimates***) and a more specific standard for fair value measurements (PCAOB AS 2502 [formerly AU 328]* **Auditing Fair Value Measurements and Disclosures***).*

When management's intent has significant impact on the assumptions employed in the accounting estimates, the auditor needs to also do the following:

- Review management's history of carrying out its stated intentions.
- Review written plans and other documentation, including, where applicable, formally approved budgets, authorizations or minutes.
- Inquire about management's reasons for a particular course of action.
- Review events occurring subsequent to the date of the financial statements and up to the date of the auditor's report that are relevant to the accounting estimates.
- Evaluate the entity's ability to carry out a particular course of action given its economic circumstances, including the implications of its existing commitments.

In essence, the auditor must have a sufficient basis for concluding that management has recognized the inherent uncertainty surrounding accounting estimates and has developed a well justified position, based on the relevant accounting standards, that supports management's estimates. Fair value estimates for financial assets and liabilities as well as for asset impairments provides their own unique challenges and will be covered further in Chapter 13.

Summary and Conclusion

We have described the basic approach to substantive testing of financial statements in this chapter. The auditor's strategy is simple in concept: select audit procedures that provide sufficient appropriate evidence on which to base an opinion of the fairness of management's assertions about transactions, accounts, and presentation and disclosure, both individually and for the financial statements taken as a whole. The audit program is dependent on the auditor's knowledge of current conditions and risk assessments for various components of audit risk, and reflects the auditor's materiality and tolerable error estimates, so as to provide an effective and cost-efficient method for gathering sufficient and appropriate audit evidence to support the auditor's opinion over the financial statements. Given that many of the elements of this process are subjective in nature, and new information is continuously being made available to the auditor, the audit program should be flexible so that the auditor can readily revise the program while producing a record of decisions made during the course of the audit.

In future chapters we will consider gathering and interpreting audit evidence for specific segments of the audit. Chapter 11 discusses the audit of the sales and customer service process, Chapter 12 discusses the audit of the supply chain and conversion process, and Chapter 13 discusses various resources management processes (including human resources, facilities, and financial management). For each process, we will prepare a process map; look at the significant management assertions that comprise affected transactions, accounts, and presentation and disclosure; and discuss sources and control of risks in the process. We will also discuss the types of testing decisions and choices that are described in this chapter in more detail. A key thought to keep in mind while studying future chapters is that the selection of substantive audit procedures, sample sizes, and transactions to test is risk-driven. The auditor's ultimate goal is to determine if the financial statements are free of material misstatements conditional on the knowledge obtained from strategic and process analysis including internal controls over financial reporting.

Bibliography of Relevant Literature

Research

Asare, S. K. and A. M. Wright. 2004. The Effectiveness of Alternative Risk Assessment and Program Planning Tools in a Fraud Setting. *Contemporary Accounting Research*. 21(2): 325–352.

Bedard, J. C. and L. E. Graham. 2002. The Effects of Decision Aid Orientation on Risk Factor Identification and Audit Test Planning. *Auditing: A Journal of Practice & Theory*. 21(2): 39–56.

Glover, S. M., J. Jiambalvo, and J. Kennedy. 2000. Analytical Procedures and Audit-Planning Decisions. *Auditing: A Journal of Practice & Theory*. 19(2): 27–46.

Messier, W. F., Jr. and L. A. Austen. 2000. Inherent Risk and Control Risk Assessments: Evidence on the Effect of Pervasive and Specific Risk Factors. *Auditing: A Journal of Practice & Theory.* 19(2): 119–132.

Smith, J. R., S. L. Tiras, and S. S. Vichitlekarn. 2000. The Interaction between Internal Control Risk Assessments and Substantive Testing in Audits for Fraud. *Contemporary Accounting Research.* 17(2): 327–356.

Professional Reports and Guidance

BDO Seidman LLP, Crowe Chizek and Company LLC, Deloitte & Touche LLP, Ernst & Young LLP, Grant Thornton LLP, Harbinger PLC, KPMG LLP, McGladrey & Pullen LLP, PricewaterhouseCoopers LLP, and W. F. Messier, Jr. 2004. *A Framework for Evaluating Control Exceptions and Deficiencies Version 3.* December 20. 22 pages. Located on-line at www. grantthornton.com/portal/site/gtcom/menuitem.91c078ed5 c0ef4ca80cd8710033841ca/?_vgnextoid=506aa3e0aec36010VgnVC M100000308314acRCRD&vgnextfmt=default. Accessed March 21, 2006.

Weil, J. (2004). Missing Numbers—Behind the Wave of Corporate Fraud: A Change in How Auditors Work—'Risk Based' Model Narrowed Focus of Their Procedures, Leaving Room for Trouble—A $239 Million Sticky Note. *Wall Street Journal* (March 25, 2004).

Auditing Standards

IAASB *International Standards on Auditing (ISA)* No. 200, "Overall Objectives of the Independent Auditor and the Conduct of an Audit in Accordance with International Standards on Auditing."

IAASB *International Standards on Auditing (ISA)* No. 300, "Planning an Audit of Financial Statements."

IAASB *International Standards on Auditing (ISA)* No. 315, "Identifying and Assessing the Risks of Material Misstatement through Understanding the Entity and Its Environment."

IAASB *International Standards on Auditing (ISA)* No. 320, "Materiality in Planning and Performing the Audit."

IAASB *International Standards on Auditing (ISA)* No. 330, "The Auditor's Responses to Assessed Risks."

IAASB *International Standards on Auditing (ISA)* No. 500, "Audit Evidence."

IAASB *International Standards on Auditing (ISA)* No. 540, "Auditing Accounting Estimates, Including Fair Value Accounting Estimates, and Related Disclosures."

IFAC. International Auditing and Assurance Standards Board (IAASB). 2015. *Handbook of International Quality Control, Audit, Review, Other Assurance, and Related Services Pronouncements.* New York: International Federation of Accountants.

PCAOB. *Auditing Standard* 1101 (formerly No. 8), "Audit Risk."

PCAOB. *Auditing Standard* 1105 (formerly No. 15), "Audit Evidence."

PCAOB. *Auditing Standard* 2101 (formerly No. 9), "Audit Planning."

PCAOB. *Auditing Standard* 2105 (formerly No. 11), "Consideration of Materiality in Planning and Performing an Audit."

PCAOB. *Auditing Standard* 2201 (formerly No. 5), "An Audit of Internal Control over Financial Reporting that is Integrated with An Audit of Financial Statements."

PCAOB. *Auditing Standard* 2210 (formerly No. 12), "Identifying and Assessing the Risks of Material Misstatement."

PCAOB. *Auditing Standard* 2301 (formerly No. 13), "The Auditor's Responses to the Risks of Material Misstatement."

PCAOB. *Auditing Standard* 2501 (formerly *Interim Standard* AU 342), "Auditing Accounting Estimates."

PCAOB. *Auditing Standard* 2502 (formerly *Interim Standard* AU 328), "Auditing Fair Value Measurements and Disclosures."

Notes

1   Statistical sampling of transactions will be discussed in more detail in Chapter 17.

2   The problem of auditor's underestimating risk is well described by J. Weil in a *Wall Street Journal* article entitled "Missing Numbers—Behind the Wave of Corporate Fraud: A Change in How Auditors Work—'Risk Based' Model Narrowed Focus of Their Procedures, Leaving Room for Trouble—A $239 Million Sticky Note" (March 25, 2004).

3   "Trivial" is generally accepted as being a small fraction of materiality in a quantitative sense. See BDO et al., 2004. *A Framework for Evaluating Control Exceptions and Deficiencies Version 3*. December 20. 22 pages. Located on-line at www.grantthornton.com/portal/site/gtcom/menui tem.91c078ed5c0ef4ca80cd8710033841ca/?_vgnextoid=50 6aa3e0aec36010VgnVCM100000308314acRCRD&vgnextfmt=default. Accessed March 21, 2006.

4   Even this rule is not universally followed, as some auditors do not distinguish between materiality and tolerable error—thus essentially setting them as being equal.

5   In practice most audits are planned before all control testing is completed and the program for substantive tests is based on the assumption that the level of reliance on internal control is going to be supported by the tests of controls. While this is an efficient approach to planning the audit, when a control test shows that a control cannot be relied on at the assessed level, this approach requires a large investment in revising the audit program in light of the new information of controls.

6   Different organizations have different processes. The ones we discuss here include the most common processes found in most organizations. Other processes that could be important to an organization include research and development, brand management, or mergers and acquisitions.

CHAPTER 11

Audit Testing for the Sales and Customer Service Process

Outline

Learning Goals for this Chapter

1. Apply our understanding of process analysis to the sales and customer service process.

2. Analyze the risk of material misstatement in the context of the sales and customer service process.

3. Apply our understanding of internal control over financial reporting audit to design, carry out, and evaluate tests of internal controls for the sales and customer service process.

4. Determine the level of residual risk based on outcome of internal control testing.

5. Plan substantive tests of account balances and transaction for the sales and customer service process (conditional on risk assessments).

6. Design and execute substantive tests of account balances and transactions for the sales and customer service process.

7. Document evidence related to the sales and customer service process.

8. Conclude whether an appropriate level of audit evidence has been collected to support the auditor's opinion with respect to the sales and customer service process.

Introduction

Having completed our discussion of risk assessment and planning substantive procedures, we now turn to the audit of specific processes within an organization. We will decompose the audit into core processes and then discuss the risks, controls, audit issues, and evidence pertinent to each process. Given that all significant or material transactions are affected by at least one major process, cumulative audit consideration of the processes within an organization should provide sufficient appropriate evidence (see Chapters 14 and 15) on which to base an opinion about the financial statements.

We will first consider the audit of sales and customer service in a typical manufacturing or merchandising company (see Figure 11.1). We start with this set of processes for a number of reasons. First, the activity in this process represents the "earnings process" of most companies. Second, this process has a heavy volume of routine transactions, so internal control considerations, including internal control over financial reporting and the assessment of control risk, are important. Third, sales in a retail environment can readily be generalized to sales of services (i.e., professional service time is analogous to inventory to be sold). Finally, a relatively small number of account balances are affected by the transactions (e.g., sales, receivables, cash, and inventory), so we can concentrate our discussion on the residual risks and tests associated with the activity in this process. Table 11.1 presents a summary of the accounts affected by the sales process.[1]

To facilitate our discussion, we will use a process map and internal threat analysis to highlight the important characteristics of sales and customer service that could have an impact on the conduct of the audit. In the next section, we will discuss the basic objectives and activities of sales and customer service. We will then discuss the specific transactions that occur within these

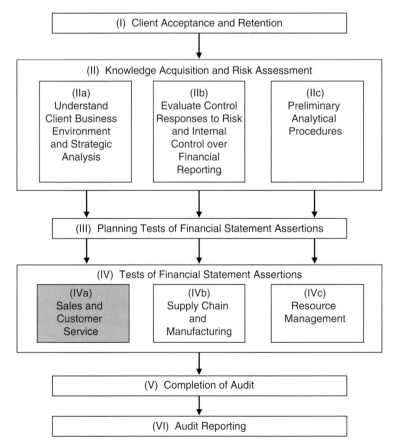

Figure 11.1 An Overview of the Audit Process

Table 11.1 *Relationships among Accounts and Processes*

Account Area or Class of Transactions	Core Processes		Resources Management Processes		
	Sales and Customer Service [Chapter 11]	Supply Chain and Production [Chapter 12]	Facilities [Chapter 13]	Human Resources [Chapters 7, 13]	Capital and Investment [Chapter 13]
Assets					
Cash and short-term investments	Cash receipts	Cash payments	Cash payments	Cash payments	Cash receipts, Cash payments, Trading securities
Receivables	Sales, Receipts, Returns, Bad debts				Investment income
Inventory	Cost of goods sold	Purchases, Production, Inventory valuation	Depreciation (product cost)	Direct labor costs	
Plant, property, and equipment including accumulate depreciation			Purchases of tangible assets, Asset disposals, Depreciation, Leased assets		
Investments					Purchase investments, Sell investments
Liabilities					
Accounts payable		Vendor payables			
Accrued liabilities	Commissions	Indirect overhead costs	Maintenance, Utilities, Leases	Wages, Benefits, Payroll taxes,	Interest, Dividends, Income taxes, Deferred tax
Debt and borrowed funds			Mortgage payable		Borrow funds, Repay debt
Paid in equity capital					Sales of equity, Repurchase of equity
Retained earnings					Dividends, Net income
Income and Expense					
Sales, revenue, and gains	Sales		Asset disposals		Investment income and gains
Cost of goods sold	Cost of goods sold	Costs of production, Cost allocation	Depreciation (product cost)	Direct labor costs	
Depreciation expense			Depreciation (period cost)		

Selling, general, and administrative expenses			Maintenance, Utilities, Operating leases	Wages and related expenses	Interest expense
Tax expense	Sales taxes		Property taxes	Payroll taxes	
Other Disclosures/ Accounts					
Other	Vendor rebates	Purchase commitments, Waste and spoilage	Interest capitalization, Impairments, Leasehold Improvements	Stock options, Pensions and post-retirement benefits	Off balance sheet items, Investment impairments

processes, the nature of process risks, and types of internal control. Finally, we will use our understanding of the process to illustrate how the auditor reaches conclusions about residual risks and designs specific tests of financial statement assertions that are related to sales and customer service.

AUTHORITATIVE GUIDANCE & STANDARDS

This chapter applies standards covered in previous chapters to a specific business process—sales and customer service. Several observations from auditing standards are included throughout the chapter (e.g., ISA 320 **Materiality in Planning and Performing an Audit***, ISA 330* **The Auditor's Responses to Assessed Risks***, ISA 500* **Audit Evidence***; AS 2105 [formerly 11]* **Consideration of Materiality in Planning and Performing an Audit***, AS 2301 [formerly 13]* **The Auditor's Responses to the Risks of Material Misstatement***, AS 1105 [formerly 15]* **Audit Evidence***). These standards provide the basic template for all evidence gathering activities in an audit and underlie much of what is discussed in Chapters 11 to 13. Rather than repeatedly refer to these standards we note at the beginning of each Chapter that they underlie the entire subject matter of the chapters.*

An Overview of Objectives and Activities Related to Sales and Customer Service

The sales and customer service process make up the set of activities by which goods and services are sold and delivered to customers in return for immediate or future payments. This process includes customer service activities both in support of sales and after sales have occurred (e.g., sales returns or warranty claims). This process does not include the acquisition or manufacture of goods and services, although sales activities can have important implications for how management approaches supply chain management and manufacturing.

Process Objectives

Figure 11.2 depicts a general process map for sales and customer service. In order to meet its sales targets, a company must design the sales and

Process Objectives

- Create product awareness within target market and enhance brand images.
- Increase customer base and the proportion of repeat customers.
- Match price and quality to achieve desired share of target market.
- Maximize revenue opportunities.
- Minimize sales returns.
- Minimize customer credit problems and collect cash on a timely basis.
- Minimize transactions costs for sales, collections, and returns.
- Continually improve customer satisfaction.
- Deliver goods and services on a timely basis.
- Minimize loss of assets due to theft or misuse.
- Capture and effectively utilize customer information.
- Capture, process, and report information necessary for process improvement

Process Activities

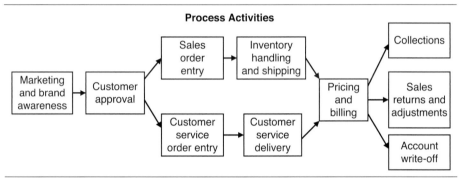

Process Data Streams

Information Feeds	Information Generation
• Strategic plan and budget	• Marketing and advertising plans
• Competitive data	• Sales forecasts
• Consumer research	• Customer transactions
• Marketing and promotion programs	• Revisions to customer files
• Customer data	• Changes in inventory levels
• Product attributes and specifications	• Customer satisfaction and retention
• Inventory levels	• Customer complaints and resolution
• Delivery options and times	• Collections, returns, write-offs
• Payment options	• Market share and related statistics
• Pricing and discount policies	
• Customer service policies	

Accounting Impact of Activities

Routine Transactions	Non-Routine Transactions	Accounting Estimates
• Sales and revenue	• Bad debt write-offs	• Bad debt expense
• Cash receipts	• Price adjustments and promotions	• Warranty claims
• Sales returns	• Valuation of returned inventory	
• Cost of goods sold	• Vendor allowances or rebates	
• Sales related expenses		
• Advertising and marketing costs		

Figure 11.2 Process Map: Sales and Customer Service

customer service process to carry out the strategy adopted by the company. Objectives mostly pertain to maximizing revenue by creating products and services that match price and quality to those demanded by customers, building a reputation for high quality or low prices, meeting or exceeding customer expectations, and delivering appropriate products or services on a timely basis. Failure to meet one or more of these objectives could lead to increased business risk for the organization, and might eventually result in organizational failure.

Process Activities

The typical activities that make up sales and customer service are indicated in Figure 11.2, although organizations design processes that are unique to their own strategy and objectives:

- **Marketing and Brand Awareness**: A company must deliver a message to prospective customers that attracts them to its products and services. Market research, advertising, telemarketing, special promotions, and brand development are ways in which a company tries to get its message to target customers. The more recognized a brand, the easier it is to get customers to consider a product. The emphasis on marketing and brand awareness is driven by the competitiveness and customer make-up within an industry. A highly competitive industry (e.g., commercial banking) or highly dispersed customer base (e.g., consumer products) requires extensive marketing and brand awareness. Conversely, a smaller industry with few customers (e.g., airplane manufacturers) places less emphasis on these activities.[2]

- **Customer Approval:** If marketing and advertising are effective, customers will wish to purchase the company's products and services. However, customers must be screened and approved to assure that they are legitimate and have the ability to pay for products and services. Customer approval may be simple, as in obtaining a credit card authorization, or can be more complex, as when the company extends credit directly to the customer. Minimizing credit risks is an important objective of this activity. Customer screening becomes even more important in an on-line environment, where credit card fraud and identity theft can be serious problems.

- **Sales Order Entry**: Once a customer is approved, the details of the transaction must be determined. The customer's desires can be communicated by personal visit (e.g., to a retail store), letter, telephone call, customer purchase order, or web site, and are matched to the available products and services.

- **Inventory Handling and Shipping**: Inventory is selected, packaged, and prepared for shipment. Items may be picked up by customers, or shipped by mail, parcel post, or company delivery vehicles. The choice of distribution channel will impact the actual steps performed in the process. Timely and error-free shipments are an important objective of this activity.

- **Customer Service Order Entry**: In the case of after sales services, schedules must be assigned and arrangements made for performance of the service. If the service involves repairs, parts need to be obtained. For warranty work, authorization is needed to perform the service at no charge to the customer.

- **Customer Service Delivery:** The timely provision of quality customer service can greatly influence customer satisfaction. Given that customer

[i]EXAMPLE

Many retailers have both a physical location and an on-line site, but in some cases retailers may only exist on-line without a physical retail location. The extent to which technology is used to process orders can vary dramatically across such organizations. Some retailers use a web site to provide product information but not to accept customer orders (e.g., car manufacturers). Others accept on-line order entry on the web site, but they do not allow on-line orders to link to internal systems so that on-line orders must be transferred or processed manually (some travel booking web sites need manual intervention to confirm certain types of travel or lodging reservations). The most sophisticated on-line retailers (e.g., Amazon.com) link on-line activity directly to internal systems to control product movement, order processing, and supply chain activity. The complexity of these different approaches varies significantly and can affect the auditor's evaluation of process risks.

service requires the interaction of company personnel with customers, the staff's professionalism, training, and general demeanor can have a direct impact on achieving organizational objectives.

- **Pricing and Billing**: Appropriate prices must be assigned to goods and services and communicated to customers. Pricing can range from quite simple to very complex. Most grocery stores, convenience stores, bookshops, and electronics stores set prices based on manufacturer suggestions and local competition. More complicated is pricing of airline or insurance services, situations in which every individual customer may receive a different price based on sophisticated analysis by the company.

- **Collection**: Payments from customers are received in various forms, including cash, checks, gift certificates, credit memos, in-house credit, and payments from third parties (e.g., bank credit cards, PayPal). These payments must be captured, protected from theft and credited to the appropriate customer.

- **Sales Adjustments:** Sales returns are the most common form of adjustment. Incoming merchandise must be processed and inspected, and proper refunds or credits issued to customers. Another example of a sales adjustment is a retroactive price change.

- **Account Write-Offs**: In the event that a customer is unable to pay amounts owed, a process should exist to attempt collection and to authorize removal of receivables in the event that collection is impossible.

The complexity of these processes will depend on the strategic and process decisions of the organization. Some of the decisions that could affect these activities include:

- The marketing strategy of the company (Advertising? Special promotions?)
- The method of delivery of goods or services (Customer pick-up or delivery?)
- The timing and form of customers' payments (Is cash involved?)
- Policies on sales returns and adjustments (Return to store or mail-in?)
- The extent of computerization in transaction processing (Web-based?)

For example, organizations can adopt different strategies for marketing products, ranging from subtle media exposure to print advertising and from web-site popups to televised infomercials. Similarly, distribution channels can differ across companies; for example, the delivery of merchandise is much different for a retail company with physical stores than it is for an on-line retailer. At the same time, the handling of customer payments is different for cash purchases, credit card charges, web based intermediaries like PayPal, and direct company credit. Returns may require significant inventory handling and repackaging. Finally, the extent to which computers automate transaction processing affects how a process is performed[i].

The information flows associated with sales and customer service are illustrated in Figure 11.2. Information requirements focus on competitor, customer, and product data as well as on pricing, payment, and delivery policies. Information outputs from the process include marketing activities, transaction data, and changes to customer and product records. Feeding

(ii)**EXAMPLE**

A drop in demand for a product may necessitate a change in restocking procedures. The sooner information related to a change in demand can be communicated along the supply chain; the less likely excess inventory will build up at the company or the supplier. In a similar vein, the better the ability to capture pricing information from competitors and feed it into its marketing efforts, the better able the company is to nimbly respond to competitive pressures. Airlines, booksellers, and consumer electronics retailers are particularly effective at tracking competitor pricing.

information from marketing and sales into planning and production activities is particularly important to facilitate the organization's response to changed market and competitive conditions[ii].

Transactions Arising from Sales and Customer Service Process

A number of accounts and transactions are affected by the sales and customer service process, as indicated in Figure 11.2. The most common transactions in this process are sales, receipts, returns, and bad debts. The key steps in handling sales, collections, and related transactions are described in Table 11.2 and discussed below.[3]

Table 11.2 *Summary of Sales and Customer Service Activities*

Process/Activity	Documents	Journals, Ledgers and Records Used	Typical Journal Entry
SALE TRANSACTION			
Sales order entry: An incoming communication from a prospective customer begins the sales process.	Customer purchase order (external) Sales order (internal)		
Credit approval: The customer is investigated to determine if sale on credit is appropriate.		Approved customer list	
Shipping: Items to be purchased are prepared for delivery or pickup.	Bill of lading (internal)		
Pricing/Billing: Appropriate pricing assigned and total billing amount computed.	Sales invoice (internal)	Price list Sales journal	
Receivable posting: Credit sales are posted to appropriate receivable accounts (e.g., customer or credit card agency).		Receivable posting: Credit sales are posted to appropriate receivable accounts (e.g., customer or credit card agency).	
General accounting: The sale, receivable and reduction of inventory are recorded in the appropriate accounts.	Journal entry ticket (internal)	General ledger	Dr. Accounts Receivable Cr. Sales
COLLECTION TRANSACTION			
Receipt capture: Payments are opened, identified, and separated from other documents. A cash prelist is prepared.	Customer check (external) Remittance advice (internal)	Cash prelist	
Receipt processing: Customer and payment information is verified and receipts are deposited.	Deposit slip (internal)	Cash receipts journal	
Receivable posting: Payments are posted to the payer's account.		Accounts receivable subsidiary ledger	
General accounting: Payments are recorded in the appropriate accounts.	Journal entry ticket (internal)	General ledger	Dr. Cash Cr. Accounts Receivable

(Continued)

Table 11.2 *(Continued)*

Process/Activity	Documents	Journals, Ledgers and Records Used	Typical Journal Entry
SALES RETURN TRANSACTION			
Returns processing: Returned goods are processed and an appropriate refund or credit issued to the customer.	Credit memo (internal) Inventory ticket (internal)	Sales returns journal	
Receivable posting: Credit is entered into payer's account (e.g., customer or credit card agency).		Accounts receivable subsidiary ledger	
General accounting: The return of goods and the refund are recorded in the appropriate accounts.	Journal entry ticket (internal)	General ledger	Dr. Sales Returns Cr. Accounts Receivable
BAD DEBT WRITE-OFF			
Uncollectible account processing: Overdue accounts are reviewed and uncollectible accounts removed.	Write-off authorization (internal)		
Receivable posting: Amounts to be written off are removed from customer balances.		Accounts receivable subsidiary ledger	
General accounting: Write-offs of account balances are recorded in the appropriate accounts.	Journal entry ticket (internal)	General ledger	Dr. Bad Debt Allowance Cr. Accounts Receivable
BAD DEBT ESTIMATION			
Estimation: Future bad debts are estimated from payment history and financial status of customers.	Worksheet (internal)	Aged receivables trial balance	
General accounting: Estimated bad debt expense is recorded in the appropriate accounts.	Journal entry ticket (internal)	General ledger	Dr. Bad Debt Expense Cr. Bad Debt Allowance

Sales: A *sales* transaction for a manufacturer typically starts with sales order entry, which produces a *sales order* that is forwarded to the credit department for approval. The approved sales order then serves as an authorization for shipping. The shipping department will release the requested items and prepare a *shipping document* (often called a *bill of lading*) as evidence of the shipment. The shipping document becomes the basis for billing the customer, via a *sales invoice*, after prices and terms have been determined. Sales invoices are separately posted to the *accounts receivable ledger* and accumulated in the *sales journal* (which is usually the basis for recording sales).

The key event in the sales process is the delivery of the goods to the customer. At this point, the earnings process is substantially complete and the company should recognize the occurrence of a sale transaction. The shipping document (or bill of lading) is the boundary document for the transaction. In many systems, however, the invoice is used to recognize sales because prices are not usually entered on shipping documents.

Organizations that primarily sell goods and services to other businesses, or that sell to on-line customers, primarily conduct sales through automated processes, including **electronic data interchange (EDI) systems**. These systems link sales and inventory systems together so that suppliers of goods are authorized to ship new inventory to a customer when certain conditions occur (a low level of inventory on hand) rather than having to wait to receive a formal sales order. Furthermore, the shipment of goods triggers the subsequent cash collection process without separate sales invoices being sent (although for on-line sales, customers are usually sent e-mail notification of shipments).

Collections: **Cash receipts** encompass all payments received from customers. Incoming payments in the form of cash or checks must be captured by the system, credited to the proper account, and deposited in a bank. Most companies use **remittance advices** for customers to send with their payments to facilitate proper processing. Returned remittance advices are the boundary documents proving the receipt of a payment. Incoming payments are accumulated on a **cash prelist** by the mail-room (or other recipient) and then passed on for further processing. Checks are separated from remittance advices and deposited. Payments are entered in the **cash receipts journal**—the basis for recognition of receipts in the general ledger—and are posted to customers' accounts. Posting of customer balances and preparation of the cash receipts journal is often computerized, whereas the initial processing of incoming receipts is done manually[(iii)].

Organizations that primarily sell goods and services to other businesses or that sell to on-line customers primarily receive payments electronically through **electronic funds transfers (EFTs).** For business-to-business (B2B) transactions, such transfers typically involve the customer's bank sending a cash payment electronically to the seller's bank. A confirmation of the transfer is also sent directly to the company receiving the payment (also electronically). When utilized as part of an EDI system, the transfer occurs based on pre-specified terms that have been built into the system (e.g., payment upon presentment). Overall, automated systems that involve both the sales and collections process can dramatically reduce the cost of transaction processing for both the seller and buyer.

Sales Returns: The key activities in the sales return process are refunding customer payments or granting customer credit, and restocking returned goods in inventory (if they can be resold). Typically, a sales return will be evidenced by a **credit memo** and, possibly, a separate **inventory ticket** to show receipt of merchandise.

Bad Debt Estimation: As discussed in Chapter 9, various estimates need to be made by management. On a periodic basis, typically when financial statements are prepared, a company will assess the realizable value of existing receivables. Based on previous experience and current economic conditions, the company will predict what portion of receivables will become uncollectible even though they may not be overdue at the moment. This is an example of an estimate where the purpose is to forecast the result of a transaction that has already occurred. An estimate of uncollectible accounts is usually developed based on a review of different categories of accounts included in the **accounts receivable subsidiary ledger**. Typically,

[(iii)]EXAMPLE

Wal-Mart requires all of its suppliers worldwide to be part of its extensive EDI system. The company's sales system is linked to its ordering and collections systems so that when goods are sold to consumers in stores, suppliers are notified electronically that Wal-Mart has made a sale and that the supplier should ship new goods to replace what has been sold (i.e., the sales order for the supplier is generated automatically based on Wal-Mart's sales records).

accounts are classified by the time that has passed since a sale was made using an **accounts receivable aging schedule.** For example, a retailer might estimate that 2 percent of all current accounts are uncollectible, but estimate that 10 percent of accounts more than 30 days past due are uncollectible, 40 percent of accounts more than 60 days past due are uncollectible, and so on. The financial statements are then adjusted to reflect the resulting estimate of bad debts.

Bad Debt Write-Offs: Delinquent customer accounts should be periodically reviewed and removed from the receivables ledger if they are deemed to be uncollectible. The write-off of an account is evidenced by a **write-off authorization**. The write-off of an account does not mean that collection efforts cease, only that the accounts receivable balance should be adjusted to reflect its realizable value. Accounts that are subsequently collected can be reinstated as the need arises. This process is different from bad debt estimation in that direct write-offs are non-routine transactions that require specific investigation and authorization. This process is meant to ensure that proper measures are taken to collect overdue accounts, whereas bad debt estimation is performed to ensure that expenses are properly matched with revenues in each reporting period.

Vendor Allowances and Rebates: Retailers often have a choice of products to sell, manufacturers to deal with, and may have concerns about whether products that are selected will be sold at a price that provides an adequate margin to justify the decision to stock the product. To encourage retailers to carry their product, manufacturers will often provide **vendor allowances or rebates**.

These allowances or rebates may serve as an incentive for a retailer to sell an item or to allocate it prominent display space. They may also be used to share any loss that arises from discounting slow-moving inventory. Vendor allowances and rebates may take many forms: (1) a direct reduction in the amount owed by the retailer to the manufacturer, (2) a discount on future purchases from the manufacturer, or (3) vendor payments for joint vendor–retailer advertising. Regardless of the form of the rebate, accounting rules require that these allowances be recorded as a reduction in costs of goods sold in the period in which the deal is negotiated[iv].

Risk Assessment for Sales and Customer Service

An internal threat analysis used for risk assessment in sales and customer service is illustrated in Table 11.3. Column 1 of Table 11.3 lists a number of risks that could arise within sales and customer service. A number of potential process risks are identified in the first column and then linked to possible entity level and process level controls that could be used to mitigate and monitor the risks. The list of risks is not intended to be comprehensive and could differ across organizations depending on the design of their sales and customer service activities. Furthermore, the controls are intended to be illustrative rather than complete.

Table 11.3 *Risk Assessment: Sales and Customer Service*

Process Risks	Entity and Process Level Controls Linked to Risks	Performance Measures
(1) Failure to provide unique product value.	• *Consumer research.* • *Research on competition.* • *Clear strategy and goals.* • *Effective capital budgeting procedures.* • *Specific guidelines for product introduction and evaluation.*	• *Market share by product line.* • *Price point relative to competition.* • *New customer acquisition rate.*
(2) Failure to respond to customer needs.	• Send monthly statements to customers. • *Establish system for obtaining satisfaction ratings and feedback from customers.*	• *Customer satisfaction ratings.* • *Customer retention rates.* • Transaction cycle time. • Processing time.
(3) Excessive credit risk.	• Segregate credit approval from sales processing. • Maintain and monitor current credit limits for approved customers. • Perform credit checks on new customers. • Review existing accounts for potential collection problems. • Maintain history of bad debt experiences.	• Delinquency rates. • Percentage of receivables written off. • Receivable turnover and time-to-collect. • Average age of customer balances. • Average customer balances.
(4) Failure to deliver product or service on a timely basis.	• Maintain a file of open orders and review for completion. • *Utilize alternative shipping channels.* • *Maintain contingency plans.*	• Transaction cycle time. • *Shipping and on-time delivery statistics.* • *Frequency of product shortages or partial shipments.*
(5) Unauthorized, incorrect or inappropriate shipments.	• Shipment authorized by credit and sales departments. • Shipments verified against supporting documentation.	• Number of incorrect shipments. • Merchandise returns. • Customer complaints related to delivery.
(6) Inaccurate or unauthorized pricing.	• Maintain master price list. • Establish standard payment terms. • Automate pricing and billing information.	• *Percentage of transactions with price adjustments.* • *Average size of price adjustments.* • Number of pricing errors.
(7) Excessive returns or price adjustments.	• Establish clear policy and procedures for accepting returns. • *Monitor competitor offers.*	• Merchandise returns as a percentage of sales. • Average cost per return.
(8) Excessive fraud, inventory shrinkage or theft.	• Control access to inventory. • Establish clear lines of responsibilities and authority over transaction processing. • Segregate incompatible activities. • Establish procedures for handling cash receipts. • Independent authorization of unusual transactions or account write-offs.	• Shrinkage statistics. • Differences between perpetual inventory records and actual counts. • Time to collect statistics. • Delinquency rates.
(9) Inaccurate information processing.	• Proper completion and verification of supporting documents. • Appropriate segregation of duties across activities. • Use of standard control numbers for accounts, products, etc. • Update files and accounting records on a timely basis.	• Percentage of transactions subject to processing errors. • Size of transaction adjustments. • Number of transaction adjustments.

(Continued)

Table 11.3 *(Continued)*

Process Risks	Entity and Process Level Controls Linked to Risks	Performance Measures
(10) Failure to capture desired information.	• Use and verify prenumbered documents for transactions. • Record all events and transactions on a timely basis.	• Number of missing documents from sequence. • Number of missing fields in customer records.
(11) Excessive customer service costs.	• *Proper training of customer service personnel.* • *Establish policies on appropriate customer service levels and monitor performance.*	• *Service costs as a percentage of sales.* • *Service costs per customer.* • Merchandise return rates. • Warranty claims.
(12) Failure to link supply chain and production to sales activity.	• *Supply chain integration and information sharing.* • *Sales forecasting and joint marketing/production planning.* • *Establish standards for supplier qualifications.*	• *Percentage of product shortages.* • *Length of product backlog.* • *Time delay in filling backlog.*
(13) Improper accounting for vendor allowances or rebates.	• Document vendor allowance agreements. • Monitor vendor allowances on a per buyer basis. • Establish vendor allowance policies (e.g., discounts, advertising, etc.).	• Vendor allowances per buyer. • Total vendor allowances compared to competitors.

Note: Items in *italics* tend to be more rarely examined in practice.

Potential sources of risk can interact to influence the existence and significance of actual risks within a process. Some risks may affect multiple areas of an organization. Furthermore, strengths in one area may offset weaknesses in other areas. For example, effective process design and use of technology could partially compensate for poorly trained or unethical employees. Similarly, regulatory attention can offset a tendency toward operational inefficiency or ineffectiveness. In the case that management is incompetent, employees are poorly trained and motivated, process technology is inadequate, or operations are poorly structured, the level of process risk would be significantly heightened. Of particular importance to the auditor is the interaction of technology and information risks, especially as it affects the flow of information within the process and the links to financial reporting.

Analysis of Process Controls

Different types of controls may be used to mitigate different risks. Recall from our earlier discussions that the company has four options for responding to a specific risk: accept, avoid, share, or reduce[v].

Column 2 of Table 11.3 describes the process controls that could be used to address process risk. Examples in the sales and customer service process include:

1. Segregation of duties: Some duties within a process are likely to be incompatible, and failure to achieve adequate separation of these activities could create opportunities to commit fraud or allow processing errors to go undetected. For sales and customer service, we should see a number of duties separated:

   (1) Credit approval and sales entry,

   (2) Cash receipt handling and receivable posting, and

[v]**EXAMPLE**

Accepting credit cards (e.g., Visa) is one way to share credit risk with another party. Implementing strict guidelines for granting credit to a customer and placing limits on the amount of credit awarded to individual customers are ways to reduce or control credit risk internally.

(3) Data processing and transaction authorization.

2. Processing controls: These controls reflect a broad range of procedures including required authorizations, use of adequate documents and records, and independent verification of information. For sales and customer service, appropriate authorization procedures should be specified for granting credit, setting prices, releasing shipments, and accepting sales returns. Appropriate documents should be used within the process including order entry forms, shipping documents, invoices, and remittance advices, all of which should be prenumbered and used in sequence (see Table 11.2). Finally, there are numerous aspects of the process that may be subject to independent verification including reviewing and comparing documents for discrepancies, checking batch and control totals (see Chapter 7), monitoring open transactions, and investigating customer complaints or discrepancies. Many of these procedures are directly relevant to the auditor's evaluation of internal control over financial reporting.

3. Physical controls: Limiting access to tangible assets, cash, and accounting records is helpful for minimizing risks arising from unauthorized decisions or actions. The receipt of cash is an area where physical control is particularly critical.

Many of the controls described in Table 11.3 may be either manual or automated. Controls related to transaction documentation and verification are especially amenable to computerization. The selection of control procedures for a process depends on the structure of the process, the significance of the various risks, and the cost of implementing specific controls. Given that every company has a slightly different set of activities and risks, each will have a slightly different set of controls. Many controls may be adapted to different risks. The controls listed in Table 11.3 provide a good starting point for an auditor's analysis, although not all procedures will be applicable to, or needed by, all companies.

Entity Level Controls over Sales and Customer Service

Box 11.1 "Testing Internal Controls Related To Sales And Customer Service" describes entity level controls that might be effective for reducing the risks related to sales and customer service. In sales and customer service the entity level controls might include controls for actively monitoring risk conditions and timely responses to increased risk. Within sales and customer service processes, the auditor should expect to see effective monitoring of the following:

- Competition (e.g., new products and marketing efforts).
- Customer attributes (e.g., tastes).
- Technological advances.
- Operational effectiveness (e.g., risks affecting delivery performance, employee morale, customer returns, and processing errors).
- Overall performance (e.g., sales and profitability relative to targets).

BOX 11.1 TESTING INTERNAL CONTROLS RELATED TO SALES AND CUSTOMER SERVICE

Entity Level Controls: Performance Reviews and Overall Process Management

- *Review policies for establishing strategy, goals, and budgets for marketing, product innovation, customer service, and sales activity.*

- *Evaluate whether policies and decisions related to sales and customer service are consistent with the overall strategy and objectives of the organization.*

- *Review and evaluate internal analyses related to competitors, customers, marketing efforts, and market conditions.*

- *Examine documentation in support of key decisions related to sales and customer service.*

- *Review sales and marketing plans and budgets and verify that variances have been investigated.*

- *Review receivables reports and verify timely handling of adjustments and bad debts.*

- *Evaluate competence and training of key individuals within the process.*

- *Discuss performance measures and process evaluation with appropriate management and evaluate whether process oversight is effective.*

- *Identify and review appropriate performance indicators relevant to key process risks.*

Detailed Internal Controls over Financial Reporting

Information Processing Controls

Proper Authorization Procedures

- *Verify existence and use of general authorization related to prices (master price list), credit approval (approved customer lists and credit limits), shipping and payment terms and account classifications (chart of accounts).*

- *Review the process for revising general authorizations.*

- *Obtain a sample of sales documents and verify that all required approvals are properly noted on the documents.*

Use of Adequate Documents and Records

- *Verify that documents are prenumbered and used in sequence including shipping documents, sales invoices, and receipt lists.*

Independent Verification of Employee Responsibilities

- *Verify that all exception reports and computer edit listings are followed up and cleared on a timely basis.*

- *Obtain a sample of sales documents and verify that all required verifications are properly noted on the documents, including evidence of posting.*

- *Obtain sample of receipt lists and remittance advices and verify that all required verifications are properly noted on the documents, including evidence of posting.*

- *Verify that proper reconciliations are performed on a timely basis for (1) sales journal and receivable postings, (2) receipts journal and receivable postings, and (3) bank reconciliations and receipts journal.*

Physical Controls

- *Observe a sample of facilities and client personnel for control over access to assets, documents, and records.*

Segregation of Duties and Process Design

- *Verify that appropriate segregation of duties exists for sales activities.*

- *Discuss work responsibilities with employees assigned to transaction processing and evaluate effectiveness and consistency of individual responsibilities and authority.*

- *Examine procedures manuals, personnel policies, organization charts, the chart of accounts, and other documents and records used in the system.*

- *Identify and evaluate significant changes within the process occurring in the past year.*

One specific type of entity level control would be review of management's monitoring controls such as performance indicators. Appropriate performance indicators for the identified process risks are listed in Table 11.3 in the third column. These measures cover a number of areas including:

- Financial performance: Sales levels and profitability provide an indication of the overall success of sales and customer service. Therefore, the auditor should examine growth in sales, trends in profitability, and profit margin ratios.

- Market performance: Statistics on market share and customer satisfaction provide direct measures of how the market views the company's sales and service efforts. Customer acquisition and retention rates can be particularly useful in gauging market reactions.

- Process performance: In general, financial and market performance are driven by process performance. Consequently, statistics for delivery time, transaction closure rates, costs per transaction, and delivery error rates are particularly helpful.

In deciding which performance indicators to examine and evaluate, the auditor must consider both the cost of obtaining the information and the reliability of the information. Unless a company has a well-developed and fully integrated information system, such as an ERP system, some of the measures identified in Table 11.3 may be difficult to obtain. Financial results extracted from the basic accounting system are likely to be the most reliable performance measures, whereas operating statistics that are generated from other systems or using standalone spreadsheets may be less reliable. Performance measures that are subjective in nature (e.g., customer satisfaction and employee morale) are also potentially unreliable unless gathered in a systematic and rigorous manner.

An auditor would examine the key performance measures for specific risks that are of concern (i.e., potential residual risks). For example, declining market share, deteriorating customer satisfaction, and increased delivery and service delays could indicate heightened process risk. To illustrate, consider the situation where the rate of customer delinquency is increasing, receivable turnover is decreasing, sales adjustments are increasing, and customer complaints are on the rise. This pattern of results would suggest weaknesses in the collection of receivables that have been billed to customers. The auditor would need to consider the implications of high residual credit risk. Presumably, the auditor would then expect that bad debt expense or sales returns should increase and the percentage of receivables reserved against future losses should be growing. These expectations could be compared with actual results to evaluate the risk of material misstatement for relevant financial statement assertions, e.g., the valuation of receivables.

Negative performance indicators can also put stress on credit managers to improve performance by becoming overly aggressive with customers or imposing overly strict conditions on customer credit. Worse still, managers may attempt to disguise actual results. These behavior patterns are not in the best interests of the company and could have important implications for the auditor's assessment of the control environment. In short, a pattern of negative performance measures would lead to increased risk assessments for some aspects of sales and customer service.

Analysis of Internal Control over Financial Reporting

Of particular concern to most auditors are process controls affecting financial reporting. Because most audit-sensitive processes generate transactions that are included in the financial statements, the auditor must be concerned that transaction processing is accurate. Table 11.4 lists a number of controls and associated management assertions at the account level that would be appropriate for sales and customer service processes.

Sales: The critical controls for sales are those related to shipping, pricing, and billing. The utmost concern to the auditor is that all sales are recorded (completeness), all recorded sales represent sales to genuine customers (existence), and that the valuation of transactions accurately reflects the quantity shipped, the prices charged, and the payment terms (accuracy). Other controls address the creditworthiness of customers and the accuracy and timeliness of transaction posting (cut-off and classification). Because sales transactions tend to be routine for many organizations, auditors should expect the presence of many automated controls for sales. In fact, auditors should be wary of any system that contains material manual journal entries for sales. At a minimum, the organization should have well-designed controls to prevent and detect any unauthorized or unreasonable adjusting entries to sales.

Receipts: The most critical concern for receipts is control over cash and checks upon taking possession and prior to deposit in order to minimize the chance that receipts may be lost or misappropriated (occurrence). The immediate creation of a cash list by the cashier or mailroom clerk opening the mail is essential for capturing transactions (completeness). After the list is prepared, misappropriation of cash or checks is difficult because missing

Table 11.4 *Internal Controls over Financial Reporting for Sales-Related Transactions*

Transaction	Management Assertion	Typical Internal Controls for Sales-related Transactions (with relevant management assertions in parentheses)
Sales	Occurrence (O) Completeness (C) Accuracy (A) Cut-off (T) Classification (CL)	Maintain a list of approved customers (O, C, CL). Segregate credit approval from sales activity (O, C, A). Maintain up-to-date approved credit limits for existing customers (A). Use prenumbered sales, shipping, and billing documents in sequence (O, C, A, T). Utilize automated system (e.g., point-of-sale system) to track all sales by operations personnel, including any discounts offered, etc. (O, C, A, T, CL). Provide indication of credit approval in documentation (O). Verify quantities shipped against the shipping document and sales order (O, C, A, T). Provide indication of shipment in documentation (O, C, T, CL). Verify prices charged for items shipped (O, C, A). Verify extensions and totals on invoice (C, A). Post transactions on a timely basis (O, C, A, T, CL). Use control and hash totals to verify accuracy of postings (C, A). Customer account numbers and product numbers should contain check digits (C, A). Match and verify all documents (O, C, A, T). Maintain up-to-date chart of accounts (C, A, CL). Reconcile general ledger totals and activity with subsidiary ledger and supporting journals (C, A, T, CL). Utilize automated systems to post all routine sales transactions with proper access controls for enabling adjusting journal entries (O, C, A). Review all adjusting journal entries prior to entering (O, C, A, T, CL). Investigate unusual entries to accounts (O, C, A T, CL).
Cash receipts	Occurrence (O) Completeness (C) Accuracy (A) Cut-off (T) Classification (CL)	Obtain item counts of incoming payments (C, A, T). Automate receipts through use of electronic funds transfers handled by qualified third-parties (e.g., banks, PayPal) (C, A, T). Separate initial handling of receipts from other accounting functions and sales-related activities (O, C A). Prepare list of all cash receipts immediately (O, C, A, T). Do not accept cash payments through mail (O, C, A). Use prenumbered receipts for cash transactions (O, C, T). Restrictively endorse all checks received as "for deposit only" (O, C). Use lock box system (O, C). Compare amount received to amount per remittance advice (O, C, A). Separate checks from remittance advices and prepare timely bank deposit (O, C, T). Verify that payments agree with quoted terms (e.g., discounts, time period, interest) (O, C, A, T). Post transactions on a timely basis (C, T). Use control and hash totals to verify accuracy of postings (C, A). Reconcile bank accounts independently of receipt processing and posting (O, C, A). Reconcile general ledger totals and activity with subsidiary ledger and supporting journals and records (e.g., bank deposits, cash listing) (C, A, T, CL). Send monthly statements to customers (O, C, T).

(Continued)

Table 11.4 *(Continued)*

Transaction	Management Assertion	Typical Internal Controls for Sales-related Transactions (with relevant management assertions in parentheses)
Sales return processing	Occurrence (O) Completeness (C) Accuracy (A) Cut-off (T) Classification (CL)	Use prenumbered credit memos (C). Record credit memos on a timely basis (T). Require approval of sales returns by operations personnel not directly interacting with customers (O, C). Segregate preparation of credit memos from cash receipt processing (O, C). Prepare receiving reports (prenumbered) of returned goods on a timely basis (O, C, T). Reconcile amounts per credit memo with documentation of original sale and "cancel" original sales documents to prevent duplicate returns (O, C, A).
Write-off processing	Occurrence (O) Completeness (C) Accuracy (A) Cut-off (T) Classification (CL)	Prepare an aged receivables trial balance on a regular basis (C, A, T, CL). Review overdue accounts periodically (O, T, CL). Keep customer correspondence files related to overdue amounts current (O, C, T, CL). Approve write-offs by someone independent of the sales and cash receipt functions. Use prenumbered documents to evidence write-offs (C, T).
Bad debt estimation	Occurrence (O) Completeness (C) Accuracy (A) Cut-off (T) Classification (CL)	Maintain bad debt historical data (A). Review assumptions underlying estimation procedures for appropriateness (O, C, A). Review calculation procedures for deriving estimates, possibly automating them based on estimation assumptions as inputs to the system (C, A).

(vi)EXAMPLE

Many previous accounting frauds involve fictitious sales throughout the year that are "hidden" by creating adjusting journal entries to write-off fictitious sales or transfer them to other accounts. Another common accounting problem arises when an organization sells service contracts that extend over a period of time at the same time a product is sold. It is then important that the sales price of the bundled products and services be properly allocated to current and future revenue.

funds will create a discrepancy between the receipt list and subsequent processing. Additionally, customers are encouraged to return a remittance advice with a payment to minimize the risk of incorrect processing or posting (completeness, accuracy, and classification).

An alternative to direct handling of cash receipts by the company is use of a third party receipt service, such as a bank, or on-line transfer of funds. The former system requires customers to mail payments directly to the company's bank. The processing of receipts becomes the bank's responsibility and many of the control procedures listed for receipts then become unnecessary. The bank provides a report to the company listing the customers and the amounts of the receipts, which the company can use to post its accounts (occurrence, completeness, accuracy). Of course, the bank charges a fee for this service and the cost of using the bank has to be weighed against the improvement in control that is gained(vi).

Sales Adjustments and Bad Debts: Still other controls pertain to the risks arising from sales adjustments and bad debts. Proper authorization procedures are particularly important for sales adjustments and bad debts (occurrence). Additionally, accurate processing of adjustments and write-offs is fostered through the use of appropriate documents and records (e.g., credit memos) and independent verification of individual transactions and transaction batches (completeness, accuracy, cut-off, classification).

A company may have different systems and controls to respond to different situations and events. One type of transaction may be well controlled (e.g., mail-orders), whereas another may be subject to significant processing errors (e.g., cash sales with immediate delivery). It is the responsibility of the auditor to develop an adequate understanding of processing controls and controls over financial reporting to support an assessment of control risk for key assertions affected by a process. When assessing control risk, the auditor must consider all possible circumstances, not just the most common. An organization implementing a large number of the procedures listed in Box 11.1 "Testing Internal Controls Related To Sales And Customer Service" and Table 11.4 would probably have moderate-to-low control risk for most assertions related to sales and customer service, especially if many of the controls are embedded in a well-designed, automated information system. Absence of such controls may indicate the existence of a significant deficiency in internal control over financial reporting.

Testing Internal Control over Financial Reporting

The purpose of tests of controls in a GAAS Audit is for the auditor to obtain support for the auditor's decision that the auditor can rely on important internal controls to reduce the risk of material misstatement. Not all identified controls need to be tested by the auditor. The controls of primary importance for all audits are those that shift risk from a significant level to an acceptable level. Some examples of controls that can be tested in the sales and customer service process are described in Box 11.1 "Testing Internal Controls Related To Sales And Customer Service" and Table 11.4. Tests of controls related to sales and customer service tend to emphasize proper authorization of transactions, including the establishment of credit, the release of inventory, the pricing of inventory, the billing of customers, and the timing of payment. The auditor would also want to know how the company initiates, approves, and implements changes to these authorization policies.

Many of the control tests involve interviewing individuals within the process. The auditor needs to clearly understand what each person does, how he or she fits into the overall structure of the process, and whether he or she has the training and expertise to effectively perform his or her tasks. Obtaining this information usually involves interviewing numerous staff, line, and low-level managerial personnel as part of a walkthrough of the process. Although individual responses do not provide strong evidence of process effectiveness, the overall consistency of the information, especially if provided from multiple individuals as part of a well-planned interview program (as discussed in Chapter 9), can provide assurance about the effectiveness of controls.

Auditors commonly examine a sample of transactions for documentary evidence of proper approval and processing. For example, the auditor could look at the credit manager's sign-off on a sales order to verify that credit has been approved. Proper release of goods for shipment may be evidenced by the warehouse supervisor's signature on the shipping document. This type of evidence must be interpreted carefully, however, because signatures and initials do not guarantee that the transaction was actually processed correctly. That is, a credit manager may sign off on a sale without actually doing a credit check.

Other forms of documentation include obtaining exception reports (especially if generated by an automated system) and determining whether problems are handled promptly and appropriately, reviewing official policies and comparing them for consistency with information obtained from process personnel, and examining internal reports used for monitoring process performance. The last form of documentation is particularly important because it highlights that the performance measures, if effectively monitored and acted upon by management, can be a strong source of evidence about the effectiveness of internal control.

In some situations, it is possible to observe process personnel in the performance of their duties. Observation should be as unobtrusive as possible to obtain an accurate impression of the seriousness and reliability of the personnel responsible for a key control. Also, observation may need to be repeated under different conditions and at different times, especially if the client has a change in personnel related to important controls.

The current trend of linking information systems across organizations is changing the way that auditors think about documents and organizational boundaries. Customers and suppliers use electronic data interface (EDI) to improve the efficiency of transaction processing and to reduce the costs of holding and moving inventory. In an EDI system, major suppliers of an organization directly monitor inventory levels at the customer and determine what and when to ship to the customer. Sales orders are nearly instantaneous, including the electronic transfer of funds (EFT) to make payments, and avoid traditional (and cumbersome) procurement processes and documents. Although the use of information technology and general authorization of transactions improves the efficiency of a process, electronic linkages make the supplier and customer much more dependent on each other. Integrated systems are one form of a strategic alliance in which information processing risks of one party become information processing risks of the other party, meaning that auditors must consider such risks *for both organizations*.

For automated systems, it may not be possible to test controls without involving an information systems (IT) assurance expert. Most large accounting firms have a specialized group of information systems experts who are qualified to examine technical documentation and analyze program code to determine whether automated controls are well designed and operating effectively. For public company audits, it is now expected that at least one member of the engagement team will have such specialized expertise.

Control Tests of Sales Transactions

Figure 11.3 provides examples of control tests that could be performed in the sales and customer service process classified by type of control activity (i.e., authorization, adequate documents and records, etc). Recall that we discussed the testing of controls over sales in detail as part of the JJ Mean Company example in Chapter 7. Figure 7.3 documents the sales internal controls in a flowchart; Table 7.3 employs an Internal Control Questionnaire to document specific controls, relates them to management assertions and documents weaknesses in the controls that are specific to the example company. Table 7.4 demonstrates how internal controls are then selected for testing as well as the implications for substantive tests where controls are not well designed or inefficient to test. The related discussion in Chapter 7 under the heading of "An Example of Internal Control Evaluation and Control Risk Assessment" should be reviewed to refresh your memory of the nature of control testing over the sales process.

Conclusions about Residual Risks from Sales and Customer Service

After completing a process map and internal threat analysis, the auditor should have adequate knowledge and evidence to assess the residual risks in a process that are potentially significant. Risk assessments are documented in a risk map as illustrated in Figure 11.3 for a few of the risks we have discussed related to sales and customer service. The initial assessment of a risk is indicated by a box. Risks that are located in the upper right of the graph are considered to be potentially significant residual risks. These residual risks are then considered by the auditor in developing his or her risk of material misstatement at the assertion level within the sales and customer service process. Risk reduction due to internal control is indicated by shifting a risk down and to the left. When risks are reduced due to controls, especially controls related to financial reporting, the auditor must **test the controls** to support the risk reduction that is being relied upon in planning the audit's substantive tests. Final risk assessments, after consideration of tests of controls (both entity level and process level), are indicated with a star.

Identifying Significant Residual Risks

Our example in Figure 11.3 indicates that risks from excess returns (risk 7) are reduced to an acceptable level by internal control. Tests of controls for excess returns would be performed by reviewing the company's returns policy and interviewing appropriate process personnel to verify that it is applied effectively. Also, documents could be examined for a sample of unusual sales returns. Figure 11.3 indicates that controls over information processing are

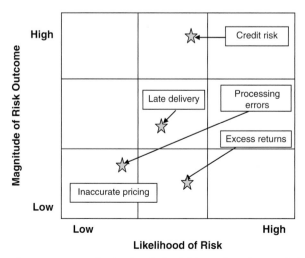

For ease of exposition, not all risks identified in Table 11.3 have been included in the risk map. This does not imply that omitted risks are less important. The risks that are included were chosen for illustrative purposes only.

Figure 11.3 Assessment of Process Risks for Sales and Customer Service*

particularly important (e.g., see risk 9 in Table 11.3). Since these controls are likely to pertain to financial reporting, the auditor would test the most important procedures, including verifying documentation and observing segregation of duties if necessary.

It is also important to note when controls do not need to be tested. For example, controls over credit risk may not need to be tested in a GAAS Audit because they may not reduce the risk associated with collectability of accounts receivable to an acceptable level. There will be significant residual credit risk in any event.

The risk map depicted in Figure 11.3 provides the support necessary to reach conclusions about residual risks related to sales and customer service. In this example credit risk would be classified as a residual risk that potentially leads to risk of material misstatement with respect to account receivable balances. The auditor must analyze the implications of this risk for the conduct of the audit and subsequent tests of financial statement assertions. As previously noted, residual risks can affect the auditor's assessment of expected financial results, the quality of the control environment, the viability of the company, or the likelihood of accounting misstatements.

A high level of credit risk in a firm suggests that receivables and bad debts could have high risk of material misstatement related to the valuation assertion. This analysis conditions the auditor's expectations about the collectability of receivables. Furthermore, these risks would cause the auditor to design tests of the affected financial statement assertions to gather enough evidence to conclude that the assertions in question were not materially misstated. In the remainder of this chapter, we will discuss substantive tests that can be used if specific financial statement assertions related to sales and receivables have a high risk of material misstatement. Given that different substantive tests are used for different assertions, the auditor selects the substantive tests that are relevant for the specific high residual risk assertions.

Planning Tests of Management Assertions: Revenue and Accounts Receivable

The purpose of substantive tests of financial statement assertions is to provide direct evidence that an account is not materially misstated. A comprehensive approach for substantive testing of accounts receivable is summarized in Table 11.5 linking management assertions to typical substantive testing procedures. Substantive audit procedures for revenue and receivables include substantive analytical procedures and various types of tests of details:

- Tests of sales transactions.
- Tests of the accuracy of the aged receivables trial balance.
- Confirmations.
- Cut-off tests.

Table 11.5 *Substantive Tests for Accounts Receivable Account Assertions*

Management Assertion	Typical Substantive Audit Procedures
Existence: All recorded transactions related to receivables occurred and recorded receivables exist.	• Confirm accounts receivable and follow up on exceptions and nonresponses. • Vouch a sample of sales and collection transactions from the period.
Completeness: All receivable transactions and balances have been recorded.	• Confirm accounts receivable and follow up on exceptions and nonresponses. • Vouch a sample of sales and collection transactions from the period.
Valuation: Transaction detail included in subsidiary journals and ledgers agrees with the general ledger balances related to receivables.	• Obtain an aged receivable trial balance as of the close of business on the last day of the fiscal period. • Test the accuracy of the aged trial balance. • Reconcile the total per the aged trial balance with the receivable balance per the general ledger. • Select a sample of accounts in the aged trial balance and test the aging by examining the appropriate supporting documentation. • Reconcile activity per the sales journal, cash receipts journal and postings to the accounts receivable subsidiary ledger with recorded activity in the general ledger receivables account.
Valuation: Transactions have been recorded in the proper period.	• Vouch transactions (sales, receipts, returns) prior to and after the fiscal year end and determine if they have been recorded in the proper period.
Valuation: Receivables are recorded at the appropriate gross amount and uncollectible amounts have been properly estimated.	• Confirm accounts receivable and follow up on exceptions and nonresponses. • Examine supporting documentation of delinquent accounts and make an assessment of the likelihood of collection. • Develop an estimate of future uncollectible amounts. • Vouch a sample of sales and collection transactions from the period. • Vouch cash receipts subsequent to year end for indications of collectability of delinquent accounts.
Valuation: Receivables are properly classified.	• Examine aged trial balance for unusual accounts that should be reclassified (credit balances, related parties, notes receivable).
Ownership: Receivable balances are owned by the company.	• Review Board of Directors' minutes, bank confirmations, attorney letters, and other correspondence to identify receivables have been factored. • Obtain representations from management about ownership of receivables.

- Tests of revenue recognition.
- Tests of receivable valuation.

This list of procedures is intended to be very broad and few engagements would require extensive use of all of these tests unless the risk of material misstatement was considered to be high for a large number of assertions. Also, the extent of the procedures (i.e., sample size in Chapter 17) would be adjusted for assessed risk levels. Some of the identified audit procedures provide evidence relevant to multiple assertions (e.g., confirmations test existence *and* valuation), whereas other procedures pertain to a single assertion (e.g., testing the accuracy of the aged trial balance).

Substantive Analytical Procedures

Expectations for many sales and collection-related accounts can be reasonably estimated using the client's financial and operating data. For example, if the company is able to provide reliable data for the number of units sold, the auditor can develop an estimate of sales revenue by multiplying the units sold by average prices. The reasonableness of revenues can then be tested by comparing this estimate with recorded sales.

AUTHORITATIVE GUIDANCE & STANDARDS

Professional standards (i.e., IAASB International Standards on Auditing [ISA] 520, Analytical Procedures and PCAOB Auditing Standard 2305 [formerly AU 329] Substantive Analytical Procedures) provide overall guidance on the use of substantive analytical procedures as audit evidence. Chapter 9 provides an in-depth discussion of the strengths and weaknesses of these procedures overall.

Consider sales commissions as an example: If the company pays a 10 percent commission on sales—as verified against published employment policies— and total sales are $125,000, the auditor would estimate commission expense to be $12,500. If the company has recorded commission expense of approximately $12,500, the auditor could conclude that the account balance is reasonably accurate and may perform no further testing. What does the auditor do if the recorded commission expense is much lower, perhaps $8,500? In that situation, further investigation is needed to determine the cause of the discrepancy.

To gather additional evidence, the first step should be to determine if the estimation method is reasonable. For example, the auditor may not know that there are actually two commission rates, with a lower rate of 5 percent being used for some products. With that new information, the auditor could re-estimate commission expense:

	10% rate	5% rate
Sales revenue subject to commission	$70,000	$55,000
Commission rate	× 10%	× 5%
	$7,000	$2,750

The total estimated commission is now $9,750, which is closer to the recorded balance of $8,500. This result may or may not be acceptable to the auditor; however, the fact that the estimate still exceeds the actual balance by 14.7 percent could concern the auditor since the difference may be due to unrecorded commissions. If the auditor is aware that the client records commissions when they are paid at the time of the bi-weekly or monthly payroll, the results may suggest that the year-end accrual of commissions' payable has not yet been recorded.

Further refinement of the estimate could be obtained by breaking sales down by location or product line. A well-accepted principle underlying substantive analytical procedures is that the finer the level of detail that is analyzed, the more likely the auditor is to spot any problems or misstatements that may exist. However, the auditor must keep in mind that each refinement of the computation requires more information. Additionally, the reliability of the information used as input must be considered. As the level of detail of the computation increases, so does the amount of effort needed to perform the analytical procedure.[4]

Substantive Tests of Transactions

Typical substantive tests of sales transactions are described in Box 11.2 "Substantive Tests of Management Assertions Related to Sales and Receipts Transactions." Most of these tests rely heavily on the documents and records produced during transaction processing. The auditor may be able to combine selected tests of transactions and tests of controls. For example, the auditor can verify approvals on documents (test of controls) at the same time that sales prices, quantities, and extensions are being verified (substantive test of transactions). These tests are referred to as *dual-purpose tests* because they facilitate simultaneous testing of the effectiveness of controls and the accuracy of transactions.

BOX 11.2 SUBSTANTIVE TESTS OF MANAGEMENT ASSERTIONS RELATED TO SALES AND RECEIPTS TRANSACTIONS

Sales Processing

Occurrence, Accuracy, Timing, Classification: *Select a sample of sales transactions from the sales journal. Obtain the related invoices along with all supporting documentation.*

Perform the following tests and note any exceptions found:

* *Trace customer to approved customer list and compare to approved credit limits.*
* *Compare quantities per sales order, shipping document, and invoice.*
* *Trace price to appropriate master price list.*
* *Recompute extensions and footing of invoice.*
* *Trace invoice to proper inclusion in the sales journal.*
* *Compare date shipped per shipping document to date posted to the sales journal.*
* *Trace invoice to proper posting in the accounts receivable subsidiary ledger.*
* *Test accuracy of customer record in the subsidiary ledger.*
* *Vouch subsequent payment of invoice including validity of discounts taken and interest charged (if any).*
* *Test the accuracy of the sales journal. This may be done on a sample basis by selecting a few days and testing the daily totals and then aggregating the daily totals to test the period totals.**

Completeness: *Select a sample of shipping documents from the prenumbered sequence and trace to proper inclusion in the sales journal, noting the existence of an invoice and the date of posting.*

Receipt Processing

Occurrence, Accuracy, Timing, Classification: *Select a sample of receipt transactions from the cash receipts journal and obtain the related remittance advices and other supporting documentation. Perform the following tests and note any exceptions found:*

- *Trace the remittance advice to proper inclusion in the appropriate receipt listing.*
- *Trace the remittance advice to proper inclusion in the appropriate duplicate deposit slip.*
- *Trace the remittance advice to proper and timely posting to the accounts receivable subsidiary ledger.*

Completeness, Accuracy: *Test the accuracy of the cash receipts journal. This may be done on a sample basis. Compare daily totals to totals per the receipt listing and deposit slip.*

*Note that this test could also be performed as a substantive test of account balances if the test is performed after year end and the entire period is included in the test.

AUTHORITATIVE GUIDANCE & STANDARDS

Dual-purpose tests are discussed as part of the standard on performing procedures in response to assessed risks (ISA 330, AS 2301).

The testing of the occurrence/existence assertion for sales transactions requires a different approach than the testing of the completeness assertion. For the occurrence/existence assertion, the auditor starts with the transactions that have been recorded as evidence in the detailed sales records (i.e., the sale transactions listed in a Sale Journal or Cash Receipts Journal that link to the recorded amounts in the financial statements). The auditor selects a sample of transactions from those listed in the primary transaction journals and examines all supporting documentation for the transactions selected. This approach is particularly useful for testing occurrence, accuracy, classification, and cut-off.

To test the completeness assertion the auditor starts with the original customer order documents (e.g., a purchase order from a customer) that indicates a customer has ordered a particular good or service. The auditor's goal is to select from among company created documents that are prepared closest to the point of initiation for a transaction. The documents are then traced to the primary journal listing all transactions (e.g., the Sales Journal) to see if the transaction has been properly included. For example, an auditor might draw a sample of sales orders from customers and trace the items to proper inclusion in the appropriate transaction journal.

The auditor must be confident that he or she has identified the appropriate population to examine and that the sample is representative of the entire population. For example, if the auditor is selecting sales from the Sales Journal, he or she would want to be assured that the entire list of sales is available for sample selection.[5] Figure 11.4 graphically summarizes the need to sample from two different sources in order to test for both the occurrence/existence and the completeness management assertions.

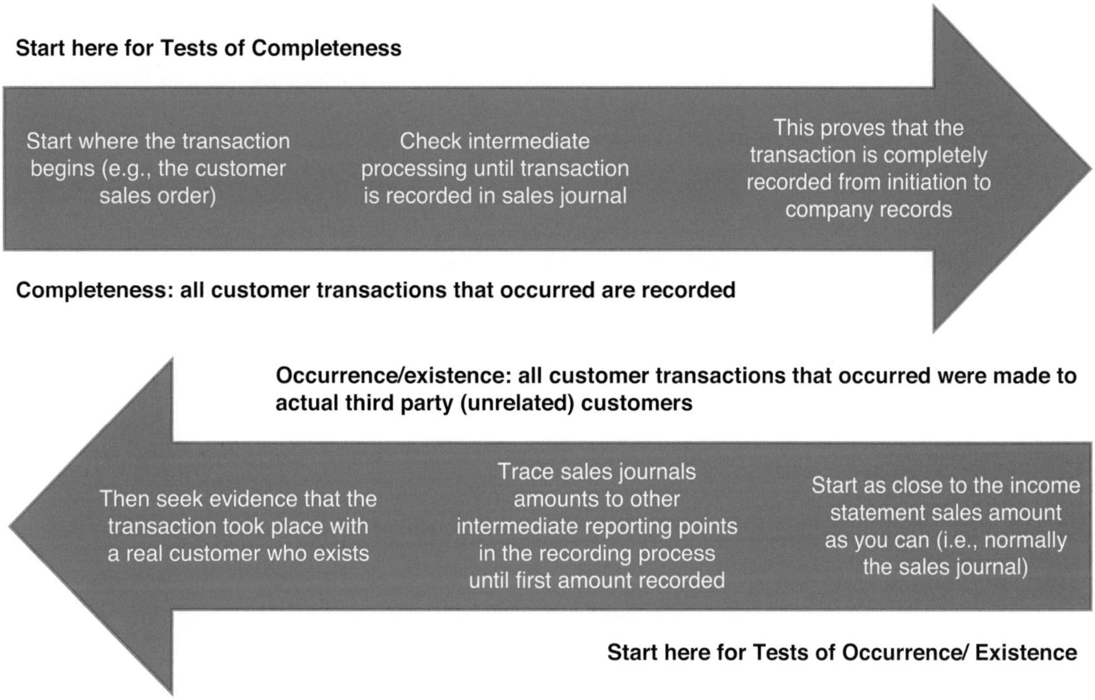

Start here for Tests of Completeness

Start where the transaction begins (e.g., the customer sales order)

Check intermediate processing until transaction is recorded in sales journal

This proves that the transaction is completely recorded from initiation to company records

Completeness: all customer transactions that occurred are recorded

Occurrence/existence: all customer transactions that occurred were made to actual third party (unrelated) customers

Then seek evidence that the transaction took place with a real customer who exists

Trace sales journals amounts to other intermediate reporting points in the recording process until first amount recorded

Start as close to the income statement sales amount as you can (i.e., normally the sales journal)

Start here for Tests of Occurrence/ Existence

Figure 11.4 Direction of Testing for Occurrence/Existence and Completeness Management Assertions Related to Sales Transactions

Substantive Tests of the Aged Receivables Trial Balance

The purpose of testing the aged trial balance is to assure the auditor that all receivables have been identified and that the details in the subsidiary ledger agree with the general ledger. The auditor could test the subtotals per the aged trial balance and reconcile those totals with summary totals in the general ledger. Additionally, the auditor might test the aging of individual customer accounts in order to determine if the client has accurately identified accounts that are overdue, as this information is also important for the auditor's assessment of the allowance for uncollectible accounts. These types of tests are becoming less common since such accounting operations are generally performed by computer. However, auditors should always use professional judgment to assess the reasonableness of assumptions used to estimate bad debts.

Confirmations

Confirmations are considered to provide high-quality evidence because they are obtained from sources outside the company. Confirmation of accounts receivables is mandatory in all engagements in the US and Canada but is not required if (1) receivables are not material to the financial statements, (2) the use of confirmations would not be effective, or (3) the auditor has assessed risk of material misstatements related to receivables at a low enough level that sufficient appropriate evidence can be obtained from other tests and procedures. The use of confirmations is often a time-consuming and costly process, and the reliability of the evidence may not be as good as hoped. Key decisions by the auditor about the confirmation process can have a significant impact on the quality and cost of evidence from confirmations.

AUTHORITATIVE GUIDANCE & STANDARDS

ISA 505 **External Confirmations** *provides international guidance on confirmations of all types, including accounts receivable. ISA 505 does not mandate confirmation of accounts receivables but many national audit standard setters require such confirmations with limited exceptions. Current PCAOB standard AS 2310 (formerly AU 330)* **The Confirmation Process** *differs from ISA 505 on many of the detailed issues but the substance is similar. The PCAOB is proposing to release a revised standard for discussion in 2016 after an attempt in 2010 to propose revisions was not well received in the comment process. The 2010 PCAOB discussion paper included questions of whether broader guidance is needed beyond just receivables, similar to the scope of ISA 505.*

The first decision that an auditor makes is whether to use the positive or negative form of confirmation. When the auditor uses a ***positive confirmation***, he or she expects an answer from a customer either confirming or disconfirming facts about their account and will evaluate the evidence received based on the nature of the response. In the event the customer disagrees with the account balance or other information about their account, the auditor must use alternative procedures to verify the information. When the auditor uses a ***negative confirmation***, he or she expects a response only when the customer *disagrees* with the reported balance. No response from a customer is considered to be evidence that the balance is valid but does not imply that the account is correctly stated. Positive confirmations are considered to be more reliable than negative confirmations and are preferred by auditors when large balances are being confirmed, risk of material misstatements are considered to be high, or there is a question about the recipient's willingness or ability to respond.

Once the decision is made to use positive or negative confirmations, or a combination of both, the auditor (or the client under the auditor's direction) prepares the confirmation requests.[6] A sample of a positive confirmation is presented in Figure 11.5. A confirmation request should originate from the client but the response should be returned to the auditor. The recorded balance (e.g., $5,237) is indicated in the request. An alternative method that is occasionally used, especially with very large balances, is to leave the amount blank and have the customer enter the balance according to his or her records. If the auditor uses the negative form, the bottom of the request would direct the recipient to respond only if he or she disagreed with the indicated balance (thus, a negative confirmation cannot be blank).

Next, the auditor chooses the customers to whom to send confirmation requests. The selection of accounts to confirm should be made by the auditor, not management. The size and selection of the sample will depend on residual risk, the materiality of receivables (in total and individually), the

---

Jones Manufacturing, Inc.
Gainesville, Florida

January 6, 20x8

Brown & Son
2020 N. Market Street
Gainesville, FL 32602

Dear Sirs:

Our financial statements are currently being examined by the auditing firm of Smith & Company, CPAs (Gainesville, Florida). In connection with this examination, we ask that you examine the information provided below related to your account with us. Please confirm directly to our auditors whether you agree or disagree with the correctness of this information.

This is not a request for payment. Please do not send payment to our auditors. Your prompt attention to this request is greatly appreciated. A stamped, self-addressed envelope is enclosed for your reply.

Edgar Jones
Edgar Jones, Controller

Smith and Company, CPAs
Gainesville, Florida

Please check one of the following:

_____ The balance of **$5,237** owed by us to Jones Manufacturing as of December 31, 20x7 is correct.

_____ The balance of **$5,237** is not correct for the reasons noted below:

_____
_____
_____

Date: _____   Signed: _____

Figure 11.5 *Example of Accounts Receivable Positive Confirmation*

number of accounts, the number of sales personnel handling customer accounts, the level of desired detection risk, the results of other audit tests, and results obtained in prior years. For example, if there are a few large accounts that make up most of the receivables balance, a few positive confirmations may suffice.

After the auditor has made the relevant decisions concerning the use of confirmations, a number of practical considerations must be taken into account. It is critical that the auditor maintain control over the confirmations at all times. Confirmations that are accessible to client personnel are of questionable value as audit evidence because the auditor cannot be assured that the responses have not been improperly altered. The auditor can have the client prepare the confirmations but must check each request for accuracy and maintain strict control over them thereafter. This means that the auditor should personally mail the requests outside the client's facilities. Also, confirmations should be returned directly to the auditor's office.

The auditor should maintain a control list of mailed confirmation requests, including the date sent and date returned. For positive confirmations, the auditor should send second and third requests if no response is received. The control list should document the nature of the response (i.e., agreement or disagreement with the reported balance). Finally, the control list is used to compute the percentage of accounts receivable that are actually confirmed.

If the auditor is unable to obtain a response to a positive confirmation request, alternative procedures should be performed to determine if the customer's balance is correctly stated. The alternative procedures typically involve examining supporting documentation of sales (similar to tests of transactions), customer correspondence (for evidence of disputes), and receipts subsequent to year-end that indicate the customer has paid the balance. Requests that are returned by the post office as being undeliverable may indicate that the client's billing system is out-of-date or the customer does not exist. In either case, the auditor must be concerned with the implications of such evidence as it relates to the existence and valuation of receivables and potential problems in the internal control system.

In recent years other approaches to confirming accounts receivable have been increasingly used by auditors and permitted by standard setters. For electronic confirmations (e.g., by FAX or email), control may appear to be less than with traditional postal mail approaches to confirmations as they may cause the auditor unfamiliar problems with authenticity of the response or the authority of the respondent, and making alterations to a confirmation more difficult to detect. An electronic confirmation process might use encryption and electronic digital signatures to validate the identity of the sender of information. Further, commercial companies like Confirmation.com can establish secure systems that will electronically connect an auditor with various client customers in a secure electronic environment. However, standard setters still clearly state that an oral confirmation via a telephone or Skype conversation is not sufficient evidence to claim an account has been confirmed.

Finally, the auditor must follow up on every response that indicates possible disagreement between the client and the customer. Many of these disagreements will be due to timing differences (e.g., the customer's check is in the mail or a shipment is in transit). The explanations for these differences must be clearly documented but they are not considered misstatements. Some differences may reflect actual errors in the client's records, e.g., a sale recorded at an incorrect amount or a payment received that was not posted to the customer's account. The accounting records should be adjusted for these errors and the auditor should consider the impact of errors on the overall risk of material misstatement.

To illustrate, if the auditor sent positive confirmations to 20 percent of large accounts and negative confirmations to 5 percent of small accounts, the auditor's assessment of potential misstatement must consider the results obtained for each group. If there were errors detected totaling $25,000 in the large balances and $1,000 in the small balances, the auditor could estimate the total misstatement of accounts receivable as follows:

Large balances: $125,000 ($25,000/0.2; sample is 20% of large balances)

Small balances: $20,000 ($1,000/0.05; sample is 5% of small balances)

Total estimated A/R misstatement: $145,000 3% of $5 million balance

However, because the auditor did not look at all items in the account, the $145,000 estimate could be either too high or too low because there may be a range of possible misstatements in an account. Consequently, the auditor must use professional judgment in projecting identified misstatements to the entire account.[7]

Cut-Off Tests

The purpose of cut-off tests is to determine if the client has recorded transactions in the correct period. The general approach for cut-off tests is to examine documentation for transactions (sales, receipts, or returns) that occur just before and just after the end of the fiscal year. Auditors should observe the last shipping document(s) sent on the last day of the fiscal year—often this procedure is performed in conjunction with year-end inventory observation since shipping usually occurs at the warehouse where inventory is counted. This type of test is facilitated if the company uses prenumbered documents in sequence and can readily determine the last document number used in the period. The auditor will almost always test the timing of the largest transactions around the end of the year, but the auditor may perform more extensive cut-off tests when risk of material misstatement related to timing is high. Cut-off tests for sales returns can be particularly important because they may indicate fictitious sales or sales that should not be recognized due to a customer's right to return the merchandise[vii].

[vii] **EXAMPLE**

Companies in high-tech industries are notorious for shipping a great deal of merchandise at the end of the fiscal year in order to pump up recorded sales—a procedure commonly known as **channel stuffing**. *The returns of that merchandise are often significant and may not occur until two or three months after year end, just after the audit opinion has been signed and the financial statements released.*

Tests of Revenue Recognition

One of the most important and common risks of significant misstatement involves revenue recognition. Because no other class of transactions on the income statement receives more attention by users of financial statements, organizations face a great deal of pressure to conform to expectations about revenues and, in many cases, appropriately recognizing revenue can be a fairly complex process. Accordingly, the procedures employed to test the recognition of revenue during the sales process are very important for auditors. The issue of revenue recognition will become increasingly challenging for (viii)**EXAMPLE**

Major warehouse retailers, such as Costco, have an automated point-of-sales system that tracks all sales across all warehouse locations on a real-time basis. Prices for goods are input into the system at the corporate level to ensure that all consumers receive the same prices, reducing the risk of price discrimination. Further, should adjustments to sales prices need to occur, the system tracks the employee who overrides the system to ensure that no unusual transactions are recorded. Often, only a supervisor can access the point-of-sales system to enable an override (e.g., a key must be inserted in the system or a password entered). To test the effectiveness of the system, an auditor could test the controls of the system to ensure that they are operating effectively. Also, the auditor could examine all adjustments to the system for a sample of days throughout the year and at the end of the reporting period, noting any unusual adjustments.

(ix)**EXAMPLE**

Several US retailers, including Best Buy, were forced to restate reported earnings because they had been improperly recognizing revenue associated with fees received for joining "rewards" programs, in which customers pay a fee to receive future discounts on items when purchases reach certain levels. Organizations like Best Buy were recognizing the fees as revenue when they were collected, instead of deferring the revenue and recognizing it evenly throughout the period of time covered by the fees.

auditors as more organizations develop innovative ways to foster customer loyalty (e.g., frequent shopper clubs) and customer sales and service become more dependent on strategic alliances (e.g., airline code sharing).

AUTHORITATIVE GUIDANCE & STANDARDS

Both the International Accounting Standards Board (IASB) and the US Financial Accounting Standards Board (FASB) have recently passed new revenue recognition standards (IFRS 15 and FASB Topic 606). These standards involve substantially new concepts in revenue recognition especially for bundled goods and services. While mandatory adoption of the new standard is not until 2019, early adoption may occur in 2017. A new accounting standard does not change the auditor's responsibility to carry out tests of revenue recognition; the complexity of the new revenue standard will likely require significant additional audit resources in the years of transition.

Because of an organization's motivation to misstate revenue—revenue recognition frauds have been among the most prevalent form of material fraud over the past fifty years—auditors should generally consider the risk of material misstatement associated with revenue recognition during the mandatory brainstorming session required for all audits. To assess fraud risk, auditors should develop a sufficient understanding of the revenue generating process for clients and the accounting policies and procedures employed for recognizing revenue. For organizations in which revenues are generated via routine transactions, auditors should expect to find highly automated systems in place that capture revenue (e.g., an integrated ERP sales process that links together a network of point-of-sales systems at retail outlets). These systems should have well-documented and effective automated controls ensuring that sales are recorded at the point in time when title transfers and at the correct sales price. It should prevent unauthorized users from accessing sales data and should facilitate recording the sale of the right items at the right prices. Furthermore, the organization should have effective controls in place restricting the creation of adjusting journal entries used to supplement the automated process for recording sales[viii].

Auditors should be concerned about errors (and even fraud) when revenue recognition is difficult to calculate. This condition can occur for transactions that are not common within an industry or there are non-routine sales transactions that involve complex issues, such as difficult decisions determining when title transfers. For example, many organizations in a highly competitive marketplace use various strategies to develop customer loyalty. Costco generates a material portion of its revenues by charging customers annual membership fees for the right to shop in the store. These membership fees are collected up-front, but the revenue should not be recognized until they are earned; that is, one-twelfth of the fee should be recognized each month following collection. Accordingly, auditors should gather sufficient evidence related to complex revenue recognition transactions to adequately assess whether conditions exist to recognize revenue[ix].

Tests of Accounting Estimates: Uncollectible Amounts

The auditor should determine if recorded receivables have been adequately adjusted to reflect an estimate for potentially uncollectible amounts. Because the auditor cannot predict the future, the identification of uncollectible accounts requires careful analysis and judgment. The auditor will typically undertake two types of substantive tests for assessing uncollectible balances.

AUTHORITATIVE GUIDANCE & STANDARDS

ISA 540 **Auditing Accounting Estimates, Including Fair Value Accounting Estimates, and Related Disclosures** *provides numerous references to the auditor making inquiries to client management and others as well as using analytical procedures in the audit of accounting estimates including fair value measurements in the financial statements. PCAOB Standards provide separate standards for auditing accounting estimates (AS 2501 [formerly AU 342]* **Auditing Accounting Estimates***) and a more specific standard for fair value measurements (AS 2502 [formerly AU 328]* **Auditing Fair Value Measurements and Disclosures***). See Chapter 9 for more details.*

One procedure is to examine the documentation of large balances, especially those that are already delinquent, to determine if the amounts will ultimately be paid by the customer. Transactions that are in dispute or customers that are in fiscal distress (e.g., bankruptcy) indicate a lower likelihood of collection. Also, the auditor can vouch cash receipts occurring after year end to determine if the customer has made any payments on the account because an actual payment is the best evidence that the receivable is collectible. Based on the review of the files, the auditor may judge that a portion of some accounts will not be paid. The amounts would be aggregated for all customers and compared to the recorded value of allowance for bad debts.

Another way to test bad debts is to directly estimate the level of bad debts using the information included in the aged trial balance. The longer an account is overdue, the less likely it is that the amount will be collected and the higher the percentage of an account that should be reserved against future losses. The percentage of accounts deemed uncollectible should be based on historical experience modified for current economic circumstances and changes in the company's credit policies. To facilitate this process, the auditor often keeps year-to-year records about the client's collection history.

To illustrate, consider the following computation of expected bad debts based on the age of receivables and historical delinquency rates:

Aging category	Receivable amounts	Delinquency rate	Potential bad debts
Current balances (less than 30 days since date of sale)	$100,000	2%	$2,000
30 days past due (less than 60 days since date of sale)	40,000	4%	1,600
60 days past due (less than 90 days since date of sale)	20,000	15%	3,000
90 days past due (less than 120 days since date of sale)	10,000	50%	5,000
Auditor's estimate of uncollectible amounts			$11,600

The auditor's estimate would be compared with the recorded value of the allowance for uncollectible accounts to assess whether the allowance is adequate. If we assume that the client has a credit balance of $8,000 in the allowance, the auditor might suggest an adjustment of $3,600. However, because the auditor's estimate is subject to estimation uncertainty, it is not possible to conclude that the company actually has a $3,600 error. The auditor in this case needs to consider the following:

- How did management develop the estimate and were the procedures consistent with prior years.
- Where did management's assumptions differ from the auditor's and why?
- How did management deal with the estimation uncertainty given these differences?

All of these inquiries need to be documented. Finally, the auditor has to reach a conclusion about the reasonableness of management's estimate by considering the current economic conditions of the client and industry. If the auditor concludes that his estimate has a range of possible values that are equally likely then the amount of the misstatement would be the difference between management's recorded estimate and the closest number in the range of reasonable amounts the auditor has developed.

Summary and Conclusion

We have discussed a broad approach for auditing sales and customer service in this chapter. A common theme presented in this book is that the tests of financial statement assertions should follow directly from the auditor's risk assessments and their impact on specific assertions related to transactions, accounts, and disclosures. For that purpose, we used a process map and internal threat analysis to evaluate process objectives, activities, risks, process controls, entity level controls, and internal controls over financial reporting. We used the results of the process analysis to assess residual risks and analyze how residual risks would affect the risk of material misstatement and the conduct of the audit, focusing on the tests of financial statement assertions affected by sales and customer service. Finally, we discussed specific substantive tests that could be performed when the risk of material misstatement is considered high for assertions related to sales and receivables.

The extent of testing applied to receivable balances depends on the risk of material misstatement assessments made by the auditor. When risk is low for the majority of receivable assertions, the auditor might disregard many of the tests listed in Table 11.5. Testing would be focused on a few large or unusual items. When inherent or control risk is high for a significant number of the receivable assertions, the auditor would increase the nature and extent testing. Consequently, the selection of substantive testing procedures will vary across clients. Auditors can adjust their substantive audit testing by choosing to perform certain procedures but not others, by increasing or decreasing the sample size of items examined, or by adjusting the timing of the performance of procedures.[8] These types of choices are illustrated for assertions related to receivables in Table 11.6 for two levels

Table 11.6 *Substantive Tests of Management Assertions Related to Accounts Receivable for Different Levels of Risk of Material Misstatement*

Type of Substantive Procedure	High Detection Risk Case (Low risk of material misstatement)	Low Detection Risk Case (High risk of material misstatement)
Tests of transactions	Moderate tests as described in "Substantive Tests of Management Assertions Related to Sales and Receipts Transactions" section, mostly performed prior to year end.	Extensive tests as described in "Substantive Tests of Management Assertions Related to Sales and Receipts Transactions" section, many performed after year end.
Test of accuracy of aged trial balance	Minimal or no testing. Totals traced to the general ledger.	Summary totals tested in detail. Some accounts traced to supporting documentation to test aging.
Confirmations	Small sample of positive confirmations; moderate sample of negative confirmations; may be done at interim date rather than year-end. Reduced testing of nonresponses to positive confirmations	Large sample of positive confirmations as of year-end. Extensive testing of nonresponses to positive confirmations.
Cut-off tests	Minimal or no testing.	Tests of year-end transactions on a sample basis.
Estimation of bad debt expense	Substantive analytical procedures performed using data from aged trial balance and historical loss rates.	Substantive analytical procedures supported by detailed examination of customer files related to large accounts which are at risk of loss.

of risk of material misstatement. Regardless of the level of substantive testing deemed necessary, the auditor will need to fully document the process analysis, the conclusions about residual risks, and the results of substantive testing.

Appendix A: Planning Tests of Financial Statement Assertions Related to Cash Balances

The sales and customer service process also has a significant effect on the cash balances of a company, mainly through cash receipts. A company may have "cash" in different forms: coins and currency, general checking accounts, imprest checking accounts, and money market accounts. Most companies maintain a general disbursement account for processing receipts and disbursements. Payroll disbursements are often made from a separate account that allows for separate levels of control over the payroll system that may differ from general disbursements made by the company. Cash is usually a relatively small portion of a company's balance sheet but takes on greater importance because of the large volume of transactions that flow through the account. Although internal control over cash is usually quite effective in most organizations, there are a number of procedures that are traditionally used to audit cash. Cash is a relatively easy account to audit, and the auditor can usually achieve very low detection risk quite easily. A general approach for the substantive testing of cash balances is outlined in Table 11.7. The primary procedures to test financial assertions related to cash include the following test of details:

- Test of cash receipts.
- Bank confirmations.
- Bank reconciliations.
- Proof of cash.
- Tests of interfund transfers.

Table 11.7 *Substantive Tests for Cash Account Assertions*

Management Assertion	Typical Substantive Audit Procedures
Existence: Cash on hand and cash in bank exists.	• Count cash on hand. • Review and test bank reconciliations. • Prepare and verify an interfund transfer schedule. • Test cash receipt and disbursement transactions.
Completeness: All cash assets of the company are included in the general ledger.	• Review board minutes for indications of new or closed accounts. • Review cash disbursements to identify accounts used. • Obtain representation from management concerning the existence of bank accounts and locations that cash is stored. • Prepare and verify an interfund transfer schedule. • Test cash receipt and disbursement transactions.
Valuation: Cash balances reconcile with cash on hand and cash in bank.	• Obtain and foot bank reconciliations for all bank accounts. • Trace balance per bank to bank statement and bank confirmation. • Trace balance per books to the general ledger. • Count cash on hand and compare the total to the general ledger.
Valuation: Cash balances are correctly valued.	• Obtain and verify bank reconciliations. • Obtain and verify proof of cash. • Test cash receipt and disbursement transactions. • Vouch selected reconciling items in the bank reconciliations.
Valuation: Cash balances are correctly classified.	• Review bank reconciliations and confirmations for items requiring reclassification (e.g., credit balances, compensating balances).
Valuation: Cash receipts and disbursements are recorded in the proper period.	• Obtain bank cut-off statement. • Obtain and verify bank reconciliations. • Obtain and verify proof of cash. • Perform cash receipt and disbursement cut-off tests. • Vouch selected reconciling items in the bank reconciliations.
Ownership: Cash balances are owned by the company.	• Obtain and review bank confirmation for pledged balances or compensating balances. • Prepare and verify an interfund transfer schedule. • Obtain representation from management concerning potential commitments, claims, or liens on bank accounts.

Tests of Cash Receipts

The primary transactions affecting the cash account are cash receipts and disbursements. Cash receipts arise naturally as part of sales and customer service processes and can be tested using the procedures listed in "Substantive Tests of Management Assertions Related to Sales and Receipts Transactions" section. Tests of cash receipts focus on proper identification, processing, and deposit of receipts on a timely basis.[9]

Bank Confirmations

A **bank confirmation** is a standardized request from an auditor to a client's bankers for the confirmation of checking or other deposit accounts. The confirmation may also provide information concerning loans or lines of credit to the client, loans guaranteed by the client (a contingent liability), and assets pledged as collateral. A sample of a bank confirmation request is presented in Figure 11.6. As is the case with all confirmations, the request comes from the client but is returned to the auditor. Bank confirmations are usually sent out blank—without either account numbers or balances on them.

Bank Reconciliations

The purpose of a **bank reconciliation** is to identify any discrepancies between the cash balance recorded on the books at a point in time and the balance according to the bank as of the same point in time, as illustrated in Figure 11.7. The auditor obtains reconciliations for bank accounts that have heavy activity or large balances. Bank reconciliations may be prepared by the auditor, or prepared by the client's personnel (as part of the client's internal control procedures) and checked by the auditor.

Reconciling items represent transactions that have been recorded by either the bank or the company but not both. For example, checks issued by the company that have not yet cleared the bank will cause the bank balance to be higher than the book balance. Similarly, if the bank has added interest to the company's account, but the company is unaware of the amount, the bank balance will exceed the book balance. There are four types of reconciling items:

Reconciling items to the book balance:	
Debits to books not recorded by bank	*Deposits in transit not yet received by bank*
Credits to books not recorded by bank	*Outstanding checks not yet paid by bank*
Reconciling items to the bank balance:	
Debits by bank not recorded on books	*Bank fees*
	Checks deposited by company returned due to insufficient funds of check writer
Credits by bank not recorded on books	*Interest earned on bank balances*
	Collections from customers by bank on behalf of company

STANDARD FORM TO CONFIRM ACCOUNT
BALANCE INFORMATION WITH FINANCIAL INSTITUTIONS

_____

Customer Name

We have provided to our accountants the following information as of the close of business on _____, 20___, regarding our deposit and loan balances. Please confirm the accuracy of the information, noting any exceptions to the information provided. If the balances have been left blank, please complete this form by furnishing the balance in the appropriate space below. Although we do not request nor expect you to conduct a comprehensive, detailed search of your records, if during the process of completing this confirmation additional information about other deposit and loan accounts we may have with you comes to your attention, please include such information below. Please use the enclosed envelope to return the form directly to our auditors.

Financial   [
Institution's [
Name and [
Address   [

]
]
]
]

1. At the close of business on the date listed above, our records indicated the following deposit balance(s):

Account Name	Account No.	Interest Rate	Balance

2. We were directly liable to the financial institution for loans at the close of business on the date listed above as follows:

Account No./ Description	Balance	Date Due	Interest Rate	Date Through Which Interest Paid	Description of Collateral

_____   _____
(Customer's Authorized Signature)   (Date)

The information presented above by the customer is in agreement with our records. Although we have not conducted a comprehensive, detailed search of our records, no other deposit or loan accounts have come to our attention except as noted below.

_____   _____
(Financial Institution Authorized Signature)   (Date)

_____
(Title)

Exceptions and/or Comments

Please return this form directly to our auditor: [   ]

Figure 11.6 Example of a Standard Bank Confirmation

```
┌──────────────────────────────────────────────────────────────────┐
│                                                      A-1           │
│                   Jones Manufacturing, Inc.                        │
│              Bank Reconciliation—Sunshine Bank    PBC    WRK       │
│                        12/31/x7                          1/24/x8   │
├──────────────────────────────────────────────────────────────────┤
│                                                                    │
│  Balance per Bank, 12/31/x7                        2,000  A-1-1    │
│                                                                    │
│  Deduct: Outstanding checks                                        │
│     #126, 12/26                        800  ✓                      │
│                                                                    │
│     #129, 12/30                        200  ✓                      │
│                                                                    │
│     #130, 12/30                      1,200  ✓                      │
│                                                                    │
│     #131, 12/30                      1,250  ✓     3,450   T        │
│                                                  ───────           │
│  Adjusted Bank Balance                          (1,450)  T        │
│                                                  ═══════           │
│                                                                    │
│  Balance per Books, 12/31/x7                    (1,500)  A-1-2     │
│                                                                    │
│  Unrecorded adjustments:                                          │
│     Interest credited by bank                        50  ~  AJE1   │
│                                                  ───────           │
│  Adjusted Book Balance                          (1,450)  T  AJE2   │
│                                                  ═══════           │
│                                                                    │
│  T  Footed and total agrees.                                      │
│                                                                    │
│  ✓  Traced outstanding checks to cash disbursements journal for 12/x7 and bank │
│     cut-off statement for 1/10/x8 received directly from bank. Amounts agree.  │
│                                                                    │
│  ~  Traced bank adjustments to bank statement as of 12/31/x7. Amounts agree.   │
│                                                                    │
│  NOTE: Check #131 was the last check issued in December, 20x7.     │
│                                                                    │
└──────────────────────────────────────────────────────────────────┘
```

Figure 11.7 Example of Bank Reconciliation

Reconciling items to the bank balance represent transactions that have not been recorded by the company and may necessitate an adjusting entry to correct the cash balances of the company.

Bank reconciliations may be prepared in various formats. The format used in Figure 11.7 reconciles both the book and bank balance to an adjusted balance that is "correct" in the sense that it represents the amount that should be reported on the balance sheet. An alternative is to start with the bank balance and reconcile it to the book balance. The format used in Figure 11.7 has the advantage of highlighting the items that may not have been recorded by the company.

Auditors verify the accuracy of bank reconciliations by performing a number of relatively simple tests. First, the auditor tests the accuracy of the schedule. The auditor then compares the reconciling items for the books with internal supporting documents and records. Finally, the reconciling items for the bank are compared with supporting documentation from the bank. Properly prepared and verified bank reconciliations result in a very low detection risk for cash assertions.

Proof of Cash

In situations where control risk for cash is high, the auditor may also wish to prepare a **proof of cash** for one or more of the company's bank accounts. A proof of cash can be prepared for any period of time, such as a month or year. A proof of cash starts with normal bank reconciliations at two points in time and then reconciles the receipts and disbursements across time. A simple proof of cash for Jones Manufacturing is illustrated in Figure 11.8. The last column of the schedule contains the same information as the bank reconciliation presented in Figure 11.7 but in a slightly different form. To facilitate the example, the bank reconciliation for the beginning of the period (12/31/x6) is also presented. The middle two columns include detailed information about cash receipts and disbursements affecting the account according to the bank and the company respectively.

To see how the proof of cash works, consider the $10,000 deposit in transit included in the 20x6 reconciliation. This is added to the bank balance in order to reconcile with the book balance on 12/31/x6. However, when we examine the second column, we are looking at the receipts for 20x7. This $10,000 would be listed as a receipt by the bank in 20x7, but the company recorded it in 20x6. Therefore, the $10,000 must be subtracted from the receipts per the bank in order to reconcile with the receipts per the books.[10] Next, consider the $3,450 in outstanding checks on 12/31/x7 (the last column). Here we see the item subtracted from the bank balance to reconcile with the book balance. Because the disbursement is recorded in 20x7 by the company, but after 12/31/x7 by the bank, the $3,450 must be added to the disbursements per the bank in order to reconcile with the disbursements per the books.

The receipts and disbursements according to the bank can be traced to the bank statements for the period under consideration and the receipts and disbursements per the books can be traced to the appropriate transaction

---

A-1-2

Jones Manufacturing, Inc.
Proof of Cash—Sunshine Bank
12/31/x7   PBC   *WRK*
1/24/x8

	12/31/x6	Cash-In	Cash-Out	12/31/x7
Balance per bank	5,000 ✓	939,000 ~	942,000 ~	2,000 **R**
Deposit in transit	10,000 ✓	(10,000)		
Outstanding checks: 20x6	(13,200) ✓		(13,200)	
Outstanding checks: 20x7			3,450	(3,450) **R**
Other reconciling items		(50)		(50) **R**
Balance per books	1,800 ✓	928,950 **✗**	932,250 **✗**	(1,500) **R**
	T	**T**	**T**	**T**
				A-1

T Footed and total agrees.

R Traced to and agrees with 20x7 bank reconciliation (see **A-1**) and cross-footings verified.

✓ Traced to and agrees with bank reconciliation in prior year's workpapers.

✗ Traced to and agrees with cash receipts journal (Cash in) or cash disbursements journal (Cash out).

~ Traced to and agrees with totals per bank statements.

Figure 11.8 Example of Proof of Cash

journals. Every reconciling item in the first and last columns (the point-in-time reconciliations) has a complementary item in the receipt or disbursement columns. If cash balances are correct, the receipts and disbursement columns should balance, providing evidence that cash transactions have been properly recorded by the company.

Tests of Interfund Transfers

Another significant concern the auditor has related to cash is the transfer of funds between bank accounts near the end of the year. Such transfers, called *interfund transfers*, represent a deposit to one account of the company and a withdrawal from another account. Both sides of the transfer affect accounts held by the company, so that if the transaction is not properly recorded, the same money may be accidentally recorded in two different accounts at the same time, or in no accounts at all. The problem of double-counting transfers is called *kiting*, and can occur when the deposit in one account is recorded earlier than the withdrawal from the other account.

Interfund transfers are tested using an *interfund transfer schedule* as illustrated in Table 11.8. This schedule illustrates five interfund transfers at or

Table 11.8 *Example of Test of Interfund Transfers*

Description	Amount	(A) Date per Books: Cash Out	(B) Date per Books: Cash In	(C) Date per Bank: Cash Out	(D) Date per Bank: Cash In	Implications
Bank 1 to Bank 2	$100,000	12/31/x7	12/31/x7	1/2/x8	1/3/x8	Payout Bank: Outstanding check Deposit Bank: Deposit in transit Books: None
Bank 2 to Bank 3	50,000	12/31/x7	1/3/x8	12/31/x7	1/3/x8	Payout Bank: None Deposit Bank: None Books: Error (Unrecorded transfer)
Bank 3 to Bank 4	20,000	1/3/x8	12/31/x7	1/3/x8	12/31/x7	Payout Bank: None Deposit Bank: None Books: Error (Kiting)
Bank 4 to Bank 5	120,000	1/3/x8	1/3/x8	12/31/x7	1/3/x8	Payout Bank: None Deposit Bank: None Books: Error (Unrecorded payment)
Bank 5 to Bank 6	70,000	1/3/x8	1/3/x8	1/3/x8	12/31/x7	Payout Bank: None Deposit Bank: None Books: Error (Unrecorded deposit)

Rules of Analysis:

Difference between A and C: Reconciling Item for Disbursing Bank
- If A is sooner than C: Outstanding check
- If C is sooner than A: Unrecorded disbursement (error)

Difference between B and D: Reconciling Item for Receiving Bank
- If B is sooner than D: Deposit in transit
- If D is sooner than B: Unrecorded deposit (error)

Difference between A and B: Error to books
- If A is sooner than B: Unrecorded transfer (error)
- If B is sooner than A: Duplicate cash—kiting (error)

Kiting, if done intentionally by the client, is an illegal act, and the auditor should consider the implications for the entire audit. In the late 1970s, the brokerage firm of E. F. Hutton was discovered to be running a giant kiting scheme involving hundreds of banks and hundreds of millions of dollars, resulting in the receipt of millions of dollars in interest income they did not deserve.

near year end. The schedule lists the date of deposit per the books (column B) and per the bank (column D), and the date of withdrawal per the books (column A) and per the bank (column C). If the dates in all four columns fall in the same fiscal period, the transfer is correctly recorded.

Transfer errors arise when the dates in the various columns fall in different fiscal periods. Four possible problems are summarized under the "Rules of Analysis" in Table 11.8. For a transfer to be correctly recorded, A and B must be in the same period and at the same time or earlier than C and D. Some of the potential problems would be revealed by a well-prepared bank reconciliation alone. However, the interfund transfer schedule reveals two problems not detectable with a standard bank reconciliation: kiting and unrecorded cash. Kiting occurs when the date in column B is in an earlier period than the date in column A. This occurs for the $20,000 transfer from Bank 3 to Bank 4. Because the deposit is recorded for Bank 4 in 20x7 but the withdrawal is not recorded for Bank 3 until 20x8, the $20,000 is included in both accounts as of 12/31/x7. If A is in a period earlier than B, cash will not be recorded in any account, which is also an error(x).

Conclusion

Cash is an area where most companies have excellent internal control, so many of the procedures listed in Table 11.7 would probably be unnecessary for most clients. The cash tests described in this chapter are used less and less as information systems improve and the cash disbursements process is increasingly automated. However, confirmations should almost always be obtained from the client's primary financial institutions. In the cases where inherent or control risk is high for a number of cash assertions, or there is a concern about the risk of fraud related to cash balances, other procedures can be performed to obtain evidence that cash is not materially misstated.

Appendix B: An Overview of Working Paper Documentation Techniques

The Need for Documentation

The auditor is required to prepare **audit documentation** that indicates that he or she has complied with all appropriate elements of generally accepted auditing standards. One purpose of preparing documentation of audit work is to demonstrate that the auditor has obtained sufficient, appropriate evidence upon which to base an opinion about the financial statements. Each and every audit working paper prepared by an auditor will be unique, depending on the assertions being tested and the nature of the evidence obtained. Accounting firms vary in terms of how they utilize audit documentation, ranging from fully automated systems of files (including scanned documents) to folders containing **working papers** (consisting of schedules, memos, and copies of client documents).

AUTHORITATIVE GUIDANCE & STANDARDS

*Both the IAASB and the PCAOB have made improvements in working
paper documentation a priority in their recent standard setting activities.
ISA 230 and AS 1215 (formerly 3), both entitled* **Audit Documentation,**
*entail a substantial increase in the amount of prescription around audit
documentation that is required. One major difference is the time allowed
for audit file finalization after the audit report has been issued. ISA 230
had a sixty day post audit requirement whereas the PCAOB standard only
allows forty-five days. Further both standards require that subsequent to
that time, no material can be discarded from the file until the retention
period (the length of time that the auditor must keep the file) is expired
(five years in ISA 230 and seven years in AS 1215). Much of the emphasis
around documentation at the PCAOB arises from its inspection division that
wants the audit file documentation to be as standard as possible so as to
increase its efficiency. Regulators in other countries (e.g., Canada's Public
Accountability Board) have made similar requests to the IAASB
for the same reasons.*

Audit documentation is typically organized into *files* or binders classified by
audit area (e.g., process or account). Auditors generally use two types of files:
current files and permanent files. Historically, files were actually on paper
but modern audit systems now consist of primarily electronic files. Some
important documents, like contracts, may still be retained on paper but even
those are increasingly being scanned and preserved electronically.

Current files contain the documentation of the work that has been performed
during the current audit. For example, the documentation of receivables
confirmation may be in one current file, whereas bank reconciliations and
confirmations for cash may be in another.

A current file usually includes a *lead sheet* that lists all of the accounts in
the general ledger that relate to a specific line in the financial statements.
For example, there may be many different inventory accounts used by
a company for control purposes. The lead sheet for inventory lists the
different types of inventory that appear as separate accounts in the general
ledger but that are added together and reported as a single line item in
the balance sheet. Following the lead sheet will be other working papers
that contain the evidence in support of the balances. For example, the
documentation illustrated in Figures 11.7 and 11.8 would be in the current
file for cash.

Permanent files contain information that is of ongoing interest to the auditor
from one year to the next. This set of files will contain information about the
client's accounting and control system, various legal documents (e.g., leases,
notes payable), minutes from Board of Directors meetings, organization
charts for the client, a chart of accounts, and results from prior-year audits.
The prior-year results will include summary information on errors found, as
well as the final financial statements and data needed for evaluating historical
trends (e.g., bad debt history for receivables).

Audit Documentation Identification

Individual files (or working papers) are used to document the work performed in an audit engagement based on a few general guidelines that most auditors follow. First, every document should be clearly identified, including the identity of the client, the year being audited, and the purpose of the document. This information usually appears in the heading of the document. Referring again to Figures 11.7 and 11.8, we see two illustrations of the basic format of audit documentation. Both contain a clear statement of the nature of the audit test, the client, and the period under examination. The top of the documents also includes an indication of who performed the audit work. In these two cases, the auditor has initialed the upper right corner "WRK" and indicated the date that the work was performed (1/24/x8 in both cases).

The letters "PBC" at the left of the "WRK" notation stand for "Prepared By Client," which means that the client, rather than the auditor, has initially prepared this schedule. Of course, the auditor is responsible for verifying that the information contained in the schedule is accurate. However, it is usually more efficient to have the client search out the relevant information and prepare the schedule for the auditor's examination.

Paperless Audits

Many public accounting firms have converted all or part of their audit documentation to automated working papers. There are a wide number of alternatives for firms to select from when designing an automated audit documentation system, but there are several features that are common across systems used in audit practice. Typically, files are stored on centralized servers that can be accessed by multiple engagement team members at the same time. Auditors who work on information can choose to synchronize their updates with the information stored in the master file. That way, if two individuals are working on the same file, the system can force individuals to reconcile information that might become inconsistent. The primary benefit of having working papers stored on a centralized server is that engagement team members can be in different locations when working on the same engagement.

Another important benefit of most automated audit documentation systems is that the system can be designed as a decision aid for ensuring that engagement team members adequately follow the firm's audit approach while conducting the audit. For example, if the firm's audit approach dictates that auditors conduct substantive tests of details for any account in which there is a high level of residual risk, the system can require that audit documentation for a substantive test of details be completed before allowing an auditor to sign off on the account. Furthermore, many auditing firms have designed pop-up screens to enable auditors to seek guidance while they are performing audit procedures.

Automated audit documentation also greatly enhances the review process, both for detail review of working papers and for general review by partners. Checking to see which areas have been completed and cross-referencing audit areas is much easier when the reviewer is able to gain quick access to other areas of an audit (as opposed to having to search through multiple working papers stored in various binders). The review process is further expedited because the reviewer can access the files from offsite locations.

Documentation Referencing

Another feature of audit documentation is the letter-number code in the upper right corner. These codes are called *indices* or *references*. Every document should be identified by a unique index so that they can be maintained in a logical order. In our example, the bank reconciliation is indexed as A-1 and the proof of cash is indexed as A-1-2. Indices are often specified as a letter followed by one or more numbers. The letter indicates the general area of audit work (e.g., "A" indicates cash in this case), and the numbers indicate the intended order of pages. Different letters would be used for other areas in the audit (e.g., the letter B could be used to indicate receivables, C to indicate inventory, and so on).

The structure of a current file for cash is depicted in Figure 11.9. In our example, the cash lead sheet would be placed in the front of the current file for cash and indexed as *A*. An index may have one or more numbers appended to the first letter. The bank reconciliation for Sunshine Bank is indexed as A-1 followed by the related bank confirmation, which is indexed as A-1-1. This tells the auditor that schedule A-1-1 relates to, and follows, schedule A-1 and precedes A-2 (which contains the bank reconciliation for Island Bank). This method of indexing is quite flexible and allows the insertion of additional documents without renumbering all the pages in the file.

Cross References

A significant advantage of indexing documents is that information that appears on more than one schedule can be easily cross-referenced. That is, the auditor, when reading one schedule, can be alerted that certain information on that schedule also relates to, and appears on, another schedule. Returning to Figure 11.7, we see the index A-1-1 entered next to the $2,000 balance per bank as of 12/31/x7. This tells the reader that further information related to that number appears on schedule A-1-1, which would be the bank's confirmation of the account balance (not presented here). We also see the index A entered next to the balance per books. This would be a cross-reference to the lead schedule for cash that lists all of the bank accounts and other forms of cash that the company owns. Cross-references should be circular. That is, the auditor should also see cross-references to schedule A-1 on schedules A (the lead sheet, see Figure 11.9) and A-1-1 (the bank confirmation, not presented).

Another form of cross-reference is illustrated with the letters AJE in Figure 11.7. These references refer to adjusting entries to correct the company's records. All adjusting entries identified during the course of an engagement should be summarized on a single schedule. In our example, we see that AJE1 is necessary to correct for the unrecorded interest income. AJE2 is necessary to reclassify the net credit balance as a payable. The full details of both adjusting entries would appear on the summary listing of adjusting entries.

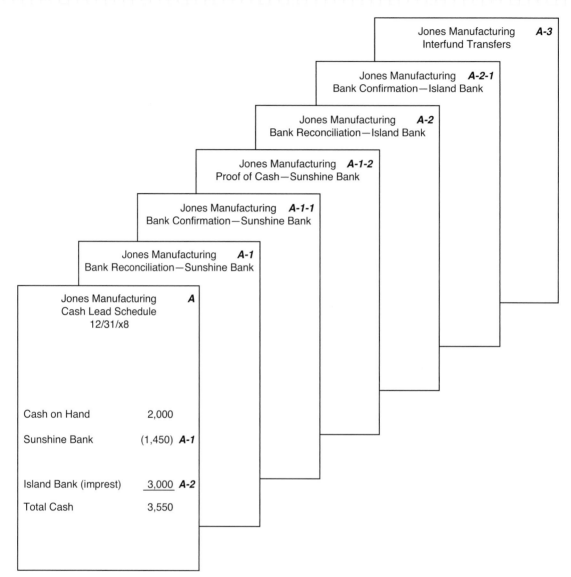

Figure 11.9 *Structure of the Current File for Cash*

Tickmarks

The auditor uses ***tickmarks*** to indicate the tests that were used to verify the information contained in an audit document. For example, in Figure 11.7 we see the symbol √. This symbol appears next to the amounts of outstanding checks listed and again at the bottom of the schedule. Reading the explanation at the bottom, we see that the symbol means that the outstanding checks have been compared with the disbursements journal and the bank cut-off statement. If these comparisons had revealed any discrepancies, the auditor would make a note of the problem and propose an adjusting entry to the client to correct the accounting. Two other tickmarks—*T* and ∼ —are used on A-1 and explain other tests that were performed. Turning to Figure 11.8 (A-1-2), we see the same symbols as on A-1 but the interpretation for 3 is different than on the prior schedule. We also see two other tickmarks that were not used before—*R* and *✗*. Tickmarks can be of various shapes and sizes, but they should be easy to distinguish one from another so as to avoid undue confusion. In addition, every tickmark used on a page should be explained by a note somewhere on the same page (usually at the bottom).[11]

Conclusion

The documentation of audit work and testing performed by an auditor is extremely important. Audit documentation is intended to be the written record of the auditor's efforts. The tests performed, evidence gathered, and conclusions reached should be documented in such a way that other readers have no trouble understanding the work performed. Audit documentation is intended to be flexible so as to be easily adapted to many diverse situations. Finally, audit documentation should be neat, complete, and clear. Audit documentation is increasingly becoming electronic. This makes it easier to prepare, correct, and store audit documentation. It also makes it easier for different people to work on the same schedule, even if separated geographically. As electronic audit documentation becomes the norm in the profession, the organization, cross-referencing, and handling of files will change accordingly.

Bibliography of Relevant Literature

Research

Engle, T. J. and J. E. Hunton. 2001. The Effects of Small Monetary Incentives on Response Quality and Rates in Positive Confirmation of Account Receivable Balances. *Auditing—A Journal of Practice & Theory.* 20(1): 157–168.

Auditing Standards

Committee of Sponsoring Organizations of the Treadway Commission (COSO). 1992. *Internal Control—Integrated Framework.* New York: COSO.

Committee of Sponsoring Organizations of the Treadway Commission (COSO). 2006. *Internal Control: An Integrated Framework: Guidance for Smaller Public Companies.* New York: COSO.

Committee of Sponsoring Organizations of the Treadway Commission (COSO). 2013. *Internal Control—Integrated Framework.* New York: COSO.

FASB Financial Accounting Standards Topic 606, *"Revenue from Contracts with Customers."*

IAASB *International Standards on Auditing (ISA)* No. 200, "Overall Objectives of the Independent Auditor and the Conduct of an Audit in Accordance with International Standards on Auditing."

IAASB *International Standards on Auditing (ISA)* No. 230, "Audit Documentation."

IAASB *International Standards on Auditing (ISA)* No. 240, "The Auditor's Responsibilities Relating to Fraud in an Audit of Financial Statements."

IAASB *International Standards on Auditing (ISA)* No. 250, "Consideration of Laws and Regulations in an Audit of Financial Statements."

IAASB *International Standards on Auditing (ISA)* No. 300, "Planning an Audit of Financial Statements."

IAASB *International Standards on Auditing (ISA)* No. 315, "Identifying and Assessing the Risks of Material Misstatement through Understanding the Entity and Its Environment."

IAASB *International Standards on Auditing (ISA)* No. 320, "Materiality in Planning and Performing an Audit."

IAASB *International Standards on Auditing (ISA)* No. 330, "The Auditor's Responses to Assessed Risks."

IAASB *International Standards on Auditing (ISA)* No. 500, "Audit Evidence."

IAASB *International Standards on Auditing (ISA)* No. 505, "External Confirmations."

IAASB *International Standards on Auditing (ISA)* No. 520, "Analytical Procedures."

IAASB *International Standards on Auditing (ISA)* No. 540, "Auditing Accounting Estimates, Including Fair Value Accounting Estimates, and Related Disclosures."

IAASB *International Standards on Auditing (ISA)* No. 570, "Going Concern."

IFAC. International Auditing and Assurance Standards Board (IAASB). 2014. *Handbook of International Quality Control, Audit, Review, Other Assurance, and Related Services Pronouncements.* New York: International Federation of Accountants.

IFRS International Financial Reporting Standard 15. "*Revenue from Contracts with Customers*".

PCAOB. *Auditing Standard* 1101 (formerly No. 8), "Audit Risk."

PCAOB. *Auditing Standard* 1105 (formerly No. 15), "Audit Evidence."

PCAOB. *Auditing Standard* 1215 (formerly No. 3), "Audit Documentation."

PCAOB. *Auditing Standard* 2101 (formerly No. 9), "Audit Planning."

PCAOB. *Auditing Standard* 2105 (formerly No. 11), "Consideration of Materiality in Planning and Performing an Audit."

PCAOB. *Auditing Standard* 2201 (formerly No. 5), "An Audit of Internal Control over Financial Reporting that is Integrated with An Audit of Financial Statements."

PCAOB. *Auditing Standard* 2210 (formerly No. 12), "Identifying and Assessing the Risks of Material Misstatement."

PCAOB. *Auditing Standard* 2301 (formerly No. 13), "The Auditor's Responses to the Risks of Material Misstatement."

PCAOB. *Auditing Standard* 2305 (formerly *Interim Standard* AU 329) "Substantive Analytical Procedures."

PCAOB. *Auditing Standard* 2310 (formerly *Interim Standard* AU 330), "The Confirmation Process."

PCAOB. *Auditing Standard* 2401 (formerly *Interim Standard* AU 316), "Consideration of Fraud in a Financial Statement Audit."

PCAOB. *Auditing Standard* 2405 (formerly *Interim Standard* AU 317), "Illegal Acts by Clients."

PCAOB. *Auditing Standard* 2415 (formerly *Interim Standard* AU 341), "Consideration of an Entity's Ability to Continue as a Going Concern."

PCAOB. *Auditing Standard* 2501 (formerly *Interim Standard* AU 342), "Auditing Accounting Estimates."

PCAOB. *Auditing Standard* 2502 (formerly *Interim Standard* AU 328), "Auditing Fair Value Measurements and Disclosures."

PCAOB *Auditing Standard* 2810 (formerly No. 14), "Evaluating Audit Results."

SEC, *Staff Accounting Bulletin* No. 99, "Materiality."

Notes

1 The material in this chapter could also be applied to a service organization such as an accounting firm.

2 Two other processes could be incorporated into our discussion of marketing and sales: brand management and product development. These processes are beyond the scope of this text.

3 The acquisition of advertising and marketing resources, such as television time, newspaper space, advertising graphics, and so on, can be considered to be part of the company's supply chain (see Chapter 12).

4 In general, samples can be obtained randomly or judgmentally (which is discussed in more detail in Chapter 17). A random sample requires the auditor to generate a set of random numbers that correspond to the numerical sequence of the transactions being examined. A judgmental sample emphasizes transactions that are of specific interest to the auditor, such as large transactions or transactions near year end.

5 Another analytical technique is the use of regression analysis as discussed in Chapter 9. For example, a regression model could be developed that predicts the level of a company's sales as a function of various economic variables which are external to the company (e.g., interest rates, unemployment rates, inflation rates, number of housing starts). Such models have the advantage of being theoretically sound and free of potential bias that might arise from using the company's internal information (which may not be accurate). One potential drawback of such models is that their level of precision may not be adequate to generate truly meaningful estimates (i.e., the margin of error may be large). Another potential drawback is that the cost and effort of acquiring the data and building the model may be large, although most computer audit programs provide this facility as a standard feature in their software.

6 For example, an auditor may decide to use positive confirmations for large balances and negative confirmations for a sample of small accounts.

7 Alternatively, the auditor might compute an average dollar misstatement per customer confirmation sent and multiply that amount by the

total number of customers in each sample to arrive at an expected misstatement.

8 The timing of audit procedures has a direct impact on the detection risk achieved through those procedures. For example, confirmation of receivables usually occurs at year end because those are the balances that are of direct interest to the auditor. However, if risk of material misstatement is considered to be low, the auditor could choose to perform confirmation work at an earlier date as a matter of convenience (i.e., there is one less thing to do after year end when there is a great deal of time pressure to complete the audit). Usually made from an imprest account that is maintained at a constant level and replenished each time payroll checks are issued. A company may have petty cash at multiple locations, but the amounts tend to be small. Finally, a company may maintain a savings or money market account for temporary investment of excess cash.

9 Tests of cash disbursements are discussed in Chapter 12 as part of supply-chain management.

10 The analysis could also start with the receipts per the books and work to the receipts per the bank. In that case, the $10,000 would be added to the receipts per the books.

11 Standardized tickmarks are occasionally used when a tickmark is specified as meaning the same thing on every document.

CHAPTER 12

Audit Testing for the Supply Chain and Production Process

Outline

- Introduction
- An Overview of Objectives and Activities Related to Supply Chain and Production Management
  - o Process Objectives
  - o Process Activities
- Transactions Arising from Supply Chain and Production Management
  - o Purchases
  - o Disbursements
  - o Production
- Risk Assessment for Supply Chain and Production Management
  - o Analysis of Process Controls
- Entity Level Controls Affecting Supply Chain and Production Management Process
- Analysis of Internal Control over Financial Reporting
  - o Testing Internal Control over Financial Reporting
  - o Conclusions about Residual Risks from Supply Chain and Production Management
  - o Identifying Significant Residual Risks
- Planning Tests of Management Assertions: Purchases and Accounts Payable
  - o Substantive Analytical Procedures
  - o Tests of Purchase and Disbursement Transactions
  - o Tests of Accounts Payable Trial Balance
  - o Tests for Unrecorded Liabilities
  - o Confirmation of Payables
- Planning Tests of Management Assertions: Inventory
  - o Substantive Analytical Procedures
  - o Tests of Inventory Purchases, Conversion, and Movement

- o   Inspection or Observation of the Inventory Count
- o   Inventory Price Tests and Tests of Estimates: Obsolescence
- o   Tests of Inventory Compilation
- o   Cut-Off Tests
- •   Summary and Conclusion
- •   Bibliography of Relevant Literature

Learning Goals for this Chapter

1.   Apply our understanding of process analysis to the supply chain and production process.

2.   Analyze the risk of material misstatement in the context of the supply chain and production process.

3.   Apply our understanding of internal control over financial reporting audit to design, carry out and evaluate tests of internal controls for the supply chain and production process.

4.   Determine level of residual risk based on outcome of internal control testing.

5.   Plan substantive tests of account balances and transaction for the supply chain and production process.

6.   Design and execute substantive tests of account balances and transaction for the supply chain and production process.

7.   Conclude whether an appropriate level of audit evidence has been collected to support the auditor's opinion with respect to the supply chain and production process.

Introduction

Most organizations create value by obtaining resources from suppliers and transforming those resources into goods and services that are demanded by customers. An organization can develop and sustain a competitive advantage over its competition by managing supply and production in ways that are difficult for others to duplicate. For example, a company could develop proprietary production technology (e.g., high-tech manufacturers). Additionally, a company can use innovative ways to manage its supply chain by identifying and managing effective alliances with suppliers. In fact, supply chain integration and management is widely regarded as one of the most important aspects of sustaining competitive advantages in today's interconnected, global economy. Due to the importance of supply chain management to the success of most organizations, we make it the focus of this chapter (see Figure 12.1).

This chapter is similar in structure to the last chapter. We will use a process map and internal threat analysis to highlight the important characteristics of supply chain and production management that could have an impact on the

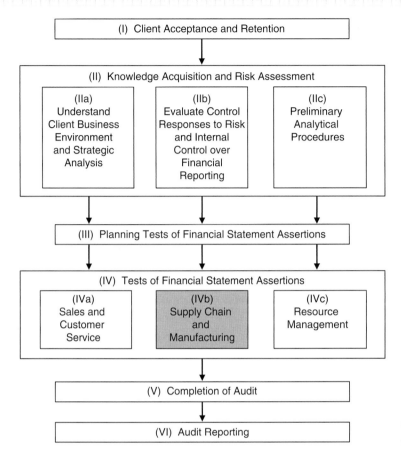

Figure 12.1 An Overview of the Audit Process

conduct of the audit. In the next section, we will discuss the basic objectives and activities of the supply chain and production. We will then discuss the transactions that occur within these processes, the nature of process risks, the process controls, entity level controls that affect control in this process and detailed within process internal controls over financial reporting. Table 12.1 presents a summary of the accounts affected by the supply chain and production process. Finally, we will use our understanding of the process to illustrate how the auditor reaches conclusions about residual risks, their implications for risk of material misstatement and designs specific tests of management assertions that are related to supply chain and production management.

AUTHORITATIVE GUIDANCE & STANDARDS

This chapter applies standards covered in previous chapters to a specific business process— supply chain management. Several observations from auditing standards are included throughout the chapter (e.g., ISA 320 **Materiality in Planning and Performing an Audit,** *ISA 330* **The Auditor's Responses to Assessed Risks,** *ISA 500* **Audit Evidence;** *AS 2105 [formerly 11]* **Consideration of Materiality in Planning and Performing an Audit,** *AS 2301 [formerly 13]* **The Auditor's Responses to the Risks of Material**

Table 12.1 *Relationships among Accounts and Processes*

Account Area or Class of Transactions	Core Processes		Resources Management Processes		
	Sales and Customer Service [Chapter 11]	Supply Chain and Production [Chapter 12]	Facilities [Chapter 13]	Human Resources [Chapters 7, 13]	Capital and Investment [Chapter 13]
Assets					
Cash and short-term investments	Cash receipts	Cash payments	Cash payments	Cash payments	Cash receipts, Cash payments, Trading securities
Receivables	Sales, Receipts, Returns, Bad debts				Investment income
Inventory	Cost of goods sold	Purchases, Production, Inventory valuation	Depreciation (product cost)	Direct labor costs	
Plant, property, and equipment including accumulate depreciation			Purchases of tangible assets, Asset disposals, Depreciation, Leased assets		
Investments					Purchase investments, Sell investments
Liabilities					
Accounts payable		Vendor payables			
Accrued liabilities	Commissions	Indirect overhead costs	Maintenance, Utilities, Leases	Wages, Benefits, Payroll taxes,	Interest, Dividends, Income taxes, Deferred tax
Debt and borrowed funds			Mortgage payable		Borrow funds, Repay debt
Paid in equity capital					Sales of equity, Repurchase of equity
Retained earnings					Dividends, Net income
Income and Expense					
Sales, revenue and gains	Sales		Asset disposals		Investment income and gains
Cost of goods sold	Cost of goods sold	Costs of production, Cost allocation	Depreciation (product cost)	Direct labor costs	
Depreciation expense			Depreciation (period cost)		

	Core Processes		Resources Management Processes		
Selling, general and administrative expenses			Maintenance, Utilities, Operating leases	Wages and related expenses	Interest expense
Tax expense	Sales taxes		Property taxes	Payroll taxes	
Other Disclosures/Accounts					
Other	Vendor rebates	Purchase commitments, Waste and spoilage	Interest capitalization, Impairments, Leasehold Improvements	Stock options, Pensions and post-retirement benefits	Off balance sheet items, Investment impairments

Misstatement, *AS 1105 [formerly 15]* **Audit Evidence**). *These standards provide the basic template for all evidence gathering activities in an audit and underlie much of what is discussed in Chapters 11 to 13. Rather than repeatedly refer to these standards we note at the beginning of each chapter that they underlie the entire subject matter of the chapters.*

An Overview of Objectives and Activities Related to Supply Chain and Production Management

The supply chain and production management process consists of the set of activities by which resources used in production are obtained and transformed into products and services to be sold to customers. This process includes design, procurement, purchasing, materials handling, and storage of raw materials and components. It also includes the myriad aspects of production—fabrication, assembly, finishing, and packaging. The process does not include the acquisition or maintenance of physical plant or management of the labor force (both are resource management processes to be discussed in Chapter 13). The process links directly to the marketing, sales, and distribution process discussed in Chapter 11. In fact, supply chain management and production can have a direct effect on marketing and sales because production problems may lead to inventory shortages (affecting delivery) or product quality (affecting customer service). In service firms, while the acquisition of human resources is done via resource management processes, the management of professionals is considered to be part of the production process. Indeed, failure to adequately manage the time of professionals may result in lost opportunities in much the same way that an empty seat on a plane represents lost revenue to an airline.

Process Objectives

The specific objectives of the supply chain and production management process critically depend on the strategy adopted by the firm to add value.

For example, a firm adopting a small market, high quality manufacturing process might configure its production processes quite differently than a broad market, low cost producer would. Figure 12.2 depicts the general process map for the supply chain and production process (note that it would need to be tailored in light of the specifics of the strategy to a much greater extent than sales and customer service process would). The overall objective of supply chain and production management is to assure that the organization can manufacture products as efficiently and effectively as possible. This overall objective can be decomposed into a number of very specific concerns related to procurement, materials handling, assembly, and packaging. Particularly important is ensuring the availability of materials, achieving efficiency of communications within the supply chain, facilitating efficient material handling and production, maintaining quality, and minimizing costs. These objectives will also facilitate marketing and sales objectives, and should result in achieving profitability goals. It is also

---

Process Objectives (dependent in part on strategic choices of client)

• Identify legitimate resource needs.
• Establish reliable supply chain meeting quality, cost, and delivery needs.
• Obtain resources at the best price given quality and other constraints.
• Minimize production costs.
• Ensure availability of resources at time and place needed.
• Minimize procurement and transaction costs.
• Minimize storage and handling costs.
• Protect resources and inventory from loss or unauthorized use.
• Make payments for legitimate obligations only.
• Produce goods and services that meet cost and quality targets.
• Maximize use of capacity.
• Minimize and control spoiled and defective units and properly handle by-products.
• Minimize and control waste.
• Capture and effectively utilize supplier and production information.
• Capture, process, and report information necessary for process improvement.

Process Activities

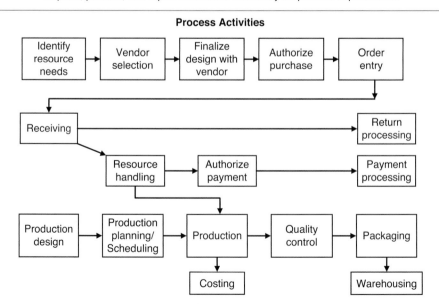

Process Data Streams

Information Feeds	Information Generation
• Strategic plan and budget	• Approved suppliers
• Material and component requirements	• Material requisitions
• Cost targets and procurement policies	• Material and component acquisitions
• Quality standards	• Contract terms and negotiated prices
• Manufacturing specifications	• Supplier performance measures
• Vendor history and profiles	• Standard cost schedules
• Sales forecasts and customer orders	• Production plan and schedule
• Capacity parameters	• Production statistics
• Inventory levels	• Payments
	• Delivery schedules
	• Changes in inventory levels and costs

Accounting Impact of Activities

Routine Transactions	Non-routine Transactions	Accounting Estimates
• Purchases	• Long-term supplier	• Inventory valuation/
• Material receipts	contracts	obsolescence
• Disbursements	• Standard cost	• Environmental
• Production	revisions	cleanup costs
• Transfer pricing	• Commodity hedging	• Vendor allowances
• Cost allocation	• Vendor returns and	or rebates accrual
• Spoilage	adjustments	
• Defective units		
• By-products		
• Waste and disposal		

Figure 12.2 Process Map: Supply Chain and Production Management

important that information about the process be used to improve process efficiency and facilitate effective decision making.

Process Activities

The typical activities that make up supply chain and production management are indicated in Figure 12.2. Although these activities would need to be tailored in light of the organization's strategic decisions (e.g., niche quality versus low cost), each step is necessary to achieve the objectives of the process.

- **Identification of resource needs**: Materials and components required for production are identified by management, engineers, and production planners based on current and future production plans. This activity involves assessing what components are needed, in what quantities, and at what point in time. For new materials, choices about quality, timing, and cost will impact what resources are to be obtained. In some situations, suppliers may be actively involved in designing or selecting the material or component that is needed. In the case of existing materials, inventory is monitored and appropriate action taken if supplies on hand fall below desired levels[i].

- **Vendor Selection:** Potential suppliers are identified and screened to determine those that potentially meet the quality, cost, payment, and delivery requirements of the company. Reliability and prior

[i]**EXAMPLE**

In the automotive industry, parts suppliers work with major car manufacturers to design and improve components that go into a new car. For example, different cars may require different sizes or shapes of filters, which are designed to meet the space and engineering requirements of the vehicle.

experience may have a significant impact on the acceptability of a specific vendor. Once selected, vendors may collaborate with the company on the specifications and design of materials to be supplied by the vendor.

- **Purchase Authorization:** The quantity, price, payment terms, and delivery schedule must be negotiated with the supplier. In many cases, purchase authorization will result in a long-term contract to provide a steady supply of materials or components. One-time or infrequent purchases may be handled differently each time.

- **Order Entry:** Specific transaction details are prepared and transmitted to the vendor for a purchase. Purchase orders can be prepared internally and sent to the supplier on a periodic basis. Alternatively, in the case of a long-term agreement, vendors can use technology to monitor inventory levels at the company and automatically ship materials when inventory falls below a specified level.

- **Receiving:** Incoming shipments are inspected, verified against internal documents, and accepted (or rejected). Shipments can arrive by public post or vendor shipping, or can be picked up by the organization's own personnel. In a just-in-time inventory system, inspection may be minimal due to the trust placed in the underlying relationship with the supplier.

- **Resource Handling:** Incoming shipments are prepared for movement or storage within the organization. Materials are often received at a central location, at which point they may be placed into general warehouse storage or moved to other company locations (e.g., retail locations). In a just-in-time environment, materials and components may go directly from receiving into production.

- **Authorize Payment:** Payments for shipments received are authorized according to organizational policies (e.g., taking discounts, avoiding interest or late fees).

- **Payment Processing:** Payments are prepared, approved, and forwarded to the vendor. Payments can be made by check or electronic funds transfer. In an integrated supply chain, payments may be tendered electronically upon delivery from the supplier.

- **Return Processing:** If incoming shipments are not acceptable (e.g., they do not meet quality specifications), they are returned to the vendor rather than placed in storage. Vendors should make appropriate billing adjustments for returned materials.

- **Production Design:** The arrangement of the factory and the production specifications of machinery will impact the materials and components needed for the production process. Size, shape, and packaging of materials and components can influence the way production is organized and impact the efficiency of the production process[ii].

- **Production Planning:** Not all products are exactly the same, and similar products may vary in size, shape, or color (e.g., consumer products like toothpaste). Production of different versions of products needs to be scheduled and may require changes to the assembly line. Changing an assembly line from one version of a product to another may be time consuming and costly. This activity is even more critical in a job order environment where each product or group of products is different and frequent changes are needed in the production process (e.g., furniture).

- **Production:** The fabrication, assembly, and completion of products and services are often the core activities in supply chain and production management. Production is the activity where resource inputs are transformed into new products. A main concern of production is tracking the stage of completion of work-in process or the location of inventory as it moves throughout the supply chain. This allows the organization to monitor cycle time within the process.

- **Quality Control:** Quality testing and inspection is often a necessary step in the production process to assure that quality standards are consistently achieved. Quality rejects can be reworked or treated as waste. Failure to assure product quality can have a negative impact on customer service.

- **Packaging:** This activity includes boxing, shrink-wrapping, and bundling finished goods for sale, shipment to customers, or storage in company facilities. Protection from accidental damage during movement and shipping is an important concern of packaging activities.

- **Warehousing:** Finished goods are stored until delivered to customers or shipped to retail outlets. Inventory in the warehouse should be protected from unauthorized use or accidental damage. Information systems should be able to track the location of inventory as it is moved through and around storage facilities.

- **Costing:** Tracking the costs of production is the purpose of cost accounting and can be a complex challenge for accountants. Allocating overhead costs, estimating labor costs, tracking material usage, and computing standard costs are part of this activity. The primary concern of costing is to assign a reasonable cost to specific units of production. There are many different ways to perform product costing depending on the objectives of management (e.g., direct costing, ABC costing, absorption costing).

The complexity of these activities will depend on the various strategic and process decisions made by the organization. Some of the decisions and circumstances that could affect these activities include:

- The nature of materials and components being purchased.
- The use of technology to integrate the supply chain.
- The method of delivery.
- The complexity of the production process (including extent of automation).
- The frequency of production changes.
- The complexity of standard costs.

- The nature of regulations in countries where products are produced or transferred as components to be included in finished products.
- The nature and volume of waste, defective units, and by-products.

For example, hazardous or perishable materials may require special handling arrangements. Deliveries made by third parties or the vendor can be handled on the loading dock, but materials to be picked up by the company necessitate acquisition of transportation services. Obviously, the more complex production and costing, the more challenging the process will be to manage. Managing waste can also be challenging, especially if it can have a negative impact on the environment. By-products and reworked units are potentially valuable to the company and also must be handled appropriately.

Of particular importance to the supply chain is the degree of integration with vendors. Current technology is allowing more and more companies to link information systems across the supply chain to improve the flow of information between suppliers and customers. These links can be made through proprietary networks (so-called electronic data interfaces or EDI) or across the Internet by establishing an electronic market where vendors and customers can interact. One advantage of supply chain integration is that it reduces transaction costs since paper flows are reduced and redundant procedures are eliminated. Integration also facilitates a just-in-time approach to inventory flows and reduces the level of excess inventory held across the entire supply chain, thus cutting storage and carrying costs. The primary disadvantage of supply chain integration is that it reduces the flexibility of a company to change suppliers when performance, quality, or price, become unacceptable. This inflexibility is exacerbated when suppliers have designed the components being supplied. Often, manufacturers are unable to switch suppliers until new designs replace current products, allowing a change in suppliers (e.g., automotive companies typically introduce new or redesigned models every three to four years).

The information requirements and output of supply chain and production management are described in Figure 12.2. Key information requirements include production specifications, inventory levels, supply channels, and sales forecasts. Production planning and material acquisitions are critically dependent on accurate sales forecasting if the company wishes to avoid either material shortages or excesses. Information output includes purchase and transaction data, production schedules, and supplier statistics. Production schedules may affect marketing and sales activities. Supplier statistics can be used to renegotiate contracts and alter the relationships in the supply chain, including dropping poorly performing vendors[iii].

Transactions Arising from Supply Chain and Production Management

The supply chain and production process potentially affects a broad range of accounts and transactions, as indicated in Figure 12.2. In general, the

[iii]**EXAMPLE**

A trend in consumer product manufacturing, especially clothing, is to send slightly defective units or products that do not quite meet quality standards to "outlet" stores, usually located in special shopping centers or malls. This is one way that a company obtains maximum value for its products. These products are usually labeled as "irregular" to avoid conflicts with local stores selling the same products at full retail prices. Outlet stores are also used to dispose of slow moving or outdated merchandise that retailers wish to remove to make space for newer products. By bringing this merchandise together into an outlet store, a manufacturer or retailer is able to dispose efficiently of excess inventory while minimizing the impact on its primary retail sales.

key transactions arising in this process are purchasing, disbursements, and production. The execution of these transactions is illustrated in Table 12.2 and discussed below.

Table 12.2 *Summary Supply Chain and Production Activities*

PROCESS/Activity	Documents	Journals, Ledgers, and Records Used	Typical Journal Entry
PURCHASES			
Requisitioning: Request for material or component purchase.	Purchase requisition (internal)		
Purchasing: Order transmitted to appropriate supplier based on open contracts or new supplier selection.	Purchase order (internal) Contract (external)	Approved vendor list	
Receiving: Resources are received and placed in storage or delivered to the requisitioning department.	Receiving report (internal) Bill of lading (external)	Receiving report journal	
Payable recognition: Liability recognized based on receipt of shipment and vendor invoice.	Vendor's invoice or statement (external) Voucher (internal)	Purchases journal **or** Voucher register	
Payable posting: The liability is posted to the appropriate vendor account.*		Accounts payable subsidiary ledger	
General accounting: The purchase, payable and asset or expense is recorded in the appropriate accounts.	Journal entry ticket (internal)	General ledger	Dr. Expenses Dr. Purchases (or inventory) Dr. Assets Cr. Accounts Payable
DISBURSEMENTS			
Check preparation: Liability identified for payment and a disbursement is prepared.	Check (internal) EFT authorization (internal)	Cash disbursements journal Check register	
Payment authorization: The payment is reviewed, authorized, and transmitted to the vendor.			
Payable posting: The payment is debited to the appropriate vendor account.		Accounts payable subsidiary ledger	
General accounting: The payment is recorded in the appropriate accounts.	Journal entry ticket (internal)	General ledger	Dr. Accounts Payable Dr. Accrued Liabilities Cr. Cash
PRODUCTION			
Start of production: Materials and components are placed into the manufacturing process.	Materials requisition (internal)	Raw materials perpetual inventory	Dr. Work-in-Process Cr. Raw Materials
Production: Machining and assembly of products.	Job cost ticket (internal) Work ticket (internal)		

(Continued)

Table 12.2 *(Continued)*

PROCESS/Activity	Documents	Journals, Ledgers and Records Used	Typical Journal Entry

Cost assignment: Costs of goods are determined and assigned to units.	Job cost ticket (internal)	Standard cost computations
		
		Overhead cost records
			Dr. Work-in-Process
			  Cr. Direct Labor
			    Applied**
			Dr. Work-in-Process
			  Cr. Overhead
			    Applied***

Finished Goods: Transfer of inventory to storage.			Dr. Finished Goods Cr. Work-in-Process

*A company that uses a voucher system may not maintain an accounts payable subsidiary ledger. Instead, the voucher register is used as the summary record of liabilities.

**The amount of labor assigned to work-in-process is usually based on standard cost computations but may be based on actual costs (as in a job cost system). In either case, a separate account is used to record direct labor costs that have been incurred. The balance of direct labor applied can be compared with the balance of actual direct labor on a periodic basis to determine if the company is assigning too much or too little direct labor to the units of production. If direct labor applied is significantly different from direct labor incurred, standard costs may not be reasonable under current economic conditions.

***The amount of overhead assigned to work-in-process is usually based on standard cost computations. A separate account is used to record overhead costs that have been incurred. The balance of overhead applied can be compared with the balance of actual overhead on a periodic basis to determine if the company is assigning too much or too little overhead to the units of production. If overhead applied is significantly different from overhead incurred, standard costs may not be reasonable under current economic conditions

Purchases

Material purchases may be initiated by a *purchase requisition* from the production department or because inventory reaches a restocking point that triggers an automatic reorder. The placement of an order is usually evidenced by the completion of a *purchase order*, although standing orders for some resources (e.g., long-term purchase contracts, utilities, or other monthly services) may obviate the need for a purchase order. Subsequent delivery of materials is evidenced by a *receiving report*. The *vendor's invoice* (and the receiving report) is the basis for recognizing a liability via the preparation of a *voucher*.[1]

The voucher and the appropriate supporting documents (e.g., purchase requisition, purchase order, receiving report, and the vendor's invoice/statement) are together referred to as a *voucher package,* which forms the basis for posting to the *voucher register*, *accounts payable subsidiary ledger,* and general ledger. The voucher register lists all vouchers in numerical order and the subsidiary ledger lists liabilities by vendor. A given vendor may have multiple vouchers outstanding at any point in time. The purchase process can be readily automated if both the supplier and the buyer allow electronic orders to flow between the computer systems of the respective organizations.

The key event in the purchasing process is the delivery (or, in some cases, shipment) of resources to the company. At this point, a liability exists that is owed to the supplier (vendor). This means that the receiving report (or shipping notification) is the boundary document representing a liability. In many systems, however, the vendor's invoice or monthly statement is used to record the liability because it contains complete information about prices and totals. This situation could lead to a delay in the recognition of liabilities and represents a potential timing problem for the auditor. This delay could be extensive, especially if liabilities are posted only on receipt of vendors' monthly statements. Again, with electronic data interchange all of this can be set up so that most of these handling steps can be eliminated from the buyer's system.

Disbursements

The disbursement process comprises the activities for paying vendors for goods and services. Payment terms and the availability of cash will determine when checks are prepared or funds transferred. A **check register** lists the checks issued on a specific account in sequence of issue. A **cash disbursements journal** is used to list all payments in chronological order. Once a check is prepared, the supporting documents (e.g., the voucher package) and the unsigned check are sent to an appropriate corporate official (typically the treasurer) for approval (signature) and mailing. Information contained in the cash disbursements journal is used to update the accounts payable subsidiary ledger and the general ledger. The key event in the process is the delivery of a check to the vendor, usually by mail, but increasingly through electronic funds transfer, which can be automated using electronic data interchange. At that point, the liability is satisfied.[2]

AUTHORITATIVE GUIDANCE & STANDARDS

Because cash disbursements can be paid in response to fictitious purchases or based on inappropriate dealings with vendors (ISA 240 **The Auditor's Responsibilities Relating to Fraud in an Audit of Financial Statements,** *PCAOB AS 2401 (formerly AU 316)* **Consideration of Fraud in a Financial Statement Audit***), auditors focus on the existence assertion when examining disbursements.*

Production

Production involves the internal movement and transformation of materials and components to produce goods and services for sale. Production activities do not usually generate transactions with outside parties once the raw materials or components have been supplied.[3] Inventory related accounts include Supplies Inventory, Raw Materials Inventory, Work-In-Process Inventory, Finished Goods Inventory, and Cost of Goods Sold. In order to effectively manage inventory, however, a company will typically use other accounts for accumulating costs to be assigned to individual units of inventory. Accounts used for cost assignment include Raw Materials Used, Direct Labor Applied, Direct Labor Incurred, Factory Overhead Applied, Factory Overhead Incurred, and Cost of Goods Manufactured. Other accounts may be needed to record waste, defective units, or by-products or variances from standard costs.

Of importance to the accounting function is the point at which inventory is transformed from raw materials to work-in-process, and from work-in-process to finished goods. Also of importance is the way in which the cost accounting

Table 12.3 *Perpetual Inventory Record*

PRODUCT: *K3456, Gasket Cover*							
Date	Document Reference	Unit Cost In	Unit Cost Out	Number In	Number Out	Balance (units)	Balance (cost)
1/1/x7	Balance					120	$1,218
1/15/x7	RR 10292	10.40		1000		1120	11,618
1/25/x7	SI 90927		10.37		320	800	8,300
2/3/x7	RR 10333	10.67		800		1600	16,836
2/27/x7	SI 91233		10.52		440	1160	12,207
3/15/x7	SI 91444		10.52		235	925	9,735
3/22/x7	RR 10568	10.95		750		1675	17,948

system assigns labor and overhead costs to work-in-process. A company may use a job cost system, a process cost system, or an activity-based cost system, but the issue is essentially the same from the auditor's point of view—determining the appropriate cost of inventory as it is transformed by the manufacturing process. The system should provide a reasonable basis to track the physical movement of inventory, the assignment of labor and overhead costs to units, and the proper classification of units at each stage of the process. Central to the process is the **perpetual inventory system**. An example of a traditional perpetual inventory record to track inventory levels is shown in Table 12.3.

Risk Assessment for Supply Chain and Production Management

An internal threat analysis used for risk assessment of supply chain and production management is illustrated in Table 12.4. A number of potential risks are identified in the first column and then linked to entity level and process level controls that could be used to mitigate and monitor the risks. This list is not intended to be exhaustive, and process risks could vary across organizations due to differences in the activities within the process. Furthermore, the controls are not intended to be comprehensive.

Table 12.4 *Risk Assessment: Supply Chain and Production Management*

Process Risks	Entity and Process Level Controls Linked to Risks	Performance Measures
(1) Failing to select an appropriate supplier or obtain an adequate supply of appropriate resources.	• Forecast resource needs based on sales and link to procurement activities. • Investigate suppliers. • Long-term contracts covering supply of key materials and components. • Electronic interface with suppliers. • Establish back-up suppliers. • Periodically review open purchase orders. • Just-in-time inventory system.	• Financial ratios of suppliers • Number of suppliers. • Supplier on-time performance. • Frequency of material outages. • Days lost to material shortages. • Production versus forecast.

Process Risks	Entity and Process Level Controls Linked to Risks	Performance Measures
(2) Acquiring unneeded or excess resources.	<ul><li>Monitor inventory levels.</li><li>Automated replenishment system.</li><li>Segregate purchase authorization from other activities.</li><li>Independent verification of purchases.</li><li>Just-in-time inventory system.</li></ul>	<ul><li>Material turnover.</li><li>Rate of material spoilage or obsolescence.</li><li>Production versus forecast.</li></ul>
(3) Purchases that do not meet quality, price, payment, or delivery specifications.	<ul><li>General authorization for routine purchases.</li><li>Specific authorization procedures for unusual or high-value resources.</li><li>Long-term contracts covering supply of key materials and components.</li><li>Independent verification of purchases.</li><li>Quality inspection prior to acceptance of shipment.</li></ul>	<ul><li>Supplier reject or defect rates.</li><li>Supplier on-time delivery statistics.</li><li>Material costs.</li><li>Purchase order error rates.</li><li>Material price and usage variances.</li><li>External quality ratings.</li><li>Customer complaints.</li></ul>
(4) Excess transaction processing costs.	<ul><li>Electronic processing of purchase transactions.</li><li>Establish process for routine purchases.</li><li>Monitor process performance.</li></ul>	<ul><li>Processing cost per purchase transaction.</li><li>Percentage of purchases in electronic form.</li><li>Percentage of payments in electronic form.</li></ul>
(5) Damage or spoilage of materials after receipt.	<ul><li>Adequate personnel training.</li><li>Schedule deliveries to allow time for proper handling.</li><li>Establish proper handling procedures by type of material.</li><li>Well-designed layout for receiving area.</li></ul>	<ul><li>Material usage variances.</li><li>Value of purchase returns.</li><li>Costs of material spoilage.</li></ul>
(6) Unauthorized use or loss of resources including inventory shrinkage.	<ul><li>Physical security.</li><li>Movement of inventory only upon appropriate authorization.</li><li>Periodic book to physical inventory reconciliation.</li><li>Background checks of personnel.</li></ul>	<ul><li>Inventory shrinkage.</li><li>Book to physical discrepancies in inventory.</li></ul>
(7) Acceptance of unauthorized or inappropriate shipments.	<ul><li>Quality inspection at time of receipt.</li><li>Do not accept unknown shipments.</li></ul>	<ul><li>Value of purchase returns.</li><li>Frequency of rejected deliveries.</li></ul>
(8) Unauthorized or inappropriate payments.	<ul><li>Payments generated upon completion of appropriate documentation.</li><li>Cancel supporting documentation upon payment to avoid duplication.</li><li>Security over checks, check writing equipment, and check signing plates.</li><li>Independent handling and verification of payments.</li></ul>	<ul><li>Frequency and number of payments without full documentation.</li><li>Frequency and number of vendor complaints.</li><li>Cash losses.</li><li>Percentage of payments made electronically.</li></ul>
(9) Inaccurate information processing.	<ul><li>Proper completion and verification of supporting documents.</li><li>Appropriate segregation of duties across activities.</li><li>Use of standard control numbers for parts, vendors, products, etc.</li><li>Update files and accounting records on a timely basis.</li></ul>	<ul><li>Percent of transactions subject to processing errors.</li><li>Size of transaction adjustments.</li><li>Number of transaction adjustments.</li></ul>

(Continued)

Table 12.4 *(Continued)*

Process Risks	Entity and Process Level Controls Linked to Risks	Performance Measures
(10) Failure to capture desired information.	• Use and verify pre-numbered documents for transactions. • Record all events and transactions on a timely basis.	• Number of missing documents from sequence. • Number of missing fields in purchase, vendor or inventory record.
(11) Inaccurate valuation of liabilities.	• Verify recorded liabilities and vendor's invoice against supporting documentation. • Use of voucher system for obligations. • Pre-numbered vouchers used in sequence.	• Number and amount of billing adjustments. • Frequency and resolution of billing disputes. • Missing voucher numbers. • Number of warranty claims/recalls
(12) Failure to pay obligations on a timely basis.	• Use automated payment timing system. • Pay bills upon presentment. • Follow up on vendor correspondence or complaints.	• Value of lost discounts. • Vendor finance charges. • Payable turnover rate.
(13) Inefficient production design resulting in increased long-term costs.	• Research into production best practices. • Competitive research. • Adequate internal R&D. • Effective capital budgeting procedures.	• Production variances. • Changeover times. • Production cycle time per production stage. • Material usage versus planned. • Time lost to maintenance and equipment failure.
(14) Inefficient production planning resulting in increased costs.	• Use of materials resource planning technology. • Use of production scheduling technology. • Monitoring of frequency and efficiency of production changeovers.	• Percent of capacity used. • Frequency of changeover. • Changeover times.
(15) Poor quality products due to production problems.	• Monitor defect and rework rates. • Timely intervention upon detection of quality problems.	• Product reject rates. • Product rework rates. • Cost of rework.
(16) Excess spoilage or waste.	• Monitor spoilage and waste rates against targets. • Timely intervention in process.	• Cost of waste and spoilage. • Volume of waste and spoilage.
(17) Improper handling of spoilage and waste.	• Establish procedures and guidelines for disposal of wastes. • Long-term contract with reputable waste disposal company.	• Cost of waste disposal. • Fines or citations for improper waste disposal.
(18) Inappropriate or inaccurate cost allocation and standard costing.	• Cost allocations verified against supporting documentation. • Review and authorization of standard costs. • Monitoring of standard cost variances for systematic discrepancies.	• Production costs actual versus budget. • Production cost variances.
(19) Excess storage or transportation costs.	• Monitor turnover statistics. • Link sales forecasts to materials orders. • Just-in-time inventory systems. • Use of material resource planning technology.	• Finished goods turnover. • Days' supply on hand. • Warehousing and shipping costs.

Process risks affecting supply chain and production management can come from a number of sources. Notice that a specific risk can be associated with many different causes. The more causes that interact to affect a risk within a process, the more likely it is that the risk will become a problem. For example, the risk that the company fails to obtain an adequate supply of materials delivered on a timely basis could be due to weak management (leadership), poor planning, inadequate information systems, or human error. As is the case in most processes, technology, human resource, and information risks are of particular importance to the auditor because their interaction has a direct impact on the quality of information that is generated within a process.

Analysis of Process Controls

As in prior examples, different types of controls can be used to mitigate different risks. The decision to accept, avoid, transfer, or reduce a risk is part of the overall design of the process and should follow from the strategy and objectives adopted by the organization. For example, the use of technology to integrate the supply chain may reduce many risks (e.g., delays in deliveries) but also creates other information processing and security risks (e.g., external hacking) that are not present in an isolated internal system. Furthermore, the controls that are available in a complex technology environment are different from those that can be used in a simpler, partially manual, system[iv].

Column 2 of Table 12.4 describes numerous controls that might be effective for reducing risks related to supply chain and production management:

- **Segregation of Duties**: Incompatible duties that are important to segregate within the supply chain and production process include (1) production design and planning; (2) soliciting and selecting potential suppliers; (3) authorizing purchases, handling inventory, accounting for inventory activity; and (4) authorizing disbursements and processing disbursements.

- **Processing Controls**: There is a broad range of processing controls that can be implemented in the supply chain or as part of production depending on the specific activities and steps of the process. Important authorization steps include selecting suppliers, ordering inventory, accepting shipments, controlling production, warehousing finished goods, handling waste and spoilage, and processing disbursements. Appropriate documents that should be used within the process include purchase orders, receiving reports, vouchers, checks, inventory movement documents,[4] and job tickets (see Table 12.4). Most of these documents should be pre-numbered and used in sequence. Key journals and ledgers include the payable ledger or voucher register, the cash disbursement journal, standard cost schedules, and perpetual inventory

---

[iv]EXAMPLE

As part of supply chain management, many companies have adopted a policy of immediate electronic funds transfer to suppliers upon electronic presentation of an invoice. Because billing and payment are fully automated, many of the normal steps in a traditional disbursement process are eliminated. This approach may increase some risks (unauthorized payments) but reduce other risks (e.g., billing errors and late payments). The net reduction in administrative costs and the increased predictability of cash flows result in savings to both the vendor and the customer.

records. Numerous independent verifications can be performed within the process, including periodic physical inventories, checking documents for discrepancies, comparing batch and control totals, and investigating unusual events. Many of these procedures are directly relevant to the auditor's evaluation of internal control over financial reporting.

- **Physical Controls**: Limiting access to inventory and cash are obvious controls. It is also important to limit access to documents, records, and computerized systems that could be used to authorize inappropriate movement of inventory or access to cash (e.g., blank checks).

BOX 12.1 TESTING INTERNAL CONTROLS RELATED TO SUPPLY CHAIN AND PRODUCTION MANAGEMENT

Entity Level Controls

Performance Reviews and Overall Process Management

- *Review policies for establishing strategy, goals and budgets for supply chain management and production.*
- *Evaluate whether policies and decisions related to supply chain management and production are consistent with the overall strategy and objectives of the organization.*
- *Review and evaluate internal analyses on competitors, production trends, and technology.*
- *Examine documentation in support of key decisions related to supply chain management and production.*
- *Review acquisitions, expense, and cash budgets, and verify that variances have been investigated.*
- *Review payables reports and verify proper and timely handling of adjustments.*
- *Review that standard costs are developed based on an in-depth analysis of product design, resource needs, and the production process.*
- *Verify that cost accounting variances are monitored and resolved on a timely basis.*
- *Verify that slow-moving inventory is monitored and realizability is periodically assessed.*
- *Verify that waste, scrap, and by-products are monitored for disposal.*
- *Evaluate the competence and training of key individuals within the process.*
- *Discuss performance measures and process evaluation with appropriate management personnel and evaluate whether process oversight is effective.*
- *Identify and review appropriate process performance indicators relevant to key risks.*

Detailed Internal Controls over Financial Reporting

Information Processing Controls

Proper Authorization Procedures

- *Verify existence of general authorization for purchasing goods and services (e.g., purchasing policy manuals, purchasing limits, standardized quality requirements, standardized payment terms).*

- *Review the process for revising general purchasing authorizations.*
- *Re-perform information systems commands associated with automated controls to ensure that they are operating effectively (with assistance of IT Assurance specialist).*
- *Obtain a sample of vouchers and verify that all required approvals are present.*
- *Obtain a sample of disbursement checks and verify that all required approvals are present.*
- *Verify that the movement/transformation of inventory is properly authorized (including new acquisitions, materials placed in process, and sales).*
- *Verify that standard costs are properly authorized.*
- *Verify that dispositions of obsolete inventory are properly authorized and recorded.*
- *Verify that dispositions of waste, scrap, and by-products are properly authorized.*

Use of Adequate Documents and Records

- *Verify that documents are pre-numbered and used in sequence including purchase orders, receiving reports, vouchers, checks, time cards, job tickets, and inventory movement documents.*
- *Observe that master inventory files are maintained on a perpetual basis.*

Independent Verification of Employee Responsibilities

- *Verify that all exception reports and computer edit listings are investigated and cleared on a timely basis.*
- *Obtain a sample of vouchers and verify that all supporting documents are present and that verifications are noted on supporting documents.**
- *Obtain a sample of general disbursement checks and verify that all supporting documents are present and that verifications are noted on supporting documents.*
- *Verify that the proper reconciliations are performed on a timely basis and exceptions fully investigated, including (1) bank reconciliations with the check register, (2) voucher journal with payable postings, (3) perpetual records with physical counts and general ledger activity, and (4) standard cost calculations and overhead allocations with actual results.*

Physical Controls

- *Observe facilities and client personnel for proper physical controls (e.g., locks, security cameras, etc.) over assets, documents and records.*

Segregation of Duties

- *Verify that proper segregation of duties exists for purchasing, production, and accounting activities.*
- *Discuss work responsibilities with employees assigned to transaction*

processing and evaluate effectiveness and consistency of individual responsibilities.

- *Examine procedures manuals, personnel policies, organization charts, the chart of accounts, and other documents and records used in the system.*
- *Identify and evaluate significant changes within the process occurring during the year.*
  - o *Observe personnel in the performance of their duties related to the approval and verification of transactions, including:*
  - o *Review and follow up on open orders.*
  - o *Preparation of receiving reports and verification of incoming shipments.*
  - o *Movement of goods out of receiving to storage or other departments.*
  - o *Check preparation and approval.*
  - o *Cancellation of supporting documents upon payment to vendor.*
  - o *Check distribution.*

Note:

* The same samples of vouchers and checks can be used to test both authorization and various independent verifications.

The extent to which these controls are used, how frequently they are used, and whether they are automated depends on the specific design of the process. Not all organizations will need to use all controls as some may be redundant or a specific risk may not be significant to the organization.

Entity Level Controls Affecting Supply Chain and Production Management Process

Box 12.1 "Testing Internal Controls Related to Supply Chain and Production Management" describes entity level controls that might be effective for reducing the risks related to the supply chain and production management process. Entity level controls that might affect the process include monitoring controls (e.g., performance measures) over such areas as:

- Inventory levels.
- Supplier performance (quality, service, processing errors, and timeliness).
- Levels of waste and spoilage.
- Product quality.
- Technological developments impacting the supply chain and production.
- Production efficiency and operational effectiveness.

Appropriate performance indicators that could be monitored for the identified process risks are listed in Table 12.4 in the fourth column. These measures cover four broad categories including:

1. Supplier performance: quality, timeliness, cost, shortages.

2. Inventory handling and usage: inventory levels, damage, waste, spoilage, defects.

3. Inventory costs: standard costs, variances, production efficiency, cycle times.

4. Transaction processing: error rates, processing costs.

Given the relative importance of measuring inventory costs, most manufacturers have relatively well-developed cost data on production and inventory that the auditor can use to evaluate process risks. However, nonfinancial data on supplier performance may not be integrated into the accounting system and may be difficult to obtain unless an organization has a highly integrated ERP system. The auditor must consider the reliability of information generated outside the accounting system (or alternatively perform procedures to reconcile this information to that contained in the accounting system or have the IT Assurance auditor who is a member of the team provide such assurance) before placing weight on it as evidence about process risks.

The interpretation of performance indicators may require that the auditor consider a number of measures jointly in order to identify patterns or trends in process performance. For example, a decrease in the quality of materials delivered by suppliers could be evidenced by higher delivery reject rates, discrepancies between materials ordered and delivered, material usage variances, external reports on product quality, or customer complaints. At the same time, the deterioration in quality of materials or components can also show up in higher rates of defects, increased material waste, or more frequent production stops to adjust machinery to handle the material. Seeing evidence of such problems will affect how the auditor approaches the tests of internal controls as well as the nature of the substantive testing that he or she plans to do.

Analysis of Internal Control over Financial Reporting

Controls over the reliability of information are particularly important to the auditor's analysis. Table 12.5 identifies a number of accounting controls, discussed below, that could be potentially relevant to purchases, disbursements, and inventory.

Purchases: The most critical controls for supply chain management focus on the proper selection of suppliers, authorization of purchases, and completeness of liabilities. Key internal controls related to financial reporting include the following:

- Suppliers should be selected only after careful review of operational and financial historical performance of alternative potential suppliers. Supplier evaluation should be segregated from supplier selection. Only appropriate purchases of materials should be made, and disbursements should be in accordance with the terms of an approved acquisition.

Table 12.5 *Internal Controls over Financial Reporting For Purchases And Production*

Activity	Management Assertions	Typical Internal Controls for Purchases and Production
Purchases	Occurrence (O) Completeness (C) Accuracy (A) Cut-off (T) Classification (CL)	• Segregate purchase accounting from purchasing and production. (O, C, A) • Maintain an up-to-date list of approved vendors and parts/supplies to be acquired. (O, C, CL) • Use pre-numbered requisitions, purchase orders, and receiving reports. (O, C, A, T) • Independently review and provide indication of approval of purchase orders. (O, A) • Verify incoming shipments against purchase orders and document discrepancies. (O, C, A, T) • Vendor invoices and/or vendor statements sent directly to payable department. (C, A) • Prices, quantities, payment terms, extensions and totals per the vendor's invoice verified against other transaction documents and company policies. (O, C, A) • Review expense or asset classification for each expenditure. (CL) • Reconcile monthly vendor statements against individual transaction activity (purchases and payments). (C, A, T) • Maintain a file of unpaid liabilities arranged by due date. (A, T, CL) • Post transactions on a timely basis. (O, C, A, T, CL) • Use control and hash totals to verify accuracy of postings. (C, A) • Maintain an up-to-date chart of accounts. (C, A, CL) • Maintain policy on expense recognition for assets of small value. (CL) • Reconcile general ledger totals and activity with the subsidiary ledger and supporting journals. (A, T) • Review all adjusting journal entries prior to posting. (O, C, A, T, CL). • Investigate unusual entries to accounts. (O, C, A T, CL)
Disbursements	Occurrence (O) Completeness (C) Accuracy (A) Cut-off (T) Classification (CL)	• Separate disbursement accounting from check preparation (treasury), purchasing, payable recognition and posting. (O, C, A) • Use pre-numbered checks or electronic funds transfers for payments. (O, C, A, T) • Cancel supporting documents related to disbursements to avoid duplicate payment. (O, C, A, T) • Use check writing machine or computer-generated checks with appropriate safeguards. (O, A) • Immediately void spoiled checks. (O, C, A, T) • Verify amount and detail of checks against supporting documents. (O, C, A, T) • Post transactions on a timely basis. (O, C, A, T, CL) • Use control and hash totals to verify accuracy of postings. (C, A) • Reconcile bank accounts independently of the cash disbursement process. (O, C, A, T) • Account for the sequence of checks used and follow up on stale checks outstanding. (C, A, T) • Reconcile general ledger totals and activity with subsidiary ledger and supporting journals with special attention to unpaid balances. (O, C, A, T)

Production	Occurrence (O)	• Segregate inventory accounting from purchase authorization and handling of inventory. (O, C, A)
	Completeness (C)	• Track costs by product (including materials, labor and overhead costs). (O, C, A)
	Accuracy (A)	• Establish standard costs based on analysis of product design, resource needs, and the production process. (C, A, CL)
	Cut-off (T)	• Evaluate standard costs against actual costs. (C, A, CL)
	Classification (CL)	• Monitor cost variances and investigate on a timely basis. (C, A)
		• Monitor slow-moving inventory and assess its realizability. (O, C, A, CL)
		• Monitor and properly account for disposal of waste, scrap, and by-products. (O, C, A, T, CL)
		• Maintain adequate perpetual records. (O, C, A, T)
		• Maintain a comprehensive chart of accounts for production-related activity. (C, A, T)
		• Use pre-numbered transfer/work documents to account for conversion of materials into finished goods and related movement through the production process. (C, A, T, CL)
		• Periodically reconcile perpetual records with general ledger activity and physical counts. (C, A, T, CL)
		• Reconcile and adjust actual versus applied overhead as needed. (C, A, T, CL)

- Existence or validity is less a concern because recognition of fictitious liabilities is not common except in the case of related party transactions (see Chapter 4).

- Proper valuation is facilitated by timely completion of a pre-numbered receiving report. Verification of the vendor's invoice by comparison with receiving reports and other supporting documents is also helpful.

- Timing is important because liabilities may not be recorded until a vendor's invoice is received. The most important control in this respect is the timely preparation of a voucher. In electronic data interchange systems the opposite might occur, goods are not yet received yet the supplier triggers an electronic payment.

- Classification is also important because of the large number of expense and asset accounts that can be affected by procurement. A formal accounting policy defining the separation of assets from expenses assists in proper classification of expenditures.

- Independent review of account classifications for reasonableness, the use of check digits or hash totals, and the use of computerized posting tend to increase the reliability of transaction processing.

Disbursements: Cash payments should be tightly controlled to avoid improper use of cash and to assure that liabilities are paid at the proper amount. Key internal controls related to financial reporting include the following:

- The most critical control element for disbursements is authorization, with separation of check preparation from purchasing and payment authorization. This separation facilitates the independent review of payments to assure that they are proper and accurate. Checks are often prepared electronically and signed using a check-signing machine. The current trend toward electronic funds transfer is reducing the need for manual controls over check preparation but creates a need for other types of controls (e.g., security and data integrity) that often will require evaluation by an IT specialist.

- Payable postings should be verified.
- Documents supporting disbursements should be canceled after payment to assure that the same liability is not paid twice.

Inventory: Controls over inventory emphasize the flow and cost of inventory in the system because management needs to know who has what inventory, and for what purpose, at each stage of processing. Key internal controls related to financial reporting include the following:

- The perpetual inventory system is the key element for establishing control over inventory.
- A periodic physical verification is also an important source of control over inventory.
- Internal control is also needed in the area of waste and scrap (and possibly by-products). Scrap usually has a positive market value and should be processed and sold to a recycler. Waste is more problematic because its disposal may require compliance with complex environmental laws.

Not all controls within an audit-sensitive process are of interest to the auditor— only those that contribute to a reduction of significant residual risks or control risk related to specific financial reporting assertions. It is the auditor's responsibility to obtain an adequate understanding of process controls including controls over financial reporting so as to have a basis for his or her conclusions about control risk for specific audit objectives. Important controls that contribute to significant risk reduction will be subject to additional testing to obtain evidence that they are effective.

Testing Internal Control over Financial Reporting

Tests of controls that could be used for the supply chain and production management process divided into entity level controls and detailed ICOFR process level controls are described in Box 12.1 "Testing Internal Controls Related to Supply Chain and Production Management." These tests may not apply to all organizations and need to be adapted to the specific circumstances of a system and the auditor's risk assessments. Tests of controls related to the supply chain and production tend to emphasize proper authorization of transactions, evidence that transaction amounts have been properly verified, and evidence that production costs are properly tracked and estimated. The auditor should first determine that the company has appropriate policies regarding purchasing, including assessing the need for goods and services, the selection of vendors, the negotiation of prices and terms, and the receipt of goods and services. The organization should also have clear-cut policies regarding the preparation and authorization of disbursements. Furthermore, the organization should have a well-designed information system for tracking production and allocating overhead costs. Finally, the auditor should examine the process by which these policies are updated.

The auditor has three basic approaches for determining if existing policies are being properly applied. The first is to interview company employees and observe them in the performance of their duties. Recall the cautions in Chapter 9 about the reliability of inquiry and how to enhance its reliability. Observation may be particularly useful for assessing the handling and movement of inventory during receiving and production. Observation should be as unobtrusive as possible and may need to be repeated under different conditions and at different times, especially if the client has a change in personnel or procedures.

The second approach is to obtain documentary evidence of the performance of control procedures. Documentation can include internal analyses, exception reports, internal memos and communications, procedures manuals, programming codes for production and inventory management systems, and transaction documents. The auditor will usually verify that pre-numbered documents are being properly used in sequence. The auditor may then select a sample of acquisitions and disbursements and examine evidence that the appropriate authorizations are present and that required reviews have been performed by responsible personnel. For example, the auditor could look at the purchasing department's sign-off on a purchase order to verify that appropriate quality, prices, and terms have been obtained. Proper receipt of goods may be evidenced by the warehouse supervisor's signature or initials on the receiving report. For disbursements, the auditor may examine canceled checks and supporting documents to ascertain that all proper authorizations are present. The results from vouching tests must be interpreted carefully, however, because signatures and initials do not guarantee that a transaction was processed correctly.

The third approach is to re-perform controls to see that they are operating properly. Re-performance is used to test automated controls embedded in complex inventory systems, electronic data interchange (EDI) systems, or integrated enterprise resource planning systems. To test automated controls, auditors will send test items through the system to ensure that controls are operating effectively. Basically, automated controls should prevent commands from being performed that are outside limits established within the system (e.g., fictitious vendor numbers, product costing outside of standard costing amounts). These tests are often performed by IT assurance specialists who are members of the audit team.

Perpetual inventory records are a critical element for controlling the movement of materials and the production of inventory. Accurate accounting for and control over inventory requires that perpetual inventory records be accurate. Such control is becoming even more critical as manufacturers move to just-in-time inventory systems, establish computerized data links with suppliers, and try to minimize the carrying costs of inventory on hand. The client (and the auditor) will periodically observe inventory to determine if the perpetual records are accurate. The more reliable the perpetual records are, the more comfort the auditor has that inventory balances are correctly stated.

Figure 12.3 illustrates that a number of process risks have been substantially reduced by process controls in our example, including the risk of receiving poor quality materials, excess spoilage, unrecorded liabilities, and processing errors. The latter two risks are particularly important because they directly impact the reliability of financial information. To test controls over material quality, the auditor could review the vendor approval and purchase authorization process by conducting interviews with key personnel, examining long-term purchase contracts, and documenting and understanding inspection processes during receipt of shipments at the client.[5] To test controls over information processing and recognition of liabilities, the auditor could test individual purchase transactions using the procedures described in Box 12.1 "Testing Internal Controls Related to Supply Chain and Production Management." Additional tests would be performed for controls over excess spoilage. Controls related to poor production design would not be needed since the risk is not significant. Figure 12.3 suggests that the auditor believes there are no effective controls over production scheduling and the controls for avoiding material shortages are not effective enough to justify further examination (i.e., the risk remains high in spite of the control assessment).

Conclusions about Residual Risks from Supply Chain and Production Management

Our analysis thus far can be summarized as follows with its implications for the financial statement transactions cycles and accounts: High residual risk of poor quality materials would cause the auditor to adjust expectations about costs, margins, and cost variances. The risk could also impact assertions related to the valuation of inventory or the valuation of warranty reserves. Finally, the residual risk might create stress or pressure on management to compensate in ways that are inappropriate or not in the best interests of the organization, including the possibility of manipulating

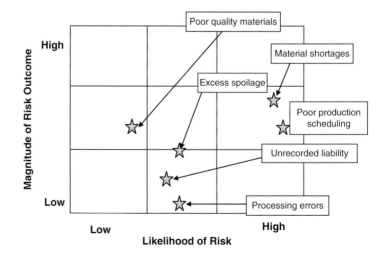

Figure 12.3 *Assessment of Process Risks for Supply Chain and Production Management**

*For ease of exposition, not all risks identified in Box 12.1 "Testing Internal Controls Related to Supply Chain and Production Management" have been included in the risk map. This does not imply that omitted risks are less important. The risks that are included were chosen for illustrative purposes only

performance measures to disguise the problem. Seven of the risks identified in Table 12.4 are included in Figure 12.3 to illustrate how process risk mapping after testing controls can be formatted graphically. Risks in the upper right-hand portion of the chart remain significant residual risks, thus having the potential for high risk of material misstatement. We see that many of these risks have been reduced to an acceptable level (lower left portion) due to entity level controls, process controls and internal controls over financial reporting. Of course, if the auditor is going to rely on these controls to reduce substantive testing then the controls must be tested to an extent necessary to support the auditor's reduction of control risk.

Identifying Significant Residual Risks

Figure 12.3 indicates that the risk of errors in information processing, unrecorded liabilities, or lost inventory appear to be low. However, these areas are often the focus of a great deal of an auditor's substantive testing. If controls are effectively designed and tested then the amount of substantive testing in those areas should be reduced. As discussed in Chapter 10, this is an example of how decisions to rely on controls (or not) affects the extent of substantive tests.

In our example, it is shortages of material and poor production scheduling that represent significant residual risks. These are the risks that suggest areas that might lead to high risk of material misstatement for specific assertions the auditor should consider in further detail.

The risk of inadequate materials will condition the auditor's expectations about a number of performance measures. Costs would be higher (due to the allocation of fixed costs over fewer units produced), inventory turnover would be higher due to lower levels of inventory, and order backlogs would be longer. Material shortages may impact the valuation of long-term contracts that would necessitate additional substantive testing or disclosures. If the company decided to use forward contracts or other forms of derivatives to manage the risks associated with obtaining a steady supply of materials, the auditor would need to consider testing the financial reporting and disclosure impact of such arrangements. Furthermore, problems associated with an inadequate supply of materials could cause deterioration in the control environment. Procurement managers might choose to deal with less reputable or reliable suppliers in order to obtain adequate supplies, or might accept lower quality materials. In the worst case, managers might manipulate inventory and production information in order to hide the problems.

Although poor production scheduling is considered to be a potentially likely risk as indicated in Figure 12.3, the magnitude of its impact is considered to be relatively low. Consequently, the auditor would devote moderate attention to this risk. The risk will probably affect the auditor's expectations about costs, margins, and plant utilization, but probably will not have a significant impact on material financial statement assertions. The auditor's testing related to this risk could be limited to substantive analytical procedures and would not involve either tests of transactions or other substantive tests.

In the remainder of this chapter, we will discuss substantive tests that can be used if specific financial statement assertions related to the supply chain or production are considered to have high inherent or control risk. These tests specifically apply to accounts payable and inventory. Different substantive tests are used for different assertions, so the auditor will select the substantive tests that are relevant for the specific assertions that have high risk.

Planning Tests of Management Assertions: Purchases and Accounts Payable

Supply chain activities generate purchase transactions, which usually create liabilities that are reported on the balance sheet. The purpose of substantive tests of accounts payable is to verify the completeness and valuation of the company's obligations. Auditors are also concerned about completeness and understandability assertions related to presentation and disclosure. A comprehensive approach for testing accounts payable is presented in Table 12.6. The primary substantive tests for purchases and payables include substantive analytical procedures and various test of details such as:

- Tests of purchase and disbursement transactions.
- Tests of the Accounts Payable Trial Balance.
- Tests for unrecorded liabilities.
- Confirmation of payables.

Most of these audit procedures will provide evidence for more than one assertion. Very few clients would need all these tests unless they had very high risk of material misstatement for numerous management assertions related to purchases and accounts payable.

Substantive Analytical Procedures

Substantive analytical procedures are especially useful for testing expense accounts that arise from procurement activities. For some accounts, substantive analytical procedures may be the only tests that are necessary. Different analytical approaches are used for different accounts depending on the nature of the account balance and the level of precision desired. As usual, the greater level of detailed analysis that can be done, assuming accurate expectations can be developed, the better the evidence that can be obtained from substantive analytical procedures. When available, auditors should analyze significant expenses by time period, by location, or by product line. Analytical approaches that are frequently used by an auditor include:

- **Trend Analysis of Expenses:** Expenses can be analyzed in absolute amount or relative to a logical base such as sales revenue. Expenses that are essentially fixed and invariant to volume can be expected to change little over time. Other expenses can be expected to be stable

Table 12.6 *Substantive Tests of Accounts Payable Account**

Management Assertion	Typical Substantive Audit Procedures
Existence: All recorded transactions related to accounts payable occurred and recorded payables exist.	• Confirm payable balances with vendors and follow up on exceptions and nonresponses. • Vouch a sample of purchases and disbursements from the period.
Completeness: All existing accounts payable transactions and balances have been recorded.	• Confirm payable balances (including some zero balance accounts) with vendors and follow up on exceptions and nonresponses. • Select a sample of receiving reports prepared shortly before and after year end and trace to proper inclusion in the voucher register and accounts payable subsidiary ledger. • Vouch payments made shortly before and after year end to determine if liabilities and payments have been recorded in the proper period. • Vouch a sample of purchases and disbursements from the period.
Valuation: Transaction detail included in subsidiary journals and ledgers agrees with the general ledger balances for accounts payable.	• Obtain an accounts payable trial balance as of the end of the fiscal period. • Test the accuracy of the trial balance. • Reconcile the totals per the trial balance with the balance per the general ledger and the accounts payable subsidiary ledger. • Select a sample of accounts in the trial balance and trace to the accounts payable subsidiary ledger. • Reconcile activity per the purchases journal, cash disbursements journal and accounts payable subsidiary ledger with recorded activity in the general ledger.
Valuation: Accounts payable are recorded at the appropriate amounts.	• Select a sample of recorded liabilities from the trial balance and trace to appropriate supporting documentation, including vendors' statements. • Confirm payable balances with vendors and follow up on exceptions and nonresponses. • Vouch a sample of purchases and disbursements from the period.
Valuation: Accounts payable are properly classified.	• Examine the accounts payable trial balance for items to be reclassified (e.g., debit balances, notes payable).
Valuation: Transactions affecting accounts payable have been recorded in the proper period.	• Vouch payments made shortly before and after year end to determine if liabilities and payments have been recorded in the proper period. • Perform inventory cut-off tests and physical observation of inventory at year end (see Figure 12.3).

*The auditor would also use a disclosures checklist and management representation letter to help ensure that assertions related to presentation and disclosure of purchases transactions and accounts payable are fairly stated.

relative to some base. For example, expenses such as utilities and materials or supplies can be expected to increase as production activity increases.

• **Direct Estimation of Expenses:** Some expenses may be directly estimated using client operating data about units, time, or volume of transactions. For example, if the auditor knows that a company received 1,000 shipments and the average shipping cost of a purchase is $25 (both numbers are process related performance indicators), an estimate of total shipping costs can be computed, in this case, $25,000. If this result is close to the recorded balance, it represents reasonable evidence that the account is correctly stated.

- **Ratio Analysis:** A number of ratios based on financial and operating data can be examined to identify unusual changes in operating patterns that might indicate the existence of a misstatement in an account balance. For example, actual production costs per unit can be compared with standard costs to evaluate the accuracy of reported inventory balances.

AUTHORITATIVE GUIDANCE & STANDARDS

Professional standards (i.e., IAASB ISA 520, **Analytical Procedures** *and PCAOB AS 2305 [formerly AU 329]* **Substantive Analytical Procedures**) *provide overall guidance on the use of substantive analytical procedures as audit evidence. Chapter 9 provides an in-depth discussion of the strengths and weaknesses of these procedures overall.*

Regardless of the method(s) used, the auditor ultimately has to make a judgment as to whether differences between recorded account balances and the auditor's expectations are important. The auditor's expectation should be conditioned on the knowledge obtained about strategic and process risks obtained during the risk assessment phase of the audit. The auditor's response to an apparent discrepancy between expected and actual results will depend on the size, direction, and possible explanations of the difference. Divergence from expectations may indicate a change in operations (e.g., adding productive capacity), a change in accounting method (e.g., FIFO inventory to weighted average), or a misstatement in an account balance. If a difference seems significant, the auditor will need to further investigate the account.[6]

Tests of Purchase and Disbursement Transactions

An illustration of the appropriate tests of transactions for purchases and disbursements is provided in Box 12.2 "Substantive Tests of Transactions Related to Supply Chain And Production Management." Recall from Figure 11.4, the starting point for tests of transactions depends on whether the test is for existence (occurrence) versus completeness. The assertions of occurrence (existence), accuracy, timing, and classification are tested using a sample taken from the population of recorded documents supporting each type of transaction. The appropriate sample for purchases is selected from recorded vouchers; for disbursements, the sample is selected from recorded checks. The sample for tests of transactions can be the same as that used for tests of controls (i.e., dual-purpose tests). The supporting documentation is reviewed to make sure that all information is consistent and recorded properly at the correct amount, in the right account, and in the correct time period. Accuracy is verified by testing the summary journals and ledgers, that is, the voucher register or purchases journal, and the cash disbursements journal or check register. Key totals should also be traced to the appropriate accounts in the general ledger. Completeness of accounts payable is tested by selecting a sample of receiving reports from the period, with specific focus on the time around the end of the fiscal year, verifying supporting documentation, and tracing the transactions to proper inclusion in the voucher register.

BOX 12.2   SUBSTANTIVE TESTS OF TRANSACTIONS RELATED TO SUPPLY CHAIN AND PRODUCTION MANAGEMENT

Purchases

Occurrence, Accuracy, Timing, Classification

- Review the voucher register and/or purchases journal for large or unusual transactions to be examined in detail.

- Select a sample of purchase transactions from the voucher register.* Obtain the related vouchers and all appropriate supporting documents (purchase requisition, purchase order, contract, receiving report, and vendor invoice and/or vendor statement). Perform the following tests and note any exceptions found:

  o Trace vendor to the approved vendor list.

  o Compare quantities per the purchase requisition, purchase order, receiving report, and vendor's invoice.

  o Review price per vendor's invoice for accuracy (e.g., by reference to published price list or contract terms).

  o Re-compute extensions and footings on vendor invoice and/or statement.

  o Compare totals per vendor's invoice and/or statement to the voucher.

  o Trace voucher to proper inclusion in the voucher register.

  o Compare receiving date per receiving report to posting date per the voucher register.

  o Trace voucher to proper posting in the accounts payable subsidiary ledger.

  o Review asset/expense classification for reasonableness.

  o Trace inventory items and quantities to proper inclusion in the perpetual inventory records.

  o Test accuracy of vendor account in the subsidiary ledger.

  o Vouch subsequent payment to vendor noting validity of discounts taken and interest paid (if any).

Accuracy: *Test the accuracy of the voucher register (or purchases journal). Take a sample by selecting a few days (or other distinct subsection of the journal) and testing daily totals and then aggregating daily totals to test the period totals. Trace totals to proper inclusion in the general ledger.*

Completeness: *Select a sample of receiving documents from the pre-numbered sequence and trace to proper inclusion in the voucher register, noting the existence of a corresponding voucher and other supporting documentation and the date of posting (as compared to the date on the receiving report).*

Disbursements
Occurrence, Accuracy, Timing, Classification

- Review the cash disbursements journal and/or check register for large or unusual transactions to be examined in detail.

- *Select a sample of disbursement transactions from the cash disbursements journal.** Obtain the voucher package in support of the disbursement. Perform the following tests and note any exceptions:*
  - o *Review and compare the information in the supporting documents.*
  - o *Verify that the amount of payment is consistent with vendor billings and payment terms (e.g., discounts, interest).*
  - o *Examine the canceled check for payee, proper signature, vendor endorsement, and bank stamp.*
  - o *Compare date on check to cancellation date for possible indications of held checks.*
  - o *Trace check to proper posting in the accounts payable subsidiary ledger.*

Completeness, Accuracy: Test a sample of the accuracy of the cash disbursements journal (and check register if desired). IT Assurance using CAATs may be able to do 100%. Trace totals to proper inclusion in the general ledger.***

Notes:

* Alternatively, the sample can be selected from the purchases journal as long as the documents are pre-numbered, used in sequence and traceable to inclusion in the accounts payable subsidiary ledger.

** Alternatively, the sample can be taken from the check register if the company uses only one general disbursement account.

*** The preparation of bank reconciliations for the audit of cash (see Chapter 11 Appendix) also provides evidence concerning the completeness of disbursements.

Tests of Accounts Payable Trial Balance

The primary test of accuracy involves obtaining a trial balance listing recorded accounts payable by vendor or voucher. This schedule should be footed and reconciled with the general ledger payable balance. This schedule should also be reviewed for unusual items that may need to be reclassified or that require further explanation.

Tests for Unrecorded Liabilities

A common substantive test for accounts payable is the search for unrecorded liabilities. This test is really a form of cut-off test. Typically, the auditor will select a sample of disbursements that have been made since the end of the fiscal year, examine the supporting documentation, determine if the payment is for a liability that existed at year end, and then determine if an actual liability had been recorded for the item. The auditor would propose adjustments to the account balance for any unrecorded liabilities that are detected. The size of the transactions tested after year end will depend on the auditor's assessment of the risk of material misstatement for liability assertions.[7]

Confirmation of Payables

Auditors may also confirm accounts payable balances with vendors. The use of confirmations for payables is not required by any national standard setter

---

Jones Manufacturing, Inc.
Gainesville, Florida

January 6, 20x6

Brown & Son
2020 N. Market Street
Gainesville, FL 326002

Dear Sirs:

Our financial statements are currently being examined by the auditing firm
of Smith & Company, CPAs (Gainesville, Florida). In connection with this
examination, we ask that you provide them with the following information:

- An itemized statement of accounts payable owed to you by our company
  as of December 31, 20x5.
- An itemized list of notes payable, acceptance or any other obligations
  owed to you by our company as of December 31, 20x5.
- An itemized list of merchandise that is in our possession on consignment
  from you as of December 31, 20x5.

Please reply directly to Smith & Company. An addressed return envelope
has been enclosed for your convenience. Thank you for your assistance
with this request.

Sincerely,

Edgar Jones

Edgar Jones, Controllers

Figure 12.4 *Sample Confirmation for Accounts Payable*

and is much less common than the confirmation of receivables. Confirmations for payables are almost always sent out in the positive or blank form (i.e., negative confirmations are not used). A sample payable confirmation is presented in Figure 12.4. The confirmation also asks for information on formal financing arrangements (notes and acceptances) and inventory on consignment. This information is useful for auditing other assertions but is not directly pertinent to accounts payable.

AUTHORITATIVE GUIDANCE & STANDARDS

ISA 505 **External Confirmations** *and PCAOB AS 2310 (formerly AU 330)* **The Confirmation Process** *provide guidance on confirmations of all types, including accounts payable as well as guidance as to what to do if confirmations are not returned. The PCAOB is proposing to release a revised standard for discussion in 2016 after an attempt in 2010 to propose revisions was not well received in the comment process. The 2010 PCAOB discussion paper included questions of whether broader guidance is needed beyond just receivables, similar to the scope of ISA 505.*

The confirmation of payables presents a unique challenge to the auditor since the use of the payables trial balance to determine the population of accounts to be sampled is problematic. In general, in tests of payables, the auditor is looking for unrecorded or understated liabilities, and selecting accounts to confirm from among those that are already recorded is not likely to produce adequate evidence to satisfy the completeness objective. However, the trial balance is often the only alternative for selecting the sample. As a result, the auditor will supplement the selection of accounts from the trial balance with a selection of vendors that have a zero (or small) balance at year end but with which the company does business on a regular basis.

Non-responses, and responses that indicate disagreement with the client's records, should be investigated by the auditor. Typically, the auditor examines documentation supporting the recorded liabilities and cross-references confirmation results to the vouching tests for unrecorded liabilities.

The extent of testing applied to liability assertions depends on the risk of material misstatement as assessed by the auditor. When risk is low for the majority of payable assertions, the auditor might avoid most of the tests described in Table 12.6 and limit testing to a few large purchase transactions and payments made after the end of the year. When the risk of material misstatement is high for most payable assertions, the auditor will perform more of these substantive tests, and use larger sample sizes for the tests of transactions and unrecorded liabilities.

Planning Tests of Management Assertions: Inventory

Inventory is usually a highly material element in the financial statements of a manufacturing or merchandising company. Furthermore, inventory is often considered to be a high business risk because of the inherent complexity of the activities related to production and the direct control that management can exercise over inventory transactions and valuations. When a company is going through a rough period, inventory manipulations often become an easy way to boost earnings and present a good appearance on the financial statements (e.g., overstating ending inventory balances at year end usually results in an overstatement of income for the year[(v)(vi)]).

These cases are illustrative of an unfortunately large number of cases where auditors have been fooled about the levels of inventory held by a company. The common lesson from cases of this type is that inventory is an area where the auditor must be especially skeptical. The complexity of inventory and the potential for management override of control systems increases the risk that material misstatements and fraud can occur in inventory transactions.

The auditor's key concerns (i.e., key management assertions to test) related to inventory are that inventory exists, is properly valued at the lower-of-cost-or-market is recorded in the proper period, and is accurately summarized in the accounts. Completeness is usually less of a concern unless inventory is stored at distant or independent locations, or has been shipped on consignment. Classification can also be an important issue for auditors to consider when there is significant work-in-process, in which case the stage of completion can significantly affect the carrying value of inventory (and thus the cost of goods sold and reported earnings[(vii)]).

A comprehensive set of substantive tests for inventory are described in Table 12.7. The primary procedures to test assertions related to inventory include substantive analytical procedures and various tests of details:

- Tests of inventory purchases, conversion, and movement.
- Inspection/observation of inventory.

[(v)]**EXAMPLE**

MiniScribe Corp. This defunct company was a manufacturer of computer disk drives that was accused of "perpetrating a massive fraud" to improperly boost net income by manipulating inventory balances. In 1986 alone, the company was forced to record a $10 million reduction in income when fraudulent activity related to sales and inventory was detected by the auditor. One fraudulent technique used by the company was to warehouse, or even ship, bricks disguised in computer boxes. Another deception was facilitated by creating a computer program, called "Cook Book," to inflate the year-end inventory data. (The Wall Street Journal, May 14, 1992.)

Table 12.7 *Substantive Tests of Inventory**

Management Assertion	Typical Audit Procedures
Existence: All recorded transactions related to inventory occurred; recorded inventory exists and properly reflect inventory in transit or held on consignment from other parties.	• Observe periodic inventory (see Box 12.3 "Auditor's Role in Inventory Counts: Inspection/Observation Procedures and Subsequent Compilation Tests"). • Confirm the existence of inventory in the hands of third parties (e.g., consignments, independent warehouses). • Perform substantive analytical procedures. • Perform tests of sales (Chapter 11) and purchases (Box 12.2 "Substantive Tests of Transactions Related to Supply Chain And Production Management").
Completeness: All existing inventory transactions and balances have been recorded and properly reflect inventory in transit, held on consignment by other parties or stored in independent warehouses.	• Observe periodic inventory (see Box 12.3 "Auditor's Role in Inventory Counts: Inspection/Observation Procedures and Subsequent Compilation Tests"). • Confirm the existence of inventory in the hands of third parties (e.g., consignments, independent warehouses). • Review consignment and purchase commitments or other inventory arrangements. • Perform substantive analytical procedures. • Perform tests of sales (Chapter 11) and purchases (Box 12.2 "Substantive Tests of Transactions Related to Supply Chain And Production Management").
Ownership: Inventory balances are owned by the company.	• Confirm the existence of inventory in the hands of third parties (e.g., consignments, independent warehouses). • Obtain a representation letter from management regarding ownership of inventory. • Review Board of Directors' minutes, legal letters, contracts, etc., for evidence of pledging or other potential claims of ownership on inventory.
Valuation: Inventory balances are recorded at the proper amounts using an appropriate accounting method with proper allocation of indirect manufacturing costs, and considering possible reductions in the realizable value of inventory on hand.	• Observe periodic inventory (see Box 12.3 "Auditor's Role in Inventory Counts: Inspection/Observation Procedures and Subsequent Compilation Tests"). • Perform substantive analytical procedures on inventory and related accounts at a detailed level (e.g., product). • Perform price tests on items in inventory (e.g., purchase prices, standard costs). • Test the computation and application of overhead allocations and standard costs. • Test the realizability of recorded inventory values. • Perform tests of sales (Chapter 11) and purchases (Box 12.2 "Substantive Tests of Transactions Related to Supply Chain And Production Management").
Valuation: Transaction detail included in subsidiary journals and ledgers agrees with the general ledger balances related to inventory.	• Test accuracy of inventory listing and trace items to proper inclusion in the perpetual inventory records. • Test the accuracy of perpetual inventory records. • Reconcile totals per inventory listing to balance of inventory per the general ledger. • Trace test counts from inventory observation to proper inclusion in the inventory listing.

(Continued)

(vii)EXAMPLE

Fashion retailers like Federated Department Stores (e.g., Macy's, Bloomingdales) must deal with difficult valuation issues for much of their inventory. Buyers for a department store often negotiate revised payment terms with vendors after merchandise has been sold based on the prices that the store was actually able to obtain when merchandise was sold to end-customers. Further complicating the process is that the cost associated with "suggested retail price" rarely is the market cost when products are sold. As goods continually are marked down (i.e., as items go "on sale"), lower-of-cost-or-market accounting requires that retailers realize markdown losses in conjunction with the markdowns. As a result, the auditors of a fashion retailer will devote significant time to the valuation assertion associated with inventory and cost of goods sold.

Table 12.7 (*Continued*)

Management Assertion	Typical Audit Procedures
Valuation: Inventory balances and related costs are properly classified.	• Review consignment and purchase commitments or other inventory arrangements. • Review production variances for proper disposition. • Perform substantive analytical procedures. • Verify stage of completion for work-in-process.
Valuation: Transactions affecting inventory have been recorded in the proper period.	• Observe periodic inventory (see Box 12.3 "Auditor's Role in Inventory Counts: Inspection/Observation Procedures and Subsequent Compilation Tests"). • Perform cut-off tests for receipt and shipment of goods.

Note: *To test assertions associated with presentation and disclosure related to inventory, auditors review consignment and purchase commitments or other inventory arrangements, complete disclosure checklist for inventory, obtain a representation letter from management regarding disclosure of inventory, and review proposed disclosures for accuracy.

• Inventory price tests and tests of accounting estimates for obsolescence.
• Tests of inventory compilation.
• Cut-off tests.

AUTHORITATIVE GUIDANCE & STANDARDS

*Standards (ISA 501 **Audit Evidence—Specific Considerations for Selected Items** and PCAOB AS 2510 [formerly AU 331] **Auditing Inventories**) state that auditors generally should perform an inspection of physical inventory to test its existence and completeness. This evidence is gathered at the same time that the auditor performs an observation of the client's periodic inventory count.*

Substantive Analytical Procedures

Substantive analytical procedures can be useful for testing the valuation of inventory, especially if there is a question about potential impairment of value. Sales can be analyzed by location or branch to identify those that are experiencing problems. For example, if the client is able to track performance results by product line, then analysis of sales, costs of sales, gross margins, and inventory turnover ratios for each product can be very useful for assessing the realizability of inventory balances. Items that have very low margins or turnover rates are candidates for write-down to the lower-of-cost-or-market If capitalized inventory costs in a manufacturing firm exceed the revenue generated for a reasonable period of time, the auditor could suggest the write-off of excess cost. An example of this type of analysis is presented in Table 12.8. In this example, the auditor uses a simple rule of thumb to write off any inventory exceeding one year's sales. A more complex analysis might be used to generate a more precise estimate of the amount of obsolete inventory if the auditor felt that the risk of material misstatement was high for inventory valuation. For example, many technology products become obsolete and virtually unsalable in a very short time period.

Table 12.8 *Substantive Analytical Procedure to Test Inventory Obsolescence*

Jones Manufacturing, Inc. Substantive Analysis of Inventory Turnover For Year Ended 12/31/x6				PBC			C-4 WRK 1/24/x7	
Item No.	Current-Year Sales		Year-End Inventory		Turnover Ratio		Proposed Adjustment	
X445	$121,345	☐	$86,376	☐	1.40	*R*	0	*T*
Y357	354,435	☐	110,888	☐	3.20	*R*	0	*T*
J665	12,478	☐	32,688	☐	0.38	*R*	20,000	*T*
D112	659,999	☐	186,974	☐	3.53	*R*	0	*T*
F145	634	☐	25,487	☐	0.02	*R*	25,487	*T*
A129	175,886	☐	121,456	☐	1.45	*R*	0	*T*
L089	76,479	☐	27,599	☐	2.77	*R*	0	*T*
			Total proposed adjustment				45,487	AJE 8
							T	
	NOTE: Per discussion with controller, the company agrees to write off any inventory costs in excess of one year's supply. See **AJE #8** for effect of $45,487 adjustment to inventory.							
	T	Footed and cross-footed without exception.						
	☐	Traced to and agrees with sales report classified by product line.						
	☐	Traced to and agrees with year-end perpetual inventory records.						
	R	Recomputed without exception.						

Substantive analytical procedures are also useful for assessing the reasonableness of overhead allocations and standard costs. Overhead and labor allocated to individual units of production can be estimated using aggregate costs incurred and total production data by product line to determine if the labor and overhead components of standard costs are reasonable. Furthermore, the company's own variances for over- and under applied overhead can be reviewed by the auditor for disposition and adjustment of inventory carrying costs.

A third possible substantive analytical procedure is the comparison of quantities on hand between the current and prior year by product line. Such a comparison may reveal unexplained inventory build-ups that may indicate problems with the existence or validity of inventory or cut-off problems related to inventory receipts and shipments. Alternatively, inventory levels that are unusually low or nonexistent may indicate problems with the completeness of inventory.

Tests of Inventory Purchases, Conversion, and Movement

There are few tests of transactions that are routinely performed for inventory movement and conversion because production does not involve an exchange with external parties. The results from sales and purchase tests, however, are relevant to inventory management given that they usually increase or decrease inventory levels. If the auditor wishes, sales and purchase tests can be augmented with tests of internal movement and conversion of inventory. For example, movement of materials into production can be tested for proper inclusion in work-in-process, and job tickets can be tested for appropriate standard costs.

Inspection or Observation of Inventory Count

The process for inventory count inspection (also known as observation) is described in Box 12.3 "Auditor's Role in Inventory Counts: Inspection/Observation Procedures and Subsequent Compilation Tests" below. Although inventory is physically inspected in most engagements, the nature and extent of the inspection can vary a great deal. At one extreme is the situation where client controls are weak and the auditor is very concerned about the existence and valuation of inventory. In these cases, the auditor will primarily conduct substantive tests by performing a large number of test counts (inventory inspections) and personally visit all significant inventory locations. At the other extreme is the situation where client controls are strong or inventory is inspected by internal auditors or a third party inventory service. Under these conditions, the auditor will perform mainly tests of controls over the client's inventory inspection with minimal test counts, a few visits to selected locations, and observation that client personnel are adhering to approved inventory instructions.

BOX 12.3   AUDITOR'S ROLE IN INVENTORY COUNTS: INSPECTION/OBSERVATION PROCEDURES AND SUBSEQUENT COMPILATION TESTS

Preliminary

1. *Review client's inventory procedures prior to the date of the inventory. Tour facilities where inventory is stored. Determine if all inventory locations are to be counted by client. Be sure that the following controls are used by the client during the client's conduct of the inventory count:*

   - *Client count teams should consist of two people to ensure accurate counts.*
   - *Client count teams should have clearly delimited areas of responsibility.*
   - *Pre-numbered, two-part tags for entering counts should be used and attached to inventory that has been counted.*
   - *A separate review (by the client supervisor) should be performed to ensure that inventory is counted and tagged.*
   - *Movement of inventory and personnel should be limited during counts.*
   - *Arrangements should be made for specific handling of shipments made or received during the count process.*

Conduct of Inventory Inspection/Observation

2. *Observe the client's personnel in the execution of the inventory counts. By observing the client perform inventory counts (a control test) the auditor can justify performing less inspection/observation of actual inventory (a substantive test).*

3. *Randomly select a sample of completed tags and verify the accuracy of the item description and quantities. (These tags should be noted for follow-up when the inventory listing is prepared.)*

4. *Inspect inventory on hand and note any indications that inventory appears to be obsolete, scrap, or on consignment.*

5. *Assess reasonableness of percentage completed or stage of completion assigned to work-in-process.*

6. *Survey areas where client counts have been completed to ensure that all inventory has been counted and tagged. Only after auditor agrees that the count is complete should the client personnel pull the tags.*

7. *After client tag pulling is complete, auditor should survey areas to ensure that all tags have been pulled.*

8. *Note the sequence numbers of all tags used in the count process at each location.*

9. *Note the number of the last receiving and shipping reports used for subsequent follow-up in cut-off tests.*

Test of Inventory Compilation

10. *Obtain a complete client prepared list of inventory quantities listed by tag number and test its accuracy.*

11. *Trace inventory tags the auditor observed during test counts to proper inclusion in the client's inventory listing.*

12. *Verify completeness and validity of tags listed in the client's compilation report against tag numbers the auditor observed being used in actual count process.*

13. *Compare quantities per inventory listing to quantities per perpetual inventory records and note disposition of any inconsistencies.*

14. *Perform price tests on a sample of items in inventory (for a test of lower-of-cost-or-market value of inventory).*

15. *Test the accuracy of the compilation and reconcile with the general ledger accounts.*

During inventory observation, it is important that the auditor obtain assurance that all items are accurately counted by the client and included in the overall client prepared inventory compilation. To facilitate this objective, the auditor should make sure inventory is not moved around during the count, that all storage areas are counted, that newly arriving shipments are properly included in the count, that outgoing shipments are excluded, and that the actual counts are carefully conducted. The use of pre-numbered inventory tags and auditor oversight of count teams are extremely important to achieving an accurate and complete count. The auditor's test counts should be traced to the subsequent client prepared inventory compilation. The compilation should be tested for accuracy and reconciled with the general ledger. An example of the type of documentation that might be used for testing the compilation of inventory quantities and inventory test counts is presented in Table 12.9.

Table 12.9 *Inventory Count List**

Jones Manufacturing, Inc. Inventory Count List For Year Ended 12/31/x6				PBC	C-3 WRK 1/24/x7
Inventory Item No.	**Item Description**	**Tag No.**	**Count per Physical Inventory**	**Count per Perpetual Inventory**	**Difference**
X3467	Sheet metal	1345	232 ☐		
		1346	145 ☐		
		1349	<u>155</u>		
			532 *T*	542 ☐	(10) *T a*
V33356	Copper tubing	1093	987	988 ☐	(1) *T a*
R34347	Gaskets	0567	57		
		0577	<u>94</u>	151 ☐	0 *T*
			151 *T*		
D41123	Clamps	2112	1046 ☐		
		2133	1077		
		2134	<u>845</u>		
			2968 *T*	2710 ☐	258 *T a*
F49990	Porcelain fixtures	1856	124		
		1876	<u>324</u> ☐		
			448 *T*	443 ☐	5 *T b*
	T	Footed and cross-footed without exception.			
	☐	Traced to and agrees with test counts performed by Joe Smith at time of physical inventory observation on 12/31/x6.			
	☐	Traced to and agrees with perpetual inventory as of 12/31/x6.			
	a	Perpetual inventory records adjusted to reflect this difference.			
	b	Difference due to inventory count error. Perpetual inventory records are correct.			

* This working paper assumes the lead schedule for inventory is indexed as C.

Finally, auditors should be alert for valuation issues when conducting an inventory inspection. Typically, auditors test the existence of inventory by tracing inventory from accounting records to its location in the warehouse, and test completeness by tracing inventory from the warehouse to accounting records. Auditors should open boxes, make sure that there are no "holes" (i.e., missing boxes in the middle) for large quantities of boxes stacked on large skids, and make sure that the inventory being counted is saleable. Further, auditors should be alert for inventory that is segregated or has a large amount of dust accumulated on it. These conditions suggest that the associated inventory might not be ready for sale. This so-called "white glove test" helps auditors assess the presence of obsolete inventory that might need to be marked down to lower of cost or market.

Young auditors are often under the impression, prior to their first inventory inspection or observation, that it is their job to carry out the inventory count. While the auditors will make test counts, the extent of which will depend on the risk of material misstatement assessed with respect to the assertion of inventory existence, it is management's job to ensure that the inventory is properly counted. The auditor is present mainly to observe the process and to ensure that it is carried out in a manner that can be relied upon to produce an accurate number to support the assertion of the existence of inventory as well as potentially give the eagle-eyed auditor insights into obsolescence and potential fraud.

Inventory Price Tests and Tests of Estimates: Obsolescence

Once the auditor is satisfied that the accounting records accurately report the quantity of inventory on hand, the next step is to determine what cost should be assigned to the units. This process depends on three key factors: the inventory method being used for purchased inventory, the existence of manufactured inventory, and the possibility of obsolescence.

- **Purchased Inventory**: Costs for purchased inventory (including raw materials used in production) should be traced to appropriate vendor invoices consistent with the accounting method being used. If the company uses FIFO, inventory on hand should be priced using the most recent vendor invoices. The auditor must be careful to examine enough invoices to cover all units on hand. For example, if there are 100 units but the most recent invoice was for only 60 units, older invoice(s) must also be examined to determine the cost of the other 40 units.

- **Manufactured Inventory**: Costs for manufactured inventory must be traced to the appropriate standard costs for each product. The computation and reasonableness of standard costs should be tested and the level of actual versus absorbed overhead should be reviewed to ensure that all proper product costs have been included in the unit cost. The stage or percentage of completion for work-in-process must also be verified to ensure that the proper portion of finished cost is assigned to those units.

- **Tests for Obsolescence**: If there is a question of the realizability of inventory due to price declines, the auditor should examine the unit costs in relation to the potential selling price of the inventory. This is another example of an accounting estimate where management needs to forecast future events, i.e., the expected price of future sales of inventory, particularly if prices are likely to be reduced. The process employed is the same as any other accounting estimate including first obtaining management's estimate of obsolescence, how management arrived at that estimate, what assumptions management has made, and whether they are different from the auditor's. If the selling price of a product minus selling expenses and a reasonable profit margin is less than its carrying cost by the auditor's estimate, and the auditor is not persuaded that management's estimate is justified, the auditor should suggest that inventory be written down to its net realizable value per the auditor's estimate.[8] Again, as with any estimate if there is a range of values that the auditor believes are equally likely, then the proposed adjustment would be from the nearest point in the range to management's estimate.

Tests of Inventory Compilation

If the auditor is satisfied that inventory quantities and unit costs are reasonable, the next step is to test the accuracy of the compilation of the final balance by footing and cross-footing the inventory listing. This test can be performed manually or by using computer-assisted techniques. The total per the inventory listing should be tied to the perpetual inventory records and reconciled with the inventory accounts included in the general ledger. The auditor should also verify that inventory is properly classified and disclosed in categories such as raw material, work-in-process, finished goods, and supplies (which is not manufacturing inventory).

Cut-Off Tests

The auditor should test the cut-off of inventory. These tests can usually be performed in conjunction with the inspection (or observation) of inventory and the cut-off tests for sales and purchases. The critical issue is to determine whether the company has properly included or excluded inventory on hand, in transit, or stored at independent warehouses. If inventory is observed at year end, the auditor can observe whether inventory is included or not included in the counts as is appropriate under the circumstances. The auditor should also identify the number of the last shipping and receiving documents used in order to facilitate the vouching cut-off tests for sales and purchases.

Although inventory is typically observed and price tests are usually performed on most engagements involving a material amount of inventory, the auditor has a great deal of flexibility in the scope of these tests. When the client's information system for inventory is reliable and provides highly detailed inventory data by product line, substantive analytical procedures become a viable and effective method for obtaining evidence about the accuracy of inventory balances. When control risk is low or high-quality substantive analytical procedures are available, the auditor can use smaller sample sizes for price tests or can perform the inventory observation and price tests at an interim date. Price tests are particularly problematic in companies selling large numbers of different products because the projection of small discrepancies to the entire population of transactions may indicate a material misstatement. As a result, auditors must carefully consider the sample size for these tests in order to obtain the needed degree of assurance.

Summary and Conclusion

We have discussed a broad range of issues related to the audit of the supply chain and production management process. We used a process map and internal threat analysis to evaluate process objectives, activities, risks, process controls, entity level controls, and internal controls over financial reporting. We used the results of the process analysis to assess residual risks and analyze how residual risks would affect the risk of material misstatement, hence the conduct of the audit, in this chapter focusing on the tests of management assertions affected by supply chain and production process.

The most common transactions occurring in the supply chain and production will affect either accounts payable or inventory, or both. An auditor can select among numerous substantive tests to examine assertions related to these accounts. The nature and extent of substantive testing for payables and inventory depends on the assessed level of the risk of material misstatement for each assertion. Table 12.10 illustrates how the various substantive tests described in this chapter might be adapted under different risk conditions. Ultimately, the auditor must decide which of these tests to perform on a given client and the extent of testing needed to gather adequate evidence to support the audit opinion.

Table 12.10 *Substantive Tests of Management Assertions for Different Levels of Risk of Material Misstatement*

Type of Procedure	High Detection Risk Case (Low Risk of Material Misstatement)	Low Detection Risk Case (High Risk of Material Misstatement)
Accounts Payable		
Tests of transactions	Moderate tests as described in Box 12.2 "Substantive Tests of Transactions Related to Supply Chain and Production Management," mostly performed at interim dates.	Extensive tests as described in Box 12.2 "Substantive Tests of Transactions Related to Supply Chain and Production Management," many performed after year end.
Test of accuracy of the accounts payable trial balance	Minimal or no testing. Totals traced to general ledger.	Trial balance footed and reconciled with the general ledger with some accounts traced to the subsidiary ledger.
Confirmations	Few (if any) confirmations used.	Many confirmations used at year end.
Tests for unrecorded liabilities	Moderate vouching tests of cash disbursements after year end.	Extensive vouching tests of cash disbursements after year end.
Inventory		
Tests of transactions	Minimal to no testing.	Moderate testing of inventory movements and cost assignment.
Observation of inventory	Performed as a test of controls with minimal test counts performed by auditor.	Extensive test counts performed by auditor.
Inventory price tests	Moderate testing of purchase prices and standard costs.	Extensive testing of purchase prices (e.g., acquisition cost) and standard costs. Detailed testing of standard costs for a sample of products.
Tests of inventory compilation	Minimal tests. Reconciliation of total inventory with inventory compilation, perpetual inventory records and general ledger.	Moderate to extensive tests of footings and cross-footings. Reconciliation of individual products with perpetual records and total inventory with general ledger.
Cut-off tests.	Minimal testing. Transactions tested based on size.	Moderate to extensive sample of transactions tested.

Bibliography of Relevant Literature

Research

Johnston, H., W. D. Lindsay and F. Phillips. 2003. Undetected Deviations in Tests of Controls: Experimental Evidence of Non-sampling Risk. *Canadian Accounting Perspectives.* 2(2): 113–134.

Auditing Standards

IAASB *International Standards on Auditing (ISA)* No. 240, "The Auditor's Responsibilities Relating to Fraud in an Audit of Financial Statements."

IAASB *International Standards on Auditing (ISA)* No. 300, "Planning an Audit of Financial Statements."

IAASB *International Standards on Auditing (ISA)* No. 320, "Materiality in Planning and Performing an Audit."

IAASB *International Standards on Auditing (ISA)* No. 330, "The Auditor's Responses to Assessed Risks."

IAASB *International Standards on Auditing (ISA)* No. 500, "Audit Evidence."

IAASB *International Standards on Auditing (ISA)* No. 501, "Audit Evidence – Specific Considerations for Selected Items."

IAASB *International Standards on Auditing (ISA)* No. 505, "External Confirmations."

IAASB *International Standards on Auditing (ISA)* No. 520, "Analytical Procedures."

IFAC. International Auditing and Assurance Standards Board (IAASB). 2015. *Handbook of International Quality Control, Audit, Review, Other Assurance, and Related Services Pronouncements.* New York: International Federation of Accountants.

PCAOB. *Auditing Standard* 1105 (formerly No. 15), "Audit Evidence."

PCAOB. *Auditing Standard* 2101 (formerly No. 9), "Audit Planning."

PCAOB. *Auditing Standard* 2105 (formerly No. 11), "Consideration of Materiality in Planning and Performing an Audit."

PCAOB. *Auditing Standard* 2301 (formerly No. 13), "The Auditor's Responses to the Risks of Material Misstatement."

PCAOB. *Auditing Standard* 2305 (formerly *Interim Standard* AU 329), "Substantive Analytical Procedures."

PCAOB. *Auditing Standard* 2310 (formerly *Interim Standard* AU 330), "The Confirmation Process."

PCAOB. *Auditing Standard* 2401 (formerly *Interim Standard* AU 316), "Consideration of Fraud in a Financial Statement Audit."

PCAOB. *Auditing Standard* 2501 (formerly *Interim Standard* AU 342), "Auditing Accounting Estimates."

PCAOB *Auditing Standard* 2510 (formerly *Interim Standard* AU 331), "Auditing Inventories."

Notes

1 The preparation of a voucher is a common method for recording liabilities but there are other systems also used in practice.

2 A company will occasionally cut a check and hold on to it because funds are not immediately available to cover the amount. In these situations, the liability should remain on the books until the check is mailed or delivered to the vendor.

3 Exceptions include waste or by-products, both of which may involve exchanges with outside parties.

4 These may come in different forms depending on the nature of the materials being moved, e.g., work-in-process in a factory, finished goods between warehouses, or waste and by-products for disposal.

5 Under sole-sourcing contracts or many just-in-time inventory environments, inspections occur at the supplier prior to shipment to the client, and no inspections occur at the client's production facility. This process occurs because many just-in-time environments are designed such that supplier deliveries go straight from the delivery vehicle to the assembly line, with no ability for inspection ahead of time.

6 Regression analysis can also be used to develop auditor expectations for the expense amount. For example, utility expense could be estimated based on the number of days worked, the volume of production, the average weather conditions (which affect heating and cooling), the average price per kilowatt, and so on. The primary challenge for building such an expectation model is the availability of reliable data to use as input to the estimation process. See Appendix to Chapter 9 for a simple illustration of using regression analysis to develop auditor expectations.

7 The results from the vouching of subsequent cash disbursements can be supplemented with the cut-off tests performed for inventory given that the presence of many errors related to unrecorded inventory may also indicate the existence of an unrecorded account payable.

8 Preferably, the test for lower-of-cost-or-market should be applied to each product in inventory. However, many companies apply the test to overall inventory, which allows gains and losses across units to offset. This is allowed by GAAP but makes it easier to manipulate inventory as an anomalous test for any individual product can be explained away as not being representative of the category tested.

CHAPTER 13

Auditing Resource Management Processes

Outline

Learning Goals for this Chapter

1. Apply our understanding of process analysis to the property management and financial management processes.

2. Analyze the risk of material misstatement in the context of the property management and financial management processes.

3. Apply understanding of internal control over financial reporting audit to design, carry out, and evaluate tests of internal controls of the property management and financial management processes.

4. Determine the level of residual risk based on outcome of internal control testing.

5. Plan substantive tests of account balances and transaction for account balances and transaction for the property management process, the financial management process and the human resource management process (Appendix).

6. Design and execute substantive tests of account balances and transaction for the property management process, the financial management process, and the human resource management process (Appendix).

7. Conclude whether an appropriate level of audit evidence has been collected to support the auditor's opinion with respect to the property management process, the financial management process, and the human resource management process (Appendix).

Introduction

Sales and customer service, as well as supply chain management and production, are often considered the core or primary processes of most organizations. However, to be successful, all organizations need to mobilize and manage a broad variety of resources such as people, property, and capital. This chapter deals with how an organization would manage two of these important resources: long lived assets and capital (see Figure 13.1). Few organizations could succeed without effective management of these resources, and risks arising in these areas can have a significant impact on the conduct of the audit.

We first discuss the property management process. This process comprises the activities of acquiring, utilizing, and maintaining the organization's base of long lived assets. We then discuss the financial resource management process, which consists of activities for obtaining and managing cash flow and financial capital such as debt and equity. For each process, we will present a process map and prepare an internal threat analysis. After analyzing risks, controls, and performance indicators for each process, we will then discuss substantive tests that can be used to test financial statement assertions that are affected by the process.[1]

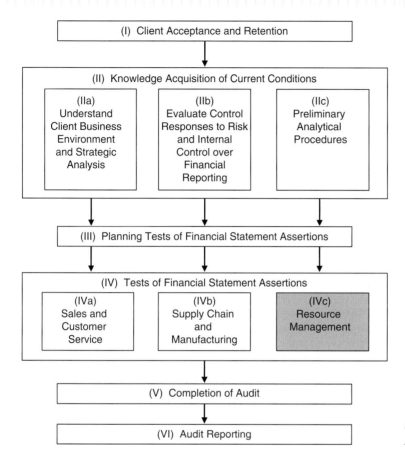

Figure 13.1 Overview of the
Audit Process

AUTHORITATIVE GUIDANCE & STANDARDS

*This chapter applies standards covered in previous chapters to three
business processes—property management, financial management,
and completes the human resources process in the Appendix. Several
observations from auditing standards are included throughout the chapter
(e.g., ISA 320* **Materiality in Planning and Performing an Audit***, ISA 330*
The Auditor's Responses to Assessed Risks*, ISA 500* **Audit Evidence***;
AS 2105 [formerly 11]* **Consideration of Materiality in Planning and
Performing an Audit***, AS 2301 [formerly 13]* **The Auditor's Responses
to the Risks of Material Misstatement***, AS 1105 [formerly 15]* **Audit
Evidence***). These standards provide the basic template for all evidence
gathering activities in an audit and underlie much of what is discussed
in Chapters 11 to 13. Rather than repeatedly refer to these standards we
note at the beginning of each chapter that they underlie the entire subject
matter of the chapters.*

Part A: Auditing the Property Management Process
Process Map

The now infamous fraud involving WorldCom, which was the final blow leading the US Congress to pass the Sarbanes-Oxley Act of 2002, was driven by a massive fraud involving property management. The fraud involved capitalization of $5 billion worth of expenses as a property account entitled "prepaid capacity." All of these amounts should have been expensed as incurred but were instead capitalized as a capital asset to be expensed over time.

The property management process is the set of activities related to acquiring, preparing, and maintaining the organization's long lived assets. Facilities include factories, warehouses, administrative offices, retail locations, equipment, computers, and vehicles. Intangible assets arise from mergers and acquisitions often bundled with the acquisition of facilities. These too need to be recorded. Maintenance and repair of assets is also part of this process. In addition, the need to assess potential impairment has become a much larger part of the audit consideration of long lived assets in recent years. The wide range of assets included in this process creates a number of challenges because acquisition and maintenance may vary greatly depending on the type of asset. Scheduling and use of the assets in operations is not part of this process and would pertain to the specific processes where the assets are used (e.g., production scheduling⁽ⁱ⁾).

Objectives: A process map for property management is presented in Figure 13.2. The primary objective of property management is to assure that the organization has the productive capacity (including purchased intangible assets) and facilities it needs to pursue its objectives and plans. In more precise terms, property management involves forecasting resource needs, acquiring appropriate resources at a reasonable cost, and maintaining facilities in appropriate working condition. Maintenance is particularly important because it is an ongoing activity and can directly affect the productivity, and even the safety, of personnel within the organization. Testing these long lived assets for impairment (another accounting estimate) has become an increasingly important part of this process. Effective and reliable information processing is also important to facilitate process improvement and to assist in the forecasting of future needs.

Activities: The physical and intangible assets of an organization provide the productive base for its operations. Even "virtual" companies need some physical facilities and equipment albeit managing their recorded intangible assets might be a much greater focus in those organizations especially ones that are active in growth via acquisition. The activities necessary to manage these resources effectively include:

- Assessing asset needs: The first step in the process is to identify the asset needs of the organization. The need for new factories, retail locations, vehicles, and computers must be evaluated. Asset needs will usually be based on forecasts, future plans, and overall strategy, including decisions about acquisition and mergers with other firms. Effective strategic planning is critical for this step of the process.

- Evaluating available resources: There are often many alternatives available once a resource need is identified. Factories can be located in different cities, states/provinces, and countries depending on factors such as logistical infrastructure, employee base, taxes, and governmental incentives. Retail locations will depend on customer traffic, accessibility, and land costs. Options also exist for more mundane assets, such as trucks

Process Objectives

- Effectively forecast and plan for current and future resource needs.
- Obtain resources that meet the technology and capacity needs of the organization.
- Maximize value of capital expenditures, including construction/remodeling.
- Establish efficient procedures for effective maintenance.
- Minimize operating costs.
- Minimize risk of asset losses or safety problems.
- Develop and implement contingency plans should major loss of property occur due to natural disaster or acts of terrorism.
- Maintain effective insurance coverage.
- Evaluate assets for impairment in values.
- Capture, process, and report information necessary for process improvement.

Process Activities

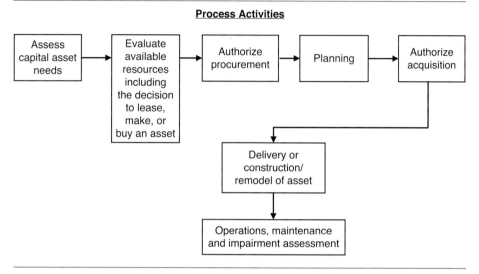

Process Data Streams

Information Feeds	Information Generation
• Strategic plans and budgets	• Acquisition decisions
• Capital budgets	• Building plans and schedules
• Capacity requirements	• Acquisition schedules
• Production specifications	• Acquisition budgets
• Suppliers/builders	• Asset acquisitions
• Location and infrastructure data	• Maintenance schedule
• Market data (e.g., costs, availability)	• Operating plans and procedures

Accounting Impact of Activities

Routine Transactions	Non-routine Transactions	Accounting Estimates
• Asset purchases*	• Asset construction/ remodeling*	• Asset impairment
• Insurance expense	• Leases*	• Self-insured losses
• Utilities expense	• Asset disposals*	• Depreciation parameters
• Maintenance expense	• Cost abatements	
• Taxes	• Interest capitalization	
• Depreciation		

Figure 13.2 *Process Map: Property Management*

* Could be either routine or non-routine depending on organization's normal activities.

or computers. Effective property management requires a full analysis of the advantages and disadvantages of the various alternatives for acquiring assets including the decision to lease, make, or buy assets with the latter including purchasing organizations as a whole to obtain access to their facilities and intangible assets.

- Authorization of procurement/acquisition: Once options have been specified and evaluated, senior management needs to make decisions concerning which options to pursue. Should a new factory be built in Tennessee or Tasmania? Should new trucks come from Volvo or General Motors? Should computers be supplied by Dell or Lenovo? Should the firm purchase another firm with the assets already in place? These decisions will be based on preliminary information and tentative negotiations with potential suppliers and acquirees.

- Planning: Formal negotiations with suppliers/acquirees will determine contract prices and terms (possibly including financing), delivery schedules or milestones, and service or warranty arrangements. Final selection of suppliers and specific models/versions/designs/floor plans will occur at this point in the process. Mergers and acquisition agreements normally involve extensive interactions with legal teams, business valuators, and other experts that determine overall purchase price and its allocation to both physical assets as well as intangibles including goodwill.

- Authorization of acquisition: Given the extensive details to be considered for most asset acquisitions, it is important that there be a separate review and approval of final plans for an acquisition. Significant asset acquisitions may involve approval by the Board of Directors. This step generally results in a signed contract with a chosen supplier and commitment to a delivery or construction schedule. Acquisitions by merger or via purchase will normally follow a similar process of approval especially the board level approval for material mergers or large scale asset acquisitions.

- Acquisition or construction/remodeling: For most assets, this step of the process involves taking delivery of the asset (e.g., vehicles, computers and furniture), physical set-up, and testing. For land or buildings, the acquisition process may be quite complex and time consuming, especially if the asset is to be constructed. Legal processes and regulatory approvals for acquisitions of other companies can often be a long and involved activity.

- Operations and maintenance: After delivery, all assets require continuous maintenance and upkeep, and occasional repairs. This is an ongoing activity in most organizations.

- Evaluation of asset impairment: Accounting standards in recent years have required that long lived assets, both tangible and intangible, be regularly evaluated for impairment of value. While this has become a routine activity in larger organizations, it is still an area for significant judgment as this is another example of an accounting estimate where valuation experts can readily disagree.

Execution of these activities may be relatively straightforward, as in the case of vehicle purchases, or may be very complex, as in the case of building a new factory or acquiring another firm. In general, the more unique the asset and the longer the lead time necessary to arrange for the acquisition, the more complex this process will be and the more things that can go wrong. Acquiring new computers usually involves no more than contacting a vendor, explaining the organization's needs, and negotiating the terms of a contract (including price, delivery and set-up, and service). Construction of a new building will involve complex planning with architects, attorneys, contractors, local government, and lenders. The tracking of costs on such a project can be a challenge, especially if construction uses internal resources (people, equipment) and funds (interest capitalization). Purchases of other firms will require legal involvement, financing considerations, and regulatory approvals in many cases.

Transactions: The information flows associated with property management are described in Figure 13.2. Information for planning and control are particularly important to this process. Effective management of property and acquisitions is dependent on the availability of appropriate information. Although the occurrence of recordable transactions is less frequent than in many processes, accounting for plant, property, equipment, and intangible assets requires a number of accounts. For tangible assets that have a limited life these accounts include accumulated depreciation.

Most companies maintain separate accounts for different types of depreciable assets. For example, separate accounts may be used for tools, equipment, buildings, and land. Assets may be further classified as manufacturing, whose depreciation is capitalized as part of the inventory, or administrative, whose depreciation is charged off as a period cost. Finally, separate accounts may be used for assets that are acquired through capital lease arrangements. Intangibles assets are similarly accounted for (i.e., the value given to patents is separated from the value of customer lists) with the residual being labeled as goodwill that has arisen through purchase. Intangible assets tend to be unique under current accounting rules in that they are only accounted for on the books of the company when they are purchased but not when they are internally generated.

In general, asset accounts are used to record additions and disposals of physical assets at cost. Accumulated depreciation is used to record periodic depreciation expense and must also be adjusted when an asset disposal occurs. Depreciation expense and gains or losses on asset disposals are included in the income statement.

A number of different types of transactions occur within the property management process including:

- Purchase of equipment or other facilities assets (e.g., shelving for a warehouse).
- Construction/remodeling of facilities (including interest capitalization).
- Operating expenses.
- Maintenance and repairs.
- Sale of assets.
- Asset leasing.

Transaction documentation will vary depending on the nature of the acquisition. Routine purchases of equipment and machinery may be very similar to acquisitions of material discussed in Chapter 12. Recurring operating expenses are handled in a similar manner. Purchases of other firms tend to be nonroutine transactions in most companies but may become routine for companies that primarily grow through acquisition of other businesses. Other transactions, such as purchase of real estate or leasing arrangements, may involve complex legal documents and contracts. Periodic adjustments to asset accounts (e.g., depreciation) may be supported by a journal entry ticket alone. Repairs and maintenance involve the additional concern that they be properly classified as assets or expenses depending on the nature of the repair.

AUTHORITATIVE GUIDANCE & STANDARDS

Overall planning guidance is given in IAASB ISA 300, **Planning an Audit of Financial Statements** *and PCAOB AS 2101 (formerly 9)* **Audit Planning.** *These standards provide the basic template for all audit planning activities.*

Internal Threat Analysis

Internal threat analysis for property management is illustrated in Table 13.1. Potential risks are described in the first column. Mitigating controls and relevant performance measures are also identified for each risk. The sources of process risks interact to influence the overall level of risks. For example, poor maintenance leading to deterioration of facilities, and possible impairment of value, can be caused by weak planning, lazy employees, or insufficient maintenance resources. The auditor should consider the interaction of risks when assessing the residual risks of a process.

Analysis of Internal Control over Financial Reporting

Table 13.1 identifies a number of controls that might be used to mitigate various property management process risks. At the entity level such controls would include performance reviews and monitoring of:

- Strategic and contingency plans.
- Forecasts of resource needs.
- Acquisition planning and identification of alternatives.
- Identification of need to carry out asset impairment tests.

At the process level more detailed control activities and controls over finanical reporting include:

- Evaluating and authorizing acquisitions, including construction.
- Conducting and authorizing contract negotiations.
- Planning and scheduling maintenance and related activities.
- Assessing asset values and amortization.
- Maintaining regulatory compliance and safety records.
- Segregation of duties: The appropriate segregation of duties for acquisitions is similar to those specified for acquisitions of material. Namely, there should be separation among need assessment, procurement and contract negotiation, acquisition authorization, asset delivery, payment authorization, and asset accounting.

Table 13.1 *Internal Threat Analysis: Property Management*

Process Risks	Controls Linked to Risks	Performance Measures
(1) Insufficient capacity.	• Long-term planning and budgeting. • Monitor current usage. • Adequate lead time for new facilities. • Establish appropriate maintenance program. • Establish back-up sources for peak loads.	• Total capacity measures. • Space utilization statistics. • Space shortages. • Revenue per square foot. • Repair costs.
(2) Excess capacity.	• Long-term planning and budgeting. • Procedures for authorizing and disposing of property. • Utilize flexible resources when possible (e.g., employee shared space)	• Space utilization statistics. • Time-in-use measures. • Revenue per square foot. • Value received for asset disposals.
(3) Impaired asset values.	• Periodic review of asset portfolio. • Independent appraisals.	• Market value of assets. • Market value per square foot. • Time-to-sell property assets. • Percent markdown on disposed assets.
(4) Excess deterioration due to poor maintenance.	• Appropriate maintenance schedules. • Outsourcing of maintenance activities. • Monitor technology and competition for possible improvements. • Provide appropriate training to personnel.	• Maintenance budgets. • Cleanliness ratings. • Equipment breakdowns. • Repair costs. • Days lost to equipment failures. • Rate of production defects due to equipment problems.
(5) Inefficient space utilization.	• Systematic plans for space usage. • Long term plans for acquisitions. • Monitor current usage. • Flexible space usage designs.	• Space utilization statistics. • Frequency and cost of reconfigurations. • Cost per square foot. • Revenue per square foot. • Square feet per employee.
(6) Casualty losses including loss of use of significant physical facilities due to natural disaster, terrorism or outbreak of hostilities.	• Periodic safety inspections. • Adequate insurance or self-insurance. • Crisis management and contingency plans. • Disaster recovery plans.	• Value of casualty losses. • Insurance claims. • Uninsured losses. • Days lost to crisis or damage conditions. • Insurance premiums and deductibles. • Tests of disaster recovery plans.
(7) Lack of resources to acquire assets.	• Effective capital budgeting. • Access to financial resources. • Effective management of cash flow. • Creative financing (e.g., leasing).	• Cost of borrowed funds for project. • Percentage of funds from outside sources. • Amount of debt service relative to cash flow from project. • Internal rate of return.
(8) Poor location selection.	• Investigate all acquisitions and location characteristics. • Negotiate arrangements with local officials. • Evaluate transportation and infrastructure of area. • Evaluate quality of local human resources.	• Cost to acquire property. • Local demographics. • Travel time to primary customers or from key suppliers. • Travel or transportation costs. • Value of incentives or abatements from local authorities.
(9) Cost overruns or delays.	• Obtain bids for acquisitions. • Establish acquisition plan and timing of milestones for completion. • Monitor acquisition costs on a timely basis.	• Actual cost compared to budget. • Days late on acquisitions. • Project progress relative to milestones.

(Continued)

Table 13.1 *(Continued)*

Process Risks	Controls Linked to Risks	Performance Measures
(10) Inaccurate information processing.	• Proper completion and verification of supporting documents. • Appropriate segregation of duties across activities. • Use of standard control numbers for parts, vendors, products, etc. • Update files and accounting records on a timely basis.	• Percent of transactions subject to processing errors. • Size of transaction adjustments. • Number of transaction adjustments.
(11) Inaccurate cost measurement.	• Establish procedures and policies for determining asset cost. • Adequate documentation of acquisitions. • Proper allocation of internal costs for acquisitions.	• Actual costs compared to budget. • Percentage of internal costs allocated to capital assets (e.g., interest). • Asset costs relative to appraised value.
(12) Improper or unauthorized usage.	• Physical security. • Proper authorization procedures. • Maintain inventory of physical assets including location information. • Periodic physical inventory observation.	• Value of lost assets. • Book to physical adjustments for physical assets.
(13) Lack of compliance with regulations (e.g., zoning, environmental)	• Monitor appropriate property regulations and environmental laws. • Periodic inspections. • Long-term planning to assure compliance with changes in regulations. • Adequate capital budgeting.	• Number of known violations. • Fines and penalties for violations. • Days lost due to violations. • Cost of environmental cleanup.
(14) Inaccurate or unreasonable amortization.	• Establish amortization policies and procedures by asset type. • Monitor economic and technology trends that may impact assets. • Comparative analysis with other organizations and competitors.	• Useful life of assets by type. • Useful lives relative to tax standards. • Useful lives relative to competitors. • Percentage of assets in use that are fully depreciated. • Average gain/loss of asset disposals.
(15) Safety hazards.	• Monitor safe and health regulations. • Perform periodic safety inspections.	• Number of worker injuries. • Cost of time lost to worker injuries. • Worker's compensation costs. • Regulatory (e.g., OSHA in USA) citations.

- Processing controls:
  - o Authorizations are needed for planning, to begin procurement and negotiations, to identify alternatives, to execute a transaction, to accept delivery, and to make payments.
  - o Adequate records and documents are needed to assure accurate accounting and are similar to those used for materials procurement and production. Some examples include procurement and purchase documents, receiving reports, vendor's invoices and statements, checks for disbursements, contracts, and internal documents for cost allocations of labor, materials, and overhead. Most companies will also maintain a ledger of long lived assets that summarizes the date they were acquired, the cost, and related depreciation information.

o Independent verifications and reconciliations over purchases, disbursements, and general ledger accounts can be used to verify accurate transaction processing.

- Physical controls: Important physical controls relate to taking possession and utilizing acquired assets. Controls should be designed to limit access and the use of assets for legitimate purposes, and to minimize the risk of casualty losses or safety hazards. Additionally, records and documents related to asset acquisitions should be properly handled and protected.

Bad decisions related to capital assets can impair the competitive position of an organization. Consequently, controls related to planning and authorization, are critical for successful and efficient property management. Given that most asset acquisitions are high value and occur infrequently, management will be actively involved so controls may be unevenly applied, adapted for each transaction, or overridden. This uneven application of controls may be problematic for organizations subject to the Integrated Audit where all material processes are expected to have adequate internal controls over financial reporting. Such inconsistent controls could be considered a control deficiency that might be significant or material.

Evaluation of Process Performance Indicators

Relevant process indicators for property management are listed in Table 13.1. These indicators can provide a source of evidence concerning risks in the property management process. However, many of these measures may not be available within the basic accounting system, so data availability and reliability may impact the auditor's ability to evaluate the performance measures. For example, measures of capacity utilization may indicate if a company has excess capacity that may need to be written off. The rate of defects in production may indicate that equipment is old and needs to be repaired or replaced, or could indicate that the equipment is being improperly utilized. In either event, the auditor would need to consider whether the observed defect rates are consistent with the standard costs of units being produced.

Tests of Financial Statement Assertions: Property, Plant Equipment, Intangible Assets, and Depreciation

Typical substantive tests for plant, property, equipment and intangible assets are summarized in Table 13.2. The approach to testing property assertions is based on the assumption that beginning asset balances were previously audited. The testing of assets then focuses on verifying current-year additions and disposals only.[2] Accumulated depreciation is verified by examining current-year disposals and performing substantive analytical procedures on current-year depreciation expense. Gains and losses on disposals are tested as part of the testing of asset disposals. Lease arrangements are also examined to determine that their treatment as capital or operating leases is appropriate. The primary substantive tests for property include:

Table 13.2 *Substantive Tests of Property, Plant, Equipment and Intangible Capital Assets Transactions, Accounts and Disclosures*

Management Assertion	Typical Substantive Audit Procedures
Accuracy/Valuation: Plant, property, equipment and intangible asset balances reconcile with subsidiary ledgers and the general ledger.	• Obtain schedules of additions and disposals of plant and equipment assets for the fiscal period and test for mechanical accuracy (including the computation of gains and losses for disposals). • Reconcile total additions and disposals with activity in the general ledger. • Tie in opening asset balances with prior-year audit results. • Re-compute balances in plant and equipment assets and accumulated depreciation using prior-year balances and current-year activity.
Existence: Recorded plant, property, and equipment exist.	• Vouch a sample of acquisitions selected from the additions schedule. • Physically observe the existence of a sample of plant and equipment assets. • Vouch a sample of disposals selected from the disposals schedule and verify supporting documentation. • Examine mergers and acquisitions documentation to ensure that plant, property, equipment, goodwill, and other intangible assets obtained as a result of such activities are properly valued and recorded on books.
Completeness: All existing plant, property, equipment, and intangible assets of the company are recorded.	• Select a sample of repairs and maintenance charges and review supporting documentation to determine that payments have been correctly recorded. • Physically observe the existence of a sample of plant and equipment assets. • Review lease agreements for possible capital leases. • Examine mergers and acquisitions documentation to ensure that plant, property, equipment, goodwill, and other intangible assets obtained as a result of such activities are properly valued and recorded on books.
Rights and obligations: Plant, property, equipment, and intangible assets are owned by the company.	• Examine vendors' invoices related to additions. • Examine mergers and acquisitions documentation to ensure that plant, property, equipment, goodwill, and other intangible assets obtained as a result of such activities are properly valued and recorded on books. • Obtain a representation letter from management pertaining to the ownership of assets. • Review minutes from Board of Directors' and management meetings to identify significant asset disposals.
Accuracy/Valuation: Plant, property, equipment and, intangible assets are correctly valued. Plant and equipment have a reasonable allowance for depreciation.	• Vouch asset additions for accuracy. • Vouch disposals for accuracy, including relief of accumulated depreciation. • Examine mergers and acquisitions documentation to ensure that plant, property, equipment, goodwill, and other intangible assets obtained as a result of such activities are properly valued and recorded on books. • Test depreciation expense and accumulated depreciation using substantive analytical procedures. • Test the computation of capitalized interest for self-constructed assets. • Where conditions suggest that tangible assets may be impaired inquire of management as to their documentation as to whether the assets are impaired. Carry out tests of management's significant assumptions in developing that assessment. • Obtain and test management's annual documentation that tests whether impairment of intangible assets with an unlimited life and allocated goodwill from acquisitions has occurred. • Confirm terms of contracts or leases.
Classification: Plant, property, equipment and, intangible asset balances are correctly classified.	• Vouch asset additions for accuracy of classification. • Examine mergers and acquisitions documentation to ensure that plant, property, equipment, goodwill, and other intangible assets obtained as a result of such activities are properly allocated and classified. • Select a sample of repairs and maintenance charges and review supporting documentation to determine that payments have been correctly classified.

Cut-off: Plant, property, equipment and intangible asset transactions are recorded in the proper period.	• Perform cut-off tests for acquisitions and disbursements and vouch transactions near year-end. • Ensure that all mergers and acquisitions activities are recorded in the correct period.
Completeness/Existence/ Valuation: All required disclosures pertaining to plant, property, equipment, and intangible asset are included in the financial statements.	• Complete a disclosure checklist for plant and equipment assets. • Consider the need for pro-forma statements and other disclosures for acquisitions and divestures that occur shortly after year-end. • Review Board of Directors' minutes, bank confirmations, attorney letters, and other correspondence for indications that assets have been pledged or leased. • Obtain representations from management about disclosures related to plant and equipment assets.

- Substantive analytical procedures.
- Tests of valuation and allocation including tests for asset impairment.
- Tests of transactions.

Substantive Analytical Procedures

Substantive analytical procedures can be very useful for testing depreciation. Most companies use a single depreciation method and classify assets into categories with a single useful life (e.g., 5, 10, or 25 years), so that the auditor can usually generate a relatively precise estimate for depreciation expense. To illustrate, assume that the client has two types of depreciable assets: buildings and equipment. The buildings are assumed to have a useful life of 30 years and the equipment has a useful life of 10 years. The auditor can estimate depreciation expense based on the average recorded cost of the assets, the useful life, and the depreciation method used by the client (assumed to be straight line in this example):

	Buildings	**Equipment**
Average balance of depreciable assets	$150,000	$80,000
Useful life	÷ 30 yrs	÷ 10 yrs
Estimated depreciation expense	$5,000	$8,000

AUTHORITATIVE GUIDANCE & STANDARDS

Professional standards (i.e., ISA 520, **Analytical Procedures** *and PCAOB AS 2305 [formerly AU 329]* **Substantive Analytical Procedures***) provide overall guidance on the use of substantive analytical procedures as audit evidence. Chapter 9 provides an in-depth discussion of the strengths and weaknesses of these procedures overall.*

The auditor estimates that depreciation should total about $13,000. If the client's records indicate depreciation that is close to that amount, the auditor would probably conclude that depreciation was properly recorded unless other evidence of a problem became available. However, if the client's records show an amount that is significantly different, the auditor would investigate the discrepancy. In such cases, the auditor would probably start by refining the estimate. For example, the auditor might need to consider additional categories of assets with different useful lives.[3] If that does not close the gap, other substantive tests of depreciation may be required (e.g., testing depreciation for specific material assets).

Other accounts where substantive analytical procedures could be useful include insurance expense, property taxes, and utilities. Repairs and maintenance expense relative to gross plant assets is also a useful measure and provides an indication of proper classification of asset-related expenditures. The strength of analytical evidence will depend on the precision of the auditor's estimate, the reliability of the information used as input to the estimation, and the size of the discrepancy between the estimate and the actual recorded value. Again, if the unexplained discrepancy is large, the auditor will need to follow up until satisfied that there is no material misstatement in the account in question.

Tests of Valuation and Allocation Including Tests for Asset Impairment

The auditor should obtain schedules of significant asset additions and disposals for each material asset account. These schedules should be tested for accuracy and the activity included in the schedules should be reconciled with what is recorded in the general ledger. An example of a schedule of additions for equipment is presented in Figure 13.3. The schedule of additions and disposals should provide the information needed to roll the balance of plant, property, and equipment forward from the beginning to the end of the year.

Auditors should also test property, plant, and equipment for impairment. For example, auditors should consider whether there are any capital assets associated with any products that have been discontinued (or for which production has been significantly reduced). In many cases, new versions of products or different products require different factory configurations or manufacturing equipment, resulting in impairments in assets previously in use. Furthermore, decisions to move physical administration, manufacturing, distribution, or retail operations likely will result in impairments to buildings, capital leases, and even land in some cases. The auditor should consider the following to aid in determining whether there has been an impairment of property, plant, and equipment:

AUTHORITATIVE GUIDANCE & STANDARDS

Held property must be tested for impairment by assessing fair values. ISA 540 **Auditing Accounting Estimates, Including Fair Value Accounting Estimates, and Related Disclosures** *provides guidance to auditors in this area. PCAOB Standards provides separate standards for auditing accounting estimates (PCAOB AS 2501 [formerly AU 342]* **Auditing Accounting Estimates***) and a more specific standard for fair value measurements (PCAOB AS 2502 [formerly AU 328]* **Auditing Fair Value Measurements and Disclosures***).*

```
                                                         F-1

                     Jones Manufacturing, Inc.
                    Analysis of Equipment Additions            WRK
                      For Year Ended 12/31/x6          PBC    1/24/x7

    Date              Description of Transaction        Amount

  1/31/x6   Purchase of furniture for factory personnel from
            Walnut Office Furniture.                    400,000 ✓

  2/20/x6   Purchase of heavy duty drill presses from Morgan
            Tool Co.                                    350,000 ✓

  3/15/x6   Purchase of production control computer
            equipment from IBM including terminals and  845,000 ✓
            network software.

  7/20/x6   Purchase and installation of conveyor belt for
            moving completed inventory from Hanover     554,000 ✓
            Systems, Inc.

  10/6/x6   Purchase of 30 delivery trucks from Johnson's
            Heavy Truck Sales and Service.             1,456,000 ✓

            Other additions (less than $100,000 each)   418,000

            Total additions to Equipment              4,023,000  F

                                                          T

        T  Footed and agrees.
        ✓  Traced to supporting documentation (voucher package).
           Verified amount of transaction and classification of asset.
           Examined supporting documentation for proper authorizations.
           No exceptions noted.
```

Figure 13.3 Audit of Plant and Equipment Additions*

- A significant decrease in market value of asset.
- A significant decline in the use of an asset or its state of disrepair.
- Adverse legal or regulatory changes that could affect the value of an asset.
- A consistent history of operating losses in the segment of the business that the assets are employed in.
- Projections of continued losses into the future in the segment of the business that the assets are employed in.

If the auditor believes that there may have been an impairment in value of property, plant, and equipment, the auditor needs to inquire of management as to their assessment of the likelihood of impairment. The auditor will need to carry out tests of management's supporting documentation that either quantifies the amount of impairment or refutes the evidence of impairment that the auditor has discovered. Testing management's support for impairment includes:

- Determining the basis that management employed to develop a fair value estimate for the assets.
- If market prices are employed, verify those prices using independent appraisals or market pricing services.
- If market prices are not available, consider the methods that management employed (i.e., the valuation techniques used) to develop that estimate.

During the early 2000s, Wal-Mart underwent a major shift in its stores, moving from discount stores to Supercenter hypermarkets that include grocery in addition to its previous product offerings. Accordingly, as Wal-Mart builds new Supercenters in the same general locations as existing discount stores, the old buildings may be impaired in an accounting sense while awaiting sale to other retailers or real estate companies.

We discuss in the next section approaches that can be employed to determine if methods used to develop a fair value estimate are supported when market prices are not available. These methods, while couched in terms of financial assets and liabilities, are similarly appropriate for testing models employed to estimate fair values of capital assets. These include methods for estimating future cash flows and developing present value estimates and methods for determining what another party would pay to acquire the asset in a non-distressed sale environment(ii).

Impairment of intangible assets that arise from acquisitions of other entities, including the portion of the purchase price allocated to goodwill, need to be assessed for impairment annually or when conditions exist that suggest a material impairment has occurred. Indications of an impairment of intangible assets would include:

- Sustained reduction in stock price.
- Significant restructuring activities.
- Loss of a material customer.

The auditor needs to understand the method (discussed latter in this chapter) that management has chosen to estimate the value of the intangible assets and assess the inputs that management has used in estimating the key factors employed in each of these models. Significant differences with management can arise over:

- Determining the reporting unit that the intangible asset is considered part of under relevant GAAP.
- Estimates about the amounts and timing of future cash flows especially assumed growth rates.
- The appropriate discount rates to be employed in calculating present value based estimates.

Considerations discussed in the Financial Management process over fair value estimates for financial assets and liabilities, especially over validating the method employed, are equally as applicable to impairment of intangible assets (see next section).

Tests of Transactions

Property management typically has relatively few routine transactions except for maintenance and basic operations, and testing for those transactions is usually minimal because the biggest cost of maintenance is payroll, which is considered in the human resource process (see Appendix and Chapters 6, 7, and 10). Smaller acquisitions for equipment and furniture may be common and subject to an overall contract so a small sample of such transactions may be tested or may be tested during the tests of purchases discussed in Chapter 12. However, many asset acquisitions are large and infrequent. The auditor will often vouch the largest asset acquisitions because they may be individually material to the financial statements. Vouching individual additions involves examining supporting documentation to verify the valuation of the asset (see notations in Figure 13.3). Confirmations for contracts and leases may be obtained and some assets may be physically examined. For assets that are self-constructed, the auditor will need to examine evidence of the materials (inventory), labor (payroll), and administrative oversight used in production, as well as the possibility that interest should be capitalized as part of the cost of the asset.

Asset disposals would be tested by examining supporting documentation and vouching receipts, with the added steps of verifying the relief of accumulated depreciation and the computation of a gain or loss on the transaction. For assets that were traded for new assets, the auditor will need to verify the proper accounting for exchanges of nonmonetary assets and cross-reference the disposal with the asset addition.

Part B: Auditing the Financial Management Process
Process Map

The purpose of the financial management process is to forecast and control the timing and nature of the company's flow of cash so as to provide adequate support for ongoing operations. The key to financial management is balancing cash inflows from operations and sources of capital against the outflows needed for operations and long-term investments. Companies raise capital by issuing equity and borrowing from diverse creditors (banks, bond holders, vendors), and make short-term investments with funds not needed immediately. In all cases these financial assets and liabilities need to be evaluated as to whether "mark to market" accounting is required for them and if so develop the appropriate fair value estimates to make any necessary adjustments that might result.

Objectives: A process map for financial management is presented in Figure 13.4. The primary objective of financial management is to manage financial resources to allow the organization to achieve its desired goals. More specifically, financial planning has the objective of effectively planning for the cash flow needs of the organization and making arrangements to assure that adequate financial resources are available. This process involves identifying potential sources of capital, minimizing the cost of the organization's capital structure, and making sure obligations can be paid on time. Another objective is to maximize the earnings on invested funds subject to the level of tolerable risk established by the board or management. Finally, given the move to "mark to market" accounting, financial management has become increasingly focused on being able to routinely generate fair value estimates as required by the appropriate accounting standards.

Activities: The key activities that comprise financial management are depicted in Figure 13.4. The importance of these activities is conditional on the strategic decisions that the organization makes concerning its capital structure, such as whether to borrow extensively or maintain a relatively debt-free balance sheet. Financial management activities include:

- Planning and budgeting: Projecting cash flows from operations is the starting point for financial planning. Strategic goals and long-term plans

Process Objectives

- Prepare accurate budgets and financial reports on a timely basis.
- Optimize capital structure given current economic environment.
- Minimize cost of capital over long term.
- Maximize return from investments for a given level of risk tolerance.
- Manage cash flows to meet obligations on a timely basis.
- Comply with obligations and terms of financing contracts.
- Record financial assets and liabilities (where required) at fair market value.
- Capture, process, and report information necessary for process improvement.

Process Activities

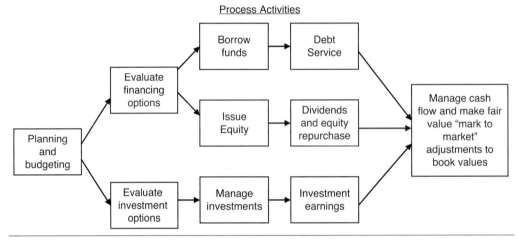

Process Data Streams

Information Feeds
- Strategic plan and budgets
- Financing sources and potential lenders
- Financial market data including stock prices, bond yields, and derivative product availability
- Capital budgets
- Cash flow requirements
- Financial asset levels
- Stock compensation plans

Information Generation
- Budgets and forecasts
- Investment transactions
- Borrowing transactions
- Risk assessments associated with investing and borrowing especially related to derivative transactions
- Equity transactions
- Investment performance
- Cost of capital
- Debt contracts and covenants
- Fair value (i.e., "mark to market") valuation reports
- Financial reports

Accounting Impact of Activities

Routine Transactions	Non-routine Transactions	Accounting Estimates
• Line of credit	• Bonds payable	• Impairment of investments
• Notes payable	• Debt retirement	• Stock compensation
• Debt payments	• Equity issues	• Cost allocation for mergers
• Interest	• Equity repurchase	• Fair value (i.e., "mark to
• Dividends	• Option grants	market") relevant financial
• Investments*	• Mergers and acquisitions	assets and liabilities.
• Sale of investments		
• Investment earnings		
• Exercise of options		

Figure 13.4 *Process Map: Financial Management*

Many companies are attempting to employ derivative products to manage risks in a way that they have not before. Hence, while some investments might be routine, others may be non-routine until sufficient organizational learning has taken place such that managing those risks has become routine.

dictate how much free cash flow the organization needs at any point in time. If cash flow is inadequate, either plans need to change or other sources of financing must be arranged. Accurate forecasting becomes the basis for critical management and board decisions about financial structure and the need for additional capital.

- Evaluating financing options: An organization can raise funds externally by borrowing or issuing equity. Borrowed funds can come from bank loans, publicly issued bonds, commercial paper, leases, or even vendors. Equity financing usually involves issuing common or preferred stock. A key management concern in this activity is monitoring the cost of capital and assessing the most reasonable source of funds.

- Borrowing funds: The key elements of this activity are identifying sources of credit and arranging acceptable terms. This activity results in the inflow of financial resources.

- Debt service: This activity involves the routine handling of periodic interest and principle payments.

- Issuing equity: Equity financing is usually more complex than borrowing because of the need for management and the Board of Directors to engage underwriters and other financial professionals. Also, public stock offerings are subject to extensive examination and regulation by government agencies, especially securities market regulators like the SEC. In addition to straight stock issues, new securities can be issued as part of stock option or employee stock purchase plans. This activity creates a cash inflow for the organization.

- Returns to shareholders: Dividends constitute the primary return to shareholders from the company. In some cases, the company may decide to repurchase some of its own shares. In both cases, the company will be making disbursements to shareholders.

- Evaluating investment options: If the company has excess financial resources that are not immediately needed for operations or long-term investments, those funds can be invested in the short term. This activity involves management and the board specifying the types of investment vehicles that are appropriate for the organization that will maximize investment returns while controlling risk. Recent developments in finance have triggered an increase in investments in complex derivatives. These types of transactions can create significant, and often misunderstood, risks to the company.

- Managing investments: The daily buying and selling of investments and the moving of financial resources are relatively routine activities. These activities can create both cash inflows and outflows.

- Investment earnings: Investments will produce returns either in the form of interest and dividends or capital gains. This activity focuses on realizing and recording investment earnings, which generally will produce a cash inflow for the company.

- Manage cash flow: The combined effect of operations, financing transactions, and investment activities determines net cash flow to the company at any point in time. The minimizing of the amount of idle financial resources while satisfying all operating and capital obligations is the purpose of cash flow management.

- Make fair value "mark to market" adjustments to book values: Accounting standards require that many financial assets and liabilities be "marked to market" requiring ongoing attention to being able to generate fair value estimates in accordance with relevant accounting standards.

The complexity of financial management will primarily depend on the capital structure of the organization and the predictability of cash flows. A company that is highly leveraged may have more difficult challenges related to financial management than one that is equity financed, especially if cash flow from operations is weak or deteriorating. Financing with bank loans and basic equity is relatively easy to manage. Financing with publicly traded debt, leases, derivatives, and hybrid securities (such as convertible bonds) increases the challenges of financial management (and accounting). Valuing all of these financial assets and liabilities in accordance with increasingly complex fair value accounting standards and making adjustments to the book values is also a great challenge for financial management.

Transactions: Financial resource management involves a broad range of potential transactions affecting numerous accounts including:

- Cash and cash equivalents.
- Short-term investments (marketable securities).
- Long-term investments.
- Notes payable.
- Debt obligations.
- Capitalized lease obligations.
- Shareholder's equity (and related accounts).

Most large financial transactions are unique and occur relatively infrequently (e.g., issuing stock). Proper processing of these transactions receives extensive scrutiny from senior management and the Board of Directors. Routine transactions such as the receipt of dividends or payment of interest are often highly automated. Proper processing and accounting for routine transactions is similar to the cash receipt and cash disbursement activities that have been discussed in earlier chapters.

Investments can be either short or long term in duration. Short-term investments are usually made with excess cash that is not needed for operations. Due to their short duration, these investments will be structured to avoid downside market risk and maximize cash earnings (e.g., interest). Long-term investments are usually undertaken for strategic purposes, for example, as a precursor to acquiring another company. These investments are probably less concerned with downside market risk and focus more on the underlying benefits of the securities acquired. Regardless of the form of the investment, the basic events are the same: Buy an investment, collect periodic earnings, and sell the investment.

An organization can borrow funds in a number of ways. Common forms of borrowed funds are bank loans (e.g., notes payable) and bonds that are issued to the public. Other forms of borrowed funds include lines of credit, leases, and specialized financial instruments. Although there is a wide disparity across types of borrowings, the basic elements of the transactions are essentially the same: Funds are received, interest is paid, and funds are returned. For example, principal repayments may be periodic or in a lump sum. Interest may be explicit and periodic, or may be implicit (as in the case of zero coupon bonds). The obligation may allow either the borrower or the lender to terminate the arrangement (e.g., through a call or prepayment provision). Some obligations may not appear on the financial statements at all as a result of specialized accounting treatment (e.g., operating leases).

A company can issue two general types of equity: common stock and preferred stock. Most equity transactions involve large amounts and must comply with complex regulations but are relatively simple from an accounting perspective (e.g., the issuance of common stock and the payment of dividends). Stock options, stock rights, and acquisitions funded with stock and convertible securities can raise some difficult accounting issues, however. The basic elements of all equity transactions are the issuance of an equity security (and the receipt of consideration), the payment of dividends and, occasionally, the repurchase/retirement of equity. Most companies maintain a **stock book**, or similar ledger, to keep track of who owns the stock of the company at any point in time. Publicly traded companies in many countries must have an independent **stock transfer agent** that handles all transactions related to who owns the stock of the company at any given time.

As financial management has grown in sophistication over the past two decades, financial managers have taken advantage of complex financial derivatives that change the risk profile of a debt or equity instrument. For example, a company's fixed rate long-term mortgage on a building can be converted into a variable rate demand loan via the creative use of derivative contracts. Here the auditor needs to identify the resulting risks and determine whether a specialist level assistance is needed to determine proper accounting and disclosure. Additionally, **hybrid** instruments are frequently found that have aspects of debt and equity rolled into one security. The classification of this type of instrument is problematic, as the financial accounting rules are complex in this area, and regulatory scrutiny tends to be high as these instruments are often traded on public markets.

Internal Threat Analysis

Internal threat analysis for financial management is illustrated in Table 13.3. There is a great deal of overlap among the various sources of risk. The effectiveness of planning may be particularly problematic given that performance depends on the quality of management, personnel, technology, and the process used to develop plans and budgets.

Analysis of Internal Control over Financial Reporting

Table 13.3 also identifies numerous controls that might mitigate the risks of financial management. Entity level controls include:

- Performance reviews and monitoring: Effective financial management will be facilitated if management:

Table 13.3   *Internal Threat Analysis: Financial Management*

Process Risks	Controls Linked to Risks	Performance Measures
(1) Ineffective planning and budgeting including inappropriate incentives to financial resource management.	• Establish strong financial information systems. • Establish independent budgeting and forecasting group. • Senior management actively involved in planning and budgeting. • Have budget and plans reviewed by line managers. • Establish policies for compensation of financial resources managers that does not give them incentives to invest in riskier investments than firm policy allows.	• Extent and nature of budget variances. • Number of budget amendments. • Cycle time for budget preparation. • Finance and budgeting department head count. • Cost of budgeting and planning department. • Compensation contracts for financial resource managers.
(2) Inadequate cash flow.	• Effective cash flow budgeting. • Establish adequate lines of credit. • Optimize timing of disbursements. • Optimize use of cash float.	• Cash balances. • Average draws on lines of credit. • Receivable turnover relative to payable turnover. • Amount of free cash flow. • Interest or fixed charge coverage ratio. • Level of short-term borrowings. • Bond ratings. • Market valuation of debt.
(3) Violations of debt or other agreements.	• Monitor compliance with debt covenants on timely basis. • Effective and independent internal audit group. • Proactive involvement with creditor groups.	• Number of violations. • Frequency of violations. • Level of working capital. • Interest coverage ratio. • Dividend payout rate. • Bond ratings.
(4) Inappropriate debt or equity transactions.	• Establish policies concerning acceptable terms for borrowings and equity transactions. • All debt and equity transactions approved at board level. • Engage outside experts to assist on new issues. • Monitor debt and equity position on a timely basis.	• Cost of capital. • Cost of debt. • Amount of free cash flow. • Leverage ratios. • Return on equity. • Market valuation of debt and equity. • Market "beta."
(5) Imbalance between investments and obligations or cash flow.	• Establish formal investment policies for excess cash. • Match investments to timing of cash needs. • Establish lines of credit to provide financing flexibility.	• Time to maturity of investments. • Yield on investments. • Cash flow from investing activities.
(6) Suboptimal capital structure.	• Effective financial planning and budgeting. • Engage outside experts to assist in planning. • Establish lines of credit to provide financing flexibility.	• Cost of capital. • Cost of debt. • Market valuation of debt and equity. • Market return on common shares.
(7) Excessive risk exposures (e.g., derivatives, guarantees).	• Establish formal policy on acceptable derivative investments.	• Losses due to derivatives. • Value at risk for derivatives.

	• Monitor derivative and value at risk on a timely basis. • Senior level approval of derivative transactions. • Independent appraisal and riskiness of value of derivative investments. • Effective and independent internal audit group.	• Volume of hedging activity. • Yield on derivative investments. • Yield on investments.
(8) Unauthorized or inappropriate investment transactions.	• Engage outside experts to assist with investment planning. • Establish formal policies on acceptable investment strategies. • Monitor investments on a timely basis. • Senior level approval of all non-routine investments. • Effective and independent internal audit group.	• Violations of investment guidelines. • Value at risk in investments. • Yield on investments.
(9) Unforeseen changes in market conditions which cause losses.	• Establish process to monitor and react to market changes. • Engage outside experts to assist with investment planning. • Establish policies and procedures for risk hedging activities.	• Unrealized losses. • Realized losses. • Insider trading activity. • Yield on investments.
(10) Inability to generate fair value (i.e., "mark to market") estimates on a timely and well supported basis.	• Establish process to regularly value affected assets and liabilities. • Develop process to determine and regularly review classification of asset/liability in fair value framework. • For level 2 fair value assets/liabilities develop process to approve observable market inputs equivalents used to generate fair value estimates. • For level 3 fair value assets/liabilities engage experts to develop models to support "mark to model" estimates.	• Cycle time to generate routine fair value estimates. • Inquiries about fair value disclosures and accounting from regulatory bodies.
(11) Violations of security regulations.	• Effective board and senior management oversight. • Establish formal policies and procedures for financial reporting and accounting choices. • Engage outside experts to assist with investment planning. • Effective and independent internal audit group.	• Citations from regulatory bodies. • Timeliness of required filings.

- o Monitors market conditions especially changes in the economic environment.
- o Monitors trends in financing structure and financial transactions.
- o Maintains timely cash flow budgets and forecasts.
- o Assures compliance with debt covenants and regulations.
- o Monitors the cost of capital.

o Establishes and monitors investment policies and the nature of acceptable investments.

o Periodically assesses investment performance.

More detailed process control activities, including internal controls over financial reporting, include:

- Segregation of duties: Incompatible duties related to financial management include authorization of capital structure and investment policies, authorization of investment transactions, processing of receipt and disbursement transactions, physical access to financial assets, and information processing for financial activities.

- Processing controls:

  o Authorizations are critical to financial management because transactions are often sizable and involve financial resources that are highly liquid. Individual investment and financing transactions should be subject to appropriate high-level authorization.

  o Transaction processing procedures should be established for investments, investment income, debt, debt service, equity, and dividends. The broad range of transactions may require a diverse set of procedures. Processing controls would focus on cash receipts and disbursements, as well as on the valuation of investment and financing transactions.

  o The company should maintain a complete inventory of all investments, whether held by a third party (e.g., broker) or in their own possession. These should be reviewed to determine if the investments are still appropriate and that related income is being properly recognized. For debt, special considerations should be given to retiring obligations and amortizing discounts or premiums when the effective interest rate on debt differs from the stated rate. Tracking of equity interests (e.g., to determine the owner of record for payment of a dividend) is usually facilitated by employing a **registrar** or **stock transfer agent** to monitor shareholder transactions. Generation of fair values estimates for finanical assets and liabilities that are subject to "mark to market" accounting and determination of when adjustments need to be made to carrying values.

- Physical controls: Limitations on access to investments, cash, and accounting records for these assets and liabilities are important in the financial management process.

Routine transactions such as disbursements and receipts are subject to the same controls as similar transactions in other processes. Non-routine transactions tend to be scrutinized by senior management and the Board of Directors, and controls focus on detailed valuation and authorization of such transactions.

Evaluation of Process Performance Indicators

Relevant performance indicators for financial management are listed in the last column of Table 13.3. Because most of the important indicators involve financial information, the measures are generally available and reliable. These performance measures can provide the auditor with a wealth of evidence about the financial management process. For example, many companies carefully monitor their external bond ratings to make sure that they can obtain the best possible terms when borrowing money. The downgrade of a company's bond rating can have a serious impact on its cost of capital and its profitability.

Tests of Financial Statement Assertions: Investments, Borrowed Funds, and Equity

Substantive Tests for Investments

The audit procedures that are appropriate for testing investment balances are summarized in Table 13.4. The primary substantive audit tests that are performed are:

- Confirmation or physical observation to establish validity (existence) of investments.
- Tests of market value for possible unrealized losses including the need to develop fair value estimates for those investments required to be "marked to market."
- Tests of documentation for current-period acquisitions or dispositions.
- Substantive analytical procedures to test the reasonableness of interest and dividend income.

The actual scope of the substantive tests will depend on the risk of material misstatement for investments and the materiality of investment balances to the financial statements.

The key assertions related to investments are existence/occurrence and valuation. Existence can be determined via physical examination of actual securities or via confirmation with independent fiduciaries (e.g., brokers). Valuation of investments is particularly important because of the accounting treatment of unrealized losses and the need for certain financial assets to be "marked to market." Verification of valuation may present problems to the auditor if market values are not readily determinable for some investments. The fair value hierarchy provides guidance to those auditors working under IFRS and FASB accounting standards as to what approaches are permitted when liquid active markets (denoted as Level 1 in the hierarchy) are not available (see Box 13.1 "Fair Value Hierarchy in IFRS 13 and SFAS 157"). Carrying out procedures to determine if management estimates of fair value are appropriate can be complex especially for Level 3 fair value estimates where the inputs to the model used to develop the hypothetical fair value estimates area not readily observable and the model employed to generate the values may be a proprietary model developed by the client and its experts. Box 13.2 "Judging the Reasonableness of Fair Value Estimates Made by Management" and Box 13.3 "Auditor Considerations when Client Employs a Model to Develop Fair Value Estimates" provide guidance for assessing management estimates when models are employed to generate hypothetical fair value estimates for investments.

Table 13.4   *Substantive Tests for Assertions about Investment Transactions, Accounts, and Disclosures*

Management Assertion	Typical Audit Procedures
Valuation and Allocation: Transaction detail included in subsidiary journals and ledgers agrees with the general ledger balances related to investments.	• Reconcile detailed investment listings with the general ledger. • Reconcile brokerage statements (or other independent investment listings) with detailed investment listings and the general ledger. • Test accuracy of detailed investment listings, including related income.
Existence: All recorded transactions related to investments occurred and recorded investments exist.	• Confirm securities held by broker or other fiduciary. • Physically inspect securities on hand. • Perform substantive analytical procedures to test investment income.
Completeness: All existing investment transactions including derivative transaction and balances have been recorded.	• Review bank confirmations, brokerage confirmations, Board of Directors minutes, attorney letters, etc., for indications of unrecorded investments especially for derivative products. • Perform substantive analytical procedures to test balance of investments relative to investment income. • Obtain representation letter concerning completeness of detailed investment listings.
Rights and obligations: Investment balances are owned by the company.	• Confirm the existence of investments in the hands of third parties. • Obtain a representation letter from management regarding ownership of investments. • Review Board of Directors' minutes, legal letters, contracts, etc., for evidence of pledging or other potential claims of ownership on investments.
Accuracy/Valuation: Investment balances are recorded at amounts properly reflecting their realizable value and where appropriate have been "marked to market."	• Vouch a sample of investment purchases. • Vouch a sample of investment sales. • Re-compute gains and losses on investment sales. • Review accounting methods used for handling investment securities (e.g., lower of cost or market vs. equity). • Review estimates of fair value following "mark to market" valuation approach. • Assess realizability of securities held at year end. • Perform substantive analytical procedures to test investment income.
Valuation and Allocation: Investment balances and related costs are properly classified.	• Review investment listings for unusual items that should be reclassified. • Review and test management policy for classifying securities as short-term, long-term, or held for sale. • Review methods employed to develop fair value estimates including determining fair value hierarchy level. • Obtain independent valuations for Level 1 fair values from valuation experts or services that are independent from client management. • Review inputs to Level 2 fair value estimates and computations including appropriateness of any models employed to generate Level 2 estimates. • Review the models employed and the inputs to the models used to determine Level 3 fair value estimates including reasonableness of data and methods employed to make those estimates. • Obtain representation letter concerning classification policy.
Cut-off: Transactions affecting investments have been recorded in the proper period.	• Perform cash receipt cut-off tests for investment sales and investment income. • Perform cash disbursement cutoff tests for investment purchases. • Perform substantive analytical procedures to test investment income.
Completeness/ Existence/ Valuation/ and Understandability: All required disclosures pertaining to investment balances are included in the financial statements.	• Complete disclosure checklist for investments. • Ensure all relevant fair value disclosures have been made. • Obtain representation letter from management regarding disclosure of investments. • Review proposed disclosures for accuracy.

BOX 13.1   FAIR VALUE HIERARCHY IN IFRS 13 AND SFAS 157

A fair value estimate is defined as "the price that would be received to sell an asset or paid to transfer a liability in an orderly transaction between market participants at the measurement date." IFRS 13 **Fair Value Measurement** *and SFAS 157* **Fair Value Measurements** *describe the general principles to be used in all other standards when implementing fair value (or "mark to market") estimates. This hierarchy is not a choice of levels. Rather, the level in the hierarchy that applies to a specific asset or liability depends on the data that is available for valuing the related asset or liability.*

- **Level 1** *refers to cases in which the market prices for the identical assets or liabilities are readily available from active liquid markets.*

- **Level 2** *refers to cases in which hypothetical market prices must be estimated based on observable inputs from other market transactions in active liquid markets. Normally Level 2 is implemented by employing those observed inputs using by a well-accepted and broadly employed model to derive an estimate of fair value.*

- **Level 3** *involves estimation based on unobservable inputs. These unobservable (in the market) inputs shall reflect management's assumptions about the assumptions that market participants would make in pricing the asset or liability. Then a model, often developed by management as there are normally not well-accepted and broadly employed models used in valuing this particular type of asset or liability, is used in conjunction with the unobservable inputs that management has estimated to develop a hypothetical market price that is used as an estimate of the fair value of the asset or liability.*

In Level 2 and Level 3 estimates, either an income approach (present value of future estimated cash flows) or a market approach (what a market participant would pay to transfer the liability or purchase the asset) can be employed.

BOX 13.2   JUDGING THE REASONABLENESS OF FAIR VALUE ESTIMATES MADE BY MANAGEMENT

Matters that the auditor may consider in evaluating the reasonableness of assumptions used by management underlying fair value accounting estimates include:

- *Where relevant, whether and, if so, how management has incorporated market-specific inputs into the development of assumptions.*

- *Whether the assumptions are consistent with observable market conditions, and the characteristics of the asset or liability being measured at fair value.*

- *Whether the sources of market-participant assumptions are relevant and reliable, and how management has selected the assumptions to use when a number of different market participant assumptions exist.*

- *Where appropriate, whether and, if so, how management considered assumptions used in, or information about, comparable transactions, assets or liabilities.*

BOX 13.3   AUDITOR CONSIDERATIONS WHEN CLIENT EMPLOYS A MODEL TO DEVELOP FAIR VALUE ESTIMATES

Panel A: Where fair value accounting estimates are based on models (Level 2 and Level 3 in the Fair Value Hierarchy) the auditor should consider:

- *Management's rationale for the method selected is reasonable.*

- *Management has sufficiently evaluated and appropriately applied the criteria, if any, provided in the applicable financial reporting framework to support the selected method.*

- *The method is appropriate in the circumstances given the nature of the asset or liability being estimated and the requirements of the applicable financial reporting framework relevant to accounting estimates.*

- *The method is appropriate in relation to the business, industry, and environment in which the entity operates.*

Panel B: Where the auditor has decided to test the model, the auditor should consider:

- *That the model is validated prior to usage, with periodic reviews to ensure it is still suitable for its intended use. The entity's validation process may include evaluation of:*

  o *The model's theoretical soundness and mathematical integrity, including the appropriateness of model parameters.*

  o *The consistency and completeness of the model's inputs with market practices.*

  o *The model's output as compared to actual transactions.*

- *Appropriate change control policies and procedures exist.*

- *The model is periodically calibrated and tested for validity, particularly when inputs are unobservable (as in Level 3 models).*

- *Adjustments are made to the output of the model, including in the case of fair value accounting estimates, whether such adjustments reflect the assumptions marketplace participants would use in similar circumstances.*

- *The model is adequately documented; including the model's intended applications and limitations and its key parameters, required inputs, and results of any validation analysis performed.*

Panel C: Where fair value accounting estimates are based on unobservable inputs (Level 3 in the Fair Value Hierarchy), matters that the auditor may consider include:

- *Management's identification of the characteristics of marketplace participants relevant to the accounting estimate.*

- *Modifications management has made to their assumptions to reflect its view of assumptions marketplace participants would use.*

- *Whether management has incorporated the best information available in the circumstances.*

- *Where applicable, how management assumptions take account of comparable transactions, assets, or liabilities.*

AUTHORITATIVE GUIDANCE & STANDARDS

ISA 505 **External Confirmations** *and PCAOB AS 2310 (formerly AU 330)*
The Confirmation Process *provide guidance on confirmations of all
types, including accounts payable as well as guidance as to what to do if
confirmations are not returned.*

Classification of investments is also critical due to the different accounting
treatments allowed for different types of investment securities.[4] Cut-
offs are usually a concern only in regard to the accrual of investment
income. Finally, disclosure requirements are extensive for financial
instruments, and some derivatives that involve material amounts can readily
be hidden for substantial periods of time if proper authorization controls are
not in place.[5]

AUTHORITATIVE GUIDANCE & STANDARDS

*Held investments and other financial assets and liabilities must be marked
to market under both IFRS (e.g., IFRS 13* **Fair Value Measurement***) and
FASB (e.g., SFAS 157* **Fair Value Measurements***) accounting standards.
While this is relatively straightforward for financial assets with active liquid
markets other financial assets and liabilities need to have estimates of
fair value made falling under the general rubic of accounting estimates.
Furthermore, equity investments must be tested for impairment by
assessing fair values. ISA 540 and AS2501 and 2502 provide guidance to
auditors in this area.*

Substantive Tests for Borrowed Funds

In general, transactions related to borrowed funds are infrequent but
large. Typical audit procedures related to borrowed funds are described in
Table13.5. The primary substantive tests for borrowed funds are:

- Confirmations from banks and known creditors to establish validity and
  completeness of obligations.

- Examination of legal documents to test valuation and disclosure of
  obligations.

- Cut-off tests for unrecorded liabilities (especially interest accruals and
  derivative transactions).

- Substantive analytical procedures to test interest expense.

- Assessment of the reasonableness and extent of disclosures.

- Assessment of those financial instruments that need to be "marked to
  market" and require the generation of fair value estimates.

The auditor must also test for compliance with debt covenants, violations of
which may create contingent liabilities for the company or affect the timing
(and classification) of obligations.[6] Finally, off-balance sheet obligations must

Table 13.5 *Substantive Tests for Assertions about Borrowed Funds Transactions, Accounts, and Disclosures*

Management Assertion	Typical Audit Procedures
Valuation and Allocation: Transaction detail included in subsidiary journals and ledgers agrees with the general ledger balances related to borrowed funds (debt, lines of credit, and notes payable).	• Obtain a listing of all known obligations (notes payable, capital leases, lines of credit, bonds, etc.) and tie into the general ledger. • Reconcile subsidiary records (e.g., for notes payable) with the general ledger.
Existence: All recorded transactions related to borrowed funds occurred and recorded obligations exist.	• Examine the supporting documentation for a sample of recorded obligations. • Confirm obligations and terms with creditors. • Examine Board of Directors' minutes for authorization of borrowings.
Completeness: All existing borrowed funds and obligations have been recorded.	• Examine payments subsequent to year end for indication of obligations not recorded at year end especially for obligations that are unrecorded but existed at year-end. • Obtain and review a standard bank confirmation for indications of unrecorded obligations. • Confirm zero-balance accounts with known creditors. • Obtain representation letter from management regarding the completeness of borrowed funds.
Valuation and allocation: Borrowed funds are recorded at the proper amounts including where appropriate valued employing fair values (i.e., mark to market) accounting standards.	• Examine supporting documentation for recorded obligations and determine that interest expense, interest payable, current balance of principal, and long-term balance of principal are correctly recorded. • Review estimates of fair value for each major liability class following "mark to market" valuation approach. • Perform substantive analytical procedures to test interest expense. • Re-compute balances for obligations that are issued at a discount, have non-market interest rates, or do not have a stated face value (e.g., capital leases). • Re-compute actual interest expense using interest rates and balances of borrowed funds for a sample of obligations. • Confirm obligations and terms with creditors.
Valuation and Allocation: Borrowed funds are properly classified.	• Scan the list of obligations for items that are unusual and may require reclassification. • Examine supporting documentation for recorded obligations and determine that current and long-term portions of principal are correctly classified. • Review methods employed to develop fair value estimates including determining fair value hierarchy level. • Obtain independent valuations for Level 1 fair values from valuation experts or services that are independent from client management. • Review inputs to Level 2 fair value estimates and computations including appropriateness of any models employed to generate Level 2 estimates. • Review the models employed and the inputs to the models used to determine Level 3 fair value estimates including reasonableness of data and methods employed to make those estimates. • Obtain representation letter concerning classification policy.
Cut-off/Valuation: Transactions related to borrowed funds (including interest expense and payments) have been recorded in the proper period.	• Examine payments subsequent to year end for indication of obligations not recorded at year end. • Perform substantive analytical procedures to test interest expense. • Re-compute actual interest expense using interest rates and balances of borrowed funds for a sample of obligations. • Scan journal entries related to interest expense for evidence of timely recognition.

Completeness/ Valuation/ and Understandability: All required disclosures pertaining to borrowed funds are included in the financial statements.	• Complete a disclosure checklist related to borrowed funds. • Ensure all relevant fair value disclosures have been made • Obtain representation letter from management regarding disclosure of borrowed funds. • Review proposed disclosures for accuracy.

be reviewed to assure proper disclosure in the financial statements. The extent and nature of substantive tests performed for borrowed funds will be related primarily to the complexity of financing arrangements.

The auditor's primary concerns related to borrowed funds are that all such arrangements are recorded (completeness) on a timely basis (cut-off) at a proper amount (valuation and allocation) and fully disclosed in accordance with appropriate accounting principles (presentation and disclosure). Completeness and cut-offs are usually tested with confirmations and as part of the general search for unrecorded and contingent liabilities (see Chapter 14). Valuation is usually determined via examination of supporting documentation, especially related legal documents. Valuation of those financial liabilities that are subject to "mark to market" accounting includes the need to generate fair value estimates (Box 13.2 "Judging the Reasonableness of Fair Value Estimates Made by Management") employing analogous procedures (Box 13.3 "Auditor Considerations when Client Employs a Model to Develop Fair Value Estimates") to those for financial assets (Box 13.1 "Fair Value Hierarchy in IFRS 13 and SFAS 157"). Proper disclosure is achieved through a careful examination of confirmations and legal documents, and consideration of appropriate reporting standards.

AUTHORITATIVE GUIDANCE & STANDARDS

ISA 505 provides guidance on confirmations of all types, including debt. These standards note that the requests for confirmation related to debt should be directed to those within the organization expected to have knowledge about the information. For example, to confirm information about waivers related to debt covenants, the confirmation should be directed to an official of the creditor with the knowledge and authority to respond to the confirmation. There are no equivalent PCAOB standards.

Substantive Tests for Equity

Equity transactions also tend to be infrequent but large. Typical substantive tests related to equity are summarized in Table 13.6. The primary audit tests are:

• Confirmation of existence, completeness, and valuation of equity with the independent registrar or transfer agent.

• Examination of Board of Directors' minutes for authorization and details about current-period transactions, particularly the authorization of dividends.

- Substantive analytical procedures to test dividend accruals and totals.
- Assessment of the reasonableness and extent of disclosures.

In general, the audit of equity is usually a minor portion of the audit unless there have been complex transactions, such as a merger executed via a stock swap, or the company uses esoteric equity arrangements.

The auditor's primary concerns related to equity are completeness and cut-offs of equity transactions, such as new issues, splits, and dividends. Given the divergence between the date of record and the date of execution/clearing for many equity transactions, auditors must be careful to determine that equity transactions are recorded in the proper period. It is important to remember that the buying and selling of stock between investors does not affect the accounts of the company. Such transactions are of interest to the company only in regard to who actually owns stock at a point in time and should receive dividends upon the date of record. The valuation of equity transactions is also of concern to the auditor, especially for complex transactions that involve deferred compensation, hybrid securities, or derivatives. In addition, while normally rarer than for financial assets and liabilities, for certain equity instruments there is also the need to consider whether they need to be "marked to market" or are subject to requirements for disclosures of fair value following the fair value hierarchy (see Box 13.1 "Fair Value Hierarchy in IFRS 13 and SFAS 157"). Finally, disclosure requirements for equity are extensive and must be evaluated by the auditor.

Table 13.6 *Substantive Tests for Assertions about Equity Transactions, Accounts, and Disclosures*

Management Assertion	Typical Audit Procedures
Valuation and Allocation: Transaction detail included in subsidiary journals and ledgers agrees with the general ledger balances related to equity.	• Reconcile the type and number of shares issued per the stock book with the general ledger. • Analyze current-year stock activity and trace to proper inclusion in the general ledger. • Confirm details of outstanding equity with outside parties (e.g., registrars, stock transfer agents, trustee for employee stock ownership plans).
Existence: All recorded transactions related to equity occurred and recorded equity balances exist.	• Perform substantive analytical procedures. • Analyze current-year equity activity. • Confirm details of current-year activity with outside parties (e.g., underwriters, stock transfer agents, trustee for employee stock ownership plans). • Review Board of Directors' minutes for date and amount of dividend declarations, stock splits, stock dividends, option grants, and treasury stock acquisitions. • Vouch selected equity transactions.
Completeness: All existing equity transactions and balances have been recorded.	
Valuation and Allocation: Equity balances are recorded at the proper amounts.	
Valuation and Allocation: Equity balances are properly classified.	
Cut-off: Equity transactions (including dividend declarations) have been recorded in the proper period.	
Completeness/ Valuation/ Understandability: All required disclosures pertaining to equity balances are included in the financial statements.	• Complete a disclosure checklist related to equity. • Obtain representation letter from management regarding disclosure of equity, especially stock compensation arrangements. • Review proposed disclosures for accuracy.

Summary and Conclusion

In this chapter, we discussed the audit of the facilities and financial management processes. These are considered critical resource management processes in most organizations. In each case, we discussed a process map for the process and analyzed the internal threats to the process. Residual risks identified during process analysis would be linked to financial statement assertions with high risk of material misstatement and appropriate substantive procedures selected to test high-risk assertions. Potential substantive tests for assertions affected by each process were discussed in detail.

The most common transactions occurring in facilities management would affect property and equipment assets and related depreciation; and in financial resource management, they would affect long-term debt, equity, and investments. These processes are generally characterized by large and infrequent transactions where controls may be performed on an ad hoc basis. Under the Integrated Audit, however, the auditor needs to consider the controls over financial reporting for all material processes, and as these transactions tend to be material, the auditor needs to examine the controls over the various resource management processes.

Traditionally, because many of the facilities and financial management transactions are large and material, the auditor has focused on refining substantive tests to be used to examine assertions related to these accounts. Table 13.7 illustrates how the various substantive tests described in this chapter might be adapted under different risk conditions. Substantive testing related to facilities and financial management tends to focus on year-end balances and activity such as acquisitions and disposals and issuances of debt and equity in financial management. Ultimately, the auditor must decide which of these tests to perform on a given client and the extent of testing needed to gather adequate evidence to support the audit opinion.

Table 13.7 *Tests of Financial Statement Assertions at Different Levels of Risk of Material Misstatement for Resource Management Processes*

Type of Procedure	High Detection Risk Case (Low risk of material misstatement)	Low Detection Risk Case (High risk of material misstatement)
Plant, Property, and Equipment		
Tests of additions	Vouch a small sample of additions (stratified by size) with few or no physical inspections of assets.	A large sample of additions vouched and physically examined.
Tests of disposals	A small sample of disposals vouched.	A large sample of disposals vouched.
Tests of repairs expense	Tested by review of repairs expense account.	Tested by review and vouching of repairs expense account.
Tests of impairment	Tested by review of management documentation supporting decision to record impairment or to refute assumption that asset may be impaired.	Tested by review of management documentation supplemented by the employment of an independent valuation expert to test the models and assumptions that management has employed in its tests of impairments.

(Continued)

Table 13.7   *(Continued)*

Type of Procedure	High Detection Risk Case (Low risk of material misstatement)	Low Detection Risk Case (High risk of material misstatement)
Tests of depreciation	Tested with substantive analytical procedure.	Tested with substantive analytical procedure and supplemented with tests of depreciation for individual assets.
Investments, Borrowed Funds and Equity		
Investments	Vouch large purchases or sales. Obtain confirmations from external parties pertaining to assets held. Test overall market value of investment portfolio. Use substantive analytical procedures to test investment income. Review procedures for making fair value estimates.	Vouch numerous sales and disposal transactions. Obtain confirmations from external parties pertaining to assets held. Physically examine investments on hand. Test overall market value of investment portfolio and vouch market value of specific items. Use substantive analytical procedures supplemented by tests of transactions to test investment income. Detailed testing of fair value estimates especially for Level 2 and Level 3 estimates that are most open to manipulation.
Borrowed Funds	Minimal vouching of large borrowings and payoffs. Confirm obligations with outside parties. Scan post-year end disbursements journal for unrecorded liabilities. Use substantive analytical procedures to test interest expense and accruals. Review procedures for making fair value estimates.	Moderate to extensive vouching of borrowings, interest, and payoffs. Confirm many obligations with outside parties. Perform extensive search for unrecorded liabilities. Use substantive analytical procedures to test interest expense and accruals supplemented by extensive tests of transactions. Detailed testing of fair value estimates especially for Level 2 and Level 3 estimates that are most open to manipulation.
Equity	Verify authorization of equity transactions. Review proper accounting for equity transactions. Vouch a few large transactions.	Verify authorization of all equity transactions. Perform tests of transactions on all significant transactions. Confirm all equity position with appropriate outside parties.

Appendix: Substantive Tests for Transactions and Accounts in Human Resource Management

The human resource management process is likely to be a critical process in most service firms as people are the key to delivering services. We previously presented a process map and internal threat analysis for human resource management (see Chapter 6). The human resource management process comprises the set of activities that an organization uses to recruit and coordinate its employees from the newest hire in the proverbial "mailroom" to the chief executive officer hired from outside the company. This process includes recruiting and hiring, setting work hours, training, payroll processing, and employee evaluation. It also includes the activities for terminating an employee, which may occur as a result of voluntary departures, layoffs, retirement, death, or disability. We can now discuss the nature of substantive tests that may be applied to transactions and accounts affected by the human resource process.

Human Resource Transactions

As previously discussed in Chapter 6, the key transactions related to human resource management include hiring, managing, and compensating employees. The process map and example process risks were presented there and repeated here in Figure 13.5 "Process Map: Human Resource Management" and Table 13.8. The emphasis of payroll processing is on the periodic preparation of payroll and the proper classification of the resulting expenditures. The steps for processing payroll are indicated in Table 13.9. Hourly employees traditionally use **time cards** to check in and out of work, but electronic swipe cards are increasingly used to track employee work hours. The time recorded using these cards becomes the basis for computing an employee's gross pay. Hourly employees may also complete a manual or electronic **time report** or **job ticket** that describes exactly what they did during a given pay period. This information is needed to assure that payroll expenditures can be debited to the appropriate expense or asset account. Salaried employees are usually not asked to complete time cards but are often required to complete a time report for each pay period.

Payroll computations are based on authorized wage and salary scales and appropriate deductions. Gross payroll reflects total wages earned prior to deductions; net payroll reflects the amount actually paid to an employee after considering all mandatory and voluntary deductions. Employee **paychecks** or other pay records (i.e., direct deposit documents) are prepared, approved, and distributed to the employees.[7] Payroll information is summarized in the **payroll register**, including gross pay, taxes, deductions, and net pay, which becomes the basis for making entries to the general ledger and preparing payroll tax returns that are filed with various taxing authorities (e.g., local, state/provincial, and federal/national governments).

The key event of this process is the completion of service by the employees. Each day, hour, and minute that an employee works adds to the amount of the company's liability to that employee. However, because payroll costs are usually recorded when employees are paid (i.e., on a periodic basis), a timing issue can arise when the end of a fiscal period does not coincide with the end of a pay period. This also applies to payroll taxes and other personnel expenses, such as vacation time, that accrue but that may be paid much later. As with other disbursements, the key event for satisfaction of the liability is the delivery of a check.

Tests of Financial Statement Assertions: Payroll and Accrued Liabilities

As with all processes, the auditor considers the results of strategic and process analysis, evaluates and tests controls, and monitors performance indicators in order to assess the residual risks related to human resources that may have an impact on the conduct of the audit. As seen in earlier chapters, the auditor would assess the frequency and magnitude of the risks and summarize the results using a risk map with supporting documentation (see Figures 6.3 and 6.4 in Chapter 6). In the event that

---

Process Objectives

- Identify and acquire adequate human resources.
- Attract and hire highly skilled, loyal, and motivated employees.
- Provide adequate training for employees.
- Establish policies and procedures for managing, evaluating, and compensating employees.
- Effectively manage employee turnover.
- Comply with workplace health and safety regulations.
- Compile, process, and report information necessary for process improvement.

Process Activities

- Identify human resource needs.
- Authorize hiring.
- Recruiting.
- Hiring.
- Training and motivation.
- Payroll processing.
- Employee evaluation.
- Promotion and changes to compensation.
- Employee termination.

Process Data Streams

Information Feeds	Information Generation
• Strategic plans and budgets	• Personnel files
• Recruitment needs and hiring requests	• Tax forms
• Position descriptions	• Employment contracts
• Work force regulations	• Human resource procedures
• Tax regulations	• Performance evaluations/reviews
• Union contracts	• Contract revisions
• Labor market statistics and demographics	• Training schedules
	• Payroll data and costs
	• Payroll tax remittances

Accounting Impact of Activities

Routine Transactions	Non-routine Transactions	Accounting Estimates
• Recruiting and hiring expenses	• Pensions, health care, and other post-retirement costs	• Pension accruals
• Payroll		• Postretirement benefit accruals
• Benefits	• Bonuses	• Self-insured medical or workers' compensation obligations
• Payroll taxes	• Employee terminations	
• Training costs	• Employee deaths	
• Employee retirements	• Disability claims	
	• Employment litigation	

Figure 13.5 *Process Map: Human Resource Management*

Table 13.8 *Risk Assessment: Human Resource Management*

Process Risks	Potential Audit Implications
PR1: Lack of personnel with appropriate skills.	• Expectations: High levels of process errors and related costs. • Viability: Risk of failure if critical skills missing. • Control environment: Lack of personnel may cause processes to be ineffective or segregation of duties to be bypassed.
PR2: Excess or unneeded personnel.	• Expectations: High overhead or administrative costs. • Audit risk: Proper allocation of excess labor costs, especially if related to production (standard costs).
PR3: Discriminatory employment practices.	• Audit risk: Contingent liabilities due to litigation. • Control environment: Attitudes of management and employees toward fellow employees may have implications for approach to financial reporting.
PR4: Excess costs of recruiting and hiring.	• Expectations: High overhead or administrative costs. • Audit risk: Cost allocation, especially related to production.
PR5: Errors in payroll authorizations (pay rates, taxes, time).	• Audit risk: Errors in payroll related transactions and accounts. • Control environment: Heightened control risk related to payroll transactions. • Client need: Improved procedures for payroll authorizations.
PR6: Errors in payroll processing.	• Audit risk: Errors in payroll related transactions and accounts. • Control environment: Heightened control risk related to payroll transactions. • Client need: Improved procedures for payroll processing.
PR7: Low employee morale.	• Expectations: Increased costs related to poor worker performance, e.g., direct labor or product defects. • Control environment: Disgruntled employees may be ineffective or act against interests of company.
PR8: Violations of employment laws.	• Audit risk: Contingent liabilities due to fines and penalties. • Control environment: May indicate attitudes towards regulation in general (including financial reporting). • Client need: Process improvement to assure compliance with labor laws.
PR9: Failure to provide adequate feedback or training for improvement.	• Control environment: Disgruntled employees may be ineffective or act against interests of company.
PR10: Unplanned loss of critical personnel or excessive turnover.	• Viability: Risk of failure if critical personnel depart. • Control environment: If losses are critical to financial reporting, there may be a pervasive effect on levels of control risk.

Table 13.9 *Summary of Payroll Activities*

PROCESS/Activity	Documents	Journals, Ledgers, and Records Used	Typical Journal Entry
Hiring: Recruiting new employees based on company needs and policies.	Employment application (internal)	Job descriptions and guidelines	
Personnel: Maintain accurate records on all personnel including pay rates, deduction authorization, tax information, and fitness reports.	Pay rate authorizations (internal) Tax forms (external) Deduction authorizations (external)	Employee master file	
Employee time reporting: Employees report time spent on job-related activities with frequency and level of detail dependent on nature of employment.	*Hourly workers:* Time cards (internal) Job tickets *Salaried workers:* Time report (internal)		
Payroll preparation: Payroll costs are computed and disbursements are prepared.	Check (internal) EFT authorization (internal)	Payroll register Labor distribution report	
Payroll distribution: Payroll disbursements are delivered to employees, by check, cash, or direct deposit.		*(Documents may be provided by service organization if payroll processing is outsourced)*	
General accounting: Payroll expenditures and liabilities are recorded in the appropriate accounts.	Journal entry ticket (internal) Tax forms (internal)	General ledger	Dr. Payroll Expenses Dr. Assets (inventory) Cr. Cash Cr. Accrued Liabilities

residual risks result in high risk of material misstatement for one or more financial statement assertions, the auditor would perform substantive testing relevant to the assertion.

For example, the auditor might conclude that controls over authorization of overtime were not adequate leading to excess overtime payments to employees. This might be revealed by performance measures of overtime hours worked and could lead to a drop in employee morale and increased employee turnover. Some employees could take advantage of the poor controls to inflate their paychecks by working unnecessary hours. Furthermore, the organization might conclude from all the overtime that it needs to expand the workforce, ultimately leading to increased personnel costs and underutilization of the workforce.

The auditor would analyze the implications of this residual risk and could come to a number of conclusions. First, the risk would condition the auditor's expectations about labor costs, margins, administrative expenses, benefit costs, and payroll taxes. Second, if the problem is severe and compounds through the addition of excess labor, the long-term fiscal health of the company may be threatened as its cost structure becomes non-competitive. The pressure on costs and margins could also create problems in the control environment as management takes steps to cope with the problem, possibly creating a discriminatory or threatening environment. The pressure could also result in a confrontational relationship between management and labor. Finally, the high residual risk could have an impact on specific financial statement assertions, such as benefit accruals, standard cost estimates, or termination payouts. If financial statement assertions are deemed to have high risk of material misstatement, substantive tests will be used to minimize detection risk for the affected assertion. Basic substantive tests for payroll and related liabilities are summarized in Table 13.10 and include:

- Tests of transactions.
- Substantive analytical procedures.
- Cut-off tests.
- Confirmation of obligations.

Tests of Transactions

Payroll transactions are generally routine but voluminous. Furthermore, except for certain pension, health, and post-retirement obligations, and accrued vacation time, liabilities related to payroll tend to be small and very short term. Consequently, payroll testing tends to focus on transactions rather than balances. Box 13.4 "Tests of Transactions for Payroll" describes general procedures for testing payroll transactions, which emphasize authorization and valuation of payroll expenditures. In situations where payroll is prepared by a third party service organization, these tests may be unnecessary or impossible to perform, in which case the auditor would obtain a report on internal control within the service organization prepared by that organization's auditor.

Table 13.10 *Audit Objectives and Related Evidence for Payroll-Related Transactions, Accounts, and Disclosures*

Management Assertion	Typical Audit Procedures
Accuracy/Valuation: Payroll registers and related liability records agree with balances in the general ledger.	• Verify the accuracy of a sample of payroll registers and trace payroll totals to proper inclusion in general ledger accounts. • Verify the accuracy of general ledger balances. • Reconcile subsidiary records with general ledger including records provided by third party services providers.
Existence/Occurrence: Payroll related obligations are for work rendered by actual employees.	• Perform tests of transactions on payroll disbursements including records provided by the third party service providers. • Vouch payments to taxing authorities and other entities for payroll related expenditures (e.g., health insurance premiums).
Completeness: All payroll related obligations are recorded.	• Perform tests of transactions on time cards and time reports. • Perform search for unrecorded payroll liabilities (e.g., year-end bonuses, unrecorded commissions).

(Continued)

Table 13.10 *(Continued)*

Management Assertion	Typical Audit Procedures
Accuracy/Valuation: Payroll related obligations are recorded at the proper amounts including authorized and mandated deductions.	• Perform tests of transactions on payroll disbursements. • Verify and vouch amounts included in payroll tax returns. • Perform substantive analytical procedures on payroll expenses and obligations. • Obtain actuarial report for pension, health, or post-retirement benefits. • Re-compute pension, benefit, and vacation/sick leave expenses and obligations.
Cut-off/Valuation: All payroll related obligations have been recorded including vacation accruals.	• Review end-of-year payroll and determine if appropriate accruals have been made. • Perform substantive analytical procedures on year-end balances.
Classification/Valuation: Personnel costs and obligations are recorded in the proper accounts.	• Verify classification of accrued liabilities and labor costs as part of tests of transactions. • Review year-end accrual balances for proper classification.
Completeness/Understandability: All disclosures related to personnel and payroll obligations are properly included in the financial statements.	• Complete a disclosure checklist for payroll and benefit costs and obligations. • Review Board of Directors' minutes, bank confirmations, attorney letters, and other correspondence for indications that compensation plans have changed or other payroll related information. • Obtain representations from management about disclosures related to payroll and benefits.

Note: The ownership management assertion does not apply to payroll related liabilities.

BOX 13.4 TESTS OF TRANSACTIONS FOR PAYROLL

Payroll Processing
Occurrence and Accuracy

• *Review the payroll register(s) for large and unusual transactions to be examined via vouching to source documents.*

• *Select a sample of payroll disbursement transactions from the payroll register. Obtain the supporting documentation for the disbursements. Perform the following tests and note any exceptions:*

  o *Compare time cards to compensated time per the payroll register.*

  o *Trace the pay rates and deductions to proper authorizations in personnel files.*

  o *Test accuracy of gross pay, deductions and net pay per employee.*

  o *Examine canceled checks for payee, amount, proper signature, employee endorsement, bank cancellation, and date of deposit.*

  o *Reconcile hours per the time card and hours per the job ticket/time report.*

  o *Trace cost allocation to the labor distribution report.*

Note: Salaried workers would be vouched to an approved salary contract or agreement.

Completeness and Accuracy

- Test the accuracy of the payroll register (all tests apply whether this is generated internally or by a third party service provider) on a sample basis. Trace totals to proper inclusion in the general ledger.

- Test the accuracy of the labor distribution report on a sample basis. Trace totals to proper inclusion in the general ledger.

- Reconcile totals per the labor distribution report with totals per the payroll register.

AUTHORITATIVE GUIDANCE & STANDARDS

There are specific auditing standards applicable to the audit of a data processing service organization. See PCAOB AS 2601 **Service Organizations**, also known as SAS 70. ISA 402 **Audit Considerations Relating to an Entity Using a Service Organization** recognizes the need to use such a report when third party service organizations carry out material activities on behalf of the organization. The International Standard on Assurance Engagements ISAE 3402, **Assurance Reports on Controls at a Service Organization** provides the international standard in this area which while similar to AS 2601 differs in many details. This area is normally covered in an IT Assurance course and is beyond the scope of this text. Some national standard setters have developed their own alternative that is a mixture of the two standards (e.g., Canada has CSAE 3416 **Reporting on Controls at a Service Organization**).

Substantive Analytical Procedures

Many payroll expenses are amenable to estimation using substantive analytical procedures. Given the easy accessibility of information on the number of employees, workloads, pay scales, authorized deductions, and tax rates, many expenses may be computed directly by the auditor. For example, payroll tax expense can be estimated by multiplying the statutory rate for social security and unemployment taxes times the total payroll for the period. Substantive analytical procedures could also be used to calculate year-end balances for accumulated sick leave or vacation pay that might not be paid out until future periods. Accrued payroll taxes may also be tested in this way.

Cut-Off Tests

Cut-off tests are particularly effective for accrued liabilities related to payroll because either the end of the fiscal year corresponds with the end of a pay period or the payroll period ends shortly after the end of the year. The analysis of accrued liabilities is illustrated in Figure 13.6. Given that the beginning balance is known, payments can be verified with tests of transactions, and expenses can be estimated using substantive analytical procedures, it is relatively easy to compute the year-end balance. Additionally, the year-end balance can be subject to a cut-off test based on the payroll data for the period which includes the fiscal year end. To illustrate, assume that the fiscal year end is December 31, and the payroll covers the two-week period ending January 8. By implication, eight days of the payroll period pertain to the New Year and six days to the prior year. Therefore, the balance sheet as of December 31, should include a liability for six-fourteenths of the payroll computed for January 8. If the total payroll is $100,000, the accrued liability on December 31, would be $42,857.[8]

Confirmation of Obligations

Some obligations arising from payroll are effectively tested by obtaining confirmations from outside parties. Pension liabilities and obligations related to post-retirement benefits should be confirmed with an actuary or insurance company, depending on the structure of the plan. If the company maintains a pension fund for its employees, the current balance of obligations and related disclosures should be confirmed with the administrator of the plan. Similarly, obligations for health insurance or other employee benefits can be confirmed directly with the providers of the coverage or benefit.

The selection of appropriate substantive tests depends on the linkage between residual risk from the process and inherent and control risks for specific assertions. Payroll costs and liabilities are generally considered to be routine transactions so issues related to validity, completeness, and valuation of basic payroll usually have low inherent or control risk. However, audit risk often arises related to the valuation of long-term liabilities such as pensions and the related disclosures that are required for financial reporting.

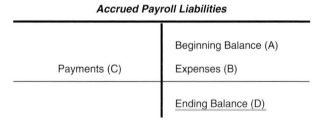

Accrued Payroll Liabilities

Payments (C)	Beginning Balance (A)
	Expenses (B)
	Ending Balance (D)

Tests of Account Details

(A) Trace to prior-year financial statements or audit results.
(B) Expenses are usually recomputed or estimated using substantive analytical procedures. Expenses may be tested through examination of transactions included in the related expense account (e.g., Payroll Tax Expense).
(C) Tests of transactions can be used to test payments throughout the period.
(D) Test accuracy of account balance. Vouch and review individually significant transactions that are included in the year-end balance. Payroll information for the last pay period in the fiscal year can be traced to proper inclusion in the liability account. Since pay periods rarely coincide with the fiscal year end, the amounts reported in the payroll register and payroll tax returns may need to be pro-rated to obtain the proper cut-off.

Figure 13.6 Substantive Testing for Accrued Payroll Liabilities

Bibliography of Relevant Literature

Accounting Standards

FASB *Statement* No. 107, "Disclosures about the Fair Value of Financial Instruments."

FASB *Statement* No. 115, "Accounting for Certain Investments in Debt and Equity Securities."

FASB *Statement* No. 157, "Fair Value Measurements."

IFRS 13, "Fair Value Measurement."

IFRS IAS 32, "Financial Instruments: Disclosure and Presentation."

IFRS IAS 39, "Financial Instruments: Recognition and Measurement."

Auditing Standards

Canadian Auditing and Assurance Standards Board. *Canadian Standard on Assurance Engagements (CSAE)* No. 3416, "Reporting on Controls at a Service Organization."

IAASB *International Standards on Auditing (ISA)* No. 300, "Planning an Audit of Financial Statements."

IAASB *International Standards on Auditing (ISA)* No. 320, "Materiality in Planning and Performing an Audit."

IAASB *International Standards on Auditing (ISA)* No. 330, "The Auditor's Responses to Assessed Risks."

IAASB *International Standards on Auditing (ISA)* No. 402, "Audit Considerations Relating to an Entity Using a Service Organization."

IAASB *International Standards on Auditing (ISA)* No. 500, "Audit Evidence."

IAASB *International Standards on Auditing (ISA)* No. 505, "External Confirmations."

IAASB *International Standards on Auditing (ISA)* No. 520, "Analytical Procedures."

IAASB *International Standards on Auditing (ISA)* No. 540, "Auditing Accounting Estimates, Including Fair Value Accounting Estimates, and Related Disclosures."

IAASB *International Standard on Assurance Engagements* (ISAE) No. 3402, "Assurance Reports on Controls at a Service Organization."

IFAC. International Auditing and Assurance Standards Board (IAASB). 2015. *Handbook of International Quality Control, Audit, Review, Other Assurance, and Related Services Pronouncements.* New York: International Federation of Accountants.

PCAOB. *Auditing Standard* 1105 (formerly No. 15), "Audit Evidence."

PCAOB. *Auditing Standard* 2101 (formerly No. 9), "Audit Planning."

PCAOB. *Auditing Standard* 2105 (formerly No. 11), "Consideration of Materiality in Planning and Performing an Audit."

PCAOB. *Auditing Standard* 2301 (formerly No. 13), "The Auditor's Responses to the Risks of Material Misstatement."

PCAOB. *Auditing Standard* 2305 (formerly *Interim Standard* AU 329), "Substantive Analytical Procedures."

PCAOB. *Auditing Standard* 2310 (formerly *Interim Standard* AU 330), "The Confirmation Process."

PCAOB. *Auditing Standard* 2501 (formerly *Interim Standard* AU 342), "Auditing Accounting Estimates."

PCAOB. *Auditing Standard* 2502 (formerly *Interim Standard* AU 328), "Auditing Fair Value Measurements and Disclosures."

PCAOB *Auditing Standard* 2601 (formerly *Interim Standard* AU 324 also known as SAS 70), "Service Organizations."

SOX Sarbanes-Oxley Act - Library of Congress. 2002. House Resolution Number 3763, An Act to protect investors by improving the accuracy and reliability of corporate disclosures made pursuant to the securities laws, and for other purposes (*The Sarbanes-Oxley Act of 2002*). www.libraryofcongress.gov.

Notes

1   Human resource management is another important resource management process. We introduced the process map for human resource management in Chapter 6. In the Appendix to this chapter, we discuss the nature of testing for transactions and accounts related to human resource management.

2   If the opening balance for plant, property, and equipment has not been audited, the auditor would probably need to obtain a trial balance of all assets included in the account(s). This schedule would need to be tested for accuracy and individual assets would be tested using vouching (valuation) and physical examination (existence).

3   Estimated depreciation expenses may need to be computed separately for each category of asset. The auditor would also have to include depreciation charged to inventory and cost of goods sold when assessing the reasonableness of the estimate.

4   FASB Statement No. 115, "Accounting for Certain Investments in Debt and Equity Securities," requires different accounting treatments for investments classified as "held to maturity," "trading securities," or "available for sale," which is similar to the treatment prescribed in IAS 39, "Financial Instruments: Recognition and Measurement."

5   For example, see FASB Statement No. 107, "Disclosures about the Fair Value of Financial Instruments" and IAS 32, "Financial Instruments: Disclosure and Presentation."

6   Violation of a covenant in a loan agreement could result in the obligation being due and payable immediately. Lenders do not often enforce such contract provisions but the potential contingent liability arising from acceleration of loans is important to the disclosure and classification audit objectives.

7   Direct deposit of payroll into employee bank accounts is becoming more common. In a direct deposit system, paper checks are not needed and payroll distribution is performed electronically. However, most countries still require that employers provide some form of written "pay advice" to their employees summarizing the gross pay and various deductions to arrive at net pay deposited to bank account.

8   The liability would need to be classified into appropriate accounts related to taxes, wages, and deductions, but the separate accounts would likely be aggregated for financial statement presentation.

CHAPTER 14

Completing the Audit I
Final Evidence Aggregation and Analysis

Outline

- Introduction
- An Overview of Final Evidence Aggregation and Finalization of the Financial Statements
- Group Audits or Audits of Consolidated Financial Statements
  - o Consolidation Issues
  - o Part of an Audit Performed by a Different Auditor
- Final Analytical Review—Business Measurement Analysis
  - o Evaluating Performance: Financial Performance Measures
  - o Evaluating Performance: Nonfinancial Performance Measures
  - o Business Measurement Analysis Based on the Balanced Scorecard
- Evaluation of Potential Going Concern Issues
  - o Assessing the Risk of Financial Failure
  - o Considering Management Responses to Going Concern Threats
- Accounting Choices and the Quality of Earnings
  - o The Impact of Accounting Choices, Policies, and Procedures
  - o Seven Ways Accounting Choices Can Lower Earnings Quality
  - o Assessing Earnings Quality
- Completion Procedures
  - o Review for Contingent Liabilities
  - o Attorney (Legal) Confirmations
  - o Review of Subsequent Events
  - o Representation Letters
- Final Evidence in Integrated Audits about Internal Control over Financial Reporting
- Final Evaluation of Audit Evidence
  - o Evaluation of Presentation and Disclosure Assertions
  - o Review of Accounting Estimates
  - o Review of Audit Documentation and Conclusions

    o Client Negotiation and Resolution of Misstatements

    o Final Technical Review

- Summary and Conclusion
- Bibliography of Relevant Literature
- **On-line Appendix:** Comprehensive Approach to Business Measurement: An Example

Learning Goals for this Chapter

1. Identify the steps that the auditor must undertake to finalize the audit in preparation for issuing the auditor's report.
2. Understand the complexities of group audits and the responsibilities of the group auditor.
3. Complete the final analytical review procedures in preparation for the audit opinion.
4. Evaluate the signs that the client is not a going concern and the effects that such a determination will have on the audit.
5. Understand the meaning of the term "earnings quality" and how the auditor's final evidence evaluation allows the auditor to prepare to discuss earnings quality with those charged with governance.
6. Learn how to identify, classify, and evaluate the accounting implications for different events that occur after year-end but before the auditor's report is issued.
7. Understand the need for adjustments to the financial statements as a result of the audit and techniques for negotiating those adjustments with the client.

Introduction

In this chapter, we begin our discussion of the final phase of the audit process. During the final stages of an engagement, the auditor evaluates the evidence he or she has collected and compares it with the set of financial statements and related disclosures prepared by management (see Figure 14.1). As part of this final process we also consider guidance on the audits of "groups" of companies, i.e., companies that have multiple legal or operating entities either domestically or around the world. These group audit requirements, while always considered good practices, have raised the bar in terms of how such large-scale audits must be planned, carried out, and most importantly, concluded. No matter what the size or complexity of the audit, this finalization process reflects the auditor's judgments and decisions about residual risks, the effectiveness of internal controls, the risk of material misstatement, and the evidence gathered to test management's assertions about transactions, accounts, and presentation and disclosure. At this stage the auditor considers the appropriateness of the client's accounting policies and choices and evaluates the overall quality of the information contained in the financial

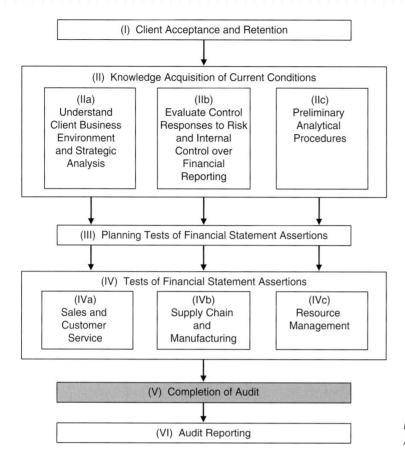

Figure 14.1 *Overview of the Audit Process*

statements. Most of the material in this chapter is equally applicable to GAAS Audits and to Integrated Audits except where noted. Finally, we look at certain audit wrap-up procedures that are designed to assure that the conclusions are appropriate and based on a full understanding of all available information.

An Overview of Final Evidence Aggregation and Finalization of the Financial Statements

After an auditor completes the strategic and business process analyses, including evaluating the financial reporting process, the next step is to aggregate all of the evidence gathered about management assertions for specific classes of transactions. The purpose of this effort is to assess whether the auditor's individual conclusions are supported by the evidence and are consistent across classes of transactions and accounts. The aggregation of evidence is particularly important when the audit is conducted by a large number of auditors or involves different audit teams in different locations.

There are a number of basic procedures that an auditor will use during the aggregation process:

- Obtain audit workpapers and audit evidence from multiple locations and multiple audit teams.
- Review the workpapers for accuracy of testing and completeness of evidence according to the audit plan.
- Reconcile the line items in the financial statements to the underlying account detail.
- Test consolidated financial statements provided by the client.
- Review the appropriateness of accounting policies used by the client.
- Perform final audit wrap-up procedures.
- Evaluate the overall reasonableness of reported earnings (often referred to as earnings quality).
- Verify the accuracy of information included in footnote disclosures and review the wording of disclosures for understandability and reasonableness.

AUTHORITATIVE GUIDANCE & STANDARDS

This chapter focuses on end of audit issues that must be settled before determining the nature of the audit opinion that is covered in Chapter 15. Key standards in this area are ISA 450 **Evaluation of Misstatements Identified during the Audit** *and PCAOB AS 2810 (formerly 14)* **Evaluating Audit Results.**

(i)EXAMPLE

The aggregation process can be particularly challenging for auditors of a multinational organization with multiple subsidiaries in a multitude of countries and statements in different currency units that need to be translated to a common currency. In such companies, the consolidated financial statements should be reconciled to the subsidiary financial statements and the auditor needs to carefully test the translation and aggregation process that management employs. Failure by management to have such a reconciliation process and related controls would be considered a material weakness in an Integrated Audit. More importantly, it highlights that errors in the consolidation process could go undetected and uncorrected, resulting in a material misstatement in the financial statements.

A particularly important element of the process is to test the grouping of individual accounts into line items to be reported in the financial statements. Most companies are structured as a set of strategic business units that are managed separately and are treated as separate units for the purpose of financial reporting. Hence, the preparation of the final financial statements that are publicly released is a two-stage process: (1) finalize the financial statements for each operating unit, and (2) compile the final financial statements for the entity as a whole (including consolidating subsidiary or division statements). The second step of this process occurs near the reporting deadline and is often done under time pressure. The process may involve significant manual entry and re-entry of data that could result in the introduction of errors. More importantly, the pressure and dynamic nature of this process may provide unprincipled management with an opportunity to manipulate the results.

The process of testing management's compilation of financial statements is relatively straightforward but a necessary step in the audit. For example, re-computing the total of all accounts that comprise a line item and then checking the accuracy of any rounding (e.g., to the nearest million dollars) assures that the client has not misclassified accounts or introduced an erroneous or fraudulent component to the line item. Although this process seems rather basic, auditors occasionally encounter clients where this last step of the accounting process is performed in a sloppy manner. For example, the final aggregation of accounts and business units may be accomplished with a spreadsheet that is susceptible to error due to the manual input of a large volume of data(i). Thus, while the transactions and accounts may be free of material error, the final tally of line items can introduce error into the financial statements.

Group Audits or Audits of Consolidated Financial Statements

Historically, auditing standard setters and regulators had looked at an audit as an audit and did not prescribe special standards for audits of large or complex entities unless the auditor relied on auditors outside his or her audit firm. However, to ensure the consolidation process was appropriately audited, guidance has been added to focus on issues associated with consolidation. In addition, in large audits sometimes auditors from different audit firms may be engaged to audit components of one overall entity. This is becoming increasingly frequent in a multi-national business world and is fueled by differences across countries in the way they structure and regulate the auditing profession.

AUTHORITATIVE GUIDANCE & STANDARDS

Auditing standards on group (consolidated financial statement) audits are found in ISA 600 **Special Considerations—Audits of Group Financial Statements (Including the Work of Component Auditors)** *and PCAOB AS 1205 (formerly AU 543)* **Part of Audit Performed by Other Independent Auditors.** *Depending on the options selected under the Integrated Audit, the amount of work carried out by a GAAS Auditor might be considerably greater than that carried out by the auditor in an Integrated Audit.*

Consolidation Issues

The auditor is responsible for obtaining an understanding of entity-wide controls over the consolidation process and is responsible for testing those controls themselves or in conjunction with the auditor of any of the individual components of the entity. If controls cannot be relied upon, then the auditor will need to consider if substantive tests of the consolidation process itself can provide appropriate evidence to support the group (consolidated) financial statements. Among the issues that the auditor needs to be alert for in this phase of the audit are:

- Differences in accounting policies across components or differences in accounting policies between one component and the rest of the group.
- Differences, if any, in the reporting period of the component versus the group. This can arise for components in countries where the statutory reporting date is different from the group (consolidated) financial statement date.
- The appropriateness, completeness, and accuracy of consolidation adjustments and reclassifications[ii].

(ii)EXAMPLE

While the WorldCom financial statement frauds led to the then largest bankruptcy in US history in 2002, the fraud was committed, in part, by one simple adjustment. During the consolidation of international and domestic operations, adjustments were entered into the system to reallocate expenses to fixed assets, resulting in grossly overstated net income.

Part of an Audit Performed by a Different Auditor

Audits that span multiple countries may need to enlist the work of multiple audit firms. Many of these audit firms are from an affiliated group, for example, the members of a Big 4 network. However, because of unique licensing laws in some countries, or local market preferences, some components of a larger audit entity may be audited by unaffiliated or local firms. This phenomenon is increasing as a result of new national or regional (e.g., European Union) regulations related to audit firm rotation. That is, in some countries, a company must periodically hire new auditors for a component operating in that country even though the auditor of the parent company may not change or is headquartered in a jurisdiction that does not require the parent company auditor to rotate. In addition, auditors may utilize other auditing firms to conduct a significant portion of the audit of component entities. As a result, reliance on component auditors is becoming increasingly common. The accounting scandals at Ahold and Pamalat were blamed, in part, on the group level auditor lacking direct access to the books and records of significant components of the entity and not providing adequate supervision of the detail work of the component auditor. As a result of these types of problems, international standards now require specific procedures for group audits. In a GAAS Audit, the group auditor is designated as the auditor that will be signing the opinion on the overall group (consolidated) financial statements.

AUTHORITATIVE GUIDANCE & STANDARDS TERMINOLOGY ALERT

Under PCAOB AS 1205 the group auditor is referred to as the principal auditor. We shall use the term IAASB term group auditor in the text except where referring specifically to the Integrated Audit. In the cases where the auditor carrying out an Integrated Audit does not apportion responsibility to another audit firm or specifically mention reliance on another audit firm in the Audit Opinion, the responsibilities of the PCAOB principal auditor and the IAASB group auditor are the same.

Some specific responsibilities that are assigned to the group auditor in a GAAS Audit include:

- The group auditor is required to be satisfied that all group and component auditors have appropriate competence and capabilities.

- The group auditor must take overall responsibility for the direction, supervision, and performance of the group audit.

- The group auditor must consider the added risk of material misstatements that is due to the component auditor not detecting an error during the conduct of the component audit that would be material to the financial statements at the group level.

- The group auditor has to communicate clearly about the scope, timing, and findings of audit work done by a component auditor.

With respect to the competence and capabilities of the component auditor, the group auditor must:

- Understand whether the component auditor understands and will comply with ethical requirements including independence.

- Have an understanding of the auditing and other standards applicable to the group audit (e.g., if local GAAP is significantly different from IFRS does the auditor understand those differences?).

- Have sufficient industry expertise and other special skills needed to effectively conduct the component audit.

- Understand and determine how to compensate for any restrictions, due to law or regulation, which would preclude the group auditor having access to any significant audit documentation or evidence related to the component audit.

Beyond these specific issues, all of the remaining material in this chapter is as applicable to group audits as it is to single location audits that are based on GAAS. The main complexities involve the time, distance, and communication that are needed to ensure that all the steps are completed in a timely manner. The responsibility to manage the overall audit process for the components is now explicitly assigned to the group auditor. If the group auditor has doubts about his or her ability to carry out these responsibilities, the auditor should not accept the engagement. If these doubts arise later in the audit process, and the auditor cannot find the means to reduce these doubts to an appropriate level, the auditor needs to consider resigning from the audit. In the end, the audit opinion for the group and all components is the responsibility of the group auditor and does not mention if any component audit work has been performed by other audit firms.

A significant difference arises for an Integrated Audit conducted under US standards when it comes to reporting on group audits. Under US standards, the principal auditor is permitted to refer to the component auditor in the auditor's report if they wish. This means the group auditor is not taking responsibility for the component auditor's work. Even if the principal auditor decides to make this reference, the principal auditor still has to evaluate the competence and capabilities of the component auditor and take appropriate measures to assure the coordination of the group and component audit activities, especially regarding matters affecting the consolidating or combining of accounts in the financial statements. However, the principal auditor who decides to refer to the component auditor in the Integrated Audit report has no further responsibilities for the overall group audit. Of course, the principal auditor has to deal with the practical need to ensure coordination of the audits but other responsibilities (e.g., taking formal responsibility for the overall supervision of the audit, etc.) is not required. If the principal auditor in an Integrated Audit decides to not refer to the component auditor in the audit report, then the responsibilities of the principal (group) auditor are the same as under a GAAS Audit.

Final Analytical Review—Business Measurement Analysis

Once the financial statements have been compiled, auditors are required to perform a final analytical review. To facilitate this review, we will elaborate on our approach for analytical procedures that was presented in Chapter 9. We refer to this review as ***business measurement analysis***, which constitutes the use of financial and nonfinancial performance measures to evaluate the status and performance of an organization. Auditors use business measurement techniques to compare the performance of a company with what the auditor expects based on previous strategic analysis, process analysis, and the detailed audit testing that has been carried out. After completing risk assessment, control testing, and substantive procedures, the auditor must address whether the financial statements capture the underlying business reality of the organization consistent with what the auditor knows about its activities and circumstances. That is, the auditor should give careful consideration to whether his or her analysis of business performance is consistent with the performance portrayed in the financial statements under generally accepted accounting principles.

AUTHORITATIVE GUIDANCE & STANDARDS

The key audit standards addressed are for final overall analytical procedures (ISA 520 **Analytical Procedures***, AS 2810) and for evaluation of audit misstatements and evidence evaluation (ISA 450, AS 2810).*

Business measurement analysis helps the auditor to integrate the evidence from all the procedures performed during the course of the audit to provide a final test of whether the financial statements are misleading. Furthermore, this review may reveal results that are still unexplained or inconsistent with the auditor's understanding of the firm's economic reality and should be subject to further review and inquiry by the auditor. We suggest a seven-step approach in Box 14.1 "Business Measurement Analysis: A 7-Step Process for Final Analytical Review," and we have provided a comprehensive example to apply this approach as an on-line supplement.

BOX 14.1   BUSINESS MEASUREMENT ANALYSIS: A 7-STEP PROCESS FOR FINAL ANALYTICAL REVIEW

PURPOSE: *To use business measurement analysis as a final review of the compiled financial statements to assure that reported results are consistent with the auditor's understanding of the organization's environments, risks, processes and activities, and economic events.*

> **STEP 1: Identify aspects of performance to be evaluated.**
>
> **STEP 2: Review the facts relevant to the analysis:** *This information comes from the auditor's review of the client's environment, strategic analysis, process analysis, and audit testing.*

STEP 3: Identify relevant business measurements: *The auditor must decide what attributes to measure. These are the financial and nonfinancial results included in the balanced scorecard.*

STEP 4: Obtain data and perform computations.

STEP 5: Impose structure: *The Balanced Scorecard is a useful technique for organizing results.*

STEP 6: Analyze: *Analyze each of the business measurements for deviations from expectations.*

STEP 7: Conclude: *Construct a cohesive explanation of the numerical data, which incorporates all of the numerical data, facts, and circumstances that are known about the company, and determine the implications for the audit, including the potential need for additional testing or inquiry.*

AUTHORITATIVE GUIDANCE & STANDARDS

IAASB ISA 720 (Revised) **The Auditor's Responsibilities Relating to Other Information in Documents containing the Audited Financial Statements** *expands the traditional auditor responsibility in reading other information in annual report like documents from ensuring there are no material inconsistencies between the information in the financial statements and in the information in the annual report or similar document (ISA 720* **The Auditor's Responsibilities Relating to Other Information in Documents containing the Audited Financial Statements** *and PCAOB 2710 [formerly AU 550]* **Other Information In Documents Containing Audited Financial Statements***). Under ISA 720 (Revised) the auditor is also responsible for reading the other information in light of the knowledge obtained during the audit, not just limited to the financial statements, but the broader knowledge gained during the audit. The procedures in this section and discussed in the on-line appendix would aid the auditor in carrying out this responsibility. For more details see Chapter 15.*

(iii)EXAMPLE

Most US based fashion retailers' value inventory using the retail form of last-in, first-out (Retail LIFO).[1] However, US fashion retailer Nordstrom utilizes the retail first-in, first-out (FIFO) method. Although in many years there might be no difference, users will be unsure whether differences in key ratios are due to different accounting methods for inventory. For example, Nordstrom reported gross margin percentages of 36.1 percent, 34.6 percent, and 33.2 percent for fiscal years 2004, 2003, and 2002 respectively. Federated Department Stores (i.e., Macy's), which uses retail LIFO, reported gross margin percentages of 40.5 percent, 40.4 percent, and 40 percent for the same three years. Accordingly, users cannot tell whether Federated was more profitable because of better operations or because the retail LIFO method resulted in more favorable results.

Evaluating Performance: Financial Performance Measures

Business measurement analysis usually starts with measures of financial performance for the period being examined. However, before examining specific financial measures of performance, it is important for the auditor to understand the significant accounting policies and practices that the client used during the period and the accounting methods generally used within the industry. The auditor should consider the degree of aggressiveness or conservatism reflected in management's choices of accounting policies and practices. In particular, the auditor should consider revenue recognition as this is an area of frequent abuse by some companies and has been a major area for accounting fraud(iii).

Once the auditor understands the key accounting policies in use, the next step is to examine an extensive set of financial measures and ratios that are typically available for a client. Most large public accounting firms have databases that allow very detailed ratio analyses within and between industries to benchmark a client's performance. Should the accounting policies of the client diverge significantly from industry norms, the auditor may need to adjust the client's financial results to be on a comparative basis with the accounting policies that are typical for the industry. The pro forma results can then be compared with industry benchmarks. Of course, the auditor must also consider why the company is at variance with industry practice and make sure that this is clear to the readers of the financial statements.

Financial analysis may reveal areas where the company's results are inconsistent or suspicious, even after all audit tests have been conducted. In such cases, the auditor needs to follow up with management about the unexpected results and possibly revisit some substantive testing to verify the accuracy of the numbers (and any explanation provided by management). These issues, arising late in the audit process, should also be discussed with the Audit Committee when the draft auditor's report is discussed. See Chapter 15 for further discussion of these communications.

Evaluating Performance: Nonfinancial Performance Measures

Auditors also obtain a great deal of nonfinancial performance data during the course of the audit. Much of this data will originate in key business processes. Nonfinancial performance measures provide additional support for the financial results and allow the auditor to develop a deeper understanding of the conditions that underlie the company's performance. That is, the auditor can gain deeper insight into the relationship between the financial and nonfinancial performance measures to better assess the reasonableness of the financial statement amounts and related disclosures. Nonfinancial performance measures are usually related to specific processes within a company. Thus, the auditor needs to capture nonfinancial performance data as part of business process analysis (Chapter 6). An auditor is usually constrained in the analysis of nonfinancial data by the accounting system of the client—the auditor cannot analyze data that is not available[iv].

The auditor must also be aware of the possibility that nonfinancial data is unreliable, especially if it comes from a source other than the client's accounting system. On the other hand, management is much less likely (or able) to manipulate nonfinancial data than financial data since much of the data is handled by individuals outside of the accounting area. Hence, the auditor needs to make a trade-off of financial and nonfinancial data based on the perceived reliability of each. This might require the auditor to commission the IT Assurance specialist on the team to carry out additional work on the integrity of the systems that produce the nonfinancial data so that the auditor can rely on it. The auditor's ultimate goal is to link the nonfinancial performance measures to the financial performance measures with the following question in mind: Are the nonfinancial performance measures consistent with the reported financial results?

[iv]EXAMPLE

Consider a client that has limited financial resources and therefore has not invested heavily in new production capability. The company is producing its products with the same technology that the company employed ten years ago. An analysis of the nonfinancial performance measures is consistent with these limited resources (e.g., measures of machine down time are increasing each year). The financial statements, however, show a lower percentage of repairs and maintenance expense to gross fixed assets than in previous years. This scenario indicates an inconsistency that needs to be resolved, possibly including the use of additional substantive audit procedures, in order to ensure that repair and maintenance expenditures were not being capitalized as fixed assets.

Business Measurement Analysis Based on the Balanced Scorecard

Business measurement analysis produces a lot of data that must be interpreted and analyzed by the auditor. Accountants are accustomed to using financial statements to organize financial data into a coherent picture. A similar technique would be useful for auditors who analyze a great deal of nonfinancial data along with the financial data. We use a variation of the balanced scorecard as presented in Figure 14.2.

The following four perspectives comprise the balanced scorecard we use for business measurement analysis:

1. Financial: This perspective reflects the investors' viewpoint and measures the overall financial performance of the organization.

2. Market: This perspective reflects customers' viewpoints and measures the success of the organization in obtaining and satisfying its customer base.

3. Core processes: This perspective reflects an internal viewpoint, focusing on the performance of the core processes that create value (e.g., products and services).

4. Resource management processes: This perspective reflects a combined external/internal viewpoint, focusing on the performance of resource management processes and interactions with external resource providers (e.g., labor, vendors).[2]

The auditor's use of a scorecard to organize his or her audit evidence does not require that the client management have a balanced scorecard system in place, just that the client has enough performance-related data to facilitate a comprehensive and meaningful analysis.

A balanced scorecard approach highlights to the auditor that performance in one area of the client can affect or relate to outcomes in other areas. For example, employee problems may be revealed by performance indicators related to human resource management (e.g., a drop in training statistics or deteriorating employee morale). These indicators could be leading warnings of problems in core processes (e.g., decreased quality as employees are less

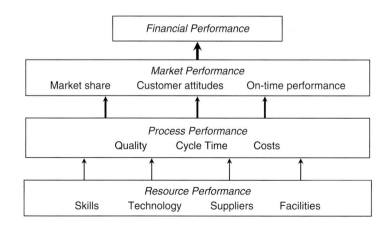

Figure 14.2 The Balanced Scorecard Model

(v)EXAMPLE

Appropriate performance measures for human resource management include employee productivity, morale, turnover, and competencies. These attributes could be important if employee turnover occurs in sensitive areas of the company such as accounting or R&D. These attributes would also be particularly important for assessing the risks and potential for success of a professional services firm. The historical level of employee turnover in major accounting firms and the increasing cost of developing experienced personnel have created challenges for firms as they manage their most critical knowledge assets—people.

careful in their jobs) or market performance (e.g., customer satisfaction can be dragged down by interactions with unhappy or surly employees). Eventually, problems in resource or core processes are likely to show up as negative financial results, such as decreased revenue, slower growth, higher sales returns and allowances, and increased warranty claims. Within each of the four dimensions, the auditor will identify a mix of financial and nonfinancial performance measures to measure and monitor over time, normally based on the set of measures that the client has available or has agreed to collect for the auditor.

Process and Resource Performance: Table 14.1 identifies a number of possible performance indicators that might be appropriate for core and resource processes. Performance measurement for core processes tends to focus on the quality, timeliness, and cost of process activities. In general, deterioration in any one attribute of a process could lead to poor market performance and weak financial results. Common cost measurement problems include determining the factors that actually drive costs higher or lower and allocating those costs to specific activities and products. Quality can be measured in a number of ways, including defect rates, product yields, waste rates, product returns, and warranty costs. Cycle time is important for assessing process performance. Although traditional financial reporting systems typically do not track time, most enterprise risk management systems track cycle times(v).

Table 14.1 *Measuring Process and Resource Performance*

Core Processes	Resource Management Processes
Process Time: • Time to market • Operating cycle • Turnover	Human Resources: • Employee productivity • Employee attitudes • Employee turnover • Employee competencies
Process Cost: • Cost drivers • Cost allocations • Cost per activity	Information Technology: • Reliability of information • Timeliness of information • System development
Process Quality: • Defect rates • Product yields • Scrap/waste rates • Product returns • Warranty costs	Property: • Facility acquisition • Facility utilization • Facility maintenance • Facility reliability
	Supply Chain: • Delivery performance • Service performance • Quality • Costs
	Financial: • Cost of capital • Cash reserves • Cash float • Taxes • Cost of transaction processing

Market Performance: Figure 14.3 summarizes the relationship between key measures of market success. Market performance and customer attitudes are reflected in total market share. Better products and services (which depend on the core and resource processes) usually lead to a larger market share. Market share is the net result of the rate at which customers are acquired and retained (or lost). Generally, the acquisition and retention of customers is driven by customer satisfaction, which can be a critical leading indicator of future problems. Highly sophisticated companies can track the profitability of individual customers in order to guide future sales and marketing efforts. Other market performance measures that might be of interest to a client include brand awareness, the rate of success at introducing new products, and revenue growth (total and by product line[(vi)]).

Financial Performance: Figure 14.4 provides an overview of the financial perspective, listing the relationships among standard financial ratios that have been previously discussed in Chapter 9. Return on equity can be decomposed into two components: (1) return on assets, which measures the profit generated given the asset base of the company, and (2) financial leverage (debt/assets), which measures the extent of debt financing used by the company. Return on assets can be further decomposed into various asset turnover ratios (e.g., receivables, inventory, PPE) and profit measures (e.g., net income/sales).

The relationship between ROA and ROE is particularly important for many clients. This relationship is directly affected by the amount of debt that

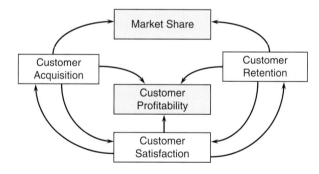

Figure 14.3 Measuring Market Performance

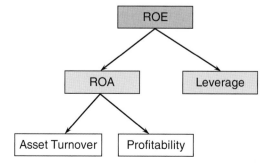

Figure 14.4 Measuring Financial Performance

a company has issued. When a highly leveraged company has a good year, shareholders benefit. When it has a bad year, however, the leveraged company has trouble and the shareholders suffer. This pattern of results occurs because the debt holders must be paid regardless of whether the client has a good or bad year. If ROA is greater than the fixed rate paid to debt holders, ROE will exceed ROA. On the other hand, if ROA is less than the fixed rate, ROE will be less than ROA.

Evaluation of Potential Going Concern Issues

Business measurement analysis leads us naturally into one of the most difficult judgments that an auditor must deal with in the course of the audit, which is to identify the conditions or events that suggest an organization is in danger of going bankrupt or experiencing severe financial distress. Such conditions or events call into question one of the underlying basic assumptions of accounting, that the entity will continue as a going concern (i.e., continue to exist) for *at least* twelve months (or twelve months in the case of PCAOB standards for US audits) after the date of the financial statements being audited.[3] After management and the auditor investigate the conditions that might lead to uncertainty about the organization's ability to continue, they then must decide if the disclosures in the financial statements adequately reflect the nature of any existing material uncertainty that may exist.

Business measurement analysis provides an excellent foundation on which to base an assessment of the likelihood of a company failing in the short term. The auditor uses a four-step process for assessing whether there is substantial doubt about whether an organization will be able to continue as a going concern:

1. Obtain management's assessment of the ability of the entity to continue as a going concern likelihood and supporting analyses (if any). Such an assessment is required under IFRS. For other systems of accountings standards, there is a presumption that management has done such an analysis. However, the auditor must also consider the competence and depth of management's analysis (i.e., is management too quick to assume the going concern assumption is satisfied in their organization).

2. Consider management's assessment in light of any audit evidence that indicates that the entity's ability to continue as a going concern is questionable, i.e., that is there is a materiality uncertainty about the entity's continued existence.

3. If the ability of the entity to continue as a going concern is uncertain, obtain and evaluate management's plan to mitigate the identified conditions causing the concern.

4. Determine if management's plan is adequate and appropriate for the circumstances and assess the likelihood that the company will suffer financial distress even if management's plan is successful.

AUTHORITATIVE GUIDANCE & STANDARDS

Auditing standards (e.g., ISA 570 **Going Concern** *[including ISA 570 {Revised}] and PCAOB AS 2415 [formerly AU 341]* **The Auditor's Consideration of an Entity's Ability to Continue as a Going Concern)** *require auditors to perform the procedures to assess an entity's ability to continue as a going concern, which is an underlying assumption of GAAP. ISA 570 requires the auditor to be proactive throughout the audit in considering whether the entity is a going concern. AS 2415 requires that an auditor should consider at the end of the audit whether there is any indication from the procedures performed that an entity is not able to continue as a going concern for the next twelve months.*

Assessing the Risk of Financial Failure

During the course of the audit—strategic analysis, process analysis, business measurement analysis—the auditor needs to be alert for warning signals of potential financial problems for the client. Some of the more common signals of financial distress include negative information about (1) company finances, (2) company operations, and (3) other issues. Examples of these warning signs include:

1. **Financial:**

   - Fixed-term borrowings approaching maturity without realistic prospects of renewal or repayment; or excessive reliance on short-term borrowings to finance long-term assets.
   - Indications of withdrawal of financial support by creditors.
   - Negative operating cash flows indicated by historical or prospective financial statements.
   - Substantial operating losses or significant deterioration in the value of assets used to generate cash flows.
   - Arrears or discontinuance of dividends.
   - Inability to pay creditors on due dates.
   - Inability to comply with the terms of loan agreements.
   - Change from credit to cash-on-delivery transactions with suppliers.
   - Inability to obtain financing for essential new product development or other essential investments.

2. **Operations:**

   - Management intentions to liquidate the entity or to cease operations.
   - Loss of key management without replacement.
   - Loss of a major market, key customer(s), franchise, license, or principal supplier(s).
   - Labor difficulties.
   - Shortages of important supplies.
   - Emergence of a highly successful competitor.

3. **Other:**

- Non-compliance with capital or other statutory requirements.
- Pending legal or regulatory proceedings against the entity that may, if successful, result in claims that the entity is unlikely to be able to satisfy.
- Changes in law or regulation or government policy expected to adversely affect the entity.
- Uninsured or underinsured catastrophes when they occur.

In addition to the above warning signs, an auditor can also use the results of business measurement analysis to obtain a broader understanding of the financial status of an organization. An organization that is not profitable and has serious cash flow problems is a likely candidate for financial distress. Consequently, auditors often look at profitability, leverage, and solvency ratios in order to identify conditions that may indicate current or future financial distress. Many of the ratios that are useful for this purpose were discussed in Chapter 9:[4]

- Current or quick ratio.
- Debt ratio.
- Interest coverage ratio.
- Total asset turnover.
- Return on assets.
- Profit margin.

However, the fact that some ratios may have values that are worrisome does not automatically imply financial distress. All ratios and facts must be considered together by the auditor. Such a judgment is highly subjective, requires extensive experience, and should be made with utmost care.

Considering Management Responses to Going Concern Threats

Under IFRS accounting standards, management needs to assess the ability of their firm to continue as a going concern. However, in many cases management will not carry out a formal assessment unless there is a reason to consider that the entity may suffer serious financial problems. The auditor should routinely inquire about the existence of such an assessment. If the auditor has doubts about the company continuing as a going concern, and if management has not performed such an assessment, the auditor should request that management carry out such an assessment. If the auditor and management disagree about whether the facts support a determination that there is a material uncertainty about the ability of the entity to continue as going concern, the auditor may need to modify their audit opinion (see Chapter 15). Even if the auditor and management agree there is a material uncertainty about the ability of the entity to continue as a going concern, the auditor has to consider if management has adequately disclosed the uncertainty in the notes to the financial statements. Further, the auditor has to determine if the material uncertainty is significant enough to warrant the auditor adding an emphasis of matter to the audit report so as to refer the reader explicitly to the disclosure by management. As will be discussed in Chapter 15, this type of emphasis is not considered a qualified opinion and does not change the interpretation of an unqualified audit opinion in reference to the financial statements. However, the emphasis of a matter does draw the attention of the reader to specific information that the auditor believes is fundamental to understanding the financial statements.

If management or the auditor believes there is a material uncertainty about the entity's ability to continue as a going concern, the auditor needs to determine management's intentions for dealing with the underlying problems. Management may have plans that are designed to mitigate a perceived going concern issue that might include:

- Plans for disposal of extraneous assets.
- Restructuring of financing.
- Acquisition of new financing.
- Reduction or deferral of expenditures.

The auditor should evaluate management's plans to determine the likelihood that those plans will rectify the organization's problems. Not all management plans will be successful. Furthermore, asset disposals may be a good source of cash but cannot be repeated and may have a negative impact on operations by reducing capacity that could be needed in the future. Cost and expenditure deferrals must also be considered with care. The reduction of costs without serious evaluation of the underlying activities of the organization may create problems in the future as the organization tries to cope with new challenges with fewer resources. Finally, acquisition of new financing, or restructuring of existing financing arrangements, may be possible, but the auditor must evaluate whether the company will be able to meet its new obligations.

Overall the auditor has to seriously scrutinize management's plans to deal with potential going concern issues. The auditor's evaluation could include:

- Analyzing and discussing cash flow, profit, and other relevant forecasts with management.
- Analyzing and discussing the entity's latest available interim financial statements.
- Reading the terms of debentures and loan agreements and determining whether any have been breached.
- Reading minutes of the meetings of shareholders, those charged with governance and relevant committees for reference to financing difficulties.
- Inquiring of the entity's legal counsel regarding the existence of litigation and claims and the reasonableness of management's assessments of their outcome and estimation of their financial implications.
- Confirming the existence, legality, and enforceability of arrangements to provide or maintain financial support with other parties, and assessing the financial ability of such parties to provide additional funds.
- Evaluating the entity's plans to deal with unfilled customer orders.
- Performing audit procedures regarding subsequent events to identify those that either mitigate or otherwise affect the entity's ability to continue as a going concern.

- Confirming the existence, terms and adequacy of borrowing facilities or lines of credit.
- Obtaining and reviewing reports of regulatory actions.
- Determining the adequacy of support for any planned disposals of assets.

Ultimately, if the entity's survival continues to be in serious doubt after considering management plans, the auditor will conclude that going concern basis of accounting is not appropriate for this entity. At that point, the most likely outcome is that the auditor modifies his or her audit opinion as is discussed in Chapter 15. A less likely alternative would have management prepare financial statements that are under a basis of accounting that takes into consideration the problem of continued existence (this is known as liquidation accounting) and the auditor could audit and opine on those statements.

If management's plans and the auditor's own analysis suggest that the going concern basis for accounting is appropriate, the auditor then needs to assess if the conclusion is a "close call." In other words, the audit evidence supports the going concern basis of accounting but it took extensive analysis by management and the auditor about the conditions related to the uncertainty to convince the auditor the organization could continue. Under ISA 570 (Revised), the auditor is now required to consider whether management has provided sufficient disclosure in the financial statement notes about the underlying events and conditions so that a reader can reach their own conclusion about the likelihood of financial distress in the future.[5] This is a new requirement and requires significant judgment by the auditor to determine if additional disclosures by management are warranted. Should such disclosures be required by the auditor and management declines to make them, then the auditor needs to consider whether a modified (i.e., qualified) opinion is necessary as will be discussed in Chapter 15.

Overall, the auditor is confronted with a dilemma anytime that conditions or events arise that suggest a material uncertainty may exist about an entity's ability to continue as a going concern. If the opinion is not modified and the organization subsequently fails, the auditor will be subject to criticism, regulatory investigation, and possible litigation. If the auditor does modify the opinion, investors and creditors may be so sensitized to the possible risk that they become leery of dealing with the organization, triggering the failure that was feared. Maintaining a balance between conservatism and fairness to the client is a difficult challenge to the auditor. Unfortunately, there have been a number of infamous cases in the past where an auditor gave a clean opinion to a company only to have the company declare bankruptcy shortly after the release of the financial statements[(vii)].

Accounting Choices and the Quality of Earnings

The financial statements are a set of complex documents intended to communicate the financial performance and status of the organization to

(vii)EXAMPLE

In early 2009, in the aftermath of the financial crisis of 2007–8, the fragile state of the international economy led the Australian Institute of Company Directors and the Australian Audit and Assurance Standards Board to issue guidance for directors and auditors in assessing going concern conditions or events for Australian companies. Based on this added guidance, the rate of going concern modified opinions spiked from 15 percent of public companies in June 2008 to 25 percent of public companies at December 31, 2009. The rate fell back to 18 percent by June 2009. This increase in going concern modified opinions occurred despite the fact that the Australian economy was one of the few in the industrial world that was not materially affected by the fiscal crisis.

interested readers. However, even after all the numbers and disclosures have been audited, a final question may arise as to the general quality of the information included in a financial report. ***Earnings quality*** is much debated in accounting, as is its inverse, ***earnings management***. Box 14.2 "Alternative Definitions for Earnings Management" presents three separate definitions of earnings management. A simple definition of earnings is "the amount that can be consumed during the period, while leaving the firm equally as well off at the beginning and end of the period."[6] All three earnings management definitions are consistent with this definition of earnings, as all three imply some deviation in reported earnings from the amount that can be consumed leaving the entity as well off at the end of the period as at the beginning.

BOX 14.2   ALTERNATIVE DEFINITIONS FOR EARNINGS MANAGEMENT

1. *Managing earnings is "the process of taking deliberate steps within the constraints of generally accepted accounting principles to bring about a desired level of reported earnings." (Davidson, Stickney and Weil [1987], cited in Schipper [1989] p. 92).*

2. *Managing earnings is "a purposeful intervention in the external financial reporting process, with the intent of obtaining some private gain (as opposed to say, merely facilitating the neutral operation of the process)." ... "A minor extension of this definition would encompass "real" earnings management, accomplished by timing investment or financing decisions to alter reported earnings or some subset of it." Schipper (1989) p. 92.*

3. *"Earnings management occurs when managers use judgment in financial reporting and in structuring transactions to alter financial reports to either mislead some stakeholders about the underlying economic performance of the company or to influence contractual outcomes that depend on reported accounting numbers." Healy and Wahlen (1999, p. 368).*

AUTHORITATIVE GUIDANCE & STANDARDS

Auditing standards (ISA 260, **Communication with Those Charged with Governance** *and PCAOB AS 1301 [formerly 16]* **Communications with Audit Committees***) require the auditor to discuss a number of issues with the Audit Committee (known more generally as "those charged with governance"), including a discussion of the qualitative aspects of the client's financial accounting policy selection and the overall nature of the "quality" of the financial reporting.*

At least three major groups care about earnings quality. First, the company's shareholders make judgments about management and whether to continue to invest in the company. Second, potential shareholders may purchase stock in the company based on their expectations of future earnings, which they forecast based on current earnings. Third, other stakeholders may enter into contracts with the entity. These stakeholders include managers (who are frequently compensated based on reported

Leases are complex transactions that can be structured in different ways in order to arrive at a desired accounting result. Many leases are long term in nature and are, in substance, purchase transactions. However, leases can often be structured such that the underlying asset and debt are not recorded on the balance sheet of the lessee, relieving the company of the need to compute depreciation on the asset while hiding the debt off the balance sheet. Accounting rules and regulations attempt to separate such capital leases from short-term operating leases, but companies can be very creative in getting around the rules. Consequently, management can usually obtain an arrangement with a seller/lessor such that a transaction is structured in the most advantageous manner.

In a large-scale survey of audit partners and senior managers at one of the Big 4 firms, a team of accounting professors found that audit partners and managers could readily identify transactions that they knew that client management had structured so as to get the accounting treatment that they wanted. Furthermore, the authors reported that the greatest challenge the auditors faced was reining in management earnings being carried out via structured transactions that met the letter, if not the spirit, of written accounting rules.[7]

earnings) and creditors (who evaluate their credit risk based on earnings). Finally, in the big picture there are losses to society based on the inefficient allocation of scarce capital to firms whose poor performance is masked via earnings management. This behavior results in losses to investors and lending institutions, which can have a dampening effect on the entire economy.

The Impact of Accounting Choices, Policies, and Procedures

Although accounting is viewed as a technical topic in which precise measurement is an important part of effective accounting (and auditing), there also is a significant judgmental aspect of accounting involving the way that management interprets the economics underlying a transaction and the wording of accounting standards. For this aspect, accounting becomes a judgment exercise full of choices that affect the numbers reported in financial statements. Generally accepted accounting principles (GAAP) often provide options for reporting a specific type of transaction; for example, inventory can be accounted for using weighted average (which generally reduces earnings), FIFO (which usually yields higher earnings), or some other accounting method (like LIFO in the US, which generally reduces earnings below weighed average). Furthermore, management can often structure transactions to achieve a desired accounting result and to portray transactions in the best possible light[(viii)].

Financial statements are the responsibility of management, and management makes the decisions about how to structure transactions and account for them. Given the flexibility of many accounting standards and the control of the underlying transactions, management may be able to manipulate financial results using accounting legerdemain. Auditors have the responsibility to provide an objective evaluation of the reasonableness of accounting choices made by management. If a client's accounting choices are excessively aggressive in maximizing reported earnings, the auditor must consider whether management is behaving appropriately, and whether some of the accounting choices cross the line from acceptable to inappropriate. Furthermore, just because a selected accounting treatment is acceptable within the standards does not mean that it is fair or desirable. Many abuses of financial reporting in the past few years were technically "correct" but ethically indefensible as they did not portray the underlying economics of a transaction or events appropriately. Consequently, the auditor must maintain his or her skepticism when considering the appropriateness of management's accounting choices.

Auditors should pay careful attention to the current environment and conditions in which an organization operates when evaluating the accounting policies and procedures chosen by management. For example, when investors and market analysts place pressure on management to improve earnings, there is a heightened probability that the organization will structure transactions to achieve a desired accounting result. This issue becomes even more important when management decides to change accounting methods for previously existing transactions. In that case, the auditor should be clear as to the reason for the change[(ix)].

Seven Ways Accounting Choices Can Lower Earnings Quality

Box 14.3 "Financial 'Shenanigans' that Produce Lower Quality Earnings" illustrates seven ways that the accrual accounting system can be used to manage earnings. Indeed, some market observers go as far as to call these techniques "financial shenanigans." Although all these techniques reduce the information quality of reported results, many of them do not cross the line into fraudulent behavior unless they are a blatant and deceptive misrepresentation of economic facts. For example, recording nonexistent revenue is fraudulent, but shifting real revenue between periods may not be because it may be a legitimate use of management discretion under GAAP. Even if the auditor wishes to challenge these behaviors, management can often hide behind the technical rules of GAAP. By first considering whether management's proposed accounting treatment of a transaction reflects its economic reality, the auditor shifts the focus of the discussion from technical accounting requirements to whether compliance with formal requirements is appropriate. Sometimes the only way that management's decisions can be judged is by considering if they are consistent across time.

BOX 14.3   FINANCIAL "SHENANIGANS" THAT PRODUCE LOWER QUALITY EARNINGS*

1. *Record revenue too soon or of questionable quality:*
   a. *Recording revenue when material future services remain to be provided*
   b. *Recording revenue when the customer is not obligated to pay for goods or services received*

2. *Recording fictitious revenue:*
   a. *Recording cash received in lending transactions as revenue*
   b. *Recording as revenue supplier rebates tied to future required purchases*

3. *Boosting income with onetime gains:*
   a. *Selling assets valued at historical cost to produce accounting gains*
   b. *Using investment income to increase operating revenue or decrease operating expenses*

4. *Shifting current expenses to a later or earlier period:*
   a. *Capitalizing normal operating costs*
   b. *Amortizing costs too slowly*
   c. *Failing to write down or write off impaired assets*

5. *Failing to record or improperly reducing liabilities:*
   a. *Reducing liabilities by changing accounting assumptions*
   b. *Failing to record expenses and related liabilities when future obligations remain*

6. *Shifting current revenue to a later period:*
   a. *Creating reserves around times of infrequent activity (e.g., mergers) and releasing them into income in a later period*

7. Shifting future expenses to the current period as a special charge:

   a. Improperly inflating a write-down or write-off so future expenses will be understated

   b. Accelerating discretionary expenses that will benefit future period's performance to current period

Drawn from Howard Schilit (2002) Financial Shenanigans. Second edition. *McGraw-Hill: New York, pp. 24–25.*

Section 204 of the Sarbanes-Oxley Act of 2002 addresses this issue by focusing on the practice of structuring transactions simply to enable preferred GAAP accounting. In the wake of Enron and other frauds, the Sarbanes-Oxley Act now requires auditors of US registrants to discuss disagreements about accounting for transactions with the Audit Committee. Should auditors believe that the form of the transaction does not correspond appropriately with its substance, they should document their concerns and present them to the Audit Committee. Because the Audit Committee is accountable for financial reporting for the company (i.e., it can be held personally liable), auditors now have more leverage in convincing clients to account for transactions in ways that are less aggressive and more transparent than the extreme limits of GAAP might allow.

AUTHORITATIVE GUIDANCE & STANDARDS

The US SEC's Staff Accounting Bulletin 99 **Materiality** *requires US-registered public companies to correct all material misstatements as well as immaterial but intentional misstatements. SAB 99 lays out a number of qualitative issues for an auditor to consider in evaluating whether a misstatement is material. The SEC issued SAB 99 as a response to perceived earnings management in which organizations claimed that improper accounting policies and practices were justified because the amounts were not material to the financial statements taken as a whole. AS 2810 makes it clear that the auditor must note all misstatements except those that are truly trivial and report the same to management.*

Assessing Earnings Quality

Earnings quality is most often associated with conservative accounting policies, that is, recognizing expenses and losses as soon as they are identified and delaying revenue recognition and gains until realization is certain. However, the nature of double entry accounting means that what is conservative in one period may reverse and become aggressive in a subsequent period; for example, increasing depreciation expense in the early years of an asset's life using an accelerated method results in larger earnings being reported in later years. To help evaluate the appropriateness of a company's accounting choices, the auditor should evaluate the client's **quality of earnings** based on the following circumstances:

- Correlation with underlying economic activity: Financial results should relate to the underlying condition of the industry. Record profits in a time of recession are suspicious and may indicate potential earnings manipulation.

- Permanence and sustainability: Companies may recognize one-time transactions to achieve certain financial goals or to maintain trends in a consistent direction, such as recording a gain on the sale of plant assets. Earnings quality is decreased in such cases because results do not reflect underlying operating patterns and the transactions may not be repeatable in the future.

- Relationship with market valuation: Inconsistency between the valuation of a company's stock and its underlying performance could indicate low-quality earnings. The auditor should question whether the market is reacting to information outside the context of the financial statements that might be relevant to financial reporting.

- Extent and impact of discretionary accruals: As noted above, management's decisions regarding accounting methods, estimates, and accruals will have an impact on the quality of the company's earnings. To the extent that aggressive choices are used to artificially inflate financial results, earnings quality will be reduced.

- Transparency and completeness of disclosures: The openness and understandability of financial disclosures provides an indication of management's willingness to communicate effectively with shareholders and analysts.

- Impact on corporate image: Management often considers how financial information reflects on the company in a broader sense. A company earning monopoly profits may wish to use very conservative accounting techniques to reduce reported income and minimize the notice that apparently unconscionable earnings would draw from the media, tax authorities, and regulatory agencies.

- Handling of "bad" news: The way that management communicates bad news about the organization can be revealing of its attitudes towards financial reporting. Attempts to sugar-coat the news or to compound losses with unnecessary write-offs, both indicate potentially poorer earnings quality.

The auditor will need to take these considerations into account when the financial statements are compiled and subject to final review. Although these indicators of earnings quality are useful for auditors, economic circumstances in an industry do not always foster smooth accounting results. In those cases, the auditor must also be aware of the possibility that management may use accounting tricks to mask volatile conditions to present an illusion of high quality earnings[x].

Completion Procedures

After all necessary risk assessments and tests of management assertions have been completed, the auditor performs a final set of procedures designed

[x]EXAMPLE

In prior editions of this book we commented on GE's well-deserved reputation for earnings management. This came to a crashing halt in 2009 when the US SEC investigation of GE's earnings management activities resulted in GE, while accepting no guilt, paying a $50 million (US) fine to the US SEC. GE restated earnings from 2001 to 2005 in 2007.[8]

to eliminate open items and assure that all available information has been appropriately considered. The auditor also wants to make sure that all professional standards have been followed and that the financial statements are complete. A number of procedures facilitate the completion process. The key procedures are:

- Review contingent losses.
- Obtain an attorney (legal) confirmation letter.
- Review subsequent events.
- Obtain a representation letter from management.
- Complete final evaluation of evidence and finalize financial statements.

Review for Contingent Liabilities

Near the end of the engagement, the auditor should identify and evaluate potential contingent liabilities that may have an impact on the financial statements. Virtually all organizations are exposed to potential losses that are contingent on future events. An extreme example is an insurance company that is in the business of assessing and measuring future losses arising from insured risks. More typical are contingent losses arising from uncollectible customer accounts. Contingent liabilities that impact most organizations include:

- Losses associated with litigation.
- Losses associated with disputes with regulatory bodies.
- Income tax liabilities in dispute.
- Warranty expenses.
- Guarantees of third-party debt.
- Losses on purchase commitments.
- Compensated absences (e.g., vacation or sick leave).
- Losses on receivables sold with recourse.

Management has the ultimate responsibility to prepare and present any estimates required for full and fair disclosure of contingent liabilities. Consistent with its responsibilities, management is expected to identify needed estimates and develop an estimation technique that considers appropriate assumptions, data, computational models, and GAAP requirements. The auditor has the responsibility to identify potential contingent liabilities, assess the likelihood and manner in which they will be resolved, evaluate the proper accounting treatment, and test the reasonableness of resulting estimates.

AUTHORITATIVE GUIDANCE & STANDARDS

Accounting standards for contingent liabilities are found in IFRS IAS 37 **Provisions, Contingent Liabilities, and Contingent Assets** *and FASB Statement No. 5* **Accounting for Contingencies.** *Various observers have noted that the thresholds for accrual and disclosure seem to vary substantially between companies under IAS 37 and companies under*

SFAS 5. In particular, the requirement to accrue the loss and loss the potential for loss due to lawsuits is interpreted as being near certain under SFAS 5 whereas it is considered to be "more likely than not" under IAS 37. This likely results in a substantial reporting and disclosure difference between financial statements prepared under US GAAP and those prepared under International GAAP. The accounting described below is consistent with IAS 37.

The accounting standards for contingent losses identify three possible treatments for contingencies depending on the likelihood of occurrence and the measurability of the impact on the financial statements:

- Accrue the loss: A contingent loss must be accrued if the loss is **probable** and **reasonably estimable**. A loss is considered probable if it is likely to occur. The loss is reasonably estimable if a specific value or range of values can be determined. If the loss is likely to fall within a range of values, the lower end of the range is used.

- Disclose the loss: If a contingency is probable but cannot reasonably be estimated, the nature of the contingency should be disclosed in the financial statements. Disclosure is also appropriate if the contingency is considered to be **reasonably possible**, which is defined as less than probable.

- No accounting recognition: Contingencies considered to be remote need not be mentioned at all.

The auditor's primary objective in the area of contingent losses is to verify that the client has properly disclosed and accounted for all contingent losses. As a result, the completeness and valuation assertions are considered most important. The auditor performs the following procedures to search for and assess contingent losses:

- Inquire of management about the existence of contingent losses.

- Review prior-year working papers for previously existing contingencies and follow up on their resolution in the current year.

- Review regulatory and tax filings for potential claims.

- Review the minutes of meetings of the Board of Directors for indications of potential contingent losses (e.g., purchase commitments).

- Analyze legal expenditures and review legal invoices for ongoing or unasserted legal claims.

- Obtain attorney confirmations from all attorneys providing services to the organization.

- Review estimates related to identified contingencies in accordance with the appropriate auditing standards.

- Review other company disclosures, including corporate sustainability reports or other press releases.

The risk of a contingent loss estimate being misstated is directly affected by the complexity of the estimate being made, the availability and reliability of data used to make the estimate, the nature of assumptions used, and the degree of uncertainty surrounding future events. For example, environmental liabilities arising from the clean-up of toxic land sites may be extremely difficult to estimate due to the long lead time of the clean-up process, the uncertainty surrounding who pays, and the changing nature of clean-up technology.

Attorney (Legal) Confirmations

Some of the best, but most problematic, sources of evidence related to contingent losses are **attorney confirmations**, also referred to as **legal letters**. An attorney confirmation can be an excellent source of evidence because it comes from a party who is intimately involved with existing and **unasserted claims** against the company.[9] On the other hand, the evidence is often difficult to interpret because attorneys are hesitant to reveal facts or conditions they feel are covered by confidentiality rules. Attorneys generally resist making precise estimates about the amount or likelihood of potential losses that may result from litigation. Yet auditing standards require that the auditor seek direct communication with the entity's external legal counsel.

In order to overcome some of these problems, attorney associations and national auditing standard setters have agreed to policies concerning an attorney's responses to a request for information from an auditor. An example of an attorney confirmation is presented in Figure 14.5. The auditor is primarily interested in the existence of conditions giving rise to a contingent loss, the period in which the event(s) occurred, the probability of ultimate loss, and the amount (or range) of potential losses that may be incurred. To obtain this information, management prepares a list of potential claims which is then forwarded to the company's law firms for confirmation and evaluation with a copy to the auditor. The formal request asks the attorney to provide the following:

- Information about pending claims identified by management and confirmation of relevant facts including:
  - o Nature of the claim against the company.
  - o Status of the case.
  - o Planned client actions.
  - o Assessment of the likelihood and amount of unfavorable outcomes.
- Information about unasserted claims identified by management including confirmation of relevant facts.
- Information about *omitted* claims that are pending or unasserted of which the attorney is aware but that have not been specifically identified by management in the confirmation request. If the attorney knows of no omitted claims, he is asked for a specific statement to that effect.

AUTHORITATIVE GUIDANCE & STANDARDS

Attorney confirmation, as noted in the text, is a major piece of audit evidence about the existence of many contingent liabilities related to outstanding legal actions. Auditing standards for such letters are contained in ISA 501 **Audit Evidence—Specific Considerations for Selected Items** *and PCAOB AS 2505 (formerly AU 337)* **Inquiry of a Client's Lawyer**

Johnson Pharmaceuticals, Inc.

Mr. Jonathan Orwell   (Date)
Orwell, Orwell & Hatchburg, Attorneys at Law
45 N. Main Street

Dear Mr. Orwell:

In connection with the audit of our annual financial statements as of December 31, 20x7, management has prepared a description and evaluation of certain contingencies. This list has been furnished to our auditors, Smith & Company. Included on the list are the following matters with which you have been engaged and to which you have devoted substantive attention on behalf of Johnson Pharmaceuticals in the form of legal consultation or representation. These contingencies are considered to be material to the fair presentation of our financial statements. Your response should include matters that existed at December 31, 20x7 and during the period from that date to the date of the completion of your response.

Pending or Threatened Litigation: The following litigation has been identified as pending or threatened:

> [A list of pending or threatened matters would be provided including the nature of litigation, the current status and progress of the case, management's actual or intended response (e.g., vigorous defense or out-of-court settlement) and an estimate of the likelihood and amount (if possible) of an unfavorable outcome.]

Please furnish our auditors such explanation, if any, that you consider necessary to supplement the foregoing information, including an explanation of those matters as to which your views may differ from those stated and an identification of the omission of any pending or threatened litigation, claims and assessments or a statement that the list of such matters is complete.

Unasserted Claims and Assessments: The following matters have been identified as giving rise to possible unasserted claims or assessments:

> [A list of unasserted matters would be provided including the nature of the matter, management's actual or intended response and an estimate of the likelihood and amount (if possible) of an unfavorable outcome.]

Please furnish our auditors such explanation, if any, that you consider necessary to supplement the foregoing information, including an explanation of those matters as to which your views may differ from those stated.

We understand that whenever, in the course of performing legal services for us with respect to a matter recognized to involve an unasserted possible claim or assessment that may call for financial statement disclosure, if you have formed a professional opinion that we should disclose or consider disclosure concerning such possible claim or assessment, as a matter of professional responsibility to us, you will so advise us and will consult with us. Please specifically confirm to our auditors that our understanding is correct.

Please specifically identify any limitations to your response and the nature of those limitations.

Respectfully,

Samuel Johnson
President, Johnson Pharmaceuticals, Inc.

Figure 14.5 *Example of Legal Inquiry Letter*

Concerning Litigation, Claims, and Assessments. *Because most countries legal environment differs somewhat, there are normally country specific addendums to ISA 501. For example, the Canadian Auditing and Assurance Board created AUG-46* **Communications with Law Firms Under New Accounting and Auditing Standards** *as a means of offering local implementation guidance as to how this ISA should be implemented in the Canadian context in addition to incorporating the Joint Policy Statement on Legal Letters developed with the Canadian Bar Association as an appendix to the Canadian version of ISA 501 denoted CAS 501.*

Because the request comes from the client directly to the attorney and the reply is addressed to the client with a copy directly to the auditor, confidentiality, and in some countries the concept of attorney-client privilege, is maintained by this process. This process, while it might seem awkward, is in place so that the auditor directly obtains the evidence required by direct communication with the attorney.

Under the commonly agreed upon guidelines between the accounting and legal profession, the attorney may provide the requested information subject to some limitations: (1) the information is limited to those cases for which the law firm has been substantively consulted, and (2) the response may also emphasize the inherent uncertainties related to facts and conclusions subject to adjudication. If a law firm that is substantively involved in a case does not respond to the request for information, the auditor should consider this a potential scope limitation. A lawyer is required by legal professional ethics to withdraw from providing services to a client if the client will not fully disclose all material lawsuits to the auditor. Thus, the auditor should be extremely suspicious if the law firm withdraws from a client engagement after the legal letter has been sent.

Review of Subsequent Events

The auditor must consider any events, conditions, or information that arise after year-end that may have implications for the reporting of financial results as of the end of the fiscal year. For example, the bankruptcy of a major customer in January indicates that the customer's receivable balance as of December 31 may not be collectible and should be considered a potential bad debt. Such an event provides evidence on the valuation of receivables. Similarly, much of the testing for unrecorded liabilities involves examining disbursements that occur after the end of the year. The auditor should explicitly consider evidence about subsequent events as part of the substantive testing of financial statement assertions and disclosures.

AUTHORITATIVE GUIDANCE & STANDARDS

Auditing standards for ensuring that subsequent events are properly accounted for and disclosed are contained in ISA 560 **Subsequent Events** *and PCAOB AS 2801 (formerly AU 560)* **Subsequent Events.** *There are differences between the ISA and PCAOB standards about the dates of audit reports as will be discussed in Chapter 15 in more detail. This difference will* *impact the period of time under which the auditor is responsible for updating his or her knowledge of subsequent events. However, the procedures and processes employed by the auditor are the same under both standards.*

Figure 14.6 depicts the period subsequent to year-end during which events are potentially significant to the auditor. Auditors are responsible for evaluating events that occur before the end of the subsequent events period, which is also the report date on the auditors' report. In general, two types of subsequent events are of interest to the auditor:

1. **Events requiring an adjustment to the financial statements:** These are events that provide information about circumstances that existed as of the fiscal year end, for example, the bankruptcy of a major customer suggests that any receivables from that customer may be uncollectible. Other examples include settlement of litigation, which provides evidence about the amount of loss related to a contingent liability, and the disposal of assets at a significant loss, which provides evidence about the impairment of those assets at year-end.[10]

2. **Events requiring disclosure in the financial statements:** These are events that have occurred since the end of the year but do not directly relate to the year-end balances. A presumption is made that knowledge of these events has a strong influence on how the financial statements are interpreted and that the readers of the financial statements would be adversely affected if they were not told about these events. Examples include business acquisitions or large casualty losses occurring after year-end[(xi)].

Because the annual report is issued after the review of subsequent events has been completed, companies sometimes have a subsequent event that occurs outside the review period but prior to the release of the financial statements. In this scenario, auditors traditionally have had a choice, to expand the subsequent events review for all possible subsequent events and re-date the audit report or re-open the audit for the subsequent event only and issue the audit report as a **dual date report**. The report will be signed and dated with the same date as before, but a second date will be indicated that relates to the disclosure describing the subsequent event that occurred after the end of the subsequent events review. An alternative under recent

[(xi)]**EXAMPLE**

To distinguish between events requiring an adjustment to the financial statements versus events requiring disclosure, consider companies impacted by the severe earthquakes in California and Japan in the mid-1990s and the tsunami in Southeast Asia in 2004. Both earthquakes occurred in January, which was subsequent to year-end for those companies with a calendar fiscal year. Thus, losses associated with the earthquakes would have been disclosed as a subsequent event for the prior fiscal year. Conversely, the tsunami occurred in late December, which would require affected organizations with a December year-end to adjust the financial statements for any losses relating to the disaster.

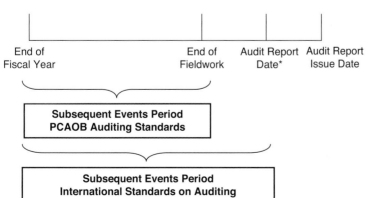

Figure 14.6 Subsequent Events Period

* Date when Board of Directors accepts finalized financial statements and approves them for release.

international audit standards is for the auditor to add a paragraph entitled "Emphasis of Matters" to the audit opinion to explain the subsequent event and the extent of auditor procedures with respect to it.

Representation Letters

The auditor should obtain a **representation letter** from management at the end of the audit. The purpose of the representation letter is to document management's responses to a number of critical inquiries (e.g., the nature of related parties, commitments and contingencies, asset valuations), ensure that those inquiries have been correctly understood, and impress on management its responsibility for all information included in the financial statements. A representation letter does not replace other forms of audit testing but does provide an effective method for avoiding misunderstandings about management's responsibilities or the meaning of important information provided by management to the auditor. In addition, because the letter forces management to document the information provided to the auditor, the letter provides a written record of any misrepresentations that management may have made, giving the auditor some defense against charges of negligence in the event of an audit failure.

(xii)EXAMPLE

While obtaining signed letters of representation from management is often seen as a routine part of the audit that may not always be so. The Chief Financial Officer of Livent, a Canadian based producer of Broadway and Broadway touring productions found to commit a major accounting fraud, would not sign the management representation letter. She insisted that her superiors, the CEO and the COO, sign the letter. The CFO, who was also a former audit partner of the firm that audited Livent, contended that she not signing the letter was her signal to the auditors that she did not believe in the representations that were contained in the letter. In the end that did not stop the local professional accounting institute from fining her and suspending her from practice for two years. She was also found guilty of one felony count for violation of US security laws.

AUTHORITATIVE GUIDANCE & STANDARDS

Auditing standards on management representation letters are found in ISA 580 **Written Representations** *and PCAOB AS 2805 (formerly AU 333)* **Management Representations.** *Further, the Sarbanes-Oxley Act (Section 302) requires the CEO and CFO of US-registered public companies to sign a certification that they have read and concur with the financial statements.*

A simple representation letter is presented in Figure 14.7. The letter is addressed to the auditor and dated as near as possible to, but not after, the audit report date (currently the end of audit fieldwork). The CEO and/or CFO sign the letter. Management refusal to provide a representation letter represents a scope limitation that may justify a disclaimer of opinion or withdrawal from the engagement. The following items must be covered in the representation letter for the preparation and presentation of the financial statements in accordance with the applicable financial reporting framework. Management must assert that they have:

- Designed, implemented and maintained internal control relevant to the preparation and presentation of financial statements that are free from material misstatement, whether due to fraud or error.
- Provided all information, such as records and documentation, and other matters that are relevant to the preparation and presentation of the financial statements.
- Document any additional information that the auditor has requested.
- Allowed the auditor unrestricted access to those within the entity from whom the auditor determines it necessary to obtain audit evidence(xii).

Johnson Pharmaceuticals, Inc.

Date

Ms. Roberta Smith, CA
333 E. University Avenue

Dear Ms. Smith:

In connection with your audit of the financial statements for Johnson Pharmaceutical, Inc. as of December 31, 20x7, and the period then ended for the purpose of expressing an opinion as to whether the financial statements present fairly, in all material respects, the financial position, results of operations and cash flows of Johnson Pharmaceuticals Inc. in conformity with generally accepted accounting principles, we confirm, to the best of our knowledge and belief, the following representations made to you during your audit.

- We are responsible for the fair presentation in the financial statements of financial position, results of operations, and cash flows in conformity with generally accepted accounting principles.

- We have made available to you (1) all financial records and related data, and (2) complete minutes for meetings of directors, shareholders, and committees of directors.

- There has been no (1) fraud involving management or employees who have a significant role in internal control of the company, (2) fraud involving employees that could have a material effect on the financial statements. or (3) communications from regulatory agencies concerning noncompliance with, or deficiencies in, financial reporting practices that could have a material effect on the financial statements.

- The effect of any uncorrected misstatements identified during the audit is not material to the latest period, either individually or in the aggregate.

- We have no plans or intentions that may materially affect the carrying value or classification of assets. [Details can be added for specific items such as intent to hold noncurrent investments to maturity or intent to dispose of idle property.]

- The following have been properly recorded and disclosed in the financial statements:

    1. Related party transactions and related amounts receivable or payable, including sales, purchases, loans, transfers, leasing arrangements, and guarantees.
    2. Capital stock repurchase options or agreements or capital stock reserved for options, warrants, conversions, or other requirements.
    3. Arrangements with financial institutions involving compensating balances or other arrangements involving restrictions on cash balances and line-of-credit or similar arrangements.
    4. Agreements to repurchase assets previously sold.
    5. Guarantees under which the company is contingently liable.
    6. Significant estimates and material concentrations known to management

- There are no (1) violations or possible violations of laws or regulations whose effects should be considered for disclosure in the financial statements or as a basis for recording a loss contingency, or (2) other material liabilities or gain or loss contingencies that are required to be accrued or disclosed by accounting standards.

- There are no unasserted claims or assessments that our lawyer has advised us are probable of assertion and must be disclosed in accordance with accounting standards.

- There are no material transactions that have not been properly recorded in the accounting records underlying the financial statements.

- Provision, when material, has been made to reduce excess or obsolete inventories to their estimated net realizable value.

- The company has satisfactory title to all owned assets, and there are no undisclosed liens or encumbrances on such assets nor has any asset been pledged.

(Continued)

- Provision has been made for any material loss to be sustained in the fulfillment of, or from the inability to fulfill, any sales commitments.

- Provision has been made for any material loss to be sustained as a result of purchase commitments for inventory quantities in excess of normal requirements or at prices in excess of the prevailing market prices.

- We have complied with all aspects of contractual agreements that would have a material effect on the financial statements in the event of noncompliance. [Specific debt covenants may be addressed if particularly important.]

- No events have occurred subsequent to the balance sheet date that would require adjustments to, or disclosure in, the financial statements.

Respectfully,

_____   _____
Samuel Smith, President   Victoria Rose, Controller

Figure 14.7 Example of Representation Letter

(xiii)EXAMPLE

In 2004, Deloitte & Touche resigned from the audit of Molex, a global electronic components company based in Illinois, because Molex's Audit Committee and Board of Directors unanimously rejected Deloitte's demand that both the CEO and CFO be removed as officers of the company. This demand was based on two issues. First, the CFO had knowledge of misstatements in the financial statements yet indicated in the management representation letter (which she signed) that no misstatements existed. Second, the CEO signed the management representation letter but admitted that he had not read the letter before signing it. Ernst & Young later accepted the client, but only after the Audit Committee and Board of Directors reversed their earlier decision and removed both individuals as officers of Molex.

Depending on the circumstances of the audit, the following representations may also need to be included in management's letter but could be included in separate management representations as they are part of other standards:

- The completeness of financial records, documents, minutes of board meetings, and regulatory reports made available to the auditor.

- The absence of unrecorded errors or transactions related to the financial statements and management's belief that the effect of any uncorrected errors is immaterial.

- The completeness of information pertaining to related party transactions.

- The completeness of information pertaining to subsequent events and uncertainties.

- Information about fraud that may have occurred.

- Management plans that might have an impact on the valuation or classification of transactions.

- Possession of legal title of assets and liens against assets.

- Information about issues that may require disclosure or accounting recognition including significant estimates, risk and uncertainties, regulatory noncompliance, unasserted claims, and contingent losses.

In a large, multinational organization, there may be representation letters for separate business units within the corporation. Auditors should be alert to situations where a financial manager at the business unit level refuses to sign a representation letter even though senior management is willing. This may indicate that the business unit manager has concerns about senior management's representations. This possibility should be considered a serious problem for the auditor. Furthermore, the auditor should not simply accept that it is corporate policy to only have senior management sign representation letters(xiii).

Final Evidence in Integrated Audits about Internal Control over Financial Reporting

Integrated Audits require that the auditor obtain additional management representations directly related to the effectiveness of internal control over financial reporting including:

- Acknowledging management's responsibility for establishing and maintaining effective internal control over financial reporting.

- Stating that management has performed an evaluation and made an assessment of the effectiveness of the company's internal control over financial reporting and specifying the control criteria.

- Stating that management did not use the auditor's procedures performed during the audits of internal control over financial reporting or the financial statements as part of the basis for management's assessment of the effectiveness of internal control over financial reporting.

- Stating management's conclusion, as set forth in its assessment, about the effectiveness of the company's internal control over financial reporting based on the control criteria as of a specified date.

- Stating that management has disclosed to the auditor all deficiencies in the design or operation of internal control over financial reporting identified as part of management's evaluation, including separately disclosing to the auditor all such deficiencies that it believes to be significant deficiencies or material weaknesses in internal control over financial reporting.

- Describing any fraud resulting in a material misstatement to the company's financial statements and any other fraud that does not result in a material misstatement to the company's financial statements but involves senior management or management or other employees who have a significant role in the company's internal control over financial reporting.

- Stating whether control deficiencies identified and communicated to the Audit Committee during previous engagements have been resolved, and specifically identifying any that have not.

- Stating whether there were, subsequent to the date being reported on, any changes in internal control over financial reporting or other factors that might significantly affect internal control over financial reporting, including any corrective actions taken by management with regard to significant deficiencies and material weaknesses.

ICOFR effectiveness audits, just like financial statement audits, are subject to requirements for subsequent events procedures up to the date of the audit report. In general, the auditor follows analogous procedures for subsequent events for the GAAS Audit and has similar responsibilities for information about control conditions existing as at year end and for information about changes in controls after year end. In particular the auditor should consider internal audit reports issued during the subsequent events period, regulatory agency reports related to internal control over financial reporting, and information obtained about the company's internal control over financial reporting obtained through other engagements.

Final Evaluation of Audit Evidence

The final evaluation of audit evidence is designed to provide a last check on the work of the auditor, to make sure that all pieces of the audit lead to the same conclusion, and to assure that no important matters have been overlooked.

Evaluation of Presentation and Disclosure Assertions

Although the audit steps associated with management assertions about transactions and accounts take most of the time required in the audit, auditors also have the responsibility of evaluating the final presentation and disclosure of the information in the financial statements. Given that the information included in the financial statements is often highly aggregated and involves a great deal of textual information, the auditor must evaluate each financial statement line item and disclosure, and the financial statements as a whole, to ensure that the presentation and disclosure assertions are valid.

Occurrence and Rights and Obligations: Most of the testing of ownership and rights and obligations is completed as part of the tests of transactions and accounts. As a consequence, the evaluation of the disclosure of occurrence and rights and obligations usually entails a review of the textual disclosures to make sure they do not contradict the results of the other audit tests and that there are no disclosures that have been overlooked by management. If management has added new disclosures that were not previously examined, the auditor must undertake additional procedures to ensure that the presentation and disclosure assertions are valid for these items. Often this is done by comparing the proposed disclosures with practices of leading companies in the industry that are acknowledged by financial analysts and others as providing full disclosure. The national or international offices of most firms have data bases of such disclosures and frequently these are being made assessable to local audit teams to aid in determining if disclosures proposed by management are sufficient.

AUTHORITATIVE GUIDANCE & STANDARDS

While no new standards were created, the IAASB recently completed a set of amendments to ten standards including ISA 700. These changes, individually and collectively, emphasize that the auditor's requirement to ensure proper presentation and disclosures in the financial statements is actively considered at every stage of the audit—from entering the engagement through to the finalization of the auditor's report. Hence, while the auditor has always examined management's assertions related to presentation and disclosure, the new requirements emphasize the need for complete and understandable disclosures as part of the auditor's responsibility in evaluating the fairness of the financial statements.

Completeness and the Use of a Disclosure Checklist: A particularly challenging aspect of the presentation and disclosure assertions is the need to evaluate whether the disclosures in the financial statements are

(xiv)EXAMPLE

Many industries have complex and unusual accounting rules for reporting transactions that are unique to the industry. In the US, the AICPA publishes a series of industry guidebooks in areas such as banking, insurance, and health care due to the unique financial reporting practices in those industries. For example, in the insurance industry, customers pay for an insurance policy when it is issued but may not make a claim against that policy for many years (if ever). This creates a unique accounting challenge for the insurance company because the premiums collected are a form of deferred revenue and the "cost" of the services rendered to the customers may not be known for a very long time. As a result, the insurance industry has developed specialized techniques for estimating the portion of premiums that are "earned" in any given year and the matching "losses" that might occur in the future as a result of issuing the policy.

complete, that is, all required disclosures are included. To help ensure that all necessary disclosures are complete, auditors often utilize a **disclosure checklist** that includes all potentially required disclosures, including specific requirements for public companies or companies in an industry that has specialized practices. Completion of such a checklist helps the auditor identify any disclosures that may have been overlooked in the preparation of the financial statements. Further, the use of databases, as described in the previous paragraph, allows for concrete examples of high quality disclosures to be readily assessed and compared to the proposed disclosures of the client in question[xiv].

Accuracy, Valuation, Classification, and Understandability: Another important consideration for auditors is that management might use the final financial statements to alter transaction or account information that has already been audited. For example, management might accidentally or intentionally alter otherwise accurate transaction and account data when aggregating it for financial statement presentation, especially when consolidated accounts are drawn up after the individual corporate accounts are audited. Thus, as previously noted, the auditor must test the accuracy of the management's process for producing the final financial statements.

Furthermore, management may try to influence the interpretation of reported results through misleading, vague, or intentionally complex descriptions in the footnotes. Auditors must carefully read all financial statement disclosures to ensure that they can be understood by reasonably astute financial statement users, especially when disclosures involve complex business transactions combined with complicated reporting regulations. For example, financial derivatives are highly complex transactions in their own right, and the accounting for such transactions is just as complex and requires significant expertise by the auditor to evaluate and verify[xv].

Review of Accounting Estimates

AUTHORITATIVE GUIDANCE & STANDARDS

ISA 540 **Auditing Accounting Estimates, Including Fair Value Accounting Estimates, and Related Disclosures** *provides guidance to auditors in this area. PCAOB Interim Standards provides separate standards for auditing accounting estimates (PCAOB AS 2501 [formerly AU 342]* **Auditing Accounting Estimates***) and a more specific standard for fair value measurements (PCAOB AS 2502 [formerly AU 328]* **Auditing Fair Value Measurements and Disclosures***).*

One of the most difficult judgments to review is the conclusions of staff auditors about the acceptability of accounting estimates made by management. We introduced the issues surrounding accounting estimates in Chapter 9, and the special nature of the substantive tests that are needed for accounting estimates in Chapter 10, applying them where appropriate in Chapters 11 to 13. At this stage of the audit the auditor is interested in whether management has adequately addressed the estimation uncertainty that is inherent in high risk accounting estimates. Should the auditor conclude that

[xv]**EXAMPLE**

One of the primary problems with the financial reporting by Enron was the incredibly complex disclosures found in the company's footnotes surrounding the accounting treatment of off balance sheet special purpose entities (SPEs) where the company was able to hide much of its accumulated financial loss and funnel cash to corporate executives. Many analysts (and possibly auditors) were hard-pressed to interpret the information contained in these disclosures, which may have been intentionally written to disguise financial and operating activities that the company did not want external readers to know about.

management has not adequately addressed the estimation uncertainty, then the auditor needs to develop a range of estimates to which he/she can compare management's estimates. This may be the case, for example, where the auditor concludes that:

- Sufficient appropriate audit evidence could not be obtained through the auditor's evaluation of how management has addressed the effects of estimation uncertainty.
- It is necessary to explore further the degree of estimation uncertainty associated with an accounting estimate, for example, where the auditor is aware of wide variation in outcomes for similar accounting estimates in similar circumstances.
- It is unlikely that other audit evidence can be obtained, for example, through the review of events occurring up to the date of the auditor's report.

The auditor may develop a point estimate or a range in a number of ways including:

- Using a commercially available, proprietary, or auditor developed model that is appropriate for the industry.
- Evaluating management's assumptions or outcomes, for example, by introducing a different set of assumptions.
- Employing or engaging a person with specialized expertise to develop or execute test the assumptions or outcomes of management's estimation process.
- Making reference to other comparable conditions, transactions, or events, or, where relevant, markets for comparable assets or liabilities.

The auditor has to obtain a sufficient understanding of the assumptions or method used by management in making their accounting estimate as it may assist the auditor to understand and evaluate any significant differences of their estimates from management's estimate. If there still exists a difference between management's estimates and the auditor's estimate or range of estimates, the procedures discussed in the next section on accounting negotiation are likely to be employed.

In addition to individual accounting estimates, the auditor is also interested in whether there are signs of significant management bias in the overall estimation process. Such bias may be difficult to detect at an account level. To identify whether there are indicators of possible management bias, the auditor needs to look at the broad picture, taking into account all accounting estimates, i.e., bias may be identifiable only may be identifiable only when considered in the aggregate of groups of accounting estimates or all accounting estimates. The auditor may develop a tool or a template that will include all accounting estimates to enable the auditor to determine if there is a pattern in the way management estimates are made. In other words, does this pattern meet management's objective in recording higher revenue, greater profitability, lower liabilities, etc.?

The susceptibility of an accounting estimate to management bias increases with the degree of estimation uncertainty involved in making it. To identify whether there are indicators of possible management bias, the auditor may consider the following indicators:

- Changes in an accounting estimate, or the method for making it, when management has subjectively determined that there has been a change in circumstances related to the estimate.

- Use of an entity's own assumptions for fair value accounting estimates when they are inconsistent with observable marketplace assumptions.

- Selection or construction of significant assumptions that yield a point estimate favorable for management objectives.

- Selection of a point estimate that may indicate a pattern of optimism or pessimism.

The auditor evaluates the reasonableness of the estimates based on the audit evidence obtained and using professional skepticism and his/her expertise (e.g., understanding of the entity and its industry), including relevant experts within the audit firm or hired independently by the auditor.

Review of Audit Documentation and Conclusions

One of the most prevalent quality control techniques used by auditors is the review of the documentation of audit evidence obtained during the engagement by senior members of the audit team. Audit documentation may be reviewed two or three times during the course of the audit. Work initially performed by staff accountants is usually reviewed on a detailed basis by senior accountants and on a general basis by managers. Work performed by senior accountants is usually reviewed on a detailed basis by managers and possibly on a general basis by partners. Ultimately, the responsibility for the overall quality of the work in the engagement rests with the partner in charge of the engagement team; however, partners often focus their reviews on key accounting issues and highly material transactions, accounts, or disclosures. If the reviewer has a question about the evidence contained in the documentation, an effort must be made to resolve the issue. Questions raised during reviews may cause the auditor to gather additional evidence. The audit report should not be issued until all questions raised during the review have been appropriately addressed by the members of the audit team, then reviewed again by the reviewer and accepted as being complete.

Client Negotiation and Resolution of Misstatements

As a result of audit testing, the auditor may discover misstatements of financial information or lack of or unclear relevant disclosures. As the audit is executed, proposed audit adjustments for known errors should be accumulated for disposition at the end of the engagement. An example of an error summary worksheet is presented in Figure 14.8. These misstatements will differ on a number of dimensions:

- Size relative to materiality.

- Degree of objectivity (e.g., objective error in a transaction versus subjective difference in opinion about the valuation of an account or on the clarity of a disclosure).

Figure 14.8 *Example of Error Summary Worksheet*

Jones Manufacturing, Inc.
Summary of Unadjusted Audit Differences
12/31/x6

X-1

WRK
1/24/x7

W/P Ref	Description	Total	Assets	Liability	Revenue	Expense
				Effect on Accounts: Debit (Credit)		
C-2	To restate inventory for inventory on hand per physical observation	10,000	(10,000)			10,000 ✓
B-3	To reflect expected bad debts	8,000	(8,000)			8,000
I-4	To accrue investment income	5,500	5,500		(5,500)	
L-3	To accrue unrecorded liabilities	20,000		(20,000)		20,000 ✓
F-2	To record repairs that should be capitalized	3,500	3,500			(3,500)
	Total effect of audit differences		(9,000)	(20,000)	(5,500)	34,500
			T	T	T	T
	Total unadjusted audit differences		(9,000)	0	(5,500)	15,500
			T	T	T	T

✓ Adjustment booked by client and reflected in financial statements
T Footed without exception

Conclusion:
After booking all individually material adjustments (denoted with a ✓), the net effect of all other unadjusted differences is deemed to be immaterial. Adjustment of further items is passed.

- Impact on financial statements (e.g., increase or decrease of net income).
- Implications for overall audit risk (e.g., unintentional errors versus fraudulent behavior).

Auditors propose adjustments to management that they feel should be made to the financial statements. Ultimately, the financial statements are the responsibility of management and the auditor cannot change the numbers; management must do so. Adjustments that are material and objective will likely be posted to the financial statements with a minimum of argument from management. However, management may debate adjustments that they believe are immaterial, have offsetting effects, involve subjective estimates or changes in wording. If management is unwilling to correct the financial statements for adjustments that the auditor deems to be material misstatements, the auditor can issue a qualified audit opinion or resign. Before resorting to such options, however, most auditors try to resolve the issues through negotiation.

The process of negotiating financial adjustments with management can be complex and difficult. There may be audit differences where the auditor and management can honestly disagree because they are subjective in nature or based on predictions about the future. In these cases, there may be a number of alternative resolutions that are equally defensible. Both the auditor and management have their own interests in the outcome of the audit process and are entitled to their own position on an issue, but this will influence each side's willingness to resolve audit differences. Understanding the position and views of the other side in a negotiation process increases the likelihood of a positive outcome from the process. More specifically, the likelihood of a mutually satisfactory outcome to the negotiation process will depend on:

- Commitment to principles or objectives relevant to the issue in question: Both management and the auditor have legitimate goals and principles driving their behavior that can cause them to disagree over specific matters. For example, the auditor will have a strong commitment to professional standards and the more that an audit difference is perceived to be in violation of those standards, the more firm the auditor's position will be regarding making an adjustment. Management may be committed to organizational success, and the more that an audit difference reflects weak performance, the more management may resist making the adjustment.

- Perceived fairness: The more that each side perceives that it has been treated fairly, the more understanding it will be of the other side's position. Compromise may be appropriate for audit differences that are subjective and uncertain, especially if management's assumptions are reasonable, albeit different, from those of the auditor.

- Effectiveness of communication: The better each party is able to communicate its objectives, principles, needs, desires, and potential areas for compromise, the more likely the groups are to reach a mutually agreeable solution. Knowing the potential limits of the other side's position helps to avoid unproductive ultimatums and a collapse of the negotiation process. For example, trying to force an auditor to accept an accounting treatment that is clearly in violation of GAAP and for which objective evidence exists, increases the likelihood that the auditor will be forced to resign or issue a qualified opinion.

- Strength of relationship: If the auditor and management have mutual respect and do not wish to jeopardize an ongoing professional relationship, they will be more likely to achieve a cooperative solution. However, the auditor should be careful to not allow the relationship with the client to undermine the auditor's compliance with professional standards relating to objectivity and independence.

In the example presented in Figure 14.8, the adjustments for inventory and unrecorded liabilities have been recorded in the financial statements, probably because they are large and objectively determined. The adjustment for bad debt expense is subjective and may be difficult to justify to management if the estimation is based on assumptions that are debatable. Furthermore, when netted against the two other errors, the net result is an immaterial amount. Consequently, three adjustments are **waived** by the auditor, meaning that the auditor does not insist on their correction in the financial statements.

For audits of registered public companies in the US, the Sarbanes-Oxley Act is believed to have strengthened the auditor's negotiation power with management. Under the law, auditors are required to discuss with the Audit Committee any disagreements with management regarding accounting policies or application of principles. Thus, should management not agree to a proposed audit adjustment and be unable to convince the auditor that it has valid reasons for doing so, the auditor will provide this information to the Audit Committee, which then must decide whether or not to force management to make the adjustment. Should the Audit Committee agree with management, the auditor could choose to issue a qualified opinion or to resign, where allowed by law. Because the Sarbanes-Oxley Act makes Audit Committee members individually liable for misstated financial statements, Audit Committees are expected to be reluctant to side with management in such disputes. Nevertheless, negotiation can still be expected to occur, even though the bargaining power has shifted towards the auditor in these situations.

AUTHORITATIVE GUIDANCE & STANDARDS

For US-registered public companies, the Sarbanes-Oxley Act requires that auditors meet with the Audit Committee to discuss all disagreements with management related to accounting policies or application of principles. The Audit Committee must then decide how to resolve the issues. However, the auditor always has the final say as to the opinions provided in the audit report.

Final Technical Review

As one last check on the accuracy of the financial statements, an audit partner who has not been involved in the engagement, often referred to as the **concurring (or review) partner**, will perform a review of the statements, supporting documentation, and audit conclusions. The primary purpose of this review is to determine if the engagement complies with all relevant auditing standards. Because the individual performing the review is not close to the engagement, the documentation must present the sole basis for reaching a conclusion. In this way, the audit firm has assurance that the workpapers adequately support the conclusion that generally accepted accounting principles (GAAP) have been correctly applied and that the data in the financial statements has been subjected to adequate audit verification. Absent any problems arising from the final technical review, the audit is essentially complete and the audit report can be issued.

AUTHORITATIVE GUIDANCE & STANDARDS

The requirement for concurring partner review (called the engagement quality control reviewer in the standard) of completed audits of financial statements is found in the International Standard on Quality Control (ISQC) 1 **Quality Control for Firms that Perform Audits and Reviews of Financial Statements, and Other Assurance and Related Services Engagements** *and in ISA 220* **Quality Control for an Audit of Financial Statements.** *Similar requirements are found in PCAOB Statement on Quality Control Standards (SQCS) QC 20* **System of Quality Control for a CPA Firm's Accounting and Auditing Practice** *and in PCAOB AS 1220 (formerly No. 7)* **Engagement Quality Review.**

Summary and Conclusion

In this chapter, we discussed the process of aggregating audit evidence and preparing the financial statements based on the results of the audit. If there are unresolved issues, unanswered questions, or unclear results, the auditor should consider additional testing and inquiry to resolve these remaining issues. The additional audit work might include more extensive review by senior audit personnel of the results of procedures conducted to date or more extensive substantive procedures in order to collect additional evidence to determine whether an account or balance is correctly stated. We also discussed wrap-up procedures whose objective is to bring together and integrate the vast amount of audit evidence obtained by the auditor in order to reach an overall conclusion about the fairness of the financial statements taken as a whole. In performing these procedures, the auditor is making sure that the evidence is consistent and complete, and fully supports the overall conclusions. In the next chapter we will discuss the nature of auditor reports that are generated once the audit is complete as well as the other reporting requirements that the auditor has to the client, especially those charged with governance.

Bibliography of Relevant Literature

Research

Davidson, S, Stickney, C.P. and Weil, R.L. (1987). *Accounting, the Language of Business* cited in Schipper, K. (1989), Commentary on Earnings Management. *Accounting Horizons*, 3: 91–102.

Fisher, Dan. (2009). Accounting Tricks Catch Up with GE. *Forbes*. August 4, 2009. www.forbes.com/2009/08/04/ge-immelt-sec-earnings-business-beltway-ge.html. Accessed on April 21, 2016

Healy, P. M. and Wahlen, J. M. (1999). A Review of the Earnings Management Literature and Its Implications for Standard Setting. *Accounting Horizons*, 13(4): 365–383.

Hicks, J. R. (1946). "Income" = Chapter XIV of *Value and Capital* (2nd Edition), Oxford: Clarendon Press.

Nelson, Mark W., John A. Elliott, and Robin L. Tarpley (2002). Evidence from Auditors about Managers' and Auditors' Earnings Management Decisions. *The Accounting Review*: Supplement, 7(1): 175–202.

Schilit, H. (2002) *Financial Shenanigans. Second edition.* McGraw-Hill: New York, pp. 24–25.

Accounting Standards

FASB *Statement* No. 5, "Accounting for Contingencies."

Securities and Exchange Commission (SEC). 1999. *Staff Accounting Bulletin No. 99*, "Materiality."

IFRS IAS 37 "Provisions, Contingent Liabilities and Contingent Assets."

Auditing Standards

Canadian Auditing and Assurance Services Board, *Assurance and Related Service Guideline,* AuG-46, "Communications with Law Firms under New Accounting and Auditing Standards."

IAASB *International Standards on Auditing (ISA)* No. 220, "Quality Control for an Audit of Financial Statements."

IAASB *International Standards on Auditing (ISA)* No. 260, "Communication with Those Charged with Governance."

IAASB *International Standards on Auditing (ISA)* No. 450, "Evaluation of Misstatements Identified during the Audit."

IAASB *International Standards on Auditing (ISA)* No. 501, "Audit Evidence—Specific Considerations for Selected Items."

IAASB *International Standards on Auditing (ISA)* No. 520, "Analytical Procedures."

IAASB *International Standards on Auditing (ISA)* No. 540, "Auditing Accounting Estimates, Including Fair Value Accounting Estimates, and Related Disclosures."

IAASB *International Standards on Auditing (ISA)* No. 560, "Subsequent Events"

IAASB *International Standards on Auditing (ISA)* No. 570, "Going Concern."

IAASB *International Standards on Auditing (ISA)* No. 570 (Revised), "Going Concern."

IAASB *International Standards on Auditing (ISA)* No 580, "Written Representations."

IAASB *International Standards on Auditing (ISA)* No 600, "Special Considerations—Audits of Group Financial Statements (Including the Work of Component Auditors)."

IAASB *International Standards on Auditing (ISA)* No. 700, "Forming an Opinion and Reporting on Financial Statements."

IAASB *International Standards on Auditing (ISA)* No. 720, "The Auditor's Responsibilities Relating to Other Information in Documents containing the Audited Financial Statements."

IAASB *International Standards on Auditing (ISA)* No. 720 (Revised), "The Auditor's Responsibilities Relating to Other Information."

IAASB *International Standard on Quality Control (ISQC)* No. 1. "Quality Control for Firms that Perform Audits and Reviews of Financial Statements, and Other Assurance and Related Services Engagements."

IFAC. International Auditing and Assurance Standards Board (IAASB). 2015. *Handbook of International Quality Control, Audit, Review, Other Assurance, and Related Services Pronouncements.* New York: International Federation of Accountants.

PCAOB *Auditing Standard* 1205 (formerly AU 543), "Part of Audit Performed by Other Independent Auditors."

PCAOB. *Auditing Standard* 1220 (formerly No. 7), "Engagement Quality Review."

PCAOB. *Auditing Standard* 1301 (formerly No. 16), "Communications with Audit Committees."

PCAOB *Auditing Standard* 2415 (formerly AU 341), "The Auditor's Consideration of an Entity's Ability to Continue as a Going Concern."

PCAOB. *Auditing Standard* 2501 (formerly *Interim Standard* AU 342), "Auditing Accounting Estimates."

PCAOB. *Auditing Standard* 2502 (formerly *Interim Standard* AU 328), "Auditing Fair Value Measurements and Disclosures."

PCAOB *Auditing Standard* 2505 (formerly AU 337), "Inquiry of a Client's Lawyer Concerning Litigation, Claims, and Assessments."

PCAOB *Auditing Standard* 2710 (formerly AU 550), "Other Information in Documents Containing Audited Financial Statements."

PCAOB *Auditing Standard* 2801 (formerly AU 560), "Subsequent Events."

PCAOB. *Auditing Standard* 2805 (formerly AU 333), "Management Representations."

PCAOB. *Auditing Standard* 2810 (formerly No. 14), "Evaluating Audit Results."

PCAOB. *Statement on Quality Control Standards* (SQCS) QC 20, "*System of Quality Control for a CPA Firm's Accounting and Auditing Practice.*"

SOX Sarbanes-Oxley Act - Library of Congress. 2002. House Resolution Number 3763, An Act to protect investors by improving the accuracy and reliability of corporate disclosures made pursuant to the securities laws, and for other purposes (*The Sarbanes-Oxley Act of 2002*). www.libraryofcongress.gov.

Notes

1 LIFO is a permitted inventory accounting method under US GAAP but is not permitted under IFRS.
2 The four fold classification of the balanced scorecard is not a requirement. The number and nature of the categories that the auditor or client management might choose to use is based on the facts and circumstances of the client.
3 The period of the auditor's responsibility for evaluating going concern may differ depending on the laws of the country involved or regulations.
4 See Chapter 9 for formulas to compute these ratios.
5 ISA 570 (Revised) covers the same matters as ISA 570 with an added focus on explicitly reporting, as part of the Auditor's Report, on whether the going concern assumption is warranted. See Chapter 15 for reporting details.
6 In the tradition of Sir John Hicks (Hicks, J.R. [1946], 'Income' = Chapter XIV of *Value and Capital* (2nd Edition: Oxford: Clarendon Press) albeit this exact wording is not found there or anywhere in his writings but is attributed to him by accounting standard setters in the US and internationally.
7 Mark W. Nelson, John A. Elliott, and Robin L. Tarpley (2002) Evidence from Auditors about Managers' and Auditors' Earnings Management

Decisions. *The Accounting Review*: Supplement 2002, Vol. 77, No. s-1, 175–202.

8 Fisher, Dan. 2009. Accounting Tricks Catch Up with GE. *Forbes*. August 4, 2009.

9 Unasserted claims are potential losses arising from events that have already occurred and are expected to result in a lawsuit against the organization. For example, tort injuries have a three year statute of limitations, so a claim could be asserted up to three years after the event occurred.

10 The assumption made in the example of assets sold at a loss is that the loss existed as at the end of the fiscal year but the existence or amount of the loss was uncertain at that time. The actual sale after the year end provides evidence about the amount of loss that had already occurred.

CHAPTER 15

Completing the Audit II
Audit Reporting

Outline

Learning Goals for this Chapter

1. Understand the auditor's requirements for reporting to the Audit Committee, or more broadly, those charged with governance, under both a GAAS Audit and an Integrated Audit.
2. Describe the major parts of an auditor's report and identify their importance to the reader of the financial statements

3. Understand the types of modifications that can be made to the standard unqualified auditor's report in both a GAAS Audit and an Integrated Audit based on the evidence that the auditor has collected.

4. Determine the auditor's opinion that should be rendered in specific circumstances based on the final review of audit evidence.

5. Identify other matters that should be included in the auditor's report that do not result in a modification to the auditor's opinion.

6. Identify the reporting choices available under an Integrated Audit for the auditor's reports on ICOFR and the financial statements.

Introduction

This chapter discusses the various ways in which the auditor communicates the results of the audit to interested parties. There are at least two major constituencies that the auditor reports to: (1) those charged with governance of the entity, and (2) readers of the general purpose financial statements. In addition, the auditor communicates various incidental findings based on the audit that may be of interest to management so that management can improve the running of the business. We are at what Figure 15.1 illustrates

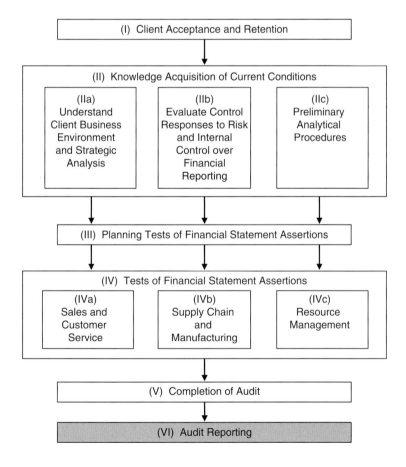

Figure 15.1 An Overview
of the Audit Process

as the final phase of the audit as this reporting process represents the culmination of all the activities outlined in Chapters 3 to 14.

We start by considering the communications that the auditor makes to internal parties, especially those charged with governance of the entity as well as management. These parties can respond to the auditor's findings by making changes to the financial statements or taking other actions that may influence the auditor's final assessment of the fairness of the financial statements. After considering reporting to internal parties, we then focus on the primary form of external communication, the auditor's report, which is distributed along with the financial statements to external stakeholders.

We introduced the subject matter of the auditor's report, the audit opinion on the financial statements, in Chapter 3, but we did not study at that time the complete report in which the opinion is included. That report is the focus of this chapter. In addition to the audit report about the fairness of the financial statements, auditors of companies that are publicly registered in the US also issue reports related to internal control over financial reporting that may be integrated with the auditor's report on the financial statements.

Communications of Audit Results to Those Charged with Governance and Management

Most entities have a governing body (e.g., Board of Directors) that oversees the entity's management. The Board of Directors, or similar governance group, normally delegates to management the responsibility for carrying out the day to day operations of the entity as well as making recommendations to the board for major strategic decisions. As can be seen in Figure 15.2, in a public company the shareholders elect a Board of Directors that hires, fires, and compensates the top management of the company. The Board of Directors in many countries is characterized as being the ultimate internal control authority in the company albeit there are countries that have separate governance boards and management boards (e.g., Germany is the best known example of the two board system). The view that the board is the ultimate authority within the company leads to the suggestion that

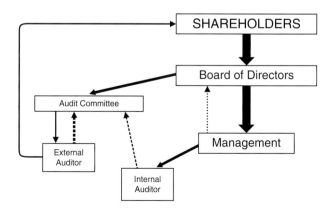

Figure 15.2 Governance Structure of a Typical Public Company

ineffective governance practices may indicate that the auditor should not accept the audit in the first place (see Chapter 4).

The board normally—and by law in many countries—sets up a subcommittee known as the Audit Committee that is responsible for oversight of the financial reporting process on behalf of the full board. This oversight includes the hiring, firing and compensation of the external auditor as well as acting on behalf of the board in its interactions with the external auditor (and frequently with the internal auditor as well). Non-publicly traded companies may not be required to have Audit Committees, although in many countries influenced by the British legal system, there is a requirement for all limited liability entities to have an Audit Committee. Because of the diversity of nomenclature standard setters have coined the term "those charged with governance" as a catch-all term to apply no matter what the actual name of the governance body.

Throughout the rest of this chapter we will call "those charged with governance" the "Audit Committee" while recognizing that the auditor is responsible to the entire Board of Directors and in some countries (e.g., many of the Nordic countries) is directly responsible to the shareholders. The separation between the entire board and Audit Committee means that the auditor needs to also consider whether the Audit Committee is fully informing the Board of Directors of what the auditor is reporting. If the auditor believes the Audit Committee is not performing that responsibility, the auditor has a duty to report to the full board directly.

AUTHORITATIVE GUIDANCE & STANDARDS

The first part of the chapter covers material related to reporting to those charged with governance (e.g., the Audit Committee) to set the stage for the external reporting on the financial statements (and effectiveness of internal control over financial reporting in the US) of the second part of the chapter. Relevant standards are ISA 260 (Revised) **Communication with those Charged with Governance** *and ISA 265* **Communicating Deficiencies in Internal Control to those Charged with Governance and Management;** *and PCAOB AS 2201 (formerly No. 5)* **An Audit of Internal Control over Financial Reporting that is Integrated with An Audit of Financial Statements** *and AS 1301 (formerly 16)* **Communications with Audit Committees.** *For reporting to management the relevant standards are ISA 265 and AS 2201 and AS 1305 (formerly AU 325)* **Communications about Control Deficiencies in an Audit of Financial Statements.**

Formal Reporting to the Audit Committee or "Those Charged with Governance"

Ideally, the members of the Audit Committee should not hold management positions within the entity as that would result in the auditor reporting *about* management *to* management. In public companies it is generally required that the entire membership of the Audit Committee is made up of independent (also known as nonexecutive) directors whose only connection with the company is the shares that they own and the fees (if any) they received as corporate directors. Box 15.1 "Matters for the Auditor to Communicate with Those Charged with Governance" outlines the set of communications that the auditor is responsible for making to the Audit Committee during the course of the audit.

> ## BOX 15.1   MATTERS FOR THE AUDITOR TO COMMUNICATE WITH THOSE CHARGED WITH GOVERNANCE
>
> - *The auditor's responsibilities in relation to the financial statement audit include:*
>   - o *Communicating that ISAs are the basis for all reports to those charged with governance and that the ISAs may not satisfy all the needs of those charged with governance.*
>   - o *Auditor independence from the client and how the auditor has ascertained this has happened and is maintained over the course of the audit.*
>   - o *The name of the audit engagement partner who will be named in the auditor's report.*
> - *Planned scope and timing of the audit:*
>   - o *Significant risk identified by the auditors and how the auditor plans to address the significant risks of material misstatement, whether due to fraud or error.*
>   - o *The auditor's approach to internal control relevant to the audit.*
>   - o *The application of the concept of materiality in the context of an audit.*
>   - o *The nature and extent of specialized skill or knowledge needed to perform the planned audit procedures or evaluate the audit results, including the use of an auditor's experts.*
>   - o *The use of internal auditors as part of the audit.*
> - *Findings related to the audit about qualitative aspects of accounting practices:*
>   - o *The auditor's subjective opinion about the adequacy of the disclosures about estimation uncertainty surrounding accounting estimates in the financial statements and management's processes and judgments associated with arriving at estimates including the reasonableness of management's assumptions.*
>   - o *The auditor's opinion about the appropriateness versus the acceptability under GAAP of key entity accounting policies especially when there are controversial or emerging areas of accounting practices.*
> - *Significant difficulties encountered during the audit:*
>   - o *Significant delays by management, the unavailability of entity personnel, or an unwillingness by management to provide information necessary for the auditor to perform the auditor's procedures.*
>   - o *An unreasonably brief time within which to complete the audit.*
>   - o *Extensive unexpected effort required to obtain sufficient appropriate audit evidence or the unavailability of expected information.*

- o *Restrictions imposed on the auditor by management that did not lead to a scope limitation but caused the auditor to have to work around these restrictions.*
- o *Management's unwillingness to make or extend its assessment of the entity's ability to continue as a going concern when requested.*
- *Significant matters discussed with management:*
  - o *Significant events or transactions during the year.*
  - o *Any occasions where the auditor knows management has communicated with another audit or about accounting or auditing issues.*
  - o *Discussions about fees and reappointment.*
  - o *Differences in opinion after discussion with management after all facts about a transaction or event have been ascertained.*
- *Matters related to the content of the auditor's report including:*
  - o *Nature of the opinion including any modifications or emphasis of matters that will be included in the final report especially if a material uncertainty with respect to going concern is going to be communicated.*
  - o *For public companies—key audit matters to be communicated in the report.*

Box 15.2 "Auditor's Elicitation of the Views of Those Charged with Governance about Matters Related to the Audit" makes it clear that the auditor is required to engage the members of the Audit Committee in a discussion about appropriate financial reporting and the need for proper internal controls over financial reporting. In other words the relationship between the auditor and the Audit Committee is not a one-sided communication effort from the auditor to the Committee. Indeed, "robust discussion" should occur between the Audit Committee members and the auditor.[1] Since standards require, as shown in Box 15.1 "Matters for the Auditor to Communicate with Those Charged with Governance" and Box 15.2 "Auditor's Elicitation of the Views of Those Charged with Governance about Matters Related to the Audit," that the auditor involve the Audit Committee in planning the audit, the auditor needs to meet with the Audit Committee twice a year at a minimum. For publicly traded companies more frequent meetings, at least quarterly, are the norm.

> **BOX 15.2 AUDITOR'S ELICITATION OF THE VIEWS OF THOSE CHARGED WITH GOVERNANCE ABOUT MATTERS RELATED TO THE AUDIT**

- *May want to seek the views of those charged with governance about:*
  - o *The appropriate person(s) in the entity's governance structure with whom to communicate.*
  - o *The allocation of responsibilities between those charged with governance and management.*
  - o *The entity's objectives and strategies, and the related business risks that may result in material misstatements.*

o   Matters those charged with governance consider warrant particular attention during the audit, and any areas where they request additional procedures to be undertaken.

o   Significant communications with regulators.

- Based on this discussion the auditor's objective is to understand the attitudes and awareness of those charged with governance regarding:

o   Importance of internal control to those charged with governance and how these seek to have oversight of the effectiveness of internal control.

o   The involvement with and awareness of accounting standards, corporate governance practices, exchange listing rules (where appropriate).

- Considering the response of those charged with governance to:

o   Any modifications the auditor is proposing to the unqualified auditor's report.

o   Discussion about the communication of material uncertainty with respect to going concern as an emphasis of matter.

o   The nature and extent of the auditor's communication of key audit matters (for public company audits).

The matters the auditor discusses with the Audit Committee as the audit report is finalized concentrate on what has been learned and observed while carrying out the audit. One purpose of these communications is to assure that the Audit Committee is informed of problems encountered during the audit. Conflicts with management or difficulties resolving auditing issues can be communicated directly to the committee in this way. At least three areas are discussed:

1. The substance of the audited financial statements:

    - The nature of significant accounting policies and procedures used in preparing the financial statements. The auditor should also comment about whether management has adopted what the auditor believes to be the most appropriate policies, not just policies that are acceptable under GAAP (i.e., known as the "qualitative aspects of financial reporting").

    - Management judgments related to significant accounting estimates and their disclosure in the notes to the financial statements

    - The nature and resolution of significant auditor proposed adjustments including immaterial differences that were not corrected by management

    - The nature and resolution of disagreements with management concerning accounting issues, estimates, and the scope of audit evidence, including whether management has consultations with other independent accountants or auditors about these matters.

    - Whether there are any material differences between the audited financial statements and other disclosures (e.g., other information such as management's discussion and analysis).

2. Internal control problems encountered:

    -   Any deficiencies in internal controls found during the audit that caused the auditor to have to change the audit plan previously communicated to the Audit Committee, and a summary of the adjustments to that audit plan to deal with the unanticipated deficiencies.

    -   In the case of an **Integrated Audit,** the auditor should report all significant deficiencies to the Audit Committee (see "Audit Reporting in an Integrated Audit" later in this chapter for more details).

3. The nature of the relationship with management:

    -   Difficulties encountered during the engagement, such as management delays in providing information, missing documents and records, unreasonable management timetables for carrying out the audit, lack of access to documents and records, or lack of expected assistance by client personnel.

    -   Any restrictions that management placed on the auditor in carrying out the audit even if the auditor was able to work around those restrictions to issue an unqualified opinion.

These communications may be oral or written (in the US written is required) and must be documented in the working papers. In public companies it is generally required that these matters be communicated prior to the finalization of the auditor's report and timely communication is required for audits of all types of entities.

Reports on Internal Control Issues Discovered as Part of the GAAS Audit

As the auditor is not required to audit ICOFR effectiveness in a GAAS Audit, the auditor does not provide an opinion on ICOFR. However, the auditor may come across matters related to internal control that should be communicated to the client's Audit Committee and management. The auditor is not required in a GAAS Audit to plan the engagement to uncover possible significant control deficiencies. However, in the execution of the auditor's procedures, especially process analysis and obtaining an understanding of internal control, such deficiencies may be discovered with respect to design effectiveness. Further, if in a GAAS Audit reliance is placed on controls to reduce the level of substantive testing, control testing may reveal weaknesses in the working of the tested controls (see Chapters 6 and 7).

The discovery of a significant deficiency requires written communication to the Audit Committee and management. While standard-setters prefer the auditor to issue a written report for any communications about internal control, it is only required in writing in the US. The report should indicate that it is based on an audit whose purpose was to report on the financial statements and does not provide assurance about the overall effectiveness of internal control. The report should include a definition of significant deficiencies that would be reported if incidentally found during the GAAS Audit. Additionally, the report should contain a statement limiting the distribution of any communication about internal control effectiveness to within the client's organization (i.e., the communication is not intended for external parties such as shareholders).

In general, the auditor should avoid issuing a report stating no significant deficiencies were found as the GAAS Audit is not designed to detect deficiencies in internal control. However, under a very limited set of conditions the auditor may issue a report about what the auditor found. In such a report, the auditor clearly indicates that he or she was not engaged to examine the effectiveness of internal controls; expresses no opinion on internal control effectiveness; defines significant control deficiencies that would be reported if found; states as a factual matter the auditor did not find any significant deficiencies in internal controls during the GAAS Audit; and finally cautions that the GAAS Audit was not designed to discover significant deficiencies. Further, the auditor must clearly restrict the report's circulation to management, the Audit Committee and those charged with governance and if required by law, the particular third party that the report is being sent to.

Reporting Matters to Audit Committees about the Effectiveness of Internal Control over Financial Reporting as Part of an Integrated Audit

Given the deeper knowledge about internal control that the auditor obtains in an Integrated Audit, an auditor has more in-depth knowledge of the state of an entity's controls to convey to the Audit Committee than in a GAAS Audit, at least for those controls in place as of year-end. Any material weakness detected in the Integrated Audit that results in an adverse opinion on effectiveness of ICOFR will be communicated to the Audit Committee and management in detail. This communication should include the circumstances surrounding the material weakness and include a discussion of how the auditor was able to deal with the ineffectiveness of the controls in reaching an opinion on the financial statements, or explain how the control weakness led to a modification of the auditor's report on the financial statements.

In addition to material weaknesses that are publicly reported, the auditor must also report to the Audit Committee any deficiencies or combinations of deficiencies that meet the definition of significant deficiency in ICOFR that was discussed in Chapter 8. The auditor will explain how the audit of the financial statements was modified to cope with the deficiency so that the auditor could obtain sufficient evidence on which to base an opinion about the fairness of the financial statements, especially the accounts affected by the significant deficiency. US regulators require that all reports to the Audit Committee about ICOFR deficiencies must be in writing. Further, if the auditor is going to issue a management letter (see the next section for details about this letter) the auditor must inform the Audit Committee that such a letter has been sent to management.

Management Letters

In either a GAAS or Integrated Audit, the auditor may wish to bring other issues to the attention of management. These could include inconsequential control or operating issues that the auditor observed that did not impact internal control reporting or the financial statements. During strategic and process analysis, numerous client concerns, issues, or comments may have been identified as a result of analyzing risks, controls, and performance indicators. Such matters are usually communicated via a ***management letter***. Often they are used to convey minor control issues that have been discovered that lower level management should be made aware of at the divisional or strategic business unit level. In this case, the auditor wants to ensure that higher level management knows these concerns exist even though they are not significant enough to have a material impact on the overall audited financial statements.

In addition to this function, management letters serve another function in audits where the strict public company independence rules do not apply to public accounting firms. Here management letters are also used as suggestions to management that are meant to enable the company to improve performance in some way. In general, such issues relate to ways in which the company can more effectively or efficiently run its operations. Topics can range from operational and administrative procedures to strategic policies. There is no required format for communicating these issues, but the letter should clearly state the purpose, the fact that no assurance is provided on the included matters, and the limitations on distribution.

External Communication of Audit Results

The primary external communication prepared by the auditor is the formal auditor's report(s). If a GAAS Audit of the financial statements has been performed, the form of report will depend on the outcome of that audit; the completeness, credibility, and persuasiveness of the evidence obtained; the compliance (or lack thereof) with GAAP and GAAS; and management's willingness to adjust the financial statements for known errors. We introduced the opinion paragraph in Chapter 4 and now elaborate on the overall report that contains the opinion.

AUTHORITATIVE GUIDANCE & STANDARDS

This section covers audit reports over financial statements for GAAS Audits prepared under IAASB standards (ISA 570 [Revised] **Going Concern***, ISA 700 [Revised]* **Forming an Opinion and Reporting on Financial Statements***, ISA 701* **Communicating Key Audit Matters in the Independent Auditor's Report***, ISA 705 [Revised]* **Modifications to the Opinion in The Independent Auditor's Report***, ISA 706 [Revised]* **Emphasis of Matter Paragraphs and Other Matter Paragraphs in The Independent Auditor's Report** *and ISA 720 [Revised]* **The Auditor's Responsibilities Relating to Other Information***). The form of the auditor's report on the financial statements under IAASB standards and the form of the report for those firms audited under PCAOB standards are already quite different due to changes made by the IAASB in 2007 and changes made by the PCAOB to put into effect its auditor reporting requirements about effective ICOFR. The two audit reports are likely to diverge further as the IAASB's auditor's report is significantly updated for* *audits of financial statements for fiscal years ending on or after December 15, 2016 (this report is covered in this text).[2] As will be discussed later in the chapter there is some early movement toward convergence of the reporting models. An on-line appendix is available that covers reporting under the previous set of ISAs 570, 700, 705, and 706 (all with the same title as above) and ISA 720* **The Auditor's Responsibilities Relating to Other Information in Documents Containing Audit Financial Statements.**

Components of an Auditor's Report in a GAAS Audit

Box 15.3 "Key Components of a GAAS Auditor's Report" highlights the six key components of the auditor's report, although not all components are needed in every report. At a minimum the auditor's report for a publicly traded company must contain:

- An opinion paragraph and the basis for that opinion.
- Key audit matters.
- Other information (unless there are material matters to report then it is to appear before key audit matters).
- Responsibilities of management and those charged with governance.
- Auditor responsibilities for the audit of the financial statement.

BOX 15.3   KEY COMPONENTS OF A GAAS AUDITOR'S REPORT

Types of opinion and basis for that opinion:

- *Opinion (unmodified or unqualified or "clean"—see Box 15.5 "Standard (Unqualified) Auditor's Report for a GAAS Audit," page 555).*
- *Qualified Opinion (see Box 15.7 "Auditor's Report Qualified for Scope Limitation in A GAAS Audit—Changed Sections Only" and Box 15.8 "Auditor's Report Qualified for Departure from GAAP in a GAAS Audit—Changed Sections Only," pages 565 and 567).*
- *Adverse Opinion (see Box 15.9 "Auditor's Adverse Report in a GAAS Audit—Changed Sections Only," see page 569).*
- *Disclaimer of Opinion (see Box 15.10 "Auditor's Denial of Opinion Due to Scope Limitation in a GAAS Audit—Changed Sections Only," page 570).*

Emphasis of matter (where applicable—see Box 15.11 "Examples of Key Audit Matters Disclosed in an Auditor's Report," page 572). Examples:

- *When a financial reporting framework prescribed by law or regulation would be unacceptable but for the fact that it is prescribed by law or regulation.*
- *To alert users that the financial statements are prepared in accordance with a special purpose framework.*
- *When facts become known to the auditor after the date of the auditor's report and the auditor provides a new or amended auditor's report (i.e., subsequent events).*
- *An uncertainty relating to the future outcome of exceptional litigation or regulatory action.*

- *A significant subsequent event that occurs between the date of the financial statements and the date of the auditor's report.*
- *Early application (where permitted) of a new accounting standard that has a material effect on the financial statements.*
- *A major catastrophe that has had, or continues to have, a significant effect on the entity's financial position.*

Key audit matters (where applicable—see Box 15.11 "Examples of Key Audit Matters Disclosed in an Auditor's Report")

Other Information (where applicable – see Box 15.5 "Standard (Unqualified) Auditor's Report for a GAAS Audit")

Responsibilities of management and those charged with governance for the financial statements (see Box 15.5 "Standard (Unqualified) Auditor's Report for a GAAS Audit" for full description).

- *To prepare the financial statements in accordance with GAAP.*
- *Assess the entity's ability to continue as a going concern.*
- *Identify those who have oversight of management with respect to these responsibilities.*

Auditor responsibilities for the audit of financial statements (See Box 15.5 "Standard (Unqualified) Auditor's Report for a GAAS Audit" for a full description).

- *State the audit's objective of reasonable assurance, what reasonable assurance means, and describe materiality.*
- *State that the audit involves professional judgment and that there are risks of not detecting material misstatements, especially there are higher risks for not detecting such misstatement with respect to fraud.*
- *State the limited goal of examining internal control for purposes of carrying out the audit, not to provide an opinion on internal control effectiveness.*

Report on other legal or regulatory requirements:

- *Matters that due to local laws and regulations that the auditor is required to report on as part of the auditor's report.*

Box 15.4 "Structure of the Auditor's Report" outlines a comprehensive set of headings for the components of the auditor's report. Note that the headings (or similarly worded headings) in bold are mandatory under international reporting standards (e.g., **OPINION**). Box 15.5 "Standard (Unqualified) Auditor's Report for a GAAS Audit" provides the detailed wording of that report.

BOX 15.4   STRUCTURE OF THE AUDITOR'S REPORT

Independent Auditor's Report*

Addressee

Report on the Audit of Financial Statements (if required due to the existence of a final report section entitled "Report on Other Legal and Regulatory Requirements" as illustrated below in italics)

Opinion

Basis for Opinion

Emphasis of Matters *(including, where needed, materiality uncertainty with respect to going concern assumption)*

Key Audit Matters *(for public companies and where otherwise required by local law)*

Other Information *(for entities that prepare an annual report or similar document)*

Responsibilities of Management and Those Charged with Governance for Financial Statements

Auditor's Responsibilities for Audit of Financial Statements**

Report on Other Legal and Regulatory Requirements (if required then a first header is required before the **Opinion** heading of "Report on the Audit of Financial Statements" as illustrated above)

Identification of audit engagement partner.

Signature of Auditor and/or audit firm with identification of audit partner

Address of Audit

Date of Auditor's Report

** **Items in bold** are required report or section headings*

** Item that is permitted to be included by reference to an appendix to the report or a publicly available web site maintained by an "appropriate authority" that is designated by law, regulation, or national audit standard setters.

> ### BOX 15.5   STANDARD (UNQUALIFIED) AUDITOR'S REPORT FOR A GAAS AUDIT
>
> **Independent Auditor's Report**
>
> [Appropriate Addressee]
>
> *Opinion**
>
> *We have audited the financial statements of ABC Company (the Company), which comprise the statement of financial position as at December 31, 20X1, and the statement of comprehensive income, statement of changes in equity, and statement of cash flows for the year then ended, and notes to the financial statements, including a summary of significant accounting policies.*
>
> *In our opinion, the accompanying financial statements present fairly, in all material respects, (or give a true and fair view of) the financial position of the Company as at December 31, 20X1, and (of) its financial performance and its cash flows for the year then ended in accordance with International Financial Reporting Standards (IFRSs).*
>
> *Basis for Opinion*
>
> *We conducted our audit in accordance with International Standards on Auditing (ISAs). Our responsibilities under those standards are further*

described in the Auditor's Responsibilities for the Audit of the Financial Statements section of our report. We are independent of the Company in accordance with the ethical requirements that are relevant to our audit of the financial statements in [jurisdiction], and we have fulfilled our other ethical responsibilities in accordance with these requirements. We believe that the audit evidence we have obtained is sufficient and appropriate to provide a basis for our opinion.

Other Information [where an annual report or similar document is prepared by client]

Management is responsible for other information. The other information comprises that found in the Company's Annual Report to Shareholders but does not include the financial statements and the auditor's report thereon.

Our opinion on the financial statements does not cover the other information and we do not express any form of assurance conclusion thereon.

In connection with our audit of the financial statements, our responsibility is to read the other information and, in doing so, consider whether the other information is materially inconsistent with the financial statements or our knowledge obtained in the audit or otherwise appears to be materially misstated. If, based on the work we have performed, we conclude that there is a material misstatement of this other information, we are required to report that fact. We have nothing to report in this regard.

Responsibilities of Management and Those Charged with Governance for the Financial Statements

Management is responsible for the preparation and fair presentation of the financial statements in accordance with IFRSs, and for such internal control as management determines is necessary to enable the preparation of financial statements that are free from material misstatement, whether due to fraud or error.

In preparing the financial statements, management is responsible for assessing the Company's ability to continue as a going concern, disclosing, as applicable, matters related to going concern and using the going concern basis of accounting unless management either intends to liquidate the Company or to cease operations, or has no realistic alternative but to do so.***

Those charged with governance are responsible for overseeing the Company's financial reporting process.

Auditor's Responsibilities for the Audit of the Financial Statements**

Our objectives are to obtain reasonable assurance about whether the financial statements as a whole are free from material misstatement, whether due to fraud or error, and to issue an auditor's report that includes our opinion. Reasonable assurance is a high level of assurance, but is not a guarantee that an audit conducted in accordance with ISAs will always detect a material misstatement when it exists. Misstatements can arise *from fraud or error and are considered material if, individually or in the aggregate, they could reasonably be expected to influence the economic decisions of users taken on the basis of these financial statements.*

As part of an audit in accordance with ISAs, we exercise professional judgment and maintain professional skepticism throughout the audit. We also:

- *Identify and assess the risks of material misstatement of the financial statements, whether due to fraud or error, design and perform audit procedures responsive to those risks, and obtain audit evidence that is sufficient and appropriate to provide a basis for our opinion. The risk of not detecting a material misstatement resulting from fraud is higher than for one resulting from error, as fraud may involve collusion, forgery, intentional omissions, misrepresentations, or the override of internal control.*

- *Obtain an understanding of internal control relevant to the audit in order to design audit procedures that are appropriate in the circumstances, but not for the purpose of expressing an opinion on the effectiveness of the Company's internal control.*

- *Evaluate the appropriateness of accounting policies used and the reasonableness of accounting estimates and related disclosures made by management.*

- *Conclude on the appropriateness of management's use of the going concern basis of accounting and, based on the audit evidence obtained, whether a material uncertainty exists related to events or conditions that may cast significant doubt on the Company's ability to continue as a going concern. If we conclude that a material uncertainty exists, we are required to draw attention in our auditor's report to the related disclosures in the financial statements or, if such disclosures are inadequate, to modify our opinion. Our conclusions are based on the audit evidence obtained up to the date of our auditor's report. However, future events or conditions may cause the Company to cease to continue as a going concern.****

- *Evaluate the overall presentation, structure and content of the financial statements, including the disclosures, and whether the financial statements represent the underlying transactions and events in a manner that achieves fair presentation.*

We communicate with those charged with governance regarding, among other matters, the planned scope and timing of the audit and significant audit findings, including any significant deficiencies in internal control that we identify during our audit.

We also provide those charged with governance with a statement that we have complied with relevant ethical requirements regarding independence, and to communicate with them all relationships and other matters that may reasonably be thought to bear on our independence, and where applicable, related safeguards.

[If key audit matters are reported—see Box 15.1 "Matters for the Auditor to Communicate with Those Charged with Governance" (page 547) then the following paragraph is included]

{From the matters communicated with those charged with governance, we determine those matters that were of most significance in the audit of the financial statements of the current period and are therefore the key audit matters. We describe these matters in our auditor's report unless law or regulation precludes public disclosure about the matter or when, in extremely rare circumstances, we determine that a matter should not be communicated in our report because the adverse consequences of doing so would reasonably be expected to outweigh the public interest benefits of such communication.}

The engagement partner on the audit resulting in this independent auditor's report is [name].

[Signature in the name of the audit firm, the personal name of the auditor, or both, as appropriate for the particular jurisdiction]

[Auditor Address]

[Date]

** **Items in bold** are required report or section headings*

** Item that is permitted to be included by reference to an appendix to the report or a publicly available web site maintained by an "appropriate authority" that is designated by law, regulation, or national audit standard setters as allowed for under ISA 700 (Revised).

*** Items that are in <u>italics and underlined</u> reflect the increased emphasis in the revised auditor's report under ISA 700 (Revised) on going concern evaluations by management and the auditor's consideration of the appropriateness of management's conclusion about going concern assumption.

The Opinion Paragraph: We introduced the opinion paragraph in Chapter 4 along with the four types of auditor opinions that can be issued for the audit of financial statements. With the movement of the opinion paragraph to the start of the auditor's report—rather than at the conclusion of the report where it has previously appeared since the auditor's report was first defined by auditing standards in the 1930s—the opinion paragraph starts by specifying the subject matter of the report, i.e., the financial statements including the footnotes.

Basis for Opinion Paragraph: The second paragraph is entitled the "Basis for Opinion" paragraph. The key items in that paragraph are the specification that the audit was carried out under International Standards on Auditing (or a country specific variant such as "Canadian Auditing Standards") and an assertion that the auditor is independent in accordance with local requirements by naming the source of those requirements. If no independence requirements exist in national law, securities regulation, or any other source then the auditor should refer to the independence requirements found in the International Ethics Standards Board Code of Ethics for Professional Accountants. The next section discusses in detail the types of opinions an auditor can render and their effects on the audit report contexts.

Explanatory Paragraph or Emphasis of Matter Paragraph: There are a number of circumstances or conditions when the auditor wishes to emphasize a matter that is "fundamental" to the reader's understanding of the financial statements while also satisfied with the overall fairness of the financial statements. Typically, the auditor will then depart from the standard unqualified report by adding a paragraph just after the Basis for Opinion section of the auditor's report. This section of the auditor's report is entitled "Emphasis of Matter" and is used to describe the reasons for the departure from the standard unqualified report. Such a paragraph will refer to a specific note in the financial statements that presents relevant facts that the reader needs to be aware of to fully understand the financial statements—a matter that the reader might easily overlook. The auditor does not add any additional commentary to the disclosure but refers the reader to the disclosure. Further, the auditor reminds the reader that this reference does not change the auditor's opinion about the financial statements.

AUTHORITATIVE GUIDANCE & STANDARDS

This section covers audit reports over financial statements for GAAS Audits prepared under IAASB standards (ISA 706 [Revised] **Emphasis of Matter Paragraphs and Other Matter Paragraphs in The Independent Auditor's Report** *and ISA 570 [Revised]* **Going Concern***).*

Examples of the Emphasis of a Matter: An auditor will occasionally wish to emphasize certain facts or conditions that may influence how a reader interprets the financial statements. The auditor might decide to emphasize that the company had significant related party transactions or that the prior year's financial statements were audited by another public accounting firm. As noted, the auditor may emphasize such a matter by adding an explanatory paragraph to the audit report. Another common matter that might be emphasized involves significant litigation. These would be called either "Emphasis of Matters" or "Other Matters" and be found in the section after the "Basis for Opinion[(i)]."

1. **Example 1—Consistency Exception:** Financial statements typically are presented on a comparative basis. For example, in most countries, public companies must present the prior-year balance sheet and income statements, and statements of retained earnings and cash flows. Sometimes a company will change the accounting policies they use for specific types of transactions, e.g., method of depreciation. Accordingly, the auditor will insert an emphasis of matter paragraph that refers the readers to the footnote that describes the effects of changing the accounting policies year over year. Two common consistency exceptions are (1) changes involving GAAP that do not require restatements of prior year financial statements, and (2) corrections of errors in prior year financial statements[(ii)].

2. **Example 2—Auditor Agrees with GAAP Departure:** In extremely rare cases, management of an organization might decide that following GAAP will mislead investors. Generally, an auditor will require the client to make adjustments to ensure conformance to GAAP or change the opinion in the

auditor's report. However, to ensure that auditors remember that the main purpose of GAAP is to provide information that is reliable and relevant to users, auditing standards allow for deviations from GAAP in situations in which auditors agree with management that the strict application of GAAP would mislead users. In such cases, the auditor's report must contain an emphasis of matter paragraph referring to the footnote that describes the departure from GAAP and noting that this departure does not affect the unqualified opinion.

Going Concern Emphasis of Matter: If the auditor has concluded that there exists substantial doubt about a client's ability to survive as a going concern for at least the next year, and the client has clearly disclosed these circumstances in the financial statements, the auditor should issue an unqualified report with an emphasis of matter paragraph. Because of the importance of drawing this matter to the reader's attention, the section highlighting this material uncertainty is labeled "Material Uncertainty Related to Going Concern" instead of the usual "Emphasis of Matter" section heading. Again, the facts related to the uncertainty should be presented in a note to the financial statements that is identified in the auditor's report. No further explanation is needed from the auditor. An illustration of a report modified for a going concern is presented in Box 15.6 "Auditor's Report Modified for Going Concern Issue for a GAAS Audit—Changes Required Only." An auditor should not use conditional language that might undermine the communication of the material uncertainty but should make it clear that the auditor is not qualifying his or her opinion.

The issues related to the auditor's assessment of the going concern assumption have led to substantial additional disclosures in the audit opinion even if there is no need for an emphasis of matter about a material uncertainty. In Box 15.5 "Standard (Unqualified) Auditor's Report for a GAAS Audit" (page 555) we highlight the sentences that refer to both management's responsibility to consider whether the entity is a going concern and the auditor's responsibility for evaluating that assessment.

BOX 15.6   AUDITOR'S REPORT MODIFIED FOR GOING CONCERN ISSUE FOR A GAAS AUDIT— CHANGES REQUIRED ONLY

Paragraph would be inserted after the **Basis for Opinion** Section.

Materiality Uncertainty Related to Going Concern

We draw attention to Note X in the financial statements which indicates that the Company incurred a net loss of ZZZ during the year ended December 31, 20X9 and, as of that date, the Company's current liabilities exceeded its total assets by ZZZ. These conditions, along with other matters as set forth in Note X, indicate the existence of a material uncertainty which may cast significant doubt about the Company's ability to continue as a going concern. Our opinion is not modified in respect of this matter.

* Adapted from ISA 705 Illustration 1 (all else as in an unqualified report).

Key Audit Matters Reporting in Public Companies: The "Key Audit Matters" section of the auditor's report is a new reporting responsibility for the auditor that commenced for public company (otherwise known as "listed companies") audit reports for fiscal years ending on or after December 15, 2016.[3] Key audit matters are a subset of the most significant issues that the auditor has reported to the Audit Committee as part of the communication with those charged with governance during the current year's audit. This is a unique requirement that only applies to audits of public companies and other entities that meet local requirements to be a "public interest entity" (PIE, e.g., financial institutions). The "Key Audit Matters" section of the report will usually be placed after the Opinion, Basis for Opinion, and Emphasis of Matters section of the report. These matters are not carried over from year to year but rather assessed anew each year. Details about key audit matters and their disclosures are found in a subsequent section of this chapter.

Other information: As a result of the fiscal crisis of 2007–09, auditing standard setters and regulators came under increasing pressure to require auditors to communicate their knowledge about the affairs of the client in more detail. Key audit matters is one response that applies primarily to public companies. A second response by standard setters was to require all auditors whose clients prepare documents that are similar to annual reports of public companies to read those reports to ensure that this other information is not misleading or inaccurate. This requirement includes considering whether the other information obscures or otherwise omits items that are necessary for the proper understanding and interpretation of the matters included in the other information. Note that this requirement is not limited to the information contained in the audited finanical statements. In particular, the auditor reads the annual report to:

- Ensure the other information does not contain any statements that were materially inconsistent with information contained in the audited finanical statements. For a matter to be considered materially inconsistent it must raise doubts about the audit conclusions, the evidence relied on by the auditor to research those conclusions, and the form of the auditor's opinion.

- Consider whether there are material misstatements of facts, i.e., statements that are factually inaccurate to the extent that the creditability of the document containing the audited finanical statements is called into question.

- Evaluate other information in light of the knowledge that the auditor has gained during the audit. The auditor needs to consider whether the other information in the annual report is materially inconsistent with the information that the auditor has gained about the business, its internal controls, its governance structure or any other matters covered by international auditing standards.

AUTHORITATIVE GUIDANCE & STANDARDS

This section covers audit reports over financial statements for GAAS Audits prepared under IAASB standards (ISA 720 [Revised] **The Auditor's Responsibilities Relating to Other Information**).

There is no requirement on the auditor to provide assurance on the other information in the annual reports other than what is needed to carry out the above three tasks. However, the auditor is responsible for publicly reporting on the procedures the auditor carried out on the other information contained in an annual report or similar document. See Box 15.5 "Standard (Unqualified) Auditor's Report for a GAAS Audit" (page 555) for the paragraph entitled "Other Information."

If the auditor discovers what appears to be a material inconsistency or a misstatement of fact, the auditor must discuss this with management and those charged with governance. Often at this stage the statements will be clarified in the annual report as requested by the auditor or additional explanations are provided by management that satisfy the auditor's concerns. However, when necessary the auditor carries out additional audit procedures to confirm whether there is in fact a material inconsistency or misstatement of fact. If the annual report is not changed to the auditor's satisfaction, then this results in a reportable condition and appropriate changes are inserted in the last line of the auditor's report on other information. Following that revision, a short added paragraph describing the inconsistency or the misstatement of fact is inserted.

While reading this other information, the auditor needs to be alert for items that appear to be a material inconsistency or misstatement of fact but actually are an indication that the audited finanical statements are misstated or the auditor's knowledge of the client appears to be in error or incomplete. Either of these conditions requires the auditor to consider whether appropriate evidence has been collected and if not, carry out additional procedures. This could result in no changes to the finanical statements, or it could lead to revision of the statements as a result of these procedures. In the latter case, if management will not revise the finanical statements in light of the results of the procedures, the auditor's opinion can be revised, including adding an emphasis of matter (an explanatory) paragraph after the basis for opinion paragraph.

Responsibilities of Management and those Charged with Governance: Box 15.1 "Matters for the Auditor to Communicate with Those Charged with Governance" (page 547) provides the standard wording of an auditor's report with respect to the responsibilities of the client. It points out that management and the board are responsible for financial reporting including the internal control needed to provide error-free financial statements whether the errors come from mistakes or fraud. To a first time reader of an auditor's report, these paragraphs may provide a brief education about the responsibilities of management, the directors and the auditors. However, it is generally recognized that this part of the report, and the following section on the Auditor's Responsibilities, are included mainly as legal "boilerplate" that are common to all auditors' reports (see Chapter 16 for details of the legal reasons this material is included).

Auditor's Responsibilities for the Audit of the Finanical Statements: Box 15.1 "Matters for the Auditor to Communicate with Those Charged with Governance" provides the standard wording on the auditor's report with respect to the auditor's responsibilities for the audit of the financial statements. The first sentence of this section refers to the concept of "reasonable assurance," defined as a "high level of assurance, but is not a guarantee" that fraud or error will be detected when they exist. The next sentence gives explicit reference to the concept of materiality and explains what it means in general terms but does not require the auditor to explicitly disclose the quantitative materiality level used on the audit. Similarly to management responsibilities, this section can be considered to also be "boilerplate" as evidenced by the flexibility an auditor is given as to where this section is reported—late in the report and by the fact that only the first paragraph of this section needs to be included in all reports. After the first paragraph, the remainder of this section of the report can be made available in an Appendix to the Report or where permitted by law or regulation on an appropriate web site that is linked to the report.

Disclosure of the Audit Engagement Partner's Name: In North America and many other parts of the world, historically the audit report was signed in the name of the audit firm without disclosure of the name of the audit engagement partner. Other parts of the world require that the audit partner either sign the report in his or her own name and on behalf of the firm or otherwise disclose the partner responsible for the audit. Under the new audit reporting model discussed in this chapter, the audit engagement partner's name must be disclosed in the text of the report where it is not part of the signature. Hence, starting in 2016, all GAAS Audits of publicly traded companies conducted under ISAs will contain a disclosure of the audit engagement partner's identity unless the exception of grave personal danger to the audit partner is used. Note, at the time of this writing, this requirement is a significant difference between audits conducted in the US and the rest of the world.

Dating of the Auditor's Report: In a GAAS Audit conducted under ISAs, the audit report date is the date that the auditor has obtained sufficient appropriate audit evidence to support the opinion on the financial statements, which includes both of the following:

- All the statements have been prepared and finalized.
- Those with authority to take responsibility for the financial statements (normally the Board of Directors, i.e., those charged with governance, but in some countries where board approval is not required then management) have asserted that they are responsible for the finalized complete set of statements including the footnotes.

Some countries require shareholder approval before the financial statements are made public (e.g., several Nordic countries have such requirements). In these cases, the second requirement is not conditional on approval by shareholders so the auditor can sign the report after the board's approval but prior to the shareholder's approval.

Subsequent Events and Dual Dating: The auditor is generally not responsible for examining events or transactions that occur after the date of the auditor's report. However, in the case where a significant event comes to the attention of the auditor after that date, but before the financial statements are released, the auditor should consider the ramifications of the event in

A common condition that leads to a dual dating scenario occurs when an organization enters into a major acquisition, such as the acquisition of another organization, subsequent to the audit report date but prior to issuing the financial statements. In these cases, the acquirer will include a footnote to the prior financial statements detailing the specifics of the transaction and any information regarding its impact on prior period financial statements. The auditor's report would include an explanatory or "emphasis of matter" paragraph directing users to the footnote and include a second date in the opinion restricted to only the information contained within the footnote.

relation to the financial statements being issued. If there is a significant issue requiring accrual or disclosure, the auditor should obtain evidence in order to evaluate the fairness of the recording and disclosure of the event. However, because such an approach involves audit work after the audit report date, the rest of the audit does not need to be updated. This situation usually leads to **dual dating** of the audit report, meaning that the auditor's report is dated as before with a notation of the later work that was performed on the isolated event. The later date pertains only to the verification of the subsequent event and related accounts and does not apply to any other events, transactions, or accounts. This distinction is usually noted by indicating that the audit report is dated "February 28, 20x9, except for Note X, as to which the date is March 4, 20x9[iii]."

Types of Opinions

In this section we consider the other three types of opinions in much more detail than in Chapter 4 along with the consequent modifications that are made in the basis for opinion paragraphs. In all three cases, note that the title of the opinion paragraph is changed to reflect opinion type change (e.g., from "Opinion" to "Qualified Opinion" and from "Basis for Opinion" to "Basis for Qualified Opinion"). First, we briefly review the unqualified opinion and then the three modifications to it.

1. Standard Unqualified (Unmodified) Auditor's Report in a GAAS Audit

After completing all planned audit work, the auditor should be able to conclude whether material management assertions are reasonable. If all material assertions related to transactions, accounts, disclosures, and the financial statements as a whole have been evaluated, the auditor can conclude that the financial statements are fairly presented. If any significant management assertion is not reasonable such that a material misstatement has been identified, the auditor cannot conclude that the financial statements are fairly presented. In either case, the auditor issues a formal report stating the nature of his or her conclusions. The auditing standards for auditor's reports are very specific and depend on national and international regulations.

AUTHORITATIVE GUIDANCE & STANDARDS

This section covers audit reports over financial statements for GAAS Audits prepared under IAASB standards (ISA 700 [Revised] **Forming an Opinion and Reporting on Financial Statements***).*

If the auditor concludes that the financial statements are fairly presented (or the alternative that is permitted by international, i.e., "true and fair") the auditor issues a **standard unqualified (or unmodified) report**. Box 15.5 "Standard (Unqualified) Auditor's Report for a GAAS Audit" (page 555) provides an example of the full ***standard unqualified (or unmodified) report***. This format is also the basis for all forms of the auditor's reports that contain modifications that might occur in conjunction with an otherwise unqualified opinion. It is also the basis for reports on public companies where additional content may be required such as a list of Key Audit Matters (to be discussed). Hence, the key term in the opinion paragraph is "present fairly." The criteria used for reaching the conclusion that the financial statements are fairly presented are based on generally accepted accounting principles (FASB, IFRS or, in some countries, national standards).

2. Qualified (Modified) Opinion

AUTHORITATIVE GUIDANCE & STANDARDS

This section covers audit reports over financial statements for GAAS Audits prepared under IAASB (ISA 705 [Revised] **Modifications to the Opinion in The Independent Auditor's Report***).*

A qualified opinion is issued when the auditor believes that the financial statements are mostly, but not completely, fairly presented. This can occur when there are scope limitations affecting the availability of evidence or isolated violations of GAAP (e.g., a departure from GAAP, inadequate disclosure). Items that could justify a qualified opinion include:

- **Scope limitation:** A scope limitation occurs when the auditor is unable to obtain sufficient, appropriate evidence on which to base an opinion. Scope limitations may be caused by the circumstances of the audit, such as an inability to observe inventory at year end or when there is inadequate evidence available to support accounting estimates involving future uncertainties. Other scope limitations may be client-imposed, such as when the client forbids communications with some customers about its receivable balance. An illustration of the changes that the auditor would make for a qualified opinion arising from a scope limitation are presented in Box 15.7 "Auditor's Report Qualified for Scope Limitation in a GAAS Audit—Changed Sections Only."

BOX 15.7   AUDITOR'S REPORT QUALIFIED FOR SCOPE LIMITATION IN A GAAS AUDIT—CHANGED SECTIONS ONLY*

Qualified Opinion

We have audited the financial statements of ABC Company (the Company), which comprise the statement of financial position as at December 31, 20X1, and the statement of comprehensive income, statement of changes in equity and statement of cash flows for the year then ended, and notes to the financial statements, including a summary of significant accounting policies.

In our opinion, except for the possible effects of the matter described in the Basis for Qualified Opinion section of our report, the financial statements present fairly, in all material respects, (or "give a true and fair view of") the financial position of ABC Company as at December 31, 20X1, and of its financial performance and its cash flows for the year then ended in accordance with International Financial Reporting Standards.

Basis for Qualified Opinion

ABC Company's investment in XYZ Company, a foreign associate acquired during the year and accounted for by the equity method, is carried at xxx on the balance sheet as at December 31, 20X1, and ABC's share of XYZ's net income of xxx is included in ABC's income for the year then ended. We were unable to obtain sufficient appropriate audit evidence about the carrying amount of ABC's investment in XYZ as at December 31, 20X1 and ABC's share of XYZ's net income for the year because we were denied access to the financial information, management, and the auditors of XYZ. Consequently, we were unable to determine whether any adjustments to these amounts were necessary.

We conducted our audit in accordance with International Standards on Auditing (ISAs). Our responsibilities under those standards are further described in the Auditor's Responsibilities for the Audit of the Financial Statements section of our report. We are independent of the Company in accordance with the ethical requirements that are relevant to our audit of the financial statements in [jurisdiction], and we have fulfilled our other ethical responsibilities in accordance with these requirements. We believe that the audit evidence we have obtained is sufficient and appropriate to provide a basis for our qualified opinion.

* Adapted from ISA 705 Illustration 3 (all else as in an unqualified report).

- **Departure from GAAP:** A departure from GAAP occurs when an improper accounting method is used. A departure from GAAP can also occur if a company is using unrealistic estimates. Examples of departures that are significant include failure to capitalize lease obligations, improper capitalization of R&D costs, or inadequate allowance for bad debts. An illustration of the changes that the auditor would make to the auditor's report for a qualified opinion due to a departure from GAAP is presented in Box 15.8 "Auditor's Report Qualified for Departure from GAAP in a GAAS Audit—Changed Sections Only." Note that the auditor should describe the effect of the departure from GAAP in quantitative terms (i.e., the numerical effects on the financial statement accounts) unless it is "impracticable" to do so. Two situations where it may be impractical to quantify a departure from GAAP include: (1) when management has not carried out the necessary computations and they are too complex for an auditor to perform without additional information that is not readily available, or (2) when the explanation of the quantitative effects would require such a lengthy explanation that it would overwhelm the content of the rest of the report.

> ## BOX 15.8   AUDITOR'S REPORT QUALIFIED FOR DEPARTURE FROM GAAP IN A GAAS AUDIT— CHANGED SECTIONS ONLY*
>
> ### Qualified Opinion
>
> *We have audited the financial statements of ABC Company (the Company), which comprise the statement of financial position as at December 31, 20X1, and the statement of comprehensive income, statement of changes in equity and statement of cash flows for the year then ended, and notes to the financial statements, including a summary of significant accounting policies.*
>
> *In our opinion, except for the effects of the matter described in the Basis for Qualified Opinion section of our report, the financial statements present fairly, in all material respects, (or "give a true and fair view of") the financial position of ABC Company as at December 31, 20X1, and of its financial performance and its cash flows for the year then ended in accordance with International Financial Reporting Standards.*
>
> ### Basis for Qualified Opinion
>
> *The company's inventories are carried in the balance sheet at xxx. Management has not stated the inventories at the lower of cost and net realizable value but has stated them solely at cost, which constitutes a departure from International Financial Reporting Standards. The company's records indicate that, had management stated the inventories at the lower of cost and net realizable value, an amount of xxx would have been required to write the inventories down to their net realizable value. Accordingly, cost of sales would have been increased by xxx, and income tax, net income, and shareholders' equity would have been reduced by xxx, xxx and xxx, respectively.*
>
> *We conducted our audit in accordance with International Standards on Auditing (ISAs). Our responsibilities under those standards are further described in the Auditor's Responsibilities for the Audit of the Financial Statements section of our report. We are independent of the Company in accordance with the ethical requirements that are relevant to our audit of the financial statements in [jurisdiction], and we have fulfilled our other ethical responsibilities in accordance with these requirements. We believe that the audit evidence we have obtained is sufficient and appropriate to provide a basis for our qualified opinion.*
>
> ** Adapted from ISA 705 Illustration 1 (all else as in an unqualified report).*

- **Inadequate disclosure:** Inadequate disclosure is another form of departure from GAAP in that the financial statements do not include all information required by appropriate authoritative accounting standards, including information about future uncertainties that should be reported in the financial statements. The auditor's report in these situations is similar to that used for other departures from GAAP. The missing information should be provided by the auditor in the explanatory paragraph if it is reasonable to do so.

AUTHORITATIVE GUIDANCE & STANDARDS

The IAASB recently completed a set of amendments to ten standards including ISA 700 and specifically created a new standard on key audit matters, ISA 701. These changes, individually and collectively, emphasize that the auditor's requirement to ensure proper presentation and disclosures in the financial statements is actively considered at every stage of the audit—from entering the engagement through to the finalization of the auditor's report. Hence, while the auditor has always examined management's assertions related to presentation and disclosure, the new requirements emphasize the need for complete and understandable disclosures as part of the auditor's responsibility in evaluating the fairness of the financial statements.

In all three situations, the condition creating the problem must be sufficiently narrow and constrained so that most of the information in the financial statements is fairly presented; that is, the problem can be isolated among a few accounts in the financial statements and does not have a pervasive impact. For this purpose, "pervasive effects on the financial statements" can be thought of as those that:

(i) *Are not confined to specific elements, accounts or items of the financial statements;*

(ii) *If so confined, represent or could represent a substantial proportion of the financial statements; or*

(iii) *In relation to disclosures, are fundamental to users' understanding of the financial statements.*

ISA 705.5a

Each of the conditions discussed above has a more extreme counterpart if the conditions causing the problem are pervasive to the financial statements and hence should receive one of the remaining two audit opinions.

3. Adverse Opinions

When the auditor concludes that the financial statements are pervasively misstated, an adverse report should be issued. This form of report might be used when the company is using the cash basis of accounting or uses other non-GAAP accounting methods that have an impact on most of the accounts in the financial statements. An example of the changes needed for an adverse auditor's report is presented in Box 15.9 "Auditor's Adverse Report in a GAAS Audit—Changed Sections Only." The type of opinion, "*Adverse Opinion,*" appears in the italicized heading before the paragraph containing the opinion. The opinion paragraph makes an assertive declaration that the financial statements are *not* fairly presented. Although rarely used by auditors, the possibility of issuing an adverse report represents one of the auditor's strongest tools for encouraging management to prepare fair financial statements in accordance with generally accepted accounting principles.

BOX 15.9   AUDITOR'S ADVERSE REPORT IN A GAAS AUDIT—CHANGED SECTIONS ONLY*

Adverse Opinion

We have audited the consolidated financial statements of ABC Company (the Company), which comprise the consolidated statement of financial position as at December 31, 20X1, and the consolidated statement of comprehensive income, consolidated statement of changes in equity and consolidated statement of cash flows for the year then ended, and notes to the consolidated financial statements, including a summary of significant accounting policies.

In our opinion, because of the significance of the matter discussed in the Basis for Adverse Opinion section of our report, the consolidated financial statements do not present fairly (or "do not give a true and fair view of") the financial position of ABC Company and its subsidiaries as at December 31, 20X1, and of their financial performance and cash flows for the year then ended in accordance with International Financial Reporting Standards.

Basis for Adverse Opinion

As explained in Note X, the company has not consolidated the financial statements of subsidiary XYZ Company it acquired during 20X1 because it has not yet been able to ascertain the fair values of certain of the subsidiary's material assets and liabilities at the acquisition date. This investment is therefore accounted for on a cost basis. Under International Financial Reporting Standards, the subsidiary should have been consolidated because it is controlled by the company. Had XYZ been consolidated, many elements in the accompanying financial statements would have been materially affected. The effects on the financial statements of the failure to consolidate have not been determined.

We conducted our audit in accordance with International Standards on Auditing (ISAs). Our responsibilities under those standards are further described in the Auditor's Responsibilities for the Audit of the Financial Statements section of our report. We are independent of the Company in accordance with the ethical requirements that are relevant to our audit of the financial statements in [jurisdiction], and we have fulfilled our other ethical responsibilities in accordance with these requirements. We believe that the audit evidence we have obtained is sufficient and appropriate to provide a basis for our adverse opinion.

* Adapted from ISA 705 Illustration 2 (all else as in an unqualified report).

---

4. Denial of Opinion

A final type of report that an auditor can issue is a denial of opinion, also referred to as a disclaimer, which is used when the auditor is either unable or unwilling to make any statement about the fairness of the financial statements. The type of opinion, "*Disclaimer of Opinion*," appears in the italicized heading before the paragraph containing the opinion. One situation where a denial is used is when there are pervasive scope limitations that preclude the auditor obtaining adequate evidence about the fairness of the financial statements. A denial or disclaimer report should not be used in lieu of an adverse report. If the auditor has evidence that the financial statements are not presented fairly, he or she cannot avoid expressing that opinion by issuing a disclaimer. An illustration of the changes needed to the auditor's report for a denial of opinion due to a scope limitation is presented in Box 15.10 "Auditor's Denial of Opinion Due to Scope Limitation in a GAAS Audit—Changed Sections Only." This report indicates that the auditor has been engaged to perform an audit but is unable to do so due to lack of evidence. A common situation where this may occur is when the auditor is unable to verify the opening balances of asset accounts. Two scope limitations that generally should result in the auditor disclaiming an opinion occur when the client does not allow the auditor access to minutes of the Board of Directors meetings or when the auditor is unable to receive a confirmation from the client's outside attorney regarding threatened or actual litigation.

BOX 15.10 AUDITOR'S DENIAL OF OPINION DUE TO SCOPE LIMITATION IN A GAAS AUDIT—CHANGED SECTIONS ONLY*

Disclaimer of Opinion

We were engaged to audit the financial statements of ABC Company (the Company), which comprise the statement of financial position as at December 31, 20X1, and the statement of comprehensive income, statement of changes in equity and statement of cash flows for the year then ended, and notes to the financial statements, including a summary of significant accounting policies.

We do not express an opinion on the accompanying financial statements of the Company. Because of the significance of the matter described in the Basis for Disclaimer of Opinion section of our report, we have not been able to obtain sufficient appropriate audit evidence to provide a basis for an audit opinion.

Basis for Disclaimer of Opinion

The Company's investment in its joint venture XYZ (Country X) Company is carried at xxx on the company's statement of financial position, which represents over 90% of the Company's net assets as at December 31, 20X1. We were not allowed access to the management and the auditors of XYZ Company, including XYZ Company's auditors' audit documentation. As a result, we were unable to determine whether any adjustments were necessary in respect of the company's proportional share of XYZ Company's assets that it controls jointly, its proportional share of XYZ Company's liabilities for which it is jointly responsible, its proportional share of XYZ Company's income and expenses for the year, and the elements making up the statement of changes in equity and cash flow statement.

[Note: The paragraph that begins with "We conducted our audit . . .." is **omitted** in this disclaimer of opinion report as the auditors were unable to carry out an audit under International Standards on Auditing.]

* Adapted from ISA 705 Illustration 4 (all else as in an unqualified report).

Key Audit Matters

AUTHORITATIVE GUIDANCE & STANDARDS

This section covers audit reports over financial statements for GAAS Audits prepared under IAASB standards (ISA 701 **Communicating Key Audit Matters in the Independent Auditor's Report**).

As noted above, the disclosure in the auditor's report of **Key Audit Matters** for public companies (and in some countries public interest entities such as large financial institutions) was a response by audit standard setters to increase the usefulness and communication ability of the audit report. However, disclosure of key audit matters does not change the auditor's responsibility to modify the opinion paragraph or add an emphasis of matter where appropriate. By placing Key Audit Matters after the opinion and the basis for opinion paragraphs the intent is to demonstrate that the material is supplemental to the audit opinion itself. To emphasize the importance of the opinion, the auditor does not report any Key Audit Matters when the auditor denies an opinion or arrives at an adverse opinion. When there are reportable matters about "Other information" that section is reported prior to Key Audit Matters as it is likely matters reported in that paragraph would highlight important inconsistencies that could affect readers' interpretation of the financial statements.

Three general types of issues that would be communicated to the Audit Committee (see Box 15.1 "Matters for the Auditor to Communicate with Those Charged with Governance" for a comprehensive list of such matters) have been identified as likely Key Audit Matters that would occur in many audits:

- Areas assessed to have high risk of material misstatement or other significant risks (see Chapters 6 and 7).

- Significant auditor judgments relating to the financial statements, including accounting estimates that have been identified as having high estimation uncertainty (see Chapter 9).

- The effects on the audit of significant events or transactions that occurred during the period (see Chapters 11 to 14).

While the matters communicated to the Audit Committee provide a starting point for assessing key audit matters to be included in the report, the auditor should only report the most significant items from that set. Significance involves the potential importance of the matter to the audit and the readers of the audit report (whereas materiality refers to the financial statements). Factors affecting significance include the relative effect on the audit (both qualitatively and quantitatively), the nature and effect of the particular accounting subject matter, and the expressed interests of intended users and recipients of the auditor's report. Each Key Audit Matter that is identified should contain:

- A description of the matter including a reference to the related disclosures (if any) in the financial report.

- The auditor's reason as to why this matter was considered one of the most significant in the audit.

- How the auditor addressed the matter in the audit including:
  - o Aspects of the auditor's response that were most relevant to the matter or the assessed risk of material misstatement.
  - o A brief overview of the audit procedures performed.
  - o An indication of the outcome of the auditor's procedures.
  - o Key observations about the matter or risk.

There is a limited exception that could preclude an auditor from reporting an identified key audit matter that would otherwise be reported. If a law or regulation prohibits the disclosure then the auditor will not make the disclosure even if it qualifies as a key audit matter. Following the same logic, there may be areas where a specific law or regulation does not prohibit disclosure but where the adverse consequences of disclosure would outweigh the public benefits of communication (e.g., disclosing details of a criminal investigation or a regulatory action before such an action has been made public). However, if an entity has already disclosed the matter, this exception does not apply. Furthermore, there is a general presumption that key audit matters will be disclosed, and a decision to not do so requires the auditor to document the reasons for not disclosing.

Box 15.11 "Examples of Key Audit Matters Disclosed in an Auditor's Report" provides the introduction to the Key Audit Matters section (Panel A) and two examples from audit reports in the United Kingdom (Panels B and C) where the reporting of key audit matters was first required in 2014. These examples give a sense of the diversity of wording and practice that may evolve in reporting entity specific key audit matters.

BOX 15.11 EXAMPLES OF KEY AUDIT MATTERS DISCLOSED IN AN AUDITOR'S REPORT*

Panel A: Inserted into All Public (or Listed) Company Audit Reports after the Basis for Opinion Paragraph (or if there is one, after an Emphasis of Matter Paragraph)

Key Audit Matters

Key audit matters are those matters that, in our professional judgment, were of most significance in our audit of the financial statements in the current period. These matters were addressed in the context of our audit of the financial statements as a whole, and in forming our opinion thereon, and we do not provide a separate opinion on these matters.

Panel B: Example of a most significant audit matter related to a key event or transaction.
(Extract from the Rolls Royce plc 2013 KPMG Auditor's Report).

Recoverability of intangible assets: *(certification costs and participation fees, development expenditure and recoverable engine costs) and amounts recoverable on contracts primarily in the civil aerospace business*

The risk: *The recovery of these assets depends on a combination of achieving sufficiently profitable business in the future as well as the ability* of customers to pay amounts due under contracts often over a long period of time. Assets relating to a particular engine programme are more prone to the risk of impairment in the early years of a programme as the engine's market position is established. In addition, the pricing of business with launch customers makes assets relating to these engines more prone to the risk of impairment.

Our response: *We tested the controls designed and applied by the Group to provide assurance that the assumptions are regularly updated, that changes are monitored, scrutinised and approved by appropriate personnel and that the final assumptions used in impairment testing have been appropriately approved. We challenged the appropriateness of the key assumptions in the impairment test (including market size, market share, pricing, engine and aftermarket unit costs, individual programme assumptions, price and cost escalation, discount rate and exchange rates) focusing particularly on those assets with a higher risk of impairment (those relating to the Trent 900 programme and launch customers on the Trent 900 and 1000 programmes). Our challenge was based on our assessment of the historical accuracy of the Group's estimates in previous periods, our understanding of the commercial prospects of key engine programmes, identification and analysis of changes in assumptions from prior periods and an assessment of the consistency of assumptions across programmes and customers and comparison of assumptions with publicly available data where this was available. We considered the appropriateness of the related disclosures in note 9 to the financial statements.*

Our findings: *Our testing did not identify any deviation in the operation of controls which would have required us to amend the nature or scope of our planned detailed test work. We found that the assumptions and resulting estimates were balanced and that the disclosures in note 9 appropriately describe the inherent degree of subjectivity in the estimates and the potential impact on future periods of revisions to these estimates. We found no errors in calculations.*

Panel C: Example of area where risk of material misstatement is high (Extract from J D Weatherspoon's plc 2014 PwC Auditor's Report),

Area of focus: Impairment of property, plant and equipment

The Company has a large portfolio of pubs with a net book value of £1.1 billion. Given the size of the amounts capitalised and the risk attendant with any sizeable retail business that some units may prove to be unprofitable, we focused on the assessment made by management of any impairment of property, plant and equipment required at an individual pub level.

Our response:

We assessed management's impairment paper and underlying analysis and challenged the assumptions adopted by management in performing its review. These included discount rates and individual pub profitability forecasts. We tested the profitability forecast on an individual pub basis and focused our detailed work on those pubs which had either previously been impaired or where anticipated future cash flows suggested that a potential impairment may be required. We used our own specialized knowledge in this area and external market data to assess the appropriateness of the discount rate used.

We tested management's budgeting accuracy in respect of individual pub budgeted profit for the 2014 year end for evidence of the reliability of the Company's budgeting process.

We tested, with reference to the entire pub estate, that all pubs which initial assessments identified as potentially not generating sufficient cash to cover the capital base, were subject to more detailed scrutiny.

We discussed the action plans in place and evaluated the reasonableness of those plans, where possible, for underperforming pubs where no impairment had been booked. We also tested whether the required pub profitability improvement had ever been attained by the relevant pub historically.

In instances where pubs had been sold, or surrender premiums agreed, we agreed this back to third-party documentation.

* Source the Auditor's Report made public by each company identified above.

Audit Reporting in an Integrated Audit

AUTHORITATIVE GUIDANCE & STANDARDS

This section covers Integrated Audit reports over financial statements and effectiveness of internal control over financial reporting that are covered in AS 2201, AS 3101 (formerly AU 508) **Reports on Audited Financial Statements,** *and AS 3110 (formerly AU 530)* **Dating the Independent Auditor's Report.** *As this text is going to print, the PCAOB has proposed changes that would converge the format of their financial statement auditor's report to one that resembles the IAASB's GAAS Audit Report. An on-line appendix will be made available if the PCAOB's revised proposals are adopted (see section entitled Future Changes to the Integrated Audit Report at the end of this chapter).*

Most of the issues and options discussed regarding audit reports in a GAAS Audit apply to public companies registered with the SEC in the US, i.e., whether the auditor can issue an unqualified auditor's report that the financial statements are fairly presented. However, the form of that report is quite different from the GAAS audit report discussed above. In addition, the auditor also issues a report related to effectiveness of internal control over financial reporting (ICOFR) at year end. For most clients, audit firms combine the report on internal control over financial reporting with the report on the financial statements as is illustrated in Box 15.2 "Report Expressing an Unqualified Opinion on the Effectiveness of Internal Control over Financial Reporting and an Unqualified Opinion on the Financial Statements in an Integrated Audit." There are ten parts to the standard unqualified Integrated

Audit report used in the US (note, the headings below are not permitted in an Integrated Audit report and are provided for illustrative purposes only):

1. *Title:* Includes the word independent and registered with the PCAOB.

2. *Addressee:* The addressee is the shareholders or the Board of Directors.

3. *Introductory paragraph:* The introductory paragraph specifies the assertions that were examined (i.e., the financial statements) and the relative responsibilities of the auditor and management. An identification of the financial statements under audit as well as the internal controls over financial reporting in addition to referencing management's report on internal control. Also a statement that management is responsible for maintaining, assessing, and reporting on the effectiveness of internal control over financial reporting.

4. *Scope paragraph:* The scope paragraph provides a brief description of what the auditor has done, including the type of assurance provided and limitations associated with the audit. It also describes the extent of the audit over both the financial statements and internal control over financial reporting.

5. *Definition paragraph:* A paragraph that defines internal control over financial reporting and the auditor's responsibilities in the audit of internal control effectiveness.

6. *Inherent limitations paragraph:* A paragraph stating that, because of inherent limitations, internal control over financial reporting may not prevent or detect misstatements and that projections of any evaluation of effectiveness to future periods are subject to the risk that controls may become inadequate because of changes in conditions, or that the degree of compliance with the policies or procedures may deteriorate.

7. *Opinion paragraph:* The auditor's opinion on whether the company maintained, in all material respects, effective internal control over financial reporting as of the specified date based on the control criteria and the fairness of the financial statements in accordance with generally accepted accounting principles.

8. *Signature:* The manual or printed signature of the auditor's firm.

9. *Location:* The city and state (or city and country, in the case of non-US auditors) from which the auditor's report has been issued.

10. *Date:* The date of the report is the date on which the auditor has sufficient appropriate audit evidence on which to base the opinion, usually the end of "fieldwork" when the auditor has competed all substantive testing. This is normally at an earlier date than would be used for a GAAS Audit since it does not require approval of the financial statements by those charged with governance. This difference in dating will affect the time period for subsequent events and the period that is subject to events that are after the date of the report but before the public release of the report.

Modifications to the Standard Unqualified Integrated Audit Report: Box 15.13 "Auditor's Report Modifications for Integrated Audits—Changes To Reports Only" illustrates the same set of modifications and qualifications discussed with regard to a GAAS Audit but worded to be consistent with

> **BOX 15.12 REPORT EXPRESSING AN UNQUALIFIED OPINION ON THE EFFECTIVENESS OF INTERNAL CONTROL OVER FINANCIAL REPORTING AND AN UNQUALIFIED OPINION ON THE FINANCIAL STATEMENTS IN AN INTEGRATED AUDIT**

Report of Independent Registered Public Accounting Firm

{Introductory paragraph}*

We have audited the accompanying balance sheets of W Company as of December 31, 20X8 and 20X7, and the related statements of income, stockholders' equity and comprehensive income, and cash flows for each of the years in the three-year period ended December 31, 20X8. We also have audited W Company's internal control over financial reporting as of December 31, 20X8, based on criteria established in Internal Control – Integrated Framework issued by the Committee of Sponsoring Organizations of the Treadway Commission (COSO). W Company's management is responsible for these financial statements, for maintaining effective internal control over financial reporting, and for its assessment of the effectiveness of internal control over financial reporting, included in the accompanying [title of management's report]. Our responsibility is to express an opinion on these financial statements and an opinion on the company's internal control over financial reporting based on our audits.

{Scope paragraph}

We conducted our audits in accordance with the standards of the Public Company Accounting Oversight Board (United States). Those standards require that we plan and perform the audits to obtain reasonable assurance about whether the financial statements are free of material misstatement and whether effective internal control over financial reporting was maintained in all material respects. Our audits of the financial statements included examining, on a test basis, evidence supporting the amounts and disclosures in the financial statements, assessing the accounting principles used and significant estimates made by management, and evaluating the overall financial statement presentation. Our audit of internal control over financial reporting included obtaining an understanding of internal control over financial reporting, assessing the risk that a material weakness exists, and testing and evaluating the design and operating effectiveness of internal control based on the assessed risk. Our audits also included performing such other procedures as we considered necessary in the circumstances. We believe that our audits provide a reasonable basis for our opinions.

{Definition paragraph}

A company's internal control over financial reporting is a process designed to provide reasonable assurance regarding the reliability of financial reporting and the preparation of financial statements for external purposes in accordance with generally accepted accounting principles. A company's internal control over financial reporting includes those policies and procedures that (1) pertain to the maintenance of records that, in reasonable detail, accurately and fairly reflect the transactions and dispositions of the assets of the company; (2) provide reasonable assurance that transactions are recorded as necessary to permit preparation of financial statements in accordance with generally accepted accounting principles, and that receipts and expenditures of the company are being made only in accordance with authorizations of management and directors of the company; and (3) provide reasonable assurance regarding prevention or timely detection of unauthorized acquisition, use, or disposition of the company's assets that could have a material effect on the financial statements.

{Inherent limitations paragraph}

Because of its inherent limitations, internal control over financial reporting may not prevent or detect misstatements. Also, projections of any evaluation of effectiveness to future periods are subject to the risk that controls may become inadequate because of changes in conditions, or that the degree of compliance with the policies or procedures may deteriorate.

{Opinion paragraph}

In our opinion, the financial statements referred to above present fairly, in all material respects, the financial position of W Company as of December 31, 20X8 and 20X7, and the results of its operations and its cash flows for each of the years in the three-year period ended December 31, 20X8 in conformity with accounting principles generally accepted in the United States of America. Also in our opinion, W Company maintained, in all material respects, effective internal control over financial reporting as of December 31, 20X8, based on criteria established in Internal Control – Integrated Framework issued by the Committee of Sponsoring Organizations of the Treadway Commission (COSO).

[Signature]

[City and State or Country]

[Date]

* Headings in {italics} are for illustrative purposes only and are not allowed in the actual report.

---

the format of the US's Integrated Audit report. Panels A to D illustrate the changes to the auditor's report due to a scope limitation and departures from GAAP, followed by examples of changes to the auditor report for an adverse opinion due GAAP departures and a denial of opinion due to scope limitations. In addition, Box 15.14 "Auditor's Report Modified For Going Concern Issue Integrated Audit—Changes Required Only" illustrates the use of the emphasis of matter paragraph for the Integrated Audit.

> ### BOX 15.13   AUDITOR'S REPORT MODIFICATIONS FOR INTEGRATED AUDITS—CHANGES TO REPORTS ONLY

Panel A: Auditor's Report Qualified for Scope Limitation

Changes to report paragraph or insertion of added paragraphs

Paragraph

Scope	Except as discussed in the following paragraph, *we conducted our audit in accordance with generally accepted auditing standards … (continues with standard wording)*
Explanatory	We were unable to obtain audited financial statements supporting the Company's investment in a foreign subsidiary, the carrying value of which was stated at $1,000,000 and $1,200,000 at December 31, 20x7 and 20x6, respectively, and the equity in earnings of which was $400,000 and $200,000 which is included in the net income for 20x7 and 20x6, respectively, as described in Note X to the financial statements; nor were we able to satisfy ourselves as to the carrying value of the investment in the foreign subsidiary or the equity in its earnings by other auditing procedures.
Opinion	*In our opinion,* except for the effects of such adjustments, if any, as might have been determined to be necessary had we been able to examine evidence regarding the investment and earnings related to the foreign subsidiary discussed in the preceding paragraph. … *(continues with unqualified opinion wording)*

Panel B: Auditor's Report Qualified for Departure from GAAP

Explanatory	The Company has excluded certain lease obligations from property and debt in the accompanying financial statements that, in our opinion, should be capitalized in order to conform to generally accepted accounting principles. If these lease obligations were capitalized, property would be increased by $3,000,000 and $3,500,000, long-term debt would be increased by $3,400,000 and $3,950,000 and retained earnings would be decreased by $400,000 and $450,000 as of December 31, 20x7 and 20x6, respectively. Additionally, net income would be increased (decreased) by $400,000 and ($50,000), and earnings per share would be increased (decreased) by $0.40 and ($0.05) for the years ended December 31, 20x7 and 20x6, respectively.
Opinion	*In our* opinion, except for the effects of not capitalizing certain lease obligations as discussed in the preceding paragraph. … *(continues with unqualified opinion wording)*

Panel C: Auditor's Adverse Report

Explanatory   As discussed in Note X of the financial statements, the Company reports its financial status and results of operations on a modified cash basis. Further, the company does not capitalize most assets with long lives and, as a result, does not compute depreciation on such assets. Nor does the company accrue liabilities that may have been incurred as of year-end. Generally accepted accounting principles require that financial statements be prepared on an accrual basis with capitalization and depreciation of long-lived assets and timely accrual of incurred liabilities. Due to the pervasive nature of these violations of generally accepted accounting principles, we are unable to assess the effect of adjustments that would be needed to restate the Company's financial position and the results of operations to conform to generally accepted accounting principles.

Opinion   *In our opinion,* because of the effects of the matters discussed in the preceding paragraph, *the financial statements referred to above* **do not** *present fairly, in conformity with generally accepted accounting principles, the financial position of ABC Company as of December 31, 20x7 and 20x6, or the results of operations or its cash flows for the years then ended.*

Panel D: Auditor's Denial of Opinion Due to Scope Limitation

Intro   *We were engaged to audit the accompanying balance sheets of ABC Company, Inc. as of December 31, 20x7 and 20x6, and the related statements of income, retained earnings and cash flows for the years then ended. These financial statements are the responsibility of the Company's management.*

Explanatory   *The Company did not make a count of its physical inventory and we were not able to apply other auditing procedures to satisfy ourselves as to inventory quantities and costs. As a result, we are unable to determine whether adjustments were required in respect of recorded or unrecorded assets, recorded or unrecorded liabilities and the components making up the statements of income, retained earnings, and cash flows.*

Opinion   *In view of the possible material effects on the financial statements of the matters described in the preceding paragraph, I am unable to express an opinion whether these financial statements are presented fairly in accordance with generally accepted accounting principles.*

> **BOX 15.14 AUDITOR'S REPORT MODIFIED FOR GOING CONCERN ISSUE INTEGRATED AUDIT— CHANGES REQUIRED ONLY**
>
> {To be inserted after the opinion paragraph}
>
> *Without qualifying our opinion, we draw attention to Note X in the financial statements which indicates that the Company incurred a net loss of ZZZ during the year ended December 31, 20X9 and, as of that date, the Company's current liabilities exceeded its total assets by ZZZ. These conditions, along with other matters as set forth in Note X, indicate the existence of a material uncertainty which may cast significant doubt about the Company's ability to continue as a going concern.*
>
> ** Items in {italics} provide report placement directions only. They would not appear in the actual report.*

In an Integrated Audit, if a material weakness is discovered, the auditor must issue an adverse opinion on the effectiveness of ICOFR, i.e., there is no provision for a "qualified" opinion on the effectiveness of ICOFR. A ***material weakness*** is "a deficiency, or a combination of deficiencies, in internal control over financial reporting, such that there is a reasonable possibility that a material misstatement of the company's annual or interim financial statements will not be prevented or detected on a timely basis."

In the case of an insurmountable scope limitation that affects the evaluation of ICOFR in an Integrated Audit, the auditor should cease his or her audit and issue a disclaimer of opinion on ICOFR effectiveness. If any material weakness has been discovered prior to the cessation of the ICOFR part of the Integrated Audit, then it must be reported as part of the disclaimer. The effects of any opinion on internal control, other than unqualified, must also be disclosed with the audit report on the financial statements.

Box 15.15 "Auditor's Report Modifications in an Integrated Audit Employing Separate Opinions on the Financial Statements with an Adverse Opinion over Effectiveness of Internal Control over Financial Reporting" illustrates the two report format that is allowed by the PCAOB. In this format, the results of the audit of financial statements are reported separately from the adverse opinion on the audit of the effectiveness of internal control over financial reporting. This approach is usually preferred when auditors cannot issue an unqualified opinion on both the financial statements and the effectiveness of ICOFR. Clients prefer to have the auditor give them a combined report when the opinions on the financial statements and ICOFR effectiveness are both unqualified, but prefer two separate opinions when there is an adverse or disclaimer on opinion on ICOFR effectiveness and an unqualified opinion on the financial statements. However, the opinion on the financial statements must refer to the adverse opinion or the disclaimer of opinion over ICOFR effectiveness.

Two questions arise from the preference for separate reports: (1) How can an auditor give an unqualified opinion over the financial statements in light of an adverse opinion or a disclaimer of opinion on ICOFR effectiveness, and (2) why would clients prefer that their auditor issue separate reports

> **BOX 15.15 AUDITOR'S REPORT MODIFICATIONS IN AN INTEGRATED AUDIT EMPLOYING SEPARATE OPINIONS ON THE FINANCIAL STATEMENTS WITH AN ADVERSE OPINION OVER EFFECTIVENESS OF INTERNAL CONTROL OVER FINANCIAL REPORTING**

Panel A: Unqualified Opinion on the Financial Statements

{Introductory paragraph}*

We have audited the accompanying balance sheets of W Company as of December 31, 20x8 and 20x7, and the related statements of income, retained earnings, and cash flows for the years then ended. These financial statements are the responsibility of the Company's management. Our responsibility is to express an opinion on these financial statements based on our audits.

{Scope}

We conducted our audit in accordance with standards promulgated by the Public Company Accounting Oversight Board (United States). Those standards require that we plan and perform the audit to obtain reasonable assurance about whether the financial statements are free of material misstatement. An audit includes examining, on a test basis, evidence supporting the amounts and disclosures in the financial statements. An audit also includes assessing the accounting principles used and significant estimates made by management, as well as evaluating the overall financial statement presentation. We believe that our audits provide a reasonable basis for our opinion.

{Opinion}

In our opinion, the financial statements referred to above present fairly, in all material respects, the financial position of W Company as of December 31, 20x8 and 20x7, and the results of its operations and its cash flows for each of the years in the three-year period ended December 31, 20x8 in conformity with accounting principles generally accepted in the United States of America.

{Separate internal control opinion}

We also have audited, in accordance with the standards of the Public Company Accounting Oversight Board (United States), W Company's internal control over financial reporting as of December 31, 20x8, based on based on criteria established in Internal Control—Integrated Framework issued by the Committee of Sponsoring Organizations of the Treadway Commission (COSO) and our report dated [which should be the same as the date of the report on the financial statements] expressed an adverse opinion on the effectiveness of internal control over financial reporting.

Panel B: Adverse Opinion on Effectiveness of Internal Control over Financial Reporting due to a Material Weakness

{Introductory paragraph}*

We have audited W Company's internal control over financial reporting as of December 31, 20x8, based on criteria established in Internal

Control – Integrated Framework issued by the Committee of Sponsoring Organizations of the Treadway Commission (COSO). W Company's management is responsible for maintaining effective internal control over financial reporting, and for its assessment of the effectiveness of internal control over financial reporting, included in the accompanying [title of management's report]. Our responsibility is to express an opinion on the company's internal control over financial reporting based on our audit.

{Scope paragraph}

We conducted our audit in accordance with the standards of the Public Company Accounting Oversight Board (United States). Those standards require that we plan and perform the audit to obtain reasonable assurance about whether effective internal control over financial reporting was maintained in all material respects. Our audit of internal control over financial reporting included obtaining an understanding of internal control over financial reporting, assessing the risk that a material weakness exists, and testing and evaluating the design and operating effectiveness of internal control based on the assessed risk. Our audits also included performing such other procedures as we considered necessary in the circumstances. We believe that our audit provide a reasonable basis for our opinion.

{Definition paragraph}

A company's internal control over financial reporting is a process designed to provide reasonable assurance regarding the reliability of financial reporting and the preparation of financial statements for external purposes in accordance with generally accepted accounting principles. A company's internal control over financial reporting includes those policies and procedures that (1) pertain to the maintenance of records that, in reasonable detail, accurately and fairly reflect the transactions and dispositions of the assets of the company; (2) provide reasonable assurance that transactions are recorded as necessary to permit preparation of financial statements in accordance with generally accepted accounting principles, and that receipts and expenditures of the company are being made only in accordance with authorizations of management and directors of the company; and (3) provide reasonable assurance regarding prevention or timely detection of unauthorized acquisition, use, or disposition of the company's assets that could have a material effect on the financial statements.

{Inherent limitations paragraph}

Because of its inherent limitations, internal control over financial reporting may not prevent or detect misstatements. Also, projections of any evaluation of effectiveness to future periods are subject to the risk that controls may become inadequate because of changes in conditions, or that the degree of compliance with the policies or procedures may deteriorate.

{Explanatory paragraph}

A material weakness is a control deficiency, or combination of control deficiencies, that results in more than a remote likelihood that a

material misstatement of the annual or interim financial statements
will not be prevented or detected. The following material weakness
has been identified and included in management's assessment.
{Include a description of the material weakness and its effect on the
achievement of the objectives of the control criteria.} *This material*
weakness was considered in determining the nature, timing, and extent
of audit tests applied in our audit of the 20x8 financial statements, and
this report does not affect our report dated {date of report, which should
be the same as the date of this report on internal control} *on those*
financial statements.

{Opinion paragraph}

In our opinion, because of the effect of the material weakness
described above on the achievement of the objectives of the control
criteria, W Company has not maintained effective internal control
over financial reporting as of December 31, 20x8, based on criteria
established in Internal Control—Integrated Framework issued by the
Committee of Sponsoring Organizations of the Treadway Commission
(COSO).

* Headings in {italics} *are for illustrative purposes only and are not allowed in the*
actual report.

---

over the financial statements and effectiveness of ICOFR? In regards to
the first question, the auditor can give an unqualified opinion on the
financial statements despite ineffective internal controls if the auditor can
gain enough evidence through substantive audit procedures to conclude
that there are no material misstatements in the financial statements. In
Chapter 10 we discussed the various possible combinations of audit
approaches in a GAAS Audit that ranged from no reliance on controls
to extensive reliance on internal controls as part of the audit strategy (see
Table 10.6). While often more difficult, time consuming, and potentially
more expensive, the auditor can frequently carry out substantive tests of
balances and transactions so as to arrive at an opinion on the fairness of
the financial statements without relying on controls that are not deemed
to be effect.

In regard to the second question, many companies feel that anything
but an unqualified opinion on both ICOFR effectiveness and the financial
statements is a negative event. Theory in psychology suggests that positive
and negative outcomes occur in close proximity to each other; people
prefer to segregate the good from the bad because people often place
more emphasis on the bad outcome, overshadowing the benefit of the
good outcome. In the context of the audit report, the concern may be that
the negative report on internal control may cause readers of the financial
statements to discount the reliability of the financial statements even though
they, in theory, have been audited to the same exacting standards and level
of sufficient evidence as the financial statements that are associated with
a positive report on internal control. By separating the two opinions when
they have mixed outcomes, readers of the financial statements may be better

able to understand how the financial statements can be fairly presented in spite of the existence of one or more material weaknesses in internal control over financial reporting.

Other Modifications to the Standard Unqualified Integrated Audit Report: There are a handful of other reasons that the standard unqualified Integrated Audit report might be modified that do not lead to an adverse opinion or a disclaimer of opinion. The circumstances under which these might occur should be relatively rare but warrant brief mention:

a. Elements of management's annual report on internal control are incomplete or improperly presented.

b. The auditor decides to refer to the report of other auditors as the basis, in part, for the auditor's own report (see next section).

c. There is other information contained in the management's annual report on internal control over financial reporting that the auditor believes should be clarified.

d. Management's annual certification of internal control effectiveness that is filed with the US Securities and Exchange Commission under the Sarbanes-Oxley Act of 2002 (Section 302) is misstated.

Normally, the auditor and client management would work to resolve these matters rather than for the auditor to have to make a modification to his or her report. Nonetheless, there are exceptional circumstances under which such an accommodation cannot be reached that might lead the auditor to take such a step.

Other Information: The auditor has only very limited responsibilities for other information in an Integrated Audit, unlike the expanded role envisioned in a GAAS Audit. In particular, the auditor is limited to reading the annual reports that are made available to shareholders, and annual reports filed with the US SEC. The auditor is further limited to focusing on the financial information and its material consistency with the information in the audited financial statements. Further, if the auditor comes across what he perceives as a material misstatement of fact, the auditor is required to discuss the matter with the client. Beyond these responsibilities the auditor has no requirement to perform additional procedures to corroborate other information in the document where the audited financial statements appear. Given the limited procedures performed, the auditor does not refer to this reading of other information in the auditor's report unless it is to report on an unresolved material inconsistency as either the basis for an audit qualification or an emphasis of matter.

AUTHORITATIVE GUIDANCE & STANDARDS

The above sub-section covers the auditor's responsibility to read other information that include the audited financial statements AS 2710 (formerly AU 550) **Other Information in Documents Containing Audited Financial Statements.**

Group Audit Reporting Where There Is a Significant Component Auditor

As was noted in Chapter 14, in certain cases audits of large concerns are carried out by multiple audit firms with one audit firm being designated as the group auditor. Many organizations are highly complex and global. As a result, the audit of such an organization may require the use of different audit firms in different locations or countries. A *component auditor* is an auditor who is responsible for the audit of one portion, segment, or location within a much larger organization. The primary auditor who is responsible for the overall audit is referred to as the *group* or *principal auditor*. In a GAAS Audit, unless it is required by law or regulation, there can be no mention of the existence of a component auditor in the audit report. Hence, under international standards there can be no apportionment of responsibility for the audit opinion across multiple auditors. That is, the group auditor must accept full responsibility for signing the group (consolidated) financial statements.

AUTHORITATIVE GUIDANCE & STANDARDS— SIGNIFICANT DIFFERENCE IN IAASB AND PCAOB REQUIREMENTS ALERT

Auditing standards on group audits are found in ISA 600 **Special Considerations—Audits of Group Financial Statements (Including the Work of Component Auditors)** *and PCAOB AS 1205 (formerly AU 543)* **Part of Audit Performed by Other Independent Auditors.** *There are significant differences in reporting responsibilities across the two standards.*

In an Integrated Audit, when one accounting firm uses another firm to conduct part of the audit, there are several options for allocating responsibility among the firms, two of which require that the auditor's report be modified. First, auditors can assume full responsibility for the engagement and make no reference to the component firm in the auditor's report— resulting in a standard unqualified report. This is the *only* option allowed in a GAAS Audit. Second, auditors can choose to share responsibility. In this case, the auditor's report mentions in the introductory opinion that part of the audit was performed by another firm. Then, in the opinion paragraph, the opinion is provided on behalf of both firms. The signature, however, is only provided by the primary accounting firm (and no explicit name of the other firm is contained in the auditor's report). Third, the auditor can accept no responsibility for the work of the other auditor. This scenario often applies when a public accounting firm has not audited prior-year financial statements. In this case, the introductory opinion mentions the part of the audit performed by the other firm and refers users to the report of the other firm. In the opinion paragraph, only the part of the audit for which the primary auditor is taking responsibility is referenced. See Box 15.16 "Division of Responsibility With A Component Auditor—Component Auditor Noted but not Named in an Integrated Audit" for an example of the relevant portions of a shared audit report for an Integrated Audit.

> **BOX 15.16 DIVISION OF RESPONSIBILITY WITH A COMPONENT AUDITOR—COMPONENT AUDITOR NOTED BUT NOT NAMED IN AN INTEGRATED AUDIT**
>
> **Addition at the end of the introductory paragraph***
>
> *We did not audit the financial statements of B Company, a wholly owned subsidiary, which statements reflect total assets of $_____ and $_____ as of December 31, 20X2 and 20X1, respectively, and total revenues of $_____ and $_____ for the years then ended. Those statements were audited by other auditors whose report has been furnished to us, and our opinion, insofar as it relates to the amounts included for B Company, is based solely on the report of the other auditors.*
>
> **Addition at the end of the scope paragraph**
>
> *We believe that our audits and the report of other auditors provide a reasonable basis for our opinion.*
>
> **Change to first line of the opinion paragraph**
>
> *In our opinion,* based on our audits and the report of other auditors, *the consolidated financial statements referred to above present fairly…*
>
> ** Items in {italics} provide report placement directions only. They would not appear in the actual report.*

Discovery of a Misstatement in the Financial Statements after the Auditor's Report and Financial Statements have been Released

The auditor has no responsibility to continue to monitor a client after the date of the auditor's report. However, if information comes to the attention of the auditor that affects the reliability or interpretation of the audited financial statements, the auditor has the responsibility to determine if readers will be adversely affected by reliance on the previously released statements. In doing so, the auditor must answer "yes" to each of the following four conditions:

1. The facts were available at or before the date of the auditor's report (which may differ for a GAAS Audit and an Integrated Audit—see Chapter 14).

2. The facts are based on reliable information.

3. The effect of the facts is material to the financial statements and hence to the auditor's report.

4. Users are still relying on the auditor's report.

> **AUTHORITATIVE GUIDANCE & STANDARDS**
>
> *Auditing standards on the discovery of facts that existed as of the date of the auditor's report but were not know at the time are found in ISA 560* **Subsequent Events** *and PCAOB AS 2905 (formerly AU 561)* **Subsequent Discovery of Facts Existing at the Date of the Auditor's Report.**

If the auditor determines that readers will be adversely affected by this information, the auditor should have management modify the statements as appropriate and publicize the change to readers who may still be using the financial statements. The auditor then issues an updated report consistent with the new information. If management does not comply, the auditor has to take actions necessary to dissociate the audit firm from the financial statements. Further, the auditor would need to seek legal advice as to his or her responsibilities, especially for public companies and when the auditor knows that users are still relying on the audited financial statements.

The only exception to this requirement is if the information is received during the subsequent audit. Because the auditor is in the process of issuing a new report that covers both the subsequent year-end and the year-end containing the misstatement, the auditor can issue a report in the subsequent year based on the corrected financial statements.

Future Changes to the Integrated Audit Report

In 2016, the PCAOB issued a re-proposal of changes to their audit reporting standard AS 3101. This new proposal follows a concepts release in 2011 and an initial proposal in 2013. We will provide updated material on the book's web site should the re-proposal be adopted by the PCAOB in the near term. In summary, what the PCAOB proposes is that:

- The format of the PCAOB audit report would converge towards the format of the IAASB's GAAS Audit report discussed in this chapter in as far as it related to the financial statement audit. However, there could still be substantive wording differences as the PCAOB has not yet dealt with "going concern" issues that the IAASB included in its revised set of standards. Further, some of the language describing the auditor's and management's responsibility will not change under the PCAOB re-proposal.

- The PCAOB proposes to use the term "critical audit matters" instead of "key audit matters" in the IAASB standard. There is substantial similarity between the PCAOB definition and the IAASB's definition.

- Whether potential items that would be identified "critical audit matters" are a smaller set of items than those considered under "key audit matters" is at present not determinable.

Summary and Conclusion

After reviewing all the evidence and carrying out such negotiations with management and those charged with governance as we discussed in Chapter 14, the auditor prepares both internal and external reports about the outcome of the audit. Recent years have seen an expansion, especially in the area of public company audits, of the reporting responsibilities of the audit to both those charged with governance and more notably to the external readers of the report. It was just a few years ago (in 2007) that the unqualified report in a GAAS Audit adopted a four paragraph format that previously had been three paragraphs and, as recently as 1990, was only two paragraphs (see Chapter 15 On-line Appendix for more details about the evolution of the auditor's report). The addition of disclosures about Key Audit Matters to the GAAS Audit report will substantially expand the content of the report. In the US, the Integrated Audit reports—with combined or separate reports on effectiveness of ICOFR and the financial statements—have increased the length of the audit report. However, one downside of these reporting changes has been an increasing inconsistency between the content and structure of the audit report for public companies in the US and the audit report used in the rest of the world. At this time it appears that there is some movement toward convergence but only time will tell the degree of convergence that will eventually result for the GAAS Audit and Integrated Audit reporting models.

Bibliography of Relevant Literature

Auditing Standards

IAASB *International Standards on Auditing (ISA)* No. 260, "Communication with those Charged with Governance."

IAASB *International Standards on Auditing (ISA)* No. 260 (Revised), "Communication with those Charged with Governance."

IAASB *International Standards on Auditing (ISA)* No. 265, "Communicating Deficiencies in Internal Control to those Charged with Governance and Management."

IAASB *International Standards on Auditing (ISA)* No. 560, "Subsequent Events."

IAASB *International Standards on Auditing (ISA)* No. 570 (Revised), "Going Concern."

IAASB *International Standards on Auditing (ISA)* No. 580, "Written Representations."

IAASB *International Standards on Auditing (ISA)* No. 600, "Special Considerations—Audits of Group Financial Statements (Including the Work of Component Auditors)."

IAASB *International Standards on Auditing (ISA)* No. 700, "Forming an Opinion and Reporting on Financial Statements."

IAASB *International Standards on Auditing (ISA)* No. 700 (Revised), "Forming an Opinion and Reporting on Financial Statements."

IAASB *International Standards on Auditing (ISA)* No. 701, "Communicating Key Audit Matters in the Independent Auditor's Report."

IAASB *International Standards on Auditing (ISA)* No. 705, "Modifications to the Opinion in The Independent Auditor's Report."

IAASB *International Standards on Auditing (ISA)* No. 705 (Revised), "Modifications to the Opinion in The Independent Auditor's Report."

IAASB *International Standards on Auditing (ISA)* No. 706, "Emphasis of Matter Paragraphs and Other Matter Paragraphs in The Independent Auditor's Report."

IAASB *International Standards on Auditing (ISA)* No. 706 (Revised), "Emphasis of Matter Paragraphs and Other Matter Paragraphs in The Independent Auditor's Report."

IAASB *International Standards on Auditing (ISA)* No. 720, "The Auditor's Responsibilities Relating to Other Information in Documents Containing Audited Financial Statements."

IAASB *International Standards on Auditing (ISA)* No. 720 (Revised), "The Auditor's Responsibilities Relating to Other Information."

IFAC. International Auditing and Assurance Standards Board (IAASB). 2015. *Handbook of International Quality Control, Audit, Review, Other Assurance, and Related Services Pronouncements.* New York: International Federation of Accountants.

PCAOB *Auditing Standard* 1205 (formerly *Interim Standard* AU Section 543), "Part of Audit Performed by Other Independent Auditors."

PCAOB. *Auditing Standard* 1220 (formerly No. 7), "Engagement Quality Review."

PCAOB. *Auditing Standard* 1301 (formerly No. 16), "Communications with Audit Committees."

PCAOB *Auditing Standard* 1305 (formerly AU 325), "Communications about Control Deficiencies in an Audit of Financial Statements."

PCAOB AS 2201 (formerly No. 5) "An Audit of Internal Control over Financial Reporting that is Integrated with An Audit of Financial Statements."

PCAOB *Auditing Standard* 2415 (formerly AU 341), "The Auditor's Consideration of an Entity's Ability to Continue as a Going Concern."

PCAOB *Auditing Standard* 2710 (formerly AU 550), "Other Information in Documents Containing Audited Financial Statements."

PCAOB *Auditing Standard* 2905 (formerly AU 561), "Subsequent Discovery of Facts Existing at the Date of the Auditor's Report."

PCAOB *Auditing Standard* 3101 (formerly AU 508), "Reports on Audited Financial Statements."

PCAOB *Auditing Standard* 3110 (formerly AU 530), "Dating the Independent Auditor's Report."

Notes

1 Where such discussions do not occur, the auditor needs to consider whether such a failure in governance requires a modification to the auditor's report as scope limitation.

2 The new form of auditor's report is effective for fiscal years ending on or after December 16, 2016 internationally. However, various national standard setters who base their standards on ISAs can set a different date of adoption—normally later. For example, Canada intends to adopt these

standards effective in 2017 with early adoption of CSAs (the Canadian version of ISAs) being permitted. Until then the previous version of ISA 700 and related standards (e.g., 570, 705, 706, and 720) are in effect for that country.

3   See note 1 about differences in date of adoption of this standard by national standard setters. Furthermore, some national standard setters require key audit matters to be reported on a broader set of entities, so-called "public interest entities" (e.g., credit unions, large not for profit or non-governmental entities, etc.) than the ISA requires such reports to be made on.

CHAPTER 16

The Ethical Auditor
Factors Affecting Auditor Decision Making

Outline

Learning Goals for this Chapter

1. To review the basic concepts of ethical reasoning and apply them to the audit setting.

2. To learn about the basic human judgment errors that auditors may commit.

3. To learn how to detect and guard against these judgment errors.

4. To understand the forces on the auditor (practice inspection, peer review, codes of ethics, quality control practices) designed to bolster the auditor in making ethical judgments.

5. To understand the forces (professional, regulatory, civil law, and criminal law) that affect the auditor who does not make ethical judgments.

6. To understand the ramifications for auditors who fail to meet their professional and ethical responsibilities, including judicial and regulatory intervention.

7. To examine and understand the auditor's legal liability with respect to fraud and error.

8. To examine and understand the auditor's defenses when charged with fraud and error.

Introduction

Auditors are professionals

Professionals are people

People make mistakes

Therefore, auditors make mistakes

This compound syllogism reflects a core element of the audit process: It is grounded in the judgment of fallible humans who are subject to errors and mistakes. At its core, auditing is a process of making professional judgments. Auditors, as members of a profession, are expected to serve a role in society that is unique and transcends the individual. What an auditor does, and how he or she behaves as a professional, is generally governed by the ethical and legal precepts of the profession. The role, expectations, and governance of a profession may be based on long-standing custom or may emanate from legal requirements imposed by government. In this chapter, we start by discussing the nature of the professional environment in which an auditor fulfills his or her responsibilities. It is the existence of this professional environment that defines the nature of ethical decision making within the context of the audit.

As noted, auditors can make mistakes. While auditors undergo extensive training and are subject to a high degree of quality control, mistakes can still happen in the audit process. The audit process includes a high degree of formal structure and, increasingly, utilizes sophisticated computer technology to reduce the possibility of auditor error. However, the reality of even the most sophisticated audit technology is that the design and use of any process or system is governed by the judgments of auditors, meaning people. Numerous institutional elements of the audit profession are aimed at improving the judgment and decision making of the auditor. Indeed, one of the principal functions of an audit firm is to implement an audit process that overcomes deficiencies in individual auditor judgment. However, as events of the last few years have shown, audit firms are also subject to forces that undermine the quality of their decisions.

Beyond the audit firm there are other institutions that motivate auditors towards making ethical decisions. These include professional codes of conduct, independence rules, auditing standards, quality control standards, and inspections of audit work. Furthermore, regulatory and legal structures can be used to punish auditors who fail to live up to the precepts of the profession. Figure 16.1 illustrates the interaction of the various forces constraining auditor judgment and decision-making. The purpose of this chapter is to discuss the personal attributes and institutional forces that affect the quality of auditor judgment and decisions.

Auditing as a Profession

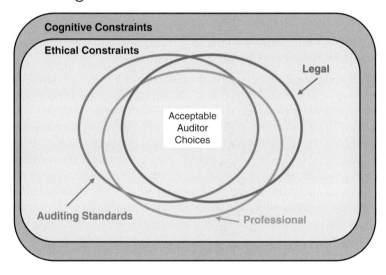

Figure 16.1 Auditor Judgment: Personal and Institutional Constraints on Auditor Choices

Source: Knechel, Issues in Accounting Education, 2000

Accountants and auditors are considered to be members of a **profession**. While the word "profession" has lost some of its meaning in recent years now that everyone from sales people to hair stylists claim to be a professional, the ideal of a being a member of a profession has some very specific consequences. The International Federation of Accountants **Code of Ethics for Professional Accountants** notes the following attributes that are the hallmark of a profession:

6. *A profession is distinguished by certain characteristics including:*

    *   *Mastery of a particular intellectual skill, acquired by training and education;*

    *   *Adherence by its members to a common code of values and conduct … , including maintaining an outlook which is essentially objective; and*

> •   *Acceptance of a duty to society as a whole ….*
>
> 7.   *Members' duty to their profession and to society may at times seem to conflict with their immediate self-interest or their duty of loyalty to their employer.*

The latter point highlights that a competent auditor must also be ethical when making the various judgments that comprise an audit because there may be times when audit decisions conflict with the individual's immediate self-interest. At the heart of ethical decision-making is consideration of others, and it normally reflects considerations broader than strict self-interest. As we noted in Chapter 1, there are various philosophical frameworks for evaluating ethical behavior:

- **Utilitarianism** involves making decisions that will increase the benefits to some while doing no harm to others.
- **Golden Rule** involves making decisions that result in treating others in a manner in which the individual making the decision would like to be treated.
- **Theory of Rights** suggests that the rights of a decision maker and other parties should be equally balanced in making a decision.
- **Theory of Justice** suggests that decisions should treat all stakeholders fairly, impartially, and equitably.
- **Enlightened Self-Interest** involves pursuing long-term self-interests and avoiding a short-term focus that might harm others.

While these views differ in the aspects of ethics they emphasize, all can lead to ethical decisions. One of the key aspects of a profession is to foster a shared ethical code among the members of the profession such that individuals will reach similar decisions when presented with a similar set of facts. Many political commentators argue that such a shared ethical framework is impossible in a diverse multi-cultural and multi-religion society that has moved away from a consensus about universal rights and wrongs to a relativist approach for judging what is "right." An opposing argument for this position is that such diversity underscores the need for an agreed upon ethical framework among those wishing to belong to a profession.

Auditing as an Ethical Judgment Process

Auditing is first and foremost a ***judgment process***. Individual auditors must exercise judgment throughout the audit process, often aided by extensive audit tools and techniques. Some examples of important judgments in the audit process include:

- Evaluating a prospective client or deciding to retain an existing client.
- Establishing materiality.
- Identifying important audit objectives.
- Assessing various types of risk.
- Allocating audit effort between tests of controls and substantive testing.
- Evaluating the effectiveness of controls.

- Evaluating fluctuations in performance indicators.
- Selecting audit procedures.
- Evaluating the competence of evidence.

Ethics and Judgment

A common thread that runs through many of the judgments made by auditors is the acquisition and evaluation of evidence. Much of the activity of an audit focuses on deciding what evidence to obtain, acquiring the evidence, and evaluating the evidence. Auditors may fail to collect appropriate evidence or misinterpret evidence because of a breakdown in the auditor's judgment. This can occur by mistake and may be due to an auditor's cognitive limitations. However, if the auditor makes good decisions about obtaining and interpreting audit evidence, what the auditor does with the evidence enters the realm of ethical reasoning. If an auditor chooses to ignore problems within a client, the auditor is breaching precepts of ethical conduct.

Auditor judgments become ethical in nature when they result in a conflict between the auditor's own self-interest and the auditor's duty to society as a whole. Consider the following situation: An auditor collects compelling evidence that suggests he or she failed to identify a material misstatement in the previous year's financial statements. This oversight may have been a failure in professional analysis due to individual cognitive limitations, e.g., evidence was overlooked or misinterpreted. Now that the auditor is aware of the problem, the auditor's choice of action creates a potential ethical dilemma. Management might point out that revelation of the problem at this time would lead to dismissal of the audit firm, hurt the auditor's career, and possibly trigger lawsuits against the audit firm. Furthermore, management may offer to correct this misstatement in the future if the auditor keeps quiet about the problem. Since no one knows about the problem, the auditor can easily delete the information from the file without his or her colleagues at the audit firm detecting it. What should the auditor do?

As this example indicates, what starts as a typical audit decision involving a series of professional judgments about collecting and interpreting audit evidence can turn into an ethical quandary for the auditor. The "right" action for the auditor to take may be readily apparent but the auditor's choice of action could be influenced by the conflict between the auditor's short-term self-interest and his duty to society[(i)].

Professional Audit Judgment and Ethical Decision Making

Decision-making is a process, whether applied by an auditor to a professional problem or applied by an individual to a personal choice. What all decisions have in common is the need to make a selection from a set of alternatives in order to achieve some desired result. Decisions come in many shapes and forms: "What car should I buy?", "What should I eat for dinner?" and "What audit opinion should I issue?" are all examples of decision problems. **Judgment** is the process by which the individual thinks about the relevant aspects of the decision problem. Errors in judgment often reveal themselves

[(i)]**EXAMPLE**

In the case of Arthur Andersen and Enron, evidence obtained through emails sent among team members suggests that certain personnel at Andersen believed that the Firm should resign from the Enron engagement because of discomfort with accounting policies related to off-balance-sheet special purpose entities (SPEs). However, others in the Firm pointed to the $50 million in annual fees being earned from contracts with Enron, and the potential for the Firm to earn $100 million in annual fees, as justification for retaining the high-risk client.

as erroneous decisions. To the extent that judgment errors can be understood and minimized, decision-making can be improved.

Deliberate decisions follow a sequential process whether the decision context is an audit or purchase of a new car. New alternatives may become available or decision criteria may change as more information becomes available, and it is common to revise judgments several times before making final decisions in an audit. The decision process typically followed when individuals are attempting to decide among multiple alternatives consists of six broad steps:

1 **Define the decision problem:** In an audit, the essential decision is whether financial statements are fairly presented. However, there are a multitude of decisions made during the execution of the audit, the cumulative effect of which will be reflected in the final opinion about the financial statements. Decisions concerning materiality, risk, and evidence are all important to the final opinion and are subject to errors in judgment.

2 **Identify the evaluation criteria:** For a financial statement audit, the evaluation criteria are embodied in GAAP and GAAS. Other decisions may be made based on assessments of materiality, risk, and the competence of evidence. Implicit in the choice of evaluation criteria is the auditor's belief that if one applies these criteria carefully, one will arrive at an ethical judgment.

3 **Weigh the relevant criteria:** Not all criteria are equally important to the decision maker. Reducing audit risk may be more important than obtaining evidence quickly, suggesting that a decision to obtain additional evidence may be more affected by the level of the achieved audit risk than by audit deadlines. Similarly, due to materiality concerns, certain aspects of GAAP may be more important than others. All of these judgments have an implicit ethical dimension in that there is a trade-off between the auditor's self-interest (i.e., performing the audit engagement faster, keeping client management happy by not proposing adjustments) and his/her duty of care to the public.

4 **Generate alternatives:** In the audit process, the alternatives for most decisions are well understood by accountants. At the highest level, the alternatives reflect the different types of audit reports that could be issued, each of which is used under fairly clear conditions. However, a decision to issue a report other than an unqualified opinion is bound to result in conflict with client management, and a conflict between the auditor's short run self-interest and his duty to society.

5 **Rate the alternatives:** Once the alternatives are identified, the decision maker must rate each of them using the defined criteria. For example, some procedures may provide more competent evidence but are costly to perform. Other procedures may be time sensitive (e.g., confirmations of receivables). These decisions implicitly include an ethical dimension in the trade-off of costs and auditor effort.

6 **Select the "best" alternative:** The selection of the best alternative follows from weighing the alternatives. In an audit, the auditor selects the best mix of evidence to achieve the desired level of audit risk. Tests of controls that mitigate risk can be an efficient source of evidence about a process; account confirmations may be used because they are considered a competent source of evidence; or a qualified opinion may be issued

because the client has failed to comply with GAAP. In the end, the auditor decides whether to base decisions on self-interest or professional duty.

In complex environments, a decision maker may not have sufficient information available to choose among alternatives or may lack experience with the decision context. In such cases, the decision maker may search for the first viable solution that is consistent with prior experience, adjusting for obvious differences in the context. For example, an auditor who has a great deal of experience in the retail industry may conclude that lower-than-expected sales during the holiday shopping season are due to a slowdown in the economy. To determine if this explanation is reasonable, the auditor will consider general economic conditions and experiences from past years. The auditor will probably not generate a comprehensive list of alternative explanations but will rely on how well available evidence confirms that the auditor understands the client and the conditions surrounding the decision context.

Table 16.1 illustrates two decisions in the audit process: Selection of an audit procedure and issuance of the audit opinion. Both require extensive professional judgment. Failures in judgment, especially if the auditor resolves judgment issues in ways that are in his or her short term self-interest, can lead to incorrect decisions, often with a negative impact on the auditor, the client, and parties relying on the financial statements. If judgment failures are substantial enough, they may cause a loss of confidence among users of financial information. If that happens, auditors will be subject to a backlash from the public. In the extreme, the value of auditing as a professional service may be undermined, essentially destroying the ability of auditors to consider themselves as members of a profession.

Table 16.1 *Audit Judgment and Decision Making: Two Examples*

Step	Audit Evidence Decision	Audit Opinion Decision
Define the choice context	What type and quantity of substantive evidence should an auditor obtain to verify the valuation assertion for accounts receivable?	What form of audit report should an auditor issue after completing the acquisition and evaluation of evidence?
Identify the evaluation criteria	(1) Time and effort to obtain evidence. (2) Relevance of evidence. (3) Availability of evidence. (4) Level of sampling risk. (5) Ease of interpretation of evidence. (6) Quality of client internal control.	(1) Compliance with GAAP. (2) Materiality. (3) Risk of undetected misstatements. (4) Risk of going concern problems. (5) Potential costs of incorrect opinion. (6) Duty to society to identify and correct misstatements.
Weight the criteria	An auditor may consider criteria (1) to be the most important consideration, with (2) a close second, but all six can be relevant to the auditor's decision. Criteria (5) may depend on the experience of the audit personnel. Criteria (4) will depend on whether a sampling approach is being used. Criteria (6) will affect the reliability of internally generated evidence.	An auditor may consider criteria (5) and (6) to be the most important consideration but all six have relevance to the auditor's decision. Criteria (1) and (2) are always important. The importance of criteria (3) and (4) will depend on whether there is any evidence to indicate that those problems may exist.
Generate alternatives	• Confirmations (positive or negative). • Vouching of sales and receipt transactions. • Analytical procedures.	• Standard unqualified opinion. • Modified unqualified opinion. • Qualified opinion. • Disclaimer.

(Continued)

Table 16.1 (Continued)

Step	Audit Evidence Decision	Audit Opinion Decision
Rate each alternative	• Confirmations: Costly to obtain, of minimal value for valuation, time sensitive (done after year end), and good when controls are poor, subject to sampling risk. • Vouching: Moderately easy to perform, not time sensitive (can be performed any time), acceptable when controls are poor, some sampling risk. • Analytical procedures: Easy to perform, good when controls are good, no sampling risk may be difficult to interpret and require other tests as follow-up, most useful after year end but can be used anytime.	• The choice of audit opinion depends on the conditions described in Chapter 15. Other than the standard unqualified opinion each of the other alternatives will normally involve an ethical balancing of management's desires and the auditor's responsibility to foster accurate financial reporting.
Select an alternative	The auditor may choose to send some positive confirmations, test a few transactions and perform extensive analytical procedures if detection risk is moderate to high.	The auditor may select the standard unqualified opinion because there is no evidence of misstatement or going concern problems, GAAP is correctly applied and the auditor has enough evidence to alleviate his or her worry about reaching the wrong conclusion.

Threats to the Quality of Individual Auditor Judgment

Detection risk arises in an engagement because of the decisions that auditors make regarding the evidence to obtain and how it should be interpreted, occasionally allowing material misstatements to go undetected. Some misstatements may be overlooked due to sampling risk, e.g., not including a misstated transaction in the sample of items to be examined. These are not necessarily decision errors since sampling risk is inherent in the audit process (i.e., there is no such thing as zero risk). However, a more significant component of detection risk is non-sampling risk and does represent decision errors by the auditor. There are four types of decision errors an auditor can make in the audit process:

1. Failure to select the appropriate audit procedures.
2. Failure to properly perform the selected audit procedures.
3. Failure to recognize that a transaction being tested is misstated.
4. Failure to remedy a detected misstatement.

Any of the above errors can be due to errors in judgment, i.e., an unintentional breakdown in auditor judgment due to individual cognitive limitations, such as not realizing that evidence suggests material financial statements misstatements. However, some of the errors could also occur as the result of ethical lapses on the part of the auditor. For example, failure to perform properly an audit procedure (or to not perform it at all) may be a willful choice by the auditor due to time pressure. Similarly, the auditor might be pressured by management to overlook known errors in the financial statements.

Concerns about Bias in Individual Professional Judgment

While auditors are generally considered rational decision-makers, extensive psychological research has shown that people make common mistakes when processing information and analyzing a specific decision. Some of the reasons why even well intentioned auditors may make mistakes in professional judgment include:

1. Auditors may not be able to define their decision problem clearly: The purpose of the audit is relatively clear-cut—to issue an opinion on the financial statements—but not all decisions are easy to specify so rigorously. How does the auditor know when enough evidence has been obtained?

2. Auditors may not be able to consider all relevant evidence and alternatives: Evidence needed for the audit may not always be available to the auditor. Information may be difficult to evaluate because it is subjective or the auditor may not have the perceptive ability to make an accurate evaluation of the evidence. In addition, auditors may become fatigued or run out of time in the course of the audit.

3. Auditors may act in a biased manner: Auditors are expected to be objective in gathering and evaluating evidence. Unfortunately, auditors, like others, often jump to conclusions based on intuition and presumptions rather than sound reasoning.

4. Auditors may not select the "best" alternative: An auditor should make decisions that are consistent with available evidence. However, auditors may not be able to identify or recall all reasonable alternatives or the related evidence in a given situation.

5. Auditors may fail to understand the dynamic nature of their clients. Organizations are constantly changing as a result of external forces, new strategies, employee turnover, new technologies, etc. Too often, auditors expect performance to be consistent over time in spite of these changes.

All people employ, whether they know it or not, three basic heuristics or ways of simplifying complex information processing tasks. These heuristics, while normally leading to acceptable decisions and judgments, can result in a number of decision biases. As auditors are people, these heuristics may also affect an auditor's professional judgment.

Availability Heuristic: An individual's ability to identify options and evaluate likely outcomes is often affected by his or her own prior experiences. A situation that is similar to something the auditor has previously encountered is likely to influence an auditor's judgment, even if the situations are not really all that similar. The *availability heuristic* reflects this tendency and can manifest in the audit in a number of ways: Auditors tend to search for similar errors to those encountered in previous audits, use the same audit procedures from one year to the next, and interpret responses to management inquiries in light of previous conversations. Table 16.2 illustrates specific ways in which the availability heuristic may affect the audit process. In all cases, the essence of this heuristic is that the auditor can think of some outcomes or conditions more easily than others can, and this affects the consideration of alternatives in the audit process[ii].

(ii)EXAMPLE

The quality of analytical procedures depends on the auditor's ability to accurately identify the cause of unusual variations in account balances or other data. Researchers have shown that auditors often have trouble identifying error-related causes, and often focus more heavily on explanations provided by management or explanations that do not suggest errors in the underlying data. Since most fluctuations are due to normal operating conditions and do not reflect errors, the easy availability of non-error explanations provided by management may distract the auditor from more serious underlying causes of a fluctuation.[1]

Table 16.2 *Examples of Judgment Biases Applied to Auditing*

Nature of Bias	Description of Bias	Example: Possible Impact on Auditing
Examples of the Availability Heuristic		
Ease of recall	Experiences that are vivid or recent are easier to remember and may be deemed to occur more frequently than those that are less vivid or recent.	An auditor who experiences a fraud at one client may think fraud is more likely to occur at all clients, even though it is a fairly rare event.
Retrievability	An individual's ability to remember specific facts may cause those facts to be perceived as more likely than those that can't be recalled.	Recalling that a client had a problem with inventory shrinkage last year may cause the auditor to concentrate on that problem and fail to consider other inventory problems that may exist.
Presumed associations	Experiencing certain facts in combination may cause a person to overestimate the likelihood that they will always occur together.	An auditor who has observed in the past that gross margin goes down when unionized employees get a raise may not adequately consider the possibility that gross margin could go down for other reasons.
Examples of the Representativeness Heuristic		
Insensitivity to base rates	Ignoring the relative frequency of a condition occurring in the general population may cause misestimation of the likelihood of that condition occurring in a specific situation.	An auditor may overestimate the risk that a client will go bankrupt because he or she fails to appreciate the relatively low frequency of bankruptcies in the entire economy.
Insensitivity to sample size	People tend to ignore the size of a sample and the fact that larger samples are generally more accurate.	When performing substantive tests of transactions, an auditor may consider a small sample to be more competent than it really is, leading to systematic under-sampling of transactions.
Misconceptions of chance	People mistakenly expect that chance will cause conditions to even out over time, i.e., people think that a random sequence will always look random.	When examining a series of sales figures, an auditor may expect to see random fluctuations that go up-down-up-down even though such a pattern is not random.
Regression to mean	Individuals tend to overestimate the likelihood that extreme conditions will repeat rather than return to something more "normal."	A client that has a large increase in sales in one period may be expected to repeat that performance in the future. This could have a negative impact on the evaluation of analytical evidence.
Conjunction fallacy	People may think that two conditions occurring together are more likely than one of the conditions occurring alone.	An auditor may believe that the combined occurrence of management fraud and contingent compensation is more likely than the occurrence of fraud irrespective of compensation arrangements.*
Examples of the Anchoring and Adjustment Heuristic		
Insufficient anchor adjustment	Initial information becomes a starting point for a decision and additional information is not adequate to compensate for the effect of the initial anchor.	An auditor uses the prior-year sample size as a starting point for performing substantive tests of transactions and fails to adequately adjust for changes in risk conditions in the current year.
Conjunctive and disjunctive events	Events that occur together are often considered to be more frequent than they actually are while events that happen independently are considered to be less frequent than they are.	In sampling transactions, an auditor may mistakenly believe that the probability of selecting 25 correct transactions in a row is higher than selecting one erroneous transaction out of 25.**

Overconfidence	Most people have unjustified faith in their ability to make accurate estimates.	An auditor may not gather enough evidence in support of an assertion or account because he or she places excessive confidence on the competence of the evidence that is already available.
Examples of Other Biases		
Confirmation	Individuals tend to search for information that supports his or her opinion and neglect or avoid information to the contrary.	If an auditor believes that the risk of misstatement for an assertion is low, he or she may search only for evidence that supports that perspective and disregard evidence to the contrary.
Hindsight ("Curse of Knowledge")	Individuals will assign a higher likelihood to the occurrence of an event after the fact than they would have before the event has occurred.	When evaluating an accounting estimate, the auditor may conclude that a client's estimate is wrong this year because it turned out to be wrong last year, even though the estimate was deemed reasonable at the time.

*In terms of probability, the conjunction fallacy states that the probability of events A and B occurring together is higher than the probability of A occurring (with or without B) or the probability of B occurring (with or without A). In the auditing example, A would be the statement "management has committed a fraud" and B would be the statement "management has contingent compensation." Obviously the probability of "management committing fraud AND management having contingent compensation" cannot be higher than the probability of "management committing fraud," since the latter statement includes all conditions in which contingent compensation is present and not present.

**If the error rate in the population is 5 percent, the probability of selecting 25 error-free transactions is 27.7 percent (0.95²⁵) while the probability of selecting one erroneous transaction out of 25 is 36.5 percent (25 ´ 0.95²⁴ ´ 0.05).

Representativeness Heuristic: Individuals often use stereotypes for evaluating new situations. Similarities between familiar and unfamiliar situations may cause an individual to judge that an unfamiliar situation is similar to a situation that has been previously encountered, and should be handled in a similar manner. This is akin to reasoning by analogy, where knowledge of one set of facts is used to interpret a different set of facts. However, this approach can lead to judgment errors when differences between the two situations are not noticed by the auditor. The ***representativeness heuristic*** may lead an auditor to use similar audit programs across multiple clients or to use a fixed formula to establish materiality for all engagements. Table 16.2 provides a number of illustrations of how representativeness may affect the audit process. The essence of this heuristic is that the auditor places undue weight on similarities across decision contexts and conditions and does not adequately consider the unique characteristics of each audit client[iii].

Anchoring and Adjustment Heuristic: In many decision contexts, an individual approaches a decision with a preconceived notion or prior expectation of the appropriate choice to make. People often use preconceived notions as a starting point when making a decision and slowly adjust their opinion as more information is obtained. However, the strength of an individual's preconceived notions may cause them to not appreciate fully the meaning of new information. The ***anchoring and adjustment heuristic*** reflects the tendency of an individual to inadequately adapt (revise) his or her position in the face of new information. This tendency can be seen in auditing when an auditor bases decisions about sample size on the prior audit and underestimates the effect of new conditions in the current year (e.g., changes to the accounting system or the competitiveness of the industry). Table 16.2 provides a number of examples of the anchoring and

[iii]**EXAMPLE**

Research has demonstrated that auditors are sensitive to the reliability of the source of evidence.[2] One study had auditors review workpapers with known errors included in the documentation. The study found that auditors reviewing audit evidence gathered by others on an engagement team tended to be more careful and thorough when they were unfamiliar with the work of the person who initially gathered the evidence. However, this increased care did not lead to the discovery of more errors in the audit work when compared with review of audit evidence prepared by people familiar to the reviewer. This suggests that although the reviewers were sensitive to the source of the audit work, they were not more effective in the audit.[3]

(iv)**EXAMPLE**

Auditors typically analyze evidence in the sequence it is received rather than waiting for all evidence to be available and then analyzing the evidence simultaneously. Numerous research studies have demonstrated that auditors are susceptible to a "recency" effect, in which the most recent evidence received has the most impact on an auditor's judgment. In fact, evidence received early in the audit process will not have the same impact on an auditor's judgments as the same evidence received late in the process. This finding can have serious implications for the audit because it suggests why two auditors can look at the same set of evidence but reach different conclusions.[4] In a separate line of research, auditors have been observed to anchor inappropriately on the unaudited book value of an account when performing analytical procedures.[5]

adjustment heuristic applied to audit judgments. The essence of this heuristic is an auditor's unwillingness to adequately adjust prior decisions in the face of new information[(iv)].

Other Biases: There are two other individual judgment biases that are applicable to audit decisions: (1) the confirmation bias, and (2) hindsight bias (also referred to as the "curse of knowledge"). They are defined and illustrated in Table 16.2. The confirmation bias is particularly important to auditors because it implies that auditors may favor evidence that supports a preconceived opinion about the financial statements. This could lead the auditor to disregard evidence that might be important.

Concerns about Ethical Reasoning in Individual Professional Judgment

Ethics is a set of moral values or principles upon which an individual bases decisions about his or her behavior. Because of ethics, an individual will place boundaries on what is acceptable behavior. Elements of ethics include honesty, integrity, fairness, respect for others, loyalty, steadfastness, and personal responsibility. These virtues are universal and most people would acknowledge the desirability of using them as a guide in one's behavior, whether in personal life or business.

Unfortunately, people are often placed in situations where they may not act consistently with what is deemed to be ethical, either by society or by their personal standards. Why do good people do questionable things? This can occur because one person's ethics may be significantly different from the norms of general society or because the person chooses to disregard ethics and make decisions that are self-centered and selfish. In other situations, ethical principles can come into conflict resulting in a trade-off among desirable virtues, for example, does one tattle on a friend who has broken a rule (loyalty versus honesty)?

There are many excuses for unethical behavior in business: "my boss told me to," "it's not my job," "it's company policy," "nobody told me not to do it" and "life is not fair" are some of the excuses one might hear when questionable behavior is revealed. In general, there are at least four reasons why an individual may choose to act in an unethical manner:

- The "everybody does it" rationalization: In some situations, the fact that many other people are acting in a specific manner, or at least the belief that they are acting that way, is often used to rationalize unethical behavior. In an audit context, the fact that some staff accountants fail to report their time may be considered justification for others not to report their time accurately.

- The "legal equals ethical" fallacy: Many difficult personal decisions come down to a person's sense of right and wrong, not an interpretation of formal laws and regulations. In an audit context, the fact that a disclosure complies with the formal requirements of GAAP does not mean that it is adequate or accurate.

- The "no one will ever know" delusion: Perhaps the strongest motivation for behaving unethically is the belief that no one will ever know, that the truth will not be detected. In an audit context, an auditor may sign off on an audit procedure without doing the work because he or she does not expect that anyone will ever find out.

- The "slap on the wrist" syndrome: Even if ethical misbehavior may be detected, individuals may feel safe to act in inappropriate ways if the perceived consequences are minimal. If auditors are not punished for ethical lapses (e.g., reduced performance evaluations, slower advancement), they are less likely to consider the ethical dimensions to their decisions.

The forces undermining ethical behavior can be quite powerful in some situations, and often lead to serious internal conflict for people. Most business relationships are built on trust; when trust is destroyed so is the business relationship. If this is not obvious then consider the poor reputations associated with used car dealers. In other words, since trust is a foundation for business, ethical behavior is good for building and maintaining business relationships. This is especially true in a profession such as accounting where the quality of the product is difficult to perceive and the main characteristic that makes accountants valuable to their clients is that they are trusted. Nevertheless, in spite of the common sense that supports ethical behavior and decisions, many situations are ethically unclear and individuals may need assistance to maintain an ethical approach to decision making.

Since auditing is a profession, there is also an institutional aspect to ethical conduct. Even a well-intentioned auditor may be susceptible to institutional forces that create a potential tension between individual ethics and organizational actions. Two important and universal forces in auditing compound this potential tension: (1) the contracting arrangement with the client, and (2) the reward system of the audit firm.

- Contracting with the client: The quality of auditor judgment may be influenced by who hires, fires, and compensates the auditor. Management often has a great deal of influence over hiring the auditor, although the arrangement must be ratified by the Board of Directors. Management may use their contracting power to try to influence the conduct and outcome of an audit, undermining the objectivity and judgment of the auditors since their personal self-interest may be served by keeping management happy. Recent audit scandals have focused public attention on the relationship between management and the auditor. The Sarbanes-Oxley Act placed the authority of hiring and compensating the auditor with the Audit Committee for US SEC registrants. Nevertheless, management will continue to influence auditor contracting since the Audit Committee will look to management for information about the auditor.

- Firm reward systems: The individual auditor's progression in the audit firm depends on at least two things: (a) perceived technical ability, and (b) ability to manage client relationships. Regarding (a), no one wants to be perceived as incompetent so an auditor may not be forthcoming in revealing an error in the conduct of an audit (especially a prior audit) for fear of punishment, loss of professional status or dismissal. Regarding (b), the loss of a significant audit client by an audit partner may be interpreted as a sign that the auditor cannot manage client relationships. Hence, the auditor has a self-interest in not raising contentious issues with client management that may lead to complaints that the auditor is "hard to get along with."

Box 16.1 "Example: Ethical Decision Making in an Audit Context" illustrates a classic ethical issue encountered by auditors where personal self-interest comes into conflict with the requirements of GAAP and GAAS. The combination of these two forces, in the absence of countervailing forces, could result in the auditor acquiescing to all but the most blatant violations of GAAP. Other common ethical dilemmas that an auditor may encounter include (1) inappropriate pressure to sell non-audit services that could undermine the objectivity of the audit, (2) alignment of interests with management rather than other stakeholders, and (3) violation of audit firm policies in order to placate client management.

BOX 16.1   EXAMPLE: ETHICAL DECISION MAKING IN AN AUDIT CONTEXT

Scenario: Jane Yardley is a senior accountant in the firm of Varnish & Co. Jane is considered a rising star in the firm and has been privately assured that she will be promoted to manager in the next two months and will receive a hefty raise. Based on this knowledge, Jane has recently acquired some of the trappings of a successful professional—a new house, an expensive car and a membership to a prestigious local country club. Jeff Smalley is a partner in the firm of Varnish & Co. and has been in charge of many of the engagements on which Jane has worked. He has a tremendous respect for Jane's capabilities and has recently requested that she be assigned to his newest client, Brown Brothers Inc.

Brown Brothers is a manufacturer of women's clothing that is sold through moderate- to low-price department stores, mostly under house brands. The company has been audited by another firm for a number of years and always received a standard unqualified opinion. The company has been profitable in the past but last year the company incurred a small loss. Due to changing fashions and an incorrect guess that miniskirts would be big sellers, the company has accumulated a significant amount of inventory in its warehouses. As a result, the company realizes it may have to report a large loss this year.

Jane has been assigned to the audit of inventory for the current year. Upon completion of the planned audit work, Jane concludes that inventory should be written down by as much as 50 percent to reflect lower-of-cost-or-market. She has prepared a memo with documentation and included it in the workpapers. Jeff, upon reviewing the inventory work, calls Jane to his office and states that he disagrees with her conclusions, does not think that a write-down is necessary and tells Jane to replace her memo with a more upbeat memo that concludes that the inventory is properly valued at cost. In support of his position, Jeff points out that the company has always been able to dispose of inventory with minimal loss and that a discounter is likely to purchase the inventory in bulk. Furthermore, the company has indicated that they will change auditors rather than record the write-down.

What should Jane do?

Reducing Ethical Dilemmas and Judgment Biases among Professionals

The long list of potential judgment errors and ethical pressures could be disconcerting to auditors if there was no way to offset these limitations on auditor judgment. An audit firm will use its training, support tools, and internal structure to reduce the potential effect ethical dilemmas and judgment biases may have on the audit process. Some of the most common techniques that are used include:

- Improving expertise: One of the most common ways to avoid judgment errors is to rely on highly educated and trained professionals. Audit firms and the accounting profession invest a huge amount of money into training audit professionals. The more familiarity an individual has with a decision situation, the more effective the auditor will be. In an audit firm, managers generally have more expertise than seniors, and seniors more expertise than staff.

- Training: Audit firms often use case-based training to improve an auditor's judgment process and to sensitize individual auditors to potential judgment biases and ethical dilemmas they may encounter. Training is an especially important element of instilling the firm's ethical values into the conduct of individual auditors.

- Framing and perspective: Changing the way an auditor looks at a decision problem may help alleviate some judgment biases. Audit firms design and structure the audit process to reduce judgment errors. For example, strategic and process analyses may reveal conditions that suggest weaknesses in strategy, management, or financial reporting before the auditor looks at the preliminary results. A particular concern for auditors is to not start the audit thinking that the accounts are fairly stated.

- Group decision making and review of individual decisions: Almost all decisions made by auditors in the audit process are made in coordination with other members of the audit team. Group decision making has the benefit of compensating for judgment errors made by individuals. Furthermore, one auditor reviews the work of another in order to identify faulty judgments.

- Justification of decisions: Research suggests that individuals are more conscientious and less susceptible to judgment errors when they are asked to justify decisions. Audit firms and auditing standards require that auditors document their judgments about a client in writing, reducing the risk of judgment errors.

- Use of decision aids: Audit firms also develop and use decision aids that direct the gathering and evaluation of evidence in such a way that common judgment errors are avoided. For example, the use of internal control questionnaires or disclosure checklists helps the auditor to consider all relevant information. Formulas for computing materiality or sample sizes assist in the specification of information to use for a decision as well as the appropriate method for arriving at a conclusion.

- Consultations with other experts: When an auditor encounters complex or difficult issues in an audit, an expert can be brought in to provide guidance on how to handle the situation. Since the expert does not usually have any other links to the client, the auditor can use the outcome of the consultation to resist the demands of the client.

- Internal quality review: Most audit firms have an internal review process whereby specific audit decisions are evaluated with hindsight to see if they meet firm and professional standards. An auditor who knows that key audit judgments will be reviewed later will probably be less willing to succumb to client pressure, especially if such reviews affect personal rewards and advancement in the firm.

- Rewarding ethical conduct: Audit firms can reduce the likelihood of the auditor giving in to client pressure by not basing partner earnings solely on his or her current client fees, not creating incentives for audit partners to sell non-audit services, having a culture that recognizes that there can be "good" losses of clients, and by rewarding—not punishing—auditors who report their own mistakes or those of others.

All decision processes are subject to potential judgment errors and erroneous conclusions. No single technique is completely effective at eliminating such problems but the combined effect of these compensating techniques serve to significantly reduce the possibility that individual auditor judgment biases and ethical lapses will affect the outcome of the audit. Indeed, auditing research has shown when there is an appropriate match between the audit task and a properly trained, properly equipped, and properly supervised auditor, the incidence of judgmental biases and ethical lapses by individual auditors is significantly reduced.

Table 16.3 (on next page) illustrates how an ethical dilemma may be addressed given the example in Box 16.1 "Example: Ethical Decision Making in an Audit Context." Jane would try to settle the situation to the satisfaction of all parties, as best as possible, but keeping everyone happy may not be possible. Of particular relevance to this situation would be the ability to bring the issue to the entire audit team (group decision-making and review), consultations with experts on inventory valuation issues, and an environment that rewards ethical conduct. In addition, putting the issue in writing that will be subject to review at a later date will probably influence the extent to which her supervisor is willing to force the issue. However, it is always possible that Jane will be backed into a corner and will have to choose between what is "right" and what is expedient.

Institutional Forces that Reinforce Ethical Auditor Judgment

Beyond the audit firm, there are a number of professional, regulatory and other institutional forces that provide guidance on acceptable auditor judgment and conduct, and reinforce society's desire for ethical auditor judgment. Specifically, ethical conduct by an auditor is supported through a code of conduct, rules regarding auditor independence, auditing standards, quality control standards, and external inspection of audit engagements.

Table 16.3 *An Ethical Decision Process*

Step	Jane's Ethical Judgment Problem
Define the Problem	Jane believes that the company should record the 50 percent write-down but is concerned that her decision will have an adverse effect on her career and the firm.
Identify the evaluation criteria	GAAP, GAAS, Professional Codes of Conduct, legal responsibilities.
Weight the criteria	Obviously not being involved in a fraudulent situation would be paramount for Jane hence legal responsibilities and the code of ethical conduct would be important to Jane. Professional technical standards like GAAP and GAAS will heavily influence her judgment. On the other hand, keeping the client and fellow professionals happy is also a concern.
Generate alternatives	(1) Refuse to change or remove her memo. (2) Comply with Jeff Smalley's instructions. (3) Learn about and follow the firm's policy for resolving differences among members of an engagement team. (4) Go to the Board of Directors and/or Audit Committee with the story. (5) Search for alternative solutions (a compromise). (6) If a public company, consider whether to report problem to relevant regulator (e.g., the SEC). (7) Resign from the firm.
Rate each alternative Select a course of action	These alternatives are not mutually exclusive but may be pursued in sequence, with re-evaluation of the situation after each step. Alternative (3) is likely her starting point after ensuring that she has fully understood all that GAAP and GAAS has to say about the issue and considering whether the financial statements would be materially misstated if the adjustment is not made. If she gets nowhere with alternative (3) she can follow alternative (1) and have Jeff overrule her in the audit file. If that occurs than Jane should consider alternative (4) if there is an effective board/Audit Committee, or alternative (6) if it is a public company. In all these cases, except where alternative (3) works or Jane is convinced that Jeff is right because of alternative (5), then Jane should consider alternative (7), resign from the firm. Indeed, if the issue is not resolved to her satisfaction, why would Jane want to remain with an unethical firm or at least a firm that condones unethical conduct on behalf of one of its partners to retain a client?

A Code of Ethics for Professional Accountants

Auditors throughout the world must follow a code of conduct that defines unacceptable ethical behavior. The International Federation of Accountants (IFAC) requires that all member bodies adopt, except where prohibited by local law, the intent of the provisions of its "Code of Ethics for Professional Accountants." IFAC recognizes that national differences of culture, language, legal, and social systems result in each member body or country developing their own detailed ethical requirements as well as enforcement mechanisms. For example, the US representative to IFAC, the American Institute of CPAs, promulgates the **Code of Professional Conduct** that applies to all members of the AICPA who are in the public practice. The purpose of the AICPA Code is to define the minimum levels of professional responsibility and behavior that are expected of a certified public accountant in the US.

AUTHORITATIVE GUIDANCE & STANDARDS

IFAC's International Ethics Standards Board for Accountants (IESBA) Code of Ethics for Professional Accountants establishes an international minimal suggested standard for professional accountants' ethical conduct. All national level accounting bodies that are members of IFAC (e.g., the AICPA, CPA Canada, etc.) as well as local regulatory bodies (e.g., the PCAOB, the UK's Financial Reporting Council) establish mandatory ethical standards, rules, and interpretations for their own jurisdiction. For the professional accounting bodies, their codes of conduct must be at least as strict as the IESBA Code. Students are advised, for the purposes of professional examinations, to make certain of their understanding of the specific ethical rules in their jurisdiction. This book follows IESBA's Code and also incorporates relevant PCAOB requirements where they differ substantially from IESBA Code.

The fundamental principles in a code of ethical conduct based on the IFAC's IESBA's *Code* include the following:

- **Integrity:** The professional accountant must be straightforward and honest in all professional and business relationships.
- **Objectivity:** The professional accountant must not allow bias, conflict of interest, or undue influence of others to override professional or business judgments.
- **Professional Competence and Due Care**
  - o The professional accountant must maintain professional knowledge and skill at the level required to ensure competent professional services based on current developments in practice, legislation, and techniques.
  - o The professional accountant must act diligently in accordance with applicable technical and professional standards.
- **Confidentiality**
  - o The professional accountant must refrain from disclosing confidential information acquired as a result of professional and business relationships without proper and specific authority unless there is a legal or professional right or duty to disclose.
  - o The professional accountant must refrain from using confidential information acquired as a result of professional and business relationships for personal advantage or the advantage of third parties.
- **Professional behavior:** The obligation of a professional accountant to comply with relevant laws and regulations and avoid any action that discredits the profession.

Rules Regarding Auditor Independence

Auditors are expected to maintain independence from their client. An auditor must be concerned with both *independence in fact* and *independence in appearance*. Independence in appearance means that an auditor should do nothing that creates a perception that he or she has a vested interest in the outcome of an audit. The perception that an auditor is not independent, or has a potential conflict of interest in providing audit services of the highest quality, undermines the value of those services even if the auditor is completely unbiased and objective. An auditor who does not possess independence in fact may be tempted to bias the execution or conclusions of the audit.

IFAC's IESBA has developed a two-pronged approach to dealing with independence. First, there is the conceptual framework approach that provides a professional accountant with a principled basis through which to evaluate threats to independence and consider what safeguards can be put in place to reduce these threats to an appropriately low level (or as an alternative, turn down the engagement). Second, the IESBA has suggested a series of prohibitions where it believes that there can be no safeguards that are adequate to allow a professional accountant to engage in such an activity.

AUTHORITATIVE GUIDANCE & STANDARDS

IFAC's IESBA formally defines independence in its conceptual framework as:

Independence of Mind: *The state of mind that permits the expression of a conclusion without being affected by influences that compromise professional judgment, thereby allowing an individual to act with integrity and exercise objectivity and professional skepticism.*

Independence in Appearance: *The avoidance of facts and circumstances that are so significant that a reasonable and informed third party would be likely to conclude, weighing all the specific facts and circumstances, that a member of the audit team's, integrity, objectivity, or professional skepticism has been compromised.*

The framework begins by defining the nature of threats to independence that can affect a professional accountant. In general, threats to independence fall into five categories:

1. **Self-interest:** The threat that a financial or other interest will inappropriately influence the professional accountant's judgment or behavior. See Box 16.2 "Self-Interest Threats."

BOX 16.2 SELF-INTEREST THREATS*

Financial Interests

A firm, a member of the audit team, or an immediate family member shall not have:

- *A direct financial interest or material indirect financial interest in an audit client.*
- *A financial interest in an entity that the audit client also has an interest in if the interest is material to any party and the audit client can exercise significant influence over the entity.*

Partners, managerial employees who provide non-audit services and their immediate family members, shall not have:

- *A direct financial interest or material indirect financial interest in any audit client served by engagement partners located in the same office.*

Threats may be created:

- *If a member of audit team knows a close family member, or other individuals, such as professionals in the firm or close personal friends, holds a direct financial interest or material indirect financial interest in the audit client*

- *A firm's retirement benefit plan holds a direct financial interest or material indirect financial interest in an audit client*

- *A firm, a member of the audit team, or immediate family member, has a financial interest in an entity and a director, officer, or controlling owner of the audit client is also known to have a financial interest in that entity*

Loans and Guarantees

- *A firm, a member of the audit team, or an immediate family member, shall not make or guarantee a loan to an audit client.*

- *A firm shall not have a business relationship with an audit client or its management.*

- *A firm, a member of the audit team, or immediate family member, may have a loan or guarantee of a loan from a financial institution like a bank provided it is made under normal lending procedures, terms, and conditions.*

Relationships

- *The purchase of goods and services from an audit client by the firm, or a member of the audit team, or an immediate family member, does not generally create threats to independence if the transaction is in the normal course of business and at arm's length.*

- *An individual professional accountant or student who has an immediate family member who is a director, officer, or an employee with significant influence over preparation of accounting records at an audit client, shall not be a member of the audit team.*

Compensation, Evaluation, and Employment with Client Policies—Partner

- *Key audit partners shall not be evaluated on or compensated for the partner's success in selling non-assurance services to their audit clients.*

- *Key audit partners include the:*
  - *Engagement partner;*
  - *Individual responsible for the engagement quality control review;*
  - *Other audit partners on the engagement team who make key decisions or judgments on significant matters with respect to the audit.*

- *In the case of public interest entities, independence is compromised if a key audit partner or the firm's Senior or Managing Partner joins the audit client as a director or officer or an employee in a position to exert significant influence over the accounting records or financial statements for at least twelve months.*

Compensation, Evaluation, and Employment with an Audit Client—Staff

- *Firm policies and procedures shall require members of the audit team to notify the firm when entering employment negotiations with an audit client.*

- *A threat may be created if other members of the audit team are evaluated on or compensated for their success in selling non-assurance services to their audit clients.*

Gifts and Hospitality

- *A firm or member of the audit team shall not accept gifts or hospitality from an audit client unless the value is trivial and inconsequential.*

*Adapted from IESBA. 2015. Code of Conduct for Professional Accountants. *Section 290.*

---

2. **Familiarity:** The threat that due to a long or close relationship with a client, a professional accountant will be too sympathetic to their interests or too accepting of their work. See Box 16.3 "Familiarity Threats."

BOX 16.3 FAMILIARITY THREATS*

Family and Personal Relationships

- *Threats to independence are created when a member of the audit team has an immediate or close family member who is an employee in a position to exert significant influence over the client's financial position, financial performance, or cash flows.*

- *Threats to independence are created if a member of the audit team has a close relationship with a director, officer, or an employee with significant influence over preparation of accounting records at an audit client.*

- *A former member of audit team or partner of the firm shall not join an audit client as director or officer or an employee in a position to exert significant influence over the accounting records or financial statements unless:*

  o *The individual is not entitled to any benefits or payments from the firm; and*

  o *The individual does not continue to participate, or appear to participate, in the firm's business or professional activities.*

Serving as a Director or Officer

- *A partner or employee of the firm shall not serve as a director or officer of an audit client.*

Long Association of Senior Personnel

- *Using the same senior personnel on an audit engagement over a long period of time creates threats to independence.*

- *In the case of audit clients that are public interest entities**, key audit partners (see definition in Box 16.2 "Self-Interest Threats") shall rotate after seven years and shall not be a member of the engagement team or a key audit partner for the client for two years.*

- *Where continuity is especially important to audit quality, key audit partners may be, in rare cases due to unforeseen circumstances outside of the firm's control, permitted one additional year as long as threats to independence can be eliminated or reduced to an acceptable level by applying safeguards.*

- During the two year "time out" period, the individual shall not:
  - o Participate in the audit of the entity;
  - o Provide quality control for the engagement; or
  - o Consult with the engagement team or the client regarding technical or industry-specific issues, transactions or events.
- Rotation is not required if all of the following are done: the firm has only a few people with the necessary knowledge and experience to serve as a key audit partner; an independent regulator has provided an exemption from rotation in such circumstances; the independent regulator has specified alternative safeguards; and the alternative safeguards are applied.

*Adapted from IESBA. 2015. Code of Conduct for Professional Accountants. Section 290.

** Rules are generally stricter for auditors of clients that are denoted as "public interest entities." These would include all public companies and other significant firms as designated by national law or regulation (e.g., credit unions or other financial institutions)

- **Self-review**: The threat that a professional accountant will not appropriately evaluate the results of a previous judgment made or service performed on which the accountant will rely when forming a judgment as part of providing the current service. See Box 16.4 "Self-Review Threats."

BOX 16.4 SELF-REVIEW THREATS*

Management Responsibilities

A firm shall not assume a management responsibility for an audit client.

Preparing Accounting Records And Financial Statements

Audit Clients that are Public Interest Entities**

- A firm shall not provide accounting and bookkeeping services, including payroll services, to an audit client or prepare financial statements on which the firm will express an opinion or financial information that forms the basis of financial statements.
- A firm may provide services of a routine and mechanical nature for divisions or related entities if the personnel providing the service are not on the audit team and:
  - o The divisions or related entities are collectively immaterial; or
  - o The services relate to matters that are collectively immaterial to the financial statements of the division or related entity.

Audit Clients that are not Public Interest Entities

- The firm may provide services related to the preparation of accounting records and financial statements where the services are of a routine or mechanical nature. Examples include:

o   *Providing payroll services based on client-originated data;*

o   *Recording transactions for which the client has determined or approved the appropriate account classification;*

o   *Posting client-coded transaction and client approved entries to the general ledger and trial balance;*

o   *Preparing financial statements based on the trial balance.*

Emergency Situations

- *In emergency or other unusual situations when it is impractical for the audit client to make other arrangements, accounting and bookkeeping services that would otherwise be prohibited may be provided for a short period of time if those who provide the services are not on the audit team and the arrangement has been discussed with those charged with governance (e.g., Audit Committee).*

Taxation Services

Tax Return Preparation

- *Providing tax return preparation services does not generally create a threat to independence if management takes responsibility for the returns and any significant judgments made.*

Tax Calculations

Audit Clients that are Public Interest Entities**

- *A firm shall not prepare tax calculations of current and deferred tax liabilities (or assets) for the purpose of preparing accounting entries that are material to the financial statements.*

- *In emergency or unusual situations when it is impractical for the client to make other arrangements, a firm may prepare tax calculations if those who provide services are not on audit team, the services are provided only for a short period of time, and the situation is discussed with those charged with governance.*

Audit Clients that are not Public Interest Entities

- *Preparing calculations of current and deferred tax liabilities (or assets) for purpose of preparing accounting entries that will be subsequently audited by the firm creates a self-review threat that needs to be evaluated by the firm and safeguards applied when necessary.*

Tax Planning and Other Tax Advisory Services

- *A self-review threat may be created when advice will affect matters to be reflected in the financial statements.*

- *A firm shall not provide tax advice if the effectiveness of the advice depends on a particular accounting treatment or financial statement presentation and:*

   o   *The audit team has reasonable doubt as to the appropriateness of the related accounting treatment or presentation; and*

   o   *The outcome or consequence of the tax advice would have a material effect on the financial statements.*

Assistance in the Resolution of Tax Disputes

- *An advocacy or self-review threat may be created when the firm assists the audit client with the resolution of a tax dispute once the tax authorities have notified the client that they have rejected the client's arguments and the matter is being referred for determination in a formal proceeding.*

- *A firm shall not act as an advocate for the audit client before a public tribunal or court in the resolution of a tax matter if the amounts involved are material to the financial statements.*

Internal Audit Services

- *When providing internal audit services to an audit client, firm personnel shall not assume a management responsibility, and the firm shall be satisfied that:*

  o *The client designates an appropriate and competent resource to be in charge and acknowledge responsibility for internal controls;*

  o *Management or those charged with governance review, assess, and approve the scope, risk, and frequency of the services;*

  o *Management evaluates the adequacy and results;*

  o *Management decides which recommendations to implement; and*

  o *Management reports to those charged with governance the significant findings and recommendations.*

Audit Clients that are Public Interest Entities**

- *A firm shall not provide internal audit services that relate to:*

  o *A significant part of the internal controls over financial reporting;*

  o *Financial accounting systems that generate information that is, separately or in the aggregate, significant to the client's accounting records or financial statements; or*

  o *Amounts or disclosures that are, separately or in the aggregate, material to the client's financial statements.*

Valuation Services

- *Valuation services may create a self-review threat.*

Audit Clients that are not Public Interest Entities**

- *A firm shall not perform a valuation service if the valuation service has a material effect on the financial statements and the valuation involves a significant degree of subjectivity.*

Audit Clients that are Public Interest Entities

- *A firm shall not provide valuation services if the valuations would have a material effect, separately or in the aggregate, on the financial statements.*

*Adapted from IESBA. 2015. Code of Conduct for Professional Accountants. *Section 290.*

** Rules are generally stricter for auditors of clients that are denoted as "public interest entities." These would include all public companies and other significant firms as designated by national law or regulation (e.g., credit unions or other financial institutions).

- **Advocacy:** The threat that a professional accountant will promote a client's position to the point that the accountant's objectivity is compromised or the threat that a financial or other interest will inappropriately influence the professional accountant's judgment or behavior. See Box 16.5 "Advocacy and Self-Interest Threats."

BOX 16.5 ADVOCACY AND SELF-INTEREST THREATS*

Provision of Non-Assurance Services

- *Before the firm accepts an engagement to provide a non-assurance service to an audit client, a determination shall be made whether providing the service creates a threat to independence.*

IT Systems Services

- *The firm may provide the following services provided firm personnel do not assume a management responsibility:*
  - o *Designing or implementing IT systems that are unrelated to internal control over financial reporting;*
  - o *Designing or implementing IT systems that do not generate information forming a significant part of the accounting records or financial statements;*
  - o *Implementation of "off-the-shelf" accounting or financial information reporting software not developed by the firm if no significant customization is required to meet the client's needs; and*
  - o *Evaluating and making recommendations on a system designed, implemented or operated by another or the client.*

Audit Clients that are Public Interest Entities**

- *A firm shall not provide services involving the design or implementation of IT systems that:*
  - o *Form a significant part of the internal control over financial reporting; or*
  - o *Generate information that is significant to the accounting records or financial statements.*

Audit Clients that are not Public Interest Entities

- *A firm shall only provide services involving the design or implementation of IT systems that:*
  - o *Form a significant part of the internal control over financial reporting; or*
  - o *Generate information that is significant to the accounting records or financial statements when specified safeguards are put in place to ensure that the client takes responsibility for the services.*

Litigation Support Services

- *If the firm provides litigation support services involving estimating damages or other amounts that affect the financial statements, the requirements regarding valuation services shall be followed.*

Legal Services

- *A firm shall not act in an advocacy role for an audit client in resolving a dispute or litigation when the amounts involved are material to the financial statements.*

Recruiting Services

- *Providing recruiting services may create threats to independence. A firm may generally provide services such as:*
  - o *Reviewing the professional qualifications of candidates and providing advice on their suitability for a position; and*
  - o *Interviewing candidates and advising on their competence for financial accounting, administrative, or control positions.*

*Audit Clients that are Public Interest Entities***

- *A firm shall not provide the following services with respect to a director or officer of the audit client or senior management in a position to exert significant influence over the client's accounting records or financial statements:*
  - o *Searching for or seeking out candidates for such positions; and*
  - o *Undertaking reference checks of prospective candidates for such positions.*

Corporate Finance Services

- *Providing corporate finance services may create threats to independence.*
- *A firm shall not provide corporate finance advice if the effectiveness of the advice depends on a particular accounting treatment or financial statement presentation and:*
  - o *The audit team has reasonable doubt as to the appropriateness of the accounting treatment or presentation; and*
  - o *The outcome or consequence of the tax advice would have a material effect on the financial statements.*

*Adapted from IESBA. 2015. Code of Conduct for Professional Accountants. Section 290.

** Rules are generally stricter for auditors of clients that are denoted as "public interest entities." These would include all public companies and other significant firms as designated by national law or regulation (e.g., credit unions or other financial institutions).

- **Intimidation**: The threat that a professional accountant will be deterred from acting objectively because of actual or perceived pressures, including attempts to exercise undue influence over the accountant. See Box 16.6 "Intimidation and Self-Interest Threats."

The Conceptual Framework defines two broad classes of safeguards that can be employed to reduce threats to independence: (1) Safeguards created by the profession, legislation, or regulation; and (2) Safeguards in the work environment. In practice, there are a number of safeguards to independence:

BOX 16.6   INTIMIDATION AND SELF-INTEREST THREATS*

Fees—Relative Size

- Threats are created when fees from an audit client represent a large proportion of the total fees of the firm or a large proportion of the total revenue of an individual partner or an individual office of the firm.

Audit Clients that are Public Interest Entities**

- If the total fees from the client are more than 15 percent of the firm's total fees for two years, the firm shall discuss which of the following safeguards to apply with those charged with governance:

  o A pre-issuance engagement quality control review performed by a professional accountant who is not a member of the firm; or

  o A post-issuance review equivalent to an engagement quality control performed by a professional accountant who is not a member of the firm.

- If the total fees significantly exceed 15 percent of the firm's total fees, the firm shall determine whether the significance of the threat is such that a pre-issuance review is necessary.

Fees—Overdue

- A threat may be created when fees from an audit client remain unpaid for a long time. Generally, the firm is expected to require payment of any significant unpaid fees before the issue of the audit report for the following year.

Contingent Fees

- A contingent fee shall not be charged in respect of an audit engagement.

- A contingent fee shall not be charged for a non-assurance service provided to an audit client if:

  o The fee is charged by the firm and the fee is material or expected to be material to the firm;

  o The fee is charged by a network firm that participates in a significant part of the audit and the fee is material or expect to be material to the network firm; or

  o The outcome of the non-assurance service, and therefore the amount of the fee, is dependent on a future or contemporary judgment related to the audit of a material amount in the financial statements.

Actual or Threatened Litigation

- Litigation between the firm or a member of the audit team and an audit client creates a threat to independence. If safeguards do not reduce the threats to an acceptable level, the firm shall withdraw from the audit engagement.

*Adapted from IESBA. 2015. Code of Conduct for Professional Accountants. Section 290.

** Rules are generally stricter for auditors of clients that are denoted as "public interest entities." These would include all public companies and other significant firms as designated by national law or regulation (e.g., credit unions or other financial institutions).

- Regulation: The establishment of specific rules plus periodic inspection of an auditor's engagements to determine compliance with formal rules.
- Professional practice: Education, training/continuing professional education, and practical experience requirements.
- Client safeguards: Approval of non-audit services by the Audit Committee and presence of competent client management who are financially literate.
- Firm safeguards: Firm-wide standards, policies and procedures, such as monitoring of up-to-date databases of firm clients and internal quality review inspections, and engagement level policies, such as second partner review and mandatory rotation of audit team personnel.

AUTHORITATIVE STANDARDS & GUIDANCE

IFAC IESBA Code of Ethics for Professional Accountants, national auditing standard setters, SEC, PCAOB and various other regulators and legislators around the world all have rules for independence that can be quite specific and difficult to understand and apply in practice. Auditors who have questions about these issues are wise to seek counsel from appropriate sources in their firms, their local certifying body (who often provide confidential ethics hotlines), and potentially directly from the regulatory or legal oversight body.

Services prohibited by the SEC applicable to Integrated Audits: The SEC Independence Rules issued in 2000 and the Sarbanes-Oxley Independence Rules from 2002 prohibit a number of other relationships and services for public companies registered with the SEC. Other countries have passed less extensive rules. Examples of the types of relationships and services that are now prohibited for US SEC registered public companies include:

- A senior member of an audit team must wait at least a year before going to work for a client in an accounting or financial management position.
- Audit partners must periodically rotate off an engagement, typically after five years, and cannot be reassigned to the engagement for a certain amount of time.
- The Audit Committee must pre-approve all services rendered by auditors that are not part of the financial statement audit.
- Audit partners cannot be directly compensated for selling non-audit services to their audit clients.

Table 16.3 (on next page) provides examples of how the five threats to independence are enacted via prohibitions on auditors in independence rules. Figure 16.2 (on p. 620) provides a decision tree approach as to how to make decisions about how these various threats would be handled in audit practice.

Audit Firm and Audit Partner Rotation

Requirements for audit partners that are in charge of audit engagements to rotate off the audit engagement every few years have been in effect in the US since the 1970s for US-registered public companies. These partner rotations

Table 16.3 *Threats to Independence and Related Prohibitions on Services Provided by a Professional Accountant in Public Practice**

Threat to Independence	Prohibition of Services Related to Threat
Self-interest: An audit firm or individual auditor should not economically benefit from the outcome of the audit (other than a non-contingent fee).	Forbidding an auditor to have an ownership interest in a client or to loan money to a client are obvious examples. Other concerns include prohibitions on borrowing money from a client, investing in a mutual fund that invests in a client's securities, or entering into a partnership with a client to sell products or services.
Self-review: An audit firm or individual auditor should not audit his or her own work.	An auditor should not be engaged to develop and implement a client's accounting system. Nor should the auditor be involved with the valuation of potential acquisitions if those valuations may eventually be included in the financial statements.
Advocacy: An auditor should not be engaged to represent a specific accounting, tax or legal position of the company that could have an effect on the financial statements.	An auditor should not serve as a financial advisor or executive recruiter to a client.
Familiarity: The auditor should not become so close to a client that the ability to be skeptical is undermined.	Prohibitions on length that an auditor stays on the engagement. Members of the audit firm or engagement team should not have close relatives that work for the client in key accounting, financial, or data processing positions.
Intimidation: An auditor should not feel threatened by the relationship with the client.	The threat to replace the auditor if he or she does not support a specific outcome or position favored by the client. Existing litigation between a client and an auditor makes them adversaries and undermines independence.

* Adapted from IESBA. 2015. *Code of Conduct for Professional Accountants.* Section 290.

gradually became the norm around the world with Canada and New Zealand being among the first to adopt similar requirements.

AUTHORITATIVE STANDARDS & GUIDANCE

IFAC IESBA Code of Ethics for Professional Accountants, national auditing standard setters, SEC, PCAOB and various other regulators and legislators around the world all have rules relating to audit partner rotation. Recent rules passed by the European Commission require audit firm rotation.

Since the passage by the US Congress of the Sarbanes-Oxley Act of 2002, the PCAOB has required that engagement partners on publicly listed engagements rotate every five years with a five year "cooling off" period before they can return to the engagement. Further, this requirement has been expanded to include engagement quality review partners (with the same five/five rule). Other audit partners that have significant decision making roles in the audit engagement are required to rotate every seven years with a two year "cooling off" period before they can return.

Internationally audit partner rotation rules generally follow the IESBA *Code of Ethics* that requires partner rotation after seven years—the position adopted by regulators at the European Union level—with a "cooling off" period of two years. European rules apply not just to public companies but to public

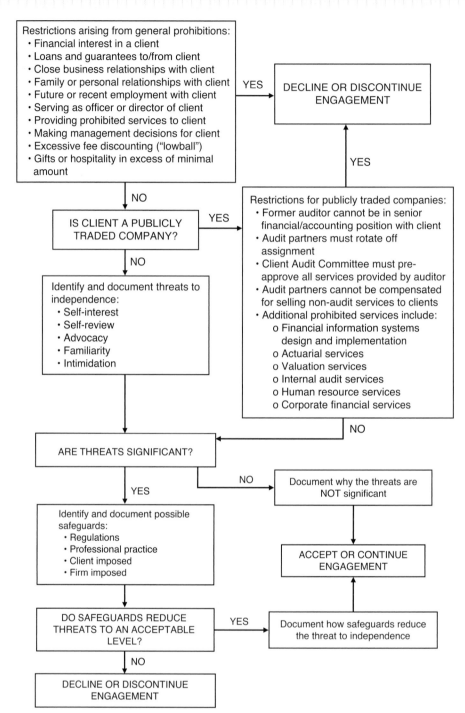

Figure 16.2 *Rules and Standards Regarding Auditor Independence: Combined Analysis of IFAC* Code of Ethics for Professional Accountants *and US SEC and PCAOB rules*

interest entities (e.g., credit unions, etc.). Further, as all national professional accounting bodies that are members of the International Federation of Accountants are committed to implementing the IESBA *Code of Ethics* as their own minimum standard, similar rules will be gradually implemented by national professional accounting bodies around the world.

A related question has repeatedly been raised whether the audit firm should change on a periodic basis rather than just the audit partner(s) for a given engagement. This issue has been raised regularly since at least the 1970s by various groups investigating financial statement frauds (e.g., the Metcalf Committee of the US Congress). This question has taken on renewed interest in recent years as the European Commission passed rules that will be phased in over several years requiring that audit firms rotate off of the audit after ten years unless certain actions are taken (e.g., putting the audit out for tender) with an absolute cap of no more than twenty-four years (e.g., where there are joint auditors). EU countries can make the initial audit firm rotation requirement shorter than ten years developing their own national laws to implement this rule. While the European rules only apply to European based public companies and their subsidiaries that are located in Europe, the effects will be felt around the world. Either the subsidiaries located outside Europe will change audit firms with the parent company or there will be an increased incidence of group audits (see discussions in Chapters 10 and 15) where the parent company auditor and the subsidiary auditor are not in the same audit network. The US PCAOB initially took a position that audit firm rotation was not going to be on their active agenda (early 2014) but recently revived the discussion in the fall of 2015

Auditing Standards

One of the roles of auditing standards is to define the process for conducting an audit. Depending on the country, auditing standards are promulgated by the profession or enacted through legislative or regulatory action (e.g., Germany). Most English-speaking countries have allowed auditors to be self-regulating subject to public oversight. However, events such as Enron and WorldCom led to the passage in the US of the Sarbanes-Oxley Act of 2002 which established the PCAOB. The PCAOB was given the option by Congress of either directly setting standards for the audits of all SEC registrants or delegating that power while retaining oversight responsibility.

The initial board decided that they would directly set the auditing standards and as an interim measure adopted existing US GAAS as promulgated by the AICPA's Auditing Standards Board (ASB). The PCAOB quickly started to set its own standards (e.g., requiring audit reports on internal control over financial reporting) and required all auditors of US traded public companies to issue auditor's reports "in accordance with the standards of the PCAOB." The PCAOB required that audit firms drop the term "generally accepted auditing standards" from the auditor's report on public companies as it felt there would be confusion with the ASB continuing to produce new standards for other than public company audits and the IAASB doing so internationally. In 2015 the PCAOB fully integrated its new standards with the legacy ASB standards to produce a standalone set of standards that we have been referring to in our authoritative standards and guidance boxes throughout the text.

Other common law countries (e.g., UK, New Zealand, and Canada) have not gone as far as the US in creating a quasi-government body to set audit standards. However, most have enhanced the oversight powers of stock exchange regulators and/or other oversight bodies that are independent of the accounting profession. Hence, while self-regulation by the profession is still the norm in most English-speaking countries, the US has joined other countries (such as many European states) that codify auditing standards into law. These code law countries codify the standards such as those from the International Auditing and Assurance Standards Board and for countries in Europe also based on European Commission directives. Even with this level of acceptance and scrutiny by lawmakers, the IAASB has found it necessary to have its parent organization, the International Federation of Accountants, establish a Public Interest Oversight Board (PIOB) that has a majority of members who are not professional accountants or auditors. The PIOB reviews all proposed auditing standards from the IAASB to ensure that they are in the public interest prior to the standards going into effect.

Audit Quality Framework and Indicators

As a response of audit standard setters and regulators to the fallout from the fiscal crisis of 2007–09, projects were undertaken to define if a quality audit engagement level in order to guide future standard setting and regulation. These efforts are also linked to the findings from engagement level inspections by the PCAOB and other national audit regulators (see later in this chapter) that suggest that there might be underlying factors, beyond specific engagement issues, that would promote or deter a quality audit from occurring.

The IAASB took a process perspective and developed a comprehensive framework (see Figure 16.3 on the following page) that focused first on the process elements (inputs, outputs, and process), then considered the interactions among the three process elements, and finally examined a variety of contextual factors (e.g., laws and regulation, GAAP adopted, etc.), including how each of the contextual factors affected the process elements and interactions among the elements. The IAASB has finalized its project as a non-authoritative framework to raise awareness about audit quality issues, stimulate discussion about these issues and focus on how audit quality could be improved.

AUTHORITATIVE GUIDANCE & STANDARDS

The IAASB and the PCAOB have both recently been interested in indicators of audit quality. The IAASB has released as part of its 2015 Handbook a supplement entitled **A Framework for Audit Quality: Key Elements that Create an Environment for Audit Quality**. *The PCAOB in 2015 released a discussion document entitled* **Concept Release on Audit Quality Indicators** *that proposes twenty-eight quantitative indicators that might be employed to judge audit quality.*

The PCAOB took the approach of developing quantitative measures of each of three main categories of audit quality—audit professionals, audit process

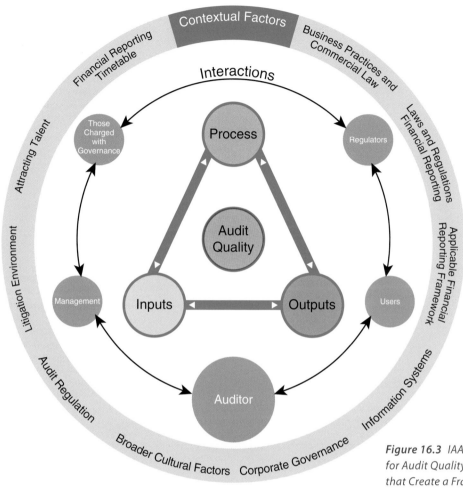

Figure 16.3 *IAASB Framework for Audit Quality: Key Elements that Create a Framework for Audit Quality*

Source: *IFAC. 2014. Framework for Audit Quality: Key Elements that Create a Framework for Audit Quality p. 5)*

and audit results. Within each of those categories they developed sub-categories (see Box 16.7 "PCAOB Quantitative Indicators of Audit Quality") and for each sub-category at least one quantitative measure. The PCAOB document, at the time of writing this book, is out for comment including looking at directions where this project might go.

BOX 16.7   PCAOB QUANTITATIVE INDICATORS OF AUDIT QUALITY*

1) *Audit professionals*

   a) Availability

      i) Staff to partner ratio

      ii) Workload of staff, managers, and partners

      iii) Availability of technical accounting, auditing, and specialized resources (e.g., IT assurance, valuation)

> b) Competence
>> i) Experience, industry expertise
>>
>> ii) Staff turnover
>>
>> iii) Staff training
>
> c) Focus
>> i) Audit hours matched to risk areas
>>
>> ii) Audit hours allocated to phases of audit

2) Audit process
> a) Tone at top—based on staff survey
>
> b) Incentives—compensation of staff and audit fee level
>
> c) Independence—compliance with detailed independence rules
>
> d) Infrastructure—dollars invested in audit support systems
>
> e) Monitoring and remediation—inspection results by regulators, audit firm's own quality inspection results

3) Audit results
> a) Financial statements—number of restatements, frauds, or other financial reporting misconduct
>
> b) Internal control—timely reporting of IC weaknesses
>
> c) Going concern—timely reporting of going concern issues
>
> d) Interactions with Audit Committee—survey of Audit Committee members
>
> e) Enforcement and Litigation—number of lawsuits

Adapted from PCAOB 2015. Concepts Release on Audit Quality Indicators. p. 13

Audit Firm Quality Control Standards

One response of professional accounting bodies to concerns about audit failure attributable to poor auditor judgment has been the establishment of standards related to quality control. The resulting **Quality Control Standards** address issues related to the management of an accounting practice so as to maximize the quality of the service that a firm delivers to its clients in compliance with all other applicable professional standards. These standards require that an accounting firm have a system of quality control for its accounting, auditing, attest, and related services. Good quality control should have the following elements (see Table 16.4):

- Firm leadership.

- Ethical requirements.

- Acceptance and continuance of clients and specific engagements.

- Human resources.

- Engagement performance.

- Monitoring of quality.

Table 16.4 *Elements of a System of Quality Control**

Elements of Quality Control	Requirements
Leadership responsibilities for quality within the firm	Policies and procedures designed to promote an internal culture recognizing that quality is essential in performing all engagements. Senior officials in the firm such as the chief executive officer (or equivalent) assume ultimate responsibility for the firm's system of quality control.
Relevant ethical requirements	Policies and procedures should be established to provide the firm with reasonable assurance that people at all organizational levels comply with relevant ethical requirements especially to maintain independence and perform all professional responsibilities with integrity and objectivity.
Acceptance and continuance of clients and specific engagements	Policies and procedures should be established for deciding whether to accept or continue a client in order to provide reasonable assurance that the firm will not associate with a client whose management lacks integrity, that the required professional services can be competently provided in compliance with relevant ethical requirements and to identify potential conflicts of interest and the resolution.
Human resources	Policies and procedures for assigning personnel to engagements should be established to provide the firm with reasonable assurance that the firm has sufficient personnel with competence, capabilities and commitment to ethical principles necessary to perform engagements in accordance with professional standards and enable the firm to issue reports that are appropriate for the circumstances.
Engagement performance	Policies and procedures should be established to provide reasonable assurance that the work performed meets all appropriate professional standards and legal and regulatory requirements with an emphasis on carrying out appropriate consultations with experts.
Monitoring	Policies and procedures for a monitoring process should be established to provide the firm with reasonable assurance that the procedures relating to the other elements of quality control are relevant, adequate, and operating effectively.

* Adapted from ISQC No. 1 and ISA 220. Similar guidance is provided by PCAOB AS 1220 and Interim Quality Control Standards.

AUTHORITATIVE GUIDANCE & STANDARDS

Standards for quality control are contained within the IAASB **International Standards on Quality Control** *and the PCAOB's* **Interim Standards on Quality Control.** *In addition, audit specific quality control standards are found in ISA 220* **Quality Control for an Audit of Financial Statements** *and PCAOB AS 1220 (formerly No. 7)* **Engagement Quality Review.**

The emphasis of these standards is on maintaining the reputation of the profession by setting minimum standards of professional behavior. In a sense, quality control standards originally represented the profession's attempt to self-police the activities of firms and individuals practicing auditing. In the US, these standards have now passed over to the PCAOB whereas in much of the rest of the world regulators are content to adopt the IAASB standards supplemented where needed (adjusted for local regulation).

Peer Reviews and Practice Inspections

Peer reviews were originally established as a self-regulatory device by the US accounting profession in response to the wave of alleged audit failures occurring in the 1970s. In the 1980s, the SEC required that an auditor of a public company be a member of the AICPA's SEC Practice Section and have a peer review every three years based on the AICPA's *Statements on Quality Control Standards*. This approach created some potential problems for the largest accounting firms since the set of potential reviewers consisted of the other large firms with which they competed. Furthermore, the SEC became concerned that the manner in which peer reviews were conducted was not rigorous, being mostly focused on descriptions of formal processes with relatively little inspection of actual audits(v).

Other countries pioneered the concept of practice inspection in the 1980s. Professional accounting bodies would hire practicing auditors as full or part time inspectors to examine the audit engagements of an accounting firm. Deficiencies could be subject to a variety of sanctions ranging from additional professional training and development to expulsion from membership in the professional body and loss of professional certifications. Like the US peer review system, this worked well for inspections of small and medium sized audit firms but the general consensus was that the practice inspectors did not have the resources to carry out meaningful inspections of international firms.

Practice inspections are now required for all firms that audit US SEC registrants. Section 104 of the Sarbanes-Oxley Act requires the PCAOB to conduct a continuing program of inspections of registered public accounting firms. In these inspections, the board assesses compliance with the Act, the rules of the board, the rules of the Securities and Exchange Commission, and professional standards, in connection with the firm's performance of audits. The board issues a report for each firm after completing the inspection. The Act requires annual inspections for firms that provide audit reports for more than 100 SEC registrants and at least triennially (every three years) for firms with fewer SEC clients. Public versions of the PCAOB reports and the audit firm's responses are posted on the PCAOB web site. In the latest year that internationally comparable statistics are available, the PCAOB inspected over 850 audit engagements across 228 audit firms. The PCAOB also inspects auditing firms located outside the US that audit US SEC registrants (over 1,200 such registrants existed as of last count by the SEC in 2004) often in cooperation with a local oversight body (e.g., the Canadian Public Accountability Board).

Internationally there are now over 40 independent regulatory bodies that carry out inspections of audit firms at the engagement level. In 2013, these bodies collectively (excluding the PCAOB) inspected nearly 1,000 audit engagements at 113 audit firms. Internationally, the Big 4 firms are normally inspected annually (44 percent of countries), with the next two largest firms normally inspected every three years (41 percent of countries) and all other firms inspected between three and five years (over 50 percent). Public reporting internationally can vary from being more detailed than the US at the audit or engagement level (e.g., UK's Financial Reporting Council) to highly aggregated such that the national regulator does not provide information on individual audit firms (e.g., Canadian Public Accountability Board).

Institutional Forces That Punish Lapses in Auditor Judgment

Regulatory Intervention

The existence of regulations and codes of conduct encourages auditors to behave in a professional and ethical manner. However, evaluation and punishment mechanisms are needed to enforce the rules when auditors violate regulations or the code of conduct. A key factor in determining the effectiveness of any regulatory rules or code of conduct is the extent to which the specific body actively polices these rules. Professional bodies are often reactive, in that they only carry out investigations of members after a complaint is filed. In some countries, like the US, professional bodies are hesitant to take any actions before related legal cases have been settled. Regulatory agencies vary as well in the extent of their policing. Some regulators are involved in or carry out inspections of audit firms whereas others do not investigate auditors until there is a reason to do so (e.g., a material restatement of a public company's financial statement or an allegation of fraud from a reputable person).

When a professional body or regulator identifies problems in a firm, some form of corrective action and/or punishment may be called for. Professional sanctions for miscreants may be as simple as a written reprimand, or may involve fines for costs, imposition of educational and professional development requirements, or expulsion as a member from the body of professionals. Regulators can usually impose similar sanctions as well as assess punitive fines, enter the enforcement action onto the public record, have the auditor or audit firm agree not to engage in the behavior again, stop the audit firm from accepting new clients for a period of time, and/or stop an individual auditor from carrying out all or certain types of audits. In the extreme, regulators can refer a matter to the criminal justice system when fraud is suspected, or can file suit on a civil basis through the court system or a quasi-judicial administrative process.

Legal Liability: Overview

In today's professional environment, an auditor is subject to potential litigation from many sources, including the client and its management, third-party users of the audited financial statements, and government agencies. Many estimates place the cost of litigation in the US between 10 and 15 percent of audit firm revenues, including insurance, defense costs, and settlement payments. In reality, the largest firms are essentially self-insured and all costs of litigation are born by the partners of the firm. While insurance is usually available for small and medium audit firms, the rate of increase in insurance costs has been as high as 100 percent per year in recent years.

In many major lawsuits, assessed damages can dwarf the audit fee realized on the engagement, rendering even a single adverse judgment potentially devastating to an accounting firm. Furthermore, the actual damages may be less significant than the threat of **punitive damages**, which are not based on the actual damages incurred by the parties involved and can be

Deloitte & Touche carried out the audit of a North Carolina reinsurance firm, Fortress Re. Fortress Re was used by four Japanese insurance companies to manage risks involving aircraft that they insured. The four planes involved in the attacks of 9/11 were all insured by these four Japanese companies. When they went to recover their losses from Fortress, it was found that the owners had pocketed over $400 million in premiums instead of maintaining the reinsurance fund. The Deloitte audit fee never exceeded $100,000 but Deloitte & Touche settled the case out of court for what the Wall Street Journal estimated to be $250 million.

assessed against an audit firm when its behavior is considered egregious. The potential assessment of punitive damages makes litigation for professional malpractice a high stakes game for all parties involved(vi).

In many cases, the auditors are thought of as a deep pocket from which to draw compensation for parties who are damaged by misstated financial reports. This reality is a simple application of economics: by the time a case is litigated, most potential defendants are bereft of financial resources to pay a judgment except the auditor, who is usually insured against malpractice losses. Furthermore, because of the concept of *joint and several liability*, the auditor can be held responsible for the entire amount of an adverse judgment even though the auditor may have been only partially responsible for the losses incurred by the plaintiff.[6] Even when an audit firm is successful in defending itself, the costs may be exorbitant(vii).

Legal Liability: Common Law

The consensus of reasoned judicial decisions and precedents that have been formalized over many years and many cases is referred to as *common law*. This body of law exists as a result of judicial, rather than legislative, actions. Lawsuits against auditors brought under common law typically draw upon either the law of contracts or the law of torts. Common law countries include most English-speaking countries. Consequently, the case law in these countries is similar, although there may be specific points of difference. In the US, most common law has developed at the state level whereas in other countries (e.g., the UK) it developed at the national level

Under the *law of contracts*, auditors who are engaged to deliver audit services are expected to comply with the terms of the contract established with the client, that is, to deliver an audit that complies with appropriate professional standards. Failure to fulfill the terms of a contract is referred to as a *breach of contract* and may be actionable in court. A client who is unhappy with the performance of the auditor can file suit claiming that the auditor has breached the contract by failing to deliver the appropriate service. Also, a *third-party beneficiary* who is named in the contract may be able to bring suit against an auditor under contract law. For example, an engagement to audit financial statements in support of a loan application with a specific bank may establish the bank as a third-party beneficiary under contract law. The suing party is referred to as the *plaintiff* and the party being sued (the auditor) is the *defendant*.

Under the *law of torts* an auditor can be sued by someone who is damaged by the production of an inferior audit. Financial institutions and vendors that lend money to a company based on audited financial statements that turn out to be materially misstated may be able to sue the auditor if balances become uncollectible, claiming that the auditor conducted a substandard audit. Similarly, equity investors who suffer a financial loss when relying on misstated financial statements may bring suit against the auditor. In these suits, the plaintiff is arguing that the auditor is the *proximate cause* of the financial loss and, therefore, should compensate the damaged parties for their losses. Cases brought under tort law usually claim that the auditor was grossly negligent, or that the auditor has committed fraud by knowingly making (or allowing) materially false misstatements in an audited financial report.

Plaintiff's keys to winning: To win a case against an auditor under common law, a plaintiff must prove that four conditions have been satisfied:

1. The financial statements of an organization were materially misleading.

2. The misstatement occurred because the auditor was negligent, grossly negligent or intentionally deceitful (the standard depends on the party bringing suit and the cause of action).

3. The plaintiff used and relied on the financial statements.

4. A loss was suffered by the plaintiff as the result of reliance on the information.

The legal basis for a suit has implications for the degree of audit misconduct that a plaintiff must demonstrate in order to win the case, as well as the defenses that an auditor can use as defendant. There are four possible standards of accountability that can be applied to the conduct of an audit in support of a plaintiff's case:

- **Negligence:** A lack of reasonable care in the conduct of the audit, either through accident or the exercise of poor judgment. The standard of comparison for determining negligence is what a competent auditor would do given a similar situation. Failure to comply with GAAS is often construed as negligence.

- **Gross negligence:** A reckless violation or disregard of auditing standards. In these situations, an auditor has made little effort to comply with appropriate professional standards.

- **Constructive fraud:** An intentional violation of auditing standards in order to avoid discovering facts that may be disagreeable is considered tantamount to fraud. Intentionally turning a blind eye to potentially questionable activity may be constructive fraud even if the auditor had no intent to deceive the users of financial statements or lacked explicit knowledge of fraud.[7]

- **Fraud:** The knowing and intentional misrepresentation of the financial statements with the complicity of the auditor.

In general, cases brought under contract law are judged against a negligence standard while cases brought under tort law are judgment against a gross negligence or constructive fraud standard. Obviously, negligence is the easiest for a plaintiff to prove and the hardest for the auditor to defend against.

Auditor Defenses: The defendant auditor has a number of defenses that can be used to counter charges of professional malpractice. The following five defenses are the most commonly used by auditors but not all defenses apply to all causes of action:

1. **No responsibility to plaintiff:** The auditor can claim that there is no "duty of care" or responsibility to the plaintiff, either because the plaintiff was not a party to the contract for services (referred to as a lack of *privity*) or because the level of service agreed to in the engagement letter was less than what is claimed in the lawsuit (e.g., the engagement was not an audit).

(vii)**EXAMPLE**

Ernst & Young (E&Y) in the UK spent £30 million pounds ($53 million US) plus thousands of hours of E&Y staff time over three years to defend itself against a £2.6 billon claim by its former client, Equitable Life, for audit work carried out in 1998 and 1999. Allegations against E&Y did not surface until 2003 and numerous leaks to news organizations suggested that Equitable's board was open to a settlement offer from E&Y to avoid a trial. E&Y proceeded to trial in early 2005 but in September Equitable Life's board withdrew the lawsuit apparently worried that under UK law it would be ordered to pay the costs of E&Y's defense if the case was decided in E&Y's favor. Equitable Life's former directors are still being sued by the new board but the claim against the auditors was dropped.

2. **Lack of reliance by the plaintiff:** The auditor can argue that the plaintiff was not aware of, or did not rely on, the information that is claimed to be misstated in the financial statements so the auditor is not responsible for losses incurred by the plaintiff.

3. **Auditor exercise of due diligence:** The auditor can claim that the conduct of the audit was effective and in compliance with all appropriate professional standards. The basis of this defense is that the audit was not substandard, notwithstanding the subsequent revelation of fraud or financial failure. This defense is most often used to counter an accusation of negligence.

4. **Lack of auditor intent to defraud:** The auditor can claim that even though some mistakes were made during the course of an audit engagement, they were "honest" mistakes and the auditor did not intentionally set out to perform a substandard audit or to defraud any parties using the financial statements. This defense can be effective against charges of gross negligence or constructive fraud.

5. **Contributory negligence by management:** This defense is based on the argument that the auditor should not be held liable for losses that are the plaintiff's own fault, that is, losses due to the action (or lack of action) of management. In these cases, the auditor claims a lack of liability because the management could have avoided the problem through their own appropriate behavior. An example where an auditor can claim contributory negligence is when the auditor alerts the company to potential problems but the management fails to take corrective action. Another example is when management intentionally deceives the auditor so as to cover up their own improper actions. This defense is useful for cases when the client firm is the plaintiff, or in jurisdictions which embrace the concept of separate and proportional liability.

The most commonly used defenses are no duty of care, lack of reliance by the plaintiff and the exercise of due diligence by the auditor. However, due diligence may be difficult to demonstrate when an actual fraudulent condition has been discovered or a company has suffered significant financial distress (e.g., recall the hindsight bias).

English-speaking countries like the UK, Ireland, Canada, Australia, and New Zealand tend to refer to precedents in each other's courts. Significant cases in the UK and other English-speaking countries are described in Table 16.5 (on next page).

The key case in the UK that led to the expansion of the ability of third parties to sue the auditor for negligence was *Hedley Byrne v. Heller & Partners (1961)*. The case did not actually involve an auditor but was brought against a merchant bank, Heller & Partners, that provided credit information about one of its clients to another bank that Heller knew would then be passed on to an unidentified customer. The House of Lords (the UK's highest court) ruled that the customer, Hedley Byrne, could sue Heller as they had a "special relationship." This doctrine was immediately applied in auditing cases both in the UK and in other English-speaking countries. Over time as litigation continued in other cases, the "special relationship" term was refined to the point that in *Anns vs. London Borough (1981)* the term was given almost

Table 16.5 *Summary of Significant Litigation against Auditors under Common Law in Other English Speaking Countries*

UK Case Name	Facts	Audit Application	Analogous Cases in Other English Speaking Countries
Hedley Bryne v. Heller & Partners	Heller & Partners, a merchant banking firm, provided incorrect data in response to a request from National Provincial Bank for credit information on Easipower Ltd. Heller & Partners knew that National would pass this information on to an unidentified customer. That customer, Hedley Bryne, employed that erroneous information to decide to extend credit to Easipower who subsequently went into liquidation.	Gave rise to the principle of foreseen third parties such that even if the auditor did not know the exact identity of the party, the auditor could be reasonably certain of knowing that such a specific party existed to whom a duty of care was owed.	Canada: *Haig v. Bamford*
JEB Fasteners v. Marks Bloom & Co.	JEB Fasteners acquired 100 percent of the shares of a privately held company relying, at least in part, on the unqualified audit opinion of Marks Bloom. The financial statements contained numerous errors including a material overstatement of inventory. When the auditor did the audit he was not aware of any takeover, although later he learned of it and cooperated with JEB by providing requested information.	Gave rise to the foreseeable class of third parties such that all potential users of financial statements that could be reasonably inferred to exist would be owed a duty of care by the auditor.	Canada: *Surrey Credit Union v. Willson* Australia: *Columbia Coffee & Tea Party v. Churchill* New Zealand: *Scott Group v. Macfarlane*
Caparo Industries v. Dickman	Existing shareholder and investor who bought additional shares based on audited statements that contained clear error (reported profits when company was in loss position).	Established the concept that the foreseeable user test should be balanced against the policy implications of an auditor being subject to an indeterminate liability for an indeterminate amount of time to an indeterminate number of parties, negating the possibility of a lawsuit against the auditor in this case.	Canada: *Hercules Management v. Ernst & Young* Australia: *Esanda Finance v. Peat Marwick Hungerfords* New Zealand: *Boyd Knight v. Purdue*

the same meaning as the US foreseeability test (see *Rosenblum*). Although the case involved no accountants, the precedent was cited extensively in litigation against auditors (see *JEB Fasteners v. Marks Bloom & Co.*)

English-speaking countries other than the US have seen judicial decisions move away from expanding the common law based duty of care to third parties who do not fit into the categories of primary beneficiaries or foreseen users. *Caparo Industries PLC v. Dickman* decided by the UK House of Lords involved Caparo Industries making a takeover bid for Fidelity PLC. After completing the takeover Caparo found that instead of a profit of £1.3 million, Fidelity had actually lost almost £0.5 million. The House of Lords devised a two-part test that has been adopted by Canadian, Australian, and New Zealand courts. The test is:

> **STEP ONE:** Is there a relationship of proximity between the parties? Put another way, are the parties' neighbors? Put another way still, is it reasonably foreseeable that carelessness by one party would adversely affect the other? If the answer is yes, then a duty of care is owed, subject to Step Two.
>
> **STEP TWO:** Are there any considerations that should limit the duty owed or eliminate it entirely?

Step one depends on the foreseeability of use and the nature of the professional relationship. In the case of a public company, the auditor knows that the results of his/her work will be communicated to known third parties or classes of third parties (e.g., potential investors). Assuming the third party can show they had a relationship, that is, the third party relied on the auditor's work and suffers a loss as a result, and that the audit is being used for the purposes for which it was prepared, then this test is readily met. Hence, for most public company auditors, the "Step One" test is met and the auditor owes a duty of care to these third parties.

The second step involves "policy considerations." In other words, is it good public policy for there to be an indeterminate amount of liability for an indeterminate amount of time to an indeterminate number of parties for auditors of public companies? The House of Lords concluded that this would likely drive audit firms out of business or to charge rates so high that only the largest client companies could afford to be publicly listed. The Lords suggested that this was not in accordance with the best interests of society and hence negated the auditor's duty of care to third parties that would lead to unbounded liability for auditors. Hence, Caparo was not allowed to sue the auditors of Fidelity. Overall, the conclusion across most other English-speaking countries is that an auditor may be sued for negligence associated with his/her work by foreseeable third parties but only when there is NOT an indeterminate amount of liability for an indeterminate amount of time to an indeterminate number of parties.

US Common Law Cases: US courts have wide latitude in determining their jurisdiction over companies that operate in the US, whether they are public or private. Hence, non-US companies who are active in the US may find themselves in a US courtroom if Americans have invested in those companies abroad, and even if the company is not registered with the US SEC. Furthermore, all public companies registered with the SEC will definitely be subject to the jurisdiction of one or more US courts. Hence, a basic understanding of US common law, especially as it differs dramatically from most other countries is relevant to auditors for any auditor who has clients operating in the US.

Table 16.6 (on next page) highlights several prominent common law cases against auditors in the US. Case law in this area was first defined by the

Table 16.6 *Summary of Significant Litigation against Auditors under US Common Law*

Case Name	Facts	Finding of Court	Significance to Audit Profession
Ultramares v. Touche, Niven & Co. (1933)	The auditor gave an unqualified opinion on the financial statements even though receivables turned out to be overstated by $1.2 million due to the recording of fictitious customers. The plaintiff lent money to the company based on the misstated financial reports.	• A third-party plaintiff cannot sue an auditor under contract law because they lack privity of contract so no breach of contract can occur relative to the third party. • A third-party plaintiff can sue the accountant using the standard of gross negligence (constructive fraud) under tort law.	• The auditing profession reworded the standard auditor's report, dropping words such as "certify" and "correct" from the opinion in the US.
McKesson-Robbins v. Price Waterhouse (1938)	An auditor gave an unqualified opinion on financial statements that included overstated assets of at least $19 million due to the recording of a nonexistent subsidiary supposedly located in Canada. The auditor did not confirm receivables nor observe inventory in Canada.	• Settled out of court.	• New audit standards were developed requiring the confirmation of receivables and the observation of inventory. • Affirmation that the auditor is hired by the shareholders of the company to protect their interests.
Rusch Factors v. Levin (1968)	The auditor was engaged at the request of a lender to audit the financial statements of a prospective borrower. A loan was granted based on the unqualified report of the auditor. The borrower subsequently was determined to be insolvent.	• The lender could be considered a primary beneficiary under the *Ultramares* precedent. • Additionally, under tort law, members of a *foreseen and limited class of persons* may be able to sue for ordinary negligence (rather than just gross negligence).	• Reduced the standard of evidence for some classes of plaintiffs, making it harder for auditors to defend against some cases brought under common law.
1136 Tenants Corporation v. Max Rothenberg and Company (1972)	An accountant was hired by an apartment co-operative to draft (not audit) financial statements and other reports for the co-op. There was no engagement letter. It was later discovered that management of the co-op was embezzling significant funds which probably would have been discovered using normal audit procedures. The accountant was aware of missing documentation for many transactions. The co-op claimed they believed they were receiving an audit.	• The auditor had performed some tests that would constitute audit procedures. • The auditor was aware of the potential problems but did not report the problems. • The accountant did not issue a disclaimer. • Auditor was held liable.	• Auditors encouraged to always obtain a clear engagement letter. • Auditors required to bring evidence of irregularities to the attention of appropriate personnel within the organization. • Accountants required to issue a disclaimer report whenever they are "associated" with financial statements (see Standards on Compilation and Review Services in Chapter 14).

(Continued)

Table 16.6 *(Continued)*

Case Name	Facts	Finding of Court	Significance to Audit Profession
Cenco v. Seidman & Seidman (1982)	Management of the company systematically overstated inventory balances in order to inflate assets. This allowed the company to file overstated fire insurance claims and to borrow money at favorable interest rates. After the fraud was discovered, the accountants settled a class action suit out of court with shareholders. New management then sued the accountant for breach of contract and gross negligence.	• The pervasive and active role of prior management in perpetrating the fraud was a valid defense against the suit filed by new management.	• Clarified the concept of contributory negligence under common law.
Rosenblum v. Adler (1983)	Giant Stores acquired H. Rosenblum in exchange for stock in Giant. When the financial statements were later discovered to be materially misstated, the stock received by the owners of Rosenblum was virtually worthless. Suit was brought against the auditors of Giant for not discovering the fraud.	• Court rejected the *Ultramares* defense of no privity of contract. • Determined that the auditor has a responsibility to all parties that they could *reasonably foresee* as using and relying on the financial statements for business purposes.	• Extended the concept of foreseeable users who can use the negligence standard under tort law.
National Medical Transportation Network v. Deloitte & Touche (1998)	The auditor was sued by the client after withdrawing from an engagement on the grounds that the CFO resigned rather than sign a representation letter and the company resisted making required adjustments to the financial statements. The company claimed that the auditor's withdrawal damaged the company's prospects for obtaining favorable financing.	• Jury found for company but California Court of Appeals overturned the decision. • Court ruled that judges should instruct juries about the professional standards applicable to an issue.	• Upheld auditor's professional rights and obligations to disassociate for cause from a client of questionable character.

Ultramares case, which found that a plaintiff must have ***privity of contract*** or be a primary beneficiary under the contract in order to sue the auditor for breach of contract. In general, a case based on contract law requires the plaintiff to demonstrate that the auditor was negligent in order to be found in breach of contract. The court also ruled that a broader class of parties can sue under common law but the standard of performance used in those cases would be gross negligence or constructive fraud. Although not a judicial decision as the auditor agreed to a large out-of-court settlement, the *McKesson-Robbins* case provides insight into what gross negligence means in the context of auditing malpractice. In this case the auditor failed to confirm receivables or inspect inventory, two procedures that are required for any audit done today.

Case law has continuously wrestled with the issue of who can sue an auditor under a negligence standard. Plaintiffs prefer the negligence standard since it is easier to prove; defendants prefer the more lenient gross negligence standard. Two cases were instrumental in broadening the class of potential litigants that could use the negligence standard. In *Rusch Factors v. Levin,* the court concluded that a primary beneficiary who is identified in the audit service contract (the engagement letter) is entitled to sue using the negligence standard even though not an official party to the contract. This decision applies to a class of parties the court described as foreseen and limited. In *Rosenblum v. Adler*, however, a New Jersey court broadened the class to include all reasonably **foreseeable users** of the financial statements whether identified or not. The precedent does not apply to all states, however, many of which follow the *Restatement (Second) of Torts*. However, since the restatement is unclear about distinguishing types of plaintiffs, states cover the full range from *Ultramares* to *Rosenblum*[8] to somewhere in between.

The other three common law cases discussed in Table 16.6 are notable because of their significance to the practice of auditing. First, the *1136 Tenants* case established the need for clear contractual arrangements with clients (engagement letters) in order to avoid misunderstandings about the level of service being provided. The second case, *Cenco v. Seidman & Seidman*, clarified the concept of contributory negligence on the part of management and emphasized that a client cannot sue the auditor for damages caused by their own actions (or inaction), especially if management was intentionally deceiving the auditor. Finally, in *National Medical Transportation Network v. Deloitte & Touche*, a California court upheld the right and obligation of an auditor to disassociate from a client of questionable integrity and emphasized that professional standards are relevant to determining the merits of a case.

To summarize the current status of auditors' legal liability under common law in the US: Parties that have privity of contract with an auditor can readily sue for damages using the negligence standard in all US states. Parties that do not have privity or are not primary beneficiaries or foreseeable users may be required to demonstrate gross negligence in order to recover damages depending on the specifics of the individual state. In either case, potentially effective defenses include lack of responsibility, lack of reliance or contributory negligence.[9]

Legal Liability: Statutory Law

Auditors are also subject to the requirements embedded in statutory law promulgated by legislative bodies. In common law countries, these laws may supplement rights and obligations established by court precedent, often expanding or limiting the rights of persons to sue an auditor. In code law countries, lawsuits are only possible when expressively permitted by statutory law. While few countries have a basis for auditor litigation in statutory law, the US has extensive experience in using civil statute law to pursue and penalize auditors who fail to meet their professional obligations. Most auditor litigation in the US falls within three sets of statutes: (1) 1933

SEC Act, (2) 1934 SEC Act, and (3) the 1970 Racketeer Influenced and Corrupt Organizations Act (RICO). All of these laws can be applied to any US SEC registered public company, including those subject to an Integrated Audit, from anywhere in the world with the exception of RICO which is limited to illegal activities committed in the US.

SEC Acts of 1933 and 1934: These statutes provide for either civil lawsuits by third parties for damages or criminal prosecutions of individuals charged with violating the statutes (covered in the next section). The ***SEC Act of 1933*** applies to companies that issue new securities for public trading. Section 11 of the Act imposes liability on parties, including underwriters and auditors, who are associated with misstatements or omissions in a registration statement prepared in conjunction with an initial public offering of securities. Section 12 imposes liabilities if a prospectus is omitted or contains incorrect information and Sections 17 and 24 cover fraudulent actions occurring in conjunction with an initial public offering.

In general, the burden of proof on the plaintiff is relatively low in cases brought under the 1933 Act. In order to win such a case, the plaintiff has to demonstrate that the financial statements were materially misstated at the time the securities were offered to the public, that the auditor was negligent, and that the plaintiff acquired the securities and suffered a loss. The plaintiff does not have to show actual reliance on the financial statements. This standard established a virtual strict liability approach to financial reporting for new issues of securities—if the statements are wrong, the auditor is likely to be held responsible. However, the auditor can use a due diligence defense in such cases.

The ***SEC Act of 1934*** extends the auditor's liability to any information that is required to be filed with the SEC, most importantly, annual financial statements. From the auditor's perspective, the key part of the statute is Rule 10b-5:

> *It shall be unlawful for any person directly or indirectly, by the use of any means or instrumentality of interstate commerce, or the mails or any facility of any national securities exchange, (a) to employ any device, scheme, or artifice to defraud, (b) to make any untrue statement of a material fact or omit to state a material fact necessary in order to make the statements made, in the light of circumstances under which they were made, not misleading, or (c) to engage in any act, practice, or course of business which operates or would operate as a fraud or deceit upon any person in connection with the purchase or sale of any security.*

Misstatements in the annual financial statements that cause damage to investors can become the basis for a cause of action against the auditor. However, plaintiffs must demonstrate reliance on the information to recover under the 1934 Act and must demonstrate that the auditor was grossly negligent. The primary defenses available for civil cases against an auditor under the 1934 Act are due diligence and lack of reliance.

Illustrative cases under SEC Acts: Cases related to the statutory law are summarized in Table 16.7. The *Yale Express* case clarified that Rule 10b-5 applies to information contained in the annual financial statements and placed a burden on the auditor to act upon information that indicates that financial statements are misstated, even if obtained after the end of fieldwork. The *BarChris* case established that compliance with professional

Table 16.7 *Summary of Significant Litigation against Auditors under US Statutory Law: Civil Actions*

Case Name	Legal Basis	Facts	Finding of Court	Significance to Audit Profession
Fischer v. Kletz "Yale Express" (1967)	SEC Act of 1934	An accountant who was involved in a consulting engagement found evidence of material misstatements in financial statements that were examined by the firm three months previously. The information was not brought to the attention of the audit team or followed up in any way.	• The court ruled that Rule 10b-5 of the SEC Act of 1934 applies to annual financial statements. • The auditor has the duty to bring irregularities to the attention of appropriate personnel. • The auditor has the duty to inform parties relying on the previous audit report of the new information.	• Clarified the application of Rule 10b-5 to the audit of financial statements. • Events subsequent to the date of the financial statements should be considered when rendering an opinion on the financial statements.
Escott v. BarChris Construction (1968)	SEC Act of 1933	The company issued convertible bonds shortly after the completion of an audit. The audit failed to detect gross overstatements in earnings due to mistreatment of sale-leaseback transactions. The company went bankrupt and the accountant was sued based on their review of the information in the proxy statements.	• Compliance with current generally accepted auditing standards is not a complete defense against charges of negligence.	• Auditors should emphasize fairness as well as GAAP in evaluating the financial statements.
Hochfelder v. Ernst & Ernst (1976)	SEC Act of 1934	Customers of an investment company were swindled by the president of the organization who misdirected certain deposits to his own use. The funds were not recorded on the books of the investment company. When the fraud was discovered, the investors sued the auditor. The trial court dismissed the action, ruling that negligence is not enough to find the auditor liable. The Court of Appeals reversed the trial court.	• The Supreme Court ruled that the application of Rule 10b-5 requires intent to deceive for the plaintiff to recover, which was absent from the case against the auditors.	• Auditors can be held liable under Rule 10b-5 of the 1934 SEC Act only when they have *scienter* ("the intent to deceive"). • The case left open the issue of reckless behavior, which is tantamount to fraud.

(Continued)

Table 16.7 *(Continued)*

Case Name	Legal Basis	Facts	Finding of Court	Significance to Audit Profession
Howard Sirota v. Solitron Devices (1982)	SEC Act of 1934	The auditor failed to detect overstatements of inventory balances that resulted in inflated earnings. A jury found the auditor guilty of "reckless behavior" but the judge overturned the decision.	• The Court of Appeals determined that the auditor should have had knowledge of the fraud. • The Court of Appeals concluded that reckless behavior constitutes intent under Rule 10b-5.	• Clarified concept of constructive fraud without intent as applied to reckless behavior of auditors.
Reves v. Ernst & Young (1993)	RICO	The auditor failed to detect behavior by management that was potentially fraudulent and led to the bankruptcy of the client (a farm co-op). Plaintiffs claimed that the firm had misvalued the company and assisted in the perpetration of a fraud.	• The Court found that the auditor must be directly and actively involved in perpetrating fraudulent activity to be accountable under RICO. Mere performance of an attest engagement does not make an auditor liable under RICO.	• Removed the overhanging threat of prosecution under RICO for mere negligence or errors in auditor judgment.

standards is not an adequate defense to all claims of negligence and that the auditor must also look to the general fairness of the financial statements when conducting the audit.

The *Hochfelder* case is important to auditors because it represented a judicial swing in their favor. The US Supreme Court concluded that auditors can be held liable under Rule 10b-5 only when they have intent to deceive readers of the financial statements. Absent intent, a plaintiff cannot recover under securities law. However, the Court went on to hint that reckless behavior by an auditor may be a basis for plaintiff relief but did not make an explicit finding on the issue. This issue was further resolved a few years later in *Howard Sirota v. Solitron Devices*, where the Court of Appeals decided that reckless behavior was tantamount to constructive fraud.

Racketeer Influenced and Corrupt Organizations Act (RICO): RICO identifies a large number of illegal activities that come under the umbrella of the act, including mail fraud and wire fraud, and plaintiffs have attempted to apply this law to instances of financial statement fraud or misstatement. In the case of outright fraud, auditors may be sued under the RICO act for treble damages. However, in *Reves v. Ernst & Young*, the US Supreme Court held that RICO does not apply to auditors unless they are actively involved in the fraudulent activity. Mere negligence, or even gross negligence, does not constitute a sustainable cause of action under RICO. Prior to this decision, the threat of treble damages was a significant incentive for auditors to settle even trivial cases out of court.

Legal Prosecution: Criminal Law

While virtually non-existent in the English-speaking world outside the US, auditors may be criminally prosecuted if their actions are in violation of criminal statutes. Most countries have the ability to charge auditors under their criminal code using laws that exist against fraud. For example, one possible area of prosecution under the Canadian Criminal Code is the following:

> Section 380 (2) Everyone who, by deceit, falsehood or other fraudulent means, whether or not it is a false pretence within the meaning of this Act, with intent to defraud, affects the public market price of stocks, shares, merchandise or anything that is offered for sale to the public is guilty of an indictable offence and liable to imprisonment for a term not exceeding ten years.

However, there are no records in Canada of the auditor of a public company being charged with criminal fraud or other criminal offenses related to his/her actions as an auditor.

The only non-US criminal prosecution of an auditor in connection with a public company audit is the Australian case of *Carter v. the Queen*. Carter, an audit partner in a predecessor firm of KPMG, was convicted in 1996 of conspiracy to defraud the public and concurring in publishing false reports in connection with the audit of Rothwells Limited, a clothing retailer turned merchant bank. While even the prosecutor noted that Carter was not motivated by greed or personal gain, the audit was so poorly carried out that it constituted criminal fraud. The court concluded that the auditor had no chance of detecting material misstatements since he relied almost entirely on management representations and obtained little or no independent evidence to verify those representations. Carter was sentenced to four years and three months in prison for his part in the fraud, and served a year.

Criminal prosecutions are rare in the US, however there are at least three sets of criminal statutes that are relevant to auditors: (1) SEC Acts of 1933 and 1934, (2) obstruction of justice laws, and (3) the Sarbanes-Oxley Act of 2002.

SEC Acts of 1933 and 1934: While rarely used, the SEC Acts of 1933 and 1934 specifically allow for criminal prosecution of auditors who are intentionally culpable in fraudulent misrepresentation of financial statements. Table 16.8 summarizes legal cases related to criminal prosecutions in the US. The first case where an auditor was criminally prosecuted was *Continental Vending*. In this case, three auditors were found guilty of constructive fraud because they wantonly ignored evidence of misrepresented related party transactions, even though there were no generally accepted reporting standards for such transactions at the time. In *National Student Marketing*, the auditors were guilty of aiding and abetting the client in executing a fraud and ended up serving prison sentences for their role in violating securities laws. These criminal prosecutions always focused on individual auditors and not the firm as a whole.

Obstruction of justice laws: The infamous criminal prosecution of the firm of Arthur Andersen that followed from the Enron accounting fraud was the first

Table 16.8 *Summary of Significant Litigation against Auditors under US Statutory Law: Criminal Actions*

Case Name	Legal Basic	Facts	Finding of Court	Significance to Audit Profession
United States v. Simon "Continental Vending" (1969)	SEC Act of 1934	The auditor was aware of a number of problems at the client including improper recognition of related party loans and loans that were secured by company stock with an inflated value. At the time, there were no generally accepted accounting principles for reporting related party transactions.	• The Court emphasized the auditor should evaluate fairness of financial reporting, not just compliance with GAAP. • Three auditors were found criminally guilty and sentenced to prison.	• Gave impetus for the development of FASB No. 57 on related party transactions. • Established the threat of criminal prosecution against auditors guilty of constructive or actual fraud.
United States v. Natelli "National Student Marketing" (1975)	SEC Act of 1934	The auditor failed to detect fictitious sales and receivables at the time of an audit. When discovered at a later date, the auditors were persuaded by the client to not reveal the information. No disclosures or adjustments were made to the financial statements in spite of the auditors' knowledge.	• The auditors were criminally guilty of constructive fraud and two individuals were sentenced to prison.	• Emphasized the threat of criminal prosecution in cases of auditor culpability in securities fraud cases.
United States vs. Arthur Andersen (2002)	US Criminal Code Section 1512	The Houston office of Andersen as well as other offices involved in the Enron audit shredded documents and destroyed electronic files that might have been pertinent to an imminent SEC investigation of Enron's accounting.	• The audit firm was found guilty of obstruction of justice in the jury trial and was ordered to pay a fine of $500,000. • The case was overturned on appeal in 2005 by the unanimous decision of the US Supreme Court based on the judge's instructions to the jury.	• The first criminal prosecution of an entire audit firm, not just the partners directly involved. • Demonstrated that audit firms (and auditors) could be criminally prosecuted for actions not directly related to the audit in question but rather how they managed their response to the potential for a government investigation.

time that the US Department of Justice decided to prosecute more than just the individual partners engaged in the alleged wrongdoing. Furthermore, it was not based on the SEC Acts but rather on an obstruction of justice statute that states in part:

Sec. 1512. Tampering with a witness, victim or an informant......

(b) Whoever knowingly uses intimidation or physical force, threatens, or corruptly persuades another person, or attempts to do so, or engages in misleading conduct toward another person, with intent to - .....

(2) cause or induce any person to - .....

(B) Alter, destroy, mutilate, or conceal an object with intent to impair the object's integrity or availability for use in an official proceeding, ...

shall be fined under this title or imprisoned for not more than ten years, or both.

Andersen was not charged with fraud or any illegal act directly related to its audit of Enron but, rather, of destroying documents in anticipation of an SEC investigation into the Andersen audit of Enron. While the US Supreme Court overturned the guilty verdict on a technical issue related to the wording of the judge's instructions to the jury, the guilty verdict meant that Andersen could not continue its audit practice and effectively shut down operations as of August 31, 2002.

Sarbanes-Oxley Act of 2002 (SOX): The provisions of SOX have been mentioned in numerous places throughout the text. This recently enacted law increased the criminal penalties under the SEC Acts from a maximum of five to ten years for most securities offenses. Furthermore, SOX made clear that actions like those taken by Andersen to shred documents in light of the imminent investigation by the SEC were illegal and could result in up to twenty years of imprisonment. Section 303 of SOX also makes it a crime "for any officer or director of an issuer to take any action to fraudulently influence, coerce, manipulate, or mislead any auditor engaged in the performance of an audit for the purpose of rendering the financial statements materially misleading."

Summary and Conclusion

In this chapter, we discussed how the audit process can be viewed as an ethical decision process carried out by a trained professional accountant as a member of the auditing profession. We documented how the unaided judgment of an auditor can be biased by a variety of information processing heuristics and biases and the conflicts caused by ethical dilemmas. We then examined how auditors constantly strive to get better at what they do. Indeed one of the principle functions of audit firms is to put processes in place that aid individual auditors in overcoming these judgment deficiencies, although firm incentives may sometimes seem to reward questionable auditor behavior.

We also examined the institutional forces that support the auditor in making ethical decisions whether they are based on professional rules or mandated by government regulation: codes of professional conduct, rules of auditor independence, audit firm and partner rotation, auditing standards, quality control frameworks and indicators, quality control standards, and peer reviews or practice inspections. Finally, we examined the institutions that exist to discourage and sanction inappropriate auditor behavior, including regulatory intervention and legal actions of either a civil or a criminal nature. The Sarbanes-Oxley Act of 2002 is the most recent development in this area and the Act will continue to influence the behavior of auditors as regulators implement rules and regulations derived from the Act.

Bibliography of Relevant Literature

Research

Asare S. and L. S. McDaniel. 1995. The Effects of Familiarity with the Preparer and Task Complexity on the Effectiveness of the Audit Review Process. *The Accounting Review*, April, 139–160.

Ashton, R. H. and A. H. Ashton. 1988. Sequential Belief Revision in Auditing. *The Accounting Review*, October: 623–641.

Blay, A.D. 2005. Independence Threats, Litigation Risk and the Auditor's Decision Process. *Contemporary Accounting Research*. 22(4): 759–789.

Chaney, P. K. 2002. Shredded Reputation: The Cost of Audit Failure. *Journal of Accounting Research*. 40(4): 1221–1245.

Donaldson, I. 2000. The Carter Case: Falling into "the Audit Gap". *Australian CPA*. 70(1): 36–39.

Erickson, M., B. W. Mayhew and W. L. Felix Jr. 2000. Why do Audits Fail? Evidence from Lincoln Savings and Loan. *Journal of Accounting Research*. 38 (1): 165–194.

Gunz, S. and S. Salterio. 2004. What if Andersen had Shredded in Toronto or Calgary? The Potential Criminal Liability of Canadian Public Accounting Firms. *Canadian Accounting Perspectives*. 3(1): 59–84.

Joyce, E. J. and G. C. Biddle. 1981. Are Auditors' Judgments Sufficiently Regressive? *Journal of Accounting Research*, Autumn: 323–349.

Kaplan, S. E. and S. M. Whitecotton. 2001. An Examination of Auditors' Reporting Intentions when another Auditor is Offered Client Employment. *Auditing: A Journal of Practice & Theory*. 20(1): 45–64.

Khurana, I. K. and K. K. Raman. 2004. Litigation Risk and Financial Reporting Credibility of Big 4 versus Non-Big 4 Audits: Evidence from Anglo-American Countries. *The Accounting Review*. 79(2): 473–495.

Kinney, W. R. Jr. and W. Uecker. 1982. Mitigating the Consequences of Anchoring in Auditor Judgments. *The Accounting Review*, January: 55–69.

Koonce, L. 1992. Explanation and Counter-Explanation during Analytical Review. *The Accounting Review*. 68(1): 59–76.

Larsson, B. 2005. Auditor Regulation and Economic Crime Policy in Sweden 1986–2000. *Accounting, Organizations and Society*. 30(2): 127–144.

Pacini, C., M. J. Martin and L. Hamilton. 2000. At the Interface of Law and Accounting: An Examination of a Trend to a Reduction in the Scope of Auditor Liability to Third Parties in Common Law Countries. *American Business Law Journal*. 37(2): 171–235.

Professional Reports and Guidance

Institute of Chartered Accountants in England & Wales Audit and Assurance Faculty. 2003. *The Audit Report and the Auditors' Duty of Care to Third Parties.* Technical Release.

Library of Congress. 2002. House Resolution Number 3763, An Act to Protect Investors by Improving the Accuracy and Reliability of Corporate Disclosures made Pursuant to the Securities Laws, and for other Purposes (*The Sarbanes-Oxley Act of 2002).* www.libraryofcongress.gov.

Metcalf Committee (US Senate Subcommittee on Reports, Accounting and Management of the Committee on Governmental Affairs). 1976. *The Accounting Establishment: A Staff Study.* www.libraryofcongress.gov.

Auditing Standards

Criminal Code of Canada. *An Act respecting the Criminal Law.* R.S.C., 1985, c. C-46. http://laws-lois.justice.gc.ca/eng/acts/C-46/page-1.html#h-1

IAASB *International Standards on Auditing* (ISA) No. 220, "Quality Control for an Audit of Financial Statements."

IAASB *International Standard on Quality Control (ISQC)* No. 1. "Quality Control for Firms that Perform Audits and Reviews of Financial Statements, and Other Assurance and Related Services Engagements."

IESBA. *Code of Conduct for Professional Accountants.* Section 290. "Independence—Audit and Review Engagements."

IFAC. International Auditing and Assurance Standards Board (IAASB). 2014. *Handbook of International Quality Control, Audit, Review, Other Assurance, and Related Services Pronouncements.* New York: International Federation of Accountants.

IFAC. International Ethics Standards Board for Accountants. 2015. *Code of Ethics for Professional Accountants.* New York: International Federation of Accountants.

Obstruction of Justice—Library of Congress. Section 1512 *Tampering with a Witness, Victim, or an Informant.* 18 U.S. Code Chapter 73 www.libraryofcongress.gov.

PCAOB. *Auditing Standard* 1220 (formerly *No. 7*), "Engagement Quality Review".

PCAOB. 2015. Concept Release on Audit Quality Indicators.

PCAOB. *Interim Quality Control Standards as amended by the PCAOB.*

PCAOB. *Statement on Quality Control Standards* (SQCS) QC 20, "System of Quality Control for a CPA Firm's Accounting and Auditing Practice."

SEC Act—Library of Congress. 1934 (as amended to 2012). *Securities Exchange Act of 1934.* June 6, 1934, ch. 404, title I, Sec. 1, 48 Stat. 881. www.libraryofcongress.gov.

Notes

1 Among the first to identify this in auditing was Lisa Koonce in her 1992 article "Explanation and Counter-Explanation during Analytical Review" *The Accounting Review*, 68(1): 59–76.

2 While many others have studied this issue the first article on this topic was "Are Auditors' Judgments Sufficiently Regressive?" by E. J. Joyce and G. C. Biddle *(Journal of Accounting Research*, Autumn 1981, pp. 323–349).

3 See "The Effects of Familiarity with the Preparer and Task Complexity on the Effectiveness of the Audit Review Process" by S. Asare and L. S. McDaniel *(The Accounting Review*, April 1995, pp. 139–160).

4 The first article to document this in auditing was "Sequential Belief Revision in Auditing" by R. H. Ashton and A. H. Ashton *(The Accounting Review*, October 1988, pp. 623–641).

5 See "Mitigating the Consequences of Anchoring in Auditor Judgments" by W. R. Kinney Jr. and W. Uecker *(The Accounting Review*, January 1982, pp. 55–69).

6 Although less common, some US states allow for separate and proportional liability, which has the effect of sharing a judgment among all guilty parties in proportion to their culpability. This is a position that is being examined in other common law countries such as the UK.

7 Many courts make no distinction between gross negligence and constructive fraud.

8 Other cases related to the foreseeable party precedent are *Citizen's State Bank v. Timm, Schmidt & Co.*, Wisconsin, 1983 and *Credit Alliance Corp. v. Arthur Andersen & Co.*, 1985.

9 Whether an auditor can use the contributory negligence defense against *new* management is subject to variations across jurisdictions.

CHAPTER 17

Interpreting Sample-Based Audit Evidence

Outline

o   Step 7: Determine the Sample Size (*n*)

o   Step 8: Select the Sample

o   Step 9: Perform the Audit Procedure and Document the Results

o   Step 10: Generalize the Sample Results to the Population

o   Step 11: Analyze Individual Errors

o   Step 12: Conclude Whether the Account Balance Tested is Acceptable

•   Judgmental Approaches to Sampling

•   Common Errors in Sampling

•   Summary and Conclusion

•   Bibliography of Relevant Literature

Learning Goals for this Material

1. To use sampling techniques to test controls and details of transactions (attributes sampling) and details of account balances (dollar unit sampling).

2. To apply general concepts of sampling to audit populations.

3. To understand when it is appropriate to employ statistical and non-statistical sampling techniques.

4. To understand non-statistical (i.e., judgmental) sampling approaches.

5. To evaluate the results of statistical and non-statistical samples.

6. To implement attribute sampling for tests of controls and transactions.

7. To implement dollar unit sampling for tests of account balances.

8. To identify and avoid common errors committed in sampling plans.

Introduction

Auditors can never examine every risk, event, or transaction that may affect the financial statements of a company, nor can they use substantive tests to verify every entry to every account in the financial statements. For companies such as Wal-Mart or Tesco, which experience millions of sales transactions, auditors may examine only a small portion of the actual recorded transactions. Auditors need to prioritize their audit efforts and focus their attention on areas where risks are most significant to the company and the risk of material misstatements is highest. The phrase "nature, extent, and timing of audit evidence" implicitly recognizes that the auditor must make tradeoffs in the type and volume of evidence obtained during the audit.

When considering tests of controls or substantive tests, an auditor will obtain *sample* evidence concerning risks, controls, transactions, or assertions being examined. **Sampling risk** is the portion of detection risk that arises because the auditor does not examine all items in a population of transactions or accounts. A well-designed approach to audit sampling can help the auditor to accurately assess and manage sampling risk. The other component of detection risk is **non-sampling risk**, which is best managed with a careful selection of the audit procedures to be performed.

AUTHORITATIVE GUIDANCE & STANDARDS

This chapter covers audit sampling, which is described in ISA 530 and PCAOB AS 2315 (formerly AU 350) both entitled **Audit Sampling.**

The Role of Sampling in an Audit

The nature and extent of sampling used by an auditor depends on the assertions being tested, the nature of the population from which the items are to be selected, and the auditor's assessment of the risk of material misstatement. Examples of common audit procedures that involve sampling include:

- Select a *sample* of weekly sales reports and review management's response to potential problems in the process (test of management controls).
- Select a *sample* of purchase requisitions and verify proper authorizations (test of process controls).
- Select a *sample* of locations and observe inventory count procedures executed by client personnel (test of process controls).
- Select a *sample* of shift changes within the factory and observe employees clocking in and out (test of process controls).
- Select a *sample* of sales invoices and test the accuracy of individual transactions by verifying quantities and prices against appropriate supporting documentation (substantive test of transactions).
- Select a *sample* of accounts receivable to be confirmed with customers (substantive test of account details).

The increased use of computer-assisted audit techniques (CAATs) enable an auditor to examine all items in a population reduces the need for sample-based tests. However, there are many process controls that cannot be tested using CAATs. For example, a CAAT test can ensure that the system produces the weekly sales reports and compares it to budget or standard, but it cannot tell if the manager actually reviewed the report, noticed a discrepancy, and acted on it to assure that the sales system is under control.

Sampling is not an end unto itself; it is the means of collecting audit evidence that is then evaluated to determine if various assertions are accurate and, in the aggregate, whether the financial statements are in accordance with GAAP. There are two ways to implement sampling once the decision to sample has been made:

- **Statistical:** The factors that are important to collecting the sample are quantified and used as input to the sampling process. As a result, the auditor can interpret the evidence collected using established statistical principles that consider the margin of error in the resulting evidence.

- **Non-statistical (judgmental):** This approach relies on the auditor's experience and judgment to determine how many sample items to select and how to interpret the sample evidence.

Many large public accounting firms have chosen to use judgmental sampling on many clients, and often use standardized sample sizes such as 25, 50, or 100 items, with the larger samples being used where the risk of material misstatement is considered to be the greatest. Where do these numbers come from? Are they reasonable? Are they big enough or too big? How much can the auditor rely on the evidence from such samples? How do auditors project the evidence from a handful of transactions to the entire population of transactions? These questions can only be answered by having a good understanding of the concepts and theory that provide the foundation on which sampling methods are based, be they statistical or judgmental.

Many audit tests are activity-dependent or transaction-dependent, meaning that a sample of items to be tested should be selected from the full set of activities or transactions that have taken place to provide evidence that the activity or recorded transaction occurred or exists (this is especially important for assets and revenue). For example, an auditor can select a sample from the sequence of prenumbered sales invoices to test that each sale was authorized, valued correctly, and made to a real customer. Other procedures are time-dependent, requiring the auditor to select periods of time to test (i.e., times to observe employee behavior or dates to test transaction totals). Still other procedures may be dependent on tangible characteristics, for example, store locations, items of inventory, or physical but movable fixed assets (furniture and fixtures).

Regardless of the actual audit procedures being performed, well-established techniques exist for improving the quality of evidence the auditor obtains through sampling. No matter how an auditor obtains a sample, it is vital that he or she interpret the results in a consistent and logical manner. The auditor should consider three issues when obtaining evidence using a sample-based audit procedure:

1. **The number of transactions or items to examine:** This decision will often be based on the risk associated with the account being audited, with larger samples being used in higher risk situations.

2. **The actual transactions or items to examine:** The selection of items to be examined can be accomplished in a number of ways depending on the composition of the activity, account balance, or nature of transaction.

3. **Interpreting the results of the sample:** The auditor makes inferences about the entire population based on the sample results. This process depends on the nature of the procedure being performed, the sampling process, and the results of the examination.

In the remainder of the chapter, we will first consider the sample selection process. We will then consider two specialized applications of statistical sampling: (1) sampling used for tests of internal controls and tests of transactions, and (2) sampling used for substantive tests of account details. For each of these approaches, we will address the questions of sample size and sample evaluation from a statistical viewpoint. We conclude the chapter with a discussion of non-statistical or judgmental sampling as well as common errors made by auditors when using sample-based evidence.

Selecting a Sample for Audit Testing

The first question an auditor must address is the size of a sample to use when gathering evidence from a larger population. The sample size for a given audit procedure will depend on two main factors:

1. **The assertion(s) being tested:** A sample-based test can be used to examine a number of attributes that might be of interest to an auditor including whether a transaction is properly authorized, meets appropriate control requirements, and is correctly valued and processed. The more significant the assertion(s) is to the overall audit, the larger the sample will be.

2. **Assessment of risk:** The higher the level of risk associated with the assertion, the larger the sample size will be for testing the attributes associated with that assertion. That is, the higher the likelihood that an audit procedure will reveal significant problems, the more items the auditor will wish to examine to have a better basis to quantify potential problems.

Once the sample size has been determined, the auditor chooses the actual items or transactions that are to be examined from the population.

Population of Prenumbered Documents

The most common application of sampling is when there are a large number of documents from which to choose. In many cases, documents are prenumbered (either preprinted on a form or numbered by the computer system), used in sequence, and the auditor knows the first and last document used in the period being audited. Then, selecting a sample to test simply involves choosing numbers that uniquely identify documents within the period. The overall goal of sample selection is to obtain a sample that is *representative* of the underlying population, i.e., the sample mirrors the entire population. If 5 percent of the transactions in the underlying population have errors, a good sample would reveal a 5 percent error rate. Of course, the auditor can never know the error rate in the population, which is why sampling is needed in the first place.

The auditor's understanding of the risk, either process- or strategic-based, and the nature of the processes and management controls designed to reduce that risk, provide the basis for evaluating the likelihood of error. A representative sample allows the auditor to accurately evaluate the amount of

AUTHORITATIVE GUIDANCE & STANDARDS

ISA 530 and PCAOB AS 2315 state that sample items should be selected in such a way that they are representative of the population, regardless of the method chosen to select the sample.

sampling risk implicit in a sampling plan. Furthermore, different approaches to sampling affect the likelihood the auditor will obtain a representative sample. The following five sampling techniques are commonly used by auditors, but the first two are most likely to result in a representative sample:

1. Random sampling.
2. Systematic sampling.
3. Block sampling.
4. Haphazard sampling.
5. Judgmental sampling.

For our discussion, assume we wish to generate a sample of ten invoices from a total population of sixty-five invoices that were prepared during one month.[1] Table 17.1 presents information on each transaction including the invoice number, the date, and the amount. This summary provides us with enough information to use any of our sampling techniques.

Table 17.1 *Sampling from a Population of Prenumbered Documents: Sales Journal Example*

Item Count	Sales Invoice Number	Date of Sale	Transaction Total	Cumulative Total
1	10394	1/2	422.28	422.28
2	10395	1/2	2,982.13	3,404.41
3	10396	1/2	1,854.92	5,259.33
4	10397	1/3	778.70	6,038.03
5	10398	1/4	2,989.73	9,027.76
6	10399	1/4	994.86	10,022.62
7	10400	1/5	1,157.55	11,180.17
8	10401	1/5	504.33	11,684.50
9	10402	1/5	2,301.01	13,985.51
10	10403	1/5	1,953.77	15,939.28
11	10404	1/5	901.86	16,841.14
12	10405	1/7	97.37	16,938.51
13	10406	1/8	2,886.61	19,825.12
14	10407	1/8	4,384.24	24,209.36
15	10408	1/8	2,863.38	27,072.74
16	10409	1/8	869.77	27,942.51
17	10410	1/8	2,414.72	30,357.23
18	10411	1/8	1,579.92	31,937.15
19	10412	1/9	770.19	32,707.34
20	10413	1/11	660.04	33,367.38
21	10414	1/12	2,683.15	36,050.53
22	10415	1/12	934.81	36,985.34
23	10416	1/12	1,177.98	38,163.32
24	10417	1/12	1,872.47	40,035.79
25	10418	1/12	317.66	40,353.45
26	10419	1/14	1,157.45	41,510.90

Item Count	Sales Invoice Number	Date of Sale	Transaction Total	Cumulative Total
27	10420	1/14	4,288.68	45,799.58
28	10421	1/15	289.35	46,088.93
29	10422	1/17	441.17	46,530.10
30	10423	1/17	178.61	46,708.71
31	10424	1/18	374.78	47,083.49
32	10425	1/18	151.07	47,234.56
33	10426	1/18	1,550.34	48,784.90
34	10427	1/18	268.64	49,053.54
35	10428	1/18	2,826.96	51,880.50
36	10429	1/18	513.93	52,394.43
37	10430	1/20	1,521.21	53,915.64
38	10431	1/20	588.92	54,504.56
39	10432	1/20	2,311.14	56,815.70
40	10433	1/21	1,072.78	57,888.48
41	10434	1/22	114.83	58,003.31
42	10435	1/23	2,467.88	60,471.19
43	10436	1/23	891.82	61,363.01
44	10437	1/23	1,257.52	62,620.53
45	10438	1/23	2,171.68	64,792.21
46	10439	1/24	88.23	64,880.44
47	10440	1/24	1,382.15	66,262.59
48	10441	1/25	2,936.26	69,198.85
49	10442	1/25	858.11	70,056.96
50	10443	1/25	1,145.88	71,202.84
51	10444	1/26	5,250.50	76,453.34
52	10445	1/28	630.16	77,083.50
53	10446	1/29	2,312.04	79,395.54
54	10447	1/29	1,740.13	81,135.67
55	10448	1/29	701.74	81,837.41
56	10449	1/30	1,187.52	83,024.93
57	10450	1/30	297.67	83,322.60
58	10451	1/30	1,192.97	84,515.57
59	10452	1/30	330.40	84,845.97
60	10453	1/30	9,639.16	94,485.13
61	10454	1/30	183.47	94,668.60
62	10455	1/30	2,230.97	96,899.57
63	10456	1/30	489.71	97,389.28
64	10457	1/30	83.63	97,472.91
65	10458	1/30	879.26	98,352.17
	Total Sales	January	98,352.17	

Random Sampling: *Random sampling* is based on the assumption that every item in the population has an equal probability of selection regardless of its individual attributes. Random sample selection is performed by obtaining a series of random numbers that uniquely identify specific items in the population. Random numbers can be generated using a computer program. For example, random numbers can be generated easily using Microsoft Office Excel (e.g., see Figure 17.1).[2] In our example, we want to select ten items selected from sixty-five invoices that are sequentially numbered from 10394 to 10458. Employing MS Excel "random number generation" data analysis program found under the "Tools" menu bar, we would select 10 as the number of random numbers to generate, over a uniform distribution (equal likelihood of selecting each invoice) for items 10394 to 10458. After sorting (and possibly removing duplicate numbers), we might get the 10 numbers indicated under "Random Sampling" in the second column of Table 17.2. These are the documents the auditor would then test. Since the numbers are selected randomly, repeating the selection process should yield a different sample (if not, then Excel is not really generating random numbers!).

Systematic Sampling: An alternative to random sample is referred to as *systematic sampling*. This approach starts with one randomly selected transaction and then uses a predetermined selection interval to identify the rest of the sample. In our example, our selection interval should be 7. This was determined by dividing the population size by the sample size and then rounding to the next larger integer (i.e., 65/10 = 6.5, rounded up to 7). The selection interval must be determined by rounding up to the nearest integer in order to assure that every item in the population has a chance of selection. We then select a starting point that falls within the first seven transactions (the interval size). An interval of 6 would not result in a representative sample because the last item in the sequence (10458) could never be chosen regardless of the starting point.

If we select the second invoice (10395) as our starting point (and this should be determined randomly), we will then select every seventh invoice thereafter until we get our sample of ten. The result of this sampling process is summarized in the third column of Table 17.2 under the heading "Systematic Sampling." A complication that can occur is that the end of the population is reached before the entire sample is selected. Whether this will happen depends on the size of the interval and the starting point. This is not a problem, however, because the auditor can simply cycle back to the beginning of the population. It should be noted that the systematic approach results in an approximately random sample as long as the starting point is selected randomly.

Block Sampling: Another way to simplify the selection process and still maintain a degree of randomness is through the use of *block sampling*. This approach assumes that the auditor will examine groups (blocks) of sequential transactions but the selection of each block will be random. The auditor must determine how many blocks to test and select as many random numbers as there are blocks. Each block consists of a randomly selected start point and the items that follow it in sequence. The block

Figure 17.1 *Random Dollars Selected by Excel Random Number Generator*

238 numbers were required based on the textbook example between 1 and 600,000 with a uniform (equal likelihood of selection) distribution. After sorting from lowest to highest, here is the sample dollars selected to identify accounts for confirmation.

1685	104190	210889	320389	407166	485464	580828
2985	106772	213361	320591	407788	486489	580902
3095	108695	214423	324491	412165	489914	582165
8698	110727	215009	324656	417658	490738	583502
9577	111185	219349	326926	419819	497531	585424
10254	113950	221162	326981	420185	510257	586120
19428	117063	223103	327311	421979	510385	591540
22779	119059	224073	329032	423023	511411	591778
23475	120286	225501	331394	423646	515293	594745
24427	123472	226691	332182	424433	515421	598627
25489	126658	229200	333097	425422	517948	
27284	130650	231800	334233	426905	520054	
32063	131767	240864	334599	427363	523844	
35707	138432	242879	335350	433241	529868	
37172	138487	244435	344707	434449	530766	
38435	147020	244453	345549	434596	535307	
39405	150462	248518	347673	438716	536827	
44606	153374	255696	348021	439009	538072	
49367	153758	259047	350713	443037	538420	
51033	153923	261043	350951	444282	539463	
51582	154015	264632	352031	450124	542320	
57222	155077	271059	353862	453200	542430	
57479	157329	272231	355821	453694	545158	
60189	162566	279611	356590	456935	546184	
60408	162896	279794	357891	459114	547282	
65133	168206	289810	361132	464461	555358	
66305	171026	292227	362047	465395	555687	
66616	171319	293893	370562	465413	556163	
68905	174780	295743	371642	466585	557299	
79232	176739	297629	375909	470138	558031	
79360	180126	298215	394110	473415	568853	
83151	180126	300467	399438	477755	569109	
87472	182342	306729	399640	478011	570611	
91336	195087	309989	400867	481289	571014	
97397	197815	310886	402936	481307	572588	
98477	198053	313669	404987	483395	575079	
100858	200378	314072	405573	483999	578576	
103934	205853	317277	406708	484402	580480	

Table 17.2 *Alternative Samples Using Different Sampling Techniques*

Sampling Technique	Random Sampling	Systematic Sampling	Block Sampling
Description	Random Number Generation from Excel for a Uniform Distribution from invoice number 10394 to 10458	Starting with the second invoice, select every seventh invoice thereafter. The starting point should be randomly selected from the first seven invoices.	Select two blocks of five invoices each. Use the random number table to select the first invoice of each block in a manner similar to random sampling. Blocks start at 10424 and 10448.
Items Selected	10398 10400 10401 10406 10407 10422 10427 10441 10447 10454	10395 10402 10409 10416 10423 10430 10437 10444 10451 10458	10424 10425 10426 10427 10428 10448 10449 10450 10451 10452
Sampling Technique	Judgmental Sampling (size)	Judgmental Sampling (time)	Haphazard Sampling
Description	Select the invoices for the ten largest sales during the period. This results in the examination of all transactions over $2,800.	Select the ten transactions that occur on or near the first and last day of the period. This results in the selection of the first five and last five invoices.	Select any ten invoices that attract the attention of the auditor.
Items Selected	10395 10398 10406 10407 10408 10420 10428 10441 10444 10453	10394 10395 10396 10397 10398 10454 10455 10456 10457 10458	Not determinable. The actual sample will vary for every auditor.

sample approach is simpler than pure random sampling but does not result in a true random sample. The more blocks that are selected, the more closely the sample will approximate a random sample. Block sampling may be appropriate in some situations where the auditor is interested in testing a sequence of transactions. The results of this selection process are summarized in the fourth column of Table 17.2 under the heading "Block Sampling."

Haphazard Sampling: *Haphazard sampling* is commonly used by auditors. Instead of formally generating random numbers, the auditor mentally generates a set of numbers that are scattered throughout the population by making up numbers within the range of interest. For example, the auditor could select ten invoices from those in Table 17.1. Another approach to haphazard sampling is used when the documents are physically available to the auditor. For example, if all the invoices are in a single file, the auditor may simply reach in and pull out ten invoices without looking at them or considering any attributes about the invoices. Finally, for tests of process controls that involve observing employee actions, the auditor might choose to perform haphazard sampling when visiting the client's facilities for other reasons (a meeting) rather than on a random basis. These techniques are not really random in any sense.

Judgmental Sampling: There are many situations where the auditor wishes to consider the attributes of the items in the population when determining which ones to examine. The consideration of transaction attributes negates the possibility of random sampling and is commonly referred to as *judgmental sampling*. This approach does not necessarily result in a representative sample, but its use is often justified because it allows the auditor to focus on items that are more likely to have problems or have a material impact on the financial statements. Common attributes that the auditor might consider when judgmentally selecting a sample include:

- **Magnitude of a transaction:** The auditor will usually care more about large transactions than about small ones because large transactions are more likely to have a material effect on the financial statements.

- **Date of a transaction:** The auditor may be concerned that transactions at the beginning and end of a period may be subject to cutoff problems and concentrate testing on those transactions.

- **Parties to the transaction:** The auditor will usually be interested in related party transactions and may select a large proportion of such transactions to test.

- **Nature of underlying assets and liabilities:** The assets obtained or liabilities incurred as a result of the transaction may be of concern to the auditor (e.g., sales to failing companies may be more likely to be uncollectible).

To illustrate the use of judgmental sampling, Table 17.2 presents two possibilities. The first sample is based on size and selects the ten largest transactions in the population. The second approach is based on time and selects the first five transactions of the period as well as the last five. Judgmental sampling can also be based on multiple attributes. For example, the auditor might select the first two transactions, the last two transactions, and the six largest transactions.

Statistical sampling had its heyday in the 1980s, but then auditors turned to judgmental sampling based on the belief that it is costly to train audit staff in the proper use of statistical sampling techniques or that it is time-consuming to rigorously select a random sample from a very large population. In addition, auditors argue that they get more competent evidence from examining transactions that are selected for specific reasons, such as their large size or susceptibility to material misstatement.

Although these arguments have some merit, the combination of mandatory ongoing training for practicing auditors and the rapid increase in the availability and decrease in the cost of computer-assisted audit tools means that they can be used to facilitate rigorous sample selection in many audits. Suggestions have recently arisen among some auditors that the Public Company Accounting Oversight Board (PCAOB) recognize the superiority of statistical sampling in situations where the auditor has no specific knowledge on which to base informed judgmental sample selection.

A Technique for Refining Sample Selection: Stratified Sampling

In some situations, an auditor may wish to split a population into smaller groups and use different sampling approaches for each group. Separating a population into subgroups for sampling purposes is referred to as **stratified sampling**. For example, the auditor may separate large transactions from small transactions and use judgmental sampling for the large transactions and random sampling for the small transactions. A similar size distinction could be made for confirmation of receivables or audits of selected branch offices. Another reason to use stratified sampling is because one subgroup of a population may be considered high risk, and the auditor will wish to sample from it very heavily, whereas another subgroup is considered low risk and will be subject to light sampling. In general, stratified sampling allows the auditor to tailor his or her sampling strategy to the characteristics of the population so as to obtain the most effective and efficient evidence. Stratified sampling can be used in conjunction with all of the sampling techniques discussed above.

Other Types of Populations

Sampling from populations consisting of items other than documents can be complicated. If no other approach is reasonable, the auditor can always use haphazard sampling. In most cases, however, the auditor may be able to assign a sequence of unique, individual reference numbers to each item in the population and then use random or systematic sampling to choose the sample items. If an auditor wishes to draw a sample of days from a specific time period, calendar dates can easily be transformed into a four-digit code that is amenable to random number generation: April 27 becomes 0427 while December 8 becomes 1208. Similarly, weeks can be represented with two-digit numbers ranging from 01 to 52.

Samples based on pages or lines within a journal or ledger are also easy to obtain because each page in the document of interest can be assigned a unique number. If transactions are listed in a book, then a numbering scheme based on page numbers and line numbers is feasible. For example, assume that warranty claims are listed in a journal that has 22 pages, and each page has 45 lines. Sampling could be performed by forming four-digit numbers based on page and line numbers. Line 10 on page 18 becomes 1810, whereas line 42 on page 7 becomes 0742. Alternatively, each page may reflect a separate date so that days can be randomly selected and then lines on the page can be selected separately.

Populations of physical items such as parts or locations are more difficult to sample because existing numbers may not be sequential. Obtaining a sample from transactions or documents that are not numbered is the most difficult. Even in these cases, though, a logical sampling approach can usually be developed. For example, if the documents are loosely gathered into a physical file, a systematic process can be used where the auditor chooses documents based on a prespecified interval.

Tests of Process Controls and Transactions: Attribute Sampling and Sample Evaluation

Some of the most common applications of sampling are for tests of internal controls and substantive tests of individual transactions. The sampling approach used for these audit procedures is designed to determine if a specific attribute of interest is present in a transaction. In general, the auditor is searching for violations of some prespecified condition that is of interest. For example, an auditor can examine a sales invoice to see if it is approved by the credit manager. Similarly, the auditor can test to see if the price on an invoice is correct when compared with a master price list. In both cases, the presence or absence of a specific condition is of interest to the auditor: the sale is either authorized or it is not; the price is either correct or it is not. Auditors refer to violations of the specified conditions as **deviations** and use **attribute sampling** to perform these types of tests. The following 12-step process facilitates the use of attribute sampling:

1. Identify the audit procedure and the purpose of the test.
2. Define the population and sample unit.
3. Define the deviation conditions.
4. Specify the tolerable deviation rate.
5. Specify the acceptable risk that the auditor's conclusion will be incorrect.
6. Estimate the expected population deviation rate.
7. Determine the sample size.
8. Select the sample.
9. Perform the audit procedure and document the results.
10. Generalize the sample results to the population.
11. Analyze individual deviations.
12. Conclude whether the assertion tested is acceptable or not.

Some of these steps may be handled by computer support software where the auditor only provides the inputs necessary for the analysis; for example, the software calculates the required sample size given inputs from the audit team.

(i)DUAL PURPOSE PROCEDURES EXAMPLE

Obtain a random sample of invoices from the invoices included in the sales journal along with the related supporting documents. The invoices should be selected using a random sample from the sequence of sales invoices for the year. Each invoice should be examined as follows:

(a) Verify that the sales order, bill of lading, and customer purchase order exist and are attached.

(b) Examine the documents for proper authorization by the credit manager.

(c) Verify that the correct price was used on the invoice by tracing unit prices to the master price list.

(d) Test the computational accuracy of the invoice.

(e) Test that the sales invoice has been properly included in the sales journal.

(f) Verify that the transaction is posted on a timely basis.

Step 1: Identify the Audit Procedure and the Purpose of the Test

The first step in any sampling process is to clearly state the purpose of the procedure and provide clear guidelines on how the test is to be performed. Failure to clearly state the purpose and nature of the audit procedure can result in an ineffective or inefficient sampling plan and inadequate or misleading evidence. For example, the purpose of the audit procedure may be to determine if sales have been recorded, classified, and summarized in accordance with management's general authorization. Sometimes multiple tests are conducted using a single sample. This is referred to as **dual purpose testing**. For example, the following combined or dual purpose audit procedure could be used to examine both internal control attributes (a, b, c) and substantive attributes (d, e, and f) of sales transactions (see "Dual Purpose Procedures Example" on the left(i)).

Step 2: Define the Population and Sample Unit

In our example, the **population** is the set of "recorded sales invoices." The **sample unit** is an individual sales invoice. Defining the population or sample unit may be more difficult in other situations. For example, if the auditor is interested in testing for completeness, he or she must determine what population to use as the basis for the sample. The population of recorded invoices would not be appropriate because they represent *recorded* transactions, and the auditor is interested in what has been *omitted*. As an alternative, completed sales orders might be used as the population for testing completeness, with the sales order being the sample unit. This approach would be effective since the population includes all potential sales, but it may be inefficient because the auditor would also have to look at sales orders that were canceled or rejected. A better sample population for testing completeness would be shipping documents because each one represents an actual delivery to a customer and a sale that should have been recorded.

Another problem with defining the population may occur when time-dependent or location-dependent samples are used. For example, if the auditor wishes to observe employees on a sample basis as they open mail containing incoming receipts, the population would be all time periods in which this activity occurs and the sample unit could be a block of time, such as one hour. Another example is testing process controls over the handling of warehouse goods in a just-in-time (JIT) environment. Here both the selection of locations and the time are critical for determining the sample.

Step 3: Define the Deviation Conditions

After clearly specifying the audit procedure to be performed, the auditor then defines the deviation conditions that are being tested. A **deviation** indicates that a process or control has failed but does not mean that the transaction is necessarily misstated. For example, failure of the credit manager to approve a sale does not mean the sale is invalid or incorrect or has been sold to someone who cannot pay. **Transaction errors** are situations where a transaction is processed improperly and may or may not result in a monetary misstatement. For example, charging a customer an incorrect low price on a sale is unfortunate, but it does not mean that the recorded amount of revenue is incorrect (i.e., the amount of revenue per the general ledger agrees with the amount per the invoice, even though the wrong price was used). Some transaction errors may cause account misstatements, for example, omission of a sales invoice from the sales journal would lead directly to an understatement of sales revenue.

Returning to our example, the auditor might identify the following conditions as being deviations or errors:

Attribute	Test for following condition	Negative outcome
(a)	Missing document	deviation
(b)	Absence of initials	deviation
(c)	Prices do not agree	deviation
(d)	Extensions are incorrect	transaction error
(e)	Invoice not included in journal	transaction error
(f)	Posting in wrong period	transaction error

The distinction between deviations and errors relates to the likelihood that an account will be misstated as a result of the condition.

Step 4: Specify the Tolerable Deviation Rate (TDR)

The **tolerable deviation rate** (TDR) is a measure of how many deviations or errors the auditor can willingly accept before concluding that the process or control is not effective. The auditor specifies a tolerable deviation rate for each of the attributes being tested. If the auditor thinks that credit approval is not an important source of audit assurance, he or she may set TDR to be high for that attribute, say 8 percent. If the auditor feels that entering incorrect prices is very significant to the audit, the TDR may be set low (e.g., 2 percent). We will see that the auditor's subsequent actions will be dictated by whether the tests reveal an actual deviation rate above or below the tolerable deviation rate. If actual deviation rates are below TDR, the auditor will then be able to conclude that the process or activity being tested is reliable, consistent with the auditor's assessment of risk.

Step 5: Specify the Acceptable Risk of Overreliance (ARO) on Controls

The **acceptable risk of overreliance** (ARO) on controls is a measure of the risk that the auditor will conclude that the actual deviation rate is below TDR when, in fact, it is higher. This situation implies that an auditor has reached an incorrect conclusion. As a practical matter, ARO measures the risk that the auditor will conclude that a given residual risk for a process or control risk for an assertion is less severe than is appropriate. Such an erroneous decision will ultimately affect the quality of the audit, as the auditor would plan the audit based on an understated assessment of the client's risks. This would probably lead to inadequate substantive testing, higher detection risk than desired, and an unknown increase in the audit risk. In practice, common values for ARO are 10, 5, and 1 percent.

Step 6: Estimate the Expected Deviation Rate (EDR)

The auditor also needs to generate a tentative estimate of the **expected deviation rate** (EDR) for the population being tested in order to calculate the desirable sample size in Step 7. One possible source of the estimate is the results from a prior audit. If similar tests were performed in the past, the actual deviation rate from those tests could be used as the estimate of the deviation rate for the current year after adjusting for any process changes (improvements) that may have been made. Another approach that may be used is to audit a small preliminary sample of transactions and use those results to estimate the EDR for the main sample to be taken later. In some cases, the auditor may simply specify the expected deviation rate as zero.

Step 7: Determine the Sample Size (n)

The sample size an auditor should use to test a specific attribute is calculated from the tolerable deviation rate (TDR), the expected deviation rate (EDR), and the acceptable risk of overreliance (ARO). Returning to our example, let's assume that the six attributes being tested have the values for TDR, EDR, and ARO described in Table 17.3. The appropriate sample size for each attribute is calculated as

$$n = R/P$$

where: n = sample size

R = Risk factor based on ARO and the expected number of errors in the sample

P = TDR – EDR (the precision gap is the difference between tolerable deviations and expected deviations)

The R-factor is based on the assumption that most audit populations will be found to be in compliance and follows a specific form of probability distribution called a "Poisson" distribution.[3] Table 17.4 presents the appropriate R-factor for various combinations of ARO (denoted "risk level" in Table 17.4) and the expected number of errors to be found in a sample. For our example, we will assume that the auditor expects one error or deviation

Table 17.3 *Calculating an Attribute Sample Size*

Attribute	TDR	EDR	P (= TDR-EDR)	ARO (Risk level)	R Factor (Table 17.4 for 1 error)	n = R/P*
(a)	5.0%	2.00%	3.0%	10.0%	3.89	130
(b)	6.0%	2.00%	4.0%	10.0%	3.89	98
(c)	5.0%	2.00%	3.0%	5.0%	4.75	159
(d)	6.0%	3.00%	3.0%	10.0%	3.89	130
(e)	3.0%	0.25%	2.75%	5.0%	4.75	173
(f)	3.0%	0.50%	2.5%	5.0%	4.75	190

* Rounding up to the next largest whole number

Table 17.4 *Determination of Factors Used for Sample Size and Error Projection Computations**

No. of Errors	Risk Level = 10% (90% confidence)		Risk Level = 5% (95% confidence)		Risk Level = 1% (99% confidence)	
	R factor	PGW factor	R factor	PGW factor	R factor	PGW factor
0	2.31	-	3.00	-	4.61	-
1	3.89	0.58	4.75	0.75	6.64	1.03
2	5.33	0.44	6.30	0.55	8.41	0.77
3	6.69	0.36	7.76	0.46	10.05	0.64
4	8.00	0.31	9.16	0.40	11.61	0.56
5	9.28	0.28	10.52	0.36	13.11	0.50
6	10.54	0.26	11.85	0.33	14.58	0.47
7	11.78	0.24	13.15	0.30	16.00	0.42
8	13.00	0.22	14.44	0.29	17.41	0.41
9	14.21	0.21	15.71	0.27	18.79	0.38
10	15.41	0.20	16.97	0.26	20.15	0.36
11	16.60	0.19	18.21	0.24	21.49	0.34
12	17.79	0.19	19.45	0.24	22.83	0.34
13	18.96	0.17	20.67	0.22	24.14	0.31
14	20.13	0.17	21.89	0.22	25.45	0.31
15	21.30	0.17	23.10	0.21	26.75	0.30

* Adapted from Guy, D. M., D. R. Carmichael, and O. R. Whittington. 2001. *Audit Sampling: An Introduction*, 5th edition. Wiley.

for each test performed. Note that this is only an assumption for our example's purposes and other expectations for deviation numbers may be appropriate depending on the purpose of the test.

We see in Table 17.3 that, all other things held constant, increasing ARO yields smaller sample sizes. Similarly, increasing TDR or reducing EDR yields smaller sample sizes. Less obvious may be the fact that the difference between TDR and EDR directly impacts the size of the sample. This can be seen by comparing attributes (a) and (d)—the difference between EDR and TDR is the same for each (3 percent), resulting in the same sample size (130). Given that the various attributes have different values for TDR, EDR, or ARO, the sample sizes for each attribute are different. However, all the tests are focused on the same sample unit (invoice), so the auditor would probably use the largest value of *n* (190) and apply all tests to all invoices.[4]

Step 8: Select the Sample

After determining the sample size, the auditor then selects the items that are to be examined. Although random sampling or systematic sampling (with a random start point) are much preferred sampling methods, the auditor might also use haphazard or judgmental sampling. However, the use of judgmental or haphazard sampling makes it harder to generalize the sample results to the population. Furthermore, the use of judgmental or haphazard sampling explicitly precludes the use of the statistical evaluation methods for generalizing the sample results described in Step 10.

Step 9: Perform the Audit Procedure and Document the Results

Once the sample is selected, the auditor then obtains the documents needed to perform the specified tests and notes any deviations or errors that are detected. The auditor's documentation of this step can vary based on individual firm practices, but it should fully describe the nature of all deviations and errors that are detected, including an explanation of the problem. For a sample size of *n*, the results of the procedures can be summarized by the *sample deviation rate* (SDR):

$$\text{SDR} = \text{Number of deviations found}/n$$

To continue with our example, we will assume that the auditor finds seven deviations: two deviations for attribute (a), three deviations for attribute (b), one deviation each for (d) and (f), and no deviations for (c) and (e). These deviations are summarized in Table 17.5.

Table 17.5 *Documenting Deviations Found via Attribute Sampling*

Johnson Pharmaceuticals Attribute Deviations for Tests of Controls and Transactions: Sales Transactions For the Year Ended 12/31/x5				*M-1* *WRK* *1/24/x7* *PBC*
Attribute Tested	**Deviation Number**	**Description of Deviation Found**	**UDR vs. TDR**	**Comments: Implications for the Audit**
(a)	1	Customer purchase order was not attached to the sales invoice because the order was received by phone.	OK (see Table 17.6)	No special audit concern. The company is not set up to handle phone orders. Suggest that management consider this in the system design.
(a)	2	The sales order was not attached. Sales clerk remembers that it was destroyed when a cup of coffee spilled on it.	OK	No special audit concern. Suggest that duplicate copies of destroyed documents be included in the files.
(b)	1	The sales transaction was not approved by the credit manager because he was on vacation at the time. There is no alternative procedure in this situation.	Too high	Indicates that the control procedure is not being applied in all cases. May result in increased problems of collection.
(b)	2	The sales transaction was not approved by the credit manager because of accidental oversight.	Too high	Indicates that the control procedure is not being applied in all cases. May result in increased problems of collection.
(b)	3	The credit manager reviewed this transaction but neglected to sign the proper place on the form.	Too high	Indicates carelessness in applying the authorization procedure. Suggest to management increasing the reliability of this process.
(d)	1	An incorrect amount of sales tax was computed on a sale made to an out-of-state customer.	OK	No special significance because this type of sale is rare and the amounts of error are small.
(f)	1	The transaction was posted to the sales journal three days later than normal as the transaction occurred at the end of business on a Friday before a holiday weekend.	OK	No special significance because this situation is a rare occurrence.

ISA 530 and PCAOB AS 2315 state that the deviation rate in the sample is the auditor's best estimate of the deviation rate in the population and should be compared to the tolerable rate for the population.

Step 10: Generalize the Sample Results to the Population

After the auditor has performed the audit procedure and tabulated the observed deviations (e.g., where the internal control has not been correctly applied or where there is a numerical error in a sales invoice), the next step is to generalize the results to the entire population.[5] Assuming a random sample and the results reported in Table 17.5, the auditor next determines if sample deviation rate (SDR) is *tolerable*; that is, is the sample deviation rate low enough to be acceptable? We rearrange our formula for sample size in order to help us evaluate the results:

$$n = R/P$$

$$P = R/n$$

where, as before, n is the actual sample size and R is the risk factor based on ARO and the number of deviations found in the sample. Table 17.4 presents the R-value for the number of deviations discovered and the planned level of ARO (denoted as "risk level" in the Table).

P captures the precision of the estimate and will be referred to as the **upper deviation limit** (UDL). The UDL is the maximum (or upper) deviation rate that an auditor can expect given the observed deviations and the auditor's acceptable risk. In other words, it includes what is more generally called the "margin for error." This means that when ARO is 5 percent, there is no more than a 5 percent chance that the true value of a deviation rate for an attribute will exceed the UDL. For example, if an auditor observes one deviation in a sample of 100 items, the sample deviation rate is 1 percent (1/100). Based on the R-factors in Table 17.4, the upper deviation rate would be 4.75 percent ($R/n = 4.75/100$) for an ARO of 5 percent (R-value for one deviation in the column headed "Risk Level = 5%"). This is the same as saying that there is a 95 percent chance that the true deviation rate is less than 4.75 percent. If our TDR is 5 percent then the control is considered effective at its assessed level (UDL < TDR).

The tolerable deviation rate is a matter of judgment by the auditor. It reflects how effective the control must be in order to reduce the risk of material misstatement to an acceptable level for the particular assertion(s) related to the test being performed. If the auditor had determined when planning the test that the acceptable TDR is 4.5 percent, then the control would *not* be considered effective at its assessed level (UDL > TDR). This difference in interpretation reinforces our earlier caution that sampling is no more than a means to an end, and what an auditor concludes depends on the level of error that is acceptable to still conclude that a control is effective or a transaction is correctly stated.

Returning to our example, the outcomes of the six attributes tests are summarized in Table 17.6.[6] For example, we see that attribute (a) had two

Table 17.6 *Evaluating Results from Attribute Sampling*

Attribute	n from Table 17.3	ARO (Risk level)	Deviations (D) found in sample	SDR = D/n	R*	UDL = R/n × 100	TDR	Conclusion
(a)	130	10.0%	2	1.52%	5.33	4.1%	5.0%	Acceptable**
(b)	98	10.0%	3	3.41%	6.69	6.8%	6.0%	Unacceptable
(c)	159	5.0%	0	0.00%	3.00	1.9%	5.0%	Acceptable
(d)	130	10.0%	1	0.76%	3.89	3.0%	6.0%	Acceptable
(e)	173	5.0%	0	0.00%	3.00	1.7%	2.0%	Acceptable
(f)	190	5.0%	1	0.64%	4.75	2.5%	3.0%	Acceptable

* Table 17.4 for ARO (risk level) planned and actual number of deviations (D) found in sample.

** TDR > UDL is means assertion is acceptable.

observed deviations in a sample of 130 at an ARO level of 10 percent, resulting in a UDL of 4.1 percent. Given that the UDL is less than the TDR of 5 percent, we can conclude that the control is effective at the planned level. The tests of attributes (c), (d), (e), and (f) are also within the acceptable TDR. However, we also see that attribute (b) has a UDL of 6.8 percent, which is greater than the TDR of 6 percent. Hence, we would conclude that the control is not effective at the planned level of reliability that was assessed during audit planning.

The auditor has a number of alternatives when the UDL exceeds TDR. One possibility is to revise either TDR or ARO upward. Such a revision after a test has been performed makes it easier to obtain a result that is acceptable to the auditor, meaning that the auditor can conclude no problems exist for a given attribute. However, this approach is highly inadvisable because the original estimates of TDR and ARO were the auditor's best judgment at the time, and revision of those values in order to obtain more acceptable test results suggests that the audit procedures may be biased. Another possibility is to increase the size of the sample used in the test, looking at additional items from the population. This approach is best employed when the UDL is very close to the TDR. If the additional items do not have any deviations, the UDL will get lower as *n* increases. This approach is acceptable when additional testing can be performed but the auditor must also be aware that additional deviations may be found which could lead to a higher value of UDL.

Step 11: Analyze Individual Deviations

The computation of UDL is only one aspect of the auditor's evaluation of the results from sample-based tests. Even if the UDL is less than TDR for all attributes, the auditor should still examine the nature of the actual deviations in the sample. One characteristic the auditor will consider is whether any of the deviations indicate fraudulent activity. A deviation that hints at possible employee or management fraud is always significant because it raises questions about the integrity of the people in the organization. Another type of deviation of interest is one that indicates a systemic problem within a process or information system. Even though a process works fine for most transactions, there may be a type or class of transactions that is routinely mishandled. For example, a company that deals primarily with credit card sales may not have a good system for handling cash receipts. Therefore, the cash sales may have a higher incidence of errors and mistakes than credit sales, and could be examined in more detail.

Step 12: Conclude Whether the Assertion Tested is Acceptable

The final step of attribute sampling is to reach an overall conclusion about the population being tested based on the sample results. For tests of internal controls, the auditor's conclusions may relate to residual risks in a process or the control risks related to financial statement assertions. For substantive tests of transactions, the conclusions drawn from sample-based tests pertain to the detection risk of specific financial statement assertions. There are three possible outcomes for a sample-based attributes test:

1. The upper deviation rate is less than the tolerable deviation rates for all attributes tested, and the individual deviations do not reveal any significant or systemic problems within the system. In this situation, the auditor would conclude that the initial risk assessments made during audit planning are correct (e.g., inherent or control risk might be low or very low).

2. The upper deviation rate is more than the tolerable deviation rate for one (or a few) attributes tested, or the analysis of individual deviations indicates some systemic problems. In this situation, the auditor might increase residual risk assessments for the affected attributes (e.g., inherent or control risk is moderate). As a result, the auditor would increase the amount of substantive testing in selected areas to reflect that some of the initial assessments of control effectiveness were not supported by the tests of controls.

3. A large number of unacceptable deviation rates are found or there are many indications of significant or systemic problems. In this situation, the auditor is likely to conclude that residual process risks are significant and not adequately controlled (e.g., inherent or control risk is high). This will lead the auditor to increase detection risk for specific assertions and significantly increase the use of substantive audit procedures. In addition, in an Integrated Audit (i.e., SOX Section 404), the auditor needs to consider whether the control problems constitute significant deficiencies or material weaknesses in internal control over financial reporting as of the end of the year.[7]

In our example (Table 17.6), we see generally good results with five of the six attributes having acceptably low deviation rates. Only attribute (b) has a deviation rate that would be considered unacceptable. Consequently, the auditor confirms his or her initial assessment of the risk of material misstatement for the assertions affected by the attributes with low deviation rates. For example, given the low incidence of unrecorded sales (attribute e), the auditor may conclude that the risk of material misstatement for the completeness of sales transactions is very low. Similarly, because there are few missing documents (attribute a), validity of sales would appear to support an assessment of low risk of material misstatement.

Valuation of sales transactions is more difficult to assess since more than one attribute affects the assertion. The low incidence of pricing errors (attribute c) indicates low valuation risk. However, at the same time, the failure of the credit manager to check transactions (attribute b) indicates that there may be a high risk of collection problems in the future. In this situation, the auditor would probably conclude that risks associated with pricing of sales are low, but additional substantive evidence will be needed to determine the appropriate level of bad debt expense for the period.

Completion of the 12-step process for attribute sampling highlights how evidence from tests of controls and individual transactions supports the auditor's assessment of residual risk. Attribute sampling is a methodical approach for testing the presence or absence of certain conditions within transactions. By relying on random sampling, a single table of computational factors, and some straightforward computations, the auditor is able to compute the best sample size consistent with the auditor's understanding of the population being tested and to generalize observed deviation rates from the sample to the entire population. Consequently, the auditor has a rigorous basis for reaching conclusions about the risks related to a process or assertion.

Tests of Account Balance Details: Dollar Unit Sampling

The second major area where an auditor can apply sampling is for substantive tests of account balances. For example, an auditor may decide to confirm selected receivable balances or verify quantities for selected items in inventory. In general, these tests are designed to detect dollar-denominated errors that may exist in a recorded account balance. The sampling approach used most often by auditors is referred to as ***dollar unit sampling*** or ***DUS***.[8] Dollar unit sampling is so-named because each dollar included in an account is considered a sample unit that can be uniquely identified and audited. Dollar unit sampling involves a 12-step process similar to attribute sampling:

1. Identify the audit procedure and purpose of the test.

2. Define the population and sample unit.

3. Define the error conditions applicable to the audit procedure.

4. Specify the tolerable error rate.

5. Specify the acceptable risk of inappropriately accepting an account as correct.

6. Estimate the expected error level and the expected tainting factor.

7. Determine the sample size.

8. Select the sample.

9. Perform the audit procedure and document the results.

10. Generalize the sample results to the population.

11. Analyze individual errors.

12. Conclude whether the account balance tested is acceptable or not.

Step 1: Identify the Audit Procedure and Purpose of the Test

The first step is to clearly identify the audit objective(s) being addressed and the audit procedure to be performed. For example, the auditor may use confirmations to test the validity and valuation of accounts receivable as discussed in Chapter 11. The auditor will rarely be able to confirm every customer's account balance. In fact, the auditor is probably most interested in the largest account balances because an overstatement of a receivable balance would probably cause an overstatement in net income. We will use the following audit procedure to illustrate the application of dollar unit sampling (see "DUS Example" on the right[(ii)]).

Step 2: Define the Population and Sample Unit

The sample unit for dollar unit sampling is a single dollar and the entire "set" of dollars that comprise an account balance is the population. An account with a balance of $1,000 consists of 1,000 sample units; an account that has a balance of $10,000 has 10,000 sample units. Any individual dollar can be selected during the sampling process, so a customer account with a large balance contains more sample units and is more likely to be selected than a small account.

This approach to defining the population and sample unit has a number of advantages. First, large accounts are more likely to be selected since they consist of more sample units. Second, any individual dollar that is sampled can be in one of two conditions, either correct or incorrect. This allows the auditor to use a sampling method similar to that used for attribute sampling. Third, this approach does not require the auditor to make any assumptions about the distribution of the errors in accounts. This advantage may not be readily apparent, but alternative approaches usually require that errors adhere to a normal distribution (bell-shaped curve).

DUS also has some disadvantages that the auditor must consider. DUS ignores accounts with a zero or credit balance. A customer who usually carries a balance may have a low balance at year end (or even a credit balance) due to an error that understates sales or overstates cash receipts. Such errors are unlikely to be detected using DUS because an account with a zero or negative balance has no sample units. This also implies that understatement

[(ii)]DUS EXAMPLE

Select a random sample of customer accounts to be confirmed. Prepare positive confirmations of account balances as of 12/31/x5 and mail out confirmations on 1/3/x6. Confirmations should be prepared by the client but reviewed and mailed by the auditor. Responses should be directed to the auditor's office address. Perform the following related procedures:

a. *Prepare a confirmation control list to facilitate documentation of the confirmation process.*

b. *Maintain a confirmation log to record when confirmations are sent and received.*

c. *Send second and third requests, if necessary.*

d. *Investigate all discrepancies identified in returned confirmations.*

e. *Prepare adjusting entries to propose to client for any detected errors.*

errors in general are less likely to be detected. An account with a balance of $1,000 that is overstated by $400 (correct balance is $600) is more likely to be selected than an account with a balance of $600 that is understated by $400 (correct balance is $1,000) even though both accounts contain a $400 error. The auditor will normally use separate procedures to test for understated receivables if deemed necessary by risk conditions.[9]

Step 3: Define the Error Conditions Applicable to the Audit Procedure

The error condition for tests of account details is usually easy to specify—the account is either correct or not. However, the sample unit is a dollar, not an account, making interpretation of the error condition more subtle. When a dollar is selected for confirmation, it is "associated" with a specific customer. In order to confirm the selected dollar, the entire customer account needs to be confirmed. That means that the actual confirmation applies to the entire account balance, for example $1,000, and the audit procedure provides evidence about more than just the sample unit selected. If an error exists in the $1,000 balance, then 1,000 sample units are considered to be in error, that is, the selected sample unit is incorrect as well as the other 999 sample units that were not selected but were covered by the confirmation.

Step 4: Specify the Tolerable Error Level (TEL)

Based on our previous discussion of materiality and tolerable error (chapter 10), we can specify the **tolerable error level** (TEL) for the account being examined, in this case accounts receivable. The tolerable error level for an account reflects the maximum size of a misstatement that could exist before the auditor would conclude that the account is materially misstated. Auditors can set tolerable errors in one of two ways: (1) by directly allocating a portion of overall materiality to the account in dollar terms, or (2) by calculating TEL as a specified percentage of the account (e.g., 5 percent, 2 percent, or 1 percent are common). Smaller values of TEL are associated with lower detection risk.

Step 5: Specify the Acceptable Risk of Incorrect Acceptance (ARIA)

The **acceptable risk of incorrect acceptance** (ARIA) reflects the maximum likelihood the auditor is willing to accept that he or she will reach an incorrect conclusion about an account that is materially misstated. ARIA is similar to detection risk but applied to a single account. Common values for ARIA are 10 percent, 5 percent, and 1 percent. When using Table 17.4, the ARIA is denoted as the "risk level."

Step 6: Estimate the Expected Error Level (EEL) and the Expected Tainting Factor (ETF)

The auditor must also generate an estimate of the **expected error level** (EEL), the auditor's best guess of the expected misstatement for the account prior to being tested. This estimate is needed in order to calculate the sample size in Step 7. One possible source of the estimate is the results from last year's audit. If similar tests were performed in the past, the actual dollar error from those tests could be used as the estimate of the dollar error for the current year. Another approach is to take a small preliminary sample, perform some audit testing, and use those results to estimate the EEL for the main sample to be taken later. In some cases, there may be little basis for estimating EEL but the auditor should be aware that higher levels of EEL increase sample sizes.

As noted above, the sample unit for DUS is an individual dollar but the actual audit procedures must be applied to some other unit, such as a customer account. That means that when an error is discovered it pertains to the entire account, both the dollars that were selected in the sample as well as those that were not. This raises the question of whether an error is attributable to the specific dollar sampled, some other dollar(s) not selected, or all dollars in the account. As a matter of simplicity, auditors assume that a discovered error in an account is equally applicable to all sample units (dollars) that comprise that account. For example, assume that a customer's account is recorded at $1,000 but is discovered to be overstated by $200. Because the overstatement represents 20 percent of the account balance, every individual dollar is assumed to be overstated by 20 percent. To look at it differently, the $200 error in an account is translated into a 20 cent error in each sample unit (dollar). The rate of misstatement (20 percent) is referred to as the **tainting factor** (TF), calculated as follows:

$$\text{Tainting Factor (TF)} = \frac{\text{Book value (BV)} - \text{Correct Audited Value}}{\text{Book Value (BV)}}$$

In order to compute the appropriate sample size for DUS, the auditor must specify the **expected tainting factor** (ETF) for the account as a whole. This reflects the auditor's conditional expectation of how large an error is likely to be, if one is discovered through an audit procedure. The value of 50 or 100 percent is often used for ETF as they are relatively conservative and result in larger sample sizes and more accurate estimates of potential misstatements.

Step 7: Determine the Sample Size (*n*)

The appropriate sample size for DUS depends on the TEL, ARIA, EEL, and ETF. Because the auditor is sampling individual dollars and each dollar is correct or incorrect, a variation of attributes sampling can be used for dollar unit sampling. The main challenge is to determine an equivalent for the R-factor that can be applied to a dollar unit sample. In general, R is based on the specified level of ARIA (denoted the "risk level" in Table 17.4) and an assumption of either zero or one or more expected errors (with zero errors being the most conservative, leading to larger sample sizes). The sample size is then computed as:

$$n = \frac{\text{BV} * \text{R} * \text{ETF}}{(\text{TEL} - \text{EEL})}$$

where BV is the book value (balance) of the account being audited. In general, sample sizes increase when ARIA is lower, ETF is larger, or TEL is smaller. A value of EEL in excess of zero will also cause sample size to increase.

For an illustration of this computation, consider the following facts for our confirmation procedure to be performed:

Book Value (BV) of accounts receivable	$600,000
Number of customers	545 individual accounts
Tolerable Error Level (TEL)	$24,000 (4%)
Expected Error Level (EEL)	$0
Expected Tainting Factor (ETF)	100%
Acceptable risk of incorrect acceptance (ARIA)	5%

We will also assume an error level of one for determining the R-factor to use in the calculation, yielding R = 4.75 based on ARIA set at 5 percent (see Table 17.4, under column entitled "Risk level = 5%" and row with one error). We can then calculate the sample size as 119 sample units as follows:

$$n = (BV^* R^* ETF)/(TEL - EEL)$$
$$= (\$600,000 \times 4.75 \times 1.00)/(\$24,000 - \$0)$$
$$= 119$$

If the expected tainting factor was 50 percent, the sample size would be half as large.

Step 8: Select the Sample

After determining the appropriate sample size, the auditor must then select the sample. Using random sampling or systematic sampling with a random start point will allow the auditor to quantify sampling risk. The use of any form of judgmental or haphazard sampling precludes the application of statistical methods for generalizing the results from a sample-based test to the population (as in Step 10). For either random or systematic sampling, the items in the population must be logically ordered, usually by account number, and a running total determined after the addition of each item. This is illustrated in Table 17.7 for the first fifteen customers in the accounts receivable ledger.

The auditor must document which accounts are selected and prepare a confirmation control sheet indicating when confirmations are sent and received. The auditor can take a random sample for the confirmation of receivables simply by generating 119 random numbers between 1 and 600,000, and then mapping them to the cumulative totals in Table 17.7.

Alternatively, the auditor can take a systematic sample with a random start point. The sample interval would be BV/(n=1) = $600,000/118 = 5085. This means that the auditor would randomly select a dollar between 1 and 5085 as the random start point and then every 5,085th dollar after that. If the start point is less than 4118, the first item selected will be the first account (132409). If the start point is larger than 4118, the first item will not be selected. Assume the auditor selects 4338 as the start point. The first account selected would be 136861 since 4338 exceeds the cumulative total of the first account but is less than the cumulative total of the second

Table 17.7 *Extracts from Dollar Unit Work Paper for Selecting Receivable Accounts to Confirm*

Item No.	Customer Number	Balance	Cumulative Total	Random Start Point Plus Interval		Balances to be Confirmed
1	132409	4,118.85	4,118.85			-
2	**136861**	9,717.34	13,836.19	4338	9423	9,717.34
3	136871	445.21	14,281.40			-
4	**136895**	7,683.03	21,964.43	14508	19593	7,683.03
5	**137127**		24,757.82	24678		2,793.39
6	**137472**	9,044.62	33,802.44	29763		9,044.62
7	137743	1,471.44	35,273.88	34848		1,471.44
8	137854	4,939.33	40,213.21	39933		4,939.33
9	**138651**	2,906.08	43,119.29			-
10	**138846**	1,433.63	44,552.92			-
11	**138988**	4,914.56	49,467.48	45018		4,914.56
12	139124	869.72	50,337.20	50103		869.72
13	**139319**	1,762.02	52,099.22			-
14	**139707**	2,738.36	54,837.58			-
15	139754	923.09	55,760.67	55188		923.09
.	.	.	.	.	.	.
.	.	.	.	.	.	.
.	.	.	.	.	.	.
	Total	**$600,000**				**$150,000**

account. The second dollar selected would be 9423 (4338 + 5085), which also pertains to customer 136861. The third dollar selected would be 14508 (9423 + 5085), falling in account number 136895. The first 11 sample units (and 9 selected accounts) are illustrated in Table 17.7. The selection process would continue in this manner until all 119 sample units (dollars) are selected.

Although the sample size is 119, the auditor would actually send out fewer than 119 confirmations because some accounts are selected more than once. We see this for items 2 and 4, but it could occur for other accounts in the population. Any account that is larger than the sample interval will always contain at least one sample unit and will be selected for confirmation no matter what the starting point for sample selection. Any account that is more than twice the sample interval will contain at least two sample units, any account larger than three times the sample interval will contain at least three sample units, and so on. The counting of the same account as multiple samples is based on the underlying theory that it is the individual dollar in the account that we are sampling, not the account itself.

Step 9: Perform the Audit Procedure and Document the Results

Regardless of the sample selection method, the auditor then sends confirmations to the individual customers within which each selected dollar is included. The auditor will keep a log of customers who respond and investigate any discrepancies noted in the confirmations. The auditor will also document if alternative procedures are performed for non-responses and prepare a summary of any errors that are detected by the audit test (see Chapter 11 for more detail). Table 17.8 describes three errors that were discovered through the confirmation of accounts receivable in our sample. The total discovered error is $1,800. Some discrepancies will not be errors from the point of view of the client. For example, a common discrepancy that occurs in receivables that is not an error is when the client adds interest to a customer's balance but the customer does not consider the interest when confirming the amount owed. Errors and non-errors must be clearly separated prior to the next step of the process.

Step 10: Generalize the Sample Results to the Population

One of the main advantages of employing statistical sampling is the ability to quantify sampling risk and calculate an upper bound on the maximum error in the population for a given level of ARIA.[10] This allows the auditor to project the detected amount of error to the population as a whole. Table 17.9 illustrates the error calculations for the example.

1. **Basic Margin of Error:** Even when an audit procedure reveals no errors, the fact that the auditor only tests a sample instead of the entire population creates a margin of error in the results. The basic margin of error in all sampling plans is always less that the tolerable error level (TEL) because of the structure of the sampling plan. The calculation of the basic margin of error is based on the R-factor for zero errors for a given level of ARIA as indicated in Table 17.4. For our example, the R-factor for zero errors is 3.00 (zero errors in column headed "Risk level = 5%"). We also assume a tainting factor of 100 percent for the basic margin of error. The basic margin of error is $15,255, which is well below the TEL of $24,000. Thus, if the auditor had detected NO errors, the account balance would be accepted as free of material misstatement.

2. **Most Likely Error:** Errors detected during the audit procedures are used to calculate the most likely (or average) error. This calculation quantifies

Table 17.8 *Summary of Confirmation Results Obtained from Dollar Unit Sampling*

Customer Number	Book Value (BV)	Corrected Audited Value (AV)	Difference = BV-AV	Tainting Percentage = Difference/BV
139834	$1,000	$500	$500	50%
140102	3,000	2,100	900	30%
140367	2,000	1,600	400	20%
Total known misstatements			$1,800	

Table 17.9 *Projection to the Population*

	(a) PGW Factor (see Table 17.4)	(b) Tainting Factor	(c) Average Sampling Interval	Subtotal (a) × (b) × (c)	Dollar value of error
Basic error margin	3.00	100%	5,085		**$15,255**
Most likely error					
Customer 139834	1.00	50%	5,085	2,543	
Customer 140102	1.00	30%	5,085	1,526	
Customer 140367	1.00	20%	5,085	1,017	**5,086**
Most likely error					**$20, 341**
Precision Interval					
Customer 139834	0.75	50%	5,085	1,907	
Customer 140102	0.55	30%	5,085	839	
Customer 140367	0.46	20%	5,085	468	**3,214**
Upper error limit (UEL)					**$23,555**

the mean amount of error in the population based on errors discovered in our sample. We list these errors from largest tainting factor to the smallest tainting factor.[11] In Table 17.9, we find the most likely amount of error due to overstatements is $5,086.

3. **Precision Interval:** The final component of the error projection is the precision interval, which reflects the sampling risk associated with the known errors. The computation of the precision interval is based on the precision gap widening (PGW) factors in Table 17.4.[12] Each error detected in the sample is assigned a different PGW factor. By convention, the first error is considered the one with the largest tainting factor (50 percent). Ordering the errors based on the tainting factor is conservative because it yields the largest precision interval. The precision interval for our example is $3,214.

AUTHORITATIVE GUIDANCE & STANDARDS

ISA 530 and PCAOB AS 2315 require the auditor to project monetary errors found in the sample to the population, regardless of the sampling method selected. The projected error should be compared to tolerable error.

Step 11: Analyze Individual Errors

In addition to generalizing the error results to the entire population, the auditor must also analyze each error to see if it has implications for the risk of material misstatement, including the risk of fraud. The auditor must be comfortable with the explanation obtained for each of the discovered errors. Errors can fall into one of three categories: random unintentional errors, systematic unintentional errors, and fraud. For errors that are considered to be unintentional and random, it is safe to draw conclusions about the entire account based on the results of the sample. Errors that are systematic mean that there is a basic flaw in the system that will lead to an error whenever certain conditions occur. These errors should be separated from the random errors and subject to separate audit testing. The remaining random errors can then be analyzed using the statistical evaluation approach described above. If the analysis reveals potential fraud, the auditor must carefully assess the extent of the problem, evaluate the implications for completing the audit, and communicate with the appropriate levels of management. The use of statistical evidence should be re-evaluated in the presence of fraud because of the intentional manipulation of the data that is the basis of the sampling plan.

Step 12: Conclude Whether the Account Balance Tested Is Acceptable

The final step in the process is to reach an overall conclusion about the account balance being examined. As indicated, the overall **Upper Error Limit** (UEL) is $23,555. Because this is less than the TEL of $24,000, the auditor can conclude that accounts receivable is not materially overstated with a 95 percent level of confidence (i.e., ARIA = 5 percent). Although understatements are usually of less concern to auditors when testing accounts receivable, a **Lower Error Limit** (LEL) should also be computed. Given that there were no understatement errors, the most likely error for understatements is 0. Therefore, the lower error limit is simply the basic margin of error, $15,255. Based on the UEL and LEL, the auditor can be 95 percent confident that the true account balance falls between $564,745 (BV − LEL) and $623,555 (BV + UEL). Because both error limits fall within the acceptable range (BV ± TEL), the auditor will conclude that accounts receivable are free of material misstatement. However, the known misstatement of $1,800 should be brought to management's attention for further action and correction.

If either UEL or LEL exceeds TEL, there exists an unacceptable risk that the account is misstated in an amount that exceeds tolerable error. If this occurs, the auditor has a number of possible responses:

- **Increase ARIA or TEL:** Either of these two actions will result in more tolerance for error, but this approach is NOT recommended on an *ex post facto* basis because it appears that the auditor is biasing the results of the tests toward accepting the client's book values.

- **Expand the Sample Size for the Audit Procedure:** If additional items can be selected and tested, the UEL may be reduced as long as no other errors are detected. This approach has two drawbacks: (1) it may not work if additional errors are detected, and (2) it may not be possible to audit additional items in the population. For example, if confirmations are being obtained as of December 31, the auditor will not know until February that there is a problem in the account. At that time, it is probably too late to obtain additional confirmations.

- **Adjust the Account Balance for Discovered (or Known) Errors:** This should be suggested to client management regardless of the TEL. The adjustment for known overstatement errors has the effect of reducing the UEL by the amount of the adjustment. In our example, the auditor can reduce UEL by $1,800 by requesting client management correct the three accounts that were found to contain errors. This reduces UEL to $21,755 ($23,555 = $1,800).

- **Adjust the Account Balance for Projected Error:** The auditor might recommend that the client reduce the balance of accounts receivable by the UEL or some portion of UEL. Such a recommendation would probably only be made when UEL exceeds TEL by an amount that is greater than the known misstatements. Making this proposal to client management has at least two drawbacks: (1) client management may balk at the idea of a large adjustment because the support for the adjustment is based on a statistical, rather than actual, measure of error, and (2) the adjustment may over-correct the problem and cause a material understatement of the account.

- **Expand Audit Testing That Focuses on Specific Problems Identified in the Sample:** The auditor might choose to perform additional tests that are focused specifically on the risks revealed by the confirmation procedures. This would provide additional evidence to the auditor as to whether the problems are universal or isolated. If the additional evidence shows that the errors in the sample are isolated and not likely to be repeated on a large scale, those errors can be removed from the statistical analysis and simply adjusted in the accounts. This approach is probably the most common approach used by auditors[iii].

- **Get the Client to Check the Entire Population:** Once the nature of the problem is diagnosed, the auditor can request that the client test the entire population to ensure all mistakes are found. If client management carries out the procedures then the auditor must take a sample and determine if management carried out the procedures correctly. The advantage of this approach is that it reduces management's reluctance to make an adjustment as the adjustment is based on known errors, not projections or sampling risks. The disadvantage of this approach is its cost, either in auditor or client time[iv].

Judgmental Approaches to Sampling

Auditors are not always willing (or able) to use formal statistical methods of sampling and sample evaluation. The auditor should consider the following characteristics when determining sample size in a judgmental approach:

- **Individually Significant Items:** Transactions that are considered to be material or significant on their own should be selected for testing. Any transaction that exceeds half of tolerable error is usually considered to be individually significant.

- **Variation of the Population:** The more variation there is in the population of items, the larger the sample should be. Variation can come in terms of size or other attributes of interest (timing, nature of transactions). The sample should be large enough to be representative of all conditions typically encountered in the population.

- **Tolerable Error Level (TEL) and Acceptable Risk of Incorrect Acceptance (ARIA):** Although these terms are not used in their statistical

(iv)EXAMPLE

Early in his career one of the authors was a senior on an audit where the inventory observation, price tests, and subsequent lack of sales all pointed to a significant amount of inventory obsolescence. The manager on the engagement, after consulting with the partner, proposed a material adjustment to the client for obsolescence (almost 30 percent of net income). The client CFO objected and decided to have his purchasing managers and inventory specialists come up with their estimate of obsolescence, rather than just relying on the CFO's computed obsolescence allowance. The CFO budgeted for an all-day meeting with the purchasing managers and inventory specialists, all who carried large binders into the meeting containing their best estimates within each of their product lines of inventory obsolescence. Within 90 minutes the CFO came out of the meeting and accepted the adjustment.

Figure 17.2 *Using Judgmental Samples in Auditing*

* Adapted from American Institute of Certified Public Accountants. 2001. Audit Sampling—An AICPA Audit Guide. AICPA: New York.

sense, the concepts apply for judgmental sampling. In general, smaller TEL and lower ARIA lead to larger samples.

- **Extent of Expected Error:** This concept is similar to EEL but is less formally stated. The more expected error there is the larger sample sizes should be.

Based on these concepts, the American Institute of Certified Public Accountants provides the following formula for determining sample size:

$$n = (BV \times \text{Assurance Factor})/\text{TEL}$$

where the **assurance factor** is selected from the possible combinations of expected error and the degree of desired assurance depicted in Panel A of Figure 17.2. The appropriate assurance factor must be judgmentally selected by the auditor based on his or her experience and the factors mentioned above. Assuming the auditor believed there was some risk of error and wanted moderate assurance about the account, the judgmental sample size for our previous example would be 100 items ($600,000 × 4.0/$24,000).

Auditors may calculate a sample size using a statistical approach but then decide to evaluate sample results employing non-statistical or judgmental means. This situation will occur when the auditor employs a judgmental or haphazard sample selection method to select the items to be tested. Although the sample is not selected randomly, the discovered errors must be projected to the entire population. Panel B of Figure 17.2 illustrates one way to project the $1,800 of errors detected by the confirmation procedures. Because the confirmed portion of the population has a 1.2 percent error rate, it is reasonable to project this error rate to the remainder of the population. The most likely error found in the population is $7,200 (1.2% × $600,000).

Another way to project the error from a judgmental sample is to compute the average error per confirmed account and then to apply that to accounts

Panel A: Assurance Factors for Judgmental Sampling*

Desired degree of audit assurance from the test sample	Little or no error expected in the account	Some error expected in the account
Substantial	3.0	6.0
Moderate	2.3	4.0
Little	1.5	3.0

Panel B: Calculation of Most Likely Error for a Judgmental Sample

Total Accounts Receivable (from Table 17.7)	$600,000
Total Accounts Receivable confirmed	150,000
Total known misstatement (from Table 17.8)	1,800

$$\text{Average sample misstatement} = \frac{\text{Total known misstatement}}{\text{Total accounts confirmed}}$$

$$= \frac{\$1,800}{150,000}$$

$$= 0.012 \text{ (or 1.2\%)}$$

Most likely error (MLE) in entire population:

$$\begin{aligned} \text{MLE} &= \text{Average Sample Misstatement} \times \text{Book Value} \\ &= 1.2\% \times \$600,000 \\ &= \$7,200 \end{aligned}$$

that have not been confirmed. In our example, the average error per account confirmed is $15.12 ($1,800 in known errors divided by 119 confirmed accounts). Projecting the error to the entire account yields a most likely error of $8,240 (545 total accounts × $15.12 per account). Although either of these estimates is reasonable, neither takes into account sampling risk. Consequently, the auditor must rely on professional judgment to determine if the estimated error is close enough to TEL to warrant additional substantive procedures.

Common Errors in Sampling

Sampling as a source of audit evidence presents the auditor with a number of difficult judgments, and there are many ways in which an auditor can bias the choice of sample size, sample selection, or interpretation of test results. Some of the more common pitfalls in acquiring and interpreting sample evidence include:

- **Sample Size is Too Small Given Reliance Placed on the Sample Results:** Average sample sizes for substantive audit procedures such as accounts receivable confirmations and inventory test counts have been steadily declining in recent years while clients have become larger and more complex.[14] The quest for efficiency in audit testing may have caused a drop in the effectiveness of sample-based testing as a result of this shrinkage.

- **Misuse of Decision Aids**: Many firms use decision aids to guide auditors in the determination of sample sizes for substantive testing. However, researchers have found that auditors who are given a decision aid may manipulate the input parameters in order to get the sample size they want.[15]

- **Influence of Irrelevant Transaction Attributes:** Research has shown that auditors reveal very subtle biases when called upon to draw a haphazard sample. Irrelevant characteristics of a transaction, such as the size, color, and location of documents, often influence the selection of items to be included in a sample. For example, the selection of accounts payable documents to be tested can be influenced by the size of the voucher package supporting a payment or the compactness of the storage space, which affects the ease with which the auditor can remove a set of documents from a cabinet. Furthermore, the physical placement of documents can influence the selection process because documents in the back of a file drawer or in a low-level file drawer are less likely to be selected than documents that are front and center in a waist-level file drawer.

- **Use of Statistical Evaluation on the Results from a Judgmental Sample:** Another common error is for an auditor to evaluate the results from a judgmental sample by employing statistical methods. This approach is inappropriate and has the appearance of rigor while lacking an adequate foundation on which to justify the projection.

- **Failure to Project Known Errors to the Population:** Failure to project known errors or an inappropriate projection method are also common problems encountered in interpreting sample evidence.[16]

In the fall of 2004, the Public Company Accounting Oversight Board (PCAOB) reported on its initial review of Big 4 audit clients, including consideration of audit sampling. The PCAOB made the following observation about one audit it examined: "In one instance, the engagement team used non-statistical audit sampling in testing the valuation of the materials inventory balance. The engagement team did not, however, project a known misstatement to the untested portion of the materials inventory balance. Such projection is necessary to evaluate whether the aggregate misstatement, which is the known misstatement plus the projected misstatement, exceeded the {tolerable error} ... In response to this comment, the engagement team projected the known misstatement to the untested portion of the materials inventory balance and determined that the aggregate misstatement exceeded the {tolerable error}." (PCAOB Release No. 104 2004-005)

Improper Omission of Isolated or Unique Errors from a Projection: Another strategy that auditors use when evaluating individual sample errors is to show that the error is isolated to a "well defined" subpopulation so as to limit the auditor's additional testing to that subpopulation, and to justify not projecting the error to the population as a whole.[17] [v]

Summary and Conclusion

Auditors can rarely examine every risk, event, or transaction that can affect the financial statements. Consequently, auditors are forced to rely on evidence obtained from sample-based audit procedures, be they tests of process controls, substantive tests of transactions, or tests of account details. In order to assure that the sampling evidence is properly obtained and evaluated, auditors have developed preferred methods for performing audit procedures that generate sample-based evidence. There are a number of techniques for selecting transactions from a large population of transactions or accounts. Random sampling or systematic sampling with a random start point is preferable in most situations, but auditors can also use random block sampling, haphazard sampling, or judgmental sampling. Different approaches are used for determining the proper sample size and evaluating the results of tests of process controls and individual transactions (attribute sampling) and tests of account balance details (dollar unit sampling). In general, the use of attribute sampling and dollar unit sampling is preferable to the use of judgmental methods when the goal is to quantify the sampling risk of an audit procedure.

Bibliography of Relevant Literature
Research

Burgstahler, D., S. Glover, and J. Jiambalvo. 2000. Error Projection and Uncertainty in Evaluation of Aggregate Error. *Auditing: A Journal of Practice & Theory.* 19(1): 79–100.

Dusenbury, R. B., J. L. Reimers, and S. W. Wheeler. 1994. The Effect of Containment Information and Error Frequency on Projection of Sample Errors to Audit Populations. *The Accounting Review.* 69(1): 257–264.

Elder, R. J. and R. D. Allen. 2003. A Longitudinal Field Investigation of Auditor Risk Assessments and Sample Size Decisions. *The Accounting Review.* 78(4): 983–1002.

Gillett, P. R. and R. P. Srivastava. 2000. Attribute Sampling: A Belief Function Approach to Statistical Audit Evidence. *Auditing: A Journal of Practice & Theory.* 19(1): 145–156.

Hall, T. W., T. L. Herron, B. J. Pierce, and T. J. Witt. 2001. The Effectiveness of Increasing Sample Size to Mitigate the Influence of Population Characteristics in Haphazard Sampling. *Auditing: A Journal of Practice & Theory.* 20(1): 169–186.

Messier, Jr, W. F., S. J. Kachelmeier, and K. L. Jensen. 2001. An Experimental Assessment of Recent Professional Developments in Nonstatistical Audit Sampling Guidance. *Auditing: A Journal of Practice & Theory.* 20(1): 81–96.

Professional Reports and Guidance

American Institute of Certified Public Accountants. 2001. *Audit Sampling: An AICPA Audit Guide.* New York: AICPA.

Guy, D. M., D. R. Carmichael, and O. R. Whittington. 2001. *Audit Sampling: An Introduction*, 5th ed. New York: Wiley.

Auditing Standards

IAASB *International Standards on Auditing (ISA)* No. 530, "Audit Sampling."

IFAC. International Auditing and Assurance Standards Board (IAASB). 2014. *Handbook of International Quality Control, Audit, Review, Other Assurance, and Related Services Pronouncements.* New York: International Federation of Accountants.

PCAOB Auditing Standard 2315 (formerly AU 350), "Audit Sampling."

PCAOB Release No. 104 2004–005 *"Report on 2003 Limited Inspection of PricewaterhouseCoopers LLP."*

SOX Sarbanes-Oxley Act-Library of Congress. 2002. House Resolution Number 3763, An Act to protect investors by improving the accuracy and reliability of corporate disclosures made pursuant to the securities laws, and for other purposes (*The Sarbanes-Oxley Act of 2002*). www.libraryofcongress.gov.

Notes

1   To keep our example manageable, we use a small population and sample, but the same techniques can apply when the population being audited numbers in the thousands or even millions of documents. In fact, in such large scale situations, sampling is a necessity.
2   Random number generation appears under the "Tools" command under the "data analysis" heading. The user must then fill in the dialogue box for "random number generation."
3   The Poisson distribution is often used to represent random events which are dichotomous, meaning they can either happen or not happen. The Poisson distribution is skewed and peaked to the right, unlike the Normal distribution (sometimes called the Bell curve), which is symmetric and peaked in the middle.
4   If the number of invoices in the sequence is less than 1,000, a slightly smaller sample may be employed by reducing the computed number by the finite correction factor. The **finite correction factor** is computed as

$$n' = \frac{n}{(1 + n/N)}$$

where N is the number of items in the entire population, n is the sample size computed using

$n = R/(TDR - EDR)$, and n' is the final sample size.

5   The generalization procedure described is only appropriate when the auditor uses random sampling, systematic sampling with a random start point, or a large number of randomly selected blocks. It is not appropriate when using judgmental or haphazard sampling as these are not *statistical* methods.

6   Our remaining discussion will be based on the sample sizes computed for each individual attribute, not the maximum sample.

7   This is an example of a situation where reliance on controls for the audit of financial statement purposes can be inconsistent with the internal control audit requirement of SOX Section 404. To reduce the number of substantive tests in the audit of financial statements, the controls need to be effective for the *entire* period under audit. Under the internal control audit requirement the controls only need to be effective as of *year-end*. Thus, it is an interesting question as to how long before year end the controls have to be put in place in order for the client to test the new controls and the auditor to opine on the client tests and satisfy himself or herself that the redesigned system will detect material errors beyond a remote likelihood.

8   The term ***monetary unit sampling*** is occasionally used synonymously with dollar unit sampling. A more general term that is used is ***sampling proportionate to size*** because the application of DUS results in large items being more likely to be selected than small items. A different approach to sampling for tests of account details is called ***variables sampling***. Variables sampling is based on the number of items in a population rather than dollars. It includes approaches to sampling that are often referred to as ***classical sampling***, which differ significantly from the sampling methods described in this chapter.

9   Another advantage of DUS that is not obvious from the exposition so far is that it usually results in smaller sample sizes than alternative approaches. Another disadvantage is that the computations for DUS can become quite complex if the population is very large.

10   For samples that are selected judgmentally, the generalization of sample results to the population should be based on the techniques described in the section "Judgmental Approaches to Sampling" later in this chapter.

11   It is necessary to separate overstatement errors from understatement errors in doing the computation of most likely error and upper error limit.

12   The PGW factors are based on the assumption that each error in the sample increases the aggregate **R**-factor for the sample. Because our example revealed three errors, the upper value of the **R**-factor is 7.76, and each error contributes to the increase in the **R**-factor from 3.0 (no errors) to 7.76. The PGW-factor is computed by taking the change in R-factor for a specific error, less 1.0. For example, the first error increases the **R**-factor from 3.00 to 4.75. Thus, the first error contributes a PGW increment of 0.75 (4.75 −3.0 −1.0). The second error increases the **R**-factor from

4.75 to 6.30 and the PGW increment is 0.55 (6.30 – 4.75 –1.0). Similarly, the incremental PGW-factor for the third error is 0.46 (7.76 –6.30 –1.0).

13   An auditor might also decide not to expand tests and wait to see what the entire set of detected and projected errors looks like for the financial statements taken as a whole. See Chapter 15 for a discussion of evaluating potential adjustments at the end of the audit. The auditor might expect that the problems that are suggested by the confirmations of receivables may be offset by other facts discovered in the course of the audit and that no adjustment may be necessary in spite of UEL exceeding TEL for a single account.

14   See "A Longitudinal Field Investigation of Auditor Risk Assessments and Sample Size Decisions," by R. J. Elder and R. D. Allen, (*The Accounting Review*. 78(4): 983–1002).

15   See "An Experimental Assessment of Recent Professional Developments in Nonstatistical Audit Sampling Guidance" by W. F. Messier, Jr., S. J. Kachelmeier, and K. L. Jensen, *Auditing: A Journal of Practice & Theory*. 20(1): 81–96

16   Researchers have found that audit seniors with more than three years of experience tend to underestimate the most likely error in the population when evaluating sample results as well as under-adjusting for the added risk that comes with any sample. See "Error Projection and Uncertainty in Evaluation of Aggregrate Error," by D. Burgstahler, S. Glover, and J. Jiambalvo, *Auditing: A Journal of Practice & Theory*. 19(1): 79–100.

17   See "The Effect of Containment Information and Error Frequency on Projection of Sample Errors to Audit Populations," by R. B. Dusenbury, J. L. Reimers, and S. W. Wheeler, *The Accounting Review*. 69(1): 257–264.

Index

Page numbers in *italics* refer to figures. Page numbers in **bold** refer to tables.